What is McGraw Hill edge™ COURSEWARE

McGraw Hill Edge Courseware is a versatile learning and assessment solution, that uses credible content and innovative pedagogies to make the readers' exam preparation journey holistic and adaptive to changing examination trends. By blending the strengths of authoritative McGraw Hill books with cutting-edge digital resources and latest updates, this Courseware offers a dynamic content solution for exam aspirants. It provides the students a thorough understanding of the subject matter, enhances learning and retention, and shares deep insights about their performance, ultimately boosting their confidence. This Courseware is at the forefront of innovation; revolutionising learning to guide learners on their path to success!

Unlock Your Potential with
McGraw Hill Edge Coursew

AF876168

Conceptual Videos
To transform complex ideas into engaging visual storytelling!

Study Aids
To simplify learning with visual summaries, mind maps, flash cards, infographics etc.

Knowledge Enrichment Content
To craft your path to success with exclusive reading materials

Questions
To practice from an extensive collection of PYQs with detailed explanations

Mock Tests
To simulate real exam conditions and boost confidence

Performance Analytics
To optimise exam preparation with data-driven insights

Live Interactive Sessions
To gain valuable insights from the author through interactive sessions

eBook Access
To conveniently access study materials anytime, anywhere

What do you get with Courseware on Polity Simplified 2e

This Courseware is a ***comprehensive and exam-focused learning resource*** meticulously crafted for UPSC/SPSC aspirants preparing for ***Prelims, Mains, and the Interview*** stage. Here's what you can expect:

- **Conceptual Videos:** Topic-wise 60+ conceptual videos by the author
- **Chapter-wise Learning Outcomes:** Structured learning outcome of every chapter for a quick overview
- **PYQs:** Access 2014–24 UPSC Questions; 300+ Prelims and 100+ Mains
- **Practice Tests:** Chapter-wise Practice Tests plus 5 Thematic Practice Tests to strengthen your exam readiness
- **Mnemonics:** Mnemonics at the end of relevant sections for easy and effective revision
- **Building Blocks for Model Introductions:** Structured Introductions to enhance Mains answer writing
- **Think About It:** Topic-wise thought-provoking questions for Mains, to foster critical thinking
- **Current Affairs:** Monthly Current Affairs updates on key topics
- **Additional Data Points:** Chapter-wise Additional Data Points to supplement and deepen subject understanding
- **Webinars:** Regular Webinars by the author and discussion on Think About It Questions

SCAN NOW

Scan this QR code to know all about this Courseware

APPEAL

COUNTER THE COUNTERFEIT & BUILD A STRONG FOUNDATION FOR SUCCESS

Books are our best friends, is the adage we have grown up with. However, the pirates of piracy are continuously forging 'our best friends'. Our books and their supplementary online resources are copyrighted, and we don't lend any right-to-copy. Piracy is synonymous to stealing books.

Knowledge comes real, let's not encourage its counterfeit. Therefore, we appeal all our readers to discourage pirated books and **choose authentic ones.**

HOW TO IDENTIFY THE PIRATED BOOKS?

1 Cover and Spine

- ☞ Look and feel (new or used book)
- ☞ Blurred images on the cover
- ☞ Hologram pasted on front
- ☞ Defective spine (wrinkles) or air pocket at its bottom
- ☞ Unclear ISBN/bar codes
- ☞ Missing/non-operational Unique Coupon Code for exclusive access to McGraw Hill Edge

2 Text/Printing/Binding

- ☞ Uneven inking of pages
- ☞ Poor quality or blurred photographs/images/charts
- ☞ Substandard paper quality and opacity
- ☞ Misaligned pages
- ☞ Missing pages
- ☞ Inferior binding quality

You can further watch this video on How to identify a pirated book

For more information about identifying piracy, visit **https://www.mheducation.co.in/piracy**

To report a pirated book, send 'Hi' on WhatsApp code given on the back cover or write to us at **support.india@mheducation.com.**

Reported pirated books are examined to combat their piracy.

Let's fight the Pirates of Piracy and resolve to go for original!

2e

COURSEWARE ON

POLITY SIMPLIFIED

For UPSC & State Civil Services Examinations

Rangarajan R

(ex-IAS, AIR - 46)

McGraw Hill Education (India) Private Limited

Published by McGraw Hill Education (India) Private Limited
Registered Office: Anjana Complex No: 5/90 A, Butt Road, St. Thomas Mount, Chennai – 600016

Courseware on Polity Simplified, 2e

Print Edition:
ISBN (13): 978-93-6444-362-3
ISBN (10): 93-6444-362-4

E-Book Edition:
ISBN (13): 978-93-6444-572-6
ISBN (10): 93-6444-572-4

1 2 3 4 5 6 7 8 9 D103074 29 28 27 26 25

Printed and bound in India.

Typeset at APS Compugraphics, 4G, PKT 2, Mayur Vihar Phase-III, Delhi 96
and printed at Rajkamal Electric Press, Kundli, Haryana-131 028.

Cover Image Source: Shutterstock
Cover Designer: Anita Kanojia

Visit us at: www.mheducation.co.in
Write to us at: support.india@mheducation.com
CIN: U80302TN2010PTC111532
Toll Free Number: 1800 103 5875

About the Author

Rangarajan R is an ex-IAS officer, a Chartered Accountant and a Cost Accountant. Starting his career in a leading global audit and consulting firm, he went on to become a corporate banker after his Chartered Accountancy with one of the largest private sector banks. He subsequently cleared the UPSC CSE, as a working professional, in his first attempt in 2005 securing AIR-46. In his role as an IAS officer, Rangarajan served in the States of Assam & Meghalaya. He has been training and inspiring civil service aspirants since 2016.

He has authored a fiction novel titled *'A Madras Mystery'*. He runs a YouTube channel @PolitySimplifiedbyRangarajan, where he discusses current events relating to Polity.

Testimonials

Rangarajan sir provides excellent guidance and motivation. I am sure his book 'Polity Simplified' will be of immense help to all the Civil Service aspirants.

Dr Mittali Sethi IAS, 2017

I have prepared with Rangarajan sir's material for Polity. It is concise and provides conceptual clarity. I am sure his book 'Polity Simplified' will be one stop solution for Civil Service aspirants.

Ms. Chatriya Kavin DJ IPS, 2023

I have prepared using 'Polity Simplified' which contains wonderful tables, flow charts and Mnemonics for Prelims. Model answers are useful for Mains. It is a one stop solution for Polity.

Dr C Vinothini IAS, 2024

Rangarajan sir's material for Polity covers the entire syllabus of UPSC in a crisp manner.

Mr. S Sivanandham IAS, 2022

I have prepared with Rangarajan sir's notes for Polity. It is simple and helps in understanding the provisions as well as analysis. I am sure his book 'Polity Simplified' will be very useful for UPSC/SPSC Prelims and Mains.

Mr. Aswin Mani Deep Kakumanu IPS, 2024

I have prepared for Polity only using Rangarajan sir's material. The book 'Polity Simplified' by him with examples, tables, flowcharts, solved previous year questions will be the best book for Civil Service aspirants.

Mr. C Saravanan IAS, 2023

I have prepared for polity using 'Polity Simplified' and notes of Rangarajan sir. It has concise content for exam preparation and is the best book for Polity.

Dr S Prashanth, IAS, 2024

To

We the People

सत्यमेव जयते

Preface to the revised 'Courseware on Polity Simplified'

The response for the first edition of 'Polity Simplified' has been quite impressive. With an aim to further improvise, simplify and facilitate the preparation of aspirants, this revised and updated edition of the '*Courseware on Polity Simplified*' has been launched. There are significant additions and improvements to the existing courseware, which makes it a one-stop solution for Prelims and Mains, which have been listed below:

1. 60+ conceptual videos have been placed alongside the relevant content in the chapters for easy viewing
2. Learning outcomes in each chapter in line with the syllabus of UPSC/State civil service examinations
3. Mnemonics at the end of relevant sections for easy revision
4. Thought Provoking Questions for Mains preparation under the tag 'Think about it' – answers to be discussed in Monthly Webinars
5. Monthly Current Affairs update to continue
6. PYQs of 2014–2024 of UPSC Preliminary examination given in the form of practice questions apart from chapter-wise practice questions
7. 5 thematic practice tests, for Preliminary examination preparation, over and above chapter wise practice questions and PYQs
8. PYQs of UPSC Mains of 2014–24 with model answers provided in edge for online reference
9. Additional Data points provided chapter-wise for easy reference including articles at a glance for each chapter in the 'edge' platform

I am sure these additional features will enhance the learning experience of all aspirants and general readers.

ACKNOWLEDGEMENTS

The aspirants whom I have trained over the years have shaped my approach towards teaching Indian Constitution and Governance in a lucid manner. This has been a great motivation for writing this book and it is reflected in the way it has been structured and written. I am thankful to all of them. I am also thankful to my student, Ms Shahida S, IRS (AIR-323, CSE 2023), who initially assisted me in this work.

I have included relevant information from various government websites and official reports of Government departments. Information and recommendations from the reports of various commissions/committees constituted by the Government from time to time have been included in various chapters. Information from news items and articles published in leading newspapers like The Hindu, The Indian

Express, The Times of India etc. have also been a source for the book. Information from various websites that deal with legal matters and the Supreme Court judgments have also been added at relevant places.

I am grateful for the support of my parents, family, and friends in my endeavours. I owe my special thanks to the team at McGraw Hill including Lalit Singh, Tanweer Ahmed, Nikhil Wadhera, Atul Gupta, Pranay Neema, Anjali Nair, Mausumi Mukherjee, Rahul Bhatadia, Sneha Roy, Tanya Jain and others for their effort and unstinted cooperation in bringing out this `Courseware on Polity Simplifed.'

April 2025 **Rangarajan R**

Preface to the First Edition

The Indian Constitution is an important part of the syllabus for the UPSC Civil Services Examination (UPSC CSE) as well as other State Public Service Commission (SPSC) examinations. These exams test the understanding of candidates on various provisions of the Constitution and the concepts underlying the same. It plays a pivotal role in the Preliminary examination stage in all exams and especially in the UPSC CSE. Answering the questions from the Constitution correctly is key to obtaining the required cut-off marks for qualifying for the Mains examination. It also plays an important role in the General Studies papers of Mains (including ethics paper in the UPSC CSE). The concepts and the provisions of the Constitution also help candidates while writing their essays on contemporary issues.

There are standard textbooks, which have been authored over the years by legal luminaries and professors on the Indian Constitution. They are valuable in helping readers understand the subject and also help candidates prepare for these exams.

Having said that, based on my own experience of having successfully cleared the UPSC CSE in 2005 (AIR-46) and training aspirants for the same exam over the last 10 years, I felt there was a need to simplify the Indian Constitution from the candidates' point of view. Many of them are from science and engineering backgrounds with no training in law and humanities. Many of the terms that are easily understood by students with a background in law are entirely new for these candidates. Even for the candidates who have a background in social science and humanities, the concepts and the provisions of the Constitution need to be explained in simpler terms with adequate examples. It starts with a simple requirement of arranging the various parts of the Constitution, not in the order as it is written for administering the country, but in an order that will help a new candidate understand it from an examination point of view.

It is with the above objective that I am writing this book as part of the McGraw Concept Series. It is a textbook, which will help any reader understand the provisions of the Constitution of India along with key underlying concepts. But over and above that, it also will serve as a guide for the candidates to grasp various aspects of the Constitution in a simple manner with adequate examples and case studies as required. The underlying background/concepts for various provisions of the Constitution are discussed with flowcharts, mind maps and tables at appropriate places. The discussion in the NCERT textbooks is also suitably covered under the respective chapters. Apart from this, there are two unique features in this book. Firstly, the key concepts and provisions in each chapter have been highlighted for better visibility. Secondly, innovative and easy to remember 'Mnemonics' for important provisions have been provided at the end of each chapter. This will enable the candidates to answer the MCQs in any Preliminary examination (UPSC and SPSC) as well as write descriptive answers in the Mains examination.

The relevant UPSC Preliminary examination questions of previous years have been solved after each chapter along with explanation. The Mains examination questions have also been presented with a model answer at the end of the respective chapters. This would help candidates in understanding the structuring and presentation that is required in the Mains examination. While the UPSC questions have been used for this exercise, this would definitely help candidates taking up any SPSC examination as well.

There are practice questions available on the 'edge' platform that will help the readers in self-assessment. The book is also supplemented with audio-visual content. Based on my experience of having conducted online classes, the key aspects and trap areas of chapters are provided in visual modules for supplementing the reading of the book. This will enhance the learning and revision experience of the readers.

With that firm belief, I welcome you to this journey of understanding Indian Polity.

ARRANGEMENTS OF CHAPTERS

Based on my experience of training aspirants for UPSC CSE, I have realised that while the Constitution has been written for the governance of the country, the candidates need to understand the same in a systematic order that makes it simpler. Hence, the arrangement of chapters in this book is different from other standard textbooks on the subject. It is based on the principle of simplifying the Constitution for the candidate. For example, after understanding the provisions in the Constitution relating to Parts I and II, the discussion will move to Parts V and VI that deal with the executive, the legislature and the judiciary. This is because executive and legislature are the organs of governance that constitute the State. Without a basic understanding of these branches, the discussion on the Fundamental Rights in Part III, enumerating the rights and also placing restrictions on the State, will not be understood in the right way. Similarly, the understanding of organs of the State is essential to appreciate the directives that have been provided in Part IV. Readers will be able to appreciate Centre-State relations, Emergency provisions etc., that are part of our federal set up only after understanding the provisions of the Union and the States with respect to the legislature and the executive. To summarise, the arrangement of chapters in this book will follow an order that will simplify the understanding process of the Indian Constitution.

Rangarajan R

Contents

CHAPTER 1

Basic Concepts

LEARNING OUTCOMES

1. Knowing the arrangement of the Constitution into Parts, Articles and Schedules
2. Exploring the key terms used in the Constitution that would facilitate better understanding while reading various chapters

The Constitution of India is one of the most important parts of the syllabus for any Public Service Commission examination. The entire governance of the country is based on this primary law of the country. Hence, it is important to understand the provisions and underlying concepts thoroughly for doing well in these examinations. Further, it will continue to be guiding force for the civil servants after they get selected into any service at the Union or the State level.

This introductory chapter is aimed at providing a basic idea about the terms that will be used in the subsequent chapters. This is provided in the beginning considering the requirement of many candidates and this will help readers appreciate these terms and the discussions in subsequent chapters.

1.1 ARRANGEMENT OF THE CONSTITUTION

The Constitution of India is arranged in the following manner. References will be made to these terms regularly as part of the discussion in subsequent chapters.

Arrangement	Explanation
Parts of the Constitution	• Parts of the Constitution are like lessons/unit in a book. Each Part deals with an individual topic or related topics. For example, Part I deals with Union and its territory; Part II deals with Citizenship; Part III deals with Fundamental rights etc. • Some of these parts are further sub-divided into chapters with each chapter dealing with a specific area within the topic. For example, Part V deals with the topic of Union; Chapter I deals with the Executive; Chapter II deals with the Parliament; Chapter IV with the Union Judiciary etc. • The Constitution is divided into 25 parts as on date (2024).

Arrangement	Explanation
Articles, clauses and sub-clauses	• Each Part of the Constitution is divided into Articles. Articles are the numbered sections under the parts of the Constitution. For example, Part I (Union and its territory) comprises Articles 1 to 4; Part II (Citizenship) comprises Articles 5 to 11; Part III (Fundamental rights) comprises Articles 12 to 35 etc. • The Articles may contain clauses that are again numbered as (1), (2), (3) etc., and sub-clauses that may be numbered as (a), (b), (c) and further into (i), (ii), (iii) etc. • The Constitution at present has around 450 articles (2024).
Schedules	• Schedules to the Constitution are similar to annexures that form part of the Constitution. • These Schedules elaborate or supplement the provisions contained in some of the Parts/Articles. For example, the First Schedule provides the list of States and Union Territories as mentioned in Article 1; the Fourth Schedule provides for the allocation of seats in Rajya Sabha to various States as mentioned in Article 80; the Tenth Schedule contains the provisions as to disqualification on the ground of defection as mentioned in Article 102 etc. • The Constitution at present has 12 schedules (2024).
Amendments	• An amendment of the Constitution is a change made to the provisions of the Constitution. An amendment may add, vary or repeal any of the provisions. • It may have the effect of amending a Part, an article or a Schedule. Amendments are carried out by the Parliament in accordance with the provisions of Article 368. • There have been 106 amendments till date (2024) of the Constitution.

1.2 GLOSSARY

It must be noted that this is not an exhaustive list but only a primary list of certain key terms. Other terms that are of legal nature will be adequately explained in the respective places of the chapters as considered necessary.

Term	Meaning
Political system and Political Science	• Political system is the form of political organisation that can be observed in a society. Various types of political system include democracy, monarchy, authoritarianism and totalitarianism. • Political science is the organised body of knowledge/discipline dealing with concepts and theories concerning the process of politics and political systems.
Organs/Branches of Governance	• There are three main branches of the government viz. the executive, the legislature and the judiciary. • The legislature is a body that enacts various laws as per the powers given to it under the Constitution. In India, the Parliament is the Union legislature and every State has its own legislature. • The executive is a branch that implements the laws and administers the government. The Union executive in India is the President, the Prime Minister and ministers while the State executive is the Governor, the Chief Minister and ministers. • The judiciary is an independent branch that is formed for interpreting the Constitution, various laws and also for delivery of justice. The judiciary in India consists of the Supreme Court, the High Courts and the lower courts.

Term	Meaning
State	• The term 'State' refers to political organisation that comprises the legislature and the executive. • In India, 'State' in this context could refer to the Union Parliament and the Union Government as well as the State Legislature and the State Governments. This term is used regularly to describe the government machinery. • When used in this context, it should not be confused with the States in our country like Uttar Pradesh, Bihar, Karnataka etc.
Laws	• Laws are enacted by Parliament and State legislatures. They derive the power to enact laws from the Constitution. Such laws are referred to as 'act' or 'statute.' Examples – Income Tax Act, GST Act, Companies Act, The Uttar Pradesh Fire Prevention and Fire Safety Act.
Case law	• The law of the country primarily consists of legal provisions as laid down in the Constitution and under various laws made by the legislature as per its powers. • Case law is the law based on judgements made by the courts in earlier cases. The Supreme Court and the High Courts interpret the Constitution while delivering judgements and they form the basis for such case laws. • Important case laws based on the Supreme Court judgements are adequately discussed in respective chapters. • The term 'Union of India' in these case laws would mean a case against the Government of India. Similarly, the name of the State is mentioned in cases involving the State governments. For example, the term 'State of Kerala' would mean a case against the Government of Kerala.
Deemed	• This is a legal term that is used in some of the provisions of the Constitution. • 'To deem' is to 'consider something as having certain characteristics'. In simple words, it means that it is legally believed to be in a particular manner. • For example, the provision that 'it is deemed to have been passed by both the Houses' would mean that 'it is legally believed to have been passed by both the Houses'.
Ceased	• The word 'cease' means 'to stop'. So, whenever the Constitution uses the term 'ceased to have effect' or 'ceased to operate' etc., it means 'stopped to have effect or operate'.
Convention/ Custom	• It means a traditional/acceptable way of doing something over a period of time. This is not a written law or a rule, but is usually followed by all, without violation. For example, the British Parliamentary system is based on the conventions and customs that have developed over the years.
Ratification	• The act of giving formal consent/approval to a contract, agreement or treaty. In the context of Constitution, it is providing approval for an amendment to the Constitution.
Notwithstanding anything in the Constitution/Part/ Chapter	• This term is used at the beginning of some of the articles of the Constitution. It means that such an article is superior to other articles of that chapter or part or entire Constitution as the case may be. In other words, in case of any inconsistency between such article and any other provision in that chapter or part or entire Constitution, such article shall prevail.

Term	Meaning
Subject to other provisions of the Constitution/Part/ Chapter	• This term is used at the beginning of some of the articles of the Constitution. It means that such an article is inferior to other articles of that chapter or part or entire Constitution as the case may be. In other words, in case of any inconsistency between such article and any other provision in that chapter or part or entire Constitution, such article shall yield to the other provision which will prevail.
Basic structure	• It was a principle that was created by the Supreme Court in the ***Kesavananda Bharati case*** law in 1973. It is a set of principles which are very basic to the Constitution that cannot be violated by the Parliament even through a constitutional amendment.

1.3 CERTAIN ADDITIONAL CONCEPTS

Elements of State

STATE

Population	In pre-democratic forms of state like absolute monarchy, people within the purview of State were called as 'subjects.' In democratic and modern societies, people are expected to participate in the affairs of the State and are called 'citizens.'
Sovereignty	It refers to undisputed legal authority of the State. It is the authority of the State to govern itself i.e., self-governing nature of the State.
Government	Element of state through which sovereign power is exercised, apparatus for functioning of the State, set of institutions and procedures for exercise of power.
Territory	It is the portion of geographic space, containing land, water and air, over which the State exercises power and control.

Difference between State and Nation

State	Nation
It is a legal and political entity. It may or may not coincide with a sense of solidarity.	Refers to psychological and emotional solidarity on various grounds like language, religion, race, customs, culture etc.
It is a territorial concept.	It is a concept of people's consciousness.

A Nation-State is a sovereign country of which most citizens are also united by factors such as language, common descent, religion or culture. India is a unique country with multiple diversities on account of language, religion and culture. However, there is also a civilisational unity in the sub-continent. Hence, many experts have opined that India is not a strict Nation-State as per western definition neither is it a State-Nation where several identities merely exist within a geographical boundary. It can be called a 'civilisational-State' where multiple languages, religion and culture co-exist connected by the civilisational history and heritage.

1.4 KEY WORDS IN MAINS QUESTIONS

UPSC has around 10–15 key words or tail words that may be asked as part of the question in Mains examination. The below table provides a broad direction about the approach to answer some of those key/tail words that are often asked in questions on Polity and Governance.

S.No.	Key Word	Broad Direction/Approach
1	Discuss	It requires discussion on various aspects relating to the topic. There may be two, three or four angles that form the sub-headings for such discussion. The conclusion can highlight your view or way forward based on such discussion.
2	Comment	It is providing a commentary by picking main points about the topic and supplementing it with your opinion. Such mains points may be 3-4 in number that can be used as sub-headings as well.
3	Enumerate	Provide details in a point-wise format. There is not much of discussion/ analysis or opinion required.
4	Elucidate	This requires providing insights or supporting the statement/hypothesis in the question. This can be considered as an 80:20 question where 80% of the answer involves supporting the statement in the question with explanations and examples. The balance 20% can summarise the counter view in brief with conclusion on a positive note.
5	(Critically) Analyse/ (Critically) Evaluate (Critically) Examine	Whether the question is to Analyse/Evaluate/Examine or to do so 'critically', answer both type of questions with a 50:50 approach. The pros and cons relating to the topic in question needs to be discussed/analysed in equal measure with conclusion on a positive note with your opinion.
6	Describe	It requires providing insights into the topic in an objective manner.
7	Summarise	To provide summary of a topic in a condensed form that focuses on main points or facts.

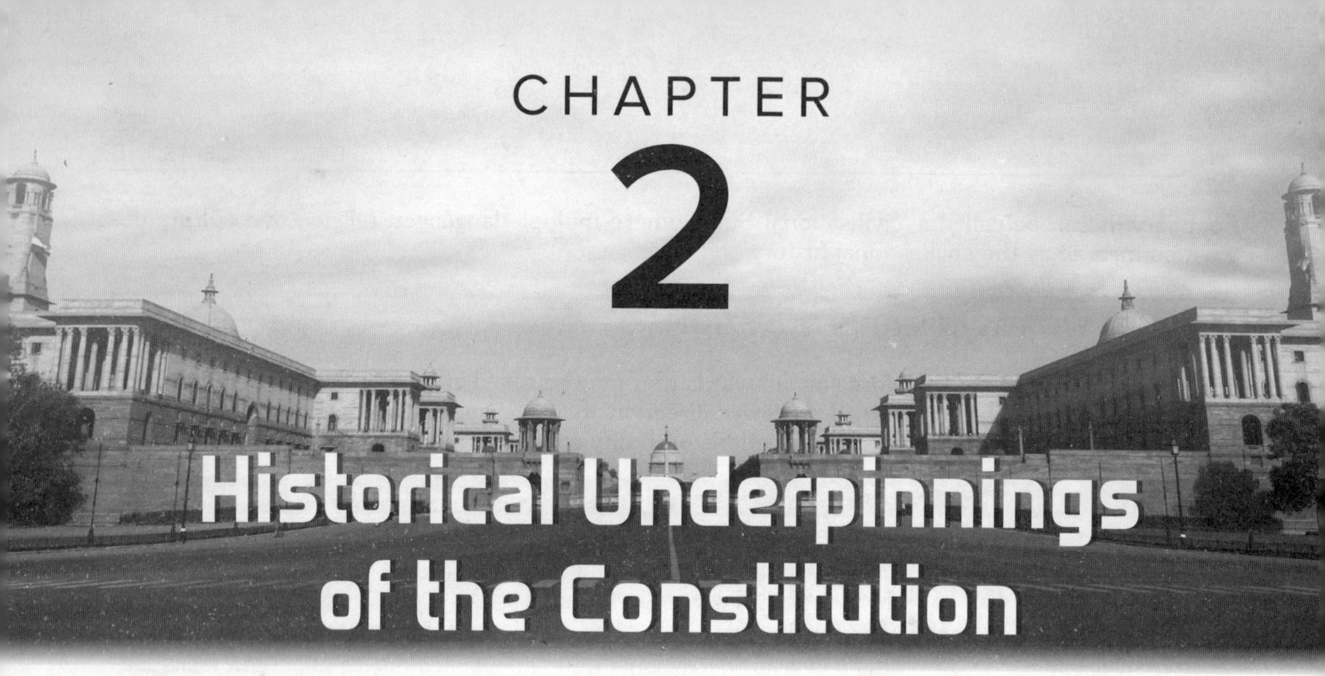

CHAPTER 2

Historical Underpinnings of the Constitution

LEARNING OUTCOMES

1. Understanding the evolution of Constitutional Governance in India during the British colonial rule
2. Gaining insight into significant laws and reforms during the British rule, and their impact on Indian governance
3. Learning about the contributions of leaders, reformers, and socio-political movements in laying the groundwork for a democratic and independent constitution
4. Exploring the formation of the Constituent assembly and its work that resulted in the adoption of our Constitution

One can trace the history of constitutional development in India from 1773 with the Regulating Act passed by the British Parliament to bring a framework to regulate the East India Company (EIC or the 'Company'). The British Parliament passed several Charter Acts to amend the Company's rule in India. These amendments provided for the historical growth of the Constitution of India and also paved the way for the development of the constituent assembly in India.

The freedom fighters of India demanded many reforms in constitutional arrangements during the colonial rule. For this purpose, the British Parliament passed the 'Government of India Act, 1858' and later three more Acts i.e., in 1861, 1892 and 1909 respectively. These Acts were enacted to amend and reform the constitutional system of India. The main objective behind these Acts was to decentralise and streamline the British administration in India. It further led to the passing of the Government of India Act, 1935 which formed the basis for many of the provisions in our Indian Constitution with respect to the executive, the legislature, the judiciary, centre-state relations, emergency provisions etc.

In this chapter, we shall understand the key provisions of various Acts starting from the Regulating Act, 1773 to the Government of India Act, 1935. These were the enactments that acted like a constitution for administering the country under the British that finally concluded with the Indian Independence Act, 1947. We shall then discuss the formation and functioning of the Constituent Assembly that prepared and adopted our Constitution.

The period of 1857–58 was a watershed moment during the British rule as the 'Sepoy Mutiny', also known as the 'First War of Independence', happened in that year. The British rule was through the EIC till 1857–58. Subsequently, the Government of India Act, 1858 was passed that dissolved the EIC and the country's administration was directly brought under the British Crown. Hence, we can broadly segregate the laws passed during the British rule for administering our country as 'pre-1857' and 'post-1857'.

Laws during British Rule	
Pre-1857 – Rule by EIC	**Post-1857 – Rule by British Crown**
1. Regulating Act, 1773	1. Government of India Act, 1858
2. Pitt's Act, 1784	2. Indian Councils Act, 1861
3. Charter Act, 1793	3. Indian Councils Act, 1892
4. Charter Act, 1813	4. Indian Councils Act, 1909
5. Charter Act, 1833	5. Government of India Act, 1919
6. Charter Act, 1853	6. Government of India Act, 1935

In the discussion about these Acts in the subsequent sections, it must be understood that the term 'British Crown' or 'Royal assent' etc., would refer to the British Government. Since the King/Queen is the ceremonial head of Britain, these terms are also used to refer to its government.

2.1 ACTS BEFORE 1857 – RULE BY EAST INDIA COMPANY (EIC)

2.1.1 Regulating Act, 1773

The Regulating Act of 1773 was the first and the most notable attempt made by the Parliament of Britain to regulate and control the affairs of the EIC in India. This Act was an important landmark in the growth of the Indian administration under the British rule. There was no dominant authority before 1773 in India. The EIC was extensively ruling over Bombay, Bengal and Madras presidencies by the headship of Governor-in-Council responsible to the Court of Directors in England. This Act recognised the political and administrative functions of the Company for the first time and laid the foundation for centralised administration.

The salient features of this Act were as follows:

1. It designated the Governor of Bengal as the 'Governor-General of Bengal' and created an advisory Executive Council of four members. The first such Governor-General to be appointed was Lord Warren Hastings.
2. This Act made the Governors of Bombay and Madras presidencies subordinate to the Governor-General of Bengal.
3. It provided for the establishment of a Supreme Court at Calcutta in 1774 consisting of a Chief Justice and three judges. Sir Elijah Impey was appointed as the first Chief Justice in 1774.
4. This Act prohibited the servants of the Company from engaging in any private trade or accepting presents or bribes from the natives.
5. This Act strengthened the control of the British Government over the Company by requiring the Court of Directors to report on the revenue, civil and military affairs in India.

The Amending Act of 1781 (Act of Settlement) was passed to address the issues in the Regulating Act of 1773. The key features of this Amending Act were as follows:

- It exempted the Governor-General, his Executive Council members and servants of the Company from the jurisdiction of the Supreme Court for their official actions. Similarly, revenue matters were also excluded from the jurisdiction of the Supreme Court.
- ***The Supreme Court was to exercise jurisdiction over all the people in Calcutta by administering their personal laws according to their religion. It meant that Hindus would be tried according to Hindu laws, Muslims according to Mohammedan laws etc.***
- The appeals from the provincial courts were to be taken up by the Governor-General in Council, who was empowered to frame regulations for provincial courts and councils.

2.1.2 Pitt's Act, 1784

This Act strengthened the position of the Governor-General in Council vis-a-vis the Supreme Court. The Company's administration was changed by this Act. The salient features of this Act were as follows:

1. It distinguished between the commercial and political functions of the Company.
2. This Act established a board for the affairs of India known as the Board of Control (BOC). The BOC consisted of a chancellor of the exchequer, a Secretary of State and four members of the Privy Council. The BOC was vested with the power of appointing any of the Company's servants.
3. The Court of Directors were bound by all orders of the Board touching the civil and military government and the revenues of India. Thus, the BOC was responsible for the civil and military government in India while the Court of Directors were mainly responsible for commercial activities. This setup was also known as 'Dual Control' or 'Double Government'.

However, this Act was significant as for the first time the Company's territory in India was called British possession in India and the British government was given supreme control over Company's affairs and its administration in the country.

There was an Act of 1786 that made the Governor-General of Bengal the Commander-in-Chief and also gave him powers to override the decision of the council in special cases.

2.1.3 Charter Act, 1793

The key features of the Charter Act, 1793 were as follows:

1. ***It gave the Governor-General more powers and control over the subordinate presidencies of Bombay and Madras.***
2. ***It extended the trade monopoly of the Company in India for another period of 20 years.***
3. It laid down that the members of the BOC and their staff would be paid out of the Indian revenues.
4. The royal approval of the British Crown was mandated for the appointment of the Governor-General, the Governors and the Commander-in-Chief.
5. The Company was empowered to give licences to individuals as well as the Company's employees to trade in India. The licences, known as 'privilege' or 'country trade', paved the way for shipments of opium to China.

MNEMONICS

Concept or Provisions	Shortcut or Mnemonics	Details to Remember
Key provisions of First three acts – 1773, 1784 and 1793	**Governor-General** of Bengal became **Supreme** and acted as **B & C** in **Dual** role (BCD) who continued playing **Monopoly for twenty years**.	• 1773 – Governor-General of Bengal and first Supreme Court established. • 1784 – Board of Control and Court of Directors resulting in Dual Control • 1793 – Trade Monopoly extended for 20 years

2.1.4 Charter Act, 1813

In England, the business interests were pressing for an end to the EIC's monopoly over trade in India because of a spirit of laissez-faire (free trade). The continental system by Napoleon also meant that the European ports were closed for Britain. Thus, the avenues for trade were reduced for the British merchants and they looked at the Indian sub-continent as an important market for their goods.

The important features of the Act were as follows:

1. ***It abolished the trade monopoly of the EIC in India i.e., the Indian trade was open to all British merchants. However, it continued the monopoly of the Company over trade in tea and trade with China.***
2. The Company was to retain the possession of territories and the revenue for 20 years more, without prejudice to the sovereignty of the Crown. It also asserted the sovereignty of the British Crown over the Company's territories in India.
3. Separate accounts were to be kept regarding commercial transactions and territorial revenues. The power of superintendence and direction of the BOC was not only defined but also enlarged considerably.
4. The regulations made by the Councils of Madras, Bombay and Calcutta were now required to be laid before the British Parliament. The constitutional position of the British territories in India was thus explicitly defined for the first time.
5. ***It allowed the Christian missionaries to come to India for the purpose of enlightening the people about Christianity.***
6. ***It provided for the spread of western education among the people of the British territories in India.***

2.1.5 Charter Act, 1833

The key features of this Act were as follows:

1. ***It made the Governor-General of Bengal the Governor-General of India*** and vested in him all civil and military powers. ***Lord William Bentinck was the first Governor-General of India.***
2. This Act deprived the Governors of Bombay and Madras of their legislative powers. The Governor-General of India had exclusive legislative powers for the whole of British India. The council was to consist of totally four members, of whom one was a Law member who could

attend the council meetings only when it performed legislative functions. When the council performed executive functions, it consisted of Governor-General and three members.

3. The Act abolished the Company's trading monopoly completely. ***The EIC was no longer a commercial body but only an administrative body.***
4. This Act was an attempt to introduce a system of open competition for the selection of civil servants and stated that the Indians should not be debarred from holding any place, office or employment under the Company. However, after opposition from the Court of Directors, this provision was not implemented under this Act but was later implemented in 1854.

2.1.6 Charter Act, 1853

Under the Charter Act of 1853, the road to the final surrender of authority by the EIC was initiated. This Act allowed the Company to govern only until Parliament shall otherwise provide. This Act was a significant constitutional landmark in India. The key features of the Act were as follows:

1. This Act for the first time separated the legislative and the executive functions of the Governor-General in Council. Thus, it laid the foundation for a parliamentary system of government.
2. This Act provided for addition of six new members declared as legislative councillors. By this Act, the legislative wing of the council worked as a mini-parliament.
3. By this Act local representatives in the Indian Legislative Council were introduced – four representative members drawn from among the Company's servants appointed by the local governments of Bengal, Bombay, Madras and Agra.
4. This Act introduced an open competition system of selection and recruitment of civil servants. It was also thrown open to Indians and the Macaulay Committee was appointed in 1854.

MNEMONICS

Concept or Provisions	Shortcut or Mnemonics	Details to Remember
Key provisions of next 3 acts – 1813, 1833 & 1853	**No Monopoly except while having Chinese Tea** and stopped that also after **becoming Governor-General of India** and laid **foundation for Parliament**.	• 1813 – Abolished trade monopoly except trade in tea and trade with China. • 1833 – Governor-General of Bengal made Governor-General of India; EIC only administrative body. • 1853 – Separated legislative and executive functions and laid foundation for Parliamentary system of Government.

2.2 ACTS AFTER 1857 – RULE BY BRITISH CROWN

The 'First War of Independence' or the 'Sepoy Mutiny' that happened in 1857 resulted in the dissolution of EIC and assumption of the entire administration of the country directly under the British Government.

2.2.1 Government of India Act, 1858

The Government of India Act, 1858 ended the Company rule and transferred the government of the country directly to the British Crown. The Company rule was, thus, ended and the administration was carried out in the name of the Crown through the Secretary of State.

The Secretary assumed the powers of the Company's Board of Directors (BOD) as well as the BOC. The Secretary of State, accountable to the British Parliament was to be supported by the ***Council of India comprising fifteen members.*** The Crown was required to appoint eight members for the Council, while the BOD was to elect the remaining seven. The main features of this Act were as follows:

1. It made the administration of the country unitary as well as rigidly centralised. Though the territory was divided into provinces with a Governor or Lieutenant Governor headed by his Executive Council, yet the provincial governments were mere agents of the Government at the centre. They had to function under the superintendence, direction and control of the Governor-General in all matters related to the governance of the province.
2. The Governor-General was designated as Viceroy and Governor-General of India, commonly shortened to Viceroy of India. The Governor-General was as such for the provinces and he acted as the Viceroy for the Princely States. Lord Canning was made the first viceroy of India.
3. It made no provision for the separation of functions. The entire authority for the governance of India like civil, military, executive and legislative was handed over to the Governor-General in Council, who was accountable to the Secretary of State.
4. The Secretary of State had complete control over the Indian administration. The BOC and the Court of Directors were abolished and their powers were transferred to the Secretary of State of India and the Indian Council.

2.2.2 Indian Councils Act, 1861

The Indian Councils Act, 1861 made various contributions to the process of making the Constitution of India. The main features of the Act were as follows:

1. It introduced a representative institution in India for the first time. ***As per this Act, the Executive Council of the Viceroy was to comprise of some Indians as nonofficial members in connection with the legislative business.***
2. It initiated the process of decentralisation by restoring the legislative powers to the Bombay and Madras presidencies. It established new legislative councils for Bengal (1862), North-Western Frontier Province (1866) and Punjab (1897).
3. The Act gave powers to the Governor-General to enact rules for convenient transaction of business in the Council. It also empowered the Governor-General/Viceroy to issue ordinances during an emergency, valid up to 6 months, without the approval of Legislative Council.
4. ***Another feature of the Act was its statutory recognition of the portfolio system.*** Under this system, a member of the Viceroy's Council was made in-charge of one or more departments of the Government. He was authorised to issue orders on behalf of the Council on matters relating to his department(s). With this, the foundation of the cabinet form of government was formed in India.

2.2.3 Indian Councils Act, 1892

The Indian Councils Act of 1892 was the first result of the Indian National Congress (INC) which was formed in 1885. The legislative reforms introduced under the Act of 1861 did not meet the aspirations of the people of India. The non-official Indians were mainly comprised of big zamindars, Indian princes or retired officials, who were entirely unaware of the problems of the common man. Thus, the people of India were not happy. The Act of 1892 was to address some of these issues. The main features of this Act were as follows:

1. The Act enlarged the Legislative Council's working in India, both central and provincial, by increasing the number of additional (non-official) members though official majority was maintained.
2. The electoral system was introduced in India by this Act in 1892. Though the word 'election' was not used in the Act and the term used was 'nomination'. The non-official members were nominated as follows:
   - In the Central Legislative Council by the Viceroy on the recommendation of the Provincial Legislative Councils and Bengal Chamber of Commerce;
   - In the Provincial Legislative Councils by the Governors on the recommendation of district boards, municipalities, trade associations, universities etc.
3. This Act gave more powers to the Legislative Councils. The members of the Council were allowed to discuss the budget and also put questions to the executive councillors.

2.2.4 Indian Councils Act, 1909

Indian Councils Act, 1909 was also known as Morley–Minto Reforms. This Act was passed 17 years after the passage of the Indian Councils Act of 1892. It was the next step of the constitutional reform in India by the British Government. Lord Morley, the Secretary of State for India, announced that his government wished to create new reforms for India, wherein the locals would be granted more power in legislative affairs. Lord Minto was the Viceroy of India at that time. The important features of the Act were as follows:

THINK ABOUT IT

Do you agree that the Indian Councils Act, 1909 sowed the seeds for partition of the country? Analyse by citing the key provisions of the Act.

1. This Act simplified the election of Indians in Legislative Councils. Prior to this, some Indians were nominated to Legislative Councils, majority of which remained under the appointments of the British government. This Act introduced the electoral principle discussing the framework for a parliamentary system. Local bodies would elect an electoral college, which in turn would elect the members of provincial legislatures, who in turn would elect members of the central legislature.
2. This Act increased the number of members of the Legislative Council at the Centre from 16 to 60. The size of the Councils of provinces was enlarged by including non-official members. The functions of the Legislative Councils were increased by this Act. It allowed the members to discuss the budget and move resolutions, ask supplementary questions, discuss matters of public interest, etc.
3. The official majority was retained in the Central Legislative Council. However, in provinces, non-official members formed the majority.
4. *This Act granted the Muslims the right of a 'separate electorate'.* This meant that from the constituencies reserved for Muslims, the members were to be elected only by Muslims.

5. This Act provided for the association of Indians with the Executive Councils of the Viceroy and Governors. ***Satyendra Prasad Sinha became the first Indian to join the Viceroy's Executive Council.*** He was appointed as the law member.

2.2.5 Government of India Act, 1919

The British Government, on 20 August 1917, proclaimed various objectives to introduce a responsible government in India. This was famously known as the 'August Declaration'. For this, the British Parliament enacted the Government of India Act, 1919 which came into force in 1921. The Act embodied the reforms recommended in the joint report of Sir Edwin Montagu (who was the Secretary of State for India) and Lord Chelmsford (who was the Viceroy of India). Hence, it is also known as Montagu–Chelmsford Reforms.

It was passed to expand the participation of the natives in the Government of India. The Act broadly emphasised on the dual form of government, called 'Diarchy', for major provinces. The key features of the Act were as follows:

1. It separated the subjects as central and provincial, thereby reducing the central control over provinces. The central and provincial legislatures were authorised to make laws on their respective list of subjects. However, it must be noted that this was through a scheme of delegation (and not a federal setup) and the structure of government continued to be unitary.
2. It further divided the provincial subjects into two categories – 'transferred' and 'reserved'. This system was known as 'Diarchy (Dyarchy)'. The transferred subjects were to be administered by the Governor with the aid of Ministers responsible to the Legislative Council. Subjects in the 'transferred' list included education, health, local government, industry, religious endowments etc. The reserved subjects, on the other hand, were to be administered by the Governor and his Executive Council without being responsible to the Legislative Council. These subjects included law and order, irrigation, finance, land revenue etc.
3. It introduced bicameralism and direct elections in the country. The Central Parliament was a bicameral legislature consisting of an Upper House (Council of States) and a Lower House (Legislative Assembly). The majority of members of both the Houses were chosen by direct election. It granted franchise to a limited number of people on the basis of property, tax or education.
4. The Central Legislative Assembly had 145 members of whom 41 were nominated and the rest were elected. The Council of States had 60 members of whom 34 were elected and 26 nominated.
5. It required that three of the six members of the Viceroy's Executive Council (other than the Commander-in-Chief) were to be Indian.
6. It extended the principle of communal representation by providing separate electorates for Sikhs, Indian Christians, Anglo-Indians and Europeans.
7. It provided for the establishment of a public service commission. Hence, a Central Public Service Commission was set up in 1926 for recruiting civil servants.
8. It separated, for the first time, provincial budgets from the central budget and authorised the provincial legislatures to enact their budgets.
9. It provided for the appointment of a statutory commission to inquire into and report on its working after ten years of its coming into force.

THINK ABOUT IT

To what extent did the Government of India Act, 1919, succeed in introducing a representative government in India, and how did its limitations influence the demand for greater self-governance?

2.2.6 Government of India Act, 1935

Simon Commission

In November 1927 (two years before schedule), the British Government appointed a statutory commission, known as Simon Commission, as envisaged by the Government of India Act, 1919 to make an enquiry in the functioning of the Act. Sir John Simon was the chairman of the commission, which consisted of members who were all British. All the parties in India boycotted the commission. The commission gave its final report in 1930. This report was given consideration at the round table conferences that created a 'white paper'. The 'White Paper on Constitutional Reforms' was examined by a joint select committee of the British Parliament. The committee presented a draft bill on 5 February 1935. The recommendations of this committee were incorporated in the Government of India Act, 1935.

Communal Award

In August 1932, Ramsay McDonald, the British Prime Minister, announced a scheme of representation of the minorities, which came to be known as the 'Communal Award'. The award while continuing with separate electorates for the Muslims, Sikhs, Indian Christians, Anglo-Indians and Europeans (that were present from the previous Acts), also extended it to the depressed classes (presently the Scheduled Castes). Mahatma Gandhi was not in favour of this extension of the principle of the communal representation to the depressed classes as he feared that it would disintegrate the Hindu society. He undertook fast unto death in Yerawada jail at Poona to get the award modified. Lastly, there was an agreement between the leaders of the Congress and the depressed classes. This agreement is known as *'Poona Pact'*. This agreement continued with a common electorate for Hindus and reserved seats to the depressed classes in India. This was also incorporated in the Government of India Act, 1935.

The Government of India Act, 1935 was another landmark towards a completely responsible Government in India. The key features of the Act were as follows:

1. **Establishment of federal features with provincial autonomy** – This Act provided for the establishment of an All-India Federation comprising the provinces and princely states as units. Though the Act advocated the provinces and the princely states as units in the federation, it was optional for the princely states to accept this provision. The princely states did not join the federation as envisaged in the Act and hence the federation envisaged by the Act was not operational. It was a federal setup only with respect to the provinces.

   The legislative powers were divided between the Provinces and the Centre into three lists. These were the Federal list, the Provincial list and the Concurrent list. The Federal list for the centre consisted of 59 items such as external affairs; currency and coinage; naval, military and air forces; and census, etc. The Provincial list consisted of 54 items which dealt with subjects such as police, provincial public services, education etc. The Concurrent list comprised of 36 items dealing with subjects like criminal law and procedure, civil procedure, marriage and divorce, and abortion etc. The residuary powers were given to the Governor-General.

2. **Introduction of provincial autonomy** – This Act provided provincial autonomy which was introduced in April 1937. Within its well-defined sphere, the provinces were no longer delegates of the central government but were autonomous units of the administration. The executive

authority of a province was to be exercised by a Governor on behalf of the Crown and not as a subordinate of the Governor-General. The Governor acted in consultation with the ministers who were accountable to the legislature. However, the Governor was given some supplementary powers which could be exercised by him at his 'discretion' or in the exercise of his 'individual decision' in certain matters without taking advice from the ministers. The governors were given special responsibilities to act in their individual judgement and assume all powers in the case of a breakdown of constitutional machinery.

3. **Diarchy at the centre** – The Act abolished diarchy in the provinces and introduced the system of diarchy at the centre. According to this system, the administration of defence, external affairs, ecclesiastical affairs, and of tribal areas, was to be made by the Governor-General in his discretion with the help of 'counsellors' appointed by him. These counsellors were not responsible to the legislature. With regards to matters other than the above-reserved subjects, the Governor-General was to act on the advice of a council of ministers who were responsible to the legislature. However, this provision of diarchy at the centre was never operationalised.
4. **Introduction of bicameralism in provinces** – ***It also introduced bicameralism in six out of eleven provinces***, and these provinces were Assam, Bombay, Bengal, Bihar, Madras and the United Provinces. It would consist of a legislative council and a legislative assembly.
5. **Replacement of Indian Council** – This Act replaced the Council of India set up under the Government of India Act, 1858. In its place, few advisors were nominated to assist the Secretary of State for India.
6. **The enlarged electorate** – This Act lowered the franchise qualification thereby enlarging the electorate. Around ten per cent of the population got the right to vote for the provincial legislatures. It provided reserved seats for Scheduled Castes under common/general electorate. It also provided reserved seats for women and labour through separate electorates. 'Communal representation' with separate electorates for various religious minorities continued in this Act.
7. **Establishment of a federal court** – This Act established a federal court with both original and appellate jurisdiction.
8. **Establishment of Reserve Bank** – This Act provided for the establishment of a Reserve Bank of India (RBI) to control the financial condition and currency of the country. The Reserve Bank of India was established in 1935 under the RBI Act, 1934.
9. **Federal and Provincial Service Commissions** – This Act provided for the establishment of Federal Public Service Commission and Provincial Public Service Commissions.

It must be noted that many administrative provisions of the Indian Constitution with respect to the executive, the legislature, the judiciary, centre-state relations etc., have been modelled on the basis of the provisions of the Government of India Act, 1935.

MNEMONICS

Concept or Provisions	Shortcut or Mnemonics	Details to Remember
Key provisions of three acts – 1909, 1919 & 1935	**M**anaging **D**irector distributed the **P**owers.	• 1909 – Separate electorate for **M**uslims • 1919 – **D**yarchy at provinces with transferred and reserved subjects • 1935 – **P**rovincial autonomy with distribution of powers between Centre and provinces.

2.2.7 Indian Independence Act, 1947

In 1942, the British set up the Cripps Mission under the chairmanship of Stafford Cripps. The Mission provided a proposal for an elected body to frame a new constitution for India. However, the proposals of the Mission were rejected by all political parties in India including the Indian National Congress (INC) and Muslim League.

In 1945, the *Cabinet Mission* was set up based on which the Constituent Assembly of India was elected. However, the proposal of the Cabinet Mission for unified India failed and the country was partitioned based on the basis of the proposal of the '*Mountbatten Plan*' that was announced in June 1947.

The British Prime Minister Clement Attlee, on 20 February 1947, officially declared that the British rule in India would end by 30 June 1948. In June 1947, the then Viceroy of India, Lord Mountbatten, came up with a plan to partition India into two separate countries viz. India and Pakistan. This was accepted by the INC and the Muslim League. The Indian Independence Act, 1947 was passed by the British Parliament that officially announced the independence of India and the partition of India.

The key features of the Act were as follows:

1. Two separate dominions of India and Pakistan came into existence on 15 August 1947.
2. It abolished the post of Viceroy. There was one Governor-General for each dominion to be appointed by the British King on the advice of the dominion cabinet. However, the British Government had no responsibility with respect to the Government of India or Pakistan.
3. The constituent assemblies of the two dominions were to frame the Constitution of the two countries. They would also work as a constitution making body and a legislative body till the constitutions were adopted and enforced.
4. The Indian princely states were free to join either dominions or remain independent.
5. It dropped the title of Emperor of India from the royal titles of the King of England.
6. It discontinued the appointment of Civil Service and reservation of post by the Secretary of State for India.
7. The Office of Secretary of State for India was ended, and its functions were transferred to the Secretary of State for Commonwealth Affairs.

2.3 CONSTITUENT ASSEMBLY AND MAKING OF THE CONSTITUTION

2.3.1 Creation and Composition of the Constituent Assembly

In 1934, the idea of the Constituent Assembly for India was put forward for the first time by M. N. Roy. He was the pioneer of the communist movement in India. In 1935, the INC officially demanded for setting of a constituent assembly to frame the Constitution of India. Pandit Jawaharlal Nehru, in 1938, on behalf of INC demanded that the Constitution of free India must be framed without any outside intervention and that the Constituent Assembly must be elected on the basis of adult franchise.

Scan the QR code for conceptual video on 'Historical underpinnings of the Constitution'

Mc Graw Hill edge

The Constituent Assembly was elected as per the scheme formulated by the Cabinet Mission Plan. The key features of this scheme were as follows:

1. The total membership of the Assembly was to be 389. It would consist of 292 members to be elected by Provincial legislative assemblies; 93 members to represent the Princely states and 4 members to represent the Chief Commissioners' provinces.
2. The provinces and princely states were to be allotted seats in proportion to their population with roughly one seat being allotted for every ten-lakh population.
3. In the Provinces, the seats were divided amongst Muslims, Sikhs and General (other than Muslims and Sikhs) in proportion to their population. The representatives of each community were to be elected by the members of that community in the provincial legislative assemblies.
4. The representatives of the princely states were nominated by the heads of the princely states.
5. However, as a result of the partition under the Mountbatten Plan of 3 June 1947, a separate Constituent Assembly was set up for Pakistan and representatives of some provinces and princely states ceased to be members of the Assembly. As a result, the membership of the Assembly was reduced to 299 (229 from the British Provinces and 70 from the Princely States).

Provinces

- (a) Seats were divided amongst Muslims, Sikhs and General
  (b) Members elected by Provincial assemblies
- (a) Originally 292 members
  (b) After partition reduced to 229 members

Princely States

- (a) Members to be nominated by the heads of the Princely states
- (a) Originally 93 members
  (b) After partition reduced to 70 members

2.3.2 Working of the Constituent Assembly

The Constituent Assembly met for the first time in New Delhi on 9 December 1946. Dr. Sachchidananda Sinha was elected as the temporary Chairman of the Assembly for two days. Dr. Rajendra Prasad was elected as its President on 11 December 1946.

Jawaharlal Nehru moved the '*Objectives Resolution*' in the Assembly on 13 December 1946 that was finally adopted by the Assembly on 22 January 1947. It set out the key objectives that the Constitution of Sovereign Republic of our country will have that will be the basis for future governance of the country. The Preamble to our Constitution is modelled on the basis of this 'Objectives Resolution'.

THINK ABOUT IT

What were some of the criticisms against the formation of the Constituent Assembly? How did the diverse composition of the Constituent Assembly ensure that the Indian Constitution reflected the aspirations of all sections of society?

The Constituent Assembly took almost 3 years (2 years, 11 months and 18 days to be precise) to complete its historic task of drafting the Constitution for Independent India. During this period, it held 11 sessions covering a total of 165 days.

Some of the important committees of the Constituent Assembly and their Chairman were as follows:

Name of the Committee	Chairman
Drafting Committee	B. R. Ambedkar
Union Powers Committee	Jawaharlal Nehru
Union Constitution Committee	Jawaharlal Nehru
Provincial Constitution Committee	Vallabhbhai Patel
States Committee	Jawaharlal Nehru
Committee on the Rules of Procedure	Rajendra Prasad
Steering Committee	Rajendra Prasad
Finance and Staff Committee	Rajendra Prasad
Ad hoc Committee on the National Flag	Rajendra Prasad
Committee on the Functions of the Constituent Assembly	G. V. Mavalankar
Advisory Committee on Fundamental Rights, Minorities and Tribal and Excluded Areas	Vallabhbhai Patel
Fundamental Rights Sub-Committee	J. B. Kripalani
Credential Committee	Alladi Krishnaswami Ayyar
House Committee	B. Pattabhi Sitaramayya
Order of Business Committee	K. M. Munsi
North-East Frontier Tribal Areas and Assam Excluded and Partially Excluded Areas Sub-Committee	Gopinath Bordoloi
Excluded and Partially Excluded Areas (Other than those in Assam) Sub-Committee	A. V. Thakkar
Minorities Sub-Committee	H.C. Mukherjee
Linguistic Provinces Commission	S.K. Dar
Adhoc Committee on Citizenship	S. Varadachari

The Drafting Committee was the most important Committee that was constituted on 29 August 1947. It consisted of seven members, with Dr. B. R. Ambedkar as its Chairman. This Committee, after taking into consideration the proposals of various other committees (as mentioned above), published the first draft in February 1948. People of India were given eight months' time to discuss the draft and propose amendments. The second draft was published in October 1948.

Dr. Ambedkar introduced the final draft of the Constitution in the Assembly on 4 November 1948. There was an overall discussion on the draft for five days thereafter. The second reading (i.e., clause by clause reading) was carried out between November 1948 and October 1949. The third reading (i.e., final passage of the constitution) started on 14 November 1949 and the motion to adopt the Constitution was declared as passed on 26 November 1949. This is the date that is reflected in our Preamble as the date of enactment and adoption of the Constitution. Out of the 299 members of the Assembly, 284 were present on that date and appended their signatures to the Constitution.

Some of the provisions relating to citizenship, elections, provisional parliament, temporary and transitional provisions came into force immediately on ***26 November 1949***. However, the bulk of the Constitution came into force on ***26 January 1950*** which is mentioned as the ***'date of its commencement'*** in the Constitution. This date was chosen due to the historical significance of 26 January that was celebrated as 'Poorna Swaraj' day in 1930 following the resolution of the Lahore Session of the INC.

Additional Functions of the Constituent Assembly

1. Adopted the National Flag on 22 July 1947.
2. Ratified India's membership of the Commonwealth in May 1949.
3. Adopted the National Anthem and National Song on 24 January 1950.
4. Elected Dr. Rajendra Prasad as the first President on 24 January 1950.
5. The constituent assembly also acted as the legislative body for Independent India (Dominion Legislature) after August 1947, enacting ordinary laws for the country. Whenever, it performed this legislative role, it was presided over by G.V. Mavalankar who was elected as a Speaker for the Dominion Legislature. It continued as the provisional Parliament of India from January 26, 1950 till the formation of new Parliament, after the first general elections in 1951–52.

The Constituent Assembly of India has had its fair share of criticism on various grounds. Some of the important criticisms against the Assembly were as follows:

- It was not an entirely representative body as its members were not directly elected by the people but indirectly elected by members of the provincial legislative assemblies.
- It was dominated by the members of the Congress Party and was also dominated by Hindus.
- It was dominated by lawyers and politicians without adequate representation to other sections of the society.
- It took enormous amount of time to complete the drafting of the Constitution.

However, it must be noted that the Assembly consisted of representatives of all religions including Scheduled Castes, Scheduled Tribes and women. It included all important personalities of the freedom struggle whose main aim was to provide a constitution that would act as the basis for democratic governance while protecting the rights of individuals and minorities.

MAINS STARTER

Area	Building Blocks For Model Introductions
Rule under the East India Company	The Britishers ruled India through the East India Company without any legislative framework till 1773. The first legislation to govern India was the Regulating Act, 1773, which continued the rule under East India Company. The powers and role of the Company were gradually reduced and the administration was directly brought under the British Crown in 1858.
Government of India Act, 1858	The GoI Act, 1858 was a significant legislation enacted after the first war of independence that shook the British empire. It brought the administration of the country directly under the British crown and provided for strict control under the Secretary of State and Governor-General in council.

Area	Building Blocks For Model Introductions
Indian Councils Act, 1909	The Indian Councils Act, 1909, enacted based on the Morley-Minto reforms, was a significant milestone in providing more powers to the locals in the administration of the country. However, it also sowed the seeds for partition by providing separate electorate for Muslims.
Government of India Act, 1919	The GoI Act, 1919, enacted based on the Montagu-Chelmsford reforms, was a significant milestone that expanded the participation of locals in governance of the country. It introduced 'Diarchy' in major provinces through a scheme of delegation.
Government of India Act, 1935	The GoI Act, 1935 was a landmark legislation towards a completely responsible government. It established federal features with provincial autonomy. This Act forms the basis for many aspects of our Constitution.
Constituent Assembly	The Constituent assembly was elected by the members of provincial assemblies and had nominated members from the Princely states. It had representatives from all communities and sections of the society, including many of our freedom fighters, who deliberated and adopted our Constitution.

UPSC Previous Years' Questions of Preliminary Examination

1. Who was the Provisional President of the Constituent Assembly before Dr. Rajendra Prasad took over? **[2024]**

(a) C. Rajagopalachari (b) Dr. B.R. Ambadkar
(c) T.T. Krishnamachari (d) Dr. Sachchidananda Sinha

Solution: (d)

Explanation: As discussed in Section 2.3.2, Dr. Sachchidananda Sinha was temporary Chairman for two days from Dec 9 to 11, 1946 before Rajendra Prasad was elected.

2. With reference to the Government of India Act, 1935, consider the following statements: **[2024]**

1. It provided for the establishment of an All-India Federation based on the union of the British Indian Provinces and Princely States.
2. Defence and Foreign Affairs were kept under the control of the federal legislature.

Which of the statements given above is/are correct?

(a) 1 only (b) 2 only
(c) Both 1 and 2 (d) Neither 1 nor 2

Solution: (c)

Explanation: As discussed in Section 2.2.6, both statements are correct. GoI Act, 1935 provided for the establishment of All-India federation that included both provinces and princely states. However, princely states did not join the federation. External affairs, defence, currency and coinage were all part of the Federal list and federal legislature.

3. By which one of the following Acts was the Governor General of Bengal designated as the Governor General of India? **[2023]**

(a) The Regulating Act (b) The Pitt's India Act
(c) The Charter Act of 1793 (d) The Charter Act of 1833

Solution: (d)

Explanation: As discussed in Section 2.1.5, the answer is (d).

4. In the Government of India Act, 1919, the functions of the provincial government were divided into 'Reserved' and 'Transferred' subjects. Which of the following were treated as 'Reserved' subjects? **[2022]**

1. Administration of Justice
2. Local self-government
3. Land revenue
4. Police

Select the correct answer using the code given below:

(a) 1, 2 and 3 (b) 2, 3 and 4 (c) 1, 3 and 4 (d) 1, 2 and 4

Solution: (c)

Explanation: As discussed in Section 2.2.5, under the salient features of GOI Act, 1919, items in the 'transferred' list included education, health, local government, industry, religious endowments etc. Hence, by eliminating item 2 i.e., Local self-government, we can arrive at the answer for list of 'Reserved' subjects in the options which are 1, 3 and 4 and hence the answer is (c).

5. With reference to the proposal of Cripps Mission, consider the following statements: **[2022]**

1. The Constituent Assembly would have members nominated by the Provincial assemblies as well as the princely states.
2. Any province, which is not prepared to accept the new constitution would have the right to sign a separate agreement with Britain regarding its future status.

Which of the statements given above is/are correct?

(a) 1 only (b) 2 only (c) Both 1 and 2 (d) Neither 1 nor 2

Solution: (b)

Explanation: As discussed in Section 2.2.7, the Cripps Mission provided a proposal for a Constituent Assembly whose members would be partly elected by the provincial assemblies and partly nominated by the princely states. Hence, statement 1 is incorrect. Statement 2 is correct as per the proposal of Cripps Mission and hence the answer is (b).

UPSC Previous Years' Questions of Main Examination

1. Did the Government of India Act, 1935 lay down a federal constitution? Discuss. [2016]

Approach: The key aspects of GOI Act, 1935 that aimed at setting up a federation and how it materialised only with respect to provinces and not with respect to princely states needs to be discussed.

MODEL ANSWER

The Government of India Act, 1935 was a landmark legislation towards a completely responsible Government in India.

Federation as envisaged in GOI Act, 1935

- This Act provided for the establishment of an All-India Federation comprising the provinces and princely states as units.
- Though the Act advocated the provinces and the princely states as units in a federation, it was optional for the princely states to accept this provision.
- The princely states did not join the federation as envisaged in the Act and hence the federation envisaged by the Act was not operational. It was a federal setup only with respect to the provinces.

Federal setup with respect to Provinces

- The legislative powers were divided between the Provinces and the Centre into three lists. These were the Federal list, the Provincial list and the Concurrent list.
- The Federal list for the centre consisted of 59 items such as external affairs; currency and coinage; naval, military and air forces; and Census etc.
- The Provincial list consisted of 54 items which dealt with subjects such as police, provincial public services and education etc.
- The Concurrent list comprised of 36 items dealing with subjects like criminal law and procedure, civil procedure, marriage and divorces, and abortion etc.
- The Residuary powers were given to the Governor General.
- It also provided for a setting up of a Federal Court to adjudicate dispute between the Centre and the provinces.

Thus, the GOI Act, 1935 laid the foundation for a federation and many of the features of our federal setup in the Constitution are modelled on the basis of GOI Act, 1935.

CHAPTER 3

Preamble

LEARNING OUTCOMES

1. Understanding the purpose of Preamble and explaining its significance
2. Learning Key Phrases and implications of terms like Sovereign, Socialist, Secular, Democratic, and Republic
3. Identifying and analysing core ideals enshrined in the Preamble – such as Justice, Liberty, Equality, and Fraternity
4. Interpreting the Preamble's Legal Standing, examining the judicial interpretation and its significance
5. Exploring historical context of Preamble and its role in reflecting the aspirations of the Constituent Assembly
6. Preamble's continuing relevance as a guide to nation's progress

The term 'Preamble' refers to the introduction or the preface to the Constitution. It contains the essence of a country's Constitution and its cardinal features. It reflects the philosophy, goals, aspirations and minds of the makers of the Constitution of India. It acts as the fountainhead for all aspects of the governance in India.

The Preamble is based on the 'Objectives Resolution' which was moved by Pandit Jawaharlal Nehru in the Constituent Assembly in December 1946 that was adopted in January 1947. The Preamble so far has been amended only once in 1976 by the 42nd Constitutional Amendment Act, to add three new words – Socialist, Secular and Integrity.

The Preamble to our Constitution reads,

WE, THE PEOPLE OF INDIA, having solemnly resolved to constitute India into a SOVEREIGN SOCIALIST SECULAR DEMOCRATIC REPUBLIC and to secure to all its citizens:

JUSTICE, social, economic and political;

LIBERTY of thought, expression, belief, faith and worship;

EQUALITY of status and of opportunity and to promote among them all;

FRATERNITY assuring the dignity of the individual and the unity and integrity of the Nation;

IN OUR CONSTITUENT ASSEMBLY this twenty-sixth day of November, 1949, do HEREBY ADOPT, ENACT AND GIVE TO OURSELVES THIS CONSTITUTION.

The Preamble to our Constitution serves two main purposes

(a) It indicates the source from which the Constitution derives its authority i.e., 'We the people';

(b) It also states the objectives or aims that the Constitution seeks to establish and achieve for the country.

The date of adoption of the Preamble and the Constitution of India is 26 November 1949 while the date of commencement of the Constitution is 26 January 1950.

3.1 KEY ADJECTIVES DESCRIBING INDIA AND THEIR SIGNIFICANCE

1. Sovereign

It implies that India is an independent State and not subject to any other power. It is not a dominion or dependency as was under the British colonial regime. For example, as on date, countries like Hong Kong or Taiwan, are not sovereign nations, as they are special administrative regions under China and are under overall Chinese control. As a sovereign nation, India is free from external influence and can enact its laws and policies (for both internal and external affairs). It can also freely join or relinquish membership of any international organisation and this does not undermine the status of being a sovereign nation.

2. Socialist

The makers of our Constitution consciously avoided the word 'socialist' in the Preamble as they felt that determining the economic and social ideal of a country in its Constitution's preamble was not appropriate. It was felt that people should decide what suits them according to time and age. However, it was added by the 42nd Amendment Act of 1976.

The word 'socialist' indicates a commitment to establish a welfare state by reducing inequalities in the society and eliminating societal ills like poverty, illiteracy and exploitation. Indian version of socialism is 'Democratic Socialism' where both the government and the private enterprise coexist.

3. Secular

Indian secularism is different from western secularism where the State and Religion are strictly separated and the government does not interfere in religious affairs. However, in India, the State enjoys the power to regulate the economic, financial, political and secular aspects associated with religious practice. Further, it can also provide for social welfare and reform or throw open the Hindu religious institutions of public character to all sections of Hindus. Hence, in the Constituent Assembly debates, the amendment to introduce the word 'secular' in the Preamble was not accepted as the Indian idea of secularism does not fit into the Western concept of secularism.

Further, various provisions of the Constitution already bring out the secular credentials of the Constitution. Articles 25–28 guarantee the fundamental right to freedom of religion to all persons in the country. Articles 15 and 16 stipulate that there shall be no discrimination only on the basis of religion by the State in its affairs or public employment.

However, the word 'secular' was added through the 42nd Amendment Act in 1976. The Constitution envisages India as a secular nation having no State religion and equal treatment of all religions by the State while dealing with them. Secularism has also been described as a 'Basic Structure' in the S. R. Bommai judgement by the Supreme Court.

A country based on its outlook towards religion can be classified as:

(a) Atheistic State (which is anti-religion) like China.

(b) Theocratic State (which is pro-religion and declares one religion as state religion) like Bangladesh, Pakistan, Burma, and Sri Lanka.

(c) Secular State (neutral towards all religions and does not have a state religion) like USA, India.

4. Democratic

Democracy means the governance of the country in the hands of the people. It guarantees rights for the people and enables checks and balance on all institutions of the country. Major elements of democracy include the rule of law, universal adult franchise, periodic elections and absence of discrimination.

> **THINK ABOUT IT**
>
> The Preamble declares India as a Sovereign, Socialist, Secular, Democratic, Republic. How do you interpret the relevance of each of these terms in today's context?

Democracy – Types and Essential Conditions

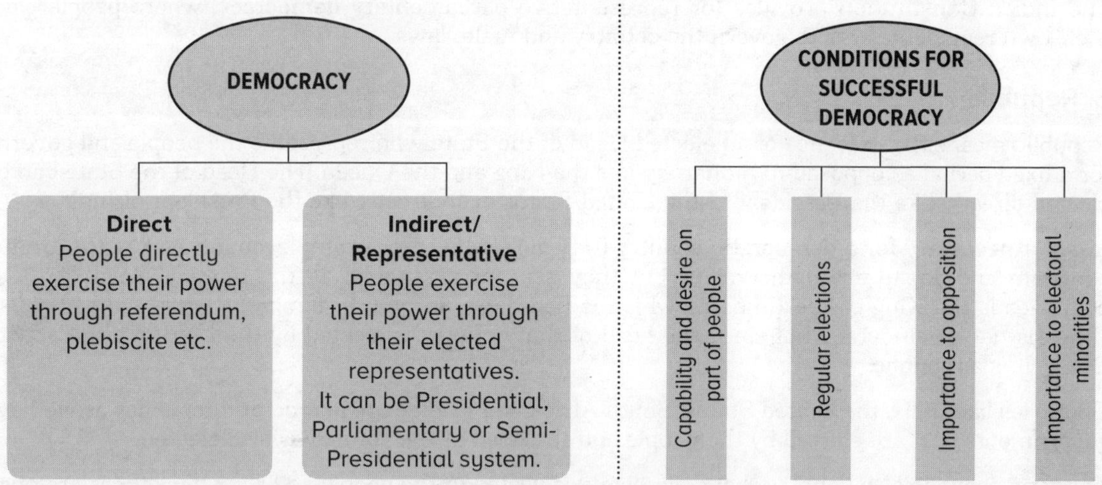

Various forms of Direct Democracy	
Type	**Brief Description**
Referendum	• Procedure where an issue is presented to the people for their verdict. • Also, when decision is taken by legislature but can be enforced only when the people have given their approval – eg: Constitutional amendments.
Initiative	Refers to a device where a group proposes a law or even a constitutional amendment supported by the signatures of specified number of people. In some cases, first submitted to the legislature.
Recall	Certain number of voters can propose the removal of an elected representative and final decision is taken after a popular vote.
Plebiscite	Direct popular vote on a matter of importance (like geographical boundaries) but chiefly in order to create a more or less permanent political condition.

Plebiscite is usually a onetime affair while referendum, initiative, and recall are in operation continuously.

Analysis of Democracy		
Importance	**Criticisms**	**Outcomes**
• Responds to needs of people • Accountability and transparency • Consultation and discussion in resolution of conflicts • Promotes equality and dignity of individual • Room to correct mistakes	• Instability • Political competition and powerplay • Majoritarianism • Corruption • Lack of knowledge of average voters	• Accountability and responsiveness • Economic growth • Reduction of inequality and poverty • Accommodation of social diversity • Freedom of citizens

It must be noted that in modern nation-states, the democracy that is practised is representative in nature considering the population and size of the countries. However, some countries still retain a direct form of democracy for deciding on specific political questions like change in the Constitution.

The Indian Constitution provides for representative parliamentary democracy, where people elect their own representatives to govern the country and make laws.

5. Republic

Republic means the presence of an elected Head of the State who represents the people and governs for a fixed period as opposed to monarchy like the King and the Queen. The Head of the State can be elected directly like the President of the United States or indirectly like the President of India.

It is not necessary for a democratic country to be a republic. For example, countries like the United Kingdom and Japan are democracies but they are not a republic as the nominal head of those countries is the King or the Emperor which is hereditary in nature. Similarly, while a country like China is not a democracy but since the head of that country is elected by the Communist Party of China, it is a republic.

Countries like India, the United States, South Africa and France are democratic republics as we have governments that are elected by the people and the head of the country is also elected.

The term republic also denotes that sovereignty is vested in the people and all public offices are open to all citizens of the country without any discrimination.

3.2 OBJECTIVES OF THE PREAMBLE

The various objectives of the Preamble can be summarised as Justice, Liberty, Equality and Fraternity. The key discussion points relating to each of these objectives, is summarised in the table below.

Objectives	Key Discussion Points
Justice	• In simple terms justice means fairness. The Preamble envisions three types of justice – social, economic and political. • SOCIAL JUSTICE: It denotes equal treatment of all citizens without any social discrimination based on caste, race, colour, religion, sex, etc. It also reflects the ideal to remove any social imbalance through appropriate measures. The provision of reservation for the backward classes and the abolition of untouchability are examples of provisions to achieve social justice.

Objectives	Key Discussion Points
	• ECONOMIC JUSTICE: It denotes non-discrimination in the matters of economic opportunities and equitable distribution of resources. It reflects the ideals of welfare state. Some examples of measures aimed at economic justice include the MGNREGA scheme (rural employment guarantee program) and various poverty alleviation schemes. • POLITICAL JUSTICE: It implies that all citizens should have equal political rights, equal access to all political offices and equal voice in government. Universal adult franchise, NOTA (introduced based on Peoples' Union for Civil Liberties case, 2013), right to know the antecedents of candidates by making public their nomination papers etc. (introduced based on Association for Democratic Reforms case, 2002) are examples of measures aimed at political justice. • The ideal of justice was borrowed from the Constitution of erstwhile USSR in the aftermath of Russian revolution. The Directive Principles of State policy (Part IV) of the Constitution is primarily aimed at securing social, economic and political justice for the citizens.
Liberty	• Liberty means absence of constraints by the State on the activities of individuals and at the same time providing opportunities for overall development. • The Preamble envisages liberty of thought, expression, belief, faith and worship. These are guaranteed through various fundamental rights between Articles 19 and 30. • However, these rights are not absolute and must be enjoyed within reasonable limits prescribed by law.
Equality	• It refers to absence of special privileges to any section of the society and provision of adequate opportunities for all individuals without any discrimination. • The Constitution ensures for all citizens of India, equality of status and opportunities in civic, political and economic spheres. Equality is guaranteed through various fundamental rights between Articles 14 and 18.
Fraternity	• It refers to the sense of brotherhood. The abolition of untouchability is to ensure fraternity amongst all citizens. • It is also stressed through Article 51A of Fundamental Duties. Fraternity ensures the dignity of the individuals and unity and integrity of the nation. • Unity refers to a situation where people are in agreement and work together as a unit. Integrity is being undivided.

THINK ABOUT IT

Can our nation truly achieve Justice, Liberty, Equality, and Fraternity as envisioned in the Preamble? What are the challenges in realising these ideals?

3.3 LEGAL STATUS OF THE PREAMBLE

There have been various Supreme Court judgements that have deliberated and decided on the status of the Preamble to our Constitution. These case laws have been summarised below.

(a) In the **Berubari case** of 1960, the Supreme Court held that the Preamble is not a part of the Constitution and thus not a source of any substantive power.

(b) However, in the **Kesavananda Bharati case** of 1973, the Supreme Court reversed its earlier opinion and said that the Preamble is a part of the Constitution and the Constitution should be read and interpreted in the light of the vision envisioned in the Preamble. It also held that the Preamble is subject to the amending power of the Parliament as any other provision of the Constitution.

(c) Further in the **S. R. Bommai case** ***(1994)***, the Supreme Court reiterated that the Preamble is a part of the 'Basic Structure' of the Constitution.

(d) In LIC case (1995), the Supreme Court reiterated that the Preamble is an integral part of the Constitution.

(e) In November 2024, the Supreme Court dismissed petitions filed by former MP Subramanian Swamy, advocate Ashwin Upadhyay and others, seeking removal of words socialism and secularism from the Preamble. The Court reiterated that socialism and secularism are part of basic structure. India has its own brand of socialism (welfare state) and secularism (equal respect for all religions without discrimination). It reiterated the Parliament's amending power including the Preamble as laid down in Kesavananda Bharati case.

Scan the QR code for conceptual video on Preamble

Mc Graw Hill edge

To summarise, the present legal status of the Preamble is as follows:

- Presently, the Preamble is an integral part of the Constitution and it can be amended by the Parliament under Article 368 without violating the basic structure.
- The Preamble is neither a source nor a limitation on the powers of the Parliament. It is not enforceable/non-justiciable by itself in a court of law.
- Nevertheless, it is crucial in interpreting various other provisions of the Constitution.

MNEMONICS

Concept or Provisions	Shortcut or Mnemonics	Details to Remember
Three words added in 1976 by 42nd amendment	• **S**mall **S**cale **I**ndustry – **SSI**	**S**ocialist, **S**ecular and **I**ntegrity
Preamble: Part of Constitution or not	• **B**achan does **Not Part**y • **K**eshav **Part**ies but **not independently**	**B**erubari case – **Not a part of** the Constitution **Kesavananda Bharati** Case – **Part** of the Constitution, but **not enforceable independently** by itself though used for interpreting other parts.

3.4 HISTORICAL CONTEXT AND CONTINUING RELEVANCE

The Constituent Assembly debated the Preamble at the end in October 1949 after the second reading (clause by clause adoption of articles) of the entire Constitution was complete. This reflects the philosophy in the minds of the Constitution makers towards the ideals and objectives for the nation. It reflects the vision and aspirations of the founding fathers of our Constitution.

In various judgements, including as recently as November 2024, the Supreme Court has held the Preamble and its content to be an integral part of the Constitution. It continues to have relevance by reminding the objectives we seek to achieve as a nation as well as its use in interpreting various provisions of the Constitution.

THINK ABOUT IT

Does the Preamble merely serve as an introduction to the Constitution, or is it a living guide in shaping India's policies and governance? Discuss with examples from recent events.

SUMMARY OF PREAMBLE

Adjectives describing India	Objectives of Preamble	Legal Status
• Sovereign – Independent • Socialist* – Welfare state • Secular* – No religious discrimination • Democratic – Government elected by the people • Republic – Elected head for the country *Added in 1976	• Justice – Social, economic and political – Fairness in all spheres • Liberty – Freedom of speech and expression; life and liberty; to practice religion • Equality – No discrimination & equal opportunity for all • Fraternity – Assuring the dignity of individual and the unity and integrity* of the Nation. *Added in 1976	• Part of the Constitution – Kesavananda Bharati case • Not enforceable by itself • Used for interpreting the other parts of the Constitution

MAINS STARTER

Area	Building Blocks For Model Introductions
Preamble	Preamble is the introductory part of our Constitution that reflects the philosophy of our polity. It declares the nature of our Indian State and also objectives we seek to achieve. This has been declared as a basic structure of the Constitution in S R Bommai case.
Nature/ Description of India in the Preamble	The Preamble declares India as a sovereign, socialist, secular, democratic, republic. This brings out the nature of our Indian State. Most of these aspects have been declared as basic structure of our Constitution in various cases by the Supreme Court.
Objectives of the Preamble	The Preamble spells out the objectives that the Constitution seeks to achieve viz., Justice, Liberty, Equality and Fraternity. Most of these aspects have been declared as basic structure of our Constitution in various cases by the Supreme Court.

UPSC Previous Years' Questions of Preliminary Examination

1. What was the exact Constitutional status of India on 26 January 1950? **(2021)**
(a) A Democratic Republic
(b) A Sovereign Democratic Republic
(c) A Sovereign Secular Democratic Republic
(d) A Sovereign Socialist Secular Democratic Republic

Solution: (b)

Explanation: The words Socialist and Secular were added to the Preamble in the 42nd Constitutional Amendment Act of 1976. Hence, the status at the time of commencement of the Constitution was a 'Sovereign Democratic Republic' and the answer is (b).

2. The Preamble to the Constitution of India is **(2020)**
(a) A part of the Constitution but has no legal effect
(b) Not a part of the Constitution and has no legal effect
(c) A part of the Constitution and has the same legal effect as any other part
(d) A part of the Constitution but has no legal effect independently of other parts

Solution: (d)

Explanation: While in the Berubari case, the Supreme Court had held that the Preamble is not a part of the Constitution, it was overturned in the Kesavananda Bharati case when the Supreme Court declared that the Preamble is a part of the Constitution. However, the Preamble is not enforceable by itself but it is used to interpret other provisions of the Constitution. Thus, it has no legal effect independently of other parts and the answer is (d).

UPSC Previous Years' Questions of Main Examination

1. Discuss each adjective attached to the word 'Republic' in the Preamble. Are they defendable in the present circumstances? **[2016]**

Likely context to the question: In January 2015 on the eve of the Republic Day celebrations, the Government of India had released an advertisement with the Preamble. It contained the original version of the Preamble and hence the words 'Socialist' and 'Secular' did not find mention in the advertisement that became a talking point. This event might have been the trigger for this question.

Approach: Introduction to the Preamble followed by a discussion on each adjective and its relevance in the present circumstances. This may be provided as two separate sub-headings or provided in a tabular form as given below.

MODEL ANSWER

The Preamble declares India as a sovereign, socialist, secular, democratic, republic. This brings out the nature of our Indian State. Most of these aspects have been declared as basic structure of our Constitution in various cases by the Supreme Court.

Discussion on the adjectives and their relevance in present circumstances:

Adjectives	Discussion on the adjectives	Relevance under present circumstances
1. SOVEREIGN	It implies that India is an independent country and not subject to any other power and free to conduct its national and international affairs.	While India is a signatory to various international agreements and treaties over the years like the Paris climate agreement etc., they are voluntary in nature. Further, while we have liberalised our economy, we retain economic sovereignty.
2. SOCIALIST	Socialist means a commitment to establish a welfare state, by reducing inequalities in the society.	While we have moved to a more liberal and market-driven economy since 1991, various welfare measures like the provision of reservation, subsidies, PDS, MGNREGA etc. indicate that socialism is relevant in India.
3. SECULAR	India as a secular nation has no State religion and treats all the religions equally.	Fundamental rights of Article 25–28, the absence of discrimination on the basis of religion defends the ideal of secularism. Secularism has also been described as a 'basic structure' in the S. R. Bommai judgement.
4. DEMOCRATIC	Democracy means the governance of the country in the hands of the people. It guarantees rights for the people and enables checks and balance on all institutions of the country.	There are shortcomings due to the delayed delivery of justice, the influence of money and the muscle power in elections in our democracy. However, provisions like the rule of law, the periodic elections and smooth transfer of power, the independence of judiciary etc. uphold the democracy in India.

The Supreme Court in November 2024 had reiterated that we have our own brand of socialism (welfare State) and Secularism (equal respect to all religions without discrimination) and that they are integral to the basic structure of the Constitution.

Thus, the ideals attached to the word 'Republic' in the Preamble are defendable and relevant in the present circumstances.

CHAPTER

4

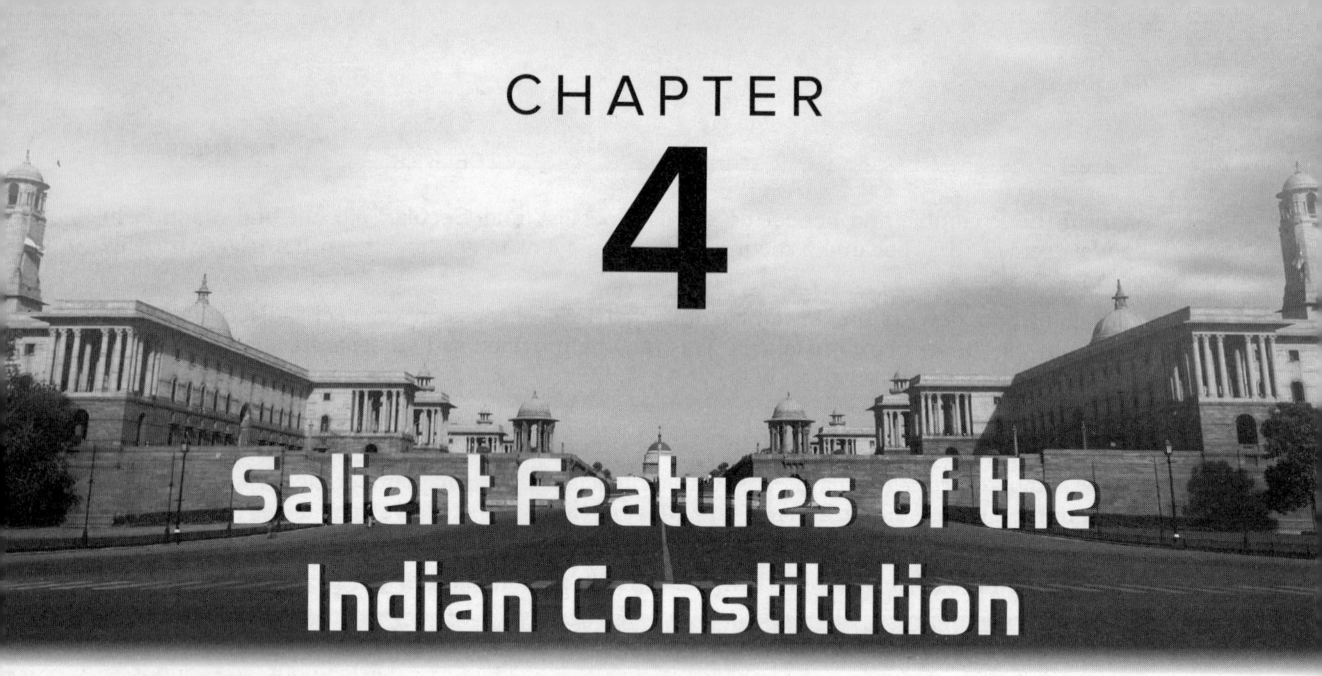

Salient Features of the Indian Constitution

LEARNING OUTCOMES

1. Knowing the role of Constituion in a democratic country like India
2. Assessing qualities of a good constitution and its categories worldwide
3. Exploring the Salient Features of Indian Constitution
4. Analysing the criticisms against the Constitution and its evolution as a 'living document'
5. Understanding the sources of Indian Constitution

The Constitution of India is the supreme law book of our country and is one of the finest-crafted constitutions in the world. The Constitution has adopted the best features of most of the major constitutions of the world as per the needs of our country. Though borrowed from various sources, the Indian Constitution has numerous salient features that distinguish it from other Constitutions.

In this chapter, we shall briefly understand the important features of our Constitution. This will provide an overall idea about the philosophy of our Constitution. It will help readers appreciate the various parts of our Constitution and to understand how they aim to achieve the objectives stated in the Preamble. We will also look at some of the criticisms against our Constitution and summarise the various sources of our Constitution at the end.

Before we understand the salient features, it is important to understand the four main functions performed by the Constitution in a democratic country like India.

1. To provide a set of basic rules that allow for minimal co-ordination amongst the members of a society (i.e., citizens of the country).
2. To specify who has the powers to make decisions in the society (country) and how the government will be constituted.
3. To set limits on what the government can impose on its citizens. It is because of such limits placed on government actions, that a constitutional government is also referred to as 'limited government.'
4. To fulfil aspirations of the society and create conditions for just society.

Some of the qualities of a good constitution are

(a) Brevity – Precise without any unnecessary provisions that can be left to ordinary legislation;
(b) Clarity – With definitive meaning for its terms;
(c) Comprehensive – That covers the powers of the government as well as rights and duties of citizens;
(d) Suitability – According to the social, cultural, economic and political conditions of the country;
(e) Stability – That allows for political and social stability; and
(f) Adaptability – That is dynamic with changing times.

Our Constitution does have these features, though there are also criticisms about the length of our constitution as well as terms that are not well defined and left to legislative and judicial interpretations.

Constitutions world-wide can be classified under the following categories:

(a) **Written and Unwritten** – Unwritten constitutions evolve over a period of time based on conventions, practices, customs and judicial decisions. Examples are the U.K., New Zealand etc. Written constitutions on the other hand are drafted by a constituent assembly or a similar authority and brought into force by adoption or promulgation. Examples are the U.S.A, India, France, Japan etc.
(b) **Federal and Unitary** – Federal Constitutions have dual governments at federal/central and provincial/State level that derive their powers directly from the Constitution. Examples are the U.S.A, India, South Africa, Germany etc. Unitary constitutions on the other hand concentrate power in the hands of central government with regional and local governments exercising such powers as are delegated to them by the centre. Examples are the U.K., Japan, France etc.
(c) **Procedural and Prescriptive** – A Procedural Constitution outlines the structure of government and sets limitations to safeguard citizens' rights, as seen in the U.S. Constitution. A Prescriptive Constitution additionally defines goals and objectives for the government, to achieve societal aspirations, as seen in the Indian Constitution.

MNEMONICS

Concept or Provisions	Shortcut or Mnemonics	Details to Remember
4 functions of the Constitution	**B**elow **P**overty **L**ine **(BPL)** **F**amily	**B – B**asic rules that allow for minimal co-ordination amongst citizens **P – P**owers to make decisions in the society & how government will be constituted **L – L**imits on what government can impose on its citizens **F – F**ulfils aspirations of the society

Constitution and Constitutionalism

Though the terms constitution and constitutionalism are closely related, there is a significant difference between the two. The presence of a constitution does not necessarily indicate that a country is governed by constitutionalism. For example, even a dictatorship like North Korea or a communist country like China have constitutions. However, constitutionalism provides for limits on the government of a country that protects the rights of its citizens. Constitutionalism requires that the country be governed by rule of law, has a democratically elected government with limits on its powers, an independent judiciary, civilian control of military and rights guaranteed for its citizens.

4.1 SALIENT FEATURES

1. Most Exhaustive Constitution

The Indian Constitution is one of the lengthiest written constitutions in the world. The Constitution of the United States of America contains only 7 articles while Britain has no written constitution. The Indian Constitution originally contained 395 articles divided into 22 parts and 8 schedules. Presently, it contains 25 parts, 12 schedules and about 450 articles. The numbering remains the same, but as and when the Constitution is amended, new articles or parts are added with suffix A, B, C etc.

The main reason for our long constitution is the adoption of various provisions (around 250) from the Government of India Act, 1935. Many provisions that are left to ordinary legislation in other Constitutions have been included in the Constitution of India. Further, while we are a federal country, we have one constitution for both the Union and the States, which is also a reason for the lengthy constitution.

Part	Subject	Articles
I	The Union and its territory	1–4
II	Citizenship	5–11
III	Fundamental Rights	12–35
IV	Directive Principles of State Policy	36–51
IV-A	Fundamental Duties (Added by 42nd Amendment Act, 1976)	51A
V	The Union	52–151
VI	The States	152–237
VII	Omitted (by 7th Amendment Act, 1956)	
VIII	The Union Territories	239–242
IX	The Panchayats (Added by 73rd Amendment Act, 1992)	243–243O
IX-A	The Municipalities (Added by 74th Amendment Act, 1992)	243P–243ZG
IX-B	The Co-operative societies (Added by 97th Amendment Act, 2011)	243ZH–243ZT
X	The Scheduled and Tribal Areas	244–244A
XI	Relations between the Union and the States	245–263
XII	Finance, Property, Contract and Suits	264–300A
XIII	Trade, Commerce and Intercourse within the territory of India	301–307
XIV	Services under the Union and the States	308–323

Part	Subject	Articles
XIV-A	Tribunals (Added by 42nd Amendment Act, 1976)	323A–323B
XV	Elections	324–329A
XVI	Special provisions relating to certain classes	330–342A
XVII	Official Language	343–351
XVIII	Emergency Provisions	352–360
XIX	Miscellaneous	361–367
XX	Amendment of the Constitution	368
XXI	Temporary, Transitional and Special Provisions	369–392
XXII	Short title, commencement, Authoritative text in Hindi and Repeals	393–395

(Please refer edge platform for Articles at a glance)

2. Rigidity versus Flexibility

Rigidity and flexibility are in terms of the amenability of the Constitution. Rigidity indicates that the constitutional amendment process requires special procedure and is not easy. On the other hand, flexibility indicates that it is easy to amend the Constitution like any other ordinary law.

When we look at various other Constitutions of the world, we can witness the following with respect to their amendments:

- **The United States:** The Constitution of the United States is rigid which requires 2/3rd members of the US Congress (equivalent to the Parliament of India) to agree to the amendment and it should be ratified (approved) by 3/4th of the States i.e., 38 out of 50 State legislatures. It has been amended only 27 times since 1789.
- **Japan:** The Constitution of Japan was adopted at the end of the 2nd World War in 1946. It is too rigid to amend as it requires 2/3rd members of both the Houses of Parliament to approve the amendments along with ratification by people through a referendum. As a result, the post-war constitution has not been amended even once till date.
- **British**: The British do not have a written constitution. Hence, any amendment to the laws of the Parliament is flexible as it can be amended with a simple majority.

The Indian Constitution is a blend of both rigidity and flexibility. Article 368 deals with the amendment to the Constitution. The various ways in which the Indian Constitution can be amended are

1. **Simple majority** – The majority of members present and voting: There are few provisions of the Constitution which can be changed by a simple majority in the Parliament and these are not deemed for the purpose of Article 368 as an amendment of the Constitution. For example, a State or a Union Territory (UT) can be reorganised under Article 3 by just a law of the Parliament and it has the effect of changing the First Schedule (list of States and UTs) and the Fourth Schedule (allocation of seats in the Rajya Sabha) as per Article 4. In 2014, the State of Andhra Pradesh was bifurcated into Andhra Pradesh and Telangana by a Parliamentary law called Andhra Pradesh Reorganisation Act, 2014. Similarly, the State of Jammu & Kashmir was reorganised into two UTs of J & K and Ladakh in August 2019 through a Parliamentary law. There are a few other provisions that can also be changed by a simple parliamentary law and these would be discussed in the appropriate chapters.

2. **Special majority** – The majority of the total membership of the House and by a majority of not less than 2/3rd of members of that House present and voting: Article 368 sets out the procedure for amendment of the Constitution. In respect of all provisions (other than a few items which can be changed by a simple majority), the majority required is a special majority in both Houses of the Parliament.
3. **Special majority along with ratification by at least 50% of the States** – Over and above the special majority in the Parliament for amending the Constitution, certain amendments to federal provisions also require ratification by not less than half of the States. This is required for the items like election of the President, provisions relating to the judiciary, distribution of powers between the Union and the States etc. For example, the 101st Constitutional Amendment that introduced the goods and services tax was ratified as per this requirement by more than half of the States in September 2016 before it was assented to by the President.

3. Parliamentary Democracy

Indirect or representative democracy can be mainly of two types based on the relationship between the executive and the legislature – Parliamentary and Presidential. There can be a third type, which can be called a semi-Presidential system that is practiced in countries like France and Sri Lanka. The key provisions of these types of governments are provided below.

Indirect/Representative Democracy		
Parliamentary	**Semi-Presidential**	**Presidential**
• People elect their legislators directly. The party/alliance parties with a majority in the legislature form the executive government. • The executive is accountable to the legislature. • In countries that are Republic, the President is indirectly elected and is only a nominal head of the State while the real powers lie with the council of ministers headed by the Prime Minister. The Prime Minister is the head of the Government. In monarchies like the UK and Japan, the King or the Emperor is the nominal head. • This is also known as 'dual executive'.	• President is the head of the State while the Prime Minister is usually the head of the government. • But the President usually has vast executive powers in military and diplomatic affairs. • President may also have the power to dissolve the Parliament like in the French Constitution.	• People elect both their executive head and legislators directly. • The executive is not accountable to the legislature. • President is directly elected by people and is the head of both the State and the Government. • This is also known as 'single executive'.
Examples: India, The UK, Canada and Japan	**Examples: France and Sri Lanka**	**Example: The United States of America**

Critical Analysis of Parliamentary form of Government	
Advantages	**Shortcomings**
1. There is better co-ordination between the executive and the legislature, as the former is part of the latter. The Government in power will enjoy majority support in the legislature and hence it is easier to pass laws and implement them. 2. It will be a responsible government, as the executive can be questioned by the legislature. The Parliament can discuss and keep a check on executive activities. If the Government loses the majority in the legislature, they have to resign. This also ensures that there is no authoritarianism. 3. The legislature represents diverse groups of the country through its elected MPs and MLAs. Since the executive is also formed from the legislature, it will represent its diversity as well. 4. It is more flexible, as the head of the government can be changed without any election within the term of the Parliament unlike the presidential system where the President, is elected for a fixed term and cannot be changed unless he/she is impeached.	1. There is no strict separation of powers. The ruling party will have a majority in the legislature and hence the legislature cannot always hold the executive accountable. 2. There may be a lack of expertise in the executive, as they have to necessarily be from elected members of the legislature. Hence, there is less room for experts being appointed, unlike the presidential system where the President decides on his cabinet and is free to choose experts. 3. The Parliamentary system lacks the stability inbuilt in a Presidential system. If the ruling government loses its majority, there will be a change in policy or fresh elections have to be called.

The advantages of the Parliamentary system cannot be found in the Presidential form. Likewise, the shortcomings of the Parliamentary system are addressed in a Presidential form.

THINK ABOUT IT

Parliamentary form of government has its own merits and demerits. Explain as to why our Constitution makers adopted the Parliamentary form of government? Is it advisable to shift to a Presidential form at present?

The Indian Constitution provides for a Parliamentary form of government, where the majority party in the Lower House (the Lok Sabha at the Centre/the Legislative Assembly at the States) forms the government and the council of ministers is responsible to the Lok Sabha/the Legislative Assembly. The President/the Governor is only a *de jure* head (nominal head) and the Prime Minister/the Chief Minister is the *de facto* head (real head).

Reasons to adopt a Parliamentary form of government

1. Our founding fathers believed that a Parliamentary form of government would be more responsible and democratic than the Presidential form of government.
2. Familiarity with the Parliamentary form of government during the British rule particularly after the implementation of the Government of India Act, 1935.

There have been debates in the recent past about the nature of campaign during elections taking a presidential form. While elections are fought on the strength of leadership of various parties, the local representatives and their campaign also play a crucial role in elections. The citizens look up to their MPs and MLAs to address their issues on a regular basis. Further, Parliamentary system has been declared as a basic structure of our Constitution by the Supreme Court in *Kesavananda Bharati* case.

4. Universal Adult Franchise

The Indian Constitution provides universal adult franchise to all citizens. Every citizen who is above the age of 18 years has the right to vote without any discrimination. It is one of the provisions which got passed unanimously in the Constituent Assembly without much deliberation, subsequently making the right to vote a constitutional right. By the 61st Amendment Act of 1988, the voting age was reduced to 18 years from 21 years from the year 1989.

5. Integrated and Independent Judiciary

The Constitution provides for an integrated judicial system with the Supreme Court at the top and the High Courts at the State level. The United States has a federal judicial setup, where the Supreme Court of the US is only for deciding cases on the federal Constitution and federal laws. Each State has its own Constitution and its own Supreme Court for deciding on the State's Constitution and laws. However, in India we have an integrated judicial system that will enforce both Central and State laws and the verdicts of the High Courts are subject to appeal in the Supreme Court.

The Constitution has also made the judiciary independent of the executive. Provisions like security of tenure, fixed conditions of service that cannot be altered to a disadvantage after appointment, financial security, ban on practice post-retirement etc., ensure the independence of the judiciary.

The above features relating to Parliamentary democracy, adult franchise, independent judiciary etc., fulfil the first two functions of the Constitution as mentioned in the introduction.

6. Fundamental Rights

The Constitution of India affirms the basic principle that every individual is entitled to enjoy certain basic rights and *Articles 12–35 in Part III of the Constitution deals with those rights which are known as fundamental rights.*

Scan the QR code for conceptual video on Salient features of the constitution

Originally the Constitution provided for seven fundamental rights, but now they are six in number. They are

I. *Right to Equality [Art 14–18]*
II. *Right to Freedom [Art 19–22]*
III. *Right Against Exploitation [Art 23–24]*
IV. *Right to Freedom of Religion [Art 25–28]*
V. *Cultural and Educational Rights [Art 29–30]*
VI. *Right to Constitutional Remedies [Art 32]*

The following important points with respect to the fundamental rights need to be noted:

- ❑ These rights seek to achieve the ideals of liberty and equality envisaged in the Preamble, thereby ensuring political democracy.
- ❑ These rights are in the nature of claims of citizens against the State. It places limits on what the government can impose on its citizens – (3rd function of the Constitution).
- ❑ These rights are guaranteed in the Constitution and are enforceable in a court of law. An affected person has the right to approach the Supreme Court directly for enforcement of these rights [Art 32].

7. Directive Principles of State Policy

Directive Principles of State Policy (DPSP) enumerated in Part IV of the Constitution are considered as a novel feature. These principles are in the nature of directives to the government to implement them for establishing social and economic democracy in the country.

The following important points with respect to DPSP needs to be noted:

- It seeks to achieve the ideals of social, economic and political justice embodied in the Preamble, thereby providing for social and economic democracy.
- While these directives are not enforceable in a court of law, they are nonetheless fundamental in the governance of the country. It aims to fulfil the aspirations of the society and create conditions for a just society – (4th function of the Constitution).
- The State should take these principles into account while formulating the laws.

8. Fundamental Duties

Article 51A of Part IV-A of the Constitution contains 11 fundamental duties. These duties are a reminder to the citizen that apart from enjoying the rights he/she has an obligation towards the country and fellow citizens. By performing their duties, the citizens contribute to strengthening of the social fabric of the country and its overall development in all spheres of life. ***Originally the Constitution did not contain any list of fundamental duties and they were added to the Constitution by the 42nd Amendment Act of 1976.***

However, it must be noted that these duties are not enforceable against the citizens but are ideals that they are expected to follow.

9. Panchayati Raj Institutions and Municipalities

The Panchayati Raj institutions and Municipalities were created by the 73rd and the 74th Constitutional Amendment Acts of 1992, respectively, and came into force in 1993. It added Part IX and IX-A to the Constitution. These institutions were created to provide constitutional sanction to establish 'democracy at the grassroots level as it is at the State level or National level'. It provides for a three-tier system of the local government institutions in both rural and urban areas.

10. Independent Bodies

Various constitutional and statutory bodies are created as independent bodies to strengthen democracy. In India, we have such independent constitutional bodies for conduct of elections, audit of government and for recruitment to government services. While all bodies work under the overall ambit of the Constitution, these independent bodies enjoy immunity from interference by the executive in its functioning.

This is essential for certain key functions like:

(a) Conduct of free and fair elections – Election Commission of India

(b) Audit of accounts of the Union and States – Comptroller and Auditor General

(c) Recruitment into the services of the Union and States – Union Public Service Commission and State Public Service Commissions.

The independence of these institutions is ensured through guaranteeing fixed tenure, financial independence, stringent removal procedure and restrictions on further employment with the government.

4.2 CRITICISM AGAINST THE CONSTITUTION

The Indian Constitution is a very robust law that was created by the Constituent Assembly after thorough deliberations. The legitimacy of our Constitution is due to its:

(a) mode of promulgation after detailed deliberations by experts,

(b) substantive provisions addressing various sections of the society including deprived classes and minorities, and

(c) balanced institutional design providing for checks and balance between various organs.

However, there are still certain criticisms against the Constitution that can be summarised as follows:

1. **Borrowed Constitution** – The main features of the Constitution have been borrowed from various other Constitutions. Dr. Ambedkar while answering this criticism in the Constituent Assembly said that it was not possible to create an entirely new constitution at that time in history when there were already so many other constitutions. Further, the requirements of a democratic constitution are recognised world over. The only new things can be to remove the faults and accommodate it to the needs of the country.
2. **Copy of Government of India Act, 1935** – Various critics have mentioned that the Indian Constitution is primarily a copy of the Government of India Act, 1935. Dr. Ambedkar while answering this criticism in the Constituent Assembly said that there is nothing to be ashamed of this. It is true that many of the administrative provisions relating to the executive, the legislature, the judiciary, centre–state relations and emergency provisions have been taken from the Government of India Act, 1935. However, there are also significant additions in the form of fundamental rights and DPSP that provide for a liberal and democratic constitution.
3. **Elephantine size** – It indicates the voluminous nature of our Constitution. Many aspects that are left to ordinary legislation in other constitutions have found a place in our Constitution. It is due to the (a) adoption of various provisions of the Government of India Act, 1935, (b) the geographical vastness of our country, (c) a single constitution for both the Union and the States and (d) the presence of legal luminaries in the Constituent Assembly.
4. **Un-Indian and Un-Gandhian** – It is one of the criticisms of some of the members of the Constituent Assembly who felt that the Indian Constitution does not reflect the spirit of our nation and also the ideals of Mahatma Gandhi, who advocated more autonomy to villages. It is more of a colonial document than a native one. However, the Constitution does provide for various directives in DPSP that capture the essence of our nation's spirit and ideals of Gandhi.

While there can be various criticism against our Constitution, it has stood the test of time over the last seven decades. It is a 'living document' that has evolved and adapted to the new circumstances through amendments by the Parliament and interpretations by our judiciary. Ultimately any constitution is as good as the people who implement it. Hence, our legislature and executive must uphold the constitutional values in letter and spirit.

> **THINK ABOUT IT**
>
> Though borrowed from various sources, our Constitution is unique in its content and has evolved as a 'living document' over the decades since its adoption. Analyse.

4.3 SOURCES OF OUR CONSTITUTION

As discussed in the previous section, many of the administrative aspects of our Constitution have been adopted from the Government of India Act, 1935. However, many other features of the Constitution have been adapted from various other constitutions of the world. This has been summarised in the table on the following page:

Constitution/Conventions	Key Features Adapted
British conventions	• Parliamentary form of Government • Rule of law • Institution of speaker • Law-making procedure • Parliamentary privileges
USA Constitution	• Fundamental rights based on the Bill of Rights • Power of judicial review and independence of the judiciary • Impeachment of the President, Removal of Judges • Vice-President post
Irish Constitution	• Directive principles of State policy
French Constitution	• Principles of liberty, equality and fraternity
Russian Constitution	• Principle of social, economic and political justice • Fundamental Duties
German Constitution	• Suspension of fundamental rights during emergency
Canadian Constitution	• Quasi-federal form of Government and residual powers with centre • Appointment of State governors by Centre • Advisory jurisdiction of the Supreme Court
Australian Constitution	• Concurrent list • Freedom of trade, commerce and inter-course • Joint Sitting of two houses of Parliament in case of deadlock in passage of a Bill.

MAINS STARTER

Area	Building Blocks For Model Introductions
Functions of the Constitution	The Constitution in a democratic country like India performs important functions of laying down the rules for basic co-ordination amongst citizens, powers of various institutions and setting limits on what the government can impose on citizens.
Parliamentary Democracy	India is a parliamentary democracy where the executive is part of the legislature and accountable to it.
Constitution as 'living document'	Indian Constitution is a 'living document' that has evolved and adapted to new circumstances through amendments by the Parliament and interpretations by our Judiciary.

UPSC Previous Years' Questions of Preliminary Examination

1. Which of the following statements are correct about the Constitution of India? **[2024]**
   1. Powers of the Municipalities are given in Part IX A of the Constitution.
   2. Emergency provisions are given in Part XVIII of the Constitution.
   3. Provisions related to the amendment of the Constitution are given in Part XX of the Constitution.

   Select the answer using the code given below:
   (a) 1 and 2 only
   (b) 2 and 3 only
   (c) 1 and 3 only
   (d) 1, 2 and 3

   Solution: (d)

   > ***Explanation:*** As provided in the table listing the parts of the Constitution in Section 4.1, all three statements are correct.

2. Which one of the following statements best reflects the Chief purpose of the 'Constitution' of a country? **[2023]**
   (a) It determines the objective for the making of necessary laws.
   (b) It enables the creation of political offices and a government.
   (c) It defines and limits the powers of government.
   (d) It secures social justice, social equality and social security.

   Solution: (c)

   > ***Explanation:*** In a country governed by a written Constitution like India, the Constitution is supreme and it places restrictions on all the other branches of government. As discussed in the introduction about the functions of the Constitution, it also places limits on what the government can impose on its citizens. This question in 2023 is in essence the same that was asked in 2020 and 2021. Hence, the correct answer is (c).

3. Constitutional government means **[2021]**
   (a) a representative government of a nation with federal structure
   (b) a government whose Head enjoys nominal powers
   (c) a government whose Head enjoys real powers
   (d) a government limited by the terms of the Constitution

   Solution: (d)

   > ***Explanation:*** This question in 2021 is in essence the same that was asked in 2023 and 2020. Hence, the correct answer is (d).

4. Which of the following 'best' defines the term 'State'? **[2021]**
   (a) A community of persons permanently occupying a definite territory independent of external control and possessing an organised government.
   (b) A politically organised people of a definite territory and possessing an authority to govern them, maintain law and order, protect their natural rights and safeguard their means of sustenance.

(c) A number of persons who have been living in a definite territory for a very long time with their own culture, tradition and government.
(d) A society permanently living in a definite territory with a central authority, an executive responsible to the central authority and an independent judiciary.

Solution: (a)

Explanation: As discussed in Chapter 1 on definition of certain key terms, State is used to refer to any country or territory with an organised government machinery. Hence, the most appropriate definition is (a).

5. A Parliamentary system of government is the one in which **[2020]**
(a) All political parties in the Parliament are represented in the government
(b) The government is responsible to the Parliament and can be removed by it
(c) The government is elected by the people and can be removed by them
(d) The government is elected by the Parliament but cannot be removed by it before the completion of the fixed term

Solution: (b)

Explanation: All political parties are not represented but only the ruling party is represented in the government. Hence, statement (a) is incorrect. The people do not elect the government directly but elect only their legislators. Hence, statement (c) is incorrect. The executive does not enjoy a fixed term in a parliamentary democracy, unlike a presidential form. Hence, option (d) is incorrect. If the government loses the majority in the Parliament, they have to step down. Therefore, the correct answer is (b).

6. A constitutional government by definition is a **[2020]**
(a) government by legislature (b) popular government
(c) multi-party government (d) limited government

Solution: (d)

Explanation: This question in 2020 is in essence the same that was asked in 2021 and 2023. Hence, the correct answer is (d).

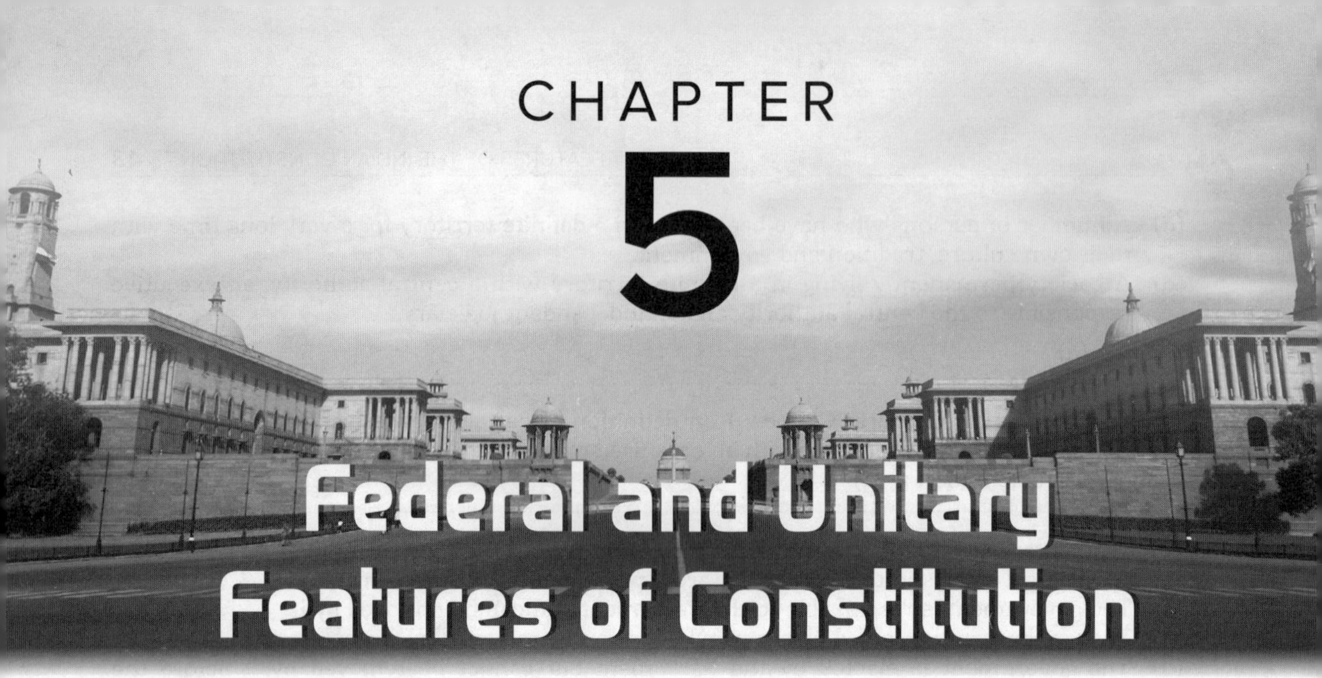

CHAPTER 5

Federal and Unitary Features of Constitution

LEARNING OUTCOMES

1. Understanding the essential features in a federal constitution
2. Federal features in the Indian Constitution
3. Unitary features in the Indian Constitution that provide the Centre with more powers
4. Understanding the conflicts in Indian federalism and its overall unique characteristics

The Government of a country can be classified as unitary or federal, based on the relationship between the Central (national) and the State (or regional) governments. When a country has two levels of government and legislature i.e., one at the centre and the other at the state/provincial level, with each deriving their powers from a written Constitution, it is a federal setup. Examples of a federal country are the United States, Germany, Australia, Canada etc. On the other hand, if there is only one central government and legislature for the whole country, and if any regional or local government derives its authority from the central government, it is a unitary setup. Examples of unitary countries are the United Kingdom, Japan, France etc.

The term 'federation' therefore implies the presence of two layers of Government, one at the central level and another at the regional/state level having autonomy in internal affairs. In a federation, the self-governing status of the component states, as well as the division of power between them and the central government, are constitutionally ensured and may not be altered by a unilateral decision of either party. The United States is the first and the oldest federation in the world. It was formed in 1776 post-American Revolution and adopted a federal Constitution in 1789. The US Constitution is considered to be the benchmark for an ideal federation. Other examples of federation include Canada, Australia, Brazil and so on.

A federation can be formed in two ways:

Integration or Aggregation	Devolution or Disaggregation
Independent States come together to form a strong and big federation.	A big country divides itself into smaller States by providing autonomy. It is done to promote regional interests and for better administration of the country.
Example: The United States of America	Example: Canada and India

The Constitution of India provides for a federal system of government. However, the term 'federation' is nowhere mentioned in the Constitution. This is because of two reasons:

- Indian federation is not the result of an agreement between the States
- Indian States have no right to secede from the Union

Thus, the Indian federation is a 'holding together' federation unlike the United States or Australian federations that are 'coming together' federations.

The discussion in this chapter is only to familiarise the reader with various federal and unitary features of the Constitution. This will provide a bird's eye view to the reader and also help in comprehending the various provisions relating to the executive, the legislature and the judiciary. However, each of these features will be discussed in further detail under the relevant chapters.

5.1 ESSENTIAL FEATURES OF A FEDERATION

The following features are essential in a federal country or a federal Constitution:

1. **Dual Government** – It refers to the presence of two layers of government, one at the Central and another at the State level.
2. **Supremacy of the Constitution** – In a federal country, there is a written Constitution that is supreme and both the federal (Union) and the State governments derive their power from the Constitution.
3. **Rigidity of the Constitution** – The method to amend the Constitution is made rigid to maintain the essence of federalism. It requires a special provision to amend the federal principle of the Constitution.
4. **Division of Powers** – The Constitution distributes the power between the Union and the State governments which act independently in their respective jurisdiction.
5. **Independent Judiciary** – One of the key features of a federation is the presence of an independent judiciary to settle the disputes between the Central and State governments or between State governments.

Process of Emergence of Federations

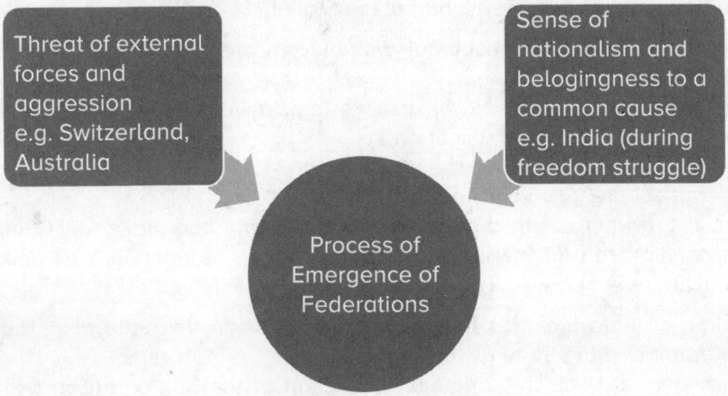

THINK ABOUT IT

A federation aims to distribute power between the Central and State governments. But, in practice, do federations always maintain a perfect balance, or does one level of government tend to dominate over time?

Forms of Power Sharing in a Federal Democracy

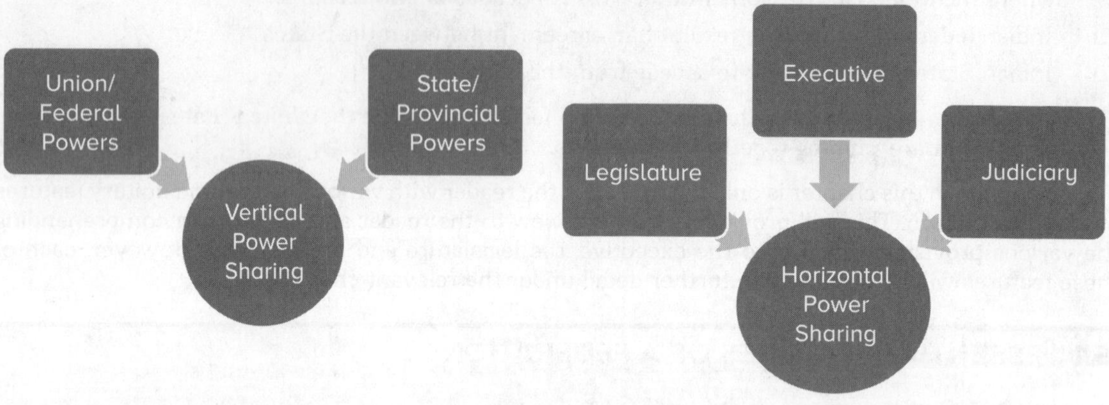

5.2 FEDERAL FEATURES OF THE INDIAN CONSTITUTION

Features	Provision in the Indian Constitution
1. Dual Government	The Indian Constitution provides for a dual government consisting of the Union government at the centre and the State governments at the State level.
2. Supremacy of the Constitution	The Indian Constitution is one of the lengthiest written Constitutions of the world consisting of around 450 articles divided into 25 parts and 12 schedules. Any act of the Parliament or State legislatures that violates the basic structure of the Constitution will be declared as *ultra vires* or unconstitutional by the courts. All organs of the State viz. the legislature, the executive and the judiciary have to act within the constitutional provisions. There is broad separation of powers between these organs while the Constitution remains supreme.
3. Rigidity of the Constitution	The Constitution of India is a blend of both rigidity and flexibility. Under Article 368, amendment of the federal provisions requires a special majority in the Parliament and ratification by at least half of the States.
4. Division of Powers	Seventh Schedule to the Indian Constitution distributes power between the Centre and States under three lists: 1. Union list – where the Centre has exclusive legislative powers [example – defence, external affairs, communication etc.] 2. State list – where the States have the power to legislate but it is not exclusive [example – agriculture, prison, fisheries etc.] 3. Concurrent list – where both the Centre and the State can make laws but in case of conflict, central laws will prevail [example – education, civil and criminal procedure etc.]
5. Independent judiciary	The Constitution of India provides for independent judiciary to settle disputes between the Centre and the State governments. Article 131 provides for exclusive original jurisdiction of the Supreme Court to resolve disputes between the Union and any State government or between State governments.

Based on the above provisions, India can be called a federal country. In *S. R. Bommai case of 1994*, 'federalism' was declared as a 'basic structure' of the Constitution. Nevertheless, India also possesses certain unitary features.

MNEMONICS

Concept or Provisions	Shortcut or Mnemonics	Details to Remember
Federal features in our Constitution	Washington **DC**^{2} (Capital of USA which is the ideal example of Federal Constitution)	**D** – **D**ual government or polity **C** – **C**onstitution that is supreme and rigid **D** – **D**ivision of powers between Centre and States as per constitution **C** – **C**ourts – Independent judiciary to settle disputes between Centre and States

5.3 UNITARY FEATURES OF THE INDIAN CONSTITUTION

Unitary features in the Indian Constitution can be described in simple terms as those provisions where the Union executive or the Parliament has more power than the State executive or legislature. There are also certain non-federal provisions as well as provisions for integrated machineries that are referred to as unitary features. It may be noted that this classification is only for ease of understanding and all the features listed below are collectively unitary features of the Constitution.

The unitary features of the Indian Constitution can be broadly studied under the following headings:

Non-federal Features and Integrated Machineries	Unitary Features – Normal Circumstances	Emergency Circumstances
• Described as the Union of States • Single Constitution • Single Citizenship • Unequal representation of States in the Rajya Sabha • Integrated Judiciary • Integrated Election Machinery • Integrated CAG	• Centre's power to reorganise States • Strong legislative power of the centre • Control over State list • All India services • Appointment of the Governor • Finance commission	• National Emergency • State Emergency • Financial Emergency

5.3.1 Non-federal Features and Integrated Machineries

The following features of the Indian Constitution are non-federal in character. These do not necessarily result in any significant additional power to the Centre over the States. However, they are not in line with ideal federal features in a country like the United States. Further, it is only the centre that can make amendments to these provisions in the Constitution, pass legislations or make appointments to some of these posts as the case may be that make these features unitary in nature.

1. Preference to Call it a Union

Article 1. Name and territory of the Union – (1) India, that is Bharat, shall be a Union of States.

In the Constituent Assembly, the Drafting Committee decided in favour of describing India as a Union, although its constitution might be federal in structure. Dr Ambedkar explained the significance of the use of the expression 'Union' instead of the expression 'Federation'.

He said that the use of the word 'Union' is deliberate. Though the country and the people may be divided into different States for convenience of administration, the country is one integral whole, its people a single people living under a single imperium (power) derived from a single source (Constitution).

2. Single Constitution

Unlike in the United States, where the States have a separate Constitution for themselves, the Constitution of India embodies the provisions for both the Union and the States and they must operate within this single framework. Any amendment to the provisions with respect to the States can also be initiated only by the Parliament.

3. Single Citizenship

Despite adopting a dual polity, the Constitution of India adopted a system of single citizenship. There is only Indian citizenship and no separate State citizenship, unlike the United States which has the system of dual citizenship i.e., national citizenship and state citizenship. Further, citizenship is a subject under the 'Union list' and only the Parliament has the power to legislate on it.

4. Unequal representation in the Rajya Sabha

In an ideal federal setup, the legislature is bicameral i.e., consisting of two Houses. One of the Houses represents the will of the people based on population, while the other represents the States' interests. In this House that represents the States, the membership is usually provided equally to all the States of the federation. For example, in the US Congress, there are two Houses namely the House of Representatives and the Senate. The number of seats in the House of Representatives varies from State to State based on their population. But the principle of equality of representation is followed in the Senate where all the States have an equal number of seats despite their population. The Senate consists of 100 members – 2 from each of the 50 States.

However, in India, the States are given representation in both the Lok Sabha and the Rajya Sabha based on their population. Hence, the number of seats varies from State to State even in the Rajya Sabha from 1 to 31.

5. Integrated Judiciary

The Constitution of India provides for an integrated judiciary with the Supreme Court at the centre and the High Courts in the States. Both Central and State laws are enforced by this integrated setup. The decisions of the High Court are subject to appeal in the Supreme Court and all High Courts have to follow the law as laid down by the Supreme Court. On the other hand, in the United States, there is a federal Supreme Court of the US to enforce federal laws and a State judiciary to enforce State laws.

Further, the judges to both the Supreme Court and the High Courts are appointed by the President. They can be removed only by the Union Parliament.

6. Integrated Audit Machinery

Article 148 of the Constitution provides for the Comptroller and Auditor General of India, who acts as the guardian of public purse and audits the entire financial system of the country. He/she audits the accounts of both the Central and State governments. However, he/she is appointed by the President and the States do not have any role in his/her appointment. The States also do not have any role in his/her removal and he/she can be removed only by the Parliament like a Judge of the Supreme Court.

7. Integrated Election Machinery

Article 324 provides for an independent Election Commission to conduct elections to both Central and State legislature. The Election Commissioners are appointed by the President and the States are not consulted before such an appointment. The States also do not have any role in the removal of Election Commissioners. The Chief Election Commissioner can be removed only by the Parliament like a Judge of the Supreme Court and the other Election Commissioners can be removed only by the President on the recommendation of the Chief Election Commissioner.

5.3.2 Unitary Features – Normal Circumstances

India is a diverse country of continental proportions. This multi-lingual, multi-cultural country required a federal polity, and our constitution-makers were aware of this requirement. Hence, they adopted a constitution that was basically federal in nature.

However, there are unitary features that are a relic of the Government of India Act, 1935. There were debates in the Constituent Assembly as to whether such provisions that were made by the British to administer a colony should find a place in the Constitution of a democratic federation. However, these unitary features were retained due to the following reasons:

- Our federation was not formed due to an agreement between erstwhile independent states or units. The country was entirely ruled by the British and after independence, we remain a united country with the States being part of it. Further, more than 500 princely states were also integrated into the existing states during independence.
- Considering the circumstances prevailing at the time of independence and also the nascent status of our democracy, it was decided that we need a strong Union to ensure the unity and integrity of the nation. Hence, these provisions were adopted with suitable modifications as required.
- The makers of the Constitution also believed that the socio-economic problems of independent India need to be addressed with a strong centre working in tandem with various States.

Scan the QR code for conceptual video on Federal and Unitary features

The features in the earlier section are non-federal in nature. However, there are provisions in the Constitution that provide disproportionate power to the Parliament and the Union executive when compared to the States. These can be broadly classified, for ease of understanding, into unitary features during normal circumstances and emergencies.

We shall now discuss the unitary features under normal circumstances.

1. Parliament's Power to Reorganise a State

Article 3 of the Constitution states that the Parliament by law can alter the territorial position of the States or Union Territories.

It must be noted that the Parliament can unilaterally reorganise a State and the State's legislature has no say in such a reorganisation. Moreover, this requires only a simple majority in the Parliament. Such a provision is unimaginable in an ideal federal setup like the United States where the federal legislature cannot alter the boundaries of the States. The American Federation has been described in its Supreme Court as 'an indestructible union composed of indestructible States'. But the Indian Constitution provides for 'an indestructible union with destructible States'.

2. Centre's Strong Legislative Powers

In the United States, the exclusive powers of the federal government are primarily in four domains – currency, telecommunication, defence and external affairs. Few concurrent subjects can be legislated by both the federal and the State governments like taxation, law enforcement and establishment of courts and chartering banks. However, the States enjoy a lot of autonomy in all the other matters. Further, any residuary power lies with the States and not with the federal government.

In India, on the contrary, the legislative power of the Union is stronger than the States. The distribution of powers under the Seventh Schedule to the Constitution is summarised below:

Union list	98 subjects	Defence, External affairs, Banking, Railways etc.
State list	59 subjects	Police, Public order, Land etc.
Concurrent list	52 subjects	Factories, Electricity, Education etc.

Further, the powers to legislate in any residuary subjects i.e., subjects which are not mentioned in any of the list in the Seventh Schedule are vested in the Parliament.

3. Centre's Power to Legislate on State Subjects

The Constitution empowers the Parliament to make laws on State subjects under certain normal circumstances:

1. Article 249: When the Rajya Sabha passes a resolution (in national interest) with a majority of not less than $2/3^{rd}$ of members present and voting;
2. Article 252: When two or more States make a joint request to the Parliament by passing resolutions in their State legislatures;
3. Article 253: When necessary to give effect to international treaties, agreements and conventions.

Under these circumstances, the Parliament takes over the legislative power of the States, which makes it a unitary feature.

4. All-India Services

At present, there are three all-India services namely the Indian Administrative Service, the Indian Police Service and the Indian Forest Service. The all-India service officers are appointed by the centre and controlled by the centre but work in the senior administrative positions in States. For example, an IAS officer, who works as a District Collector or an IPS officer, who works as a Superintendent of Police, is essentially performing the functions of the State government. However, they are employees of the Central government and the State governments cannot remove these officers from service.

5. Position of the Governor

The Governor acts as the constitutional head of a State but he/she is appointed by the President. He/she holds office during the pleasure of the President. The centre controls the affairs of the States through the office of the Governor. He/she can reserve bills passed by the State legislature for the assent of the President and can also recommend for the President's rule in case of breakdown of Constitutional machinery. This sort of arrangement again is unimaginable in an ideal federation like the United States where States enjoy complete autonomy in respect of their subjects.

6. Appointment of Finance Commission

In the Indian constitutional setup, the centre has more taxation power than States. Direct taxes are the exclusive domain of the centre and with the advent of goods and service tax, the balance of power has shifted towards the centre even in matters of indirect taxation. As per Article 280, the President appoints the Finance Commission of India once every five years for making recommendations with respect to the distribution of tax revenues between the Centre and the States. This body is entirely appointed by the centre without any role for the States in its appointment.

5.3.3 Unitary Features – Emergency Circumstances

We have discussed the unitary features that provide more power to the Centre when compared to the States under normal circumstances in the earlier section. Apart from this, there are emergency provisions that result in the Centre becoming powerful when compared to the States.

The Constitution of India provides for three types of emergencies:

1. *Article 352: Proclamation of emergency [National emergency]*
2. *Article 356: President's rule [State emergency]*
3. *Article 360: Financial emergency*

During emergency, the centre becomes all-powerful and States will come under the control of the centre. It converts the federal structure of polity into a unitary one without a formal amendment to the Constitution. This feature is borrowed from the Government of India Act of 1935 and was retained by the Constituent Assembly to safeguard the sovereignty, unity, integrity and security of the country.

MNEMONICS

Concept or Provisions	Shortcut or Mnemonics	Details to Remember
Unitary features in our Constitution	Normal and Emergency unitary features **ABCDEFG**	**A** – **A**ll India services **B** – **B**ifurcation or reorganisation of a State **C** – **C**ontrol over State list by centre **D** – **D**ivision of powers in favour of centre – Centre's strong legislative powers **E** – **E**mergency provisions – National, State and Financial **F** – **F**inance Commission appointment by centre **G** – **G**overnor appointment by centre

5.4 CONFLICTS IN INDIAN FEDERALISM

The Indian Constitution, as discussed above, provides for a federal polity but with a unitary bias. There are various conflicts in the Centre–State administration because of this 'quasi-federal' setup. Some of the key aspects of these conflicts can be summarised as follows:

1. Demand for Autonomy

(a) Many States (like Tamil Nadu, West Bengal, Kerala) and regional political parties (like DMK, Akali Dal, TMC) have demanded more autonomy for the States. They have demanded more legislative, administrative and financial powers for the States. In terms of legislative relations, it is the transfer of subjects from the Concurrent list to the State list. With respect to administrative setup, it is non-interference of the central government in the affairs of the State. Finally, in respect of financial relations, it is more taxation powers and independent sources of revenue to the States.

(b) The demand for autonomy can also be from linguistic and cultural angles. There have been agitations in the past against the imposition of Hindi in States like Tamil Nadu. In the recent past, there have been voices in some of the States against schemes like National Education Policy that is perceived as an attempt to design a unitary system for the entire nation.

2. Role of Governor and President's Rule

(a) The role of the Governor has always been a sticky point between the Centre and States especially when the ruling parties in the Centre and State are different.

(b) The imposition of the President's rule has been the most controversial unitary feature of the Indian Constitution in the past. While Dr Ambedkar was hopeful that it would remain a 'dead letter' in the Constitution, the fact is that it has been used more than 130 times till 2024, and on most occasions due to political reasons. It is only due to the safeguards provided by the Supreme Court in S. R. Bommai judgement that its misuse has been curtailed after 1994.

(c) There have been recommendations provided by the Sarkaria Commission, the Administrative Reforms Commission, the Punchhi Commission for streamlining the Centre–State relations including appointments and removal of the Governors. However, many of these recommendations have not been implemented by the centre.

3. Demand for New States

(a) There has been a demand for the creation of new States. States reorganisation happened for the first time in 1956 on linguistic lines. Subsequently, Gujarat and Maharashtra were created in 1960; Punjab and Haryana were created in 1966. There has been a demand for newer States around cultural and ethnic identities. The North-Eastern States were created from Assam starting with Nagaland in 1963 and ending with Mizoram and Arunachal Pradesh in 1987.

(b) Jharkhand, Chhattisgarh and Uttarakhand were created in 2000 due to regional demands. Similarly, Telangana was created in 2014 to fulfil a long pending aspiration of that region. Jammu & Kashmir was reorganised in 2019 into two Union territories for strategic and administrative reasons.

4. Inter-State Conflicts

Finally, apart from conflicts between the Centre and States, one of the major issues in Indian federalism is the conflicts between States. The inter-State conflicts are mainly on account of two factors – (i) Border disputes and (ii) River water disputes.

(i) **Border disputes** – Examples include disputes between Karnataka and Maharashtra over Belagavi; disputes between Kerala and Karnataka over Kasaragod etc. These are more sentimental and do not flare up into a full-blown conflict.

(ii) **River water disputes** – Inter-State river water disputes are more serious as they are concerned with the livelihood of farmers as well as the availability of drinking water to people. Some of the vexatious disputes include the Cauvery water dispute between Tamil Nadu and Karnataka; the Narmada water dispute between Gujarat, Madhya Pradesh and Maharashtra; the Sutlej water dispute between Punjab and Haryana etc.

5.5 FEDERALISM OF A NOVEL TYPE

The above discussions invariably lead to a confusion as to whether the Indian Constitution is federal or unitary in character. There have been international legal luminaries who have described the Indian Constitution and its polity in various ways. Morris Jones termed it as 'bargaining federalism' while Ivor Jennings has described it as a 'federation with strong centralising tendency'. Alexandrowicz stated that 'India is a case *sui generis* i.e., unique in character'. Granville Austin has specified that Indian federation is a new kind of federalism to meet its unique needs. K. C. Wheare described it as 'quasi-federal'.

> **THINK ABOUT IT**
>
> Indian Constitution provides for various unitary features that endow more powers on the Centre. Does it strengthen national unity or does it limit the representation of regional and cultural diversity within the federal structure? Discuss.

Dr. Ambedkar himself declared in the Constituent Assembly that the Constitution is a federal Constitution with both the Union and the States deriving their authority from it. Yet the Constitution avoids the tight mould of federalism and could be both unitary and federal according to the requirements.

The working of the Constitution over the last seven decades has highlighted the unique nature of our federal setup. The conflicts discussed in the earlier section is in itself a reflection of the strong federal spirit in our country. Further, it must be noted that while the unitary features do provide more power to the centre, they are not unilaterally used regularly. There are checks and balance to ensure that the federal spirit of the Constitution is maintained.

Apart from the 'quasi-federal' nature with respect to all the States, the Constitution has special provisions for some of the States given their social and historical circumstances. Articles 371A to 371H have special provisions, mainly for the States in North-East due to their tribal population with a distinct culture. These provisions are to protect the tribal culture of these States while providing for development and maintenance of law and order. It is because of this unique setup that Indian federalism is also referred to at times as 'asymmetrical federalism'.

Hence, India can be termed as a federal government with unitary bias, as it has all the features of federalism and at the same time provides the centre with more powers when compared to the States.

The effort at present is to move towards cooperative federalism. The following developments in the recent past strengthen the move towards cooperative federalism:

- Establishment of NITI Aayog in January 2015, in place of the erstwhile Planning Commission, with the objectives of catalysing economic development and fostering cooperative federalism. The main aim is to involve State governments in the economic policy-making process using a bottom-up approach.
- Formation of the GST Council as part of the implementation of the Goods and Services Tax in 2017. This Council has representation from the Union and all States. This is again seen as a classic example of cooperative federalism in India.

- Inter-State council has been reconstituted in May 2022 with a Standing Committee for consultation and monitoring.
- Zonal Councils being reformed to act as action platforms from erstwhile advisory role.

MAINS STARTER

Area	Building Blocks For Model Introductions
Federalism	The Indian Constitution provides for a federal polity and 'federalism' has been declared as a 'basic structure' of our Constitution in the S.R. Bommai case.
Federalism with Unitary Bias	The Indian Constitution provides for a federal polity. However, it also contains 'unitary' provisions that provide additional powers to the Centre when compared to the States.
Co-operative federalism	India is a federal country with unitary bias. However, the aim is to foster co-operative federalism between the Centre and States and amongst the States. Bodies like NITI Aayog, Inter-State Council, GST Council and Zonal Councils are aimed at strengthening co-operative federalism.

UPSC PREVIOUS YEARS' QUESTIONS OF PRELIMINARY EXAMINATION

1. Which one of the following in Indian polity is an essential feature that indicates that it is federal in character? **[2021]**
   (a) The independence of judiciary is safeguarded
   (b) The Union legislature has elected representatives from constituent units
   (c) The union cabinet can have elected representatives from regional parties
   (d) The fundamental rights are enforceable by courts of law

Solution: (a)

Explanation: As discussed in Section 5.2, independent judiciary is one of the important features of a federal polity. In India, we have an independent judiciary with the Supreme Court having the powers to settle any disputes between the centre and the states. While the other statements are correct statements, the statement that indicates our federal character is an independent judiciary. Hence, correct answer is (a).

UPSC Previous Years' Questions of Main Examination

1. Though the federal principle is dominant in our Constitution and that principle is one of its basic features, but it is equally true that federalism under the Indian Constitution leans in favour of a strong centre, a feature that militates against the concept of strong federalism. Discuss. [2014]

Approach: First part of the answer can summarise the federal features; second part of the answer can summarise the unitary features that results in a strong centre – the non-federal features need not be highlighted as it is not relevant to the question; the concluding remarks can specify steps that are being taken to strengthen cooperative federalism.

MODEL ANSWER

The Indian Constitution provides for a federal polity and federalism has been declared as a 'basic structure' of our Constitution in the S. R. Bommai case by the Supreme Court.

Federal features of the Indian Constitution

1. Dual polity – We have two layers of government at the Centre and State level.
2. Supremacy and rigidity of the Constitution – Our Constitution is supreme and all organs of the State have to act within the contours of the Constitution. Further the amendment to our Constitution requires a special majority for most items, and ratification by at least half of the states for federal items.
3. Division of powers – There is a constitutional division of powers in the Seventh Schedule between Centre and States.
4. Independent judiciary – The Supreme Court under its original jurisdiction resolves any disputes between Centre and States or between the States.

Unitary features that favour a strong centre

At the same time, there are certain provision in the Constitution which makes the centre more powerful than the States which are known as unitary features. These features can be summarised as follows:

Normal Circumstances	Emergency Circumstances
• Centre's power to reorganise State – Articles 3 and 4 • Strong legislative power of the centre when compared to states – 98 entries in Union list against 59 for States • Control over State list – Power of the Parliament to legislate on State list • All-India services – IAS, IPS, IFoS officers appointed by the Centre but working for the States • Appointment of the Governor – Agent of the Centre in the States • Finance Commission – Appointment by the Centre that recommends for distribution of revenue	• National emergency [Art 352] • State emergency [Art 356] • Financial emergency [Art 360] During emergency, the Centre becomes all powerful and States will come under the control of the Centre. It converts the federal structure of polity into a unitary one without a formal amendment to the Constitution.

Towards cooperative federalism – Despite the presence of unitary features, the Indian Constitution is federal in spirit and is not against federalism. In fact, the recent efforts are to move towards cooperative federalism to increase synergy between the Centre and States. The creation of NITI Aayog and GST Council can be seen as examples towards this effort.

CHAPTER 6

Union and its Territory

LEARNING OUTCOMES

1. Explaining the concept of India as a Union of States and knowing the components of its territory
2. Tracing the history of formation and reorganisation of States since independence
3. Analysing the power of Parliament regarding the reorganisation of a State or Union Territory and its procedural requirements

Articles 1 to 4 of Part I of the Indian Constitution deal with the Union and its territory which are summarised below.

6.1 CONSTITUTIONAL PROVISIONS

6.1.1 Union and its States

Article 1 provides that India, that is Bharat, shall be a Union of States. The Constituent Assembly decided to describe it as a Union instead of 'Federation'.

Article 1 also provides for the following:

- The States and the territories thereof shall be as specified in the First Schedule.
- The territory of India shall comprise:
  - (a) the territories of the States;
  - (b) the Union territories specified in the First Schedule; and
  - (c) such other territories as may be acquired.

Article 2 provides that the Parliament may by law admit into the Union, or establish, new States on such terms and conditions as it thinks fit. The First Schedule to the Constitution contains the list of States and Union Territories. At present, there are 28 States and 8 Union Territories.

6.1.2 Parliament's Power to form New States, Reorganise and Rename Existing States

Article 3 provides that the Parliament may by law:

(a) form a new State by separation of territory from any State or by uniting two or more States or parts of States or by uniting any territory to a part of any State;

(b) increase the area of any State;

(c) diminish the area of any State;

(d) alter the boundaries of any State;

(e) alter the name of any State.

For the above clauses, the term 'State' includes a Union Territory.

This is a unitary feature of the Indian Constitution where the Parliament has the power to reorganise any State or Union Territory.

The key provisions of Article 3 are summarised below:

(i) The Parliament may by law form a new State (or Union Territory) by dividing or merging the State(s) or the Union territories.

(ii) Such a law can be introduced in the Parliament only with the recommendation of the President.

(iii) The President shall refer the bill to the Legislature of the State for expressing its views thereon within such period as provided by the President. The view of the State Legislature though does not have any bearing on the reorganisation of the State.

(iv) The law needs to be passed only by a simple majority in the Parliament.

(v) Based on this law, the First Schedule (List of States) and the Fourth Schedule (Allocation of seats in the Rajya Sabha to States) is altered. It is not treated as an amendment to the Constitution under Art 368 [Article 4].

Evolution of States

At the time of independence, 552 princely states were part of the India territory. Five hundred forty-eight of them joined the Indian Union at the time of independence and Kashmir, Hyderabad, Junagadh and Pudukottai joined subsequently.

In June 1948, the Government of India appointed the Linguistic Provinces Commission under the chairmanship of S. K. Dhar to examine the feasibility of reorganisation of States on linguistic lines. The Commission recommended the reorganisation of States on the basis of administrative convenience rather than linguistic factor. Subsequently the JVP Committee (comprising Jawaharlal Nehru, Vallabhbhai Patel and Pattabhi Sitaramayya) was formed in 1949 that rejected language as the basis for reorganisation of States. At the time of commencement of the Constitution in 1950, there was a four-fold classification of the States and territories. Part A States - Erstwhile Governor's provinces of British India, Part B States - Erstwhile princely states with legislatures, Part C States - Erstwhile Chief Commissioner's provinces of British India and some other princely states, Part D Territory - Andaman & Nicobar Islands.

The reorganisation of States has been happening since 1953 when the first linguistic State of Andhra Pradesh was created. Subsequently in 1956 linguistic States were created based on the report of

Fazl Ali Commission. It identified the following factors to be taken into account in any scheme of reorganisation of States –

(a) Preservation and strengthening the unity and security of the country,

(b) Linguistic and cultural homogeneity,

(c) Financial, economic and administrative considerations, and

(d) Planning and promotion of welfare of people.

THINK ABOUT IT

The power of Parliament to reorganise a State is a unitary feature that can be viewed as going against the spirit of federalism which is the basic structure of the Constitution. Comment.

Thereafter, reorganisation has continued based on linguistic factors, popular agitations and political conditions. The recent reorganisations in the last decade have been creation of Telangana (2014) from Andhra Pradesh and bifurcation of the State of Jammu & Kashmir into two Union territories of Jammu & Kashmir and Ladakh (2019). While the Parliament's unilateral power to reorganise a State is a unitary feature, it must be noted that it is usually carried out only when the need arises due to local demands. In the case of reorganisation of J & K, it was due to the prevailing political situation.

Similarly, starting with the renaming of the United Provinces as 'Uttar Pradesh' in 1950, States have been renamed as per popular demands like Madras to 'Tamil Nadu' (1969), Uttaranchal to 'Uttarakhand' (2006), Orissa to 'Odisha' (2011) etc.

6.1.3 Ceding of Indian Territory or Acquisition of New Territory

There was a Presidential reference (under Article 143) in 1960 to the Supreme Court with respect to the power of the Parliament to cede (give up) any territory of the country to a foreign country or to acquire any new territory into the Indian Union. The Central government had ceded part of a territory known as Berubari Union (in West Bengal) to Pakistan through a Parliamentary law. This led to a political controversy and thereby necessitated the Presidential reference.

The Supreme Court held that the power of the Parliament to reorganise/ diminish the boundary of a State (under Article 3) does not cover cession of the Indian territory to a foreign country. Hence, the Indian territory can be ceded to a foreign country only by amending the Constitution under Article 368. The cessation of Berubari was subsequently regularised as per this opinion through the 9th Constitutional Amendment.

Scan the QR code for conceptual video on Union and its territory

McGraw Hill edge

The acquisition of Goa (1961), Daman and Diu (1961), Dadra and Nagar Haveli (1961), Puducherry (1962), Sikkim (1975), and exchange of territories between India and Bangladesh (2015) were all carried out through constitutional amendments.

On the other hand, the Supreme Court in Maganbhai Ishwarbhai Patel Vs Union of India (1969) ruled that, settlement of a boundary dispute between India and another country does not require a constitutional amendment. It can be done by executive action as it does not involve cession of Indian territory to a foreign country.

MNEMONICS

Concept or Provisions	Shortcut or Mnemonics	Details to Remember
Reorganisation of a State	**Introduce** and **RePreSent** **Simply** like **F**ast & **F**urious	**Introduce RePre** – **Introduce** only with **Re**commendation of **Pre**sident **Sent** – Refer/**Send** bill to State legislature for its views by President (though it is not binding on the Centre) **Simply** – Law to be passed by a **Simple** majority in Parliament. **FF** – **F**irst and **F**ourth schedule altered based on this law.
Exchange, Acquisition or Ceding of territory with another country	**B**lood **SMEAR** test	**B** – **B**erubari case **SM** – **S**pecial **M**ajority (constitutional amendment) for **E**xchange, **A**cquisition or **R**elinquishing (ceding) territory with another country

MAINS STARTER

Area	Building Blocks For Model Introductions
India as Union of States	The Constitution describes India as a Union of States. Though federal in character, the term 'Union' has been used deliberately instead of 'federation' to reflect the fact that our country is 'one integral whole' under a single constitution. It also reflects the fact that we are a 'holding together' federation, and not a result of an agreement between the States.
Parliament's power to reorganise States/UTs	The Parliament, through an ordinary law, can reorganise a State or a Union Territory by merging, dividing or redrawing boundaries. This is a unitary feature of the Indian Constitution. In the past, reorganisation has been carried out based on linguistic factors, popular agitations, political conditions and strategic reasons.

Register on **McGraw Hill Edge** for the following:

- Articles at a glance for this chapter
- Additional Data points for territories during commencement of Constitution; acquisition & ceding of territory and reorganisations of States/UTs since independence
- Practice questions for Preliminary examination
- Attend regular webinars by the author including discussion on **'Think about It'** questions

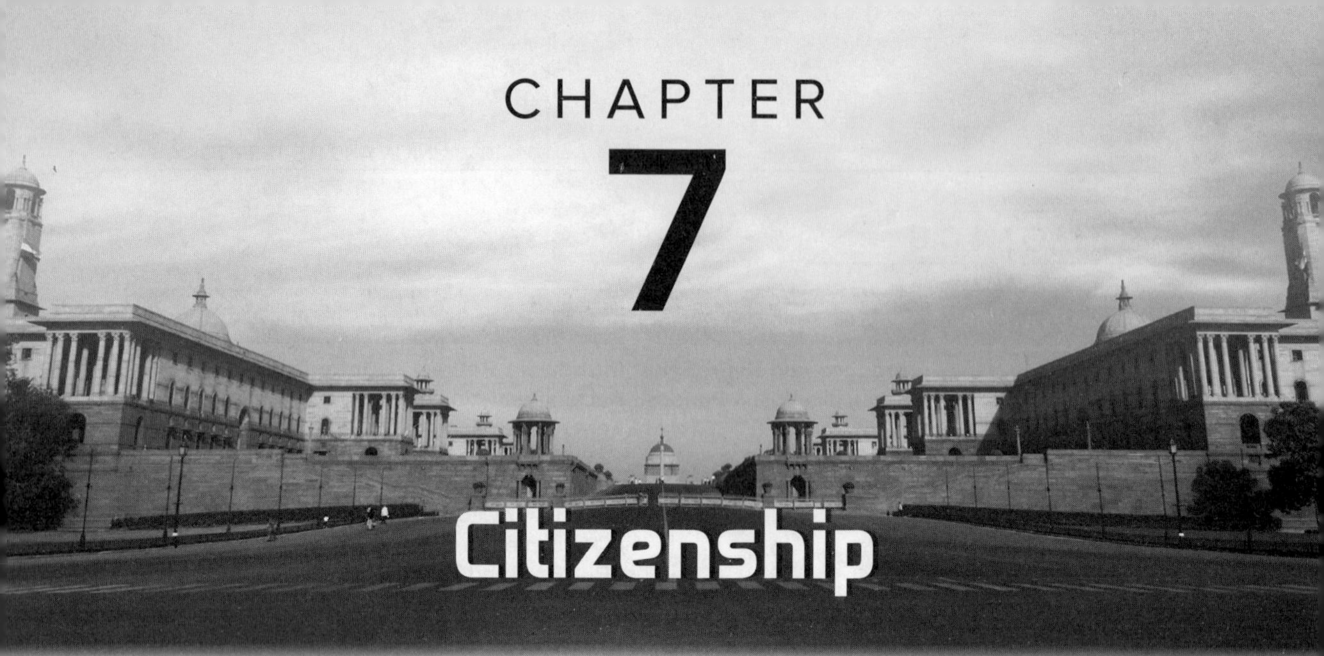

CHAPTER 7

Citizenship

LEARNING OUTCOMES

1. Understanding the concept and significance of Citizenship
2. Evaluating Parliament's power to regulate citizenship through legislation – ways of acquiring and losing citizenship
3. Overseas Citizens of India – Exploring the eligibility, restriction and cancellation
4. Knowing Citizenship Amendment Act, 2019 – its key features, rules and issues surrounding this amendment

The provisions relating to citizenship are found in Part II of the Indian Constitution between Articles 5 and 11. The Constitutional provisions identify the persons who became citizens of India at the commencement of the Constitution i.e., 26 January 1950. The provisions with respect to acquisition and loss of citizenship after the commencement of the Constitution are regulated by a Parliamentary law – The Citizenship Act, 1955. The Citizenship Act was amended in 2019 to provide accelerated citizenship to minorities from three neighbouring countries of Pakistan, Afghanistan and Bangladesh. We shall also analyse the provisions relating to this amendment at the end of the chapter.

Conceptual Points Relating to Citizenship

- Citizenship is defined as full and equal membership of a country. Equality of rights and status is one of the basic aspects of citizenship. In the words of political theorist Hannah Arendt, citizenship is the 'right to have rights.'
- In pre-democratic forms like absolute monarchy or even in colonies of imperial powers, the people within the purview of laws of the State and who were governed by it were called 'subjects.' However, citizens in modern independent nations are expected to participate in the affairs of the State. The quality and extent of participation is regarded as important for evaluating a democracy.

7.1 CONSTITUTIONAL PROVISIONS

There is only single citizenship in India, unlike the dual citizenship in the United States. The Constitutional provisions on who became a citizen of India at the commencement of the Constitution i.e., 26 January 1950 are as follows:

- Persons domiciled (residing) in India if –
  - born in the territory of India; or
  - either of whose parents was born in the territory of India; or
  - ordinarily resident in the territory of India for not less than 5 years immediately preceding such commencement [Art 5].
- Persons migrated from Pakistan if –
  - that person or any of his/her parents or grandparents were born in undivided India (as it existed during the Government of India Act, 1935) and
  - he/she has been ordinarily resident in India since 19 July 1948; or
  - he/she had migrated after 19 July 1948, he/she had been registered as a citizen of India before an appropriate authority after residing in India for at least 6 months [Art 6].
- A Person who migrated to Pakistan after 1 March 1947 but has returned to India for resettlement after residing in India for at least 6 months [Art 7].
- Person of Indian origin – Any person residing outside India, whose parents or grandparents were born in undivided India (as it existed during the Government of India Act, 1935), shall become a citizen of India if he/she is registered as a citizen by the diplomatic or consular representative of India in the country of his/her residence, whether before or after the commencement of the Constitution [Art 8].

Other provisions with respect to citizenship as per the Constitution are as follows:

- No person shall be a citizen of India if he/she has voluntarily acquired the citizenship of a foreign country [Art 9].
- Every person who is or is deemed to be a citizen of India under the provisions of Part II of the Constitution shall continue to be a citizen of India, subject to provisions of law made by the Parliament [Art 10].
- The Parliament shall have the power to make any law with respect to acquisition, termination and any other matter relating to citizenship [Art 11].

7.2 THE CITIZENSHIP ACT, 1955

The Citizenship Act 1955 was first enacted on 30 December 1955. It has been amended on six occasions thereafter in 1986, 1992, 2003, 2005, 2015 and 2019. The Citizenship Act, 1955 as amended from time to time, contains the rules for acquisition and termination of Indian Citizenship.

7.2.1 Acquisition of Citizenship

The Citizenship Act of 1955 prescribes five ways of acquiring citizenship of India, such as birth, descent, registration, naturalisation and incorporation of territory. The provisions with respect to these as per the act are summarised below.

Before understanding the key provisions of the Citizenship Act that grants citizenship of India, we need to be aware of two most important legal systems based on which citizenship rights are acquired in various countries around the world.

1. **Jus Soli** – which in Latin means 'right of soil', is a principle where a child's citizenship is determined by his or her place of birth. Examples include Canada, Mexico, etc.
2. **Jus Sanguinis** – which in Latin means 'right of blood', is a principle where a child's citizenship is determined by the citizenship of parents. Examples include India, Germany, etc.

Criteria for Citizenship	Key Provisions as per the Citizenship Act, 1955 (as amended from time to time)
Birth	• Any person born in India, ▪ on or after 26 January 1950 but prior to 1 July 1987 is a citizen by birth (based on the principle of Jus Soli). ▪ on or after 1 July 1987 is a citizen if either parent was a citizen of India at the time of the birth (based on the principle of Jus Sanguinis). ▪ on or after 3 December 2004 is a citizen if both of their parents are citizens of India or if one parent is a citizen of India and the other is not an illegal migrant at the time of their birth.
Descent	• Any person born outside India, ▪ on or after 26 January 1950 but before 10 December 1992 is citizen by descent if his/her father was a citizen of India at the time of the birth. ▪ on or after 10 December 1992 is considered as citizen if either of his/her parents is a citizen of India at the time of the birth. • Birth of the child (on or after 3 December 2004), is to be registered at an Indian consulate within 1 year of the date of birth. However, registration can be done in some circumstances after 1 year (permission of the Central Government is required in such cases). • The application for registration of the birth of a minor child must be made to an Indian consulate and must be accompanied by an undertaking in writing from the parents of such minor child that he/she does not hold a passport of another country.
Registration	• Following categories of persons can be registered as citizens of India on application by the prescribed authorities: ▪ A person of Indian origin who is ordinarily resident in India for 7 years before making an application for registration; ▪ A person who is married to a citizen of India and is ordinarily resident in India for 7 years before making an application for registration; (For the purposes of above two clauses, the person has to reside in India for a period of 12 months immediately before making the application for registration and should have resided in India for not less than 6 years out of the 8 years immediately preceding those 12 months). ▪ A person of Indian origin who is ordinarily resident in any country or place outside undivided India; ▪ Minor children of persons who are citizens of India; ▪ A person of full age (i.e., above 18 years of age) and capacity whose parents are registered as citizens of India; ▪ A person of full age and capacity who, or either of his/her parents, was earlier citizen of independent India, and has been residing in India for 1 year immediately before making an application for registration; ▪ A person of full age and capacity who has been registered as an overseas citizen of India for 5 years, and who has been residing in India for 1 year before making an application for registration. • A person shall be deemed to be of Indian origin, if he/she or either of his/her parents was born in undivided India or in such territories that became part of India after August 1947.

Criteria for Citizenship	Key Provisions as per the Citizenship Act, 1955 (as amended from time to time)
Naturalisation	• A person can acquire the citizenship of India, through naturalisation if he/she belongs to a country where the citizens of India are allowed to become subjects or citizens of that country by naturalisation. • Has been residing in India or serving the government for 12 months before the date of making application for naturalisation and should have resided in India for not less than 11 years out of the 14 years immediately preceding those 12 months. (For Hindu, Sikh, Buddhist, Jain, Parsi or Christian communities from Afghanistan, Bangladesh or Pakistan, the aggregate period of residence or service of the Government in India as required under this clause shall be 'not less than 5 years' in place of 'not less than 11 years'). • He/she is of good character • Has adequate knowledge of any language specified in the Eighth Schedule. • He/she intends to reside in India after naturalisation. • Government of India can waive all or any of the above conditions in case of a person who has rendered distinguished service in the cause of philosophy, science, literature, arts, world peace etc.
Incorporation of a territory	• If a new territory becomes a part of India, the Government of India shall specify, by an order, the persons of that territory who shall be citizens of India. • For example, the persons of Goa and Puducherry were made citizens of India by an order made when they became part of India.

Apart from the above, there are special provisions made for citizenship of immigrants into Assam as per the Assam Accord of 1985:

- All Persons of Indian Origin (PIO) who came to Assam before 1 January 1966 from Bangladesh and have been ordinarily residents in Assam since then shall be citizens from 1 January 1966.
- For PIO who came to Assam after 1 January 1966 but before 25 March 1971 from Bangladesh and who have been ordinarily residents in Assam since their entry and who has been detected as a foreigner needs to register himself/herself with the appropriate authority of the Government. Such registered persons shall be deemed to be citizens after the expiry of 10 years from the date of detection as a foreigner. Such persons during the intervening period of 10 years shall have all the rights of citizens except the right to vote.

The above two provisions were added through an amendment in 1985 to address the issues raised with respect to the influx of foreigners from Bangladesh into Assam. The Supreme Court, in October 2024, upheld these provisions that provided for a cut-off date of 25 March 1971 for persons who entered Assam from Bangladesh and who were eligible for citizenship after the expiry of 10 years from the date of detection.

THINK ABOUT IT

Acquiring Indian citizenship has moved from the principle of 'jus soli' to 'jus sanguinis'. Trace the history of the Citizenship Act in granting citizenship to people born in India and also the various methods of acquiring citizenship.

7.2.2 Loss of Citizenship

A citizen may lose their citizenship under the Citizenship Act in three ways, as summarised in the following table.

Criteria for Losing Citizenship	Key Provisions as per the Citizenship Act, 1955 (as amended from time to time)
Renunciation	• A citizen of India of full age (above 18 years) and capacity can make a declaration renouncing his/her Indian citizenship before a prescribed authority. Upon registration, he/she shall lose his/her citizenship. The registration shall however be withheld by the Central Government if the declaration is made at a time when India is engaged in a war. • When a person renounces his/her Indian Citizenship, every minor child of that person also loses Indian Citizenship. However, the child can apply within 1 year after attaining full age (18 years) and resume Indian citizenship.
Termination	• Any citizen of India ▪ who by naturalisation, registration or otherwise voluntarily acquires the citizenship of another country, shall cease to be an Indian citizen upon such acquisition, or ▪ has at any time between 26 January 1950 (commencement of the Constitution) and 30 December 1955 (commencement of the Citizenship Act) voluntarily acquired the citizenship of another country, shall cease to be an Indian citizen from the date of commencement of the Citizenship Act. • If an Indian citizen voluntarily acquires the citizenship of another country when India is engaged in any war, these provisions shall not apply until the Central Government otherwise directs.
Deprivation	• Indian citizenship can be terminated (for naturalised, registered and certain other categories of citizens under provisions of the Constitution) by the Central Government under the following circumstances: ▪ Registration or naturalisation was obtained by means of fraud or concealment of facts; or ▪ The citizen has shown disloyalty towards the Constitution; or ▪ The citizen has engaged in trade or communication with enemy during a war; or ▪ The citizen, within 5 years of registration or naturalisation, has been imprisoned in any country for not less than 2 years; or ▪ The citizen has been ordinarily resident out of India for a continuous period of 7 years.

7.2.3 Overseas Citizens of India

The L. M. Singhvi Committee was constituted in 2000 for a comprehensive study of the Indian Diaspora (people of Indian origin living abroad). This Committee recommended granting dual citizenship to persons of Indian origin. However, since our Constitution does not permit dual citizenship, the Citizenship Act was amended in 2003 to provide for the acquisition of Overseas Citizenship of India (OCI) by eligible persons. These provisions have been amended again in 2005 and 2015. The key summary of the provisions relating to OCI as on date (2024) is given below.

Persons who are Eligible for OCI and its Benefits

- OCI is offered by India to the following categories:
  - Any person of full age, (18 years and above) who is a citizen of another country but was earlier a citizen of India or eligible to be one at the time of commencement of the Constitution;
  - Any person of full age, who is a citizen of another country but belonged to a territory that became part of India after 15 August 1947;

- Persons who are minor children of the above two categories of persons;
- A person, who is a minor child, and at least one of his/her parents is a citizen of India;
- A person who is a spouse of Indian citizen or who is a spouse of an OCI cardholder whose marriage has subsisted for at least 2 years at the time of application.

❑ An OCI cardholder can open special bank accounts in India just like NRIs and make investments. OCI cardholders can also buy non-farm property and exercise ownership rights.

❑ An OCI card allows one to apply for a driver's licence, PAN card or open a bank account in India. They get the same economic, financial and educational benefits as NRIs and can also adopt children.

Restrictions for OCI Cardholders

An OCI cardholder cannot vote, hold a government job or purchase agricultural or farmland. The person can also not run for any public office (like the President, the Member of the Parliament etc.).

Cancellation of Registration of OCI Cardholders

The Central Government may cancel the registration of a person as an OCI cardholder, if it is satisfied that:

(a) the registration as an OCI cardholder was obtained by means of fraud, false representation or the concealment of any material fact; or

(b) the OCI cardholder has shown disaffection towards the Constitution of India; or

(c) the OCI cardholder has, during any war in which India may be engaged, unlawfully traded or communicated with an enemy; or

(d) the OCI cardholder has, within 5 years of registration, been sentenced to imprisonment for a term of not less than 2 years; or

(e) it is necessary so to do in the interests of the sovereignty and integrity of India, the security of India, friendly relations with any foreign country, or in the interests of the general public; or

(f) the marriage of an OCI cardholder
- has been dissolved by a competent court of law or otherwise; or
- has not been dissolved but, during the subsistence of such marriage, he/she has solemnised marriage with any other person.

An OCI cardholder may also renounce his/her OCI status by registering a declaration to that effect with the Central government. If any such person renounces his/her OCI cardholder status, the spouse of foreign origin of such person who has obtained an OCI card as well minor children of such person registered as an OCI cardholder will also cease to be OCI cardholders.

7.2.4 Citizenship (Amendment) Act, 2019

The Citizenship Act was amended in 2019 to provide accelerated citizenship to six religious minorities from neighbouring countries of Pakistan, Afghanistan and Bangladesh. This has been done to provide citizenship to persons from these countries who may have entered India due to religious persecution of minorities in these countries at various points of time.

THINK ABOUT IT

Critically analyse the provisions and rules of Citizenship Amendment Act, 2019.

The key provisions of the Citizenship (Amendment) Act (CAA 2019) are as follows:

Citizenship by naturalisation, requires any person to stay in India for 12 months consecutively before the date of application and 11 years out of immediately preceding 14 years. However, the following relaxations have been provided in CAA 2019:

- This period has been reduced to 6 years for six religious refugees – 12 months consecutively before the date of application and 5 years out of immediately preceding 14 years.
- The cut-off date for the same i.e., entry into India from these 3 countries, is 31 December 2014.
- Hindus, Sikhs, Buddhists, Jains, Parsis and Christians from Afghanistan, Pakistan and Bangladesh are the six religious refugees for whom these relaxed conditions are applicable.
- As per the Citizenship Act, illegal immigrants cannot get citizenship. But this clause has also been relaxed for these six religious groups from these three countries if they satisfy the above requirements.

SUMMARY OF OBJECTIONS TO THE AMENDMENT AND GOVERNMENT RESPONSE

Objections to the CAA, 2019	Government Response
Violates Art 14 which provides equality before law or equal protection of laws as it leaves out just Muslims and is discrimination on the basis of religion.	The classification should have nexus to the objective of the law. This law is meant to provide accelerated citizenship to minorities of neighbouring countries which have Islam as State religion. Hence, it is a reasonable classification and the exclusion of Muslims is not arbitrary. Further, the Muslims from these countries are not denied citizenship but need to go through normal rule of 12 years.
Violates Art 21 which guarantees life and liberty to every person in the country.	Same response as above.
Ignores the fact that Shias and Ahmadiyas in these neighbouring countries are persecuted. Further Rohingyas in Burma, Tamils and Muslims in Srilanka, and Christians in Bhutan are also persecuted. The Act extending accelerated citizenship to only minorities from these three countries is arbitrary.	Only the three neighbouring countries have a State religion of Islam. Hence, it addresses this issue. The fact that it does not address other issues is not a ground to say that this Act is unconstitutional. Further, there are statistics to show the decline of minorities drastically in these three countries.

Rules under Citizenship Amendment Act, 2019 (CAA, 2019)

The Central Government notified the rules under CAA, 2019 in the month of March 2024 and amended the same in August 2024. The key provisions of these rules are summarised here.

What proof required to establish country of origin?

According to the CAA Rules, a birth or educational institution certificate, identity document of any kind, any license or certificate, land or tenancy records, or any other document issued by these 3 countries, which proves the applicant was their citizen, would serve as proof of citizenship of these countries. Any document that shows that either of the parents or grandparents or great grandparents of the applicant is or had been a citizen of one of the three countries is also acceptable. These documents will be accepted even after their validity period. It will also be used to establish the religion of the applicant.

As per the amendment in August 2024 to the rules, the list of documents to establish country of origin has been expanded to include any document issued by the State or the Central government or any quasi-judicial authority in India. Further, it also enables local priests or a 'locally reputed community institution' to issue the mandatory certificates certifying the faith of an applicant.

How will the date of entry into India be established?

The cut-off date for entry into India for obtaining citizenship under CAA, 2019 is 31 December 2014.

The Rules list 20 documents, any of which would be admissible as proof of date of entry into India. These include a valid visa or residential permit issued by the Foreigners' Regional Registration Office (FRRO); slip issued by census enumerators in India; a driving licence, Aadhaar, ration card, or any letter issued by the government or a court; an Indian birth certificate; land or tenancy records; registered rent agreement; PAN card issuance document, or a document issued by the central or a State government, PSU, or bank; certificate issued by an elected member of any rural or urban body or officer thereof, or a revenue officer; a post office account; an insurance policy; utility bills; court or tribunal records; EPF documents; school leaving certificate or academic certificate; a municipality trade license; or a marriage certificate.

Who will be in charge for processing applications?

While citizenship applications were earlier made to the District Collector – who is under the administrative control of the State government – the new Rules provide for an Empowered Committee and a District Level Committee (DLC), to be instituted by the Centre, to receive and process the applications, which are to be submitted electronically.

Applications will be made to the DLC, and the final decision will be taken by the Empowered Committee. The Empowered Committee will be headed by a Director (Census Operations), and will have as its members an officer of the Subsidiary Intelligence Bureau (under the Ministry of Home Affairs) of the rank of deputy secretary or above, the Foreign Regional Registration Office (FRRO), the State Informatics Officer of the National Informatics Centre (under the Ministry of Electronics & Information Technology), and the Postmaster General (under the Union Ministry of Communications) of the State. A representative each from the State home department and the Railways will be invitees to the Committee.

The DLC shall consist of the District Informatics Officer or District Informatics Assistant of the district concerned, and a nominee of the central government. The two invitees to the committee will be a representative of the District collector's office not below the rank of Naib Tehsildar or equivalent, and the jurisdictional station master of the Railways.

The CAA, 2019 only aims to provide accelerated citizenship to immigrants from 3 neighbouring countries and as such should not result in any issues for Indian Citizens. However, the government must ensure that implementation of the above mentioned rules made under the amendment including creation of National Register of Citizens (if and when done in future) should not create any undue hardship for citizens of our country, especially Muslims, in establishing their citizenship.

Scan the QR code for conceptual video on Citizenship

McGraw Hill edge

MNEMONICS

Concept or Provisions	Shortcut or Mnemonics	Details to Remember
Acquisition and Loss of citizenship	**BIRD Not TiReD**	**B – B**irth within India with one parent being citizen and another not being an illegal immigrant **I – I**ncorporation of a territory **R – R**egistration of various categories of persons **D – D**escent of a child born to an Indian parent (one of the parents) outside India and registered within 1 year **N – N**aturalisation – anyone who has been residing in India for 1+11 years. For 6 religious communities except Muslims from 3 neighbouring countries for 1+5 years. **Loss of Citizenship** **T – T**ermination if an Indian citizen acquires citizenship of another country **R – R**enunciation of citizenship by an Indian Citizen above 18 years of age **D – D**eprivation of citizenship (of naturalised and registered citizens) by central government under certain circumstances.

MAINS STARTER

Area	Building Blocks For Model Introductions
Single citizenship	The Indian Constitution, though federal in character, provides for a single citizenship of the country and no separate citizenship of a State. Any law relating to citizenship can be passed only by the Parliament. This is a unitary feature that reflects the fact that our country is 'one integral whole' under a single constitution and single citizenship.
Citizenship Amendment Act, 2019	The Citizenship Amendment Act, 2019 (CAA, 2019) provides for accelerated citizenship to Hindus, Christians, Sikhs, Jains, Buddhists and Parsis from neighbouring countries of Pakistan, Afghanistan and Bangladesh.

UPSC Previous Years' Questions of Preliminary Examination

1. With reference to India, consider the following statements **[2021]**

1. There is only one citizenship and one domicile.
2. A citizen by birth only can become the Head of the State.
3. A foreigner once granted the citizenship cannot be deprived of it under any circumstances.

Which of the statements given above is/are correct?

(a) 1 only (b) 2 only (c) 1 and 3 only (d) 2 and 3 only

Solution: (a)

Explanation: As discussed in Section 7.1, there is only single citizenship and single domicile status (residential status) in our country and hence statement 1 is correct. In our Constitution, there is no distinction between a natural citizen or a naturalised citizen from holding public office including Head of the State and hence, statement 2 is incorrect. As discussed in Section 7.2.2, the citizenship granted to a foreigner can be deprived under specified circumstances and hence statement 3 is also incorrect and the answer is (a).

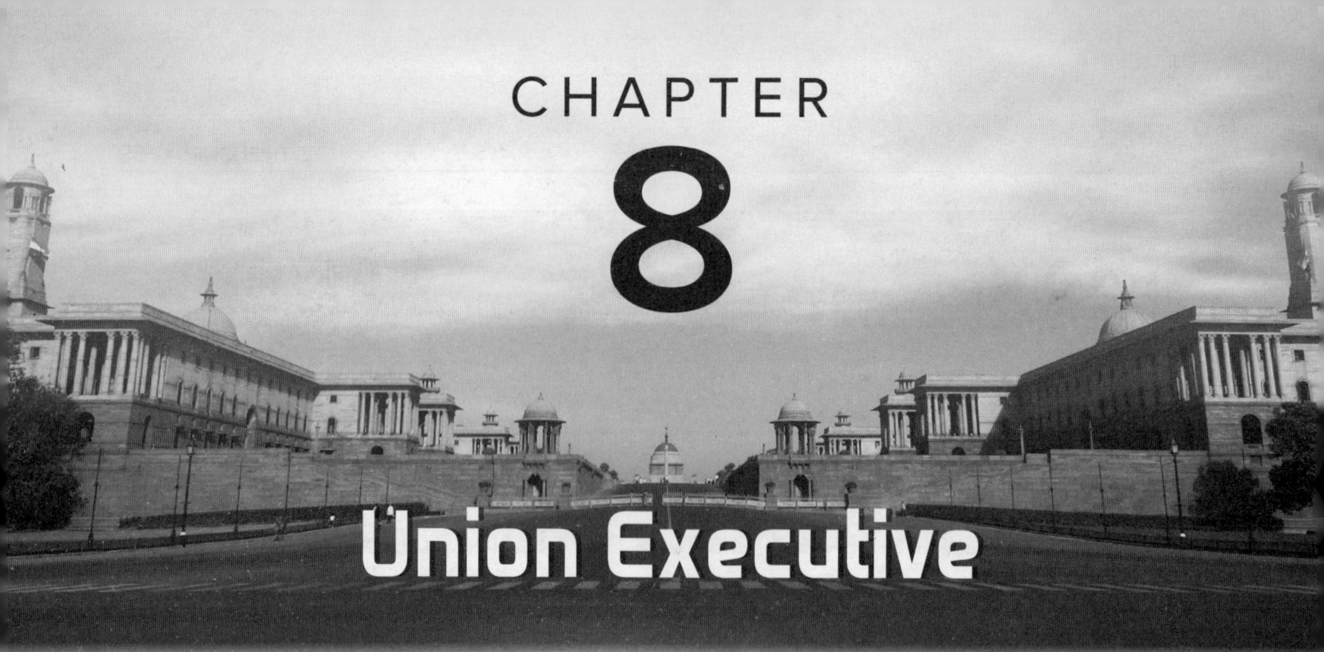

CHAPTER 8

Union Executive

LEARNING OUTCOMES

1. Understanding the Composition and Functions of the Union Executive
2. Examining the Role of the President – Required qualification, Election Process, Terms of Office and Impeachment
3. Analysing the President's Relationship with the Council of Ministers and the circumstances when the President can exercise his/her discretion
4. Exploring the President's powers including Veto, Ordinance and Pardoning power – Issues surrounding them and way forward
5. Understanding the role of Vice-President – Qualification, Election Process, Terms of Office and Removal
6. Evaluating the role of Prime Minister and Council of Ministers – Powers, Principle of Collective Responsibility, Constitution and Role of Cabinet Committees

8.1 INTRODUCTION TO THE EXECUTIVE

The Indian Constitution provides for a Parliamentary form of Government that is modelled on the British system. The Constituent Assembly debated between adoption of the Parliamentary form and the Presidential form of government before settling for the Parliamentary form of Government.

The executive branch in our country is federal in character. This means that there is an executive at the Union level for carrying out the executive functions vested in the Union as per the Constitution. There is a similar setup at each of the States for carrying out the functions vested in such States as per the Constitution. We will first discuss the provisions of the Union executive in detail. The provisions of the State executive are very similar to the Union executive with a few exceptions, which we will understand in the next chapter.

8.2 FUNCTIONS OF THE UNION EXECUTIVE

There are three main branches of Government viz., the executive, the legislature and the judiciary. The judiciary is an independent branch that is formed for interpreting the Constitution, various laws and also for the delivery of justice. The legislature and the executive are the two branches of the State that are tasked with the duties of administering the country.

In a Presidential democracy, like the United States, there is a strict separation of powers between the legislature and the executive. It is the exclusive domain of the legislature to make laws and the executive headed by the President is responsible for implementing the laws.

In a Parliamentary democracy, like India, there is no strict separation of powers but a broad mechanism of checks and balance. The executive is part of the legislature and initiates most of the legislative work. It introduces bills and gets them passed in the legislature. Thereafter, it is responsible for implementing these laws. Article 73(1) of the Constitution specifies that the executive power of the Union shall extend to the matter with respect to which the Parliament has power to make laws.

8.3 COMPOSITION OF THE UNION EXECUTIVE

The Union executive consists of the President, the Vice-President, the Council of Ministers headed by the Prime Minister and the Attorney General of India. We shall discuss in detail about the President, the Vice-President and the Council of Ministers in this chapter.

Union Executive		
President	**Vice-President**	**Council of Ministers**
• Election of the President • Qualification, conditions and term of office • Impeachment of the President • Relationship with Council of Ministers • Powers of the President	• Election of Vice-President • Removal of the Vice-President • Functions of the Vice-President	• Council of Ministers as the real executive head • Appointment of the Prime Minister and Ministers by the President • Provisions relating to ministers • Principle of collective responsibility

MNEMONICS

Concept or Provisions	Shortcut or Mnemonics	Details to Remember
Composition of Union Executive	**President and his/her deputy Counselled** the **Attorney**	Union executive consists of (a) **P**resident (b) **V**ice-President (c) **C**ouncil of Ministers (d) **A**ttorney General of India

8.4 PRESIDENT

The Constitution provides that there shall be a President of India (Art 52). The executive power of the Union is vested in the President and he/she shall exercise it directly or through officers' subordinate to him/her. He/she shall also act as the supreme command of the defence forces of the Union (Art 53).

8.4.1 Election of the President

India is a republic because it has an elected head for the country viz., the President of India. The Constitution has provided for indirect election of the President.

8.4.1.1 Electoral College

The term 'electoral college' refers to the set of people who are eligible to vote in an election. For example, in an election for the Lok Sabha or the Legislative Assembly of a State, the electoral college consists of all eligible citizens above the age of 18 whose name appears in the electoral rolls.

The electoral college for the President (Art 54) consists of:

(a) Elected Members of the Parliament; and

(b) Elected Members of Legislative Assembly of States including the Members of Legislative Assembly of National Capital Territory (NCT) of Delhi and Puducherry.

Hence, it follows that the nominated members of the Rajya Sabha do not vote in the Presidential elections. Similarly, the members of the Legislative Councils of States where they exist also do not vote in the Presidential elections. The underlying philosophy behind this electoral college is that the President of the Indian republic should be elected by only those elected representatives who are either directly or indirectly elected by the people of our country. The members of the Lok Sabha and the Legislative Assemblies of States (including NCT of Delhi and Puducherry) are elected directly by universal adult franchise. The elected members of the Rajya Sabha are elected by the elected MLAs of States (including NCT of Delhi and Puducherry).

The Legislative Assemblies of NCT of Delhi and Puducherry were added to the electoral college by the 70th amendment to the Constitution in 1992. However, the recent reorganisation of the State of Jammu & Kashmir into the Union Territories of Jammu & Kashmir (with a Legislative Assembly) and Ladakh (without a Legislative Assembly) in 2019 was carried out through a Parliamentary law as per provisions of Article 3. The inclusion of the Legislative Assembly of the Union territory of Jammu & Kashmir in the electoral college will require a Constitutional amendment of Article 54, which has not been carried out. Hence, as it stands today (2024), the elected members of the Legislative Assembly of the Union territory of Jammu & Kashmir will not be eligible to vote in the Presidential election.

8.4.1.2 Manner of Election of the President

1. The Constitution has devised a mechanism for the election of the President that provides for equal weightage to the Union and the States as a whole. The total number of elected members in the Parliament is 776 while the number of elected MLAs of all States and the Union territories of Delhi and Puducherry put together (excluding UT of J & K as explained above) is 4033. Hence, the usual principle of one vote-one value will not achieve the desired objective of providing equal weightage between the Union and all the States as a whole. Similarly, considering that different States have different populations, the value of vote of each MLA also needs to be arrived at using a formula that will provide for uniformity in the scale of representation of different States. Article 55 provides the formula to achieve this uniformity among the States inter se as well as parity between the States as a whole and the Union.

   The provisions of this (Art 55) are summarised as follows:

   (a) Each elected member of the Legislative Assembly of a State shall have as many number of votes as there are multiples of 1000 in the quotient obtained by dividing the population of the State by the total number of the elected members of the Assembly. For the purpose of this calculation, the population as per 1971 Census is considered.

In simple terms,

$$\text{Value of vote of each MLA of a State} = \frac{\text{Population of the State as per 1971 Census}}{\text{Number of elected MLAs of the State} \times 1000}$$

For example, for the State of Uttar Pradesh, the value is arrived at as follows:

$$\text{Value of vote of each MLA of Uttar Pradesh} = \frac{8,38,49,905}{403 \times 1000} = 208$$

For the State of Karnataka, the value is arrived at as follows:

$$\text{Value of vote of each MLA of Karnataka} = \frac{2,92,99,014}{224 \times 1000} = 131$$

Similarly, the values are calculated for each State based on their population (as per 1971 Census) and the number of elected MLAs. Hence, the value of vote varies for MLAs of various States. The summary of the same is given below:

Name of the State	Number of Elected MLAs	Population (1971 Census)	Value of vote of each MLA	Total value of votes for the State
(1)	(2)	(3)	(4)	(2 × 4)
ANDHRA PRADESH	175	27800586	159	27825
ARUNACHAL PRADESH	60	467511	8	480
ASSAM	126	14625152	116	14616
BIHAR	243	42126236	173	42039
CHHATTISGARH	90	11637494	129	11610
GOA	40	795120	20	800
GUJARAT	182	26697475	147	26754
HARYANA	90	10036808	112	10080
HIMACHAL PRADESH	68	3460434	51	3468
JHARKHAND	81	14227133	176	14256
KARNATAKA	224	29299014	131	29344
KERALA	140	21347375	152	21280
MADHYA PRADESH	230	30016625	131	30130
MAHARASHTRA	288	50412235	175	50400
MANIPUR	60	1072753	18	1080
MEGHALAYA	60	1011699	17	1020
MIZORAM	40	332390	8	320
NAGALAND	60	516449	9	540
ODISHA	147	21944615	149	21903
PUNJAB	117	13551060	116	13572
RAJASTHAN	200	25765806	129	25800
SIKKIM	32	209843	7	224

Name of the State	Number of Elected MLAs	Population (1971 Census)	Value of vote of each MLA	Total value of votes for the State
(1)	(2)	(3)	(4)	(2 × 4)
TAMIL NADU	234	41199168	176	41184
TELANGANA	119	15702122	132	15708
TRIPURA	60	1556342	26	1560
UTTARAKHAND	70	4491239	64	4480
UTTAR PRADESH	403	83849905	208	83824
WEST BENGAL	294	44312011	151	44394
NCT OF DELHI	70	4065698	58	4060
PUDUCHERRY	30	471707	16	480
Total	**4033**			**5,43,231**

Note: The above table is excluding 90 Assembly seats of J & K after its reorganisation into a Union territory in 2019.

(b) Each elected member of either House of Parliament shall have a value of vote that is obtained by dividing the total value of votes of all MLAs of States by the total number of elected members of both Houses of Parliament.

$$\text{Value of vote of each MP} = \frac{\text{Total value of votes of MLAs of all States}}{\text{Total number of elected members of the Parliament}}$$

$$= \frac{543231}{(543 + 233)} = 700$$

Hence, the value of vote for each MP, either from the Lok Sabha or the Rajya Sabha, is the same at 700.

The total value of votes for all MPs = 776 × 700 = **5,43,200**

As can be seen from the above calculations, this formula provides for uniformity among the States inter se as well as parity between the States as a whole and the Union.

2. The election of the President shall be held in accordance with the system of proportional representation by means of the single transferable vote and the voting at such election shall be by secret ballot.

We are all familiar with the process of General elections in our country. It is for electing members to the Lok Sabha and the State Legislative Assemblies. These elections are held according to 'plurality system', which is famously known as the 'first-past-the-post system'. In these elections for single-member constituencies, the candidate who gets more votes than any other candidate is declared elected.

However, all indirect elections in our country including the Presidential election happens in accordance with the system of proportional representation by means of the single transferable vote. Let us understand the mechanism in a simple manner taking a hypothetical example.

Let us assume, there are 100 electors (voters) in an election to elect the President and there are 4 contestants – A, B, C and D. Let us also assume for ease of calculation that the value of each vote is only 1 and so the total value of votes is also 100. Under the first-past-the-post system, the electors will cast their votes for one of the candidates and the candidate who obtains more votes than other three (maximum votes) is declared the winner. However, in proportional representation by means of the single transferable vote, voters can rank individual candidates, rather than just vote for a single candidate. The ballot paper in such an election will list down the contesting candidates and the voters can provide their first, second, third preference and so on against the names of contesting candidates. An example for the same is provided below for four voters.

Voter 1		Voter 2		Voter 3		Voter 4	
Name of candidate	Pref Rank	Name of candidate	Pref Rank	Name of candidate	Pref Rank	Name of candidate	Pref Rank
A	1	A	4	A	2	A	3
B	4	B	1	B	3	B	2
C	2	C	2	C	1	C	
D	3	D	3	D		D	1

This system does not determine the winner based on 'maximum' first preference votes, but a quota is calculated for arriving at the number of votes required for being declared elected.

$$\text{The formula for arriving at the quota is} = \frac{\text{Total number of valid votes / Value of votes polled}}{\text{Number of vacancies + 1}} + 1$$

$$\text{So, for election of the President in our example, this would be} = \frac{100}{1+1} + 1 = 51$$

Let us assume, the value of first preference votes at the end of the first round of counting is as follows:

Value of 'First' preference votes	A	B	C	D
At the end of the first round of counting	35	30	20	15

As no candidate has obtained the required quota of 51, the candidate with least first preference votes is excluded and their second preferences are transferred to the respective continuing candidates. Let us assume again that out of 15 voters who had provided their first preference to D, 5 had given second preference to A and 10 had given their second preference to B. Then this would be transferred to the respective candidates. This is the reason for the procedure to be known as proportional representation by means of 'single transferable vote'.

Particulars	A	B	C	D
Value of first preference votes for various candidates at the end of the first round of counting	35	30	20	15
Transfer of second preference votes of Candidate D (who is excluded as he obtained the least first preference votes)	5	10	-	X
Value of first preference votes at the end of the second round of counting	40	40	20	X

As no candidate has obtained the required quota of 51 even after the second round, the same process of exclusion of the candidate with least first preference vote and transfer of their second preference votes to other continuing candidates is carried out. If at the end of any count, two or more candidates have been credited with the same lowest number of votes, the candidate who had secured the lowest first preference votes (without considering any transfer) will be excluded. And if that number is also the same, the candidate to be excluded is determined by draw of lots.

Particulars	A	B	C	D
Value of first preference votes for various candidates at the end of the first round of counting	35	30	20	15
Transfer of second preference votes of Candidate D (who is excluded as he obtained the least first preference votes)	5	10	–	X
Value of first preference votes at the end of the second round of counting	40	40	20	X
Transfer of second preference votes of Candidate C (who is excluded) to continuing candidates	7	13	X	X
Value of first preference votes at the end of the third round	47	53	X	X

So, in the above example, Candidate B will be declared as the winner.

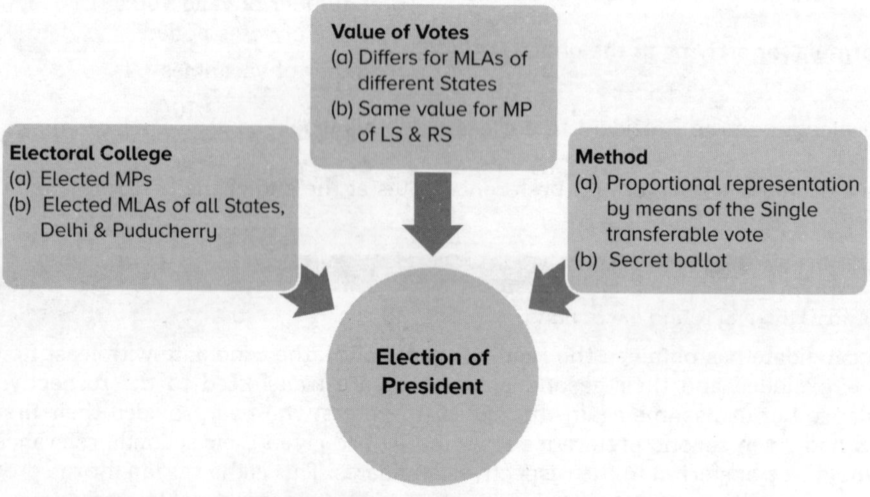

8.4.2 Qualification, Conditions and Term of Office

8.4.2.1 Qualification for Election as the President

In order to be qualified to be elected as the President, a person must:

(a) be a citizen of India;

(b) have completed the age of thirty-five years;

(c) be qualified for election as a member of the House of the People; and

(d) must not hold any 'office of profit' under the Government of India or the Government of any State or under any local or other authority subject to the control of Union/State Government.

However, a sitting President or Vice President or Governor of a State or a Minister either of the Union or a State is not considered an 'office of profit'.

8.4.2.2 Office of Profit

The term 'office of profit' has not been defined in the Constitution or in any law made by Parliament. It owes its origins to the British system under which, no person who has an office or place of profit under the King, or receives a pension from the Crown, shall be capable of serving as a member of the House of Commons. This was instituted so that there would not be any undue influence from the royal household in administrative affairs.

Disqualifying the holders of offices of profit in India is also an effort in this direction for protecting the independence of the legislators. A person may not be able to discharge his/her functions as a legislator and question the government if the government is in a position to influence him/her. This understanding has led to the development of the concept of 'office of profit'.

In India, holding an 'office of profit' is a disqualification for being President, Vice President, Governor or Members of Parliament and State Legislature. However, in respect of Members of Parliament and State Legislature, the Parliament or the State Legislature, respectively, can declare that holding certain offices will not disqualify its holders from being a member.

While there is no definition for 'office of profit', there are Supreme Court case laws that have laid down the key tests to determine whether an 'office' would constitute an 'office of profit'.

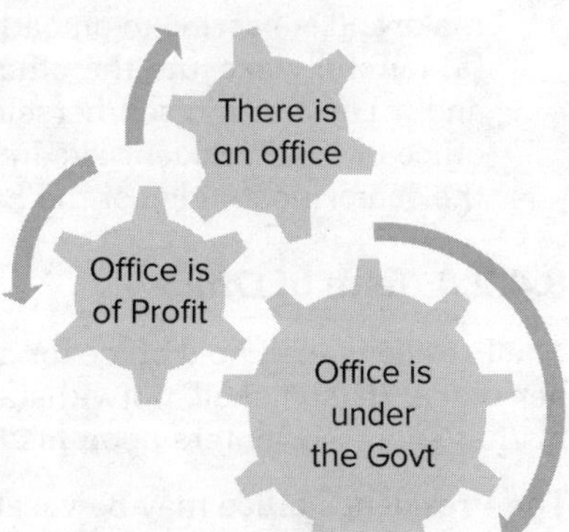

(a) There is an office
- The term 'office' refers to an employment which is permanent in nature and exists independent of the holder.
- A post which is created for doing certain duties and which is temporary in nature will not constitute an 'office'.

(b) The office is one of 'profit'
- The member should be entitled to monetary benefit because of holding that office.
- In respect of the Members of Parliament, it should be apart from the 'compensatory allowance' for certain posts that is allowed under the ***Parliament (Prevention of Disqualification) Act, 1959.***
- The monetary benefit can be in cash or even in kind – like free furnished accommodation, free air travel etc.
- As per the ruling of the Supreme Court in the case ***Jaya Bachan Vs Union of India***, it is not necessary that a person has actually received the allowances or benefits. As long as they are entitled to the same, it will constitute 'profit' whether actually received or not.

(c) The office is under the Government
- The Supreme Court through its various judgements have laid down certain tests for determining whether an office is under the Government. They can be summarised as follows:
  (1) Whether the government makes the appointment;
  (2) Whether the government has the right to remove or dismiss the office-holder;
  (3) Whether the government pays remuneration;
  (4) Whether the office-holder performs functions for the government;
  (5) Whether the government controls the duties and functions of the office-holder.

8.4.2.3 Conditions for Office of President

1. The President shall not be a member of either House of Parliament or of a House of the Legislature of any State. If any such member gets elected as the President, he/she shall be deemed to have vacated his/her seat in that House on the date on which he/she enters upon his/her office as President [Art 59].
2. The President shall be entitled without payment of rent to the use of his/her official residence and shall be also entitled to such emoluments, allowances and privileges as may be determined by the Parliament by law [Art 59].

   The Parliament has enacted the ***President's Emoluments and Pension Act, 1951***, which was amended in 2018. As per the latest amendment, the President is paid an emolument (salary) of ₹5 lakhs per month and pension for retired President is at the rate of 50% of the emoluments per month.
3. The emoluments and allowances of the President shall not be diminished during his/her term of office.
4. The President (and every person acting as President or discharging his/her functions) shall make and subscribe to an oath or affirmation. In this oath, the President swears that he/she will (a) faithfully execute the office; (b) preserve, protect and defend the Constitution and the law; and (c) devote himself/herself to the service and well-being of the people of India. This oath of office of the President is administered by the Chief Justice of India and in his/her absence, by the seniormost judge of the Supreme Court available [Art 60].

8.4.2.4 Term of Office

The President shall hold office for a term of five years from the date on which he/she enters upon his/her office. He/she shall, notwithstanding the expiration of his/her term, continue to hold office until his/her successor enters upon his/her office [Art 56].

The President's office may be vacated within the term of five years if:

(a) he/she resigns from his/her office by writing to the Vice-President or
(b) he/she is removed from office, for violation of the Constitution, by impeachment proceedings under Art 61.

Any resignation by the President shall immediately be communicated by the Vice-President to the Speaker of the Lok Sabha.

The President of India is eligible for re-election to that office [Art 57]. However, as a matter of convention, except for the first President of India, Shri Rajendra Prasad, who served two consecutive terms, no President has been re-elected to the post till date.

An election to fill a vacancy caused by the expiration of the term of office of the President shall be completed before the expiration of the term. An election to fill a vacancy in the office of the President occurring by reason of his/her death, resignation, removal or otherwise shall be held as soon as possible after, and in no case later than six months from the date of occurrence of the vacancy. The person so elected as President shall be entitled to hold office for the full term of five years from the date on which he/she enters office [Art 62].

8.4.2.5 Miscellaneous Provisions relating to Election of the President and the Vice-President

Matters relating to, or connected with, the election of a President or a Vice-President [Art 71]

(a) ***All doubts and disputes arising out of or in connection with the election of a President or a Vice-President shall be inquired into and decided by the Supreme Court whose decision shall be final.***

In 2012, the election of Pranab Mukherjee as the President was challenged in the Supreme Court by P. A. Sangma, who was the opposition candidate for that election. However, the Supreme Court later rejected the petition and did not proceed further with it.

(b) ***If the election of a person as a President or a Vice-President is declared void by the Supreme Court, acts done by him/her in the exercise and performance of the powers and duties of the office of the President or the Vice-President, as the case may be, on or before the date of the decision of the Supreme Court shall not be invalidated by reason of that declaration.***

(c) Subject to the provisions of this Constitution, the Parliament may by law regulate any matter relating to or connected with the election of a President or a Vice-President.

The Parliament has legislated '***The Presidential and Vice-Presidential Elections Act, 1952***' for the purpose of conducting elections to the post of the President and the Vice-President. Some of the key provisions of this Act are as follows:

1. The nomination paper for the Presidential candidate should have 50 electors as proposers and 50 electors as seconders – This means that out of (a) elected MLAs of various States & Union territories of Delhi and Puducherry, (b) elected MPs of the Lok Sabha and the Rajya Sabha, 50 members should propose and 50 members should second a Presidential candidate.
2. The nomination paper for a Vice-Presidential candidate should have 20 electors as proposers and 20 electors as seconders – This means that out of all MPs of the Lok Sabha and the Rajya Sabha, 20 members should propose and 20 members should second a Vice-Presidential candidate.

(d) ***The election of a person as the President or the Vice-President shall not be called in question on the ground of the existence of any vacancy for whatever reason among the members of the electoral college electing him/her.***

Scan the QR code for conceptual video on President's qualification, election and impeachment

McGraw Hill edge

8.4.3 Impeachment of the President

Procedure for impeachment of the President [Art 61]:

1. When a President is to be impeached for violation of the Constitution, the charge shall be preferred by either House of the Parliament.
2. No such charge shall be preferred unless – (a) the proposal to prefer such charge is contained in a resolution which has been moved after at least 14 days' notice in writing signed by not less than one-fourth of the total number of members of the House has been given of their intention to move the resolution, and (b) such resolution has been passed by a majority of not less than two-thirds of the total membership of the House.
3. The first House is the House that 'prefers charge' and the other House is called the 'investigating House'.
4. The 'investigating House' shall investigate the charge or cause the charge to be investigated and the President shall have the right to appear and to be represented at such investigation.
5. If as a result of the investigation a resolution is passed by a majority of not less than two-thirds of the total membership of the House by which the charge was investigated or caused to be investigated, declaring that the charge preferred against the President has been sustained, such

resolution shall have the effect of removing the President from his/her office as from the date on which the resolution is so passed.

The impeachment of the President is a ***quasi-judicial*** procedure in the Parliament. This is because, the Parliament performs an investigation on the charges against the President before voting on the resolution for his/her removal.

It should be noted that the Constitution has provided a stringent provision for the removal of the President as he/she is the highest authority in the country. The majority stipulated in each House is 2/3rd of the total membership of that house.

In the Lok Sabha, this number at present would be = 2/3 × 543 = 362

In the Rajya Sabha, this number at present would be = 2/3 × 245 = 164

So, irrespective of the number of members present and voting, the above number of votes should be cast in favour of a resolution for the impeachment of the President. This majority is specified only in Article 61 for removal of the President in the Constitution and nowhere else. It must also be noted that the Constitution of India does not provide any specific names for different types of majorities.

Here we will refer to this majority of 2/3rd of the total membership of the House in short form as 'Highest Special Majority'. It must, however, be kept in mind while answering questions in the examination that the specific majority is explained in detail at the beginning and then the short form may be used subsequently.

The following points should be kept in mind as regards impeachment of the President:

- Only the elected Members of Parliament vote in the Presidential election, while both elected and nominated members (of the Rajya Sabha) vote in the House during the impeachment proceedings.
- While the elected MLAs of various States and Union Territories of Delhi and Puducherry vote in the Presidential election, they do not have any role in the impeachment which can be carried out only by the Parliament.
- No President of India has been impeached till date.

Impeachment of President [Art 61]		
Ground	**Majority required**	**Procedure in brief**
• Violation of the Constitution • This is not defined in the Constitution but any criminal act which is against the constitutional provisions or its values will be treated as 'Violation of the Constitution'	• 2/3rd of the total membership of House (in the Lok Sabha and the Rajya Sabha) – [may be referred as 'Highest Special Majority' in this book]. • The resolution containing the proposal for removal has to be signed by not less than 1/4th of the total membership of the House preferring the charge.	• Charge may be preferred in either House. • Resolution to be passed by 'Highest Special Majority' in the House that prefers the charge. • President shall have the right to defend his/her case in the investigating House. • If the resolution is passed by 'Highest Special Majority' in the investigating House as well, the President is impeached from the date of such resolution.

8.4.4 Relationship with Council of Ministers

The Constitution specifies that all executive powers of the Union shall be vested in the President [Art 53]. The President is therefore the head of the Union executive.

However, in our Parliamentary democracy, the President is only a nominal head of the Union executive while the real executive powers are exercised by the Council of Ministers headed by the Prime Minister.

Dr. Ambedkar declared in the Constituent Assembly that the President occupies the same position as the King under the British conventions. He/she is head of the State. The President nonetheless is expected to act as a conscience keeper and 'a safety valve' for the Council of Ministers. He/she takes an oath to preserve, protect and defend the Constitution (Art 60).

Article 73(1) of the Constitution specifies that the executive power of the Union shall extend to the matter with respect to which the Parliament has the power to make laws. It may be mentioned that the executive functions refer to all the residue of governmental functions that remain after the legislative and the judicial functions. In general, the executive functions of the Union comprise policy making and its execution, carrying out various schemes for the welfare of the people, maintenance of armed forces, maintaining diplomatic relations with foreign countries etc.

8.4.4.1 Original Provisions in the Constitution

Article 74(1) of the Constitution as originally adopted read as follows:

> 'There shall be a Council of Ministers with the Prime Minister at the head to aid and advise the President'.

While, there was no express provision in the Constitution to state that the President is bound to act as per advice of the Council of Ministers, the Supreme Court had laid down in 1955 in *Ram Jawaya Vs State of Punjab*, that the President is only a nominal head and was bound to act as per advice of the Council of Ministers in both the executive and the legislative matters. This was reiterated by the Supreme Court in various subsequent decisions.

8.4.4.2 42nd and 44th Amendment to the Constitution

To amply clarify this position, Article 74(1) was amended in the 42nd Amendment Act in 1976 as follows:

> 'There shall be a Council of Ministers with the Prime Minister at the head to aid and advise the President who shall, in the exercise of his functions, act in accordance with such advice'.

In legal parlance, the word 'shall' makes it an obligation. Hence as per the amended Article, the President is bound by the advice of the Council of Ministers.

When the Janata Party Government came to power in 1978, while the above Article was retained, the 44th amendment added a proviso to Art 74(1) as follows:

> 'Provided that the President may require the Council of Ministers to reconsider such advice, either generally or otherwise, and the President shall act in accordance with the advice tendered after such reconsideration'.

Thus, the above provision provides a discretionary power to the President to require the Council of Ministers to reconsider their decision but only once. The President shall act as per the advice provided after such reconsideration, even if it is the same advice that is reiterated by the Council of Ministers.

Having said that, the President under normal course will not use this discretionary power as he/she is also aware of his/her position as only a nominal head. In fact, this provision has been used only twice in the past since 1978. President K. R. Narayanan had returned the advice provided by the Council of Ministers headed by Prime Minister I. K. Gujral in October 1997 that sought to dismiss the State Government in Uttar Pradesh and impose President's rule. A similar advice in September 1998 seeking to dismiss the State Government in Bihar and impose President's rule was again returned by him for reconsideration by the Council of Ministers headed by Prime Minister Atal Bihari Vajpayee.

In both these instances, the Council of Ministers did not send it back for approval of the President. Hence, while any such return of advice can be overruled by the Council of Ministers (as the President is bound to act as per advice tendered after reconsideration), it has been observed in the past that it has a huge moral force that resulted in the Council of Ministers not tendering the same advice again immediately.

In fact, subsequently in February 1999, after massacres of Dalits in Bihar that claimed 35 Dalit lives, the council of ministers reiterated the advice to President K R Narayanan for imposition of President's rule in the State. It was imposed in February 1999, but since the Rajya Sabha did not approve of the same, it was revoked and the same State government was reinstated in Bihar in March 1999.

8.4.5 Powers of the President

As discussed earlier, the real authority in our Parliamentary democracy lies with the Council of Ministers. However, since the President is the Constitutional head, all actions are taken in the name of the President based on ministerial advice. The key powers of the President can be summarised as follows:

President's Powers		
Administrative and Military	**Legislative**	**Judicial**
• All executive actions of the Government of India shall be expressed to be taken in the name of the President [Art 77]. • President has rule-making powers for Government of India [Art 77]. • Appointment of persons to various posts under the Constitution and other statutes. • Supreme command of the Defence forces of the Union [Art 53]	• Summoning, Prorogation of the Houses of Parliament and Dissolution of House of the People [Art 85]. • Addressing the first session of Parliament at the beginning of each year and after every General election to the House of the People [Art 87]. • Summoning joint sitting of Houses to resolve a deadlock [Art 108]. • Right to address and send messages to the Parliament [Art 86]. • Nominating 12 members to the Council of States [Art 80]. • Assent to legislation and veto power [Art 111 and 201]. • Ordinance-making power [Art 123].	• Power to grant Pardons [Art 72]. • Appointment of judges to the Supreme Court and the High Courts.

The above are the key powers of the President of India. There are also certain other powers including Emergency powers. These powers will be discussed under the relevant chapters. However, we will discuss the following three important powers in detail here – (a) Veto power, (b) Ordinance-making power, and (c) Pardoning power.

8.4.5.1 Veto Power

In simple terms, veto is the power to either reject or delay the passage of a bill. This power is usually exercised by the executive head in various countries. In Presidential democracies where there is strict separation of powers between the executive and the legislature, the executive head need to have some form of control over the legislation. For example, in the United States, the veto power of the President is justified on the grounds that any legislation should not undermine the powers of the President or should not provide for practically unimplementable provisions.

There are four types of veto across the world, which can be broadly summarised as follows:

1. Absolute veto, that is, withholding of assent to the bill passed by the legislature
   - It's an end to the legislation if vetoed and so it cannot become a law.
   - Till the year 1700, English Crown had absolute veto power over Parliament's legislation. However, owing to the development of the Parliamentary system of Government (where the Cabinet initiates almost all the legislative proposals too), this has not been in effect in Britain since 1700.
2. Qualified veto, which can be overridden by the legislature with a higher majority.
   - A veto is qualified when it can be overridden (removed) by an extraordinary majority of the legislature and can become a law.
   - The US President has Qualified veto power. If the US Congress sends a bill, the US President can return the bill within 10 days if he/she has objections. If the US Congress passes the bill again with 2/3rd majority, it becomes an Act without the President's signature.
3. Suspensive veto, which can be overridden by the legislature with an ordinary majority.
   - A veto is suspensive when it can be overridden by a simple majority of the legislature and can become a law.
   - This type of veto power belongs to the French President. The French President can resend the bill passed by the legislature for reconsideration. However, upon a reconsideration, if it is again passed by a simple majority, the President has to provide his/her assent to the bill.
4. Pocket veto, that is, taking no action on the bill passed by the legislature.
   - This is again a type of veto that is with the American President. He/she may choose to neither give his/her assent, nor return the bill within the stipulated 10 days. This happens during the last few days of the session of the Congress (the US legislature is called as the US Congress). Hence by simply delaying action on the bill during last few days of the Congress, the US President can prevent a bill from becoming a law.

Veto Power of the Indian President	
With respect to the Union bills passed by Houses of Parliament (Art 111)	**With respect to the State bills reserved for his/her consideration by a Governor (Art 201)**
It is a combination of: (a) Absolute veto – For Private members bills and under rare circumstances; (b) Suspensive veto – Used rarely; (c) Pocket veto – Under rare circumstances.	The President can exercise Absolute veto for any State bill reserved by a Governor. However, he/she exercises veto power over such reserved bills based on advice of the Union Council of Ministers.

Veto power with respect to the Union bills

As summarised above, the President has a combination of absolute, suspensive and pocket veto with respect to the Union legislation. The relevant article of the Constitution, Article 111, is reproduced below:

Art 111. Assent to Bills – When a Bill has been passed by the Houses of Parliament, it shall be presented to the President, and the President shall declare either that he/she assents to the Bill, or that he/she withholds assent therefrom:

Provided that the President may, as soon as possible after the presentation to him/her of a Bill for assent, return the Bill if it is not a Money Bill to the Houses with a message requesting that they will reconsider the Bill or any specified provisions thereof and, when a Bill is so returned, the Houses shall reconsider the Bill accordingly and if the Bill is passed again by the Houses with or without amendment and presented to the President for assent, the President shall not withhold assent therefrom.

As per the above article, the President can perform any of the following actions:

1. Assent to the Bill, which means providing approval for the bill.
2. Withhold assent to the Bill, which means rejecting the bill i.e., Absolute veto.
3. Return the Bill for reconsideration i.e., Suspensive veto.
4. The words 'as soon as possible' is provided and hence no time limit specified for returning the bill. Hence, the Indian President may keep the bill pending without returning in rare circumstances i.e., Pocket veto.

(i) Absolute veto

As discussed earlier, this was a power that was available with the King of United Kingdom till 1700. After the King was made only a nominal head, with the full responsibility and powers being vested in the Cabinet, this power has been rendered obsolete in the United Kingdom. In India, this absolute veto that was provided for in the Government of India Act, 1935 has been retained in the Constitution. However, as will be explained below, it is only in rare circumstances that the President will withhold his/her assent i.e., exercise absolute veto with respect to a Parliamentary bill.

Most of the bills introduced in the Parliament are Government bills that are introduced by Ministers. However, Private members can also introduce bills. A Private member is any member of the Parliament who is not a Minister. So, all Members of the Parliament, whether from the Lok Sabha or the Rajya Sabha, who are not ministers are Private members. Usually, unless such bills are supported by the Government of the day, it is unlikely to be passed in the Lok Sabha (as the Government will have a majority in the Lok Sabha). In the history of independent India, there have been only 14 Private member bills that have been passed by both the Houses of Parliament and enacted into a law. The last of such bills was passed in the year 1970. However, it is possible to imagine a situation where a private member bill has been passed by both the Houses but the Council of Ministers advise the President to withhold his/her assent and exercise Absolute veto.

Similarly, a situation can also be imagined where an incumbent Government introduces a government bill and it is passed by both the Houses. However, before the bill is assented to by the President, that government resigns and the new government that commands majority in the Lok Sabha may advise the President to withhold his/her assent and exercise Absolute veto.

In reality, this absolute veto has been exercised by the Indian President on two occasions as follows:

(a) In 1954, President Dr. Rajendra Prasad withheld his assent to the PEPSU (Patiala and East Punjab States Union) Appropriation Bill. The Bill was passed by the Parliament when the President's Rule was in operation in the State of PEPSU. But, when the bill was presented to the President for his assent, the President's Rule was revoked.

(b) In 1991, President R. Venkataraman withheld his assent in case of Salary, Amendments and Pension of Members of Parliament (Amendment) Bill. This Bill was passed on the last day before the Lok Sabha was dissolved after being introduced without seeking prior recommendation from the President of India as per the Constitutional requirements.

(ii) Suspensive veto

Article 111 specifies that the President may return a bill, other than a money bill, for reconsideration of the Parliament with specific or general instructions.

But, if the Houses of Parliament pass the bill again with or without any amendments and sends it back to the President, he/she shall not withhold his/her assent. This means that the President must provide his/her assent for such a bill that is returned by the Houses of Parliament. Hence, while it is a discretionary power of the President to return a bill for reconsideration, he/she can be overruled again by a simple majority of the Parliament and hence it is in the nature of Suspensive veto.

In reality it is used rarely where the President sees a compelling reason to return the bill for reconsideration. In fact, this has been exercised only once by President A. P. J. Abdul Kalam in 2006. It was an amendment to the Office of Profit Bill, 2006 that was passed by the Parliament. It protected members from disqualification on the grounds of holding certain offices with retrospective effect. President A. P. J. Kalam, returned the Bill with a message for reconsideration. However, the Bill was passed by the Parliament again without amendments and sent back to the President, which he approved as per the requirements of Article 111.

(iii) Pocket veto

In this case, the President neither assents nor rejects nor returns the bill, but simply keeps the bill pending for an indefinite period. This power of the President not to take any action (either positive or negative) on the bill is known as the pocket veto. The President can exercise this veto power as the Constitution does not prescribe any time-limit within which he/she has to take the decision with respect to a bill presented to him/her for assent. Again, this veto is exercised by the President only in rare circumstances and has been exercised only once till date by an Indian President.

In 1986, President Zail Singh exercised the pocket veto with respect to the Indian Post Office (Amendment) Bill. The bill, passed by the Rajiv Gandhi Government, imposed restrictions on the freedom of press and also gave the executive extensive powers to intercept personal communication. This bill was widely criticised and the President also felt that it violated the right to privacy of an individual. When no action was forthcoming based on his informal suggestions for changes to the bill, he simply exercised Pocket veto by doing nothing about the bill.

After three years, in 1989, the next President R. Venkataraman returned the bill for reconsideration of the Parliament and finally in 2002 this bill was dropped by the Rajya Sabha and it was never enacted into a law.

The President has no veto power in respect of a Constitutional amendment bill. The 24th Constitutional Amendment Act of 1971 made it obligatory for the President to give his/her assent to a Constitutional amendment bill.

Veto power with respect to State bills reserved by the Governor for the President's consideration

The President has veto power with respect to State legislation whenever a bill passed by the State legislature is reserved by the Governor for the Presidential assent.

A bill passed by a State legislature can become an Act only if it receives the assent of the Governor or of the President (in case the bill is reserved for the consideration of the President). When a bill, passed by a State legislature, is presented to the Governor for his/her assent, he/she has four alternatives (under Article 200 of the Constitution):

1. He/she may give his/her assent to the bill, or
2. He/she may withhold his/her assent to the bill, or
3. He/she may return the bill (if it is not a money bill) for reconsideration of the State legislature, or
4. He/she may reserve the bill for the consideration of the President.

The Governor of a State can exercise a Suspensive veto over a State bill whenever it is presented to him/her, just like the President exercises it with respect to the Union legislation. Further, under rare circumstances similar to the ones explained earlier with respect to the President, the Governor may also exercise Absolute veto or Pocket veto over the State bills.

However, the Governor further has a power to reserve any bill passed by the State Legislature for the consideration of the President. This is usually done by the Governors based on the advice of the State Council of Ministers. However, if the Governor feels that any bill passed by the State Legislature would affect the powers of the Union or contravene any of the provisions of the Constitution, he/she may use his/her discretion to reserve such a bill for the consideration of the President.

Whenever such a bill is reserved by a Governor for the consideration of the President, he/she shall act on the bill as per provisions of Article 201.

As per Article 201 when a bill passed by a State legislature is reserved for the consideration of the President,

- He/she may either give his/her assent or reject a bill that is reserved for his/her consideration.
- He/she can also return the bill (if it is not a Money Bill) with a message to the State legislature. But whenever such a bill is again passed by the State legislature with or without amendment (within 6 months) and sent back to the President, it is open for the President to assent to the bill or to withhold his/her assent.

THINK ABOUT IT

The President enjoys absolute, pocket and suspensive veto for Union bills, but they are exercised only under rare circumstances. Elucidate with examples from Indian Constitutional history.

MNEMONICS

Concept or Provisions	Shortcut or Mnemonics	Details to Remember
Veto power of President with respect to Union Bills	**A**s **S**oon as **P**ossible	President has combination of the following vetos for Union Bills: (a) **A**bsolute – rare circumstances (b) **S**uspensive – used rarely (c) **P**ocket – rare circumstances
Veto power of President with respect to State bills reserved for his/her consideration by Governor	As **Per council**	President has the following vetos that he/she can exercise for State bills reserved for his/her consideration: (a) **A**bsolute (b) **P**ocket But he/she exercises this based on the **advice of the Union Council of Ministers.**

- Hence, the President enjoys absolute veto in respect of State bills reserved for his/her consideration. It must however be noted that the President exercises this power based on the advice of the Union Council of Ministers.

8.4.5.2 Ordinance-making Power

The Ordinance-making power is legislative power vested in the hands of the executive. Such a power is unimaginable in the United States owing to the strict separation of powers between the executive and the legislature as per the Presidential system of democracy in that country. Even in the United Kingdom, with a similar Parliamentary system like India, there is no such law-making power vested in the executive.

The Ordinance-making power in India is a relic of the Government of India Act, 1935 with certain modifications, namely (a) The Ordinance power of the Governor General under the Government of India Act, 1935 was a discretionary power based on his/her 'individual judgement' while the power of the President under the Constitution is based on the advice of the Council of Ministers; (b) An Ordinance under the Constitution can be promulgated by the President only when the Houses of Parliament are not in session and it is valid for a maximum period of six weeks after reassembly of the Parliament.

Constitutional provisions with respect to Ordinance-making power

Article 123 of the Constitution provides for Ordinances to be promulgated by the President.

Art 123. Power of the President to promulgate Ordinances –

1. If at any time, except when both Houses of Parliament are in session, the President is satisfied that circumstances exist which render it necessary for him/her to take immediate action, he/she may promulgate such Ordinances as the circumstances appear to him/her to require.
   - It can be seen from the above provision that ***the President can promulgate an Ordinance only when the Parliament is not in session. It can be promulgated even if one of the two Houses is not in session.***
   - The satisfaction referred to in this clause is not the personal satisfaction of the President but it is formed based on the advice of the Council of Ministers. Further, 'immediate action' does not mean an 'Emergency' situation. It must be a situation that requires immediate legislative action that cannot await the summoning of sessions of the Parliament.
2. An Ordinance promulgated under this article shall have the same force and effect as an Act of Parliament, but *every such Ordinance* –

   (a) shall be laid before both the Houses of Parliament and ***shall cease to operate at the expiration of six weeks from the reassembly of Parliament***, or, if before the expiration of that period resolutions disapproving it are passed by both Houses, upon the passing of the second of those resolutions; and

   (b) ***may be withdrawn at any time by the President.***

   Explanation. Where the Houses of Parliament are summoned to reassemble on different dates, the period of six weeks shall be reckoned from the later of those dates for the purposes of this clause.

   - The Ordinances promulgated have the same effect as an Act of the Parliament. However, they are valid for a maximum period of six weeks from the reassembly of the Parliament.

   For example, let us assume that the Parliament was in session from 10 July to 10 August in a year. After the prorogation of session on 10 August, an Ordinance can be promulgated if there is a need. Let us assume that an Ordinance was promulgated by the President on 14 August. Let us further assume that the Parliament is summoned for the next session to be held from 1 November to 20 November. In this example, the Ordinance that was promulgated on 14 August will be valid for six weeks from the date of reassembly of 1 November i.e., it will be valid till 12 December.

- Any Ordinance promulgated has to be laid before the Houses when the Parliament reassembles. It is open for the Houses to pass a resolution disapproving of the Ordinance and if it happens, then the Ordinance will cease to have effect from the date of second of those resolutions. However, in reality it is unlikely that such a resolution will be approved by the Lok Sabha as the Council of Ministers would enjoy a majority in the Lok Sabha.
- The rules of the Lok Sabha/the Rajya Sabha further provide that whenever a Bill seeking to replace an Ordinance is introduced in the House, there shall be placed along with the Bill, a statement explaining the circumstances which had necessitated immediate legislation by an Ordinance.

3. If and so far as an Ordinance under this article makes any provision which Parliament would not under this Constitution be competent to enact, it shall be void.
   - The scope of the Ordinance-making power of the executive is co-extensive with the legislative power of the Parliament. It means that Ordinance can be promulgated by the President only for those subjects (as per the Seventh Schedule) in respect of which the Parliament has the power to make laws.
   - Further, whatever cannot be enacted as a valid law by the Parliament can also not be promulgated as an Ordinance. For example, the Parliament cannot enact a law that contravenes the Fundamental Rights as per Article 13. Hence, such a provision cannot be promulgated as an Ordinance as well by the President.

Issues with respect to Ordinance power and various case laws of the Supreme Court

The two most contentious issues with respect to Ordinances are their Constitutional validity and repeated repromulgation.

(a) Constitutional validity

In some of the earlier cases before 1970, the Supreme Court had taken a view that the courts cannot inquire into the satisfaction of the President while promulgating an Ordinance and cannot determine whether it was done in good faith.

However, in *Cooper's case*, the Supreme Court held that the satisfaction of the President can be inquired into by the courts and an Ordinance can be struck down by the courts if it was passed with mala fide intention [mala fide (opposite of bona fide) means 'with a bad intention' or 'with an intention to deceive'].

The 38th Constitutional Amendment passed in 1975, added Clause (4) to Article 123, which provided that the President's satisfaction shall be final and that Ordinances promulgated cannot be subjected to judicial review on any grounds. However, the Janata Party Government through the 44th Constitutional Amendment in 1978 overturned the above amendment. It is now a well-settled principle that Ordinance-making power is subject to judicial review.

(b) Repromulgation of Ordinances

A bigger issue with respect to Ordinances has been their misuse through repromulgation in the past. The Constitution does not prohibit repromulgation of Ordinances. As specified earlier, it only requires that the Ordinance promulgated be laid before the Houses on reassembly and the rules further require that whenever an Ordinance is proposed to be replaced by a Bill, there should be a statement explaining the circumstances which necessitated

THINK ABOUT IT

Ordinance power is a colonial relic that needs to be discontinued. Critically evaluate along with important Supreme Court judgements in connection with Ordinance making power.

legislation through Ordinance route. However, the executive in the past has misused this power and have repromulgated Ordinances without any attempt to replace them with an Act of Parliament/ State Legislature.

The Supreme Court through various judgements has laid down that repromulgation of the same Ordinances repeatedly without any valid reason is an abuse of power by the executive. The latest case to be decided by the Supreme Court with respect to Ordinances is *'Krishna Kumar Singh Vs State of Bihar (2017)'*. In this case, the Supreme Court has clearly laid down that repeated repromulgation of an Ordinance is a 'fraud on the Constitution'. The constitution may also be suitably amended to prohibit repromulgation of the same ordinance except under extraordinary circumstances.

SUMMARY OF IMPORTANT CASE LAWS WITH RESPECT TO ORDINANCE MAKING POWER

Year	Case Law	Key Points
1970	R. C. Cooper vs. Union of India	In R. C. Cooper vs. Union of India (1970) the Supreme Court, while examining the Constitutionality of the Banking Companies (Acquisition of Undertakings) Ordinance, 1969 which sought to nationalise 14 of India's largest commercial banks, held that the President's decision could be challenged on the grounds that 'immediate action' was not required; and the Ordinance had been passed primarily to by-pass debate and discussion in the legislature.
1987	D. C. Wadhwa vs. State of Bihar	It was argued in D. C. Wadhwa vs. State of Bihar (1987) that the legislative power of the executive to promulgate Ordinances is to be used in exceptional circumstances and not as a substitute for the law-making power of the legislature. Here, the Court was examining a case where a State government (under the authority of the Governor) continued to repromulgate ordinances, that is, it repeatedly issued new Ordinances to replace the old ones, instead of laying them before the State legislature. A total of around 256 Ordinances were repromulgated, some of them for as long as 14 years. The Supreme Court argued that if Ordinance making was made a usual practice, creating an 'Ordinance raj' the courts could strike down repromulgated Ordinances.
2017	Krishna Kumar Singh Vs State of Bihar	• The Supreme Court has clearly held that repromulgation of Ordinances is a fraud on the Constitution and that the judicial review can investigate whether any fraud or abuse of power has been committed. • It also specified that Ordinances will not provide enduring benefits like legislations that are passed by the legislature.

SUMMARY OF ORDINANCE MAKING POWER

Key Feature	Provisions under Constitution/Discussion Points
Requirements for promulgation of an Ordinance	• President promulgates based on advice of the Council of Ministers. • President can promulgate an Ordinance only when the Parliament is not in session. It can be promulgated even if one of the two houses is not in session.

Key Feature	Provisions under Constitution/Discussion Points
Validity	• Ordinance shall cease to operate at the expiration of six weeks from the reassembly of Parliament. • It may be withdrawn anytime by the President.
Key issues	• Constitutional validity – Ordinance power is subject to judicial review as laid down in Coopers' case. • Repromulgation of the same ordinance – Declared as a fraud on the Constitution in Krishna Kumar Singh case.

MNEMONICS

Concept or Provisions	Shortcut or Mnemonics	Details to Remember
Ordinance Power	**P**resident **O**rders food when at least **one house not in pix** that will be stale in **six**	**P**resident promulgates **O**rdinance when **both** or at **least one of the houses is not in session**. The ordinance is **valid for 6 weeks** after reassembly of the Parliament.

8.4.5.3 Pardoning Power

Pardoning power refers to the power of the President to grant a pardon for punishment and to suspend, remit or commute the sentence for a punishment. This extraordinary power, which is in the nature of a judicial power, is granted to the executive to correct any wrongs by the judiciary. Most of the world's Constitutions have such pardoning power that is bestowed on the executive. In the Indian Constitution as well, this power is provided to the President at the Union and the Governor at the States.

Scan the QR code for conceptual video on relationship of President with Council of Ministers & powers of the President

Mc Graw Hill edge

Article 72. Power of President to grant pardons, etc., and to suspend, remit or commute sentences in certain cases –

1. The President shall have the power to grant pardons, reprieves, respites or remissions of punishment or to suspend, remit or commute the sentence of any person convicted of any offence –
   (a) in all cases where the punishment or sentence is by a court-martial;
   (b) in all cases where the punishment or sentence is for an offence against any law relating to a matter to which the executive power of the Union extends;
   (c) in all cases where the sentence is a sentence of death.

Before understanding the details of pardoning power, let us briefly understand some of the terms and their meanings as applicable in a criminal case:

Term	Meaning
Accused	Person(s) who is/are charged with having committed a crime/offence.
Prosecution	This is the process by which the State tries to prove that the accused is guilty of the crime.

Term	Meaning
Trial	The hearing in a court based on which the judge decides if the accused is guilty of the crime. The accused can defend themselves against the prosecution.
Acquittal	A judgement that the accused is not guilty of the crime for which they have been charged.
Conviction	The accused is/are found to be guilty of the crime.
Sentence	The punishment given to the convict by the court. Examples – Death sentence, Life imprisonment, 10 years imprisonment, etc.

Various types of reliefs

The term 'Pardoning power' is used to refer to a group of powers/reliefs that can be provided by the President. The various types of relief that can be granted by the President are briefly explained below.

Pardon

It cancels the sentence and absolves the offender from all punishments and disqualifications. For example, a person who has been sentenced to 10 years of rigorous imprisonment can be set free with no punishment.

It must be noted that granting of pardon absolves the offender from any disqualifications as well. For example, a person convicted for a criminal offence and sentenced to a jail term of 2 years or more is disqualified from contesting elections for 6 years after his/her release. However, if such a person is pardoned, he/she is set free and is also free from any disqualifications attached.

Commutation

Commutation of sentence involves the reduction of legal penalties, especially in terms of imprisonment. Unlike a pardon, a commutation does not nullify the conviction and is often conditional. It substitutes one form of punishment with another of a lighter character.

Examples: Death sentence to life imprisonment; rigorous imprisonment (RI) to simple imprisonment; simple imprisonment to fine.

Remission

It reduces the amount of sentence without changing its character. For example, 10 years of rigorous imprisonment may be remitted to 5 years of rigorous imprisonment.

Respite

This indicates awarding a lesser sentence in place of one originally awarded due to some special fact like pregnancy of a woman offender, physical disability of the offender etc.

Reprieve

This is a postponement of a punishment. For example, the stay of execution of a sentence given due to a pending proceeding for pardon.

Extent of pardoning power – President versus Governor

- The President alone has the pardoning power in respect of punishment or sentence by court-martial. A court-martial refers to the military court for Armed forces that conduct the trial against a member of the armed forces. The pardoning power in respect of any punishment or sentence by court-martial is exclusively available to the President of India as he/she is Commander-in-chief of the armed forces. This power is not available to a Governor of a State.

- The President shall have the power to grant pardon, commutation, remission, respite or reprieve where the punishment or sentence is for an offence against a law to which the executive power of the Union extends. This basically means that in respect of offences against the laws made under the Union and Concurrent list, the President shall have pardoning power. Similarly, the Governor shall have the power to grant pardon, commutation, remission, respite or reprieve where the punishment or sentence is for an offence against a law to which the executive power of the State extends i.e., laws made under the State and Concurrent list.
- The President alone has the power to grant pardon in respect of a death sentence. However, the Governor can commute a sentence of death (into any other form of punishment).

Important Supreme Court judgements

I. In **Maru Ram v Union of India**, the Supreme Court held that the power under Article 72 is to be exercised on the advice of the Central Government and not by the President on his/her own, and that the advice of the council of ministers is binding on the President.

II. In **Kehar Singh's case**, the following principles were laid down:
   a. The convict seeking relief has no right to insist on oral hearing.
   b. No guideline needs to be laid down by the Supreme Court for the exercise of pardoning power.

III. In **Epuru Sudhakar & Anr vs Govt. of A.P. & Ors**, it was held by the Supreme Court that it is a well-set principle that a limited judicial review of the exercise of pardoning power is available to the Supreme Court and the High Courts. Granting of clemency (pardon or any other relief) by the President or the Governor can be challenged on the following grounds:
   (a) The order has been passed without application of mind. The order is mala fide.
   (b) The order has been passed on extraneous or wholly irrelevant considerations.
   (c) Relevant material has been kept out of consideration. The order suffers from arbitrariness.

IV. **In the case of Shatrughan Chauhan & Others**, in January 2014, the Supreme Court commuted the death sentence of 15 convicts to life imprisonment. Thirteen of these was on account of delay in rejecting their mercy petitions and two of them on account of mental illness of the convicts. The Supreme Court made the following observations/guidelines as part of this judgement:
   (a) The suffering that comes with anticipating death on an everyday basis amounted to torture, which was violative of the right to life under Article 21 of the Constitution. The nature of crime is irrelevant in deciding the impact of delay. An inordinate delay in deciding mercy petitions is a ground for commutation of the death penalty to life imprisonment.
   (b) Mental illness of the convict is a ground for commutation of the death penalty to life imprisonment.
   (c) There should be a minimum 14 days' notice for execution after communication of the rejection of the mercy petition to the convicts.

V. **In the case of Rajiv Gandhi's assassination**, in February 2014,
   (a) The Supreme Court commuted the death sentence of three convicts viz., Murugan, Santhan and Perarivalan, to life imprisonment citing that the 11-year delay in deciding their mercy petition by the Central government had a dehumanising effect on them.
   (b) The Court expected that the government would render advice in reasonable time to the President for taking a decision on mercy pleas and has asked the government to add a new criterion for considering commuting the death penalty to life imprisonment, i.e., the excessive delay in deciding mercy petitions.

VI. **In State of Maharashtra Vs Pradeep Yashwant Kokade & Anr**, December 2024,

(a) The Supreme Court has held that any inordinate delay in the execution of death row convicts after the rejection of mercy petitions will violate the fundamental rights under Article 21 of the Constitution. The court held that it will be a justifiable ground for commuting the death penalty to life imprisonment.

(b) The court also held a convict can move the Supreme Court under Article 32 or the High Court under Article 226 in the event of inordinate delay in the execution of death sentence, post confirmation of the sentence.

VII. **The Supreme Court in 'Laxman Naskar Vs Union of India' (2000)** had laid down five grounds on which remission is to be considered.

(a) Whether the offence is an individual act of crime without affecting the society at large?

(b) Whether there is any chance of future recurrence of committing crime?

(c) Whether the convict has lost his potentiality in committing crime?

(d) Whether there is any fruitful purpose of confining the convict anymore?

(e) Socio-economic condition of the convict's family.

Further, the Supreme Court in *'Sangeet Vs State of Haryana' (2012)* had held that a convict serving life imprisonment does not have a right to be prematurely released on completion of fourteen years in jail. The court held that remission should be granted only on a case-by-case basis.

SUMMARY OF IMPORTANT SUPREME COURT JUDGEMENTS W.R.T PARDONING POWER

Case Law	Key Judgement
Maru Ram	Pardoning power to be exercised by the President based on advice of the Council of Ministers which is binding on the President.
Epuru Sudhakar	Pardoning power is subject to judicial review.
Shatrughan Chauhan & Rajiv Gandhi assassins' case	Inordinate delay in deciding mercy petitions is a ground for commutation of death penalty to life imprisonment.

Global view of the Presidential Pardon

(i) The United States

- According to Article II Section 2 of the US Constitution the President can grant pardon except in the cases of impeachment.
- Unlike Indian President, the American President has absolute power of pardon and such power cannot be questioned or blocked by the Court or the Congress. However, the President can pardon only federal criminal offences (and not the prosecutions in various States of the US). Further, in the U.S., once the pardon is accepted, it grants relief from punishment and associated disqualifications but does not erase the conviction record.

THINK ABOUT IT

Pardoning power of the President has outlived its utility. Critically examine along with relevant rulings of the Supreme Court.

(ii) France, Germany and Russia

- In France, pardon and act of clemency are granted by the President of France who has the sole discretion and power.

- A German President has pardoning power which he/she may delegate to other authorities such as the chancellor or the minister of justice.
- An absolute power of pardon is given to the Russian President through Article 89 of its Constitution.

8.4.5.4 Overall Analysis and Way Forward

Pardoning power in modern democracies is based on the 'Royal prerogative of mercy' of the British Monarch. However, even in the U.K., the Criminal Cases Review Commission has been constituted to investigate alleged miscarriages of justice. It began its operations in 1997 and has diminished the use of royal prerogative of mercy.

The pardoning power may continue in the Constitution and Statute books to deal with exceptional cases. However, it must be exercised in a judicious manner without any nepotism, favouritism or arbitrariness. The decisions should also be taken within a reasonable time of, say, 3 months.

MNEMONICS

Concept or Provisions	Shortcut or Mnemonics	Details to Remember
Pardoning power – 5 types of Pardon and key aspect of each type	**P**an-India **C**inema was **RRR**	**P**ardon – Cancels sentence, punishment and disqualification. **C**ommute – **S**ubstitutes punishment with lighter character. **ReM**ission – **R**educes without **M**odifying character. **ReS**pite – **R**educes due to **S**pecial circumstance or fact. **ReP**rieve – Postponement of sentence pending the proceeding.

8.4.5.5 Discretionary Powers of the President

The President is the nominal head and he/she acts as per the advice of the Council of Ministers in all matters. However, under the following circumstances, the President exercises his/her discretionary powers (deciding on his/her own as to what should be done):

(a) He/she can send back the advice given to him/her by the Council of Ministers for reconsideration. In doing this, the President acts on his/her own discretion. He/She is however bound by the advice tendered to him/her after reconsideration.

(b) The President may exercise suspensive veto on bills presented to him/her (except the Money bill). In doing this, the President acts as per his/her own discretion. However, if the Parliament passes the same bill again and presents it to the President, he/she shall give his/her assent to the bill.

(c) The third situation arises in appointing the Prime Minister when no single party enjoys a majority in the Lok Sabha. In such a situation, the President has to use his/her discretion

THINK ABOUT IT

The President, though only a nominal head, holds a significant position in the Indian Constitutional framework. Comment with special reference to discretionary powers enjoyed by the President.

in appointing the Prime Minister who will enjoy the support of the majority of members in the Lok Sabha.

(d) Finally, the President may use his/her discretion before dissolving the Lok Sabha if the incumbent Council of Ministers has lost majority and advise for dissolution of the Lok Sabha.

MNEMONICS

Concept or Provisions	Shortcut or Mnemonics	Details to Remember
Discretionary powers of the President	SSS	**S** – **S**end back advice of council of ministers for reconsideration under Art 74. **S** – **S**uspensive veto over a bill presented for assent (except money bill) under Art 111. **S** – **S**ingle party or pre-poll alliance does not enjoy a majority in Lok Sabha and the President has to appoint a Prime Minister.

8.5 VICE-PRESIDENT

The Constitution provides that there shall be a Vice-President of India [Art 63].

8.5.1 Electoral College of the Vice-President

The Vice-President shall be elected by an electoral college consisting of all the members of both the Houses of Parliament in accordance with the system of proportional representation by means of the single transferable vote. Voting at such elections shall be through a secret ballot [Art 66]. While the nominated members of the Rajya Sabha do not vote in the Presidential election, they vote in the election of the Vice-President.

8.5.2 Qualification, Conditions and Term of Office

Qualification for the Vice-President

The following are the qualifications for election as the Vice-President [Art 66] –

(a) is a citizen of India;

(b) has completed the age of 35 years; and

(c) is qualified for election as a member of the Council of States.

A person shall not be eligible for election as the Vice-President if he/she holds any office of profit under the Government of India or the Government of any State or under any local or other authority subject to the control of any of the said Governments. However, a sitting President or Vice President or Governor of a State or a Minister either of the Union or a State is not considered an 'office of profit'.

As can be seen, the qualification requirements for the President and the Vice-President are similar. One difference is that the President should be qualified for election as a member of the House of the People as he/she is the overall head of the Union Executive. For the Vice-President, the requirement is that he/she should be qualified for election as a member of the Council of States as he/she acts as ex-officio Chairman of the Council of States.

Conditions and Term of Office

The Vice-President shall not be a member of either House of Parliament or of a House of the Legislature of any State, and if a member of either House of Parliament or of a House of the Legislature of any State is elected the Vice-President, he/she shall be deemed to have vacated his/her seat in that House on the date on which he/she enters upon his/her office as the Vice-President [Art 66].

Article 67 specifies that the Vice-President shall hold office for a term of five years from the date on which he/she enters upon his/her office.

An election to fill a vacancy caused by the expiration of the term of office of Vice-President shall be completed before the expiration of the term. An election to fill a vacancy in the office of the Vice-President occurring by reason of his/her death, resignation or removal, or otherwise shall be held as soon as possible after the occurrence of the vacancy, and the person elected to fill the vacancy shall be entitled to hold office for the full term of five years from the date on which he/she enters upon his/her office [Art 68].

Further provisions with respect to the term of office of the Vice-President [Art 67]:

(a) a Vice-President may, by writing under his/her hand addressed to the President, resign his/her office;

(b) a Vice-President may be removed from his/her office by a resolution of the Council of States passed by a majority of all the then members of the Council and agreed to by the House of the People; but no resolution for the purpose of this clause shall be moved unless at least 14 days' notice has been given of the intention to move the resolution;

(c) a Vice-President shall, notwithstanding the expiration of his/her term, continue to hold office until his/her successor enters upon his/her office.

The Vice-President shall make and subscribe to an oath or affirmation. In this oath, the Vice-President swears that he/she will bear true faith and allegiance to the Constitution of India as by law established and that he/she will faithfully discharge the duty upon which he/she is about to enter. This oath of office of the Vice-President is administered by the President or some person appointed in that behalf by the President [Art 69].

Removal of Vice-President

The procedure for the removal of Vice-President is stipulated in Article 67. The majority that is required for the removal of Vice-President in the Rajya Sabha is a different type of majority. It is 'majority of all the then members of the House'. We will refer to this as 'effective majority' in this book. It should then be approved by a simple majority, that is the majority of members present and voting, in the Lok Sabha.

The 'effective majority' is calculated as follows:

- All the then members of the House = Total membership (Less/-) Vacancies in the house
- The majority of all the 'then members' should vote for the removal of the Vice-President in the Rajya Sabha

Vacancies in the House may be due to death, resignation, retirement, disqualification etc., of a member. It must not be confused with members who are 'absent' from the House. Members who are not present in a particular sitting are 'absent' while vacancy may be due to any of the aforementioned reasons.

Example:

- Let us assume that on a particular day when a resolution to remove the Vice-President from his/her office is put to vote in the Rajya Sabha, there are five vacancies in the Rajya Sabha.
- All the then members of the House = Total membership (245) (Less) Vacancies (5)
- Hence all the 'then members' of the Rajya Sabha on that day is 240.
- The majority of all the 'then members' i.e., the majority of 240 which is 121 members have to vote in favour of the resolution for removing the Vice-President. So irrespective of the number of members present in the House, this 'effective majority' considering 'all the then members' of the House needs to be obtained.
- Hence, whether all 'the then' 240 members are present, or whether 160, 170 or 180 members are present, the number of votes required for the resolution to be passed in the Rajya Sabha is 121 in our example.

The Vice-President can defend his/her case in the Rajya Sabha while the resolution for his/her removal is being considered but shall not vote in such a resolution as he/she is not a member of the Rajya Sabha.

Once the resolution is passed with an 'effective majority' in the Rajya Sabha, it will be taken up in the Lok Sabha. ***The Constitution specifies that this resolution needs to be 'agreed' in the Lok Sabha.*** It means that in the Lok Sabha, this resolution for the removal of the Vice-President needs to be passed by a majority of the members present and voting. We shall refer to this as 'simple majority' in this book.

Let us assume that in our above example, the resolution is passed with the required 'effective' majority of 121 votes in the Rajya Sabha. It will then be taken up in the Lok Sabha. On the day the resolution is put to vote in the Lok Sabha, let us assume that there are 500 members who are present and voting on the resolution. The 'simple majority' required for the resolution to be passed in the Lok Sabha is the majority of 500 i.e., 500/2+1 = 251 votes.

For the first time in Indian Constitutional history, a notice for the removal of the Vice-President was issued by 60 opposition MPs in the Rajya Sabha in December 2024. The Deputy Chairman of Rajya Sabha dismissed the notice on various grounds which included, that the minimum 14 days notice under Article 67(b) for moving such a resolution cannot be complied with before the prorogation of that ongoing Parliament session.

Summary Comparison of Election and Removal Procedures of the President and the Vice-President

Particulars	President	Vice-President
Electoral college	• Elected Members of the Parliament • Elected MLAs of all States and UT of Delhi and Puducherry	• All Members of Parliament – (elected and nominated)

Particulars	President	Vice-President
Election procedure	• Proportional representation by means of the single transferable vote. However, different values are assigned for votes of MLAs of different States. The value of votes of MP is same for LS and RS. • The election is through secret ballot.	• Proportional representation by means of the single transferable vote. Each MP will have one vote-one value. • The election is through secret ballot
Grounds for removal	• Violation of the Constitution	• No specific grounds mentioned in the Constitution.
Initiation of removal procedure	• Can be initiated either in the Lok Sabha or the Rajya Sabha	• Can be initiated only in the Rajya Sabha
Majority for removal	• Highest Special Majority – 2/3rd of the total membership in each of the Houses	• Effective majority in the Rajya Sabha – Majority of 'all the then members' of the House • Simple majority in the Lok Sabha – Majority of members present and voting.

8.5.3 Functions of the Vice-President

8.5.3.1 Regular Functions of the Vice-President

- ❑ *The Vice-President shall be the ex-officio Chairman of the Council of the States [Art 64].*
- ❑ The term '*ex-officio*' is a Latin term that means 'by virtue of' or 'by reason of an office'. Hence, by the reason of a person holding the office of the Vice-President, he/she automatically becomes the Chairman of the Rajya Sabha.
- ❑ He/she conducts the proceedings of the House as per 'Rules of procedure and conduct of business in the Council of States'.
- ❑ *He/she exercises his/her casting vote in case of equality of votes in the Rajya Sabha [Art 100]. However, he/she is not entitled to vote on a resolution for his/her removal as he/she is not a member of the Rajya Sabha [Art 92].*

THINK ABOUT IT

The Vice-President, as the Chairman of Rajya Sabha, plays a crucial role in the conduct of its legislative business that has a significant impact on democratic practices. Discuss in light of recent controversies surrounding the office of the Vice-President.

- ❑ However, *during any period when the Vice-President acts as President or discharges the functions of the President under Article 65, he/she shall not perform the duties of the office of Chairman of the Council of States [Art 64].*

8.5.3.2 Vice-President to act as President or Discharge Functions of the President

- ❑ In the event of occurrence of any vacancy in the office of the President by reason of his/her death, resignation or removal, or otherwise (for example, if the President's election is set aside by the Supreme Court), the Vice-President shall act as President until the date on which a new President is elected [Art 65].
- ❑ When the President is unable to discharge his/her functions owing to absence, illness or any other cause, the Vice-President shall discharge his/her functions until the date on which the President resumes his/her duties [Art 65].

- In June 1960, when then President Dr. Rajendra Prasad was on a 15-day visit to the Soviet Union, Vice-President Dr. Radhakrishnan discharged the functions of the President.
- Similarly in May 1961, when Dr. Rajendra Prasad became seriously ill, he suggested that Vice-President Dr. Radhakrishnan should discharge the functions of President until he resumed his duties.

- In the event of occurrence of vacancy in the office of both President and Vice-President, the Chief Justice of India or the senior most Judge of the Supreme Court available shall discharge the functions of the President until a new President is elected. This situation has arisen once in independent India. When President Dr. Zakir Hussain died and Vice-President V. V. Giri resigned, Chief Justice Shri Hidyatullah discharged the functions of the President for a brief period between July and August 1969.
- Whenever the Vice-President is acting as or discharging the functions of the President, he/she shall have all the powers and immunities of the President and be entitled to the same emoluments as the President.
- The office of the Vice-President of India is modelled on the lines of American Vice-President. However, if the office of President of U.S.A. falls vacant, the Vice-President succeeds to become President and remains so for the unexpired term of his/her predecessor. However, in India, the Vice-President acts as President only till the new President is elected to maintain continuity in the highest office.

Vice-President

Qualification
(a) Citizen & 35 years of age
(b) Qualified to be a member of Rajya Sabha
(c) Does not hold an office of profit

Election
(a) Proportional representation by means of the single transferable vote
(b) Elected by all MPs (including nominated MPs of Rajya Sabha)

Removal
(a) Can be initiated only in the Rajya Sabha
(b) Majority of all the then members in Rajya Sabha and agreed by Lok Sabha
(c) VP can defend his/her case in Rajya Sabha

Functions
(a) Acts as President or discharges duties of President during vacancy or absence of President
(b) Regular function is ex-officio Chairman of Rajya Sabha

8.6 PRIME MINISTER AND COUNCIL OF MINISTERS

8.6.1 Prime Minister

The Prime Minister of India occupies an important place in the Indian Constitutional system.

- Article 74 states that, 'There shall be a Council of Ministers with the Prime Minister at the head to aid and advise the President who shall, in the exercise of his functions, act in accordance with such advice'.

- Article 75(1) deals with the appointment of the Prime Minister. It states that, 'The Prime Minister shall be appointed by the President and the other Ministers shall be appointed by the President on the advice of the Prime Minister'.
- There is no fixed term of office for the Prime Minister. He/she continues to be in office as long as their government enjoys majority in Lok Sabha. If the council of ministers loses the confidence (majority) of the Lok Sabha, the Prime Minister and the entire council of ministers resign from their office. The party/coalition with a majority in the Lok Sabha may also choose to change the Prime Minister while the government continues in power.
- Lastly, Article 78 of the Constitution lays down the duties and functions of the Prime Minister vis-à-vis the President.

The Prime Minister is called as ***'Key-stone of the Cabinet arch'***. PM is the real Chief executive while President is the Ceremonial Chief Executive.

8.6.1.1 Appointment of Prime Minister

When Single party has a majority in Lok Sabha

The Prime Minister is appointed by the President. When a party enjoys majority in the Lok Sabha, the leader chosen by that party is appointed as the Prime Minister by the President. For example, in the General elections to the Lok Sabha in 2014 and 2019, the Bhartiya Janata Party (BJP) secured a majority of its own in the Lok Sabha. The BJP MPs chose Mr. Narendra Modi as their leader and he was appointed as Prime Minister in 2014 and 2019.

When no Single party has a majority in Lok Sabha

However, in the event of no single party securing a majority of its own, the President has to decide on whom to appoint as the Prime Minister. There are no guidelines/rules laid down in the Constitution or any law for such a situation. The President, as per convention in such circumstances, invites the leader of the largest pre-poll alliance, or single largest party (where no alliance has a majority), or post-poll alliance to form the Government and appoints such leader as the Prime Minister. For example, after 2024 general elections, the BJP on its own had secured 240 seats. However, the National Democratic Alliance (NDA), which was a pre-poll alliance with parties like Telugu Desam Party, JD(U), etc., secured more than 290 seats and Mr. Narendra Modi, who was elected its leader, was again appointed as the Prime Minister. After 2004 elections, the Congress party led United Progressive Alliance secured more than 200 seats but was short of the majority mark of 272 seats. With the support of Left Parties, Samajwadi Party and Bahujan Samaj Party, it staked claim to form the Government and Dr. Manmohan Singh was appointed as the Prime Minister. Similarly, alliance governments had been formed between 1989 and 2009 and the leaders of such alliances, like Shri V. P. Singh, Shri P. V. Narasimha Rao, Shri Atal Bihari Vajpayee, Shri Deve Gowda, were appointed as the Prime Minister.

The Prime Minister may be from the Lok Sabha or the Rajya Sabha. There have been three instances in the past when the Prime Minister was from the Rajya Sabha – Smt. Indira Gandhi (1966), Shri Deve Gowda (1996) and Dr. Manmohan Singh (2004).

The President administers oaths of office and secrecy to the Prime Minister (as per the forms in the Third Schedule) at the time of his/her appointment which is similar to that of any Union Minister.

The Prime Minister continues in office as long as he/she and his/her Council of Ministers continue to enjoy a majority in the Lok Sabha. If the Council of Ministers lose majority in the Lok Sabha, the Prime Minister has to tender his/her resignation. For example, Prime Minister Shri V. P. Singh

(1990), Shri Deve Gowda (1997) and Shri Atal Bihari Vajpayee (1999) resigned after losing the majority in the Lok Sabha.

8.6.1.2 Comparison between British Prime Minister and Indian Prime Minister

The position of the Indian Prime Minister is more or less modelled on his/her British counterpart. The similarities between the Cabinet system of India and the United Kingdom can be summarised as below:

- Prime Minister is the real chief executive with the Indian President (just like the British King or Queen) being the nominal head.
- Prime Minister is in-charge of coordinating the policy of the Government and hence supervises all the departments.
- Prime Minister is the link between the President and the Council of Ministers. All the important communication to the President is made by the Prime Minister.
- Prime Minister decides on whom to appoint as Ministers in the Cabinet. He/she decides on the allocation and reshuffling of portfolios amongst them. While the President formally appoints all ministers, it is the Prime Minister who decides and advises the President on ministerial appointments and the allocation of portfolios.
- The death or resignation of the Prime Minister dissolves the entire Council of Ministers. The new Prime Minister has to be sworn-in and the Council of Ministers also needs to be again sworn-in. However, the death or resignation of any other minister creates only a vacancy in the Council of Ministers, which may be filled up by a new appointment.

However, there are differences between the two on certain aspects, which are summarised below:

Particulars	British Prime Minister	Indian Prime Minister
Head of the Council of Ministers	• British PM is not officially the head of the Council of Ministers as per their convention, though he/she is considered to be 'Primus inter pares' that means 'First among equals'.	• Indian PM as per Article 74 of the Constitution is at the head of the Council of Ministers.
Membership	• As per British convention (since 1963), the Prime Minister has to be a member of the House of Commons.	• The PM of India can be a member of either the Lok Sabha or the Rajya Sabha.

8.6.1.3 Responsibilities towards the President

Article 78 of the Constitution lays down the duties and functions of the Prime Minister vis-à-vis the President in the following words:

1. To communicate to the President all decisions of the Council of Ministers relating to the administration of the affairs of the Union and proposals for legislation;
2. To furnish such information relating to the administration of the affairs of the Union and proposals for legislation as the President may call for; and
3. If the President so requires, to submit for the consideration of the Council of Ministers any matter on which a decision has been taken by a Minister but which has not been considered by the Council.

As can be seen above, the Prime Minister is the link between the President and the Council of Ministers. While individual ministers can meet and apprise the President about their departments as required, the Prime Minister communicates all important policy decisions of the Cabinet to the President. Further, even though an individual minister has tendered any advice to the President without placing it before the Council of Ministers, the President can ask the Prime Minister to refer the matter to be considered by the Council of Ministers.

Scan the QR code for conceptual video on Vice-President and Council of Ministers

McGraw Hill edge

MNEMONICS

Concept or Provisions	Shortcut or Mnemonics	Details to Remember
Responsibilities of PM towards the President	**C**hloro**F**luoro**C**arbons (**CFC**)	**C** – **C**ommunicate to the President the decisions of council of ministers relating to administration and proposals for legislation. **F** – **F**urnish such information as the President may call for. **C** – **C**onsideration of the council of ministers – Submit any matter on which decision taken by individual minister, if asked for by the President.

8.6.2 Council of Ministers

8.6.2.1 Appointment of Ministers

- The Prime Minister is appointed by the President and all other ministers are appointed by the President on the advice of the Prime Minister [Art 75(1)].
- The President administers oath of office and oath of secrecy (as per forms in the Third Schedule) for all the Ministers who are appointed.
- The Ministers can be from either House of Parliament i.e., the Lok Sabha or the Rajya Sabha.
- A person who is not a member of either house of Parliament can also be appointed as a Minister. However, such Minister should become a member of either of the Houses within six months failing which he/she ceases to be a Minister [Art 75(5)]. For example, in May 2019 Shri S. Jaishankar was appointed as the External Affairs Minister. However, he was not a Member of Parliament at that time. He was elected to the Rajya Sabha from Gujarat in July 2019.
- The Ministers shall hold office during the pleasure of the President [Art 75(2)]. In reality, it is the Prime Minister who decides on whom to appoint or remove as Ministers. The President acts as per the advice of the Prime Minister in this regard.

- The President shall make rules for the more convenient transaction of business of the Government of India and for allocation of such business amongst Ministers [Art 77(3)].

8.6.2.2 Cabinet and Council of Ministers

- The Constitution does not classify the members of the Council of Ministers into different ranks. All this has been done informally, following the British practice. It has now got legislative sanction, so far as the Union is concerned, in Sec. 2 of the Salaries and Allowance of Ministers Act, 1952, which defines Minister as a 'Member of the Council of Ministers, by whatever name called, and includes a Deputy Minister'. According to this act, the Prime Minister and other ministers are paid salaries and allowances that are payable to a Member of Parliament. Apart from this, they get a sumptuary allowance as follows: PM – ₹3,000 per month, cabinet minister – ₹2,000 per month, Minister of State – ₹1,000 per month and deputy minister – ₹600 per month.

- Further, the rules of Lok Sabha and Rajya Sabha define a Minister to include a member of the council of ministers, a Minister of State, Deputy Minister or a Parliamentary Secretary. In Lok Sabha rules, specific mention is also made about the member of the cabinet.
- All the Ministers, however, do not belong to the same rank. They are classified under three ranks: (a) Cabinet Ministers who are 'Members of the Cabinet'; (b) Ministers of State; (c) Deputy Ministers.
- Theoretically, the full executive is the Council of Ministers, with Cabinet being one of its three components. In reality, the Cabinet is more important, influential and powerful than the full council.
- The Cabinet rank ministers are the head of their departments. They head important ministries like home, defence, finance, external affairs, railways and so on. They are members of the Cabinet and decide the important policies of the Government along with the Prime Minister.
- The Ministers of State may hold independent charge of their ministries or may be working under a Cabinet rank Minister. However, even a Minister of State holding an independent charge will not attend the Cabinet meeting unless he/she is invited specifically. The other Ministers of State (without independent charge) are attached to the Cabinet rank ministers. They may be allotted departments within the ministries or specific work by the Cabinet minister to whom they are attached.
- Deputy Ministers have no separate charge of a department and are attached to either a Cabinet rank minister or Minister of State.

- The Constitution does not stipulate a minimum number of ministers with respect to the Union Council of Ministers. However, there was a provision added by the 91st Constitutional Amendment Act in 2003 that restricts the total number of ministers including the Prime Minister to 15% of the total membership of the Lok Sabha. Further, the same amendment has also provided that a member of either house of the Parliament who has been disqualified under the Tenth Schedule for defection, shall not be appointed as a Minister for the remainder of the term unless he/she is re-elected [Art 75 (1A) & (1B)].
- A Minister is entitled to speak in both the Houses of Parliament but can vote only in the House of which he/she is a member [Art 88].

- **Caretaker Government**: The Constitution does not make any mention of caretaker government. However, it is used in common parlance on two occasions. Firstly, after the general elections, the outgoing council of ministers resign and they are asked to continue till the new Lok Sabha is constituted and the new government takes oath. This interim period, which lasts for a few days, is when the outgoing government is called in common parlance a 'caretaker government'. Such a government manages only routine activities of the government and no significant policy decisions are made. Secondly, when the incumbent government loses majority support in the Lok Sabha and no alternative government can be formed, such a government performs the routine functions as a 'caretaker government' till fresh elections are held and a new government takes office. However, it may be noted that it is still the council of ministers as per the Constitution which wields the real executive power to take any decisions relating to national security or national interest. For example, after the government, headed by Shri A B Vajpayee, lost the confidence vote in April 1999, the council of ministers resigned and were asked to continue as 'caretaker government' till fresh elections were held. However, the Kargil war of May-July 1999 was fought under the leadership of this government.

MNEMONICS

Concept or Provisions	Shortcut or Mnemonics	Details to Remember
Key provisions relating to Council of Ministers – appointments and office	APPOINTS 15%	• **APP** – **A**ppointed by **P**resident based on advice of **P**rime Minister; • **PP** – Holds office during **P**leasure of **P**resident; • **OINTS** – **O**ath **IN** **T**hird **S**chedule • **OINTS** – Member of **O**ne of the houses and **I**f **N**ot, **T**hen to become member within **S**ix months. • Total strength of council of ministers including PM not to exceed 15% of total membership of Lok Sabha.

8.6.2.3 Collective Responsibility

- Parliamentary democracy works on the principle of collective responsibility of the executive to the legislature. In our Constitution, this is reflected in Article 75(3) which states that, 'The Council of Ministers shall be collectively responsible to the House of the People'.
- Collective responsibility indicates that all the Ministers are unanimous in their support for policies of the Government. They may differ and disagree within the cabinet but once the policy is formed, everyone works for its implementation and success.
- However, unlike in Britain, the ministers do not have any legal responsibility. In Britain, every order of the King is counter-signed by the Minister who is liable in a court of law in case of any violation of law. However, in India all executive actions of the Government of India shall be expressed to be taken in the name of the President [Art 77(1)].
- The Constitution further states that all orders and instruments made and executed in the name of the President shall be authenticated in such manner as specified in the rules to be

THINK ABOUT IT

The principle of collective responsibility is the essence of Parliamentary democracy. Elucidate.

made by the President. The validity of an order or instrument so authenticated shall not be called into question [Art 77(2)].

- Article 74 further states that the courts cannot inquire into what advice was tendered by the Ministers to the President. Hence, considering all the above factors, a Minister cannot be held personally legally liable for any official act of the Government.

- The individual ministers hold their office during the pleasure of the President [Art 75(2)]. This means that they are individually responsible to the President. The real power of removing a minister lies with the Prime Minister as he/she is the one who advises the President regarding appointment of ministers.

8.6.2.4 Cabinet Committees

- Cabinet Committees are not mentioned in the Constitution but provided in 'The Government of India (Transaction of Business) Rules, 1961'.
- There are 8 Standing Cabinet Committees at present (2024) as per the First Schedule to the above said rules. These are:
    1. Appointments Committee of the Cabinet
    2. Cabinet Committee on Accommodation
    3. Cabinet Committee on Economic Affairs
    4. Cabinet Committee on Parliamentary Affairs
    5. Cabinet Committee on Political Affairs
    6. Cabinet Committee on Security
    7. Cabinet Committee on Investment and Growth
    8. Cabinet Committee on Employment and Skill Development
- The functions of these various committees are also specified in the First Schedule of the Transaction of Business Rules.
- The Prime Minister may, from time to time, add or reduce the number of cabinet committees. The Prime Minister may constitute ad-hoc committees from time to time to deal with specific issues or to devise solutions for specific problems. Six committees at present (2024) are headed by the Prime Minister. The cabinet committee on accommodation is headed by the Home Minister (Shri Amit Shah) and cabinet committee on Parliamentary affairs by the Defence Minister (Shri Rajnath Singh) as of July 2024.
- In addition to these committees, there may also be a Group of Ministers (GOM) that may be constituted for dealing with specific issues.
- Mostly these ad-hoc committees or GOM make recommendations to the Cabinet that takes the final decisions. However, the NDA government that took over in May 2014 has not been constituting GOMs like previous regimes for various matters.

Cabinet Committee	Key Functions/Role
Appointments Committee	Decides all higher-level appointments and empanelments in the Central Secretariat, PSUs, Banks and financial institutions.
Accommodation	Deals with allotment of government accommodation to Members of Parliament, central government employees, etc.
Economic Affairs	Directs and coordinates government activities in economic field.

Cabinet Committee	Key Functions/Role
Parliamentary Affairs	Watches progress of government business in Parliament to ensure smooth and efficient conduct of such business.
Political Affairs	Deals with problems relating to Centre-State relations; policy matters relating to foreign affairs that do not have external or internal security implications.
Security	Deals with issues relating to defence, law and order, internal security, atomic energy and policy matters relating to foreign affairs that have external or internal security implications.
Investment and Growth	Considers measures to promote investment and growth; sector specific reforms aimed at export promotion, import substitution and accelerating capital flows; measures to improve ease of doing business.
Employment and Skill development	Considers policies, programmes and measures for employment generation and skill development; measures aimed at increasing workforce participation of women.

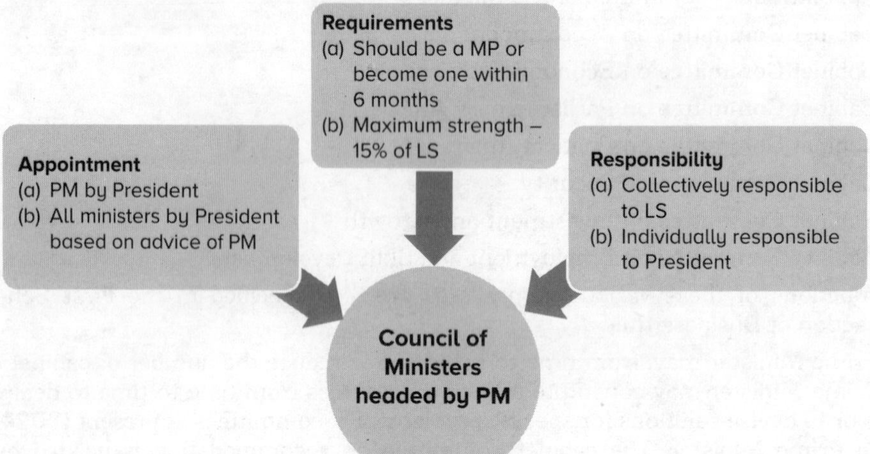

MAINS STARTER

Area	Building Blocks for Mains Answer Writing
Election of President	India is a republic with an elected President. The President is the nominal head of the Union executive and hence indirectly elected by the elected members of Parliament and State legislative assemblies [Arts 54 & 55].
Office of Profit	The term 'office of profit' is not defined in the Constitution or any other statute. It owes its origin to medieval Britain when no person who held a remunerative post with the King shall be capable of serving in the House of Commons to avoid any conflict of interest.

Area	Building Blocks for Mains Answer Writing
Relationship between President and Council of Ministers	India is a parliamentary democracy in which the President is the nominal head and the real executive powers are vested in the council of ministers who are accountable to the legislature. This is reflected in the relationship between the President and Council of Ministers as per the provisions of the Constitution [Art 74].
Veto power	Veto power is the power to either reject or delay the passage of a bill exercised by the executive head of a country. In India, which is a parliamentary democracy, the President exercises this power as a part of Parliament based on the advice of council of ministers except under exceptional circumstances where he/she could use his/her discretion [Art 111].
Ordinance making power	Ordinance making power is a legislative power vested in the hands of the executive [Art 123]. This is a relic of the Government of India Act, 1935 in the Indian Constitution. While it may seem to be against the principles of separation of powers between the legislature and the executive, it is a temporary measure to meet circumstances that need immediate action.
Pardoning power	Pardoning power is a judicial power vested in the President to grant mercy to convicts in the form of pardon, commutation, remission, etc., based on the advice of the council of ministers [Art 72]. This is based on the 'Royal prerogative of mercy' vested in the British Monarch.
Discretionary powers of the President	India is a parliamentary democracy in which the President, being the nominal head, acts on the aid and advice of the council of ministers who have the real executive powers. However, under certain exceptional circumstances, he/she exercises his/her discretionary powers.
Vice-President	The Vice-President of India is part of the Union executive and is elected by all the Members of Parliament [Art 66]. His/her normal function is to preside over the Rajya Sabha as its ex-officio Chairman [Art 64].
Prime Minister & Council of Ministers	The Council of Ministers headed by the Prime Minister is the real executive head of our country with the President being the nominal head. The Council of Ministers are collectively responsible to the Lok Sabha [Art 75(3)].

Register on **McGraw Hill Edge** for the following:

- Articles at a glance for this chapter
- Additional Data points for List of Presidents, Vice-Presidents and famous sayings about Prime Minister and Cabinet
- Practice questions for Preliminary examination including PYQ of 2014–24
- Model answers for Mains PYQ of 2014–24
- Attend regular webinars by the author including discussion on **'Think about It'** questions

UPSC Previous Years' Questions of Preliminary Examination

1. Consider the following statements: [2023]
   1. If the election of the President of India is declared void by the Supreme Court of India, all acts done by him/her in the performance of duties of his/her office of President before the date of decision become invalid.
   2. Election for the post of the President of India can be postponed on the ground that some Legislative Assemblies have been dissolved and elections are yet to take place.
   3. When a Bill is presented to the President of India, the Constitution prescribes time limits within which he/she has to declare his/her assent.

   How many of the above statements are correct?
   (a) Only one (b) Only two (c) All three (d) None

   Solution: (d)

   > ***Explanation:*** As discussed in Section 8.4.2.5, under Article 71 both statements 1 and 2 are incorrect. Under Article 111, there is no time limit prescribed for the President to declare his/her assent and hence statement 3 is also incorrect. Hence, the answer is (d).

2. Consider the following statements in respect of election to the President of India: [2023]
   1. The members nominated to either House of the Parliament or the Legislative Assemblies of States are also eligible to be included in the Electoral College.
   2. Higher the number of elective Assembly seats, higher is the value of vote of each MLA of that State.
   3. The value of vote of each MLA of Madhya Pradesh is greater than that of Kerala.
   4. The value of vote of each MLA of Puducherry is higher than that of Arunachal Pradesh because the ratio of total population to total number of elective seats in Puducherry is greater as compared to Arunachal Pradesh.

   How many of the above statements are correct?
   (a) Only one (b) Only two (c) Only three (d) All four

   Solution: (a)

   > ***Explanation:*** As discussed in Section 8.4.1.1, the electoral college for President consists of only elected members of Parliament and Legislative assemblies. Hence, Statement 1 is incorrect. As can be seen from the discussion and table given in Section 8.4.1.2, Statements 2 and 3 are also incorrect. Statement 4 is correct as can be seen in table in Section 8.4.1.2. Hence, the answer is (a).

3. Consider the following statements: [2022]
   1. The Constitution of India classifies the ministers into four ranks viz. Cabinet Minister, Minister of State with independent charge, Minister of State and Deputy Minister.
   2. The total number of ministers in the Union government, including the Prime Minister, shall not exceed 15 percent of the total number of members of the Lok Sabha.

   Which of the statements given above is/are correct?
   (a) 1 only (b) 2 only (c) Both 1 and 2 (d) Neither 1 nor 2

Solution: (b)

Explanation: As discussed in Section 8.6.2.2, the classification of ministers into various ranks is not provided in the Constitution but follows British practice. Hence, Statement 1 is incorrect. As per 91st constitutional amendment, total number of ministers including the Prime Minister shall not exceed 15% of the total membership of the Lok Sabha and hence, Statement 2 is correct and the answer is (b).

UPSC Previous Years' Questions of Main Examination

1. Discuss the role of the Vice-President of India as the Chairman of Rajya Sabha. [2022]

Approach: This is a static question that requires discussion about the duties of Vice-President as the ex-officio Chairman of Rajya Sabha.

MODEL ANSWER

The Vice-President of India is the ex-officio Chairman of Rajya Sabha [Art 64]. As Chairman of Rajya Sabha, he/she performs the following functions:

- He/she conducts the proceedings of the house as per 'Rules of procedure and conduct of business in the Council of States.'
- He/she exercises his/her casting vote in case of equality of votes in the Rajya Sabha. However, he/she is not entitled to vote on a resolution for his/her removal as he/she is not a member of the Rajya Sabha, though he/she can be present and defend his/her case.
- However, during any period when the Vice-President acts as President or discharges the functions of the President under article 65, he/she shall not perform the duties of the office of Chairman of the Council of States.
- Further, he/she takes the following decisions as Chairman:
  - Referring a bill to a Standing Committee after introduction in the Rajya Sabha if he/she considers it necessary.
  - Deciding on disqualification of any member under the Tenth Schedule of the Constitution.
  - The Chairman can name a member who disregards the authority of the Chair or obstructs the business of the house. Such a member may be suspended by a motion passed in the House.
  - Nominating the Chairperson for the 8 Departmentally related Standing Committees that function under the Rajya Sabha.

Thus, the Vice-President discharges key functions as Chairman of Rajya Sabha.

CHAPTER 9

State Executive

LEARNING OUTCOMES

1. Learning the similarities between the Union executive and State executive considering our federal polity
2. Knowing the functionalities of the office of the Governor – Appointment, tenure and qualifications
3. Exploring the discretionary powers of the Governor, issues related to it, and way forward

9.1 INTRODUCTION TO THE STATE EXECUTIVE

The executive branch in our country is federal in character. This means that there is an executive at the Union level for carrying out the executive functions vested in the Union as per the Constitution. There is a similar setup at each of the States for carrying out the functions vested in States as per the Constitution. The provisions of the State executive are very similar to the Union executive with a few exceptions, which we will understand in this chapter.

9.2 FUNCTIONS OF THE STATE EXECUTIVE

The State executive is part of the State legislature and initiates most of the legislative work. It introduces bills and gets them passed in the legislature. Thereafter, it is responsible for implementing these laws.

- Article 162 of the Constitution specifies that the executive power of the State shall extend to the matter with respect to which the Legislature of the State has the power to make laws.
- There is distribution of powers between the Union and States as per the Seventh Schedule of the Constitution. We have seen that there are three lists viz. Union, State and Concurrent. In respect of the concurrent list, both Union and States have the power to make laws but the State laws cannot be in contradiction to the Union laws.
- Article 162 that deals with the executive power of the State provides that in such concurrent list matters, the executive power of the State shall be subject to, and limited by, the executive power expressly conferred upon the Union or authorities thereof.

9.3 COMPOSITION OF THE STATE EXECUTIVE

The State executive consists of the Governor, Council of Ministers headed by the Chief Minister and the Advocate General of State. We shall discuss the similarities between the Union and State executive in a tabular form. This table will help the reader understand that majority of the provisions of State executive are very similar to the Union executive provisions. Hence, knowledge of the Union executive and understanding of the comparative table will be sufficient to know majority of the provisions of the State executive. However, there are differences between the office of the President and of a State Governor that we shall discuss in detail. We shall then summarise the provisions relating to the Council of Ministers at the State level.

State Executive	
Governor	**Council of Ministers**
• Appointment of Governor • Qualification, Conditions and Term of office • Relationship with the Council of Ministers • Powers of the Governor • Discretionary powers of the Governor	• Council of Ministers as real executive head • Appointment of Chief Minister and Ministers by Governor • Provisions relating to ministers • Principle of Collective Responsibility

9.4 COMPARISON BETWEEN UNION AND STATE EXECUTIVE

9.4.1 Similarities between President and Governor

The following table summarises the similarities between the office of the President at the Union executive level and the office of the Governor at the State executive level. As a simple thumb rule for most provisions at the State executive – the President is replaced by the Governor, the Lok Sabha is replaced by the Legislative Assembly and the Prime Minister is replaced by the Chief Minister. The reader must have noted that in the previous chapter on the Union executive (Chapter 8), examples have been provided from both the Centre and the States under various sections as the provisions are similar. The various case laws discussed are also related to both the Union and State-related matters.

There are of course differences between the way the President is elected and the Governors are appointed. The impeachment process of the President is different from the removal of Governors. The Governor enjoys certain discretionary powers under the Constitution that the President does not enjoy. These will be covered in detail in subsequent sections.

Particulars	Union Provisions w.r.t President	Similar Provisions for State w.r.t Governor
Head of the executive	The President is the nominal head of the Union executive. The real executive powers are with the Council of Ministers headed by the Prime Minister.	The Governor is the nominal head of the State executive. The real executive powers are with the Council of Ministers headed by the Chief Minister.
Key administrative powers	• All executive actions of the Government of India shall be expressed to be taken in the name of the President [Art 77]. • President has rule-making powers for the Government of India [Art 77].	• All executive actions of the Government of a State shall be expressed to be taken in the name of the Governor [Art 166]. • Governor has rule-making powers for the Government of a State [Art 166].

Particulars	Union Provisions w.r.t President	Similar Provisions for State w.r.t Governor
	• Appointment of persons to various posts under the Constitution and other statutes.	• Appointment of persons to various posts under the Constitution and other statutes.
Veto power	• The President can exercise different types of Veto – Absolute, Suspensive and Pocket – on Parliamentary bills. • He/she can also exercise absolute veto, based on the advice of the Council of Ministers, on State legislature bills reserved by the Governor of a State for his/her consideration (Article 201).	• The Governor can exercise different types of Veto – Absolute, Suspensive and Pocket – on State Legislature bills. • Additionally, he/she may also reserve a bill passed by the State Legislature for consideration of the President (Article 200).
Ordinance-making power	• The President can promulgate ordinances when both the Houses of Parliament are not in session. • The President promulgates ordinance based on the advice of the Union Council of Ministers. • The Ordinances promulgated have the same effect as an Act of Parliament. However, they are valid for a maximum period of 6 weeks from the reassembly of the Parliament. • Any Ordinance promulgated has to be laid before the Houses when the Parliament reassembles. It is open for the Houses to pass a resolution disapproving of the Ordinance and if it happens, then the Ordinance will cease to have effect from the date of second of those resolutions. • The scope of the Ordinance-making power of the Union executive is co-extensive with the legislative power of the Parliament. It means that Ordinance can be promulgated by the President only for those subjects (as per the Seventh Schedule) in respect of which the Parliament has the power to make laws. • Further, whatever cannot be enacted as a valid law by the Parliament can also not be promulgated as an Ordinance. For example, the Parliament cannot enact a law that contravenes the Fundamental Rights as per Article 13. Hence such a provision cannot be promulgated as an Ordinance by the President [Art 123].	• The Governor can promulgate ordinances when the House(s) of the State Legislature is/are not in session. • The Governor promulgates ordinances based on the advice of the State Council of Ministers. • The Ordinances promulgated have the same effect as an Act of the State Legislature. However, they are valid for a maximum period of 6 weeks from the reassembly of the State Legislature. • Any Ordinance promulgated has to be laid before the House(s) when the State Legislature reassembles. It is open for the Legislative Assembly to pass a resolution disapproving of the Ordinance and if it happens, then the Ordinance will cease to have effect from the date of such resolution by the Assembly or such resolution being agreed to by the Legislative Council (in States that have Legislative Council). • The scope of the Ordinance-making power of the State executive is co-extensive with the legislative power of the State Legislature. It means that Ordinance can be promulgated by the Governor only for those subjects (as per the Seventh Schedule) in respect of which the State Legislature has the power to make laws. • Further, whatever cannot be enacted as a valid law by the State Legislature can also not be promulgated as an Ordinance. For example, the State Legislature cannot enact a law that contravenes the Fundamental Rights as

Particulars	Union Provisions w.r.t President	Similar Provisions for State w.r.t Governor
		per Article 13. Hence such a provision cannot be promulgated as an Ordinance by the Governor. • Additionally, the Governor cannot promulgate an ordinance without the instruction of the President i.e., approval of the Central Government in the following three situations: (a) If a bill containing the same provisions would have required previous sanction of the President for its introduction in the State Legislature. For example, a bill imposing reasonable restrictions on freedom of trade in the public interest cannot be introduced in a State Legislature without the previous sanction of the President [Article 304(b)]. Such an ordinance also cannot be promulgated without instruction from the President. (b) If he/she would have deemed it necessary to reserve a bill containing the same provisions for consideration of the President. This is a discretionary power of the Governor. (c) If an Act of the State legislature containing the same provisions would have been invalid without previous assent of the President. For example, a law under the Concurrent list where State law is repugnant to a Union legislation requires previous assent of the President to be effective in the State. Such an ordinance can also be promulgated only with instruction from the President [Art 213].
Pardoning power	• The President shall have the power to grant pardon, commutation, remission, respite or reprieve where the punishment or sentence is for an offence against a law to which the executive power of the Union extends [Art 72].	• The Governor shall have the power to grant pardon, commutation, remission, respite or reprieve where the punishment or sentence is for an offence against a law to which the executive power of the State extends [Art 161]. • However, there are a few differences between Pardoning power of the President and the Governor. This has been summarised under the section – Extent of pardoning power – President versus Governor. (Refer Section 8.4.5.3.)

9.4.2 Appointment, Qualification, Condition and Term of Office of Governor

9.4.2.1 Appointment of Governor

- The Constitution provides for the post of the Governor as the Head of a State in India. The same person may be appointed as Governor for two or more States [Art 153].
- He/she is appointed by the President of India [Art 155]. He/she is both the constitutional head of a State and an agent of the Central Government in a State.
- He/she takes oath, administered by the Chief Justice of the High Court, to preserve, protect and defend the Constitution and to devote himself/herself to the service and well-being of people of the State [Art 159].
- The President may make such provision as he thinks fit for the discharge of the functions of the Governor of a State in any contingency not provided for in the Constitution.

9.4.2.2 Term of Office

- The Governor is normally appointed for a term of 5 years. However, he/she holds office during the pleasure of the President i.e., he/she can be removed by the Central Government at any point of time.
- He/she can also resign by writing to the President.
- He/she continues to be in office even after the expiration of his/her term until his/her successor enters upon his/her office [Art 156].

9.4.2.3 Governor – Issues with respect to Appointment and Removal

- The original draft of the Constituent Assembly was for elected Governor. However, it was replaced for the following important reasons:
  - Avoiding the cost and other issues of one more direct election involving millions of voters, which the country cannot afford.
  - To avoid friction between the elected Governor and elected Chief Minister as a directly elected Governor may consider himself/herself superior to the Chief Minister. This is not desirable as constitutionally, real executive power in our parliamentary democracy rests with the Council of Ministers.
  - Through appointment by the President, the Union can exercise control over States.
  - There were a few arguments advanced against nomination too in the Constituent Assembly. An appointed Governor could be a source of friction when the Centre and a State are ruled by different parties. This method of appointment of the executive head of a State by the Centre is against the federal nature of our Constitution. However, the Constituent Assembly finally settled for a nominated Governor.
- There have been many instances of friction between the Chief Minister of an elected government and the Governor of a State when the ruling party at the Centre and at a State are in opposition. However, in our parliamentary democracy, there is a need for a permanent nominal executive head and this post is filled by the Governor. This is because, all executive actions of a State are expressed to be taken in the name of the Governor. Further, in the event of failure of constitutional machinery, there will be no Council of Ministers and the executive power is exercised by the President through the Governor of a State. This role cannot be performed by the Chief Justice of a High Court as he/she is the head of judiciary in a State and there needs to be a separation between the executive and the judiciary.

- **Sarkaria Commission report** – The Sarkaria Commission, which was set up to examine Centre–State relations, suggested the following recommendations with respect to the appointment of a Governor.
  - Should be an eminent person from outside the State.
  - Must not have participated in active politics for some time before appointment.
  - Should be appointed in consultation with the Chief Minister of the State, the Vice-President of India and the Speaker of the Lok Sabha.
  - Tenure should be guaranteed except under compelling circumstances. He/she should be given an opportunity of being heard, in case of termination and the reasons for removal have to be laid before the Houses of Parliament.
  - Governor should not be eligible for any other appointment to office of profit under the Union or the State Government except the second term as Governor or Vice-President of India.

- However, in reality, most of these recommendations have not been implemented. The appointment of Governors is solely based on the decision of the Central government. The convention of appointing a person from outside the State has been followed. However, the convention of consulting the Chief Minister of the State has always not been followed.
- There have been *en masse* replacements of Governors whenever there has been a change of government at the Centre. For example, in the recent past, this happened in 2004 when the United Progressive Alliance (UPA) Government headed by the Congress, replaced almost 17 Governors who were appointed by the previous National Democratic Alliance (NDA). Again in 2014, the NDA Government headed by Bhartiya Janata Party, replaced around 7 Governors who were appointed by the previous UPA Government.
- The way forward is to implement the recommendations of the Sarkaria Commission to ensure that the office of the Governor is not embroiled in political controversies. Consultation with the Chief Minister of the State concerned before appointment may not remove all problems or issues but will at least be a good starting point to reduce friction.

9.4.2.4 Qualification and Conditions of Governor's Office

A person to be appointed as a Governor must: [Art 157 and 158]

- be a citizen of India;
- be at least 35 years old;
- not be a member of the either House of the Parliament or House of a State Legislature. If such a member is appointed as Governor, he/she is deemed to have vacated his/her seat in that House on the date on which he/she enters upon his/her office as Governor.
- not hold any other office of profit.

The Governor shall be entitled to free official residence and emoluments, allowances and privileges as determined by the Parliament, which shall not be diminished during his/her term of office [Art 158].

9.4.3 Discretionary Powers of the Governor

Article 163 of the Constitution reads as follows:

1. There shall be a Council of Ministers with the Chief Minister at the head to aid and advise the Governor in the exercise of his/her functions, except in so far as he/she is by or under this Constitution required to exercise his/her functions or any of them in his/her discretion.

I. The Constitution has 'express provisions' under certain circumstances when the Governor is required to act at his/her discretion.

There are specific provisions in the Sixth Schedule where the Governor of Assam, acts as per his/her discretion. Similarly, the Governor of a State who is appointed also as an administrator of an adjoining Union Territory shall exercise the functions as administrator independently [Art 239]. There are also 'special responsibilities' bestowed on Governors of various states like Maharashtra, Gujarat, states of North-Eastern India, Andhra Pradesh, Karnataka etc., under Articles 371 to 371J. These are for development of the backward regions of some States (Gujarat, Maharashtra, Andhra Pradesh, Telangana and Karnataka) and to deal with the law-and-order situation in some of the North-Eastern States. All these provisions are in the nature of discretionary powers of Governors with respect to those particular States or Union territories.

II. The Governors of all States enjoy the following discretionary powers under specific circumstances 'by implication':

Discretionary Powers of Governor

- Reservation of Bills passed by the State legislature for consideration of the President
- Report of breakdown of Constitutional machinery under Article 356
- Appointment of Chief Minister when no party enjoys majority in the Legislative Assembly
- Dismissal of Chief Minister and dissolution of Legislative Assembly under specific circumstances

THINK ABOUT IT

Damned if you do, damned if you don't – Nothing is more appropriate in our constitutional scheme for this statement, except the discussion surrounding the abolition of the Governor's post. Discuss the role of the Governor with the controversies surrounding this post.

(a) Reservation of a Bill passed by the State Legislature for assent of the President [Art 200]

A bill passed by a State legislature can become an Act only after it receives the assent of the Governor or of the President (in case the bill is reserved for the consideration of the President). When a bill, passed by a State legislature, is presented to the Governor for his/her assent, he/she has four alternatives (under Article 200 of the Constitution):

1. He/she may give his/her assent to the bill, or
2. He/she may withhold his/her assent to the bill, or
3. He/she may return the bill (if it is not a Money Bill) for reconsideration of the State Legislature, or
4. He/she may reserve the bill for the consideration of the President.

As can be seen from the above, the Governor of a State can exercise Suspensive veto over a State bill whenever it is presented to him/her, just like the President exercises it with respect to the Union legislation. Further, under rare circumstances, the Governor may also exercise Absolute veto or Pocket veto over the State bills.

However, the Governor further has a power to reserve any bill passed by the State Legislature for consideration of the President. This is usually done by the Governors based on the advice of the State Council of Ministers. However, if the Governor feels that any bill passed by the State Legislature would affect the powers of the Union or contravene any of the provisions of the Constitution, he/she may use his/her discretion to reserve such a bill for consideration of the President.

State Bills reserved for President's consideration under the Constitution, may be classified as follows:

1. Bills which **must be reserved** for the President's consideration. In this category come Bills –
   (i) which reduce the powers of the High Court, as to endanger the position which that Court is designed to fill (Second Proviso to Article 200);
   (ii) which relate to the imposition of taxes on water or electricity in certain cases, and attract the provisions of Clause (2) of Article 288; and
   (iii) which are Money Bills or Financial Bills passed by the State Legislature during a Financial Emergency and required to be submitted for consideration of the President as per direction [Art 360].

   The above category of bills should be reserved for consideration of the President. These are also in the nature of 'express provisions' under the Constitution where the Governor is required to act in a particular manner and must reserve the bills for consideration of the President.
2. Bills which **may be reserved** for the President's consideration and assent for specific purposes
   (i) To secure immunity from the operation of Articles 14 and 19. These are Bills for – (a) acquisition of estates, etc. [First Proviso to Article 31A(I)]; (b) giving effect to Directive Principles of State Policy [Proviso to Article 31C].
   (ii) A Bill relating to a subject enumerated in the Concurrent list, to ensure operation of its provisions despite their repugnancy to a Union law or an existing law, by securing the President's assent in terms of Article 254(2).
   (iii) Legislation imposing restrictions on trade and commerce requiring Presidential sanction under the Proviso to Article 304(b) read with Article 255.

   The above category of bills may be reserved by the Governor for the President's consideration based on the advice of the State Council of Ministers.
3. Bills which may not specifically fall under any of the above categories, yet may be reserved by the Governor for the President's consideration under Article 200.

   The above category of bills (as per point 3) may be reserved by the Governor for the consideration of the President in his/her discretion. This is very rare and the Governor may exercise his/her discretion where he/she feels that the provisions of the bill will contravene any of the provisions of the Constitution and it is prudent to reserve it for consideration of the President.

   Whenever any bill passed by the State Legislature is reserved by a Governor for assent of the President, he/she shall act on the bill as per provisions of Article 201.

Recent issues with respect to reservation of Bills by Governors

There have always been issues with respect to (a) delay in providing assent to the bills or (b) reserving bills for consideration of the President by Governors in opposition ruled States. In past few years, this issue had amplified itself due to inordinate delay in providing assent or reserving bills for consideration of the President, that are otherwise within the State domain, by Governors of opposition ruled States like Punjab, Telangana, West Bengal, Kerala and Tamil Nadu. Many of these States approached the Supreme Court for resolving this impasse. The Supreme Court had observed, while hearing these cases, that such delay/reservation of routine bills is a matter of serious concern that affects the federal structure of our country. The court had indicated in July 2024 that it would look into 'when Governors can refer bills to President.'

As discussed before, the Sarkaria Commission had recommended that the President (Central Government) should dispose of Bills reserved for consideration within a maximum period of six months. In the event of President 'withholding assent', the reasons should be communicated to the State Government wherever possible.

Scan the QR code for video on recent issues with respect to reservation of Bills by Governor

McGraw Hill edge

The Punchhi Commission had also recommended that the Governor should take a decision with respect to a Bill presented for his/her assent within a period of six months. These recommendations should be implemented, either through constitutional amendments or by issuing guidelines, in order to maintain a healthy federal set-up.

(b) Report of breakdown of constitutional machinery under Article 356

Article 356 provides for the imposition of the President's rule through a proclamation when the Government of a State cannot be carried on in accordance with the provisions of the Constitution. This proclamation may be made by the President on receipt of a report from the Governor or otherwise. Such a report will be made by the Governor against a ministry in power if it attempts to subvert the Constitution or has lost its majority in the Legislative Assembly. Obviously, this report will be made by the Governor himself/herself without any advice from the Council of Ministers. Further, if a ministry has resigned and no other party or coalition is able to form a Government, the Governor may recommend imposition of the President's rule through his/her report under Article 356.

There have been many instances of controversial misuse of powers vested in Article 356. However, after the *S. R. Bommai case* judgement in 1994 by the Supreme Court, the misuse of this power has been curtailed, as this judgement has made the Presidential proclamation under Article 356 subject to judicial review.

(c) Appointment of the Chief Minister when no party enjoys majority in the Legislative Assembly

As per Article 164 of the Constitution, the Chief Minister is appointed by the Governor. The Governor under normal circumstances will appoint the leader of the party that enjoys a majority in the Legislative Assembly as the Chief Minister. However, when there is no single party with a majority, the Governor exercises his/her discretion in appointing the Chief Minister.

The Sarkaria Commission made recommendations on the manner in which the Chief Minister may be appointed in case no party enjoyed a majority in the Assembly. If there is no such party with a majority of its own (hung assembly), the Governor should select a Chief Minister from among the following parties or group of parties in the order of preference indicated below:

1. An alliance of parties that was formed prior to the Elections.
2. The largest single party staking a claim to form the government with the support of others, including 'independents'.
3. A post-electoral coalition of parties, with all the partners in the coalition joining the Government.
4. A post-electoral alliance of parties, with some of the parties in the alliance forming a government and the remaining parties, including 'independents' supporting the Government from outside.

However, in reality the Governors, in the event of hung assembly, have appointed Chief Ministers without following any particular order to favour the party in power at the Centre.

This issue can be resolved if the recommendations as provided in the Sarkaria Commission report are issued as guidelines that need to be followed by Governors while appointing Chief Ministers in the event of no single party enjoying a majority in the Legislative Assembly.

(d) Dismissal of Chief Minister and dissolution of the Legislative Assembly

There has been no uniformity regarding the criteria adopted for the dismissal of a Chief Minister. Obviously, a Chief Minister cannot continue in office after he/she ceases to command a majority in the Legislative Assembly.

Various Governors have adopted different approaches in similar situations regarding the dissolution of the Legislative Assembly. The advice of a Chief Minister, enjoying majority support in the Assembly, is normally binding on the Governor. However, where the Chief Minister had lost such support, some Governors refused to dissolve the Legislative Assembly on his/her advice, while others in similar situations, accepted his/her advice, and dissolved the Assembly.

The Sarkaria Commission had recommended the following course of action for the above two aspects:

(i) Dismissal of Chief Minister – The Governor should dismiss a Chief Minister if he/she fails to resign after the Council of Ministers have lost majority support in the Legislative Assembly. Whether a ministry enjoys majority support or not should only be tested on the floor of the House. If the Chief Minister refuses to convene the Assembly session in order to face a confidence motion, the Governor may summon the House himself/herself and direct the Council of Ministers to prove its majority.

(ii) Dissolving Legislative Assembly – If after the resignation of an incumbent government, no viable alternative emerges that can provide a stable government, then the Governor may either dissolve the Assembly or recommend the President's rule under Article 356 depending on the circumstances.

(e) Functioning as Chancellor of Universities

Many State legislations provide that the Governor of the State by virtue of his/her office shall also be the Chancellor of various State universities. As Chancellor, the Governor takes various decisions with respect to the appointment of Vice-Chancellors and other functionaries of these State universities. The convention has been that all these decisions are made by the Governor based on the advice of the council of ministers. However, the Governors have taken such decisions on their own, especially in the recent past in opposition ruled States, that has been a subject matter of criticism and court cases. The University Grants Commission (UGC) regulations have also been subject to debate on account of such differences. All these issues should be addressed and resolved in a manner that upholds the federal nature of our polity and State's autonomy in the administration of its universities without compromising on the standards for higher education.

MNEMONICS

Concept or Provisions	Shortcut or Mnemonics	Details to Remember
Discretionary powers of the Governor	**R**eservation **A**gainst **C**ancellation **(RAC)**	• **R** – **R**eservation of Bills passed by State legislature for consideration of President. • **A** – **A**ppointment of CM when no single party or pre-poll alliance enjoys majority in the Legislative Assembly. • **C** – **C**onstitutional machinery breakdown – Report to President

9.4.4 Similarities in Council of Ministers between Union and State

The arrangement of the State executive is very similar to the Union executive as we are a federal country. The below table summarises the similarity between the Council of Ministers at the Union and the State level.

Particulars	Union Provisions w.r.t. Prime Minister and Council of Ministers	Similar Provisions for State w.r.t. Chief Minister and Council of Ministers
Appointment	The Prime Minister is appointed by the President and all other ministers are appointed by the President on the advice of the Prime Minister [Art 75]. The Prime Minister and other ministers may be from the Lok Sabha or the Rajya Sabha. The President administers oaths of office and secrecy to the Prime Minister and other ministers (as per the forms in the Third Schedule) at the time of their appointment.	The Chief Minister is appointed by the Governor and all other ministers are appointed by the Governor on the advice of the Chief Minister [Art 164]. The Chief Minister and other ministers may be from the Legislative Assembly or the Legislative Council. The Governor administers oaths of office and secrecy to the Chief Minister and other ministers (as per the forms in the Third Schedule) at the time of their appointment.
Prime Minister and Chief Minister	• Prime Minister is the real Chief executive with the President being the nominal head. • Prime Minister is in-charge of coordinating the policy of the Government and hence supervises all the departments. • Prime Minister is the link between the President and the Council of Ministers. All the important communication to the President is made by the Prime Minister. • Prime Minister decides on whom to appoint as ministers in the Cabinet. He/she decides on the allocation and reshuffling of portfolios amongst them. While the President formally appoints all ministers, it is the Prime Minister who decides and advises the President on ministerial appointments and allocation of portfolios. • The death or resignation of the Prime Minister dissolves the entire Council of Ministers. New Prime Minister has to be sworn-in and the Council of Ministers also need to be again sworn-in. However, the death or resignation of any other minister creates only a vacancy in the Council of Ministers, which may be filled up by a new appointment.	• Chief Minister is the real Chief executive with the Governor being the nominal head. • Chief Minister is in-charge of coordinating the policy of the Government and hence supervises all the departments. • Chief Minister is the link between the Governor and the Council of Ministers. All the important communication to the Governor is made by the Chief Minister. • Chief Minister decides on whom to appoint as ministers in the Cabinet. He/she decides on the allocation and reshuffling of portfolios amongst them. While the Governor formally appoints all ministers, it is the Chief Minister who decides and advises the Governor on ministerial appointments and allocation of portfolios. • The death or resignation of the Chief Minister dissolves the entire Council of Ministers. New Chief Minister has to be sworn-in and the Council of Ministers also need to be again sworn-in. However, the death or resignation of any other minister creates only a vacancy in the Council of Ministers, which may be filled up by a new appointment.

Particulars	Union Provisions w.r.t. Prime Minister and Council of Ministers	Similar Provisions for State w.r.t. Chief Minister and Council of Ministers
	• There is no fixed term of office for the Prime Minister. He/she continues to be in office as long as their government enjoys majority in Lok Sabha. If the council of ministers loses the confidence (majority) of Lok Sabha, the Prime Minister and the entire council of ministers resign from their office. The party/coalition with a majority in Lok Sabha may also choose to change the Prime Minister while the government continues in power.	• There is no fixed term of office for the Chief Minister. He/she continues to be in office as long as their government enjoys majority in the Legislative Assembly. If the council of ministers loses the confidence (majority) of the Legislative Assembly, the Chief Minister and the entire council of ministers resign from their office. The party/coalition with a majority in the Legislative Assembly may also choose to change the Chief Minister while the government continues in power.
Duties of Prime Minister/ Chief Minister	Article 78 of the Constitution lays down the duties and functions of the Prime Minister vis-à-vis the President in the following words: • To communicate to the President all decisions of the Council of Ministers relating to the administration of the affairs of the Union and proposals for legislation; • To furnish such information relating to the administration of the affairs of the Union and proposals for legislation as the President may call for; and • If the President so requires, to submit for the consideration of the Council of Ministers any matter on which a decision has been taken by a Minister but which has not been considered by the Council.	Article 167 of the Constitution lays down the duties and functions of the Chief Minister vis-à-vis the Governor in the following words: • To communicate to the Governor all decisions of the Council of Ministers relating to the administration of the affairs of the State and proposals for legislation; • To furnish such information relating to the administration of the affairs of the State and proposals for legislation as the Governor may call for; and • If the Governor so requires, to submit for the consideration of the Council of Ministers any matter on which a decision has been taken by a Minister but which has not been considered by the Council.
Council of Ministers	• A person who is not a member of either House of Parliament can also be appointed as a Minister. However, such a Minister should become a member of either of the Houses within 6 months failing which he/she ceases to be a Minister [Art 75(5)]. • The Ministers shall hold office during the pleasure of the President [Art 75(2)]. In reality, it is the Prime Minister who decides on whom to appoint or remove as Ministers. The President acts as per the advice of the Prime Minister in this regard.	• A person who is not a member of the State Legislature can also be appointed as a Minister. However, such a Minister should become a member of the State Legislature within 6 months failing which he/she ceases to be a Minister [Art 164(4)]. • The Ministers shall hold office during the pleasure of the Governor [Art 164(1)]. In reality, it is the Chief Minister who decides on whom to appoint or remove as Ministers. The Governor acts as per the advice of the Chief Minister in this regard.

Particulars	Union Provisions w.r.t. Prime Minister and Council of Ministers	Similar Provisions for State w.r.t. Chief Minister and Council of Ministers
	• The President shall make rules for the more convenient transaction of business of the Government of India and for allocation of such business amongst Ministers [Art 77(3)]. • Total number of ministers including the Prime Minister shall not exceed 15% of the total membership of the Lok Sabha. Further, a member of either House of Parliament who has been disqualified under the Tenth Schedule for defection, shall not be appointed as a Minister for the remainder of the term unless he/she is re-elected [Art 75 (1A) & (1B)]. • A Minister is entitled to speak in both the Houses of Parliament but can vote only in the House of which he/she is a member [Art 88].	• The Governor shall make rules for the more convenient transaction of business of the Government of the State and for allocation of such business amongst Ministers [Art 166(3)]. • Total number of ministers including the Chief Minister shall not exceed 15% of the total membership of the Legislative Assembly subject to a minimum of 12. Further, a member of State legislature who has been disqualified under the Tenth Schedule for defection, shall not be appointed as a Minister for the remainder of the term unless he/she is re-elected [Art 164 (1A) & (1B)]. • A Minister is entitled to speak in both the Houses of State Legislature (where there are two Houses) but can vote only in the House of which he/she is a member [Art 177].
Collective responsibility	• The Council of Ministers shall be collectively responsible to the House of the People [Art 75(3)].	• The Council of Ministers shall be collectively responsible to the Legislative Assembly of the State [Art 164(2)].

MNEMONICS

Concept or Provisions	Shortcut or Mnemonics	Details to Remember
State executive – Article numbers for important provisions similar to Union executive	Add 89 to Article number of Union executive	• **72 + 89 = 161** – Pardoning power of Governor • **73 + 89 = 162** – Extent of executive powers of the State • **74 + 89 = 163** – Council of Ministers with Chief Minister at the head to aid and advise the Governor. • **75 + 89 = 164** – Provisions with respect to appointment of Chief Minister and ministers. • **76 + 89 = 165** – Advocate General of the State • **77 + 89 = 166** – Conduct of Business of the Government of a State • **78 + 89 = 167** – Duties of the Chief Minister towards the Governor
Similarities between Union and State Executive	Many provisions similar – For example – appointment of Ministers, collective responsibility of the council of ministers, maximum strength of the council of ministers	Replace: • President with Governor • Prime Minister with Chief Minister • Lok Sabha with Legislative Assembly

Some additional points and examples for State executive are summarised below:

- In the states of Chhattisgarh, Jharkhand, Madhya Pradesh and Odisha, there shall be a minister in-charge of Tribal welfare [Art 164].
- Many smaller states like Goa, Uttarakhand, Himachal Pradesh, and states of North-East (except Assam) have total membership of the Legislative Assembly varying from 30 to 70. However, all of them have a minimum of 12 ministers (including the Chief Minister) in the Council of Ministers [Art 164(1A)].
- There have been Chief Ministers from the Legislative Council on many instances. Some of the recent ones are Mr. Yogi Adityanath (UP – 2017), Mr. Uddhav Thackeray (Maharashtra – 2019), and Mr. Nitish Kumar (Bihar – 2020).

Scan the QR code for conceptual video on State executive

MAINS STARTER

Area	Building Blocks For Model Introductions
Role of Governor	In our Parliamentary democracy, the Governor is the nominal head of the State while the real executive powers are exercised by the council of ministers. The Governor is appointed by the centre, but he acts as per the aid and advice of the council of ministers (Art 163).
Discretionary powers of Governor	The Governor in a State, being the nominal head, acts as per the aid and advice of the council of ministers. However, he enjoys discretionary powers under specific circumstances under the provisions or by implication as per the Constitution (Art 163).
Reservation of Bills by Governor	Under Article 200 of the Constitution, the Governor may refer a bill for consideration of the President under specific circumstances. He/she should compulsorily reserve if the bill derogates the powers of High Court.
Some similar areas with Union Executive	If questions from this chapter are asked on Veto power, Ordinance power, Pardoning power, relationship of Chief Minister with Governor, Chief Minister and Council of ministers, the same introductions that have been provided in Union executive (Chapter 8) can be used by replacing President with Governor, Prime Minister with Chief Minister, and Lok Sabha with Legislative Assembly.

Register on **McGraw Hill Edge** for the following:

- Articles at a glance for this chapter
- Practice questions for Preliminary examination including PYQ of 2014–24
- Model answers for Mains PYQ of 2014–24
- Attend regular webinars by the author including discussion on **'Think about It'** questions

UPSC Previous Years' Questions of Preliminary Examination

1. Which one of the following suggested that the Governor should be an eminent person from outside the State and should be a detached figure without intense political links or should not have taken part in politics in the recent past? **[2019]**
   (a) First Administrative Reforms Commission (1966)
   (b) Rajamannar Committee (1969)
   (c) Sarkaria Commission (1983)
   (d) National Commission to review the working of the Constitution (2000)

   Solution: (c)

   Explanation: As discussed in Section 9.4.2.2, Sarkaria Commission made recommendations with respect to appointment of Governors and hence the correct answer is (c).

UPSC Previous Years' Questions of Main Examination

1. Discuss the essential conditions for exercise of the legislative powers by the Governor. Discuss the legality of re-promulgation of ordinances by the Governor without placing them before the legislature. **[2022]**

   Approach: The various legislative powers of the Governor need to be discussed in the first part. The issue with re-promulgation of ordinances and the recent Supreme Court judgement in this regard needs to be the second part of the answer.

MODEL ANSWER

The legislature of a State consists of the Governor and the Legislative Assembly (and the Legislative Council in states with two houses). The Governor performs various legislative functions as listed below. It must be noted that he/she performs the following functions on the advice of the council of ministers:

1. Summoning and prorogation of house(s) of State legislature from time to time and dissolution of the Legislative assembly (Art 174).
2. Addressing the State legislature at the beginning of every year and after general election to the Legislative assembly (Art 175).
3. Giving assent to the bills passed by State legislature.
4. Reserving bills for consideration of the President – this may be done on the advice of council of ministers for laws in the concurrent list that may contain provisions repugnant to a central law or on Governor's discretion if he/she feels that such a bill requires the assent of the President (Art 200).
5. Nominating the members to Legislative council of a State (Art 171).
6. Disqualification of members from State legislature on various grounds mentioned in the Constitution and Representation of the People Act, 1951 – This is done based on the opinion provided by the Election Commission of India (Art 191).

Ordinance power and re-promulgation (Art 213)

- Ordinance power is one of the important legislative powers of the Governor that he/she exercises based on the advice of the Council of Ministers.
- An ordinance once promulgated is valid for six weeks after the reassembly of the State legislature.
- One of the important issues surrounding this power was the constant re-promulgation bypassing the State legislature. This was done because the constitution did not prohibit such a practice.
- However, in 'Krishna Kumar Singh Vs State of Bihar (2017)' case, the Supreme court has clearly laid down that repeated repromulgation of an Ordinance is a 'fraud on the Constitution.'

CHAPTER 10

Union Parliament

LEARNING OUTCOMES

1. Understanding the composition and functioning of Parliament – its structure, composition of Houses, duration, and sessions
2. Evaluating the qualifications and disqualifications for MPs
3. Examining the election, removal and functions of Officers of Parliament
4. Explaining the legislative procedures, joint sittings, and the special procedure for Money and Financial Bills
5. Assessing Parliamentary privileges – Issues and way forward
6. Analysing the mechanism for legislative control over the executive
7. Exploring the role of Parliamentary Committees

10.1 INTRODUCTION TO THE PARLIAMENT

India has the Parliamentary form of government following the British model. Parliament is the legislative arm of the democracy, to which people elect their representatives to govern the country. Unlike the Presidential form of government in the United States, there are adequate checks on the executive as they are accountable to the legislature.

The Parliament of India consists of the President of India, the Upper House or the Council of States (Rajya Sabha) and the Lower House or the House of the People (Lok Sabha). Articles between 79 and 122 in Part V of the Constitution deal with the Union Parliament.

Though the Indian President is not a member of either House of Parliament and does not attend the proceedings of either House, he/she is nevertheless an integral part of the Parliament. The Parliamentary form of government was thought to be ideal for nascent democracy like India as the executive can be held accountable for their acts of omission and commission. In the U.S., the President is not part of the U.S. Congress.

Parliament		
Composition & Duration	**Qualification & Functioning**	**Legislative Procedure**
• Composition of the Parliament, the Lok Sabha and the Rajya Sabha • Duration of the Parliament • Sessions of the Parliament	• Qualification for members • Disqualification for/of members • Officers of the Parliament • Conduct of business	• Ordinary Bill • Money Bill • Financial Bills • Joint Sitting

Apart from the above, two more important areas that need to be understood are (a) Privileges of members and of the Houses and (b) Various ways through which the legislature exercises control over the executive. These will be covered at the end of the chapter after discussion on the above three aspects. At the end, we shall discuss the role played by Parliamentary Committees.

Before the discussion on composition, duration, qualification and disqualification, functioning of the Houses and legislative procedure, let us briefly understand the key functions performed by the Parliament in India.

10.2 FUNCTIONS OF THE PARLIAMENT

The Parliament of India performs the following key functions:

1. **Legislation** – The first and foremost function of the Parliament is to make laws. It is the legislative body that enacts various Acts as well as constitutional amendments according to the requirements. The Constitution has provided for three lists in the Seventh Schedule viz. (a) Union list, (b) State list and (c) Concurrent list. The Parliament enacts laws under the Union list and can also enact laws under the Concurrent list. It can enact laws under the State list as well during specific situations including emergencies.
2. **Providing the Council of Ministers** – India is a parliamentary democracy and the executive is part of the legislature. In order to be a minister, a person should be a member of either the Lok Sabha or the Rajya Sabha. Hence, it is the Parliament that provides the Council of Ministers including the Prime Minister.
3. **Control over Council of Ministers** – The Council of Ministers are collectively responsible to the House of the People. This is the overall control that the legislature exercises over the executive and a government cannot continue in power unless it has a majority in the Lok Sabha. Apart from this, the Parliament also exercises regular control over the executive through various means including questions, discussions, motions, parliamentary committees etc.
4. **Financial control** – The executive cannot collect any taxes or incur any expenditure without the approval of the Parliament. This is the financial control that Parliament exercises and the Annual Financial Statement (Budget) is presented every year for such approval.
5. **Source of information** – People of the country elect their representatives in a representative democracy like India. It is through parliamentary debates and discussions that the policies of the government are disseminated to the public at large. Further, through questions raised by members, the government provides information on various schemes and policies that are a very important source of information for the society.
6. **Constituent, Judicial and Electoral functions** – Apart from the above functions, the Parliament also performs the following functions:
   (a) Constituent function of amending the Constitution when required under Article 368.
   (b) Judicial function when it passes resolution (i) to impeach the President or remove the Vice-President; (ii) to remove the Judges of the Supreme Court, High Court, CAG (the Comptroller and Auditor General), Chief Election Commissioner; (iii) to punish members or outsiders for breach of privileges.
   (c) Electoral function when (a) members of the Parliament elect the President and the Vice-President and (b) members of the Lok Sabha elect the Speaker, Deputy Speaker and members of the Rajya Sabha elect the Deputy Chairman.

10.3 COMPOSITION OF PARLIAMENT AND DURATION OF HOUSES

10.3.1 Constitution of Parliament

Article 79. Constitution of Parliament – There shall be a Parliament for the Union which shall consist of the President and two Houses to be known respectively as the Council of States and the House of the People.

Our Parliament consists of the President, the Council of States (Rajya Sabha) and House of the People (Lok Sabha). Though the Indian President is not a member of either House of Parliament and does not attend the proceedings of either House, he/she is nevertheless an integral part of the Parliament.

10.3.2 Composition of the Council of States (Rajya Sabha)

- *Article 80 provides for the composition of the Rajya Sabha.* The maximum strength of the Rajya Sabha is 250 members.
    - Twelve members are nominated by the President with special knowledge or personal experience in Literature, Science, Art and Social service.
    - A maximum of 238 members are representatives of States and Union Territories with Legislative Assembly i.e., Delhi, Puducherry and Jammu & Kashmir.
- The key advantages of 'Rajya Sabha' or the second chamber are:
    1. Affords protection against the despotism (absolute power) of Lok Sabha.
    2. May give representation to special interests or groups of people in a State.
    3. Nomination also affords a chance for experts to enter the legislature.

- **Allocation of seats** – The allocation of seats in the Rajya Sabha is provided in the Fourth Schedule to the Constitution – As on date the number of elected members in the Rajya Sabha is 233. Hence, the total membership of the Rajya Sabha as on date is 245 (233 elected + 12 nominated). Unlike in the United States where the 100 seats in the Senate (Upper House that is equivalent of our Rajya Sabha) are equally distributed amongst the 50 States, the number of seats in the Rajya Sabha for each State is based on population. Hence, the number of seats varies from 1 (Goa, Puducherry, States of North-East except Assam) to 31 (Uttar Pradesh).
- **Electoral college for Rajya Sabha** – The representatives of the States are elected indirectly by the elected members of the Legislative Assemblies through the method of proportional representation by means of the single transferable vote. For the Union Territories with the Legislative Assembly i.e., Delhi, Puducherry and Jammu & Kashmir, the Representation of the People Act, 1950 provides for a similar procedure of election of representatives to the Rajya Sabha.
- The following additional points need to be kept in mind with respect to the Rajya Sabha elections:
    - Through an amendment to the Representation of the People Act, 1951 in 2003, the voting in such elections is through an open ballot. To avoid cross-voting by party MLAs, they are required to show their ballot paper to authorised agent of the Party (and to no one else). Not showing the ballot paper to the authorised agent or showing it to anyone else will disqualify the vote. Independent MLAs are barred from showing their ballots to anyone.

- If any MLA votes against the instruction of the party to which he/she belongs, it will not be considered a ground for disqualification under the Tenth Schedule since it is not a vote inside the assembly.
- There is no provision for NOTA (none of the above) in the Rajya Sabha elections.
- A member who is yet to take oath as a member of the assembly is allowed to vote in the Rajya Sabha elections as this is not a legislative function inside the assembly.

10.3.3 Composition of the House of the People (Lok Sabha)

- Article 81 deals with the composition of the Lok Sabha. It provides that the maximum strength of the representatives of the Lok Sabha should not be more than 550. Of this the representatives from the States and the Union territories should not be more than 530 and 20 respectively.
  - The representatives of States shall be chosen by direct election from territorial constituencies. The representatives of Union Territories shall be chosen in a manner as provided by a law made by Parliament. The Union Territories (Direct Election to the House of the People) Act, 1965 provides for a similar procedure where representatives of Union Territories are also chosen by direct election.
  - Earlier there were two members from the Anglo-Indian community who were nominated by the President to the Lok Sabha. But the 104th Constitutional Amendment Act repealed this provision in 2020 and subsequently no Anglo-Indian member has been nominated since the 17th Lok Sabha.
- **Allocation of seats** – The seats of the Lok Sabha are allocated to the States in such a manner that the ratio between the number of seats and the population of the State is, so far as practicable, same for all States. Similarly, each State is divided into territorial constituencies in such a manner that the ratio between the population of each constituency and the number of seats allotted to it is, so far as practicable, the same throughout the State.
  - The allocation of the seats in the Lok Sabha is provided in the First Schedule to the Representation of the People Act, 1950. The ***total membership of the Lok Sabha as on date is 543.***
  - The ***28 States put together have 524 seats.*** Uttar Pradesh has the maximum number of seats at 80 while Mizoram, Nagaland and Sikkim have 1 seat each.
  - The ***8 Union Territories put together have a total of 19 seats.*** Five Union Territories including the newly formed Ladakh, have 1 seat each. National Capital Territory of Delhi has 7 seats and Jammu & Kashmir has 5 seats.
  - Article 82 of the Constitution provides that the number of seats for a State as well its division into territorial constituencies shall be readjusted after each Census. This process is known as the 'Delimitation process' and is performed by 'Delimitation Commission' that is set up under an Act of Parliament. Such an exercise was carried out after the 1951, 1961 and 1971 Census. However, it has been frozen as per 1971 Census in order to encourage population control measures so that States with higher population growth do not end up having higher number of seats. This was done through the 42nd Amendment Act till the year 2000 and was extended by the 84th Amendment Act till 2026. ***Hence, population based on which the seats are allocated refers to the population as per the 1971 Census till the first Census after 2026. The division into territorial constituencies was carried out (without changing the number of seats) as per the 2001 Census and will again be performed based on the first Census after 2026.***

> **THINK ABOUT IT**
>
> Will the 106th constitutional amendment that provides one-third reservation for women in Lok Sabha and Legislative Assemblies usher in real women's empowerment in politics? Critically analyse.

- **Electoral college for Lok Sabha** – The electoral college for the Lok Sabha is all the citizens above the age of 18 years whose name is included in the electoral rolls. The representatives of the Lok Sabha are directly elected by the people once every five years. We have the plurality system or first-past-the-post system for the election of members to the Lok Sabha when compared to the proportional representation system for the election of members to the Rajya Sabha.
- **Reservation of seats for Scheduled Castes (SC) and Scheduled Tribes (ST)** – Article 330 provides for the reservation of seats in the States for the SC and ST in the Lok Sabha in proportion to their population. ***Population for this purpose means the population as per the 2001 Census*** till the first Census after the year 2026. As on date 84 seats are reserved for the Scheduled castes and 47 seats are reserved for the Schedule tribes out of the total 543 seats. This provision of reservation for SC and ST was initially for a period of 10 years, from the commencement of the Constitution. Considering the need to continue the same, it has been extended through successive constitutional amendments up to 2030 (recently through the 104th constitutional amendment).

  This exercise is carried out by the Delimitation Commission as per the following process:
  (a) The number of constituencies to be reserved in each state is fixed depending on the proportion of SC or ST in that State.
  (b) The constituencies that have the highest proportion of ST population, are reserved for ST.
  (c) For SC, the Delimitation Commission considers two aspects: (i) picking the constituencies that have higher proportion of SC population, and (ii) spreading these constituencies in different regions of the State.
- **Reservation of seats for Women in Lok Sabha**
  - The 106th Constitutional Amendment Act (also called 'Nari Shakti Vandan Adhiniyam') that was passed by the Parliament in September 2023 provides for reservation of, as nearly as may be, 1/3rd seats in Lok Sabha for women [Art 330A].
  - This will include, as nearly as may be, 1/3rd of the seats reserved for women out of the seats reserved for Scheduled Castes and Scheduled Tribes under Article 330 [Art 330A].
  - This reservation shall come into effect after the relevant figures of the first census conducted after the commencement of this Constitutional Amendment Act is published. Based on that census, delimitation exercise will be undertaken to reserve seats for women.
  - The seats reserved for women will be rotated after every subsequent delimitation as determined by a law made by Parliament.
  - This reservation is originally provided for a period of 15 years. However, it can be continued further based on a law to be made by Parliament.
- **Critical analysis of Women's Reservation Amendment**
  - The first Bill towards women's reservation in Lok Sabha and State Assemblies was introduced in 1996. After that Bills have been introduced in 1998, 1999 and subsequently in 2008 (which was passed in the Rajya Sabha). However, due to lack of political consensus they were never finally passed by both houses and operationalised. The main advantages of this reservation and issues involved are summarised below.

Advantages	Issues/Criticisms
• The number of women MPs in the 18th Lok Sabha is 14%, which is much lesser than western democracies where it averages from 30%-45%. This reservation will ensure adequate representation for women.	• This will be implemented only after the delimitation exercise based on the first census after commencement of this Amendment Act. This process will take time and the earliest this reservation would be implemented may be for the 2029 Lok Sabha elections.

Advantages	Issues/Criticisms
• The reservation of seats for women in local bodies that has been implemented since 1993 has been instrumental in empowering them politically and it is required in the Lok Sabha and State assemblies also. • Women MPs will increase the required gender sensitivity in Parliamentary processes including legislation. • The number of women Ministers in Central and State governments is likely to increase due to their increased representation.	• Rotation of seats after each delimitation may reduce the incentive for MPs to work for their constituencies as they could be ineligible to seek re-election. • There is no reservation of seats for women belonging to Backward Classes. • Reservation of seats within political parties as followed in democracies like Australia, Sweden, UK, France, etc., may be a better method to increase the representation of women.

Despite the issues/criticisms listed above, this policy of reservation for women has been a long pending reform and will go a long way in ensuring the rightful place for women in Indian politics and governance.

Comparison of Composition of Lok Sabha and Rajya Sabha

Particulars	Lok Sabha	Rajya Sabha
Maximum number of seats	550 – 530 from States and 20 from Union Territories (UT)	250 – 12 nominated and balance to be elected
Total membership as on date (2024)	543 – 524 from States and 19 from Union Territories	245 – 12 nominated and 233 elected
Allocation	• Based on population as per 1971 census • Allocation of seats to States/Union Territories is provided in the First schedule to the Representation of the People Act, 1950	• Unequal representation based on population of each State/UT with Legislative Assembly • Allocation of seats to States/Union Territories is provided in the Fourth Schedule to the Constitution
Electoral college	• All citizens over 18 years of age, included in the electoral rolls	• Elected MLAs of the States & UTs with Legislative Assembly
Method of voting	• Secret ballot	• Open ballot
Reservation of Seats	• Reservation for SC and ST as per 2001 census population • 1/3rd reservation for women (including in seats reserved for SC and ST) – To be implemented based on the first census after commencement of the 106th Constitutional Amendment.	• No reservation

MNEMONICS

Concept or Provisions	Shortcut or Mnemonics	Details to Remember
Census for Delimitation purposes	**Numbers 1971, Others 2001**	• **Number** of seats in Lok Sabha and Legislative Assemblies – Based on 1971 census • **Others** – Boundaries of seats and reservation for SC & ST – Based on 2001 census

10.3.4 Duration of the Houses

- **Rajya Sabha**
  - The Council of States or the Rajya Sabha is the permanent house of the Parliament and is not subjected to dissolution [Art 83(1)].
  - The Constitution has not fixed the tenure for the members of the Rajya Sabha and has left it to the Parliament. Accordingly, the Parliament through the Representation of the People Act 1951 has provided the tenure of the members to be 6 years.
  - At the end of every second year, 1/3rd of the members retire and fresh elections are conducted for those 1/3rd seats falling vacant.
- **Lok Sabha**
  - The normal term of the Lok Sabha is 5 years, from the date appointed for its first meeting, after which it is subjected to automatic dissolution [Art 83(2)]. However, the President is authorised to dissolve the Lok Sabha at any time before the completion of the 5-year term.
  - Also, the term of the Lok Sabha can be extended during emergency by 1 year at a time through a law made by Parliament. However, this extension cannot continue beyond a period of 6 months after the emergency has ceased to operate [Art 83(2)].

10.3.5 Sessions of Parliament

Article 85 of the Constitution provides for sessions, prorogation and dissolution of the Houses of the Parliament by the President.

1. Summoning

- The Constitution provides that the President shall from time to time summon each House of Parliament to meet at such time and place as he/she thinks fit, but six months shall not intervene between its last sitting in one session and the date appointed for its first sitting in the next session.
- The summoning of Houses is a legislative power of the President and he/she exercises this power based on the advice of the Council of Ministers.
- While there has to be at least two sessions of the Parliament in a year as per the constitutional requirement, there are normally three sessions by convention. They are
  - Budget session [February to April]
  - Monsoon session [July and August]
  - Winter session [November and December]
- Secret Sitting – On a request made by the Leader of the House, the Speaker shall fix a day or part thereof for a secret sitting of the Lok Sabha. When the Lok Sabha sits in secret, no stranger shall be permitted except persons authorised by the Speaker. The members of Rajya Sabha may be present in their galleries. The proceedings of a secret sitting may be issued in such manner as the Speaker thinks fit but no other person shall keep a note or record any proceedings or decisions of a secret sitting. The Lok Sabha may subsequently move a motion to lift the ban on the publication of proceedings of a secret sitting.

Scan the QR code for conceptual video on Composition, Duration and Sessions of Parliament

McGraw Hill edge

2. Prorogation

- The term 'prorogue' means to discontinue without dissolution. The Constitution provides that the President may from time to time prorogue the Houses or either House.
- It refers to the termination or ending of the session. It does not affect the bills or any other business pending before the House like motions, resolutions and amendments. Only the notices pending in the House (other than those for introducing bills), lapse on prorogation of the House.

3. Adjournment

- It refers to suspension of sitting of the Parliament by the presiding officer for a definite period of time which may be hours, days or weeks.
- The Speaker (or person acting as Speaker) in case of the Lok Sabha and the Chairman (or person acting as Chairman) in case of the Rajya Sabha adjourn the House from time to time when the Parliament is in session.

4. Adjournment Sine Die

- Sine die in Latin literally means 'without day'. It refers to terminating the sitting of the Parliament by the presiding officer for an indefinite period of time.
- This is done by the presiding officer on the last scheduled date of the session. Usually after the House is adjourned sine die by the presiding officer, the President prorogues the House. However, the President, based on the advice of the council of ministers, may prorogue even an ongoing session anytime.

5. Dissolution

- Dissolution by the President ends the life of the existing House. Rajya Sabha being a permanent House is not subjected to dissolution and only the Lok Sabha is subjected to dissolution.
- The dissolution can be automatic [on expiry of 5-year tenure of the Lok Sabha] or even before the completion of 5 years.
- Under normal circumstances, the Lok Sabha is usually dissolved after the election results for a general election are declared to enable the new government to take office. For example, the first meeting of the 17th Lok Sabha was scheduled on 17 June 2019. As per Article 83, the 17th Lok Sabha would have been automatically dissolved on 16 June 2024, i.e., at the end of 5 years from the date of its first meeting. The general election for constituting the 18th Lok Sabha was held across the country during April–June 2024 and the results were declared on 04 June 2024. The outgoing NDA Council of Ministers headed by Shri Narendra Modi recommended the dissolution of the 17th Lok Sabha to the President and it was dissolved on 05 June 2024. As per Section 73 of the Representation of the People Act, 1951, a new Lok Sabha is constituted upon issue of notification by the Election Commission in the official gazette of the results of general election in all constituencies where elections were held. This list was submitted by the ECI to President on June 6, 2024 and published in the official gazette thereby constituting the 18th Lok Sabha from that date. The first meeting of the 18th Lok Sabha was held on June 24, 2024.
- The Council of Ministers enjoying a majority in the Lok Sabha may recommend dissolution of the Lok Sabha at any point of time and the President is bound to act as per such advice. For example, the 13th Lok Sabha had a term up to October 2004. However, the NDA government headed by Shri A. B. Vajpayee recommended the dissolution of the Lok Sabha 8 months before schedule and it was dissolved in February 2004.
- However, if the Council of Ministers has lost the majority in the Lok Sabha and recommends dissolution of the House, the President may use his/her discretion before acting as per such

recommendation. For example, the NDA government headed by Shri A. B. Vajpayee lost majority in the Lok Sabha when a confidence motion moved by the Council of Ministers was defeated on 17 April 1999. The Cabinet headed by Shri Vajpayee, recommended the dissolution of the Lok Sabha. However, the President did not immediately accept the recommendation but explored the possibility of an alternate government. When it was clear that no other group was able to provide an alternate government, he dissolved the Lok Sabha on 26 April 1999.

10.4 QUALIFICATION AND DISQUALIFICATION

10.4.1 Qualification for becoming a Member of Parliament

Article 84 provides for the qualification of membership of the Parliament. A person shall not be qualified to be chosen to fill a seat in the Parliament unless he/she:

(a) is a citizen of India,

(b) is, in the case of a seat in the Council of States, not less than thirty years of age and, in the case of a seat in the House of the People, not less than twenty-five years of age; and

(c) possesses such other qualifications as may be prescribed in that behalf by or under any law made by the Parliament.

Accordingly, the Parliament through the Representation of the People Act of 1951 (RPA 1951) has enlisted the following qualifications:

- For the Lok Sabha
  - He/she must be registered as an elector in a Parliamentary constituency (from anywhere in India and not necessarily the constituency in which the person is contesting).
  - He/she must be a member of Scheduled caste or a Scheduled tribe in any State or UT in order to contest in a reserved seat. Hence a Scheduled Caste (SC) candidate can contest from any seat reserved for SC and similarly a Scheduled Tribe (ST) candidate can contest from any seat reserved for ST.
  - SC or ST candidates can also contest from a general/unreserved seat.
- For Rajya Sabha elections, before 2003, the candidate must be a domicile of the State that he/she wants to represent i.e., he/she must be an elector from the State that he/she wants to represent in the Rajya Sabha. However, in 2003, the domicile requirement was dropped by amending the RPA 1951 enabling an elector to contest from any State for the Rajya Sabha. For example, Mr. P. Chidambaram (former Finance Minister), an elector from Tamil Nadu represented Maharashtra in the Rajya Sabha from 2016 to 2022. Similarly, Mr. S. Jaishankar (External Affairs Minister since 2019), an elector from New Delhi represents Gujarat in Rajya Sabha since 2019.
- This amendment was challenged in the Supreme Court in the case of ***Kuldip Nayar Vs Union of India*** on the grounds that it violates the 'basic structure' of 'Federalism'.
- However, the Supreme Court upheld the amendment on the grounds that 'residence' was never a constitutional requirement for the Rajya Sabha and was only prescribed by the Parliament. Further, it held that the Indian federation is one of its own kind. The 'Council of States' has been in existence since the Government of India Act, 1919 and acted as a House of check and balance on the popularly elected House. It also upheld the 'open ballot system' for elections to the Rajya Sabha in this case.

10.4.2 Vacation of Seat by a Member of Parliament

Article 101 provides for the grounds of vacation of seat by a Member of Parliament. This has been summarised in the table below. Out of these, it is the disqualification of MPs that requires detailed discussion that will be covered in the next section.

Ground for Vacation	Provision under Article 101	Example(s)
No simultaneous membership in both Houses	No person shall be a member of both Houses of Parliament [Art 101(1)]. • If a person is elected to both the Houses at the same time, the choice between either of the two seats should be exercised within 10 days failing which the seat in the Rajya Sabha becomes vacant [Section 68 of RPA 1951]. • If a person is already a member of one House and gets elected to the other House, his/her seat in the first House shall become vacant on the date he/ she is declared chosen to the other House [Section 69 of RPA 1951].	• Smt. Sonia Gandhi was a member of Lok Sabha from Raebareli constituency in Uttar Pradesh after the General elections in 2019. She got elected to the Rajya Sabha on 20 February 2024 and on that date, her seat in the Lok Sabha fell vacant. • Union Minister Mr Piyush Goyal was a member of Rajya Sabha from Maharashtra after being re-elected to that house in July 2022. He won the Mumbai North Lok Sabha seat in the General elections of 2024 and was declared elected on 04 June 2024. On this date, his seat in the Rajya Sabha fell vacant.
No simultaneous membership in the State Legislature and the Parliament	No person shall be a member both of the Parliament and of a House of the Legislature of a State (MP and MLA/MLC), and if a person who is a member of a State Legislature is chosen as a Member of Parliament, then, within 14 days he/ she should resign his/her seat in the State Legislature, failing which his/her seat in the Parliament becomes vacant. [Art 101(2) & Prohibition of Simultaneous Membership Rules, 1950].	• Shri Narendra Modi was an MLA in Gujarat Assembly in 2014 when he contested the Lok Sabha election. He got elected to the Lok Sabha on 16 May 2014. He resigned his MLA seat from Gujarat Assembly on 21 May 2014. • Samajwadi Party leader, Shri Akhilesh Yadav was an MLA in Uttar Pradesh Assembly since 2022. He got elected to the Lok Sabha on 04 June 2024 and resigned his MLA seat on 12 June 2024.
Vacancy due to resignation	If a member of either House of Parliament, resigns his/her seat by writing under his/ her hand addressed to the Chairman or the Speaker, as the case may be, and his/her resignation is accepted by the Chairman or the Speaker, as the case may be, his/ her seat shall thereupon become vacant [Art 101(3)]. Provided that in the case of any resignation, if the Chairman or the Speaker, as the case may be, is satisfied that such resignation is not voluntary or genuine, he/ she shall not accept such resignation.	In July 2019 around 17 rebel MLAs from ruling coalition of Congress and Janata Dal (Secular) in Karnataka had tendered their resignation to the Speaker of the Legislative Assembly. However, there were proceedings for disqualification under the Tenth Schedule that was already pending against these MLAs. Hence in the instant case, the Speaker did not accept the resignations as they were not genuine and went on to disqualify the MLAs under the anti-defection law, which was subsequently upheld by the Supreme Court.

Ground for Vacation	Provision under Article 101	Example(s)
Absence without leave of the House	If for a period of 60 days a member of either House of Parliament is absent without permission of the House from all meetings thereof, the House may declare his/her seat vacant by passing a motion [Art 110(4)]. In computing the said period of 60 days no account shall be taken of any period during which the House is prorogued or is adjourned for more than four consecutive days. Hence these 60 days are counted when the House is in session.	

10.4.3 Disqualification of a Member of Parliament

Article 102 of the Constitution deals with disqualification of Members of Parliament (MP). It provides two scenarios of grounds for disqualification. The detailed discussion on these grounds along with relevant Supreme Court judgements as well as recent examples is provided in the following sections. The summary table for reference is provided post the discussion.

10.4.3.1 Disqualification under Article 102(1)

Article 102(1) of the Constitution lays down that a person shall be disqualified for being chosen as, and for being, a member of either House of Parliament under the following circumstances. It must be noted that if a person is already suffering from any of these disqualifications, he/she will not be allowed to contest the elections to Lok Sabha or Rajya Sabha. If a sitting MP suffers from any of these disqualifications, he/she will be disqualified by the President and his/her seat shall fall vacant as per provisions of Article 101. Before deciding on any such disqualification under the following grounds, the President shall obtain the opinion of the Election Commission and shall act according to such opinion. Hence, the opinion of the Election Commission on such disqualification cases is binding on the President (Art 103).

1. If he/she holds any office of profit under the Government of India or the Government of any State, other than an office declared by the Parliament by law not to disqualify its holder.

   The Parliament has enacted a law named 'The Parliament (Prevention of Disqualification) Act, 1959' that lists down various offices that are exempted from 'office of profit'. If a person holds an office of profit other than those exempted under the said law, he/she suffers from this disqualification.

2. If he/she is of unsound mind and stands so declared by a competent court.

   This is a medical condition and if any person is declared as mentally ill, he/she suffers from this disqualification.

3. If he/she is an undischarged insolvent.

   A solvent person is someone who has the resources to repay his/her debts. An insolvent person on the other hand is a person who is unable to repay his/her debts. If a person is declared

THINK ABOUT IT

Enumerate the circumstances when a person is disqualified from becoming a Member of Parliament or for continuing as one under Article 102(1). Who decides on these disqualifications?

insolvent and has not yet been discharged from his/her liabilities by a court, he/she continues to be an undischarged insolvent and suffers from this disqualification.

4. If he/she is not a citizen of India, or has voluntarily acquired the citizenship of a foreign State, or is under any acknowledgement of allegiance or adherence to a foreign State.

   This is an issue relating to the citizenship status of an individual for which he/she suffers from disqualification.

5. If he/she is so disqualified by or under any law made by the Parliament.

   The Representation of the People Act, 1951 (RPA 1951) has listed down various circumstances that can result in disqualification of a person.

   Sections 8 to 10A of the Representation of the People Act 1951 (RPA 1951) enlists the criterion for disqualification. They are summarised as follows:

   (a) Convicted of any offence and sentenced to imprisonment for not less than 2 years [Sec 8(3)]. Such a person is disqualified for a further period of 6 years from the date of release. So, for example a person convicted for 3 years in jail for a criminal offence will be disqualified for a total period of 9 years.

   (b) However, Section 8(1) provides that a person convicted for
      (i) various heinous crimes like rape etc., under criminal laws;
      (ii) promoting enmity between different groups, for preaching and practicing social crimes like sati, untouchability etc.,
      (iii) any offence under the Prevention of Corruption Act, Foreign Exchange Management Act etc.,

      shall be disqualified for a period of 6 years from the date of release irrespective of the period of sentence. In case a person is only levied a fine for any of these offences, he/she will still be disqualified for a period of 6 years from the date of conviction. Further, Section 8(2) provides that a person convicted for contravention of any law preventing hoarding, or relating to adulteration of food/drugs, or provisions of Dowry Prohibition Act and sentenced for not less than six months, shall be disqualified for a period of 6 years from the date of release.

      Section 8(4) provided that in respect of a sitting member of Parliament or State Legislature, any disqualification on account of conviction shall not take effect for a period of 3 months from the date of conviction or if an appeal has been filed against such conviction, till such time the appeal is disposed of by the court. However, the Supreme Court in the *Lily Thomas case* in 2013 struck down this clause as unconstitutional. Hence, any member of the Parliament or the State Legislature shall stand disqualified immediately from the date of sentencing for the conviction.

   (c) Found guilty on the ground of corrupt practices during election – Under Section 8A of the Act, if a High Court finds a person guilty of corrupt electoral practice, such an order shall be placed before the President for determining the disqualification of such a person. The President shall obtain opinion from the Election Commission of India (ECI) and shall act according to such opinion for disqualifying such a person for a maximum period of 6 years from the date of such order.

   (d) Dismissed from Government service for corruption or disloyalty – Section 9 of the Act specifies that any such person shall be disqualified for a period of 5 years from the date of dismissal.

   (e) Having interest in government contracts – Section 9A stipulates that a person having interest in government contracts shall be disqualified as long as his/her interest subsists in such contracts for the supply of goods or services.

(f) A managing agent, manager or secretary of any company or corporation (other than a cooperative society) in which the appropriate Government (i.e., Central or State Government) has not less than 25% share in capital – Section 10 stipulates that such a person shall be disqualified as long as he/she continues to hold such managerial post.

(g) Failure to lodge account of election expenses within stipulated time – Section 10A stipulates that if a person fails to lodge his/her account of election expenses within the stipulated time (30 days from declaration of results with the District Election Officer) without any valid reason, the Election Commission can disqualify him/her for a period of three years.

However, Section 11 of the Representation of the People Act, 1951 provides that the ECI may remove any disqualification (except disqualification for corrupt electoral practices) or reduce the period of disqualification for reasons to be recorded in writing.

In September 2019, in the case of Shri Prem Singh Tamang, the incumbent Chief Minister of Sikkim, the ECI had reduced the period of disqualification from 6 years to 13 months using its powers under Section 11.

10.4.3.2 Disqualification under Tenth Schedule

The Constitution provides that a person shall be disqualified from being a Member of Parliament if he/she is disqualified on the ground of defection. The provision for anti-defection was added in the Tenth Schedule by the 52nd Amendment Act in 1985. The background to this amendment was the frequent defections that happened across political parties during the 1960s and 1970s. These defections created political instability in many States bringing down the elected governments. It is in this background and to ensure stability of elected governments, the 52nd constitutional amendment introduced the 'Anti-defection' law through the Tenth Schedule in 1985. The Tenth Schedule specifies that for the purpose of this schedule, a member is deemed to be a member of the political party that has set him/her up as a candidate for his/her election to the House. In this regard, we need to understand the following terms:

> **THINK ABOUT IT**
>
> The Tenth Schedule has not fulfilled the objective for which it was enacted. Comment highlighting the issues with respect to effective implementation of the Tenth Schedule.

(a) Political Party or Original Political Party is the political party that has set up a member as a candidate for election to the concerned house. The Political Party appoints the 'whip' who provides directions to the members of that party on how they should vote in the house. Thus, the Political Party comprises of the entire organisation structure of such party, including its members in the Houses of Parliament and State Legislature(s).

(b) Legislature Party refers to the members of a Political Party in a particular house of Parliament or State legislature.

The grounds for disqualification of a member under the Tenth Schedule includes:

(a) If a member of political party has voluntarily given up his/her membership of such political party.

The Supreme Court has interpreted in various judgements that 'voluntary giving up membership' does not only mean resigning from the party to which the member belongs. Actions that can be interpreted, without a formal resignation, as giving up membership can be inferred from the conduct of the member.

(b) If he/she votes or abstains from voting in such House contrary to any direction issued by the political party to which he/she belongs, without prior permission of the party and condonation of such voting or abstention within 15 days.

Each political party designates one of its members in the Lok Sabha and the Rajya Sabha as 'Chief whip'. The whip issues 'directions' on how the members belonging to the party should vote on any question before the House. If a member votes or abstains from voting contrary to such direction, they are liable for disqualification under this clause.

(c) If an independent candidate joins any political party after such election.

However, they are free to join the Council of Ministers or support the Government of any other political party without joining any political party.

(d) If a nominated member of a House joins any political party after the expiry of 6 months from the date on which he/she takes his/her seat.

As on date, there are 12 members who are nominated to the Rajya Sabha. If they are members of a political party already at the time of their nomination, they will be deemed to be members of such political party. But if they are not members of any political party at the time of their nomination, they can join any party only within 6 months and not later.

Exceptions from disqualification under the Tenth Schedule

The Tenth Schedule provides the following exceptions to the above-mentioned grounds for disqualification of members:

1. If an original political party to which a member belongs merges with another party or forms a new political party on account of such merger.
    - Then if at least 2/3rd of the members of the concerned legislature party have agreed for such merger, then they are not liable for disqualification.
    - The balance members of the original political party who have not agreed to such merger can continue to function as a separate group and are also not liable for disqualification.
    - Before 2003, the Tenth Schedule allowed for split in the legislature party where 1/3rd of the members of the legislature party could split from their original political party and claim to be a separate group. However, the 91st Constitutional Amendment of 2003 deleted this provision.
2. Any person who is elected as the Speaker or the Deputy Speaker of the Lok Sabha or a State Legislative Assembly; any person who is elected as Deputy Chairman of the Rajya Sabha or Chairman/Deputy Chairman of the Legislative Council of a State can resign from their party immediately on election to such post (to demonstrate their impartiality). They can also rejoin the same party after they demit their post and such resignation as well as rejoining will not be a ground for disqualification.

Decision under the Tenth Schedule

If any question arises as to whether a member of a House has become subject to disqualification under the Tenth Schedule, the question shall be referred for the decision of the Chairman or, as the case may be, the Speaker of such House. It must be noted that the Chairman or the Speaker cannot take suo moto cognisance of any such defection and a petition needs to be submitted to the authority to take action under the Tenth Schedule. If a question arises as to whether the Chairman or Speaker of a House has become subject to disqualification under the Tenth Schedule, the question shall be referred for the decision of such member of the House as the House may elect in this behalf.

The Supreme Court in ***Kihoto Hollahan case*** in 1992 held that such decision by the Speaker or the Chairman is subject to judicial review on the grounds of mala fide, violation of constitutional mandate, non-compliance with rules of natural justice.

In *K. M. Singh vs Manipur Speaker case* in 2020, the Supreme Court has suggested to the Parliament to amend the Tenth Schedule, to provide that a tribunal with a judge as its head be constituted for adjudicating Tenth Schedule disqualification rather than the Speaker in order to avoid any partisan behaviour. It also held that the Speaker should decide any petition for disqualification within a reasonable time and unless there are exceptional circumstances, the Speaker should decide within 3 months.

Issues with respect to the Tenth Schedule

- The Tenth Schedule was inserted to avoid instability in elected governments due to defections. However, it has been noticed in many instances in the past that the Speakers act in a partisan manner to favour the ruling party. The Dinesh Goswami Committee on electoral reforms set up in 1990 as well as the Constitution Review Commission headed by Justice Venkatachaliah set up in 2002 had recommended that the President or the Governor be made the deciding authority for any disqualification under the Tenth Schedule based on opinion obtained from the Election Commission in a similar manner to disqualifications under Article 102(1). The Supreme Court has also suggested in K. M. Singh case that an independent tribunal headed by a judge be made the deciding authority. It further specified that Speakers should decide on any disqualification petition within a period of 3 months unless there are extraordinary circumstances.
- The Tenth Schedule also limits a legislator from voting according to his/her conscience or his/her constituency's interest. It may limit the legislator from participating in debates on various bills as he/she is bound finally by the whip of the party to vote in a particular manner. The Dinesh Goswami Committee and the Law Commission in its 170th report in 1999 have suggested that the provisions of the Tenth Schedule be made applicable only when the stability of the Government is in question like vote on budget or no-confidence motion.
- The 91st constitutional amendment has deleted the provision with respect to defection by $1/3^{rd}$ of the members of a legislature party in the House from their original political party. The present exceptions to disqualification as discussed previously is applicable only in case of merger of a political party with approval by at least $2/3^{rd}$ of its members. However, the Supreme Court is yet to authoritatively decide on instances when $2/3^{rd}$ members of a legislature party defect and claim immunity from disqualification on the grounds that they represent the original political party.
- The Supreme Court, in Sadiq Ali Vs Election Commission of India (1971), laid down the 3-test formula for determining which faction is to be recognised as the original political party by the Election Commission in case of a split in the party. These are aims and objects of the party; its affairs as per the party's constitution that reflect inner party democracy; and majority in the legislative and organisation wings. However, considering lack of inner party democracy in most of the political parties in our country, decisions by the Election Commission in this regard are invariably based on only the strength of support of legislators like MPs and MLAs/MLCs for the different factions.
- The real reform to address these issues is regular inner-party elections. Various experts are of the view that the Election Commission of India should not be involved in monitoring and regulating these elections as it will drag a constitutional authority into the muddle of party politics. It is the primary members of various political parties as responsible citizenry who need to demand and operationalise such internal democracy.

Scan the QR code for conceptual video on Qualification and Disqualification for Members of Parliament

McGraw Hill edge

SUMMARY OF DISQUALIFICATION PROVISIONS

Provisions	Grounds for Disqualification	Deciding Authority
Article 102(1) read with The Representation of the People Act, 1951	A person is disqualified for being chosen as and for being a member of either House of Parliament if he/she suffers from any of the following disqualification. It means that a person who suffers from any of the following disqualification cannot contest in an election and if he/she is already a sitting member, he/she vacates his/her seat on disqualification under these grounds: 1. Holding an office of profit, unless exempted by a Parliamentary law 2. Unsound mind 3. Undischarged insolvent 4. Issues relating to citizenship 5. Disqualification under the Representation of the People Act, 1951	• Any question of disqualification under Article 102(1) shall be decided by the President based on the opinion provided by the ECI, which is binding on the President. • However, disqualification on grounds of conviction in a criminal case takes immediate effect as per the Supreme Court judgement in Lily Thomas case.
Article 102(2) read with Tenth Schedule	A Member of Parliament is subject to disqualification under 'anti-defection' law as per the Tenth Schedule. Following is the summary of the provisions of the Tenth Schedule that results in disqualification: 1. A member of a political party voluntarily gives up his/her membership of that party or votes/ abstains against the instruction of such party in the House. 2. An independent member of the House joins any political party or a nominated member of the Rajya Sabha (who is not already a member of a political party) joins a political party 6 months after taking his/her seat. Exceptions: • If a political party merges with another party or forms a new party on account of such merger, which is approved by at least 2/3rd of the members of the concerned legislature party, it is not a ground for disqualification. • The Speaker, the Deputy Speaker (of the Lok Sabha) and the Deputy Chairman (of the Rajya Sabha) may resign from their political parties on being elected to such a constitutional post and rejoin the same party after demitting office. This is not a ground for disqualification.	• The Speaker in case of the Lok Sabha and the Chairman in case of the Rajya Sabha decide on any disqualification under the Tenth Schedule. • As per the Supreme Court judgement in K. M. Singh Vs Speaker of Manipur case, the Speaker should decide on any case of disqualification within a period of 3 months unless there are extraordinary circumstances.

10.4.3.3 Suspension of Members

Procedure for Suspension under Rules of Lok Sabha and Rajya Sabha

- The Speaker of Lok Sabha/Chairman of Rajya Sabha can direct a member to withdraw immediately from the House if he/she finds the member's conduct disorderly. Such member shall remain absent during the remainder of the day's sitting [Rule 373 of Lok Sabha rules & Rule 255 of Rajya Sabha rules].
- The Speaker/Chairman can name a member who disregards the authority of Chair or abuses the rules of the House by persistently and wilfully obstructing the business of the House. Such a member may be suspended from the House, for a period not exceeding the remainder of the session, by a motion passed by the House. The House may at any time, by a motion, terminate such suspension [Rule 374 of Lok Sabha rules & Rule 256 of Rajya Sabha rules].
- In case of grave disorder, on being named by the Speaker, a member stands automatically suspended from the service of the House for five consecutive sittings or the remainder of the session, whichever is less. The House may at any time, by a motion, terminate such suspension [Rule 374A of Lok Sabha rules].

Issues with suspension and way forward

- It curbs the democratic representation of elected representatives.
- If it is targeted at only the opposition members, it can be viewed as partisan behaviour by the Speaker/Chairman and the Houses.
- It reduces scope for debate and discussion.
- The way forward is for the government to respond to the demands raised by the opposition in a timely and respectful manner. The opposition MPs should also shun unnecessary disruption. There must be dialogue and consensus building amongst different parties and groups.

Apart from suspension, expulsion is an extreme step where a member may be expelled from the House by a motion passed by the House. Expulsion is an extreme punishment and not mentioned explicitly in the Constitution. The Supreme Court in February 2025 has held that such decision of expulsion by any house of the legislature is subject to judicial review.

10.4.3.4 Salaries and Allowances

The members of either House of Parliament receive salaries and allowances as may be determined by a Parliamentary law. The Parliament enacted 'Salary, allowances and pension of Members of Parliament Act, 1954' that has been amended from time to time, with the recent amendment being in the year 2020. As per this Act, the current salary of an MP is ₹1,00,000 per month. MPs also receive constituency allowance of ₹70,000 per month and office expenses allowance of ₹60,000 per month apart from daily allowance of ₹2,000 for each day of residence on duty. They also receive pension of ₹25,000 per month, and persons who have served for more than 5 years receive an additional pension of ₹2,000 per month for every year served in excess of 5 years.

MNEMONICS

Concept or Provisions	Shortcut or Mnemonics	Details to Remember
Disqualification under Article 102(1) – 5 grounds	**OPiUM** sale by an **UND**erage **Non-citizen** resulted in **disqualification as per law by President**.	• **OP** – Office of Profit • **UM** – Unsound Mind • **UND** – Undischarged insolvent • **Non-Citizen** – Not a citizen or acquired citizenship of a foreign country • **Disqualified under law made by Parliament – RP Act, 1951** **President** decides on this disqualification as per the opinion given by the Election Commission of India.
Disqualification under Representation of the People Act, 1951	**5C1E**	• **C** – Conviction for 2 years or more and in some cases even less than 2 years – Immediate disqualification – Period of sentence + 6 years. • **C** – Corrupt practices during election – Maximum period up to 6 years. • **C** – Corruption or disloyalty – Dismissal from Government service – 5 years. • **C** – Contracts with Government – disqualified as long as interest subsists. • **C** – Company or Corporation of Government – Manager or Managing agent – disqualified as long as holding such managerial position. • **E** – Election expenses – failure to lodge within time – 3 years.
Tenth Schedule disqualification – Anti-defection law	**PP** = **VV** **PP** = **I** **PP** > **6** = **N** Exceptions (a) **2/3rd** (b) **OOPS**	• **P**olitical **P**arty (PP) member = **V**oluntary resigns or **V**otes against or abstains from voting against instruction of his/her party. • **I**ndependent member = joins any **P**olitical **P**arty • **N**ominated member = joins any **P**olitical **P**arty after 6 months Exceptions • If PP merges with another PP and agreed by 2/3rd of members of the Legislature party • Not applicable for Officers of Parliament (OOP) – Speaker, Deputy Speaker and Deputy Chairman Decision by Speaker or Chairman

10.5 OFFICERS OF PARLIAMENT AND CONDUCT OF BUSINESS

10.5.1 Officers of Parliament

Presiding Offcers of the Parliament	
Lok Sabha	**Rajya Sabha**
(a) Speaker (b) Deputy Speaker (c) Pro-tem Speaker (d) Panel of chairpersons	(a) Chairman (b) Deputy Chairman (c) Panel of vice-chairpersons

10.5.1.1 Speaker and Deputy Speaker of the Lok Sabha

Election of Speaker and Deputy Speaker

Article 93 of the Constitution provides for the position of the Speaker and the Deputy Speaker for the House of the People.

The Speaker is elected by the Lok Sabha from among its members by a simple majority and the date of election is fixed by the President. The Speaker is the Presiding officer of the Lok Sabha. He/she is the guardian of powers and privileges of the House, its members and its committees. He/she is the principal spokesperson of the House, and his/her decisions on all matters is final as far as the Houses are concerned. In 1952, 1967 and 1976, there had been voting in Lok Sabha for the election of the Speaker.

The Deputy Speaker is elected by the Lok Sabha from amongst its members by a simple majority and the date of election is fixed by the Speaker. The Deputy Speaker acts as the Presiding officer of the Lok Sabha and performs the functions of the Speaker when the latter is absent or the position of the Speaker is vacant.

Conditions of Office of Speaker and Deputy Speaker

According to Article 94, a member holding office as the Speaker or the Deputy Speaker of the House of the People shall vacate his/her office:

- If he/she ceases to be a member of the House of the People;
- May at any time, by writing under his/her hand addressed, if such member is the Speaker, to the Deputy Speaker, and if such member is the Deputy Speaker, to the Speaker, resign his/her office; and
- May be removed from his/her office by a resolution of the House of the People passed by a majority of all the then members of the House (effective majority). Such a resolution shall be moved only with a prior notice of at least 14 days. The leave (permission) for taking up such a resolution should be granted by at least 50 members of the house. If granted, the resolution will be taken up for discussion within 10 days from the date on which the leave is granted.
- The Speaker or the Deputy Speaker shall not preside over the sitting that is considering a resolution for their own removal. They can be present as a member and will have the right to speak and take part in the proceedings of the House. They can also vote in such resolution in the first instance as a member [Article 96].
- Whenever the House of the People is dissolved, the Speaker shall not vacate his/her office until immediately before the first meeting of the House of the People after the dissolution.

- The duration of the Lok Sabha is 5 years and it is usually dissolved after the results of a general election is declared to pave the way for the constitution of new Lok Sabha. The 17th Lok Sabha, was dissolved on 05 June 2024. The 18th Lok Sabha that was constituted on 06 June 2024, had its first meeting on 24 June 2024. While all the members of the 17th Lok Sabha ceased to be its members from 05 June, Shri. Om Birla, who was the Speaker of the 17th Lok Sabha, continued in his office as Speaker till immediately before the first meeting on 24 June. This provision is to ensure that the post of Speaker, who is the officer incharge for all actions of the Lok Sabha and its secretariat, is never left vacant.

THINK ABOUT IT

The functioning of the Speaker should be above political considerations. Discuss in view of critical functions performed by the Speaker as the presiding officer of Lok Sabha. What reforms are required to strengthen the independence of the Speaker?

The Speaker and the Deputy Speaker of the Lok Sabha are paid such salaries and allowances as may be fixed by the Parliament by law [Art 97]. The Parliament enacted the Salaries and Allowances of Officers of Parliament Act, 1953 that has been amended from time to time. As per this Act, the Speaker and Deputy Speaker of Lok Sabha are entitled to salary, daily allowance and constituency allowance at the same rate as payable to Members of Parliament. The Speaker is also paid a sumptuary allowance of ₹2,000 per month that is payable to a cabinet minister. The Deputy Speaker is paid ₹1,000 per month payable to a Minister of State.

Functions of Speaker and Deputy Speaker

Speaker	Deputy Speaker
• He/she is guardian of power and privileges of members. • His/her decision in all parliamentary matters is final for the members of the House. • Adjourns House or suspends the House if no quorum is maintained. • Exercise casting vote in case of a tie; cannot vote in the first instance as a member except when it is a motion for his/her removal when he/she is not presiding over the House. • Presides over joint sitting. • Certifies whether a bill is a Money Bill or not. • Decides disqualification of members on the grounds of defection under the Tenth Schedule.	• Presides over the House when the Speaker is absent or his/her post is vacant. • Whenever he/she presides over the House, he/she cannot vote in the first instance as a member.

By convention, from the 10th Lok Sabha constituted in 1991, the position of the Speaker is occupied by the ruling party and of the Deputy Speaker by the principal opposition party. However, it may be noted that there was no Deputy Speaker elected by the House during the 17th Lok Sabha (2019–2024).

Panel of Chairpersons

- While the office of the Speaker is vacant, the duties of the office shall be performed by the Deputy Speaker or, if the office of the Deputy Speaker is also vacant, by such member of the House of the People as the President may appoint for the purpose [Art 95(1)].
- During the absence of the Speaker from any sitting of the House of the People the Deputy Speaker or, if he/she is also absent, such person as may be determined by the rules of procedure

of the House, or, if no such person is present, such other person as may be determined by the House, shall act as the Speaker [Art 95(2)].

- Rules of Procedure of the Lok Sabha provides for nomination of the Chairperson who will preside over the House in the absence of both the Speaker and the Deputy Speaker as per Article 95. The rules provide that at the commencement of the Lok Sabha or from time to time, as the case may be, the Speaker shall nominate from amongst the members, a panel of not more than ten Chairpersons, anyone of whom may preside over the House in the absence of the Speaker and the Deputy Speaker.

Pro-tem Speaker

- The first meeting after the election when the Speaker and the Deputy Speaker are elected by members of the Lok Sabha is held under the senior most Member of the Lok Sabha known as Pro-tem Speaker. 'Pro-tem' in Latin refers to 'for the time being'.
- Article 95 states that when the office of the Speaker and the Deputy Speaker are vacant, such member of the House as the President may appoint shall perform the functions of the Speaker.
- The Speaker vacates the office immediately before the first meeting of the Lok Sabha after dissolution i.e., before the first meeting of the newly constituted Lok Sabha after election. At this stage, both the office of the Speaker and the Deputy Speaker fall vacant and hence the President (based on advice of the Council of Ministers) appoints one of the senior most members of the new Lok Sabha to perform the functions of the Speaker. For example, in the 18th Lok Sabha, Shri Bhartruhari Mahtab was appointed as the Pro-tem Speaker.
- The Pro-tem Speaker administers the oath to all the elected members of the Lok Sabha after which the permanent Speaker is elected by the House. This is presided over by the Pro-tem Speaker. For example, Shri Om Birla was again elected as the Speaker of the 18th Lok Sabha.
- This term 'Speaker pro-tem' is not mentioned in the Constitution or rules of Lok Sabha but is a conventional term. This office is modelled on the basis of 'Father of the House of Commons' in the U.K., who is a senior member of the House with the longest continuous service. He/She presides over the election of Speaker of the House of Commons in the U.K.

Comparison with Office of Speaker in Britain

The office of the Speaker evolved in British Parliament since 1376 CE. Till the 17th Century, the British Crown got the House of Commons (equivalent of our Lok Sabha) to elect a person whom it wanted as the Speaker and in medieval Britain, the Speaker was viewed more as an agent of the Crown. However, since middle of the 19th Century, the Speaker is considered to be an impartial presiding officer of the House of Commons.

In Britain, the Speaker once elected to his/her office, resigns from the political party to which he/she belonged. In subsequent elections to the House of Commons, he/she seeks election not as a member of any political party but as a Speaker of the House. This is to reflect his/her impartiality while presiding over the House. When an incumbent Speaker retires, a new Speaker is elected by the House and the same process is repeated.

In our Constitution, while the Tenth Schedule allows a Speaker (or the Deputy Speaker) to resign from their political party on being elected to the office of the Speaker (or the Deputy Speaker), it has been never done by any Speaker till date. Further, the Speaker contests and gets elected in a Lok Sabha election from a constituency as a member of the political party unlike in Britain where he/she does not contest under any political party label but as 'The Speaker seeking re-election'. The British practice with respect to the office of Speaker may be adopted in India as well to maintain impartiality in their functioning. This will strengthen the democratic practices in the Lok Sabha. However, till such time this is adopted, the Speaker may at least resign from their political party as provided in the Tenth Schedule to demonstrate impartiality.

10.5.1.2 Chairman and Deputy Chairman of the Rajya Sabha

Article 89 provides for the office of the Chairman and the Deputy Chairman of the Council of States.

The Vice-President of India shall be the ex officio Chairman of the Council of States. The Council of States shall, as soon as may be, choose a member by simple majority of the Council to be the Deputy Chairman.

Conditions of office of Chairman and Deputy Chairman

The ex officio Chairman of the Rajya Sabha is the Vice-President of India. If the Vice-President of India is removed from his/her office, he/she automatically ceases to be the Chairman of the Rajya Sabha as well.

According to Article 90, a member holding the office as the Deputy Chairman of the Council of States shall vacate his/her office:

- if he/she ceases to be a member of the Council;
- may at any time, by writing under his/her hand addressed to the Chairman, resign his/her office; and
- may be removed from his/her office by a resolution of the Council of States passed by a majority of all the then members of the House (effective majority). Such a resolution shall be moved only with a prior notice of at least 14 days.
- The Chairman or the Deputy Chairman shall not preside over the sitting that is considering a resolution for their own removal. They can be present and will have the right to speak and take part in the proceedings of the House. The Chairman cannot vote in the first instance as well on a resolution for the removal of the Vice-President as he/she is not a member of the Council of States. The Deputy Chairman however, can vote on a resolution for his/her removal in the first instance as a member of the Council [Article 92].

The Chairman and the Deputy Chairman of the Rajya Sabha are paid such salaries and allowances as may be fixed by the Parliament by law [Art 97]. The Parliament has enacted the Salaries and Allowances of Officers of Parliament Act, 1953 that has been amended from time to time. As per this Act, the Chairman of Rajya Sabha draws a salary of ₹4 lac per month (as amended in 2018). The Deputy Chairman is entitled to salary, daily allowance and constituency allowance at the same rate as payable to Members of Parliament. The Deputy Chairman is paid a sumptuary allowance of ₹1,000 per month payable to a Minister of State.

Functions of Chairman and Deputy Chairman

The Chairman and the Deputy Chairman of the Rajya Sabha perform similar functions to that of the Speaker and the Deputy Speaker. However, the Chairman does not certify a bill to be a Money Bill and does not preside over a joint sitting of both the Houses.

Panel of Vice Chairpersons

- While the office of the Chairman or during any period when the Vice-President is acting as, or discharging the functions of President, the duties of the office shall be performed by the Deputy Chairman. If the office of Deputy Chairman is also vacant, then by such member of the Council of States as the President may appoint for the purpose [Art 91(1)].

- During the absence of the Chairman from any sitting of the Council of States the Deputy Chairman or, if he/she is also absent, such person as may be determined by the rules of procedure of the Council, or, if no such person is present, such other person as may be determined by the Council, shall act as the Chairman [Art 91(2)].
- Rules of Procedure of Rajya Sabha provides for nomination of the Vice-Chairman who will preside over the House in the absence of both the Chairman and the Deputy Chairman as per Article 91. The rules provide that the Chairman shall, from time to time, nominate from amongst the members of the Council a panel of not more than six Vice-Chairmen, any one of whom may preside over the Council in the absence of the Chairman and the Deputy Chairman.

MNEMONICS

Concept or Provisions	Shortcut or Mnemonics	Details to Remember
Election and removal of Officers of Parliament (except Chairman of Rajya Sabha)	**Officers of Parliament** elected **simply by their house** and **removed by their house** if not **effective**	Speaker and Deputy Speaker of Lok Sabha; Deputy Chairman of Rajya Sabha – All 3 **elected by simple majority** in their respective house and **removed by effective majority** in their respective house. All 3 vote in first instance as a member on resolution for their removal.

10.5.2 Conduct of Business

10.5.2.1 Oath or Affirmation by Members

- Every member of either House of Parliament shall, before taking his/her seat, make and subscribe before the President, or some person appointed in that behalf by him/her, an oath or affirmation according to the form set out for the purpose in the Third Schedule [Art 99].
- The newly elected Members of a Lok Sabha are administered oath by the Pro-tem Speaker who is appointed by the President. Thereafter, any MP of the Lok Sabha who gets elected in a bye-election during the term of that Lok Sabha is administered oath by the Speaker of the House.
- The Chairman of the Rajya Sabha administers the oath to the new members of the Rajya Sabha whenever they are elected during the biennial election (once every 2 years) or bye-election.

10.5.2.2 Majority during Voting in Houses

- The Constitution provides that save as otherwise provided, all questions at any sitting of either House or joint sitting of the Houses shall be determined by a majority of votes of the members present and voting, other than the Speaker or person acting as the Chairman or Speaker. The Chairman or Speaker (or the person acting as such) shall not vote in the first instance but exercise a casting vote in the case of equality of votes [Art 100].
  - The above majority is what we usually refer to as 'simple majority'. Hence, as per the Constitution, unless there is a specific majority required as per the provisions of any article, the decisions of the House are arrived at with a simple majority.
  - If the Constitution provides for a specific majority – for example, for impeachment of the President the majority required is $2/3^{rd}$ of the total membership of each House (Highest

Special Majority) or for removal of the Speaker of Lok Sabha, the majority required is of all the then members of the House (effective majority) – then such a majority is required.

- The presiding officer of the House does not vote in the first instance but only votes in case of equality of votes for decisions that require simple majority. Though there are no rules to regulate the exercise of casting vote, as per British Parliamentary conventions, the presiding officer votes to maintain the status quo.
- The Houses shall have the power to act notwithstanding any vacancy in the membership and any proceeding shall be valid notwithstanding that some person who was not entitled to vote had voted in any decision.

❑ The various methods of voting adopted in the houses are briefly summarised below:

- *Voice vote* – Here, the question before the house is determined by the 'Ayes' (yes) or 'Noes' (No), as the case may be, by the Speaker/Chairman. For any question that needs to be decided by a simple majority, this is the first method by which voting happens in both houses. If the decision of the Speaker/Chairman is challenged, then the other methods are adopted.
- *Division* – This is ordered when the voice vote is challenged. Further, for questions that require special majority or effective majority, the voting happens only by this method. The most usual way of recording the vote at present is through Automatic Vote Recorder Equipment that is placed on each seat. The individual results are shown by three colours – green for 'Ayes', red for 'Noes' and yellow/amber for 'abstain'. The total result under these 3 categories is flashed on a big screen at the end of counting after which the Speaker/Chairman announces the decision.
- *Recording of votes by distribution of slips* – This is done by recording of votes on 'Ayes' and 'Noes' slip by the members. This is resorted to when there is a failure of Automatic Voter Recording Equipment or at the first session of a new Lok Sabha before seats are allotted to new members.

10.5.2.3 Quorum of the Houses

❑ Quorum is the minimum number of members who need to be present in the House during a proceeding for it to be valid.

❑ The Constitution provides that until the Parliament by law otherwise provides, the quorum to constitute a meeting of either House of Parliament shall be one-tenth of the total membership of the House [Art 100].

❑ Hence, in the Lok Sabha the number of members who need to be present for a valid quorum is 55 (one-tenth of 543) including the Speaker as he/she is a member of the House. Similarly, in the Rajya Sabha the quorum is 25 (one-tenth of 245) excluding the Chairman as he/she is not a member.

❑ If at any time during a meeting there is no required quorum, the presiding officer shall adjourn or suspend the meeting till the required quorum members assemble.

Scan the QR code for conceptual video on Officers of Parliament and Conduct of Business

Mc Graw Hill edge

10.5.2.4 Language in Parliament

❑ As per Article 120 of the Constitution, the business in Parliament shall be transacted in Hindi or in English. English was to be discontinued at the end of fifteen years from the commencement of the Constitution (1965), but it has been allowed to continue indefinitely along with Hindi under the Official Languages Act, 1963. The Chairman or Speaker may allow a member to address the House in his/her mother-tongues if they cannot adequately express themselves in Hindi or in English.

10.5.3 Leaders of Parliament

10.5.3.1 Leader of the House/Council

- As per rules of the Lok Sabha and the Rajya Sabha, the Prime Minister is the leader of the House of which he/she is a member. For example, during the 14th and 15th Lok Sabha (2004–14), when the Prime Minister of India, Dr. Manmohan Singh was a member of the Rajya Sabha, he was the leader of the Rajya Sabha. Similarly, during the 16th and 17th Lok Sabha (2014–24) when the Prime Minister, Shri Narendra Modi was a member of the Lok Sabha, he was the leader of the Lok Sabha and continues to be so in the 18th Lok Sabha (2024–29).
- In respect of the other House of which the Prime Minister is not a member, a minister who is a member of that house and nominated by the Prime Minister is the leader of that house. For example, during the 14th and 15th Lok Sabha (2004–14), Shri Pranab Mukherjee (2004–12) and Shri Sushilkumar Shinde (2012–14) were the leaders of the Lok Sabha. Similarly, during the 16th Lok Sabha (2014–19), Shri Arun Jaitley was the leader of the Rajya Sabha. Shri J P Nadda is the leader of Rajya Sabha since June 2024.

> **THINK ABOUT IT**
>
> Discuss the role of Leader of the Houses of Parliament as per rules of procedure. How critical is their role in ensuring smooth functioning of the Parliament?

- The Leader in Lok Sabha is named 'Leader of the House' and leader in Rajya Sabha is named 'Leader of the Council'. The Speaker/Chairman makes the following important decisions in consultation with the Leader of the House/Council:
  (a) Allotment of time for discussion of matters referred to in the President's address.
  (b) Arrangement of government business when Parliament is in session.
  (c) Allotting day other than Friday for transaction of private members' business.
  (d) Allotment of days for 'No-Day-Yet-Named Motions.'
  (e) Allotment of days for discussion and voting of 'Demands for grants.'
  (f) Fixing a day for secret sitting (only in Lok Sabha).

10.5.3.2 Leader of Opposition

- The leader of opposition was officially recognised for the first time in 1969 in the Lok Sabha. Subsequently 'The Salary and Allowances of Leaders of Opposition in Parliament Act, 1977' was enacted that provided a statutory status to the Leader of Opposition.
- As per this Act, 'Leader of the Opposition', in relation to either House of Parliament, means a member who is the Leader in that House of the party in opposition to the Government having the greatest numerical strength and recognised as such by the Chairman of the Council of States or the Speaker of the House of the People, as the case may be.
- Additionally, as per the existing practice, a leader of a party is recognised as 'Leader of Opposition' only if that party has at least one-tenth of the total membership of the House. This is based on a direction issued in 1950s by the Speaker for recognising a party for the purpose of allotment of seats in the Lok Sabha, time for participating in debates etc.
- The Leader of Opposition in both the Houses enjoys all the status of a cabinet rank minister.
- The Leader of Opposition in the Lok Sabha is also a member of committees that select the Chief Election Commissioner & Election Commissioners, Director of the Central Bureau of Investigation, Chief Vigilance Commissioner, members and chairperson of Central Information Commission, Lokpal etc. The Leader of Opposition in both the Houses are members of committee that selects the members and chairperson of the National Human Rights Commission.

- In Britain, the leader of opposition is known as 'Shadow Prime Minister'. He/she also appoints senior members of the opposition party to a 'shadow cabinet' that shadows the council of ministers in Government. This 'shadow cabinet' does not enjoy any executive power but scrutinises the policy of the Government and offers alternative policies. There is no such practice formally in India.

10.5.3.3 Whip

- The term 'whip' is derived from the British Parliamentary convention under which they are directed to follow the party line.
- A whip is a direction from a political party that binds the members of that party in a House to follow the instructions of the party. There are three kinds of whips that may be issued as per convention:
  - **One line whip:** It is issued to inform the members about a vote without any specific instruction to vote in a particular manner.
  - **Two-line whip:** It is issued to direct the members to be present in the House at the time of voting but no instructions are given on the voting pattern.
  - **Three-line whip:** It is issued to members directing them to vote as per the party line.
- Every party in the Lok Sabha and the Rajya Sabha appoints one of its members as 'Chief Whip' who gives the above instructions during a vote. The functions of the 'Chief Whip' also includes (a) ensuring discipline amongst party members, (b) ensuring attendance and voting as per whip issued, (c) inform the party members about the opinion of the party on various issues, (d) to supply the list of speakers on Bills and other businesses in the House to the Speaker or Chairman etc.
- If a member does not follow the instruction of the whip to vote in a particular manner, he/she is liable for disqualification under the Tenth Schedule.
- The Parliament has also enacted 'The Leaders and Chief Whips of Recognised Parties and Groups in Parliament (Facilities) Act, 1998' that provides certain telephone and secretarial facilities to Chief whips of every recognised party and recognised group in each House of the Parliament.

10.6 LEGISLATIVE PROCEDURE

The primary function of the Parliament is to make laws applicable for the entire country. Constitution in this regard provides for detailed procedure for the enactment of bills. The legislative procedure is identical in both the Houses except for Money Bills. The various bills that are enacted by the Parliament include:

(a) Ordinary bills – Bills other than those that deal with financial matters.

(b) Money Bills – Bills that contain only provisions relating to taxation, borrowing, appropriation etc., as defined under Article 110(1).

(c) Financial bills – Bills of financial nature other than Money Bills.

(d) Constitutional amendment bills – Bill to amend the Constitution.

The legislative procedure under Articles 107 to 117 deal with the first three categories of bills (a) to (c). The procedure for constitutional amendment is provided in Article 368.

10.6.1 Procedure for Introduction and Passing of Bills

Article 107 of the Constitution provides the procedure for introduction and passing of bills. These provisions are summarised in the next page:

(a) Subject to the provisions of Articles 109 and 117 with respect to Money Bills and other financial bills, a bill may be introduced in either House of Parliament.

(b) Subject to the provisions of Articles 108 (Joint sitting) and 109 (Money Bill), that have a different procedure, a bill is deemed to have been passed by the Houses of Parliament if it has been agreed to by both Houses, either without amendment or with such amendments only as are agreed to by both Houses.

A bill is said to lapse when it expires and cannot be proceeded with in the House of Parliament. Article 107 specifies the conditions with respect to lapse of bills:

(a) A bill does not lapse by reason of prorogation of the Houses of Parliament. This is specifically provided for in our Constitution since as per the British Parliamentary convention, all bills lapse (except certain public bills that can be carried over to next session based on approval by the House of Commons) on prorogation of the Parliament. However, in India prorogation does not result in lapse of bills.

(b) A bill pending in the Council of States which has not been passed by the House of the People shall not lapse on a dissolution of the House of the People. It means that a bill that has been introduced in the Rajya Sabha and pending in that House does not lapse on dissolution of the Lok Sabha.

(c) A bill which is pending in the House of the People, or which having been passed by the House of the People is pending in the Council of States, shall, subject to the provisions of Article 108 (with respect to joint sitting), lapse on a dissolution of the House of the People. It means that bills (a) introduced in the Lok Sabha and pending in that House, (b) that have been passed in the Lok Sabha and pending in the Rajya Sabha and (c) that have been passed in the Rajya Sabha and pending in the Lok Sabha, lapse on dissolution of the Lok Sabha.

(d) A bill passed by both the Houses and pending with the President for his/her assent does not lapse on dissolution of the Lok Sabha.

Bills don't lapse

- When houses are prorogued
- Bill introduced and pending in Rajya Sabha does not lapse when Lok Sabha is dissolved
- Bill passed by both houses and pending with President for assent does not lapse when Lok Sabha is dissolved

Bills lapse

- Bill pending in Lok Sabha on dissolution of Lok Sabha
- Bill passed in Lok Sabha and pending in Rajya Sabha on dissolution of Lok Sabha

MNEMONICS

Concept or Provisions	Shortcut or Mnemonics	Details to Remember
Lapse of Bills	**PORB**andar **does not lapse** All other lapse on dissolution of LS	• **P**rorogation – Does Not lapse • **O**riginated and pending in **R**ajya Sabha – Does Not lapse • **B**oth houses passed and pending with President – Does Not lapse • Pending in Lok Sabha or pending in Rajya Sabha after passed by Lok Sabha lapses on dissolution of Lok Sabha

10.6.2 Ordinary Bills

A bill is the draft of a legislative proposal. A bill is deemed to be passed by both the Houses if it has been agreed to by both Houses, either without amendment or with such amendments only as are agreed to by both Houses. It has to pass through various stages before it becomes an Act of Parliament.

This procedure is provided in the Rules of Lok Sabha and Rajya Sabha, the key points of which is summarised below.

(A) First Reading

- The legislative process starts with the introduction of a bill in either House of Parliament i.e., the Lok Sabha or the Rajya Sabha.
- A bill can be introduced either by a Minister or by a private member. In the former case it is known as a Government Bill and in the latter case it is known as a Private Member's Bill. The introduction of Private Member's Bill requires one month's notice. There is no notice period requirement provided in the rules for a Government Bill.
- It is necessary for a member-in-charge of the bill to ask for leave (permission) to introduce the bill. If leave is granted by the House, the bill is introduced. After a bill has been introduced, it is published in the Official Gazette. Even before introduction, a bill might, with the permission of the Speaker/Chairman, be published in the Gazette. In such cases, leave to introduce the bill in the House is not asked for and the bill is straightaway introduced.
- If the motion for leave (permission) to introduce a bill is opposed, the Speaker/Chairman may allow brief explanatory statement to be made by the member who opposes the motion and the member-in-charge who moved the motion. Where a motion for leave to introduce a bill is opposed on the ground that the bill initiates legislation outside the legislative competence of the House, the Speaker/Chairman may permit a full discussion thereon. Thereafter, the question is put to the vote of the House. If the House grants permission, the bill is introduced.

Reference of Bill to Standing Committee

- After a bill has been introduced, the Presiding Officer of the concerned House can refer the bill to the concerned Standing Committee for examination and to make a report thereon.
- If a bill is referred to Standing Committee, the Committee shall consider the general principles and clauses of the bill referred to them and make a report thereon. The Committee can also take expert opinion or public opinion who are interested in the measure.
- After the bill has thus been considered, the Committee submits its report to the House. The report of the Committee, being of persuasive value shall be treated as considered advice given by the Committee.

(B) Second Reading

The second reading consists of consideration of the bill which is in two stages.

First Stage

- The first stage consists of a general discussion on the bill as a whole when the principle underlying the bill is discussed.
- At this stage it is open to the House to refer the bill to a Select Committee of the House or a Joint Committee of the two

> **THINK ABOUT IT**
>
> Though the rules of legislative procedure provide for detailed scrutiny of bills before passage, the spirit of such procedure is not often followed. Comment on the issues surrounding passage of bills in Indian Parliament.

Houses or to circulate it for the purpose of eliciting opinion thereon or to straightaway take it into consideration.

- If a bill is referred to a Select/Joint Committee, the Committee considers the bill clause-by-clause just as the House does. Amendments can be moved to various clauses by members of the Committee.

Second Stage

- The second stage of the second reading consists of clause-by-clause consideration of the bill as introduced or as reported by Select/Joint Committee.
- Discussion takes place on each clause of the bill and amendments to clauses can be moved at this stage. Amendments to a clause that have been moved but not withdrawn are put to the vote of the House before the relevant clause is disposed of by the House. The amendments become part of the bill if they are accepted by a majority of members present and voting.

(c) Third Reading

- Thereafter, the member-in-charge can move that the Bill be passed. This stage is known as the third reading of the bill.
- At this stage the debate is confined to arguments either in support or rejection of the bill without referring to the details thereof further than that are absolutely necessary. In passing an ordinary bill, a simple majority of members present and voting is necessary.

Bill in the other House

- After the bill is passed by one House, it is sent to the other House for concurrence with a message to that effect, and there also it goes through the stages described above except the introduction stage.
- If both the Houses agree, then the bill is sent to the President for assent. If there is disagreement on the amendments between the two Houses, it may lead to a joint sitting. If it is passed in joint sitting, then it is sent to the President for his/her assent. Thus, no bill can become an Act without the assent of the President who is an integral part of the Parliament.

Various Stages in Passage of a Bill

First Reading
- Introduced with the permission of the house
- Speaker or Chairman may refer the Bill to Standing Committee
- Standing Committee gives report after consulting public or experts

Second Reading
- Discussion after which house may refer bill to Select/Joint Committee
- Committee will consider clause by clause and suggest amendments
- House will consider clause by clause and pass amendments

Third Reading
- Member-in-charge to move that the Bill be passed
- Debate confined to overall arguments in support or rejection of the bill
- Once passed by one house, bill goes through the stages in other house except introduction stage

Scan the QR code for conceptual video on Legislative procedure for Ordinary Bills and Joint Sitting

McGraw Hill edge

10.6.3 Joint Sitting of the Two Houses

Joint Sitting [Art 108]		
Circumstances when it can be held	**Circumstances when it cannot be held**	**Procedure**
• If a bill has been rejected by the other House. • Disagreement between the Houses as to the amendments to be made. • If more than 6 months have elapsed in the other House.	• If the bill is a Money Bill [Art 109]. • If the bill is a Constitutional amendment bill [Art 368]. • If the bill has already lapsed due to dissolution of the Lok Sabha.	• President summons joint sitting. • Presided over by the Speaker. • Requires simple majority of total members of both the houses present and voting to pass the bill.

10.6.3.1 Circumstances for a Joint Sitting

- Article 108 provides for a joint sitting. It is an extraordinary device to resolve a deadlock between the two Houses of Parliament over the passage of a bill.
- The President may summon a joint sitting of both Houses of the Parliament in the following circumstances, after a bill has been passed by one House and transmitted to the other House:
  - (a) If the bill is rejected by the other House;
  - (b) If the Houses have finally disagreed as to the amendments to be made in the bill;
  - (c) If more than 6 months elapse from the date of the reception of the bill by the other House without the bill being passed by it. While calculating the period of 6 months, no account shall be taken of any period during which the House is prorogued or adjourned for more than four consecutive days. Hence, the 6 months is calculated when the House is in session.
- The President may under the above circumstances, unless the bill has lapsed by reason of a dissolution of the House of the People, notify to the Houses by message if they are sitting or by public notification if they are not sitting, his/her intention to summon them to meet in a joint sitting for the purpose of deliberating and voting on the bill. Where the President has notified his/her intention of summoning the Houses to meet in a joint sitting, neither House shall proceed further with the bill.
- In reality, a Joint Sitting is usually called only for a government bill that has been passed by the Lok Sabha but rejected, disagreed or delayed in the Rajya Sabha.

10.6.3.2 Procedure and Other Provisions with Respect to a Joint Sitting

- If at the joint sitting of the two Houses the bill, with such amendments, if any, as are agreed to in joint sitting, is passed by a majority of the total number of members of both Houses present and voting, it shall be deemed for the purposes of this Constitution to have been passed by both Houses. Hence, the majority required is a simple majority of the total number of members (of both the Houses) present and voting in a joint sitting.
- The amendments allowed in a joint sitting are only of two types –
  - (a) If a bill passed in one House is not passed in the other House, then only such amendments that are necessary due to the delay in passage of the bill;

(b) If a bill has been passed by the other House, then only such amendments as are relevant to the matters with respect to which the Houses have not agreed.

- The Constitution provides that the President, after consultation with the Chairman of the Rajya Sabha and the Speaker of Lok Sabha, may make rules as to the procedure with respect to joint sittings [Art 118]. Accordingly, Appendix 1 of the Lok Sabha rules contains 'The Houses of Parliament (Joint Sittings and Communications) Rules'.

  (a) The Speaker of the Lok Sabha presides over a joint sitting. During the absence of the Speaker from any joint sitting, the Deputy Speaker of the Lok Sabha or, if he/she is also absent, the Deputy Chairman of the Rajya Sabha or, if he/she is also absent such other person as may be determined by the members present at the sitting, shall preside. The Chairman of the Rajya Sabha will not preside over such joint sitting under any circumstance since he/she is not a member of the Parliament.

  (b) The quorum required to constitute the joint sitting is one tenth of the total number of members of the two Houses.

- The provision of joint sitting is available only to ordinary and financial bills. It is not applicable for Money Bills that are governed by a separate procedure under Article 109. Similarly, constitutional amendment bills are governed by the procedure under Article 368 and hence a joint sitting is not applicable to such bills.

- A joint sitting may be held under this article and a bill passed thereat, notwithstanding that a dissolution of the House of the People has intervened since the President notified his/her intention to summon the Houses to meet therein. As discussed earlier, a joint sitting cannot be called if a bill has already lapsed due to dissolution of the Lok Sabha. However, after a joint sitting has been notified, if the Lok Sabha is dissolved due to any reason, the joint sitting may still be held with the members of the newly elected Lok Sabha and Rajya Sabha. But such a situation has never arisen since 1950.

10.6.3.3 Previous Instances of Joint Sitting

The requirement for a Joint Sitting will, in normal course, arise only in respect of a government bill that has been passed in the Lok Sabha, but rejected or delayed in the Rajya Sabha. The Constitution has provided for a mechanism to break the deadlock that favours the Lok Sabha (since total number of members in the Lok Sabha is 543 as against 245 in the Rajya Sabha). However, this provision has been used only on three occasions in the past.

The bills that have been passed in a joint sitting till now are:

1. Dowry Prohibition Bill, 1960
2. Banking Service Commission (Repeal) Bill, 1977
3. Prevention of Terrorism Bill, 2002

This demonstrates that though the mechanism of joint sitting can be used by a ruling government that enjoys a significant majority in the Lok Sabha, the endeavour is always to build a consensus amongst the two Houses.

MNEMONICS

Concept or Provisions	Shortcut or Mnemonics	Details to Remember
Joint Sitting	**When it can be called for** • Start **R**ecurring **D**eposit after **6 months (RD after 6 months)**	**When it can be called** • **R**ejected by other house • **D**isagreement between the two houses on the amendments • **6 months** have elapsed in other house without passing.
	When it cannot be called • If no **Money** or **lapsed**	**When it cannot be called** • If it is a **Money Bill**. • If a bill has already **lapsed due to dissolution of Lok Sabha**.

10.6.4 Money Bills

10.6.4.1 Special Procedure with Respect to Money Bills

Article 109 provides the special procedure with respect to Money Bills that is summarised below:

- A Money Bill shall not be introduced in the Council of States. It means that a Money Bill can be introduced only in the Lok Sabha.
- A Money Bill can be introduced only with the recommendation of the President [Art 117].
- After a Money Bill has been passed by the House of the People,
  - It shall be transmitted to the Council of States for its recommendations; and
  - The Council of States shall within a period of 14 days from the date of its receipt of the bill, return the bill to the House of the People with its recommendations; and
  - The House of the People may thereupon either accept or reject all or any of the recommendations of the Council of States.
- If the House of the People,
  - Accepts any of the recommendations of the Council of States, the Money Bill shall be deemed to have been passed by both Houses with the amendments recommended by the Council of States and accepted by the House of the People;
  - Does not accept any of the recommendations of the Council of States, the Money Bill shall be deemed to have been passed by both Houses in the form in which it was passed by the House of the People without any of the amendments recommended by the Council of States.
- If a Money Bill is not returned to the House of the People within the said period of 14 days, it shall be deemed to have been passed by both Houses at the expiration of the said period in the form in which it was passed by the House of the People.
- Hence, a Money Bill may be returned by Rajya Sabha to Lok Sabha without recommendations (approved/accepted) or with recommendations (suggesting changes) but cannot be amended or rejected by Rajya Sabha.

10.6.4.2 Why Special Privilege for Money Bills?

As can be seen from the above discussion, a Money Bill is under the total control of the Lok Sabha. The Rajya Sabha has only a recommendatory role in such bills and it can be overruled by the Lok Sabha. This is because the provisions of a Money Bill deal **only** with financial matters that are crucial for administration of the country. Since the elected government that enjoys majority in the Lok Sabha is responsible for administration of the country, the Constitution provides for this special procedure for Money Bills that effectively requires only the approval of Lok Sabha. It has its origin in the U.K., where, in 1911, the powers of the unelected House of Lords over the Budget were curtailed and the Budget was required to be passed only by the House of Commons that reflected the will of the people. However, it must be noted that the operative word in the below definition is the word **'only'**. Hence, bills that deal only with financial matters as per the definition are deemed to be Money Bills.

THINK ABOUT IT

Define Money Bill. What is the special procedure for its passage? What are the recent controversies surrounding the passage of money bills?

Article 110 provides the definition of a Money Bill. A bill shall be deemed to be a Money Bill if it contains *only* provisions dealing with all or any of the following matters, namely:

(a) The imposition, abolition, remission, alteration or regulation of any tax;

(b) The regulation of the borrowing of money or the giving of any guarantee by the Government of India, or the amendment of the law with respect to any financial obligations undertaken or to be undertaken by the Government of India;

(c) The custody of the Consolidated Fund or the Contingency Fund of India, the payment of moneys into or the withdrawal of moneys from any such fund;

(d) The appropriation of moneys out of the Consolidated Fund of India;

(e) The declaring of any expenditure to be expenditure charged on the Consolidated Fund of India or the increasing of the amount of any such expenditure;

(f) The receipt of money on account of the Consolidated Fund of India or the public account of India, the custody or issue of such money or the audit of the accounts of the Union or of a State; or

(g) Any matter incidental to any of the matters specified in sub-clauses (a) to (f)

However, a bill shall not be deemed to be a Money Bill only because it provides for:

- The imposition of fines or other pecuniary (monetary) penalties, or for the demand or payment of fees for licences or fees for services rendered, or
- The imposition, abolition, remission, alteration or regulation of any tax by any local authority or body for local purposes.

Hence, a bill that deals *only* with matters of finance or audit is considered as a Money Bill. In this regard, a brief explanation about the various accounts maintained by the Government, which forms part of definition of a Money Bill, is provided below:

Name of the Account	Definition and Nature of the Account	Approval of Expenditure/ Payments
Consolidated Fund of India	• All revenues received by the Government of India, all loans raised by the Government through various means, and all moneys received by the Government in repayment of loans shall form one consolidated fund to be called 'Consolidated Fund of India' [Art 266].	All the expenditure of the Government of India is made out of this fund after approval by the Parliament.

Name of the Account	Definition and Nature of the Account	Approval of Expenditure/ Payments
	• Hence all taxation revenues of the Government like Income Tax, GST etc.; non-tax revenues like fees, royalty etc.; all loans raised both internally within India and internationally; and moneys received due to repayment of loans to the Government of India are all credited to the Consolidated Fund of India. • This account is maintained with the Reserve Bank of India.	
Public Account of India	• All other moneys (other than those covered above under the Consolidated Fund) received by or on behalf of the Government of India shall be credited to the Public Account of India [Art 266]. • This consists of various amounts like Provident fund, postal savings, national small savings fund etc. These amounts are received by the Government and are to be repaid on maturity.	This account is operated by the executive and it does not require any parliamentary approval.
Contingency Fund of India	• Parliament may by law establish the 'Contingency Fund of India' into which shall be paid such sums as may be determined by Parliamentary law and the said fund shall be placed at the disposal of the President to enable to meet unforeseen expenditure pending authorisation of the Parliament [Art 267]. • Hence, the inflow into this account is through appropriation from the Consolidated Fund of India and the expenditure from this account is made by the Central Government to meet all unforeseen expenditures like natural calamities etc.	Amount is spent by the executive but is authorised by the Parliament after the expenditure is incurred.

10.6.4.3 Expenditure Charged on Consolidated Fund of India

Article 110(1)(e) stipulates that a bill that deals *only* with declaring of any expenditure to be expenditure charged on the Consolidated Fund of India or increasing such expenditure shall be a Money Bill.

Article 112(3) provides that the following expenditure shall be charged on the Consolidated Fund of India:

(a) The emoluments and allowances of the President and other expenditure relating to his/her office;

(b) The salaries and allowances of the Chairman and the Deputy Chairman of the Council of States and the Speaker and the Deputy Speaker of the House of the People;

(c) Debt charges for which the Government of India is liable including interest, sinking fund charges and redemption charges, and other expenditure relating to the raising of loans and the service and redemption of debt;

(d) The salaries, allowances and pensions payable to or in respect of Judges of the Supreme Court and the pensions payable to or in respect of Judges of any High Court;

(e) The salary, allowances and pension payable to or in respect of the Comptroller and Auditor-General of India;

(f) Any sums required to satisfy any judgment, decree or award of any court or arbitral tribunal;
(g) Any other expenditure declared by the Constitution or by the Parliament by law to be so charged.

Various other expenditure like the salaries, allowances and pension of the UPSC members; the administrative expenditure including salaries, allowances and pensions of the staff of the Supreme Court, CAG and UPSC are all charged on the Consolidated Fund of India as per various other articles of the Constitution.

The significance of expenditure 'charged' is that they are non-votable in the Parliament. They can be only discussed in the Houses of Parliament but even the Lok Sabha does not vote on these expenditures, while approving the demand for grants and the appropriation bill, and it is automatically 'charged' on the Consolidated Fund and has to be incurred.

10.6.4.4 Budget as Money Bill

The Constitution specifies that the President shall in respect of every financial year cause to be laid before both the Houses of Parliament, a statement of estimated receipts and expenditure of the Government of India that is referred to as 'annual financial statement'.

This is the Budget that is presented every year in the Parliament and is a classic example of a Money Bill. Till 2017, the Government had two separate budgets – one for the Railways and the other being a general budget. The practice of having a separate budget for the Railways considering its large size and providing for an annual contribution towards the Government exchequer was introduced in 1924. However, in 2017, the Government of India merged the Railway budget with the overall Budget.

The provisions with respect to presentation and approval of the budget are provided in Articles 112 to 116 of the Constitution. The key points with respect to these provisions along with the overall procedure for presentation and approval of budget is summarised below.

- Starting from 2017, the Budget is being presented on 1 February of every year. Earlier, it used to be presented on 28 February but since the approval of the budget by the Lok Sabha takes about 45 to 60 days, it was advanced to 1 February to enable the approvals in place before the commencement of the ensuing financial year.

- The budget documents consist of the following:
  - Annual Financial Statement
  - Demand for Grants
  - Appropriation and Finance Bill
  - Statements mandated by Fiscal Responsibility and Budget Management (FRBM) Act like macro-economic framework statement, fiscal policy strategy statement and medium-term fiscal policy statement
  - Economic survey prepared by the Finance Ministry and presented a few days before the Budget that indicates the assessment of the economy

- Annual Financial Statement
  - It shall have an analysis of the actual receipts and expenditure of the closing year and an explanation of the expenditure in the coming year along with prospects of revenue.
  - The estimates of expenditure shall show separately (a) the sums required to meet the expenditure 'charged' upon the Consolidated Fund of India and (b) the sums required to meet the expenditure proposed to be 'made' from the Consolidated Fund of India [Art

112]. Apart from the expenditure charged on the Consolidated Fund of India, all other expenditures are 'made' from the Consolidated Fund after approval by the Parliament.

- Demand for Grants
  - So much of the estimates as relates to expenditure 'charged' upon the Consolidated Fund of India shall not be submitted to vote of the Parliament but they can be discussed by either of the Houses [Art 113].
  - So much of the estimates as related to expenditure to be 'made' from the Consolidated Fund of India are submitted in the form of 'demand for grants' to the Lok Sabha and the Lok Sabha can approve, refuse or reduce such amounts [Art 113].
  - The demand for a grant shall be made only with the recommendation of the President [Art 113].
- Discussion and scrutiny by committees
  - Once the budget is presented and after its general discussion, the budget estimates with respect to various departments are referred to the department-related Standing Committees of the Parliament.
  - These committees review the estimates with respect to their respective ministries/departments and submit their report to the Lok Sabha within the stipulated time.
  - Apart from this, the Estimates Committee of Lok Sabha examines the estimates throughout the year in order to report to the House the economies and improvements, consistent with the policy underlying the estimates, that may be effected.
- Voting on demand for grants
  - Based on the report of the departmental standing committees, the demands are taken up for voting in the Lok Sabha. A demand once voted becomes a grant.
  - The voting on demand for grants is the exclusive business of the Lok Sabha and the Rajya Sabha has no role to play in it. Further, the voting is only on the demand for grants for the expenditure to be 'made' from the Consolidated Fund of India. There shall be no voting on expenditure 'charged' on the Consolidated Fund of India.
  - While voting, the members can move motions to reduce any amount of demand for grant. The motions to reduce the demand for grants are called 'cut motions' and they are of three types:
    1. Disapproval of Policy Cut – It states 'that the amount of the demand be reduced to Re. 1' which implies that the mover of the motion disapproves of the policy underlying the demand. It is open to the member to suggest an alternative policy.
    2. Economy Cut – Where the objective of the motion is to reduce the amount of expenditure, the form of the motion would be 'that the amount of the demand be reduced by a specified amount'.
    3. Token Cut – Where the objective of the motion is to express a specific grievance within the sphere of responsibility of the Government of India, the form of the motion would be 'that the amount of the demand be reduced by ₹100'.
  - The cut motions cannot be in respect of expenditure 'charged' on the Consolidated Fund as they are not subject to vote.
  - The demands are voted individually by the Lok Sabha. On the last day, all the remaining demands are put to vote by the Speaker whether they have been discussed by the members or not. This process is known as 'guillotine'.
  - Apart from demand for grants, the following types of grants are also presented in the Lok Sabha for their approval:
    1. Supplementary Grants – If the amount authorised to be spent for a particular service for the current financial year is found to be insufficient for the purpose of that year or when a need has arisen during the current financial year for supplementary or

additional expenditure upon some 'new service', the President causes to be laid before both the Houses of Parliament another statement showing the estimated amount of that expenditure. This additional demand is known as 'supplementary grant' or 'additional grant' [Art 115].

2. Excess Grants – If any money has been spent on any service during a financial year in excess of the amount granted for the service for that year, the President causes to be presented to Lok Sabha a demand for such excess [Art 115]. All cases involving such excesses are brought to the notice of the Parliament by the Comptroller and Auditor General through a report on the Appropriation Accounts. The excesses are then examined by the Public Accounts Committee which makes recommendations regarding their regularisation in its report to the House.
3. The supplementary and additional grants are presented to and passed by the House before the expenditure is incurred i.e., before the end of that financial year. The demands for excess grants on the other hand are made and approved after the expenditure has actually been incurred and after the financial year to which it relates has expired.

❑ Appropriation Bill and Finance Bill

- Once the demand for grants is voted by the Lok Sabha as per the process explained above, an Appropriation Bill is presented to provide for the appropriation out of the Consolidated Fund of India. This bill contains the grants voted by the Lok Sabha and the expenditure 'charged' on the Consolidated Fund of India as per the Budget statement. The moneys shall be withdrawn from the Consolidated Fund of India only after the passage of the Appropriation Act [Art 114].
- Neither the grants already voted by the Lok Sabha nor the expenditure charged on the Consolidated Fund can be amended when the Appropriation Bill is passed by the Lok Sabha [Art 114].
- In order to give effect to the taxation proposals, a Finance Bill is introduced in the Lok Sabha. Article 265 states that no tax shall be levied or collected except by authority of law and this bill is to obtain the approval of the Parliament for tax proposals that constitute the revenues under the Budget. The Parliament can pass an amendment for reduction or abolition of tax but not for an increase of any tax. This is because, any increase in tax can be proposed only by the executive.
- Both the Appropriation Bill and Finance Bill are Money Bills and follow the procedure for a Money Bill.

10.6.4.5 Certain other Points relating to Money Bills

❑ The Speaker of the Lok Sabha certifies a bill to be a Money Bill.

❑ There shall be endorsed on every Money Bill when it is transmitted to the Council of States under Article 109, and when it is presented to the President for assent under Article 111, the certificate of the Speaker of the House of the People signed by him/her that it is a Money Bill [Art 110].

❑ This certification of the Speaker, of a bill to be a Money Bill, shall be final as far as the Houses of Parliament are concerned. However, in the **Aadhaar case** (K.S. Puttaswamy Vs Union of India) in 2018, the Supreme Court has ruled that such a certification by the Speaker is subject to judicial review.

❑ As per provisions of Article 111, the President cannot return a Money Bill for reconsideration i.e., he/she cannot exercise suspensive veto on a Money Bill. This is due to the fact that such a bill would have been introduced only after his/her recommendation and the Lok Sabha, where the Council of Ministers enjoy a majority, is the House that has the final authority with respect to a Money Bill. The President may exercise Absolute or Pocket veto on a Money Bill only under rare circumstances (as discussed in Section 8.4.5.1).

- As per parliamentary convention, a defeat of Money Bill in the Lok Sabha leads to the resignation of the Council of Ministers.
- There is no express provision in the Constitution or the Lok Sabha rules that a Money Bill can be introduced only by a Minister. Rule 65 of the Lok Sabha rules provides that if a Private member seeks to introduce a bill that requires previous recommendation of the President for its introduction, like a Money Bill, then he/she must annex such recommendation conveyed through a Minister. However, since the President acts only as per the advice of the Council of Ministers, it is unlikely that a Money Bill can be introduced by a private member unless it has support of the ruling government.
- There have been controversies surrounding the passage of various amendments under the Money Bill route as part of the Budget. For example, in 2017, amendments to various Acts for reorganisation of tribunals like National Green Tribunal, Income Tax Appellate Tribunal were passed as part of the Money Bill during Budget. This was struck down by the Supreme Court in ***Rojer Mathew Vs South India Bank (2019)***. The Supreme Court is set to constitute a seven-judge bench for interpreting the provisions of Money Bill and the significance of word 'only' in the definition of Money Bill.

Scan the QR code for conceptual video on Money Bill and Financial Bills

McGraw Hill edge

MNEMONICS

Concept or Provisions	Shortcut or Mnemonics	Details to Remember
Money Bill procedure	• **Lok**esh sends **Money** to **Raja**, who should return it within **2 weeks (14 days)** and that may or may not be accepted by **Lok**esh.	• Can be introduced only in **Lok Sabha**. After passage of Money bill, it is sent to **Rajya Sabha** which cannot amend or reject it but only give its recommendations within **14 days**. • **Lok Sabha** may or may not accept all or any of the recommendations of Rajya Sabha. • **Money bill** is introduced only in Lok Sabha with recommendation of **President**.
Definition of Money Bill under Article 110(1)(a) to (f)	• **a** – alteration, abolition • **b** – borrowing • **c** – custody of funds • **d** – deals with appropriation • **e** – expenditure charged • **f** – finance related – receipt or issue of money & audit	(a) imposition, **a**bolition, alteration, remission or regulation of any tax; (b) regulation of **b**orrowing or guarantee relating to it; (c) **c**ustody of consolidated fund or contingency fund and payment of money or withdrawal of money from such fund; (d) appropriation out of consolidated fund; (e) declaring any **e**xpenditure to be charged on consolidated fund or increasing such expenditure; (f) receipt of money on account of consolidated fund or public account, audit of accounts of Union or a State.

MNEMONICS

Concept or Provisions	Shortcut or Mnemonics	Details to Remember
Definition of expenditure charged on consolidated fund of India [Art 112(3)]	3B & 3D 1C	Top offices of **3 B**ranches of governance; 1) Executive – President's emoluments & allowances; 2) Legislature – Speaker/Dy Speaker of LS & Chairman/Dy Chairman of RS – salaries & allowances; 3) Judiciary – Salaries & pension of judges of Supreme Court; pension of judges of High Court. **3D** 1) **D**ebt charges including sinking fund & redemption charges 2) **D**ecree, judgement or award by a court – amount required to satisfy the same 3) **D**eclared as expenditure charged by the Constitution or any law of Parliament. **1C** – CAG salaries and pension

10.6.5 Financial Bills

- Apart from Money Bills as defined under Article 110(1) that have a special procedure for its passage under Article 109, the Constitution under Article 117 provides for 'Financial Bills' that also deal with financial matters. Financial Bills are of two categories – Category A and Category B. They are also referred to as Category I and Category II bills.
- Financial Bill of Category A (or Category I)
  - It contains provisions dealing with any of the matters specified in sub-clauses (a) to (f) of clause (1) of Article 110 and other matters of general legislation [Art 117]. It should be noted that a Bill that deals '*only*' with matters specified in 110(1)(a) to (f) is a Money Bill while a Bill that deals with any of those matters along with other general matters is a Financial Bill of Category A. For example, a Bill that is passed for the acquisition of land for government projects may also contain provisions dealing with borrowings by the Government of India to meet the cost of such land acquisitions. This would fall under Financial Bill of Category A as it contains provisions dealing with borrowings [110(1)(b)] along with procedure for land acquisition.
  - Similar to the procedure with respect to introduction for a Money Bill, Financial Bill of Category A can be introduced only in the Lok Sabha and only on the recommendation of the President [Art 117].
  - However, once it has been passed by the Lok Sabha, it is like any other ordinary Bill and there is no restriction on the powers of the Rajya Sabha on such bills. If there is any disagreement between the two Houses, it can be resolved only through a joint sitting.
- Financial Bill of Category B (or Category II)
  - Those bills that involves expenditure from the Consolidated Fund of India but do not include any of the matters specified in sub-clauses (a) to (f) of clause (1) of Article 110 are classified as Financial Bill of Category B [Art 117].

- For example, the President's Emoluments and Pension Act provides for various facilities like free travel, free telephone facility etc., to retired Presidents and spouses of deceased Presidents. The provision of these facilities does not deal with any of the matters specified in Article 110(1)(a) to (f) but involve expenditure from the Consolidated Fund of India and this aspect of such a Bill would fall under Financial Bill of Category B.
- Financial Bill of Category B is like any other ordinary bill and can be introduced either in the Lok Sabha or the Rajya Sabha. President's recommendation at the time of introduction of Bill is not required. Only condition for these bills is that the President's recommendation is required before the Bill is being considered by the House where it is introduced. This Bill is passed following the procedure for any other ordinary Bill and if there is any disagreement between the two Houses, it can be resolved only through a joint sitting.

10.6.6 Comparison between Various Types of Bills

Now that we have discussed in detail the provisions and procedure for various types of Bills, the below table summarises the key points with respect to different categories of Bills.

Provisions	Ordinary Bill	Money Bill	Financial Bill Category A or I	Financial Bill Category B or II
Introduction	Either in the Lok Sabha or the Rajya Sabha	Only in the Lok Sabha	Only in the Lok Sabha	Either in the Lok Sabha or the Rajya Sabha
Recommendation	Not required	President's recommendation for introduction	President's recommendation for introduction	President's recommendation for consideration
Certification	Not applicable	Certified as Money Bill by the Speaker	Not applicable	Not applicable
Rajya Sabha role	Can amend or reject	Only 14 days to suggest recommendations	Can amend or reject	Can amend or reject
Joint sitting	In case of deadlock between two Houses	Not applicable	In case of deadlock between two Houses	In case of deadlock between two Houses
Suspensive veto by the President	Can be exercised	Cannot be exercised	Can be exercised	Can be exercised

10.6.7 Overall Issues

As we had discussed in the previous sections, the most important role of the Parliament is to legislate various laws for administration of the country. The Parliamentary committees like department-related Standing Committees and Select/Joint Committees play an important role in scrutinising various legislations during the introduction and consideration of the Bills.

However, the role of the Parliament is diminishing in the legislative process due to following reasons:

- Limited discussion
  - If the ruling party enjoys comfortable majority on its own in the Lok Sabha and also manages to garner adequate support in the Rajya Sabha, the Bills are passed without adequate

discussion. This is due to the increasing emphasis of party politics even in the Parliament and the executive capturing the imagination of people with limited role for the Parliament.
- Many significant Bills in the 16th and 17th Lok Sabha like 103rd Constitutional amendment for providing reservation to Economically Weaker Sections, Citizenship Amendment Act, Triple Talaq Act, Jammu & Kashmir Reorganisation Act etc., were passed in each of the Houses in a single day. This reduces the discussion on such significant legislations by the Parliament.

- Reduced referral to committees
  - Standing committees and select committees play an important role in scrutinising the Bills and reporting to the House(s) on key aspects and amendments required.
  - However, as against more than 60% of Bills that were referred to standing committees in the 14th and 15th Lok Sabha, less than 25% of Bills were referred in the 16th Lok Sabha and 17th Lok Sabha.
- Tenth Schedule
  - The Tenth Schedule was added in the Constitution to prevent defections from political parties. However, it also restricts the members from expressing their views against their party's instruction. This has also played a part in reducing the role of the Parliament in legislative matters.

Way Forward

- There should be adequate discussion on Bills in the Parliament before their passage. Similarly, all significant Bills should be referred to standing and/or select/joint committees during their introduction and consideration by the Houses of Parliament.
- As suggested by the Dinesh Goswami Committee and Law Commission reports, the defections under the Tenth Schedule should be made applicable only when the voting affects the stability of the Government like Budget or No-Confidence motion. This will enable the members to express themselves freely during ordinary legislation.

10.7 LEGISLATIVE CONTROL

The Parliament exercises control over the executive through various means as per the Constitution and rules of the Lok Sabha and the Rajya Sabha. The key provisions of such control are summarised here.

1. Parliamentary System

- The underlying aspect of the Parliamentary system of democracy as discussed earlier is that the legislature provides the executive and the latter is accountable to the former.
- Article 75(3) of the Constitution provides that the Council of Ministers shall be collectively responsible to the Lok Sabha. Thus, only a party or a coalition that commands majority in the Lok Sabha can be in government and this is the overall control exercised by the legislature over the executive.

2. Control through Various Legislations

- The laws made by the Parliament control the activities of the executive. For example, the Lokpal Act or Prevention of Corruption Act provides a mechanism for controlling corruption and convicting guilty public servants that include ministers.
- All schemes of the government are to be implemented by civil servants within the laws made by Parliament that acts as a control mechanism.

3. Question Hour

- The procedure relating to 'Question Hour' is provided in the rules of the Lok Sabha and the Rajya Sabha.
- The rules specify that the first hour of every sitting shall be designated for answering questions in the Lok Sabha i.e., from 11 a.m. to 12 noon. Since 2014 the question hour is from 12 noon to 1 p.m. in Rajya Sabha.
- Questions require 15 days' notice to be provided by the member asking the question. Notice of the question shall be given by the member to the Secretary-General of the House. The Secretary-General then gives the notice of question to the Minister in-charge. The Minister should get at least 5 days' notice before it is listed for answer.

- The different types of questions that can be asked to a minister are as follows:
  1. Starred question: It is one for which an oral answer is required to be given by the Minister on the floor of the House. 'Supplementary questions' may be asked by the member who raised the question based on the Minister's reply.
  2. Unstarred question: It is one for which the Minister lays on the table a written answer. No supplementary questions can be asked with regard to such questions.
  3. Short Notice question: This type of question can be asked by members on matters of public importance of an urgent nature. It is for the Speaker/Chairman to decide whether the matter is of urgent nature or not. The member has also to state reasons for asking the question while serving notice. If the Minister agrees for a reply on a specified date, it will be answered on that date.

4. Zero Hour

- This period follows the 'Question Hour' and it normally begins at noon in the Lok Sabha. Since 2014, the 'Zero Hour' is from 11 a.m. to 12 noon in the Rajya Sabha.
- This is not specified in the rules of the Lok Sabha or the Rajya Sabha and has been an Indian Parliamentary innovation since 1962.
- Usually, the members use this period to raise various issues for discussion.

5. Half-an-hour Discussion

- The Speaker/Chairman may allot half-an-hour for raising discussion on a matter of sufficient public importance which has been a subject of a recent question and the answer to which needs elucidation on a matter of fact.
- There shall be no motion or voting at the end of the discussion.

6. Calling attention Motion

- This motion is moved to call the attention of minister on a matter of urgent public importance. It is mentioned in Rules of procedure of both the Lok Sabha and the Rajya Sabha.
- There shall be no voting at the end of the discussion.

7. Adjournment Motion

- This motion can be introduced only in the Lok Sabha.
- This is moved to draw the attention of the House to a definite matter of urgent public importance.
- The Speaker will decide on the admissibility of an Adjournment motion proposed. The matter should be of urgent public importance related to a recent occurrence involving the responsibility

of the Government of India. It should be related to one matter and not involve a matter which is under adjudication in a Court of law.

- If the Speaker gives consent, the member concerned asks for the leave of the House to move the motion. If 50 members agree for the motion to be moved, then it is taken up for discussion.
- It is an extraordinary device as it interrupts the normal business of the house. The Adjournment motion is taken up by adjourning all other business and the discussion happens for a maximum period of two and a half hours.
- There shall be voting at the end of the discussion. If the motion is carried, it is an indication that the Council of Ministers do not enjoy majority in the Lok Sabha and may result in their resignation.

8. No Confidence Motion

- This motion is not mentioned in the Constitution but is mentioned in the rules of the Lok Sabha.
- There is no need to state any reason for moving this motion. This is moved against the entire Council of Ministers in the Lok Sabha.
- If 50 members demand a no-confidence motion against the Council of Ministers, it shall be admitted by the Speaker and discussion shall ensue. It concludes with the Prime Minister reply against the motion.
- The motion should be taken up for discussion within 10 days and then put to vote. If the motion is carried in the Lok Sabha, it results in the resignation of Council of Ministers.

Apart from this there can be various kinds of motions like:

- Censure motion (against a minister or group of ministers or specific policy) which may be moved by the opposition. If this motion is carried in the Lok Sabha, it is seen as a lack of confidence on an individual minister or group of ministers or a specific policy of the Government. However, the Council of Ministers technically need not resign if this motion is carried. But in reality, this motion is rarely moved and instead a no-confidence motion is moved against the entire Council of Ministers.
- 'Motion of thanks' for the President's address is moved after every general election and in the first session of each year. This is discussed in both the Houses and concludes usually with the Prime Minister's reply in both the Houses. If this motion is defeated in the Lok Sabha, it is seen as a lack of confidence on the Council of Ministers and results in their resignation.
- There can also be (a) various kinds of motions on matters of general public importance that are discussed and put to vote, (b) privilege motion for breach of parliamentary privileges by a minister or a member, (c) confidence motion that is moved by the council of ministers to prove their majority in Lok Sabha, and (d) No-Day-Yet-Named motion admitted by the Speaker or Chairman for discussion and allotted days in consultation with the Leader of the House/Council or Business advisory committee.

Summary of mechanisms for Legislative control

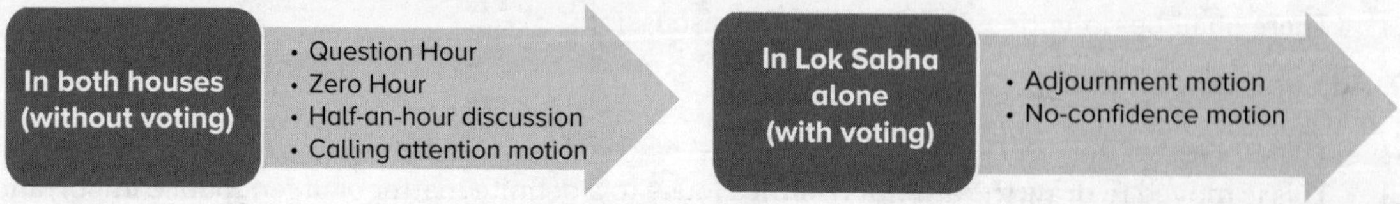

Overall issues with respect to the Parliamentary control

One of the important functions of the Parliament is to exercise control over the executive. It performs this function through various means as discussed above. However, in the recent times, the effectiveness of the Parliamentary control has reduced due to the following reasons:

1. Powerful executive – When a single party enjoys majority in the Lok Sabha, it results in lesser control of the Parliament over the executive.
2. Ordinance route – The executive resorts to promulgating ordinances that have the effect of reducing the role of the Parliament in legislation. However, with the Supreme Court judgement in *Krishna Kumar Singh* case, it is expected that the executive will not resort to repromulgation of ordinances.
3. Money Bill route – In the recent past, many legislative amendments have been clubbed along with the Money Bills presented during budget. This reduces the role of Rajya Sabha as Money Bills are under the control of the Lok Sabha where the executive always enjoys a majority.
4. Reduced role of the Parliamentary Committees – There is a considerable reduction in referring bills to the Parliamentary committees, thereby reducing the role of the Parliament in law-making process.
5. Delegated legislation – Many laws provide for rules to be made by the executive. This effectively reduces the role of the Parliament in making detailed laws and increases the power of bureaucracy.
6. Lack of effective opposition – The opposition resorts to boycott of the Houses or disrupts the proceedings for political reasons that reduces the functioning of the Parliament.

The above issues should be suitably addressed by the parties in power as well as opposition parties to maintain the importance of Parliament and its control over the executive.

10.8 PARLIAMENTARY PRIVILEGES

Parliamentary privileges are special rights, immunities and exemptions enjoyed by the two Houses of Parliament, their committees and their members. They are necessary to secure the independence and effectiveness of the Parliament. The Parliament can also extend these privileges to those who are entitled to speak and take part in the proceedings of a House like the Attorney General of India and ministers. However, the President is not entitled to these privileges though he/she is an integral part of the Parliament. However, the President enjoys certain privileges as well as immunity from criminal proceedings and arrest during his term of office, under Article 361 of the Constitution.

THINK ABOUT IT

Trace the history of Parliamentary privileges in the Indian context. Are they still required in a modern democracy?

10.8.1 History of Parliamentary Privileges

The genesis of parliamentary privileges dates back to medieval Britain i.e., between the 14th and end of 16th Century. At that time, there was always a friction between the House of Commons (elected representatives) and the King who was the real executive head. This resulted in the King arresting several members and speakers. Thus, the Parliamentary privileges evolved to protect the interest of the House of Commons and its members from the excesses of the King and the House of Lords. It must be noted that privileges were to protect the members and the House of Commons from the King and not from the people. In the recent years, the British Courts have opined that the privileges be limited to cases of clear necessity to protect the House, its members and its officers from being obstructed or interfered in the performance of their duties.

10.8.2 Parliamentary Privileges in India

Article 105 provides for privileges of the members, committees and Houses of the Parliament. It provides for the following privileges:

(a) Freedom of speech in the Parliament to members and others who have the right to speak in and take part in proceedings of the Houses or any committee of the Parliament;

(b) No member of the Parliament shall be liable to any proceedings in any court in respect of anything said or any vote given by him/her in the Parliament or any committee thereof;

(c) No person shall be liable to any proceedings in any court in respect of the publication by or under the authority of either House of Parliament of any report, paper, votes or proceedings;

(d) Apart from the above privileges, till the Parliament by law defines, the Houses of Parliament, members and committees will enjoy the privileges that were enjoyed by the House of Commons before the commencement of the Constitution.

Apart from this constitutional provision, various other sources of Parliamentary privileges include

(a) laws made by the parliament,

(b) rules of both the Houses,

(c) parliamentary conventions, and

(d) judicial interpretation.

Importance of Parliamentary privileges

- To ensure freedom of speech and expression for Members of Parliament.
- To maintain the authority and dignity of the Parliament and to protect its proceedings from external interference including courts of law.
- To exercise the constitutional functions by the parliamentarians effectively.
- To regulate the behaviour of members.

The Parliamentary privileges can be grouped under two categories – (a) Collective privileges of the Houses and (b) Individual privileges of members.

10.8.3 Collective Privileges of the Houses

These privileges are enjoyed by each House of the Parliament collectively, which includes:

- The right of the Parliament to publish its report, debates and proceedings
- The right to exclude strangers
- The right to receive information about the arrest, detention, conviction, release of the members
- It can make rules for the conduct of its business
- It can punish members and outsiders for the breach of privileges
- No legal process can be initiated on any person within the premises of the House without the permission of the presiding officer
- Courts are prohibited from inquiring into the proceedings of the House.

10.8.4 Individual Privileges of Members

These privileges are enjoyed by the members individually, which includes:

- Prohibition of arrest of members during the session and 40 days before and after the session of the Parliament. However, this is applicable only in civil cases and not in criminal or preventive detention cases.
- Freedom of speech and expression in the parliament. While freedom of speech and expression of other citizens under Article 19(1)(a) is subject to reasonable restrictions under Article 19(2), there are no such restrictions on the members for whatever is said inside Parliament. However, this freedom of speech by members is subject to rules of procedure of the Houses (Art 118) and there is also a restriction that no discussion can take place on the conduct of a Supreme Court or High Court judge except upon a motion for his/her removal (Art 121). Further, the Supreme Court in ***Sita Soren Vs Union of India (2024)*** declared that parliamentary privilege or immunity will not protect legislators who take bribes to vote or speak in Parliament or State Legislative Assemblies from criminal prosecution.
- Freedom of attendance as witness – A member cannot be summoned, without the leave of the House, to give evidence as a witness while the Parliament is in session.

The Parliament is empowered to punish the members and the outsiders for the breach of these privileges. Such punishment may be in the form of admonition, reprimand (firm warning) or even imprisonment.

10.8.5 Issues with Respect to Privileges

The history of the Parliamentary privileges dates back to medieval Britain when the House of Commons wanted to protect the interest of the House and its members from the wrongful action of the King.

In India, when the Constitution was adopted, it provided the privileges for members which includes freedom of speech and vote. The Constitution also provided that till the Parliament enacts a law to codify the privileges, the Houses and members will continue to enjoy the privileges that were enjoyed by the House of Commons before the commencement of the Constitution. In 1978, through the 44th amendment there was a cosmetic change in Article 105 to remove the reference to the House of Commons in our Constitution but the position with respect to privileges remains the same.

The Parliament has not enacted any law to codify privileges till date. This has resulted in many cases where conflict has arisen between Fundamental rights of individual citizens to express their views on the proceedings of the House and the privilege of the Houses. There have also been cases, where the Houses of Parliament or State legislature have ordered for arrest of individuals for breach of privileges.

> Scan the QR code for conceptual video on Legislative control, Parliamentary privileges and Parliamentary Committees
>
> McGraw Hill edge

The Supreme Court while delivering its opinion on a Presidential reference under Article 143 in ***Keshav Singh case*** held that wherever it appears that there is a conflict between the privileges and the provisions pertaining to fundamental rights, an attempt will have to be made to resolve the said conflict by the adoption of the rule of harmonious construction.

The Lok Sabha Committee of privileges opined in 2008 that there does not arise any occasion for codification of the Parliamentary privileges and recommended against its codification. It is the lack of political will to codify the privileges that results in avoidable conflict between the Fundamental rights of citizens and privileges of the legislature. This can be resolved by codifying the privileges through a legislation.

MNEMONICS

Concept or Provisions	Shortcut or Mnemonics	Details to Remember
Privileges of Houses collectively	Public Private Partnership for Enterprise Resource Planning **Rules:** **PPP** for **ERP Rules**	• **P** – **P**ublish its report, debate, proceedings • **P** – **P**unish members and outsiders for breach of privileges • **P** – **P**ermission of presiding officer for any action inside the house • **E** – **E**xclude strangers • **R** – **R**eceive information about arrest, detention, conviction and release of members • **P** – **P**rohibition for courts from inquiring into proceedings • **Rules** – Make **Rules** for conduct
Privileges of Individual Members	**Freedom** from **AAA**	**Freedom** from • **A**rrest in civil cases for 40 days before and after session of Parliament • **A**ttendance as witness (without permission of the House) • **A**rticle 19(2) restriction for freedom of speech (but subject to House regulations and no discussion on Judge)

10.9 PARLIAMENTARY COMMITTEES

Parliamentary committees play an important role in assisting the Parliament in legislative work and also in exercising control over the executive. The Constitution mentions about committees of Houses of Parliament in various articles and also in the Seventh Schedule.

The details about various types of committees as well as the procedure for their constitution and functioning are provided in the rules of the Lok Sabha and the Rajya Sabha. The important committees can be classified into the following three broad categories.

Committees of Parliament		
Financial Committees	**Other Permanent Committees**	**Ad Hoc Committees**
• Committee on Public Accounts • Estimates Committee • Committee on Public Undertakings	• Departmental Standing Committees • Business Advisory Committee • Committee of Privileges • Committee on Private Members' Bills and Resolutions • Committee on Government Assurances • Committee on Subordinate Legislation	• Select Committee on Bills • Joint Parliamentary Committees

10.9.1 Financial Committees

The financial committees play a vital role in exercising financial control. These are permanent committees and are constituted every year. Ministers are not elected as members of these committees.

10.9.1.1 Committee on Public Accounts

- The Committee on Public Accounts (also known as Public Accounts Committee or PAC) is constituted by the Parliament each year for examination of accounts showing the appropriation of sums granted by the Parliament for expenditure of Government of India, the annual finance accounts of Government of India, and such other accounts laid before Parliament as the Committee may deem fit such as accounts of autonomous and semi-autonomous bodies.
- The PAC is the oldest Parliamentary Committee and was first constituted in 1921. The Committee consists of 22 members, 15 members are elected by the Lok Sabha and 7 members of the Rajya Sabha are associated with it. The Speaker appoints the Chairman of the committee. As per convention, the Chairman is from the opposition party.

- The PAC scrutinises the 'Appropriation Accounts' of the Government of India and the reports of the Comptroller and Auditor General of India (CAG) thereon. The Committee is assisted by the CAG in performing its functions.
- The Committee while scrutinising the accounts and CAG reports, verifies the following:
  - that the moneys shown in the accounts as having been disbursed were legally available for, and applicable to, the service or purpose to which they have been applied or charged;
  - that the expenditure conforms to the authority which governs it; and
  - that every re-appropriation has been made in accordance with the provisions made in this behalf under rules framed by competent authority.

> **THINK ABOUT IT**
>
> The Committee on Public Accounts plays a crucial role in holding the executive accountable. Discuss its composition, functions and powers.

- The functions of the Committee extend, however, beyond the formality of expenditure to its wisdom, faithfulness and economy. The Committee thus examines cases involving losses, unimportant expenditure and financial irregularities.
- Another important function of the Committee is the discussion on points of financial discipline and principle. The Committee is not concerned with questions of policy though it is within its jurisdiction to point out whether there has been extravagance or waste in carrying out that policy.
- However, the effectiveness of the committee is limited due to the following factors:
  - It is not concerned with questions of policy, which limits its scope.
  - It conducts only a post-mortem examination of accounts after the expenditure has been incurred.
  - Its recommendations are only advisory in nature and not binding on the ministries.
- Despite the above limitations, PAC plays an important role in enforcing accountability of the executive in financial matters.
- As far as PAC's power to summon ministers is concerned, there are differing opinions. A rule of PAC states that Ministers can also be summoned with the permission of the Speaker while a direction (Direction 99) of the 'Directions of the Speaker' states that ministers cannot be summoned by financial committees including PAC either to give evidence or for consultation.

It only allows the Chairperson to have an informal discussion with a Minister, the estimates or accounts of whose Ministry were under consideration by the Committee. In the past two Joint Parliamentary Committees constituted in 1992 and 2001 have sought written information and also summoned ministers with the permission of the Speaker of Lok Sabha.

10.9.1.2 Estimates Committee

- The Estimates Committee is a Committee of Lok Sabha. The Committee consist of not more than 30 members from the Lok Sabha who shall be elected by the House every year from amongst its members and the Speaker appoints the Chairman of the committee who is invariably from the ruling party. The Rajya Sabha has no representation in this committee.
- Rules of Procedure and Conduct of Business in Lok Sabha define the scope of functions of the Committee as follows:
  - to report what economies, improvements in organisation, efficiency or administrative reform, consistent with the policy underlying the estimates, may be effected;
  - to suggest alternative policies in order to bring about efficiency and economy in administration;
  - to examine whether the money is well laid out within the limits of the policy implied in the estimates; and
  - to suggest the form in which the estimates shall be presented to the Parliament.
- The Committee continues the examination of the estimates from time to time throughout the financial year and reports to the House on its findings from time to time.
- However, the effectiveness of the committee is limited due to the following factors:
  - It is not concerned with questions of policy, which limits its scope.
  - It reviews the estimates only after they have been voted by the Lok Sabha.
  - Its recommendations are only advisory in nature and not binding on the ministries.
  - It lacks the expert assistance of CAG that is available to the PAC.
- Despite the above limitations, the Estimates Committee plays an important role in enforcing accountability of the executive in financial matters.

10.9.1.3 Committee on Public Undertakings

- India has a lot of Public Sector Undertakings (PSU) that are owned by the Government of India. A separate committee has been constituted to examine the accounts and audit reports of these PSU.
- The Committee consists of 22 members, 15 members are elected by the Lok Sabha and 7 members of the Rajya Sabha are associated with it. This committee is constituted every year and the Speaker appoints the Chairman of the committee.
- The Committee performs the following functions:
  - to examine the reports and accounts of Public Undertakings;
  - to examine the reports of the Comptroller and Auditor General of India on the Public Undertakings;
  - to examine, in the context of the autonomy and efficiency of the Public Undertakings, whether the affairs of the Public Undertakings are being managed in accordance with sound business principles and prudent commercial practices;
  - to exercise such other functions vested in the PAC and Estimates Committee in relation to public undertakings.
- The effectiveness of the committee is limited since it only carries out a post-mortem and its recommendations are advisory and not binding on the ministries.

10.9.2 Permanent Committees

10.9.2.1 Departmental Standing Committees

The department-related Standing Committees were set up in the year 1993. As on date there are 24 department-related standing committees. Out of the 24 standing committees, 8 work under the Rajya Sabha (Home affairs, Industry, Health and Family welfare etc.) and 16 work under the Lok Sabha (Defence, External affairs, Finance etc.).

These committees are constituted every year with 21 members from the Lok Sabha and 10 members from the Rajya Sabha. A Minister cannot be a member of these committees and if a member of any committee is appointed as a minister, he/she ceases to be a member of such committee. The Chairman of the committee is nominated by the Speaker for the 16 committees that function under the Lok Sabha and by the Chairman for the 8 committees that function under the Rajya Sabha.

These committees perform the following functions:

- Consider the demand for grants of concerned ministries or departments before they are discussed and voted in the Lok Sabha during the Budget process.
- Examine the Bills referred to them by the Lok Sabha or the Rajya Sabha.
- To consider annual reports of ministries/departments and make a report to the Parliament.

These committees play an important role in the Parliament due to following reasons:

- They result in effective parliamentary control over the executive due to detailed and continuous scrutiny.
- They help in exercising greater financial control over the executive due to detailed scrutiny of demand for grants before they are voted by the Lok Sabha.
- They avail public and expert opinion while making its report on various bills referred to them by the Houses.
- They provide opportunities for all members to participate in the functioning of the Parliament/ Government and contribute to it.

10.9.2.2 Other Permanent Committees

Apart from Departmental Standing Committees, there are many permanent committees that are formed in both the Lok Sabha and the Rajya Sabha. The Constitution and functioning of these committees is governed by the Rules of procedure of the Lok Sabha and the Rajya Sabha. The important committees amongst them are briefly discussed in this section.

- Business Advisory Committee – It finalises the agenda for a session and allocates time for the transaction of legislative and other business in the House. It consists of 15 members in the Lok Sabha and 11 members in the Rajya Sabha.
- Committee of Privileges – It examines the breach of privilege of the House and its members and recommends appropriate action. It consists of 15 members in the Lok Sabha and 10 members in the Rajya Sabha.
- Committee on Private Members' Bills and Resolutions – This committee is constituted in the Lok Sabha with 15 members to classify and allocate time for discussion on bills and resolutions introduced by private members. In the Rajya Sabha, the Business advisory committee performs this function.

- Committee on Government Assurances – It scrutinises the assurances, promises and undertakings given by the ministers, from time to time, on the floor of the House. It reports on the extent to which such assurances, promises and undertakings have been implemented and whether such implementation has taken place within the minimum time necessary for the purpose. It consists of 15 members in the Lok Sabha and 10 members in the Rajya Sabha.
- Committee on subordinate legislation – It examines and reports whether the powers to make regulations, rules, bye-laws that are delegated by the Parliament or under the Constitution to the Executive are properly exercised by it. It consists of 15 members in both the houses.
- Committee on Ethics – Constituted in Rajya Sabha in 1997 and as an ad hoc committee in Lok Sabha in 2000, which became a permanent committee in 2015. It inquires into complaints of alleged misconduct of members referred to it by the Speaker/Chairman. Any person can complain against a member through another member. A member himself/herself can also complain against other members. The Committee does not entertain complaints based only on media reports or on matters that are subjudice.

Apart from the above, there are other committees to inquire like the Committee on Petitions, Committees for Welfare of SCs and STs and Committee on Empowerment of Women; House-keeping Committees like House Committee, Library Committee, General Purposes Committee etc., that are constituted in both the Houses from time to time.

10.9.3 Ad hoc Committees

10.9.3.1 Select Committees

Select committees are constituted usually for reviewing a Bill during the consideration stage. The members of a Select Committee on a Bill shall be appointed by the House when a motion that the Bill be referred to a Select Committee is made.

The Select Committee shall consider the Bill clause by clause and report the amendments that are proposed by the committee in its report. The Select Committee has to submit its report within the time fixed by the House or 3 months whichever is earlier. The House may extend the time provided to the Select Committee for submitting its report.

A Select Committee of the Rajya Sabha was formed for the GST constitutional amendment bill in 2015. Such Select Committees provide valuable inputs to the House while considering the bill. However, in the recent past, the number of bills getting referred to a Select Committee has been on the decline.

10.9.3.2 Joint Parliamentary Committee

A Joint Parliamentary Committee (JPC) is constituted for a specific purpose. It is formed when motion to form such a JPC is adopted by one House and is agreed to by the other House. They are usually constituted for investigation into any matter of public importance or for reviewing a bill introduced in the Parliament.

There have been several important JPCs that have been constituted over the years for investigating into Bofors case (1987), Harshad Mehta stock market scam (1992), 2G spectrum case (2011), VVIP Chopper case (2013) etc. Recently, JPCs have been constituted for review of Personal Data Protection Bill in 2019, Waqf (Amendment) Bill, 2024 and simultaneous elections related bills in 2024.

10.10 SUMMARY AND COMPARISON BETWEEN THE LOK SABHA AND THE RAJYA SABHA

The Lok Sabha and Rajya Sabha are the two houses of Parliament. While the Parliament is the highest legislative body under the Indian Constitution, the Parliament is not sovereign in India, unlike in United Kingdom, where the British Parliament is sovereign. The sovereignty of Indian Parliament is restricted due to factors like

(a) written constitution which limits the powers of Parliament;
(b) distribution of powers between Union and States as per the constitution;
(c) restriction on the Parliament in making laws that contravene Fundamental rights; and
(d) system of judicial review by the courts.

The Constitutional position of the Rajya Sabha (as compared with the Lok Sabha) can be studied from three dimensions:

1. Where the Rajya Sabha's powers are equal to the Lok Sabha.
2. Where the Rajya Sabha is unequal with the Lok Sabha.
3. Where the Rajya Sabha has certain special powers that are not shared by the Lok Sabha.

Powers of Rajya Sabha		
Equal Status with the Lok Sabha	**Unequal status – where only Lok Sabha has powers**	**Special Powers of Rajya Sabha**
• Ordinary bills • Passage of Constitutional amendment bills • Financial bills Category A (or Category I) and Category B (or Category II) for passage (though Financial Bill category A (or Category I) can be introduced only in the Lok Sabha) • Election and impeachment of the President • Election of the Vice-President • Approval/Rejection of Ordinances promulgated by the President • Approval/Rejection of emergencies declared • Removal of Judges of the Supreme Court, High Courts, Chief Election Commissioner, CAG • Ministers can be from both the Lok Sabha and the Rajya Sabha • Consideration of various reports of Constitutional bodies	• Money Bills can be introduced only in the Lok Sabha; the Rajya Sabha has no power to amend or reject a Money Bill • The Rajya Sabha can only discuss the Budget but cannot vote on demand for grants • The Speaker of the Lok Sabha presides over a joint sitting. Further, in a joint sitting, the Lok Sabha has numerical advantage when compared to the Rajya Sabha • Resolution for discontinuance of national emergency can be passed only in the Lok Sabha • No confidence motion – Removal of Council of Ministers can be only initiated in the Lok Sabha	• The Rajya Sabha can authorise the Parliament to make a law on a subject in the State list in National interest [Art 249] • The Rajya Sabha can authorise the Parliament to create All India Services [Art 312] • At present there are 12 nominated members only in the Rajya Sabha. Two nominated Anglo-Indian members to the Lok Sabha have been discontinued from the 17th Lok Sabha through the 104th Constitutional amendment • Removal of the Vice-President (the Rajya Sabha can alone initiate removal of the Vice-President and the majority required in the Rajya Sabha is effective majority while it is simple majority in the Lok Sabha)

Comparison between Rajya Sabha and Senate in the United States

- The Rajya Sabha in the Indian Parliament is not as powerful as the Senate in the United States.
- The Senate in the United States consists of 100 members and it has equal representation of 2 members from all the 50 states unlike unequal representation in the Rajya Sabha.
- The Senate confirms appointments made by the US President to important executive positions and the judges of the Supreme Court of the United States.
- The Senate can use 'filibuster' as a tactic for delaying the passage of a bill. 'Filibuster' requires that 60 members have to vote to stop debate on a bill thereby enabling a minority of 41 members to delay its passage.

However, despite its limitations, the Rajya Sabha has significant powers in the Indian Parliament as discussed in the summary table above. It acts as check and balance on the powers of the Lok Sabha where the ruling government enjoys a majority.

MAINS STARTER

Area	Building Blocks For Model Introductions
Parliamentary democracy/ Parliamentary control/ Legislative control, etc.	India is a Parliamentary democracy in which the executive is accountable to the legislature [Art 75(3)]. Unlike a presidential democracy, it is not based on strict separation of powers between the executive and the legislature but works on the principle of 'checks and balance'.
Qualification for Parliament	The Constitution provides age, citizenship and such other qualifications as prescribed by a parliamentary law as qualifications for being a member of Parliament (Art 84). The Representation of the Peoples Act, 1951 provides that the person should be an elector from any constituency. Further, for reserved seats, at present for SC and ST, the person should belong to such category.
Disqualification for becoming or being Members of Parliament	The Constitution provides 5 grounds for disqualification which includes disqualification under a Parliamentary law [Art 102(1)]. The decision relating to such disqualification is made by the President based on the opinion of the Election Commission (Art 103). The Representation of Peoples Act, 1951 provides for disqualification on various grounds that includes conviction for a criminal offence.
Disqualification under Tenth Schedule	The disqualification for anti-defection was added in the Tenth Schedule in 1985 to prevent instability in elected governments due to defections which was the norm during the 1960s and 1970s.
Speaker's office/ post	The office of the Speaker is one of the most important offices that uphold democratic values. There are important responsibilities placed on this office that he/she is expected to perform in a non-partisan manner.
Legislative procedure	The primary function of Parliament is to enact laws. The Constitution and rules of procedure provide the detailed procedure for such law-making process.

Area	Building Blocks For Model Introductions
Money Bill procedure	The Constitution provides a special procedure for passage of money bills (Art 109). This is because such a bill contains provisions only with respect to financial matters over which the Lok Sabha, where incumbent government enjoys majority, needs to have effective control to ensure smooth administration of the country.
Joint Sitting	The Constitution provides the mechanism of Joint Sitting for passage of a bill (other than money bill) to break a deadlock between the two houses on account of rejection, disagreement or delay (Art 108).
Expenditure charged on consolidated fund	There are certain expenditures of institutions/offices that are charged on the consolidated fund in the Appropriation Bill which is not subject to vote even in the Lok Sabha [Art 112(3)]. It is a reflection of the importance or independence of such institutions.
Parliamentary privileges	Parliamentary privileges are special rights, immunities and exemptions available to houses of Parliament and its members (Art 105). They evolved in medieval Britain to protect the House of Commons and its members from excesses of the King.
Parliamentary Committees	Parliamentary committees play an important role in assisting the Parliament in legislative work and also in exercising control over the executive.

Register on **McGraw Hill Edge** for the following:

- Articles at a glance for this chapter
- Additional Data points for allocation of seats in Lok Sabha and Rajya Sabha; Durations of various Lok Sabhas with list of Speakers; List of Departmentally related standing committees under Lok Sabha and Rajya Sabha; List of No-Confidence and Confidence motions in Lok Sabha
- Practice questions for Preliminary examination including PYQ of 2014–24
- Model answers for Mains PYQ of 2014–24
- Attend regular webinars by the author including discussion on **'Think about It'** questions

UPSC Previous Years' Questions of Preliminary Examination

1. Which of the following statements about the Ethics Committee in the Lok Sabha are correct? **[2024]**

1. Initially, it was an ad-hoc Committee.
2. Only a member of the Lok Sabha can make a complaint relating to unethical conduct of a member of the Lok Sabha.
3. This Committee cannot take up any matter which is sub-judice.

Select the answer using the code given below:
(a) 1 and 2 only (b) 2 and 3 only
(c) 1 and 3 only (d) 1, 2 and 3

Solution: (c)

Explanation: Ethics Committee was first formed as an ad hoc committee in 2000 that became a permanent committee in 2015. So, statement 1 is correct. Any person can complain but only through a member of Lok Sabha. A member of Lok Sabha can also complain. So, statement 2 is incorrect. The committee does not entertain complaint only based on media reports or on matters that are sub-judice. Hence, Statement 3 is correct and answer is (c).

2. Which of the following statements are correct in respect of a Money Bill in the Parliament? **[2024]**

1. Article 109 mentions special procedure in respect of Money Bills.
2. A Money Bill shall not be introduced in the Council of States.
3. The Rajya Sabha can either approve the Bill or suggest changes but cannot reject it.
4. Amendments to a Money Bill suggested by the Rajya Sabha have to be accepted by the Lok Sabha.

Select the answer using the code given below:
(a) 1 and 2 only (b) 2 and 3 only
(c) 1, 2 and 3 (d) 1, 3 and 4

Solution: (c)

Explanation: As discussed in Section 10.6.4.1 (grey shaded area), the first three statements are correct and the fourth statement is incorrect and hence answer is (c).

3. Consider the following statements regarding 'Nari Shakti Vandan Adhiniyam': **[2024]**

1. Provisions will come into effect from the 18th Lok Sabha.
2. This will be in force for 15 years after becoming an Act.
3. There are provisions for the reservation of seats for Scheduled Castes Women within the quota reserved for the Scheduled Castes.

Which of the statements given above are correct?
(a) 1, 2 and 3 (b) 1 and 2 only
(c) 2 and 3 only (d) 1 and 3 only

Solution: (c)

Explanation: As discussed in Section 10.3.3, the 106th constitutional amendment provides for $1/3^{rd}$ seats reservation for women including quota for SC and ST women within the SC and ST quota. It is for a period of 15 years and can be extended by an Act of Parliament. Hence, statements 2 and 3 are correct. However, it did not come into effect from the 18th Lok Sabha that has been elected in June 2024, but after the first census conducted after the commencement of the 106th Amendment Act, i.e. first census after 2024. Hence, Statement 1 is incorrect and the answer is (c).

4. With reference to Union Budget, consider the following statements: **[2024]**

1. The Union Finance Minister on behalf of the Prime Minister lays the Annual Financial Statement before both the Houses of Parliament.

2. At the Union level, no demand for a grant can be made except on the recommendation of the President of India.

Which of the statements given above is/are correct.

(a) 1 only (b) 2 only
(c) Both 1 and 2 (d) Neither 1 nor 2

Solution: (b)

Explanation: As discussed in Section 10.6.4.4 – Budget as a Money Bill, Statement 1 is incorrect and Statement 2 is correct and hence answer is (b).

5. With reference to the Speaker of the Lok Sabha, consider the following statements: **[2024]**

While any resolution for the removal of the speaker of the Lok Sabha is under consideration

1. He/she shall not preside.
2. He/she shall not have the right to speak.
3. He/she shall not be entitled to vote on the resolution in the first instance.

Which of the statements given above is/are correct?

(a) 1 only (b) 1 and 2 only
(c) 2 and 3 only (d) 1, 2 and 3

Solution: (a)

Explanation: As discussed in Section 10.5.1.1 (grey shaded box), only the first statement is correct and the remaining two statements are incorrect and hence answer is (a).

6. With reference to the Indian Parliament, consider the following statements: **[2024]**

1. A bill pending in the Lok Sabha lapses on its dissolution.
2. A bill passed by the Lok Sabha and pending in the Rajya Sabha lapses on the dissolution of the Lok Sabha.
3. A bill in regard to which the President of India notified his/her intention to summon the Houses to a joint sitting lapses on the dissolution of the Lok Sabha.

Which of the statements given above is/are correct?

(a) 1 only (b) 1 and 2
(c) 2 and 3 (d) 3 only

Solution: (b)

Explanation: As discussed in Section 10.6.1 – 'Grey shaded box and mind map, the first two statements are correct and the third is incorrect and answer is (b).

7. With reference to the Parliament of India, consider the following statements: **[2024]**

1. Prorogation of a House by the President of India does not require the advice of the Council of Ministers.
2. Prorogation of a House is generally done after the House is adjourned sine die, but there is no bar to the President of India prorogating the House which is in session.
3. Dissolution of the Lok Sabha is done by the President of India who, save in exceptional circumstances, does so on the advice of the Council of ministers.

Which of the statements given above is/are correct?

(a) 1 only (b) 1 and 2

(c) 2 and 3 (d) 3 only

Solution: (c)

Explanation: As discussed in Section 10.3.5, summoning of house, prorogation of houses, is done by President based on the advice of the Council of Ministers (COM) only. Hence, Statement 1 is incorrect. Prorogation is usually done after the house is adjourned sine die, but it is not necessary and the President, based on the advice of the COM, can prorogue it earlier also. Dissolution, except when the COM have lost majority, is usually done by President again based on the advice of the COM. Hence, Statements 2 and 3 are correct.

8. With reference to Finance Bill and Money Bill in the Indian Parliament, consider the following statements: **[2023]**

1. When the Lok Sabha transmits Finance Bill to the Rajya Sabha, it can amend or reject the Bill.
2. When the Lok Sabha transmits Money Bill to the Rajya Sabha, it cannot amend or reject the Bill, it can only make recommendations.
3. In the case of disagreement between the Lok Sabha and the Rajya Sabha, there is no joint sitting for Money Bill, but a joint sitting becomes necessary for Finance Bill.

How many of the above statements are correct?

(a) Only one (b) Only two (c) All three (d) None

Solution: (b)

Explanation: The term used by UPSC is Finance Bill while it is clear from the construction of the question that it is actually referring to a Financial Bill. Based on that, as summarised in Section 10.6.6, the first two statements are correct. The third statement is incorrect, because a Joint Sitting is not absolutely necessary in the case of disagreement over a Financial Bill but may be called by the President if the council of ministers so desire. Hence, the answer is (b).

9. Which of the following is/are the exclusive power(s) of the Lok Sabha? **[2022]**

1. To ratify the declaration of emergency
2. To pass a motion of no-confidence against the council of ministers
3. To impeach the President of India

Select the correct answer using the code given below:

(a) 1 and 2 (b) 2 only (c) 1 and 3 (d) 3 only

Solution: (b)

Explanation: As discussed in the summary table in Section 10.10, in respect of Statements 1 and 3, dealing with approval of emergency and impeachment of President, both the Lok Sabha and Rajya Sabha have equal powers. The No-confidence motion can be passed only in the Lok Sabha and hence the answer is (b).

10. With reference to the anti-defection law in India, consider the following statements: **[2022]**

1. The law specifies that a nominated legislator cannot join any political party within six months of being appointed in the House.

2. The law does not provide any time frame within which the presiding officer has to decide a defection case.

Which of the statements given above is/are correct?

(a) 1 only (b) 2 only (c) Both 1 and 2 (d) Neither 1 nor 2

Solution: (b)

Explanation: As discussed in Section 10.4.3.2, the Tenth Schedule specifies that a nominated legislator can join any political party only within six months and not thereafter and hence statement 1 is incorrect. Statement 2 is correct as the Tenth Schedule has not provided any time frame within which the Speaker or Chairman has to decide on a defection case. Hence the answer is (b).

11. With reference to the Deputy speaker of Lok Sabha, consider the following statements: **[2022]**

1. As per the Rules of procedure and conduct of Business in Lok Sabha, the election of the Deputy speaker shall be held on such date as the Speaker may fix.
2. There is a mandatory provision that the election of a candidate as Deputy Speaker of Lok Sabha shall be from either the principal opposition party or the ruling party.
3. The Deputy Speaker has the same power as of the Speaker when presiding over the sitting of the House and no appeal lies against his rulings.
4. The well-established parliamentary practice regarding the appointment of Deputy Speaker is that the motion is moved by the Speaker and duly seconded by the Prime Minister.

Which of the statements given above is/are correct?

(a) 1 and 3 only (b) 1, 2 and 3 (c) 3 and 4 only (d) 2 and 4 only

Solution: (a)

Explanation: As per the rules of Lok Sabha (Rule 8), statement 1 is correct. As discussed in Section 10.5.1.1, from the 10th Lok Sabha there has been a convention that the Deputy Speaker shall belong to the principal opposition party. But it is only a convention and not a mandatory provision and hence statement 2 is incorrect. Statement 3 is correct as per rules of Lok Sabha (Rule 10). Statement 4 is incorrect since the rules of Lok Sabha specify that the motion for proposing a member as Deputy Speaker is to be moved by another member (and not the Speaker) and seconded by any other member. So, the answer is (a).

UPSC Previous Years' Questions of Main Examination

1. "The growth of cabinet system has practically resulted in the marginalisation of the parliamentary supremacy." Elucidate. **[2024]**

Approach: The essence of Parliamentary democracy where the executive is held accountable by the legislature needs to be part of the introduction. The issues and diminishing role of Parliament in recent past due to a strong executive need to be elaborated as the key word or tail word of the question is 'Elucidate'. The suggestions for strengthening parliamentary control and supremacy need to be summarised in the conclusion.

MODEL ANSWER

The Council of Ministers (executive) are collectively responsible to the Lok Sabha (legislature) in India [Art 75(3)]. The Constitution is supreme in our democracy. However, the legislature is required to exercise control and have check and balance over the executive.

However, the cabinet system of government with a strong executive has resulted in the diminishing role of Parliament.

Mechanisms for Parliament supremacy and executive accountability

Parliament is the law-making body and exercises control over the executive in various ways as follows:

- MPs question government policies and programmes during the debates while passing various bills and resolutions.
- Parliament exercises control over taxation and expenditure of the government while passing the annual budget.
- Various departmentally related standing committees and other select/joint committees peruse bills before being passed by Parliament to ensure it addresses the concerns of all stakeholders.

Issues with Parliamentary functioning

The following are the main issues that affect Parliamentary supremacy and control over the executive:

(a) Powerful executive that captures people's imagination coupled with absence of a strong opposition.

(b) Reduced role of parliamentary committees since there is reduction of reference of bills to standing or select committees. In the 16th and 17th Lok Sabha, less than 25% bills were referred to the Committees. Critical bills were passed without adequate debate in the Parliament because of the majority enjoyed by the executive.

(c) Many laws provide for rules to be made by the executive. This effectively reduces the role of Parliament in making detailed laws and increases the power of bureaucracy.

(d) Passage of various bills as 'Money Bills' even when it does not satisfy the definition of Money Bill. This reduces the role of Rajya Sabha. The Supreme Court is set to constitute a seven-judge bench to adjudicate on this matter.

The above issues need to be addressed by the government of the day and opposition parties to ensure an effective role of Parliament in law making and ensuring accountability of the executive to the Parliament.

2. Compare and contrast the British and Indian approaches to Parliamentary sovereignty. **[2023]**

Approach: Section 10.10 – Comparison between Indian and UK Parliament and restrictions on sovereignty of Indian Parliament to be the first part of the answer. Section 15.2 – Basic Structure doctrine and limitation on Indian Parliament to be the concluding part.

MODEL ANSWER

Both Britain and India are Parliamentary democracies. The Indian system is modelled on the basis of the Westminster system in UK. The law making procedure for various types of Bills under the Indian Constitution is modelled on the basis of similar system in the UK.

Comparison between British and Indian Parliament

While the Parliament is the highest legislative body in both the countries, the Parliament is not sovereign in India unlike in United Kingdom where the British Parliament is sovereign as it does not have any restrictions placed on it by a written constitution.

The sovereignty of Indian Parliament is restricted due to factors like:

(a) written constitution,
(b) distribution of powers between Union and States as per the constitution,
(c) restriction on the Parliament in making laws that contravene Fundamental rights and
(d) system of judicial review by the courts.

The courts have also propounded the 'Basic structure' doctrine under which the Indian Parliament cannot amend some of the basic features of the Constitution like Judicial review, independence of judiciary, rule of law, federalism, secularism, principle of equality, essence of fundamental rights, harmonious balance between fundamental rights and directive principles, etc.

3. (a) On what grounds a people's representative can be disqualified under the Representation of People Act, 1951? Also mention the remedies available to such person against his disqualification. **[2019]**

(b) Discuss the procedures to decide the disputes arising out of the election of a Member of the Parliament or State Legislature under The Representation of the People Act, 1951. What are the grounds on which the election of any returned candidate may be declared void? What remedy is available to the aggrieved party against the decision? Refer to the case laws. **[2022]**

Approach: This is a static question though the context may have been a current event at that time. The grounds for disqualification under the RP Act, 1951 as explained in Section 10.4.3.1 needs to be summarised and then the remedies available can be highlighted.

MODEL ANSWER

The Representation of the People Act, 1951 (RP Act, 1951) provides for various grounds on which an MP or an MLA/MLC can be disqualified.

Grounds for disqualification under the RP Act, 1951

1. Convicted of any offence and sentenced to imprisonment for not less than 2 years.
2. Found guilty on ground of corrupt practices during election.
3. Dismissed from Government service for corruption or disloyalty.
4. Having interest in Government contracts.
5. Failure to lodge account of election expenses.
6. A managing agent, manager or secretary of any Government company or corporation in which the Government has not less than 25% share.
7. Punished for preaching and practicing social crimes like sati, untouchability, dowry etc.

As per the Constitution (Articles 103 and 192), any question of disqualification under the RP Act, 1951 shall be referred for the decision of the President (in case of MP) and the Governor (in case of MLA or MLC). The President or the Governor shall, before giving decision on any such question, obtain the opinion of the Election Commission and shall act according to such opinion. The disqualification due to conviction for any criminal offence is automatic from the date of sentencing as per the Supreme Court judgement in ***Lily Thomas*** case.

Remedies available for a disqualified member

1. Any person disqualified can approach the High Court for judicial review of the decision.
2. The Election Commission on certain grounds can remove any disqualification or reduce the period of disqualification as per Section 11 of the RP Act, 1951.

In September 2019, in the case of Shri Prem Singh Tamang, the incumbent Chief Minister of Sikkim, the ECI had reduced the period of disqualification from 6 years to 13 months using its powers under Section 11 of the Representation of the People Act, 1951 (RP Act, 1951).

4. Rajya Sabha has been transformed from a 'useless stepney tyre' to the most useful supporting organ in past few decades. Highlight the factors as well as the areas in which this transformation could be visible. **[2020]**

Approach: Discussion on the composition of Rajya Sabha under Indian Constitution along with its unique powers can be the first part of the answer. Then the areas in which it has been useful in legislations and executive control in the recent decades can be discussed in the second part.

MODEL ANSWER

The Rajya Sabha represents the States in the Indian Parliament. The representation is unequal amongst the states based on their population (Art 80). However, it acts as a check and balance on the powers of Lok Sabha where the ruling government has a majority.

In the initial decades after independence, the same party had majority in both Lok Sabha and Rajya Sabha. This reduced the role of Rajya Sabha and it merely gave its stamp of approval to various laws and amendments that were introduced by the government.

Transformation of Rajya Sabha

However, with coalition governments being formed from 1990s, the role of Rajya Sabha transformed from being a 'mere stepney tyre' to a powerful supporting organ. Further, various regional parties also captured power in states like Uttar Pradesh, Tamil Nadu, Andhra Pradesh, Odisha, Haryana, Karnataka that altered the composition of the Rajya Sabha.

Some of the areas where contribution of Rajya Sabha can be seen in recent decades are as follows:

- Joint Parliamentary committees have been constituted over the years for investigating into various irregularities like Bofors case (1987), Harshad Mehta stock market scam (1992), 2G spectrum case (2011), VVIP Chopper case (2013) etc. JPCs have also been formed for Digital Personal Data Protection Bill, Waqf (Amendment) Bill and bills on simultaneous elections.
- There was a select committee of Rajya Sabha that was constituted in 2014 for the GST amendment that provided valuable inputs before the amendment was passed by Parliament.
- After more than 4 decades, a private member bill was passed with respect to Transgender rights in Rajya Sabha in the year 2015 that forced the government to bring its own bill and get the same enacted in 2019.
- Various regional and opposition party members in Rajya Sabha exercise control over the council of ministers through question hour, zero hour, calling attention motion etc.

Thus, the Rajya Sabha plays an important role in the legislative work as well as exercising control over the executive.

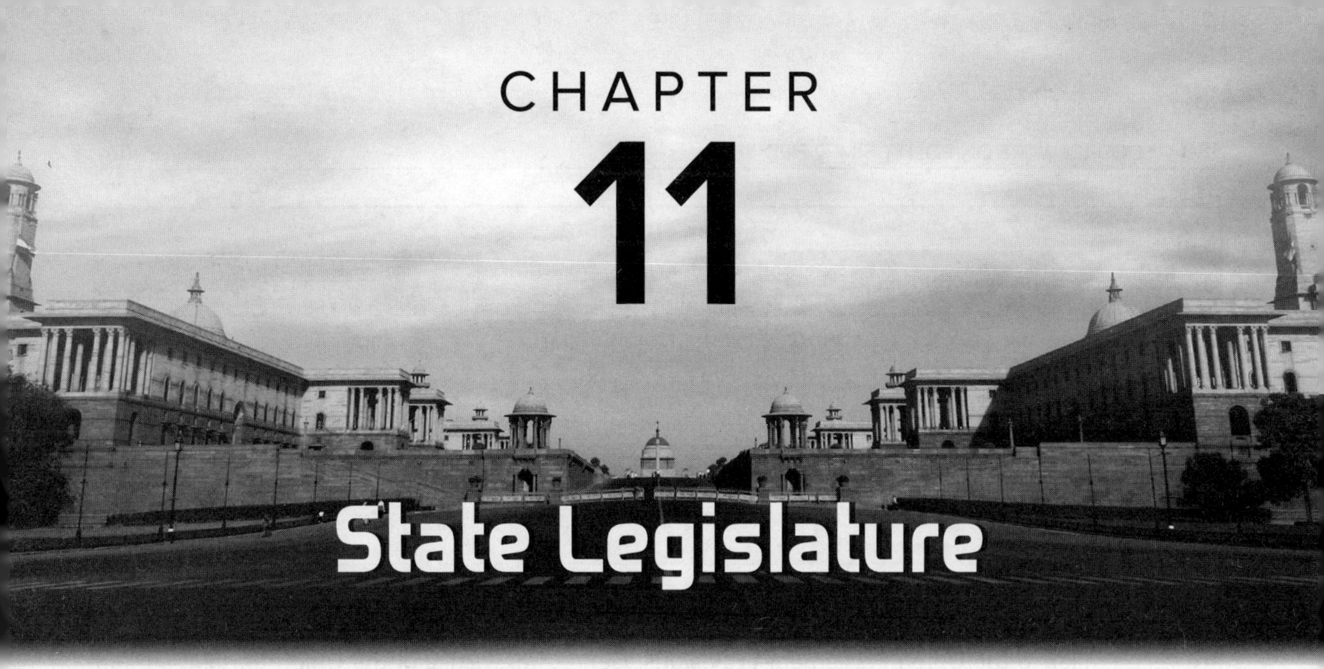

CHAPTER 11

State Legislature

LEARNING OUTCOMES

1. Understanding the structure including the roles of the Legislative Assembly and Legislative Council
2. Exploring the functional similarities between Parliament and State legislature considering our federal polity
3. Knowing Legislative Councils – Its creation, abolition, composition and limited legislative powers
4. Comprehending the utility of Legislative Councils and way forward including 2nd ARC recommendations

11.1 INTRODUCTION TO THE STATE LEGISLATURE

The legislative branch in our country is federal in character. There is a Parliament at the Union level for carrying out the legislative functions vested in the Union as per the Constitution.

As with the Parliament at the centre, the Constitution provides for a legislative body for each State which is called the State Legislature. The State Legislature usually consists of a single House called the Legislative Assembly. There may also be an upper House or Legislative Council in some States. Currently, six States have a Legislative Council which are Andhra Pradesh, Karnataka, Telangana, Maharashtra, Bihar and Uttar Pradesh. The provisions of the State Legislature are very similar to the Union Parliament with a few exceptions, which we will understand in this chapter.

11.2 COMPOSITION OF THE STATE LEGISLATURE

Articles 168 to 212 in Part VI of the Constitution deals with the organisation, composition, duration and functions of the State Legislature.

The articles that deal with State Legislature can be broadly classified for the purposes of understanding into three broad categories as provided in the table, next page (similar to the Union Parliament).

State Legislature		
Composition and Duration	**Qualification, Disqualification and Functioning of the Houses**	**Legislative Procedure**
• Composition of the State Legislature, the Legislative Assembly and the Legislative Council • Duration of the State Legislature • Sessions of the State Legislature	• Qualification for members • Disqualification for/of members • Officers of the State Legislature • Oath and affirmation • Conduct of business	• Ordinary Bill • Money Bill • Financial Bills • Limited powers of the Legislative Council

We shall discuss the similarities between the Union Parliament and the State Legislature in a tabular form. This table will help the reader understand that majority of the provisions of the State Legislature are very similar to the Union Parliament provisions. Hence, knowledge of the Union Parliament and understanding of the comparative table will be sufficient to know majority of the provisions of the State Legislature.

11.3 COMPARISON BETWEEN UNION PARLIAMENT AND THE STATE LEGISLATURE

11.3.1 Similarities between Parliament and the State Legislature

The following table summarises the similarities between the Union Parliament and the State Legislature. As a simple thumb rule for most of the provisions of the State Legislature – the President is replaced by the Governor, the Lok Sabha is replaced by the Legislative Assembly and the Rajya Sabha is replaced by the Legislative Council. The reader must have noted that in the previous chapter on Union Parliament (Chapter 10), examples have been provided from both the Centre and the States under various sections as the provisions are similar. The various case laws discussed are also related to both the Union and the State-related matters.

However, the provisions with respect to creation and abolition of the Legislative Councils in States along with its limited legislative powers when compared to the Rajya Sabha at the Centre, are different at the State Legislature level. These will be covered in detail in subsequent sections.

Particulars	Union Provisions w.r.t. Parliament	Similar Provisions for State w.r.t. State Legislature
Functions	The Parliament performs the following functions: (a) Legislative function of making laws for the whole or part of the country. (b) Provides and controls the Union Council of Ministers. (c) Financial control over revenue and expenditure of the Union Government.	The State Legislature similarly performs the following functions: (a) Legislative function of making laws for whole or part of the State. (b) Provides and controls the State Council of Ministers. (c) Financial control over revenue and expenditure of the State Government.

Particulars	Union Provisions w.r.t. Parliament	Similar Provisions for State w.r.t. State Legislature
	(d) Electoral and judicial functions – election of the President, the Vice-President, removal of judges, CAG and CEC	(d) The elected members of the State Legislative Assemblies participate in the President's election and election of the Rajya Sabha MPs from the State.
Constitution	Parliament consists of the President, the Lok Sabha and the Rajya Sabha [Art 79].	For every State there shall be a Legislature which shall consist of the Governor, and (a) in the States of Andhra Pradesh, Telangana, Bihar, Uttar Pradesh, Karnataka and Maharashtra, two Houses (b) in other States, one House. Where there are two Houses of the Legislature of a State, one shall be known as the Legislative Council and the other as the Legislative Assembly, and where there is only one House, it shall be known as the Legislative Assembly [Art 168].
Composition of Rajya Sabha/ Legislative Council	• The Rajya Sabha consists of maximum 250 members – 238 elected and 12 nominated (Total membership as on date is 245 – 233 elected and 12 nominated). • The allocation of seats is provided in the Fourth Schedule to the Indian Constitution. • The members are elected by an electoral college consisting of elected MLAs of the respective States.	• The Legislative Council in a State can be created or abolished by the Parliament [Art 169]. • The number of seats in a Legislative Council shall not exceed one-third of the total number of members in the Legislative Assembly of the State subject to a minimum of 40 members [Art 171]. • The provisions with respect to creation or abolition, composition and election of members of Legislative Council will be discussed in detail in the next Section 11.3.2.
Composition of the Lok Sabha/ Legislative Assembly	• The Lok Sabha shall consist of a maximum of 550 members – 530 from States and 20 from the Union Territories. • As on date, there are 543 elected members to the Lok Sabha. The allocation of seats in the Lok Sabha is provided in the First Schedule to the Representation of the People Act, 1950. • The nomination of 2 Anglo-Indian members to the Lok Sabha has been discontinued since January 2020 through the 104th Constitutional amendment. • The allocation of seats, at present, is based on the Census of 1971.	• The Legislative Assembly of each State shall consist of not more than 500 members and not less than 60 members [Art 170]. Some smaller States have less than 60 members like Goa (40), Mizoram (40) and Sikkim (30). • The allocation of seats in the Legislative Assemblies is provided in the Second Schedule to the Representation of the People Act, 1950. • The nomination of 1 Anglo-Indian member to the Legislative Assemblies has been discontinued through the 104th Constitutional amendment.

Particulars	Union Provisions w.r.t. Parliament	Similar Provisions for State w.r.t. State Legislature
	• The boundaries of the territorial constituencies have been redrawn based on the Census of 2001. • There is reservation for Scheduled Castes and Scheduled Tribes in the Lok Sabha in proportion to their population in each State. This is also based on the Census of 2001. • 1/3rd reservation for women in Lok Sabha (including in seats reserved for SC and ST) – To be implemented based on the first census after commencement of the 106th Constitutional Amendment.	• The allocation of seats, at present, is based on the Census of 1971. • The boundaries of the territorial constituencies have been redrawn based on the Census of 2001. • There is reservation for Scheduled Castes and Scheduled Tribes in the Legislative Assemblies in proportion to their population in each State. This is also based on the Census of 2001. • 1/3rd reservation for women in Legislative Assemblies (including in seats reserved for SC and ST) – To be implemented based on the first census after commencement of the 106th Constitutional Amendment.
Duration of Houses – Rajya Sabha/ Legislative Council	• The Council of States or the Rajya Sabha is the permanent House of the Parliament and is not subjected to dissolution. • The tenure of the members is 6 years and at the end of every second year, 1/3rd of the members retire and fresh elections are conducted for those 1/3rd seats falling vacant.	• The Legislative Council may be created or abolished by the Parliament. However, it is not subjected to dissolution [Art 172 (2)]. • The tenure of the members is 6 years and at the end of every second year, 1/3rd of the members retire and fresh elections are conducted for those 1/3rd seats falling vacant. The provisions with respect to creation or abolition, composition and election of members of the Legislative Council will be discussed in detail in the next Section 11.3.2.
Duration of Houses – Lok Sabha / Legislative Assembly	• The normal term of the Lok Sabha is 5 years after which it is subjected to automatic dissolution [Art 83(2)]. However, the President (based on advice of council of ministers) is authorised to dissolve the Lok Sabha at any time before the completion of 5-year term. • The term of the Lok Sabha can be extended during emergency by 1 year at a time through a law made by the Parliament. However, this extension cannot continue beyond a period of 6 months after the emergency has ceased to operate [Art 83(2)].	• The normal term of the Legislative Assembly is 5 years after which it is subjected to automatic dissolution [Art 172(1)]. However, the Governor (based on advice of council of ministers) is authorised to dissolve the Legislative Assembly at any time before the completion of 5-year term. • The term of Assembly can be extended during emergency by 1 year at a time through a law made by the Parliament. However, this extension cannot continue beyond a period of 6 months after the emergency has ceased to operate [Art 172(1)].

Particulars	Union Provisions w.r.t. Parliament	Similar Provisions for State w.r.t. State Legislature
Summoning, Prorogation, Adjournment and Dissolution	• The President summons and prorogues the Houses of Parliament from time to time. More than 6 months shall not intervene between two sessions. • The Speaker/Chairman adjourns the Lok Sabha/Rajya Sabha during a session. • The President may dissolve the House of People (on the advice of the Council of Ministers).	• The Governor summons and prorogues the House or Houses of State Legislature from time to time. More than 6 months shall not intervene between two sessions [Art 174]. • The Speaker/Chairman adjourns the Legislative Assembly/Legislative Council during a session. • The Governor may dissolve the Legislative Assembly (on the advice of the Council of Ministers) [Art 174].
Qualification for Membership	• Indian citizen; • 25 years of age for the Lok Sabha and 30 years of age for the Rajya Sabha; • Should be an elector from any constituency in India as per the requirement of Representation of the People Act, 1951; • The candidate has to belong to the reserved category of Scheduled Caste or Scheduled Tribe for contesting in reserved constituencies.	• Indian citizen; • 25 years of age for the Legislative Assembly and 30 years of age for the Legislative Council; • Should be an elector from any constituency in the State as per the requirement of Representation of the People Act, 1951; • The candidate has to belong to reserved category of Scheduled Caste or Scheduled Tribe for contesting in reserved constituencies [Art 173].
Vacation of Seat	• A person shall not be a member of both the Houses of Parliament. • A person shall not be a member of both a House of Parliament and a State Legislature. • A person may vacate his/her seat by resigning from the House of which he/she is a member. • If a member is absent for 60 days (when the House is in session) without the permission of the House, the House may declare his/her seat vacant.	• A person shall not be a member of both the Houses of State Legislature. • A person shall not be a member of both a State legislature and a House of Parliament. • A person may vacate his/her seat by resigning from the House of which he/she is a member. • If a member is absent for 60 days (when the House is in session) without the permission of the House, the House may declare his/her seat vacant [Art 190].
Disqualification	• A person is disqualified for being chosen as, and for being, a member under the following grounds: (a) Holding an office of profit unless it is exempted by a Parliamentary law (b) Unsound mind (c) Undischarged insolvent	• A person is disqualified for being chosen as, and for being, a member under the following grounds: (a) Holding an office of profit unless it is exempted by a law of State Legislature (b) Unsound mind (c) Undischarged insolvent

Particulars	Union Provisions w.r.t. Parliament	Similar Provisions for State w.r.t. State Legislature
	(d) Not a citizen of India or has voluntarily acquired the citizenship of any other foreign state (e) Disqualified under any law made by the Parliament i.e., The Representation of the People Act, 1951. • Any question with respect to the disqualification of a member under any of the above grounds is decided by the President as per the opinion given by the Election Commission of India. • A member shall also be subject to disqualification under the anti-defection law as per the Tenth Schedule. • Disqualification under the Tenth Schedule is decided by the Speaker of the Lok Sabha or the Chairman of the Rajya Sabha.	(d) Not a citizen of India or has voluntarily acquired the citizenship of any other foreign state (e) Disqualified under any law made by the Parliament i.e., The Representation of the People Act, 1951 [Art 191(1)]. • Any question with respect to disqualification of a member under any of the above grounds is decided by the Governor as per the opinion given by the Election Commission of India [Art 192]. • A member shall also be subject to disqualification under the anti-defection law as per the Tenth Schedule [Art 191(2)]. • Disqualification under the Tenth Schedule is decided by the Speaker of the Legislative Assembly or the Chairman of the Legislative Council.
Officers of Parliament/State Legislature	**Lok Sabha** • The Speaker and the Deputy Speaker are elected by the House by a simple majority. • The Speaker resigns by writing to the Deputy Speaker and the Deputy Speaker by writing to the Speaker. • The Speaker and the Deputy Speaker may be removed by a resolution passed by an effective majority in the House. • The Speaker/Deputy Speaker shall not preside over a meeting which considers a resolution for their removal but can participate and vote in the first instance as a member. • On dissolution of the Lok Sabha, the Speaker shall not vacate his/her office until immediately before the first meeting of the Lok Sabha after the dissolution. • If both the Speaker and the Deputy Speaker are absent, one of the Chairpersons nominated as per the rules of the Lok Sabha shall act as the Speaker.	**Legislative Assembly** • The Speaker and the Deputy Speaker are elected by the House by a simple majority [Art 178]. • The Speaker resigns by writing to the Deputy Speaker and the Deputy Speaker by writing to the Speaker [Art 179]. • The Speaker and the Deputy Speaker may be removed by a resolution passed by an effective majority in the House [Art 179]. • The Speaker/Deputy Speaker shall not preside over a meeting which considers resolution for their removal but can participate and vote in the first instance as a member [Art 181]. • On dissolution of the Legislative Assembly, the Speaker shall not vacate his/her office until immediately before the first meeting of the Legislative Assembly after the dissolution [Art 179]. • If both the Speaker and the Deputy Speaker are absent, one of the Chairpersons nominated as per rules of the Legislative Assembly shall act as the Speaker [Art 180].

Particulars	Union Provisions w.r.t. Parliament	Similar Provisions for State w.r.t. State Legislature
	• If both the Speaker and the Deputy Speaker posts are vacant, their duties are performed by such member as the President may appoint. • Pro-tem speaker is appointed by the President whenever a new Lok Sabha is constituted till the Speaker is elected by the House. **Rajya Sabha** • The Vice-President of India is the ex officio Chairman of the Rajya Sabha and the Deputy Chairman is elected by the House from amongst its members. • The provisions with respect to the Chairman and the Deputy Chairman are discussed in Section 10.5.1.2.	• If both the Speaker and the Deputy Speaker posts are vacant, their duties are performed by such member as the Governor may appoint [Art 180]. • Pro-tem speaker is appointed by the Governor whenever a new Legislative Assembly is constituted till the Speaker is elected by the House. **Legislative Council** • The Chairman and the Deputy Chairman of a Legislative Council are both members of the Council. • Articles 182 to 185 contain provisions with respect to the Chairman and the Deputy Chairman of the Legislative Council. • These provisions are similar to the provisions for the Speaker and the Deputy Speaker of the Legislative Assembly as discussed above.
Conduct of Business	• Every member of either House of the Parliament shall, before taking his/her seat, make and subscribe before the President, or some person appointed in that behalf by him/her, an oath or affirmation according to the form set out for the purpose in the Third Schedule. • Save as otherwise provided in the Constitution, all questions at any sitting of either House of the Parliament or a Joint sitting shall be decided by a simple majority. The Speaker or the Chairman shall not vote in the first instance but shall exercise a casting vote in the case of equality of votes. • The quorum to constitute a meeting of either House of the Parliament shall be one-tenth of the total membership of that House. • Language for transacting business in Parliament is Hindi or English. English was to be discontinued at the end of fifteen years from the commencement of the Constitution (1965), but it has been allowed to continue indefinitely	• Every member of the Legislative Assembly or the Legislative Council of a State shall, before taking his/her seat, make and subscribe before the Governor, or some person appointed in that behalf by him/her, an oath or affirmation according to the form set out for the purpose in the Third Schedule [Art 188]. • Save as otherwise provided in the Constitution, all questions at any sitting of a House of the Legislature of State shall be decided by simple majority. The Speaker or the Chairman shall not vote in the first instance but shall exercise a casting vote in the case of equality of votes [Art 189]. • The quorum to constitute a meeting of a House of Legislature of a State shall be one-tenth of the total membership of that House [Art 189]. • Language for transacting business in a State legislature is the official language(s) of the State or Hindi or English. English was to be discontinued at the end of fifteen years from the

Particulars	Union Provisions w.r.t. Parliament	Similar Provisions for State w.r.t. State Legislature
	along with Hindi under the Official Languages Act, 1963. The Chairman or Speaker may allow a member to address the House in his/her mother-tongue if they cannot adequately express themselves in Hindi or in English.	commencement of the Constitution (1965) (or in the case of Himachal Pradesh, Manipur, Meghalaya and Tripura – at the end of twenty-five years or in the case of Arunachal Pradesh, Goa and Mizoram – at the end of forty years), but the State legislature is authorised to decide whether to continue English even after this period. The Chairman or Speaker may allow a member to address the House in his/her mother-tongue [Art 210].
Legislative Procedure	The Legislative procedure in the Parliament with respect to Ordinary Bills, Money Bills and Financial Bills has been discussed in detail in Section 10.6.	The Legislative procedure in a State Legislature with respect to Ordinary Bills, Money Bills and Financial Bills is similar in many respects to the provisions discussed for the Parliament in Section 10.6. However, there are also limitations on the power of the Legislative Council and there is no requirement of a joint sitting in a State Legislature. The limited legislative power of the Legislative Council is discussed in Section 11.3.3. The key provisions with respect to the Legislative procedure in a State Legislature, that are similar to the Parliament, are summarised below.
Introduction of Bills	• Ordinary Bill and Financial Bill of Category B (or Category II) can be introduced in either the Lok Sabha or the Rajya Sabha. • Money Bill and Financial Bill of Category A (or Category I) can be introduced only in the Lok Sabha.	• Ordinary Bill and Financial Bill of Category B (or Category II) can be introduced in either the Legislative Assembly or the Legislative Council. • Money Bill and Financial Bill of Category A (or Category I) can be introduced only in the Legislative Assembly [Art 196, 198, 207].
Lapse of Bills	• A Bill does not lapse by reason of prorogation of the Houses of Parliament. • A Bill pending in the Council of States which has not been passed by the House of the People shall not lapse on a dissolution of the House of the People.	• A Bill pending in the Legislature of a State shall not lapse by reason of prorogation of the House or Houses thereof. • A Bill pending in the Legislative Council of a State which has not been passed by the Legislative Assembly shall not lapse on a dissolution of the Assembly.

Particulars	Union Provisions w.r.t. Parliament	Similar Provisions for State w.r.t. State Legislature
	• A Bill which is pending in the House of the People, or which having been passed by the House of the People is pending in the Council of States, shall, subject to the provisions of Article 108 (with respect to join sitting), lapse on a dissolution of the House of the People. • A Bill passed by both the Houses and pending with the President for his/her assent does not lapse on dissolution of the Lok Sabha.	• A Bill which is pending in the Legislative Assembly of a State, or which having been passed by the Legislative Assembly is pending in the Legislative Council, shall lapse on a dissolution of the Assembly [Art 196]. • A Bill passed by the House or Houses of a State Legislature and pending with the Governor for his/her assent does not lapse on dissolution of the Legislative Assembly.
Passage of Bills	• A Bill introduced in either House of the Parliament passes through the following stages: ♦ First Reading – Introduction – Reference to Standing Committee ♦ Second Reading – Consideration – Reference to Select Committee ♦ Third Reading – Passage – Final passing of the bill. • In the other House also, the bill passes through the above stages except introduction. • A Bill is deemed to have been passed by the Houses of Parliament if it has been agreed to by both Houses, either without amendment or with such amendments only as are agreed to by both Houses.	• A Bill introduced in a House of a State Legislature passes through the following stages: ♦ First Reading – Introduction – Reference to Standing Committee ♦ Second Reading – Consideration – Reference to Select Committee ♦ Third Reading – Passage – Final passing of the bill. • In a State with two Houses the bill passes through the above stages in the other House also, except introduction. • A Bill is deemed to have been passed by the Houses of State Legislature in a State with Legislative Council, if it has been agreed to by both Houses, either without amendment or with such amendments only as are agreed to by both Houses [Art 196].
Joint Sitting	• If there is a deadlock between the two Houses in passage of Ordinary or Financial Bills, it may be resolved through the mechanism of joint sitting of two Houses.	• There is restriction on powers of the Legislative Council with respect to passage of Ordinary or Financial Bills. The Legislative Assembly is the final authority as far as bills in the State Legislature are concerned and there is no requirement for joint sitting. The limited legislative power of the Legislative Council is discussed in Section 11.3.3.
Special Procedure for Money Bills	• A Money Bill can be introduced only in the Lok Sabha. The President has to recommend introduction of a Money Bill.	• A Money Bill can be introduced only in the Legislative Assembly. The Governor has to recommend introduction of a Money Bill.

Particulars	Union Provisions w.r.t. Parliament	Similar Provisions for State w.r.t. State Legislature
	• After passage by the Lok Sabha, a Money Bill is transmitted to the Rajya Sabha, which has only 14 days to provide its recommendations on such bill. A Money Bill cannot be amended or rejected by the Rajya Sabha. • The Lok Sabha may accept or reject all or any of the recommendations of the Rajya Sabha with respect to Money Bill. • A Money Bill is certified as such by the Speaker of the Lok Sabha. • The President cannot exercise Suspensive veto on a Money Bill.	• After passage by the Legislative Assembly, a Money Bill is transmitted to the Legislative Council in a State with Legislative Council, which has only 14 days to provide its recommendations on such bill. A Money Bill cannot be amended or rejected by the Legislative Council. • The Legislative Assembly may accept or reject all or any of the recommendations of the Legislative Council with respect to Money Bill [Art 198]. • A Money Bill is certified as such by the Speaker of the Legislative Assembly. • The Governor cannot exercise Suspensive veto on a Money Bill.
Various funds	There is Consolidated Fund of India, Contingency Fund of India and Public Account of India for dealing with the finances of Government of India.	Similarly, in every State, there is a Consolidated Fund of the State, Contingency Fund of the State and Public Account of the State. The provisions as discussed in Section 10.6.4.2 with respect to nature of these accounts and approval by legislature are similar at the State level.
Legislative Control	• There are various mechanisms for legislative control over the executive at the Union level like collective responsibility of the executive to the Lok Sabha, question hour, zero hour, calling attention motion, adjournment motion and no-confidence motion. • Adjournment motion and no-confidence motion can be moved only in the Lok Sabha.	• Similar mechanisms for legislative control over the executive at the State level like collective responsibility of the executive to the Legislative Assembly, question hour, zero hour, calling attention motion, adjournment motion and no-confidence motion. • Similarly, adjournment motion and no-confidence motion can be moved only in the Legislative Assembly.
Privileges	There are privileges for members individually and the House collectively of the Parliament.	There are similar privileges for members individually and the House collectively of the State Legislature [Art 194].
Committees	There are various Parliamentary Committees constituted for assisting the Houses in legislative work and also for legislative control over the executive.	Similar committees are constituted at the State Legislature for assisting the Houses in legislative work and also for legislative control over the executive.

11.3.2 Composition of the Legislative Council

Legislative Council		
Creation and Abolition	**Duration and Membership**	**Election/Nomination of Members**
• The Parliament may by law create or abolish a Legislative Council in a State. • The Parliament may pass such a law, if the Legislative Assembly of the State passes a resolution with special majority for such creation or abolition [Art 169].	• The total number of members in a Legislative Council of a State shall not exceed one-third of the total number of members in the Legislative Assembly subject to a minimum of 40 members [Art 171]. • The Legislative Council is not subject to dissolution, but as nearly as possible one-third of the members shall retire every second year as per provisions of law made by the Parliament [Art 172].	Of the total number of members in the Legislative Council of a State: 1. 1/3rd to be elected by members of local bodies in the State; 2. 1/12th to be elected by graduates for at least 3 years; 3. 1/12th to be elected by teachers for at least 3 years, not lower in standard than that of a secondary school; 4. 1/3rd to be elected by MLAs of the State; 5. 1/6th to be nominated by the Governor.

11.3.2.1 Creation and Abolition of the Legislative Councils

- The Parliament may by law provide for the abolition of the Legislative Council of a State having such a Council or for the creation of such a Council in a State having no such Council, if the Legislative Assembly of the State passes a resolution to that effect by a majority of the total membership of the Assembly and by a majority of not less than two-thirds of the members of the Assembly present and voting (special majority) [Art 169].
- No such law shall be deemed to be an amendment of the Constitution for the purposes of Article 368.
- Under the Government of India Act, 1935 the provinces of Madras (present-day Tamil Nadu, Karnataka and Andhra Pradesh), Bombay (present-day Maharashtra and Gujarat), Bengal (present-day West Bengal), the United Provinces (present-day Uttar Pradesh), Bihar and Assam had Legislative Councils.
- Our Constitution, while retaining many of the provisions relating to the Legislative Council, has also provided for their creation or abolition as per procedure given above.
- The Legislative Councils of various States that were functional were later abolished in subsequent years as indicated against them: (a) West Bengal – 1969, (b) Tamil Nadu – 1986, (c) Punjab – 1969, (d) Assam – 1969, (e) Madhya Pradesh – 1969 and (f) Uttarakhand – 2002.
- The Andhra Pradesh Legislative Council was abolished in 1985 and it was again created through an Act of Parliament in 2007.

11.3.2.2 Duration and Membership of the Legislative Councils

- Like the Rajya Sabha the Legislative Council is a continuing chamber and is not subject to dissolution.
- The total number of members in a Legislative Council of a State shall not exceed one-third of the total number of members in the Legislative Assembly subject to a minimum of 40 members.

- One-third of its members retire every second year. The vacant seats are filled up by fresh elections.

11.3.2.3 Election and Nomination of the Members

(a) as nearly as may be, 1/3rd shall be elected by members of municipalities, district boards and local authorities in the State;

(b) as nearly as may be, 1/12th shall be elected by persons residing in the State who have been graduates for at least 3 years;

(c) as nearly as may be, 1/12th shall be elected by persons who have been teachers for at least 3 years, not lower in standard than that of a secondary school;

(d) as nearly as may be, 1/3rd shall be elected by MLAs of the State from amongst persons who are not members of the Assembly;

(e) the remainder 1/6th shall be nominated by the Governor consisting of persons having special knowledge or practical experience in literature, art, science, cooperative movement and social service.

The members to be elected under (a), (b) and (c) above shall be chosen from territorial constituencies. The allocation of these seats is provided in the Third Schedule to the Representation of the People Act, 1950. The elections for members to be elected under (a), (b), (c) and (d) above shall be held in accordance with the system of proportional representation by means of the single transferable vote.

11.3.3 Restriction on Powers of the Legislative Council

The procedure for Money Bills in a State Legislature is similar to the procedure in the Parliament. However, in respect of all other types of ordinary and financial bills, there is limited power for a Legislative Council.

Article 197 provides the procedure with respect to Bills (Ordinary and Financial Bills) in a State Legislature other than Money Bills as follows:

- If after a Bill has been passed by the Legislative Assembly of a State having a Legislative Council and transmitted to the Legislative Council –

  (a) The Bill is rejected by the Council; or

  (b) More than 3 months elapse from the date on which the Bill is laid before the Council without the Bill being passed by it; or

  (c) The Bill is passed by the Council with amendments to which the Legislative Assembly does not agree;

  the Legislative Assembly may, pass the Bill again in the same or in any subsequent session with or without such amendments, if any, as have been made, suggested or agreed to by the Legislative Council and then transmit the Bill as so passed to the Legislative Council.

- If after being so passed for the second time by the Legislative Assembly and transmitted to the Legislative Council

  (a) The Bill is rejected by the Council; or

  (b) More than 1-month elapses from the date on which the Bill is laid before the Council without the Bill being passed by it; or

(c) The Bill is passed by the Council with amendments to which the Legislative Assembly does not agree;

the Bill shall be deemed to have been passed by the Houses of the Legislature of the State in the form in which it was passed by the Legislative Assembly for the second time with such amendments, if any, as have been made or suggested by the Legislative Council and agreed to by the Legislative Assembly.

- Therefore, it is clear that there is no provision for joint sitting in a State Legislature with Legislative Council. The Legislative Council can delay the passage of a Bill by 4 months (3 months for the first time + 1 month for the second time).

Certain other points with respect to Legislative Council

- The ministers in the State council of ministers including the Chief Minister can either be from Legislative Assembly or Legislative Council.
- In States with legislative council, the reports of constitutional bodies like State Finance Commission, State Public Service Commission, CAG, etc. are laid before the legislative council also.

> **THINK ABOUT IT**
>
> Discuss the utility of Legislative Councils in legislative business of State legislatures. Is it time to abolish them from existing States or create them in all States?

- An ordinary bill introduced and passed in the legislative council, when transmitted to the legislative assembly and rejected by the assembly, results in the end of the bill without any further action.
- The legislative council members do not participate in the election of the President or members of Rajya Sabha.
- The legislative council has a limited role in the ratification of constitutional amendment bills that need ratification of the State legislatures. In respect of such bills too, the will of the legislative assembly shall prevail just like other ordinary bills.

11.3.4 Utility of Legislative Councils

- The Legislative Councils are supposed to perform the function of a 'wise' chamber considering the fact that its members are elected by members of local authorities, graduates, teachers and MLAs.
- They can act as a 'check and balance' on the Legislative Assembly and provide valuable inputs during the law-making process.
- But as can be seen from the above discussion, the Legislative Councils can be created or abolished by a Parliamentary law after a resolution is passed with a special majority by the Legislative Assembly of a State. The abolition or creation in the past has been primarily for political reasons.
- Further, unlike the Rajya Sabha, the Legislative Council has restrictions on its powers and can only delay any legislation by 4 months.

> Scan the QR code for conceptual video on State Legislature
>
> McGraw Hill edge

- The 2nd Administrative Reforms Commission had suggested that the Legislative Councils be formed in all the States. However, it has also suggested that the proportion of members who are elected by local body representatives be increased (from present 1/3rd) in order to make the Legislative Councils a representative of local body requirements in the State Legislature.

MNEMONICS

Concept or Provisions	Shortcut or Mnemonics	Details to Remember
Creation/Abolition of Legislative Council and maximum membership	2/3rd and Simple majority; 1/3rd or Forty	**Creation or Abolition** • **2/3rd** – Special majority resolution in State Legislative Assembly and • **Simple majority** law to be passed in Parliament **Membership** • Maximum **1/3rd** of total number of members in the State legislative assembly subject to a minimum of **Forty**
State Legislature – Article numbers for important provisions similar to Union Parliament	Add 89 to Article number for Parliament for some important articles till Article 111 & Add 90 after that for some important Articles	**83+89 = 172** – Duration of State legislatures 84+89 = 173 – Qualification for membership 85+89 = 174 – Sessions of State legislature, Prorogation & dissolution. 88+89 = 177 – Rights of Ministers and Advocate General as respects the Houses 102+89 = 191 – Disqualification of membership 105+89 = 194 – Privileges of members of State legislature 109+89 = 198 – Special procedure for Money Bills 110+89 = 199 – Definition of Money Bills 111+89 = 200 – Assent to Bills 112+90 = 202 – Annual Financial statement 117+90 = 217 – Special provisions as to financial bills 121+90 = 211 – Restriction on discussion in State legislature about conduct of a judge 122+90 = 212 – Courts not to inquire into proceedings of State legislature 123+90 = 213 – Ordinance power of Governor
Similarities between Parliament and State Legislature	Many provisions similar – For example – Census for delimitation purposes, Disqualification of members, Election and removal of officers of State legislature, Lapse of Bills, Procedure for Money Bills.	• Replace President with Governor • Replace Lok Sabha with Legislative Assembly • Replace Rajya Sabha with Legislative Council (in States where there is a Legislative Council)

MAINS STARTER

Area	Building Blocks For Model Introductions
Legislative Council	The Parliament by ordinary law may create or abolish Legislative Council in a State, if the Legislative Assembly of the State passes a resolution to such effect by a Special majority (Art 169).
Utility of Legislative councils	Legislative Councils are supposed to act as a 'wise' chamber to complement the popularly elected Legislative Assemblies. However, the creation or abolition of legislative councils has been primarily driven by political considerations in the past. Further, it has limited legislative powers unlike the Rajya Sabha at the centre.
Presiding officers of State legislatures	The Speaker of the assembly and the Chairman of the council are the presiding officers of State legislatures. They perform an important function of maintaining order and impartiality while conducting legislative business that upholds democratic principles.
Some similar areas with Union Parliament	If various areas like composition, functioning of the legislature; special procedure for Money Bill; expenditure charged on the consolidated fund; privileges, etc. are asked from a State legislature perspective, the same introductions that have been provided in Union Parliament chapter can be used by replacing President with Governor; Lok Sabha with Legislative Assembly; Rajya Sabha with Legislative Council where appropriate.

UPSC PREVIOUS YEARS' QUESTIONS OF PRELIMINARY EXAMINATION

1. With reference to the Legislative Assembly of a State in India, consider the following statements. **[2019]**
   1. The Governor makes a customary address to members at the commencement of the first session of the year.
   2. When a State Legislature does not have a rule on a particular matter, it follows the Lok Sabha rule on that matter.

Which of the statements given above is/are correct?

(a) 1 only (b) 2 only (c) Both 1 and 2 (d) Neither 1 nor 2

Solution: (c)

Explanation: As per Article 176(1), the Governor addresses the House(s) of the State Legislature at the first session of each year. Hence, statement (1) is correct. As per convention, where there is no rule on a particular matter in the State legislature, it follows the Lok Sabha rule on such matter. Hence, the second statement is also correct and the answer is (c).

UPSC Previous Years' Questions of Main Examination

1. Discuss the role of Presiding Officers of State legislatures in maintaining order and impartiality in conducting legislative work and in facilitating best democratic practices. **[2023]**

Likely context: The delay by the speaker of Maharashtra in deciding various disqualification petitions filed by the opposition parties in that State assembly was a contentious issue that was heard by the Supreme Court on multiple occasions during 2023. This could have been the likely trigger for the question.

Approach: Summarise the role of presiding officers in the introduction. Then discuss the issues and way forward. The content for this is as discussed under relevant sections in Chapter 10 – Union Parliament (as the provisions and case laws are similar for both centre and States considering our federal set-up).

MODEL ANSWER

As per Part VI of the Constitution, the Speaker/Deputy Speaker of the assembly and Chairman/Deputy Chairman of the council are the presiding officers of State legislatures.

Role of Presiding officers of State Legislatures

(a) The presiding officers have powers to expel members for unruly behaviour, and adjourn the proceedings in case of disruptions.

(b) The Speaker of Legislative Assembly certifies a bill to be a Money Bill. (Art 199)

(c) It is the presiding officers who decide on Tenth Schedule disqualification.

Issues and Way Forward

It has been observed that the Presiding Officers, especially the Speaker of the Legislative Assembly, act in a partisan manner that favours the ruling party when it comes to conducting the business of the House as well as disqualification proceedings against any members. This has also been recently seen in the way the Maharashtra Assembly Speaker has not decided on disqualification petitions despite Supreme Court directives.

The Maharashtra assembly had also recently passed a resolution suspending some of its members for a period of one year which was struck down by the Supreme Court as unconstitutional and undemocratic.

The Supreme Court in K M Singh Vs Speaker of Manipur case had urged the Parliament to amend the Tenth Schedule to vest the power of deciding on disqualification petitions in an independent Tribunal.

The practice in UK House of Commons with respect to the post of Speaker may be introduced in Indian legislatures as well to maintain independence. At least the presiding officers should resign from their political parties on getting elected to that post, which is allowed as per the Tenth Schedule, to display impartiality.

2. Explain the constitutional provisions under which the Legislative Councils are established. Review the working and current status of the Legislative Councils with suitable illustrations. **[2021]**

Approach: The provisions relating to creation or abolition of the Legislative Councils as discussed in Section 11.3.2.1 needs to be first discussed. Then the limited powers of these councils as discussed in Section 11.3.3 and the points relating to utility of councils as discussed in 11.3.4 needs to be summarised.

MODEL ANSWER

Creation or abolition of the Legislative Council (Art. 169)

- As per the Constitution, the Parliament may by law provide for the abolition of the Legislative Council of a State having such a Council or for the creation of such a Council in a State having no such Council by an ordinary law.
- However, before the Parliament can pass such a law, the Legislative Assembly of the State should pass a resolution, for creation or abolition as the case may be, by a majority of the total membership of the Assembly and by a majority of not less than two-thirds of the members of the Assembly present and voting.
- Thus, it is the Parliament that has the final say in creation or abolition of a council in a state.

Limited powers of Legislative Council (Art. 197)

- If a bill passed by the Legislative Assembly is rejected or amended or kept pending for 3 months by the Council, the Assembly can once again pass the same bill or pass the bill with amendments that it is agreeing to. If again the bill is rejected or amended or kept pending for 1 month by the Council, the bill is deemed to have been passed by both the Houses as passed by the Assembly for the second time.
- Therefore, it is clear that there is no provision for joint sitting in a State Legislature with Legislative Council. The Legislative Council can delay the passage of a Bill by 4 months (3 months for the first time + 1 month for the second time).

Working and utility of Legislative Councils

- The Legislative Councils are supposed to perform the function of a 'wise' chamber considering the fact that its members are elected by members of local authorities, graduates, teachers and MLAs.

- However, the Legislative Councils can be created or abolished by the Parliamentary law after a resolution is passed with a special majority by the Legislative Assembly of a State. The abolition or creation in the past has been primarily for political reasons. For example, in the State of Andhra Pradesh, the Council was abolished in 1985 to be created again in 2007 for political reasons. The Andhra Pradesh Assembly has again passed a resolution recently for abolition of the Council for political reasons. Similarly, there are States like Tamil Nadu where the Council has been abolished in the past that are now seeking to create the same again.
- Further, unlike the Rajya Sabha, the Legislative Council has restrictions on its powers and can only delay any legislation by 4 months.
- The 2nd Administrative Reforms Commission had suggested that the Legislative Councils be formed in all the States. However, it has also suggested that the proportion of members who are elected by local body representatives be increased (from present 1/3rd) in order to make the Legislative Councils a representative of local body requirements in the State Legislature.

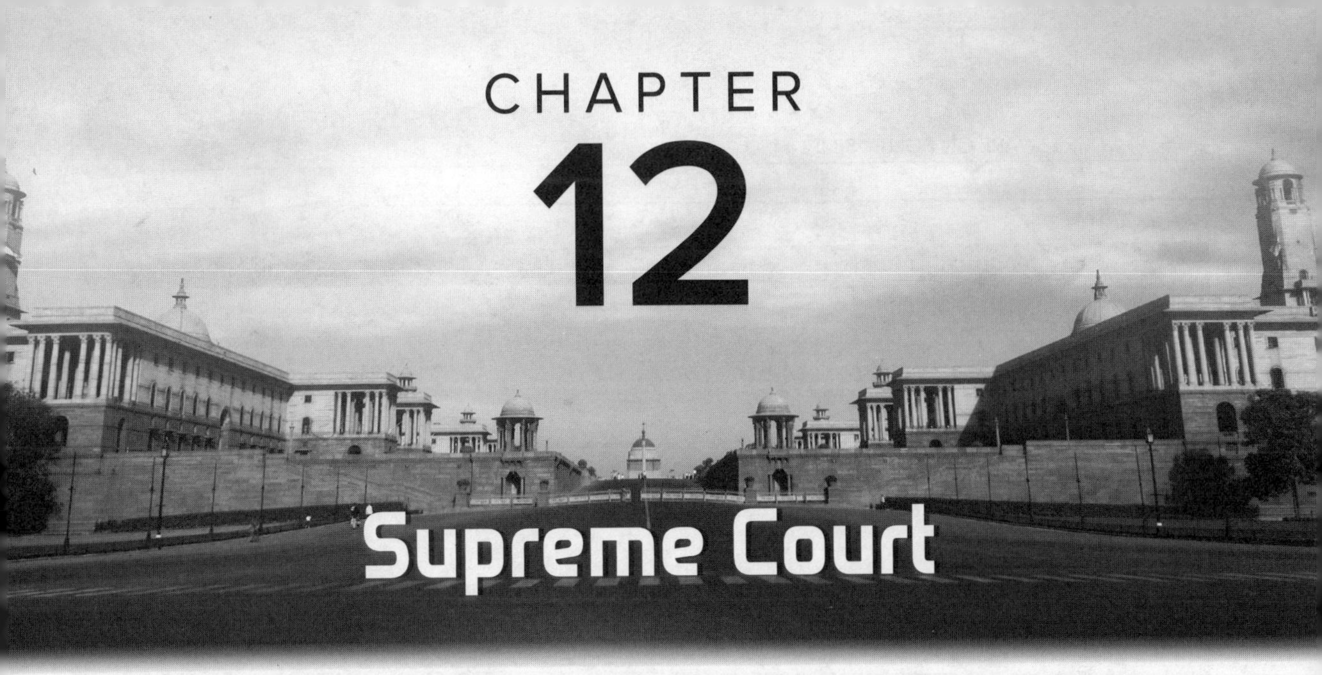

CHAPTER 12

Supreme Court

LEARNING OUTCOMES

1. Understanding the composition, qualification and tenure of Supreme Court Judges
2. Analysing the appointment process of judges and examining key case laws that led to the collegium system
3. Exploring the procedure for the removal of Supreme Court judges
4. Evaluating the constitutional safeguards ensuring the independence of the Supreme Court
5. Understanding the various jurisdictions of the Supreme Court
6. Assessing the role of the Supreme Court as the custodian of the Constitution
7. Examining the concept of judicial activism and its importance
8. Identifying the need for judicial reforms, including the establishment of an All-India Judicial Service (AIJS)

12.1 INTRODUCTION TO THE JUDICIARY

The Indian Judicial System is one of the oldest legal systems in the world. It is a part of the inheritance India received from the British after more than 200 years of their colonial rule. The same is evident from the many similarities the Indian legal system shares with the English legal system. The Constitution of India is the supreme law of the country, and has laid the framework for the Indian judicial system. Despite India adopting the features of a federal system of government like the United States, the Constitution of India has provided for the setting up of a single integrated system of the courts to administer both the Union and the State laws.

The Supreme Court is the apex court of India, followed by the various High Courts at the State level, which cater to one or more number of States. Below the High Courts exist the Subordinate Courts comprising the District Courts at the district level and the other lower courts.

Chapter IV of Part V of the Constitution deals with the Union Judiciary. It consists of Articles 124 to 147. The key provisions of the Union Judiciary i.e., the Supreme Court is as follows.

Supreme Court		
Composition	**Appointment and Removal**	**Functioning**
• Composition of the Supreme Court • Qualification for being a Judge of the Supreme Court • Conditions of office of the Supreme Court Judges	• Appointment of Judges • Removal of Judges	• Independence of the Judiciary • Jurisdiction of the Supreme Court • Supreme Court as custodian of the Constitution

12.2 COMPOSITION OF THE SUPREME COURT

12.2.1 Composition

There shall be a Supreme Court of India consisting of a Chief Justice of India and, until the Parliament by law prescribes a larger number, of not more than seven other Judges [Art 124]. Presently, as per the Supreme Court (the Number of Judges) Act of 2019, there are 34 Judges including the Chief Justice of India. The number of judges has been increased to 33 as per the recent amendment to the Supreme Court (the Number of Judges) Act in 2019.

The Supreme Court shall sit in Delhi or in such other place or places as the Chief Justice of India may, with the approval of the President from time to time appoint [Art 130].

Presently, there are no benches of the Supreme Court as on date and it sits only in Delhi. In order to reduce the pendency of cases in the Supreme Court (which stands at around 83,000 as of January 2025), there have been demands for setting up regional benches of the Court. The Parliamentary Standing Committees had recommended setting up of such regional benches in 2004, 2005, 2006 and 2008. The Law Commission in its report in 2009 had recommended four regional benches in four regions to deal with the appellate work arising out of the orders and judgements of the High Courts of the particular region. This can help in easy access to justice for the citizens and also faster disposal of cases. However, the Supreme Court has consistently held an opinion against setting up of benches in order to ensure no dilution of control. The Supreme Court could explore establishing regional benches to address the rising backlog of cases. Initially, a bench could be set up in one region, with the possibility of expansion to other regions based on a review of its effectiveness.

> **THINK ABOUT IT**
>
> What is the procedure for constituting benches of the Supreme Court? Critically evaluate its pros and cons.

The Supreme Court shall be a court of record and shall have all the powers of such a court including the power to punish for the contempt of the Court [Art 129].

12.2.2 Qualification for a Supreme Court Judge

As per Article 124(3), a person shall be qualified for appointment as a Judge of the Supreme Court if he/she fulfils the following conditions:

1. He/she is a citizen of India and,
2. Has been for at least 5 years a Judge of a High Court or of two or more such courts in succession; or
3. Has been for at least 10 years an advocate of a High Court or of two or more such courts in succession; or
4. Is, in the opinion of the President, a distinguished jurist.

12.2.3 Conditions of Office

Every Judge of the Supreme Court shall be appointed by the President by warrant under his/her hand and seal, after consultation with such Judges of the Supreme Court and of the High Courts in the States as the President may deem necessary for the purpose, and shall hold office until he/she attains the age of 65 years [Art 124]. In the case of appointment of a Judge other than the Chief Justice, the Chief Justice of India shall always be consulted.

Provided further that –

(a) A Judge may, by writing under his/her hand addressed to the President, resign his/her office;

(b) A Judge may be removed from his/her office in the manner provided in the Constitution.

Every person appointed to be a Judge of the Supreme Court shall, before he/she enters upon his/her office, make and subscribe before the President, or some person appointed in that behalf by him/her, an oath or affirmation according to the form set out for the purpose in the Third Schedule. A Judge takes an oath to bear true faith and allegiance to the Constitution; to uphold the sovereignty and integrity of India; to perform his/her duties to the best of his/her ability without fear or favour and affection or ill-will; and to uphold the Constitution and laws.

There shall be paid to the Judges of the Supreme Court such salaries as may be determined by the Parliament by law [Art 125]. As per The Supreme Court Judges (Salaries and Conditions of Service) Act, 1958 (as amended in 2018), the Chief Justice of India draws a salary of ₹2,80,000 per month and other judges ₹2,50,000 per month.

It may be noted that the Constitution neither provides for minimum age as a condition for qualification of Judges of the Supreme Court nor a fixed number of years of office (like 6 years for constitutional authorities like CAG, Election Commissioners or UPSC members). They serve from the date of their appointment till they attain the age of 65 years.

12.3 APPOINTMENT OF JUDGES

As per Article 124(2) of the Constitution every Judge of the Supreme Court shall be:

(a) appointed by the President by warrant under his/her hand and seal;

(b) after consultation with such Judges of the Supreme Court and of the High Courts in the States as the President may deem necessary for the purpose;

(c) and shall hold office until he/she attains the age of 65 years.

Provided that in the case of appointment of a Judge other than the Chief Justice, the Chief Justice of India shall always be consulted.

The procedure for appointment of judges has been subject to various cases before the Supreme Court.

12.3.1 Cases related to Appointment of Judges

12.3.1.1 First Judges Case

The majority view in the *S. P. Gupta case (famously known as the 1st Judges Case – 1981)* was that the executive should have primacy in the matter of appointment of judges, since it is accountable to the people while the judiciary has no such accountability.

12.3.1.2 Second Judges Case

In *Advocates on Record Versus Union of India 1993 case (famously known as the 2nd Judges case)*, the Supreme Court ruled that in matters relating to appointments in the Supreme Court, the opinion given by the Chief Justice of India in the consultative process has to be formed taking into account the views of the two seniormost judges of the Supreme Court. Thus, the 2nd Judges case interpreted the word 'consultation' to mean 'concurrence' and laid down the 'Collegium' process for appointment of the judges.

The other key points from the judgement of the 2nd Judges case are as follows:

- Initiation of the proposal for appointment in the case of the Supreme Court must be by the Chief Justice of India, and in the case of a High Court by the Chief Justice of that High Court; and for transfer of a Judge/Chief Justice of a High Court, the proposal has to be initiated by the Chief Justice of India.
- In the event of conflicting opinions between the constitutional functionaries i.e., the executive and the judiciary, the opinion of the judiciary symbolised by the view of the Chief Justice of India and formed in the manner indicated, has primacy.
- If a recommended candidate is not appointed on the grounds of unsuitability, the reasons must be communicated to the Chief Justice of India (CJI), allowing for reconsideration and possible withdrawal of the recommendation. However, if the CJI, after due consideration and with the unanimous agreement of the Supreme Court judges consulted, reiterates the recommendation, the appointment should be made as a matter of healthy convention.
- Appointment to the office of the Chief Justice of India should be of the seniormost Judge of the Supreme Court considered fit to hold the office.

12.3.1.3 Third Judges Case

The *3rd Judges case of 1998* is not a case but an opinion delivered by the Supreme Court of India, responding to a Presidential reference (under Article 143) on a question of law regarding the Collegium system, raised by then President of India K. R. Narayanan, in July 1998.

It upheld its view in the 2nd Judges case and increased the Collegium from CJI and 2 seniormost judges to CJI and 4 seniormost judges of Supreme Court to be consulted for the appointment of the Supreme Court judges. Usually, one of the 4 seniormost judges would succeed the CJI to be the next CJI. However, if that is not the case, the judge who is likely to be the next CJI would also be part of the Collegium. With respect to appointment of Judges of High Courts, the Collegium consists of CJI and 2 seniormost judges.

The other key points from the opinion of the 3rd Judges case are as follows:

- The recommendation of the Collegium should be based on the consensus – If CJI dissents or 2 out of 4 Judges dissent, the recommendation should not be persisted with.
- In case of non-appointment of a person recommended, the material and information conveyed by the Government of India must be placed before the Collegium. If after reconsideration, the name is unanimously reiterated by the Collegium, then that appointment must be made as a matter of 'healthy convention'. (This is reiteration of the judgement in Second Judges case).
- Merit is the main consideration, though seniority will also be given weightage.
- The High Courts not represented in the Supreme Court may also be considered while selecting between the judges who are otherwise equal in merit.

A detailed Memorandum of Procedure was finalised based on the above by the Law Ministry for appointments to the higher judiciary.

SUMMARY OF CASE LAWS RELATING TO APPOINTMENT OF JUDGES

Case Laws	Judicial Pronouncements
1st Judges case	Primacy of the executive was established.
2nd Judges case	Collegium system was created and primacy of the judiciary was established.
3rd Judges case	Reaffirmed the Collegium system by expanding the same.

The Collegium system had ensured independence of the judiciary from the executive, in the matter of appointments. However, it has its own drawbacks like lack of transparency and accountability. There is also resentment on account of alleged nepotism in this process whereby kith and kin of sitting judges are favoured for appointment to higher judiciary.

In order to overcome the shortcomings of the Collegium system, the Parliament amended the Constitution through the 99th Constitutional amendment to create the National Judicial Appointments Commission.

12.3.1.4 National Judicial Appointments Commission

National Judicial Appointments Commission (NJAC) was a proposed body which would have been responsible for making recommendations for the appointment and transfer of judges in the higher judiciary in India.

The Commission was established by amending the Constitution of India through the Constitution (99th Amendment) Act, 2014. The NJAC would have replaced the Collegium system for the appointment of judges. Along with the Constitution Amendment Act, the National Judicial Appointments Commission Act, 2014, was also passed by the Parliament of India to regulate the functions of the National Judicial Appointments Commission.

> **THINK ABOUT IT**
>
> The collegium system was introduced to protect the independence in judicial appointments. However, it is plagued with lack of transparency at present. Critically analyse the need to reform the collegium system. Should the National Judicial Appointments Commission be revived by the Parliament?

Composition

As per the amended provisions of the Constitution, the NJAC would have consisted of the following six persons:

- The Chief Justice of India as *ex-officio* Chairperson;
- Two other senior judges of the Supreme Court next to the Chief Justice of India as *ex-officio* members;
- The Union Minister of Law and Justice, ex-officio member;
- Two eminent persons to be nominated by a committee consisting of the Chief Justice of India, the Prime Minister of India and the Leader of Opposition in the Lok Sabha.

Functions of the Commission

The functions of the Commission would have included the following:

(a) Recommending persons for appointment as the Chief Justice of India, the Judges of the Supreme Court, the Chief Justices of High Courts and other Judges of High Courts.

(b) Recommending transfer of the Chief Justices and other Judges of the High Courts from one High Court to any other High Court.

However, the Supreme Court in 2015 in ***Advocates on Record Vs Union of India (now famously known as the 4th Judges case)***, struck down the 99th Constitutional Amendment Act and National Judicial Appointments Commission Act, 2014 as unconstitutional on the ground that it violates the basic structure of independence of the judiciary. The Supreme Court also acknowledged that the current Collegium process requires strengthening to ensure transparency. However, the revised Memorandum of Procedure is yet to be finally approved (as of 2024) and the process as per the existing Memorandum of Procedure continues to be followed.

12.3.2 Way Forward

Scan the QR code for conceptual video on appointment of judges

Mc Graw Hill edge

Procedure for appointment of the Judges is an important aspect for ensuring independence of the judiciary. The present Collegium system may ensure complete independence from the executive in the matter of appointments. However, the Collegium process lacks transparency and has also resulted in nepotism and favouritism in appointments. In January 2025, the Supreme Court collegium had stated that it is considering a proposal to discontinue recommending the relatives of sitting or former judges for High Court appointments. While this initiative could create more opportunities for first-generation lawyers, it also raises concerns about the potential unfair exclusion of qualified candidates solely due to their familial connections.

The way forward may be to expand the membership of a Commission like NJAC to include various stake holders like the Members of Parliament, the representatives of Lawyers etc. The CJI and other senior Judges of the Supreme Court may also be provided with a veto to have their final say in any appointment. This will make the selection process more broad-based and inclusive without compromising on independence. However, till such time there is a consensus on this aspect, the revised Memorandum of Procedure for strengthening the Collegium system should be finalised and implemented.

12.3.3 Ad hoc and Retired Judges

- When the office of the Chief Justice of India is vacant, or when the Chief Justice is unable to perform his/her duties, the President may appoint any of the other Judges as the acting Chief Justice [Art 126].
- If at any time the quorum of Judges of the Supreme Court to hold or continue any session of the Court shall not be available, the Chief Justice of India may with the previous consent of the President and after consultation with the Chief Justice of the High Court concerned, request the attendance of a Judge of a High Court, who is duly qualified for appointment as a Judge of the Supreme Court, as an ad hoc Judge for such period as may be necessary [Art 127].
- The Chief Justice of India may at any time, with the previous consent of the President, request any person who has held the office of the Judge of the Supreme Court or has held the office of the Judge of a High Court and duly qualified for appointment as a Judge of the Supreme Court, to sit and act as a Judge of the Supreme Court [Art 128].

12.4 REMOVAL OF JUDGES

12.4.1 Constitutional Provisions

- A Judge of the Supreme Court shall not be removed from his/her office except by an order of the President passed after an address by each House of the Parliament supported by a majority of the total membership of that House and by a majority of not less than two thirds of the members of that House present and voting (special majority);
- and has been presented to the President in the same session for such removal on the ground of proved misbehaviour or incapacity [Art 124(4)].

Example of calculation of 'Special majority' for removal of judges

Let us take the Rajya Sabha, for example. The total membership of the Rajya Sabha is 245 and hence majority of the total membership of the House is 123. However, for 'special majority' specified for removal of judges, the number of members voting for the resolution should be minimum 123 but should also be not less than two-thirds of members present and voting. In simple words, it is majority of the total membership (123) or two-thirds of members present and voting (as the case may be) whichever is higher. Let us take three scenarios to understand this:

Scenario	Majority of Total Membership (A)	No of Members Present and Voting	2/3rd of Members Present and Voting (B)	Majority required – (A) or (B) whichever is Higher
I	123	240	160	160
II	123	210	140	140
III	123	180	120	123

The same method will be applied in the Lok Sabha as well for calculating special majority for that house.

The Constitution does not define the terms 'proved misbehaviour' or 'incapacity'. The Supreme Court has opined in various cases that wilful misconduct in office, corruption, lack of integrity or any other offence involving moral turpitude (an immoral crime that gravely violates the sentiment or accepted standard of the community) would constitute misbehaviour. Incapacity is a medical condition that may include physical or mental incapacity.

Parliament may by law regulate the procedure for the presentation of an address and for the investigation and proof of the misbehaviour or incapacity of a Judge [Art 124(5)].

12.4.2 Procedure for Removal of Judges

The detailed procedure for removal of a Judge is provided under the Judges (Inquiry) Act, 1968.

- A notice of a motion for the removal of a Judge, if given in the Rajya Sabha, is to be signed by not less than 50 members and, if given in the Lok Sabha, by not less than 100 members of that House.
- The Chairman or the Speaker, as the case may be, after due consideration and consultation, may admit or refuse to admit the motion.
- If the motion is admitted, the Chairman or the Speaker, as the case may be, will constitute a committee of three members, one each from (a) The Chief Justice or other Judges of the Supreme Court, (b) the Chief Justices of any High Court and (c) Distinguished jurists.

- The Committee will frame definite charges against the Judge on the basis of which investigation is proposed to be held. In a case of alleged physical or mental incapacity and where such an allegation is denied, a Medical Board will be appointed for the medical examination of the Judge.
- At the conclusion of the investigation, the Committee will submit its report to the Chairman or, as the case may be, to the Speaker, stating therein its findings on each of the charges separately with such observations on the whole case as it thinks fit. The report will, thereafter, be laid before the respective House or the Houses, if the Committee has been appointed jointly by the Chairman or the Speaker.
- If the Committee absolves the Judge of any misbehaviour or incapacity, the motion pending in the respective House or Houses, as the case may be, will not be proceeded with.
- If the report of the Committee contains a finding that the Judge is guilty of any misbehaviour or suffers from any incapacity, the motion will, together with the report of the Committee, be taken up for consideration by the House or the Houses in which it is pending.
- In the event of the adoption of the motion in accordance with the constitutional provisions i.e., special majority in both the houses, the misbehaviour or incapacity of the Judge will be deemed to have been proved and an address praying for the removal of the Judge will be presented in the prescribed manner by each House of the Parliament in the same session in which the motion has been adopted.

Removal of Judges

Grounds	Majority	Detailed Procedure
• Proved misbehaviour or incapacity	• Majority of the total membership of the House and majority of not less than 2/3rd of the members present and voting (special majority). • Passed in the same session in both the Houses of the Parliament.	Judges Inquiry Act – 1968 • Rajya Sabha – 50 members; Lok Sabha – 100 members to sign the notice for removal. • Chairman/Speaker may admit or reject. • If admitted, forms a committee for investigating. • If proven, the judge may be removed by the Parliament.

12.4.3 Instances of Removal

There have been 8 instances in the past where impeachment motion has been initiated against Supreme Court/High Court judges [**refer 'Additional data point' on 'edge' for the list**]. However, no Judge has been removed till date (2024) as per the provisions of the Constitution.

Such motions for removal, being constitutional in nature, do not lapse on prorogation of the houses and may be taken up for consideration even in a subsequent session. However, after the inquiry, the motion for removal with special majority needs to be passed in both the houses in the same session.

In-house procedure of the Judiciary

The Supreme Court had laid down the guidelines in 1999 (which was made public by a Supreme Court order in 2014) for conducting in-house inquiry by the judiciary with respect to any complaint received against a Judge of the higher judiciary. The summary of such procedure is as follows:

(a) When a complaint is received against a Judge of a High Court, the CJI will decide whether the issue is frivolous (pointless or silly) or warrants an inquiry. If an inquiry is deemed necessary, the judge's initial response along with comments of the Chief Justice of the High Court concerned are taken on record.

(b) The CJI can then form a 3-member committee – 2 Chief Justices from other High Courts and 1 High Court Judge.

(c) The committee, after an inquiry, can provide a recommendation that the misconduct is serious enough to warrant removal or not serious enough.

(d) If the recommendation is for the Judge's removal, he/she will be asked to resign. If the Judge is not willing to resign, judicial work will be withdrawn from him/her. The President and Prime Minister will be informed of the findings for Parliament to initiate action for removal.

(e) If the recommendation is not for removal, the Judge would be apprised accordingly.

(f) If the complaint is against the Chief Justice of a High Court, then the committee would consist of a Supreme Court Judge and two other Chief Justices of other High Courts. If the complaint is against a Supreme Court Judge, the committee would consist of 3 Supreme Court Judges.

THINK ABOUT IT

Security of tenure is a crucial aspect for ensuring independence of constitutional authorities. In this regard, elaborate on the procedure for removal of judges of higher judiciary in India.

MNEMONICS

Concept or Provisions	Shortcut or Mnemonics	Details to Remember
Removal of Supreme Court Judge	**MISS**	Grounds • Proved **M**isbehaviour or • **I**ncapacity Procedure • **S**pecial Majority in both houses • **S**ame session

12.5 INDEPENDENCE OF THE SUPREME COURT

An independent Judiciary is a vital requirement for a functional democracy.

While the executive is accountable to the legislature and the legislature gets elected by the people every 5 years, it is the Judiciary that upholds the Constitution and Rule of law on a day-to-day basis.

The Judiciary acts as an independent branch that keeps a check and balance on the other two organs. In order to protect the Judiciary from wrongful interference by the executive as well as to ensure the financial independence of the Judges, the Constitution contains various provisions to secure the independence of Judiciary.

Scan the QR code for conceptual video on removal of judges and independence of the Supreme Court

McGraw Hill edge

The following provisions ensure independence of the Supreme Court:

(a) Every Judge of the Supreme Court shall be appointed by the President after consultation with the Judiciary/Chief Justice of India. This was provided for in the Constitution, since the Judiciary will be in a better position to assess the competence of persons to be appointed as the Judges of the Supreme Court. Now, with the Collegium system in place, the independence of the Judiciary with respect to appointments has increased even further [Art 124(2)].

(b) A Judge of the Supreme Court shall be removed from his/her office, on the grounds of proved misbehaviour or incapacity, only by both the Houses of Parliament passing a resolution with special majority in the same session [Art 124(4)].

(c) Every Judge shall be entitled to such privileges and allowances and to such rights in respect of leave of absence and pension as may from time to time be determined by or under law made by the Parliament. Neither the privileges nor the allowances of a Judge nor his/her rights in respect of leave of absence or pension shall be varied to his/her disadvantage after his/her appointment (except during a Financial emergency) [Art 125].

(d) The salaries, allowances and pensions payable to or in respect of Judges of the Supreme Court shall be charged on the Consolidated Fund of India [Art 112(3)].

(e) The administrative expenses of the Supreme Court, including all salaries, allowances and pensions payable to or in respect of the officers and servants of the Court, shall be charged upon the Consolidated Fund of India [Art 146].

(f) Restriction on discussion in Parliament – No discussion shall take place in the Parliament with respect to the conduct of any Judge of the Supreme Court or of a High Court in the discharge of his/her duties except upon a motion for the removal of the Judge [Art 121].

(g) No person who has held office as a Judge of the Supreme Court shall plead or act in any court or before any authority within the territory of India [Art 124(7)]. This restriction is laid because they should not feel obliged during the period of holding the position as a judge to any other potential employers. The other reason is that they may influence their former colleagues in the judiciary if they can appear before them as lawyers.

(h) The officers and servants of the Supreme Court are appointed by the Chief Justice of India or any other Judge or officer whom he/she may direct. The Chief Justice of India also prescribes the conditions of their service [Art 146].

(i) The jurisdiction of the Supreme Court cannot be curtailed by the Parliament. It can only extend it.

MNEMONICS

Concept or Provisions	Shortcut or Mnemonics	Details to Remember
Independence of Judiciary	2C4R	**C**ollegium – Appointment only as per recommendation of Collegium **C**harged on Consolidated Fund – Salaries, allowances, pension of Judges and all expenses of the Court **R**emoval – Only by Parliament **R**ights and privileges – cannot be varied to their disadvantage after appointment **R**estriction on discussion in Parliament – about the conduct of a Judge except when it is a motion for his/her removal **R**estriction – on appearance as a lawyer in any court after ceasing to hold office.

12.6 JURISDICTION OF THE SUPREME COURT

The Supreme Court is the apex court of the country. It has a wide range of jurisdiction or powers as per the Constitution. The various jurisdiction of the Supreme Court can be summarised as follows:

Jurisdictions	Article	Descriptions
1. Original Jurisdiction	131	Between Centre vs State or State vs State
2. Writ Jurisdiction	32	Right to move the Supreme Court for enforcement of Fundamental rights
3. Appellate Jurisdiction	132–134, 136	• Appeal in civil and criminal proceedings against judgements from any High Court • Special leave – Supreme Court in its discretion may allow appeal against any order or a judgement of any court or tribunal.
4. Advisory Jurisdiction	143	Power of the President to consult the Supreme Court
5. Review	137	Power of the Supreme Court to review its own judgements

12.6.1 Original Jurisdiction

- It means exclusive jurisdiction of the Supreme Court.
- Subject to the provisions of the Constitution, the Supreme Court shall, to the exclusion of any other court, have original jurisdiction in any dispute:
  - Between the Government of India and one more States; or
  - Between the Government of India and any State or States on one side and one or more States on the other; or
  - Between two or more States, if and in so far as the dispute involves any question (whether of law or fact) on which the existence or extent of a legal right depends [Art 131].

This jurisdiction covers dispute between (a) Central Government and one or more State Governments or (b) between two or more State Governments. This is to resolve any disputes between the executive at the Union and the State level.

However, any dispute between the Central Government and a Union Territory Government (Delhi, Puducherry and J & K) will be heard by the respective High Courts first. For example, the dispute between NCT of Delhi Government and Central Government in 2015 was first heard in the Delhi High Court.

12.6.1.1 Exceptions to Original Jurisdiction

The following are some important exceptions to the original jurisdiction of the Supreme Court:

- A dispute that arises out of a treaty or an agreement that was entered into before the commencement of the Constitution or which specifically provides that jurisdiction of the Supreme Court shall not apply to such treaty or agreement [Art 131].
- Inter-State River water disputes that are governed by a Parliamentary law [Art 262]. However, the Supreme Court does hear appeals against the orders of River water Tribunals at present.

- Matters referred to the Finance Commission and its recommendations. This view stems from the fact that the Finance Commission's recommendations are advisory in nature and reflect policy decisions made by its experts. They attain legal status only after being accepted by the Union Government and formally enacted through a Presidential order. Consequently, the recommendations themselves cannot be directly challenged in the Supreme Court. However, an alternative view holds that once a Presidential order on revenue devolution is issued, it acquires the force of law, granting legal rights to the States. Therefore, if such an order is found to violate the basic structure of federalism, it may be subject to judicial review.

12.6.2 Writ Jurisdiction

- The right to move the Supreme Court by appropriate proceedings for the enforcement of Fundamental right guaranteed in Part III under Article 32, is known as the Writ Jurisdiction of the Supreme Court.
- The Supreme Court shall have power to issue directions or orders or writs, including writs in the nature of habeas corpus, mandamus, prohibition, quo warranto and certiorari, whichever may be appropriate, for the enforcement of any of the rights conferred in Part III.

12.6.3 Appellate Jurisdiction

The Supreme Court is the highest court of appeal in the country. It hears appeals on civil, criminal and other proceedings from the judgements or orders of a High Court.

Civil matters are related to disputes such as land disputes, marriage and divorce, enforcement of contracts, taxation disputes etc. Criminal matters involve any offence under various criminal laws. Other proceedings may relate to other administrative matters of the Government.

Constitutional Cases

An appeal shall lie to the Supreme Court from any judgement, decree or final order of a High Court in the territory of India, whether in a civil, criminal or other proceeding, if the High Court certifies that the case involves a substantial question of law as to the interpretation of the Constitution [Art 132]. Thus, the Supreme Court is the final authority with respect to interpretation of the Constitution. Article 145(3) provides that there shall be a minimum of five Judges who are to sit for the purpose of deciding any case involving a substantial question of law as to the interpretation of the Constitution.

> **THINK ABOUT IT**
>
> The Supreme Court is the highest court of appeal with extraordinary powers. Discuss the appellate jurisdiction of the Supreme Court.

Civil Cases

An appeal shall lie to the Supreme Court from any judgement, decree or final order in a civil proceeding of a High Court if the High Court certifies that the case involves a substantial question of law of general importance, and in the opinion of the High Court the said question needs to be decided by the Supreme Court [Art 133].

Criminal Cases

An appeal shall lie to the Supreme Court from any judgement, final order or sentence in a criminal proceeding of a High Court if the High Court, (a) has on appeal reversed an order of acquittal of an accused person and sentenced him to death; or (b) has withdrawn for trial before itself any case from any court subordinate to its authority and has in such trial convicted the accused person and sentenced him to death; or (c) certifies that the case is a fit one for appeal to the Supreme Court [Art 134]. As per the enlarged criminal appellate jurisdiction, appeal in a criminal case will lie with the Supreme Court even where the High Court has reversed an acquittal or withdrawn any case from a subordinate court and sentenced a person to imprisonment for life or 10 years.

Article	Nature of Cases	Grounds for Appeal
132	Civil, criminal or other proceeding	Substantial question of law as to the interpretation of the Constitution.
133	Civil proceeding	Substantial question of law of general importance and the High Court is of the opinion that the question needs to be decided by the Supreme Court.
134	Criminal proceeding	Reversal of acquittal or withdrawal of the case from lower court and sentencing to death (or imprisonment for life or 10 years) by the High Court or the High Court certifies that it is a fit case for appeal.

In respect of all such above appeals, the concerned High Court has to provide a certificate for the purpose of appeal. It may do so on its own or may provide it if an application is made by the aggrieved party [Art 134A].

Special leave to appeal

Notwithstanding the various provisions with respect to appeals in different matters as discussed above, the Supreme Court may, in its discretion, grant special leave to appeal from any judgement, decree, determination, sentence or order in any cause or matter passed or made by any court or tribunal in the territory of India [Art 136].

This is an extraordinary power of the Supreme Court and it may entertain appeal on any matter from any court or tribunal except the military courts or tribunals [Art 136(2)]. However, Section 31 of the Armed Forces Tribunal Act, 2007 provides that an appeal from the order of such military tribunals can lie with the Supreme Court after the leave is granted by the Tribunal or the Supreme Court itself.

This special leave to appeal is granted by the Supreme Court only under exceptional circumstances, e.g., when principles of natural justice have not been followed or there is a miscarriage of justice.

12.6.4 Advisory Jurisdiction

If at any time it appears to the President that a question of law or fact has arisen, or is likely to arise, which is of such a nature and of such public importance that it is expedient to obtain the opinion of the Supreme Court upon it, he/she may refer the question to that Court for consideration and the Supreme Court may, after such hearing as it thinks fit, report to the President its opinion thereon [Art 143 (1)]. This is modelled on a similar provision that was contained in the Government of India Act, 1935.

Scan the QR code for conceptual video on jurisdiction of the Supreme Court

Mc Graw Hill edge

This is again a unique jurisdiction of the Indian Supreme Court that provides for an opinion from the court with respect to any Presidential reference. The following points need to be noted with respect to this advisory jurisdiction:

(a) It is not mandatory for the Supreme Court to provide its opinion. However, out of the 15 Presidential references made till 2024, the Supreme Court has declined to provide its opinion only in respect of one reference in 1993 with respect to the Rama Janma Bhumi case.

(b) However, in respect of a reference relating to a dispute for any treaty signed before commencement of the Constitution, it is mandatory for the Supreme Court to provide its opinion [Art 143(2)].

(c) The opinion given by the Supreme Court is not binding in nature but it carries a lot of legal weight as it is provided by the highest court of the country. The governments have always acted in accordance with the opinion of the court in respect of such matters e.g., Collegium process as per the opinion of the Supreme Court in the 3rd Judges case.

(d) A minimum of five Judges sit for the purpose of hearing a reference made under Article 143 [Art 145(3)].

12.6.5 Review Jurisdiction

The Supreme Court has the power to review any judgement pronounced or order made by it (Art 137). As per the Supreme Court rules, a review petition must be filed within 30 days from the date of judgement or order sought to be reviewed and must be placed before the same Bench that had delivered the decision.

A review petition is usually allowed on the following grounds – (a) discovery of new and important matter or evidence; (b) mistake or error apparent on the face of the record; and (c) any other sufficient reason.

The court may either admit or reject the review petition. However, even after dismissal of the review petition, a curative petition may be filed on limited grounds like (a) to rectify violation of principles of natural justice; (b) to cure gross miscarriage of justice; (c) to prevent abuse of the process of the court or (d) to rectify bias of the judge.

12.6.6 Other Powers

Apart from the above, the following are other important powers of the Supreme Court:

1. It is a court of record and has the power to punish for the contempt of the court. A Court of Record under Article 129 means that (a) judgements, proceedings and acts of the court are recorded for perpetuity and have evidentiary value. They are recognised as legal precedents and references and (b) the court has the power to punish for contempt. The Supreme Court has ruled that it has the power to punish not only for its own contempt but also for the contempt of High Courts, subordinate courts and tribunals in the country. Further, the power to punish for contempt is also provided in Article 142.

   As per the Contempt of Courts Act, 1971, the contempt can be civil or criminal. Civil contempt would mean wilful disobedience of any judgement or order; or wilful breach of any undertaking made to the court. Criminal contempt would mean the publication of any matter or doing an act that (a) scandalises or lowers the authority of the court; or (b) prejudices or interferes with the due course of judicial proceeding; or (c) interferes or obstructs the administration of justice.

   The court may initiate the contempt proceedings (a) suo moto; or (b) on a petition made by the Attorney General or Solicitor General; or (c) on a petition made by any person, and in case of a criminal contempt, with the consent of the Attorney General or Solicitor General.

2. The Supreme Court shall have further jurisdiction and powers with respect to any matter in the Union List as the Parliament may by law confer [Art 138].
3. The law declared by the Supreme Court shall be binding on all courts within the territory of India [Art 141]. This has resulted in the 'Doctrine of Precedence' by which a decision taken by a higher court is binding on the lower court and stands as a 'precedent' for lower court judgements. There can be (a) original precedents (which creates and applies new rules in cases where the question of law has not been decided before); (b) Authoritative or binding precedents (that are binding on lower courts); and (c) Persuasive precedents (which are not as binding as authoritative precedents but need to be given higher weightage).
4. The Supreme Court in the exercise of its jurisdiction may pass such decree or make such order as is necessary for doing complete justice in any cause or matter pending before it [Art 142] **[Refer 'Additional Data Points' on 'edge' for some recent and past important orders under Art 142]**.
5. All authorities, civil and judicial, in the territory of India shall act in aid of the Supreme Court [Art 144].
6. The Supreme Court may from time to time, with the approval of the President and subject to any Parliamentary law, make rules for regulating the practice and procedure of the court [Art 145].

12.7 GUARDIAN OF THE CONSTITUTION

The Supreme Court is the guardian or the custodian of the Constitution. There is no express provision in our Constitution empowering the courts to invalidate laws, but the Constitution has imposed definite limitations upon each organ of the State and any transgression would make the law void according to the Supreme Court (*A. K. Gopalan vs State of Madras 1950*).

Though not explicitly provided in the Constitution, 'Judicial review' has been declared as a Basic Structure of the Constitution in the Kesavananda Bharati case. It is the power of the courts to review the actions of the legislature and the executive for constitutional validity. The Supreme Court and the High Courts can strike down any law or the executive action as 'void' (not valid) if it is unconstitutional.

THINK ABOUT IT

Discuss the role of the Supreme Court as the guardian of the Indian Constitution.

Judicial review is important for the following reasons:

- To uphold the supremacy of the Constitution and the rule of law.
- To uphold the federal feature and maintain an independent balance between the Centre and the States.
- To protect fundamental rights of citizens.

We have already discussed about the various jurisdiction of the Supreme Court that provides the scope for judicial review. Similarly, the High Courts too have the power of judicial review through its various jurisdiction.

The Supreme Court is the highest court for judicial review and hence can be considered as the guardian or the custodian of the Constitution.

12.8 INDIAN AND AMERICAN SUPREME COURT COMPARISON

Both India and the United States have a federal setup in the legislative and the executive branches of the Government. However, as discussed in the introduction, the Indian judiciary is integrated in its setup unlike in the United States where the Judiciary is also federal in character.

The Indian and American Supreme Courts have the following similarities:

1. They are the highest court of the respective federations that settle any disputes between federal/central government and State governments or between State governments.
2. Both the courts have the power of judicial review that enables them to review the constitutional validity of any amendment of the Constitution as well as ordinary legislations and executive action.

The Indian Supreme Court and its American counterpart are different in terms of its jurisdiction and powers as follows:

1. In the United States, the appellate jurisdiction is confined to cases arising out of the federal relationship or those relating to the constitutional validity of laws and treaties only. However, in India, the Supreme Court is the highest court of appeal and has appellate jurisdiction over all types of cases.
2. In India, the Supreme Court has an extraordinary power without any limitation under Article 136 i.e., Special leave to allow an appeal from any court or tribunal within the territory of India. There is no such power for the American Supreme Court.
3. While the Indian Supreme Court enjoys advisory jurisdiction (Art 143), there is no such jurisdiction for American Supreme Court.
4. The American Supreme Court cannot supervise the lower courts as the American judiciary is federal in its character. On the other hand, the Indian Supreme Court is the apex court in our country that has the power of the judicial superintendence and control over all the courts and tribunals in the country.
5. The American Supreme Court has much wider power in terms of judicial review. In the US Courts, judicial review powers are wider under 'substantive due process' where the courts can review the validity of laws against unenumerated fundamental rights under the Constitution. In India, the scope of courts is a 'limited judicial review' where they can review the laws and the executive actions for the constitutional validity and 'procedural due process'.

12.9 JUDICIAL ACTIVISM

- Judicial activism believes that judges assume a role as independent policy makers or independent 'trustees' on behalf of the society, that goes beyond their traditional role as interpreters of the Constitution and laws.
- Judicial activism can also be considered as legislating from the bench.
- Failure on part of the legislative and the executive wings of the Government to provide good governance is one of the reasons for rise in judicial activism.

Judicial Activism and Judicial Review

- Judicial activism and judicial review are closely-related. It is only due to the power of judicial review, that the judiciary has interpreted the Constitution in a way that upholds rule of law and strikes down any excessive actions by the legislature or the executive. Further, judicial review has also resulted in delivery of justice to the citizens of the country while upholding the supremacy of the Constitution.

- In fact, the creation of 'basic structure' doctrine in the *Kesavananda Bharati* case is the beginning of judicial activism. In this case, the Supreme Court moved away from just a literal interpretation of the Constitution into a wider interpretation by formulating the 'basic features' in order to uphold the supremacy of the Constitution.
- However, over the period with the advent of PILs, the Supreme Court has taken up the role of not just reviewing the validity of laws or the executive action, but also providing instructions to the legislature and the executive on various issues. This expanded role is 'Judicial activism'.

Reasons for growth of Judicial activism

The expanded role of the judiciary in providing instructions to the legislature and the executive has arisen mainly due to the following reasons:

(a) Non-responsiveness of the government.

(b) Pressure on the judiciary to step in due to incompetence of the executive.

(c) Judicial enthusiasm to participate in social reform and change.

(d) Legislative vacuum left open – The Parliament and the State legislature have been hesitant or have delayed the passage of various laws with changing times. For example, it was the Supreme Court judgement that resulted in decriminalisation of homosexuality even amongst consenting adults since the Parliament was reluctant to amend the law.

(e) Authority to make final declaration as to the validity of a law.

(f) Role of the Judiciary as guardian of fundamental rights.

(g) Public confidence in the judiciary.

Public Interest Litigation

- The concept of judicial activism is closely tied to the advent of 'Public Interest Litigation' or PIL.
- A PIL is litigation for the protection of public interest. Earlier, the rule of *locus standi*, which means the right or capacity to bring an action in a court, was applicable for bringing cases in the court. It meant that only an aggrieved party could file a case in a court.
- The role of the Supreme Court of India has been further widened due to emergence of the idea of PIL. Under the principle of PIL, the petition can be filed in the court not only by the aggrieved party but also by any conscious person or organisation to seek relief on behalf of the aggrieved party. It started in 1979 with a petition filed seeking speedy justice for jail inmates in Bihar (Hussainara Khatoon Vs State of Bihar). Subsequently, since the 1980s the courts took a liberal view and took a stand that matters could be raised even without formally filing a suit. Even letters of organisations and petitions may be treated as writ petitions.
- Thus, a PIL may be introduced in a court of law by the court itself (*suo motu*) or another third party rather than the aggrieved party. For the exercise of the Court's jurisdiction, it is not necessary for the victim of the violation of his/her rights to personally approach the court. The member of the public may be a non-governmental organisation (NGO), an institution fighting for social or human rights, or an individual.
- The Supreme Court and the High Courts have given various reliefs for the poor, uneducated, disabled and helpless people under the PIL.

Judicial activism Vs Judicial overreach and Judicial restraint

- As discussed in the previous sections, judicial activism through PILs as well as many other cases have been instrumental in providing justice to the poor and the needy. It has also acted as a check and balance on the legislative and the executive organs of the State.
- Some of the examples of judicial activism resulting in constructive intervention in public issues include: (a) Binding directives issued to create accountability on public officials with respect to demolitions (2024) (b) Suo moto cognisance of rape and murder of a doctor in a Kolkata hospital and handing over the control of the hospital to CISF (2024) (c) Announcement of ex-gratia for COVID 19 victims by the Central Government (2021), (d) Framing of guidelines known as Vishaka guidelines that ensured proper treatment of women at workplace (1997), (e) Formation of SIT for probe into black money (2014) etc.
- However, when the judiciary crosses its line of activism and intrudes into policy domain, then it is considered as judicial overreach.
- Some of the examples of such judicial overreach include: (a) Ban on registration of diesel vehicles above 2000CC in NCT of Delhi that was subsequently reversed (2015), (b) Ban on sale of liquor within 500 metres of any National or State highway. It was later clarified by the Supreme Court that such ban will not apply within city limits (2016).
- The above two instances are examples of overreach because these matters are administrative that require the executive knowledge. Similarly, there are instances where the courts have interfered excessively into the legislative domain.
- In such cases, the judiciary may end up providing judgements that are beyond its competence and affect the fine balance of separation of powers between various organs i.e., the legislature, the executive and the judiciary, which is a basic feature of our Constitution.
- The remedy to avoid judicial overreach is 'Judicial restraint'. Judicial restraint is an obligation on the part of the judiciary to remain within their domain and uphold the principle of separation of powers.
- The Supreme Court itself in 2007 had called for judicial restraint and asked the courts not to take over the functions of the legislature or the executive in order to respect the separation of powers under the Constitution. It also held that the judiciary has neither the expertise, nor the resources to perform the functions of the legislature and the executive. Some recent instances of judicial restraint by the courts include:
  (a) Supriyo v. Union of India (2023): The court acknowledged the right of individuals in same-sex relationships to enjoy equal rights similar to heterosexual couples. However, it refrained from legalising same-sex marriage, stating that the matter falls within the purview of Parliament, which must deliberate on related issues and enact appropriate legislation.
  (b) In 2025, instead of issuing its own guidelines, the court directed the government to establish an expert committee to examine the challenges faced by domestic workers and formulate a law to safeguard their interests.
- Hence, while judicial activism is essential for upholding the supremacy of the Constitution and to provide justice, it should not result in judicial overreach. The courts must exercise judicial restraint while performing their functions.

Scan the QR code for conceptual video on judicial review, activism and reforms

Mc Graw Hill edge

12.10 JUDICIAL REFORMS

- The Judiciary, which is one of the three important pillars of our democracy, is the final interpreter of the Constitution and laws. As an upholder of the Rule of Law and enforcer of the right to liberty, the role of the Judiciary is sacrosanct.
- Quick delivery of justice is *sine qua non* (indispensable or absolutely essential) for efficient jurisprudence. Justice delayed is justice denied. Justice should be speedy, accessible and affordable. Our courts are today overburdened on account of the large number of cases pending before them.

Key issues facing the judiciary that require reforms

- **Pendency of cases** – There are over 5 crore cases pending in various courts throughout the country. Out of these about 62.3 lakh cases are pending in 25 High Courts as of January 2025. A whopping 4.56 crore cases are pending in the district courts across the country as of January 2025 which are short of nearly 5,250 judicial officers as of November 2024.
- Reasons for pendency of cases include
  - Increasing number of State and Central litigations.
  - Continuation of ordinary civil jurisdiction in some of the High Courts.
  - Appeals against orders of quasi-judicial forums going to the High Courts.
  - Number of revisions/appeals.
  - Frequent adjournments.
  - Indiscriminate use of writ jurisdiction.
  - Lack of adequate arrangement to monitor.

THINK ABOUT IT

Critically evaluate the long pending reform of introducing All India Judicial Service to address the issue of vacancies in lower judiciary.

- **Vacancies of Judges** – The pendency of cases is also dependent upon the number of vacancies in the courts. Out of a sanctioned strength of 1122 judges in all the High Courts, the working strength of the High Court judges throughout the country as of December 2024 was only 751. This amounts to vacancy of 371 judges. Stated otherwise, our High Courts are working with about 67% of the sanctioned capacity.
- Lack of adequate infrastructure is another reason that reduces the efficiency and speed of disposal of cases by the courts.

Steps taken to reduce pendency of cases and other reforms

- Pendency reduction campaign was initiated for the first time in July 2011. The High Courts were requested to prioritise disposal of cases that had been pending for a long duration, particularly those relating to the senior citizens and the marginalised sections of the society.
- From 2014, emphasis was laid on filling up of vacancies of the judicial officers and organisation of the Mega Lok Adalats.
- The Law Commission of India in its 230th report has also offered a long list of measures to deal with the pendency of cases. These include providing strict guidelines for the grant of adjournments, reducing the time for oral arguments unless the case involves a complicated question of law, and framing clear and decisive judgments to avoid further litigation. In addition, the courts should also seriously consider incorporating technology into the system.
- In January 2025, the Supreme Court relaxed the conditions it had earlier imposed for appointing retired judges as adhoc judges of the High Courts under Article 224A.

All India Judicial Services

- The proposal for an All-India Judicial Service (AIJS) was first suggested in 1950s by the 1st Law Commission report as a way to remove any scope for the judicial or the executive intervention in the appointments to the judiciary.
- The Constitution was amended through the 42nd Amendment Act to provide for an AIJS under Article 312. It requires an enabling resolution in the Rajya Sabha with 2/3rd of members present and voting, after which the Parliament can pass a law for creation of AIJS.
- The proposal was floated in 2012 but the draft bill was shelved after opposition from the High Court Chief Justices who labelled this an infringement of their rights.
- Advantages
    - Primarily, the direct recruitment of judges from the entry level will be handled by an independent and impartial agency through an open competition thereby ensuring fair selection of incumbents. It would help attract bright and capable young law graduates to the judiciary to take over as judges.
    - For subordinate judicial officers it would ensure equitable service conditions.
    - The measure of uniformity in the standards for selection will improve the quality of personnel in different High Courts, as one-third of the judges come there on promotion from the subordinate courts.
    - Similarly, judges of the Supreme Court are drawn from the High Courts. In this process only persons of proven competence will preside over the benches of the higher judiciary.
- Key challenges
    - A 'national exam' risks shutting out those from less privileged backgrounds from being able to enter the judicial services.
    - It may also end up not considering local laws, practices and customs which vary widely across the States, vastly increasing the costs of training for the judges selected through the mechanism.
    - Local languages and dialects would be a problem.

Even though, AIJS has lot of advantages, the Government should take necessary steps to address the challenges before bringing AIJS into functioning.

12.11 ADVOCATES OF SUPREME COURT

Senior Advocates	Section 16 of the Advocates Act refers to the separate class of 'senior advocate'. Both the Supreme Court and High Courts can confer senior designation to lawyers based on their merit, experience, special knowledge of the law and standing at the Bar. Such senior advocates get precedence in right of pre-audience in the courts above 'other advocates.'
Advocates-on-Record	As per the Supreme Court rules, no advocate other than an advocate on record shall be entitled to file an appearance or act for a party in the Supreme Court of India. No advocate other than an advocate on record can appear and plead in any matter unless he/she is instructed by an advocate-on-record. There are qualification requirements to be registered as an advocate-on-record which include practice as an advocate for four years, training under a senior advocate for one year and then passing an exam conducted by the Supreme Court.
Other advocates	They can appear and argue any matter for a party in the Supreme Court but are not entitled to file any document before the court.

MAINS STARTER

Area	Building Blocks For Model Introductions
Supreme Court seat and Benches	The Supreme Court at present sits in Delhi (Art 130). Benches may be created by the Chief Justice of India with the previous approval of the President though there are no such benches at present.
Appointment of Supreme Court Judges	The Judges to the Supreme Court are appointed by the President (executive) after consultation with the Chief Justice of India (judiciary) [Art 124]. This process has been subject to various case laws in the court that has resulted in the creation of the collegium system.
National Judicial Appointments Commission (NJAC)	NJAC was a multi-member body that was to consist of judges, union law minister and eminent persons under the 99th constitutional amendment and NJAC Act, 2014. This body was to replace the collegium process for appointment and transfer of judges to the higher judiciary. However, this amendment was struck down by the Supreme Court.
Removal of Judges	The Constitution provides a stringent process for removal of judges of higher judiciary to ensure their independence. They may be removed on the grounds of proved misbehaviour or incapacity after a resolution with special majority is passed in both the houses in the same session [Art 124].
Independence of Judiciary	An independent Judiciary is a vital requirement for a functional democracy. The Judiciary acts as an independent branch that keeps a check and balance on the other two organs, viz., Executive and Legislature.
Custodian/ Guardian of the Constitution	The Supreme Court, by virtue of its powers for settling federal disputes, judicial review and upholding fundamental rights, acts as the guardian of the Constitution.
Judicial activism	Judicial activism believes that judges assume a role as independent policy makers or independent 'trustees' on behalf of society, that goes beyond their traditional role as the interpreters of the Constitution and laws. This is primarily exercised through the Public interest litigations (PILs) that can be filed in courts by any person in respect of a matter where public interest is involved.
All India Judicial Service	The All-India Judicial Service may be instituted by a Parliamentary law after being authorised by the Rajya Sabha through a resolution passed with 2/3rd majority (Art 312). This service would be for direct recruitment of judges to the lower judiciary.

UPSC Previous Years' Questions of Preliminary Examination

1. We adopted parliamentary democracy based on the British model, but how does our model differ from that model? [2021]
   1. As regards legislation, the British Parliament is supreme or sovereign but in India, the power of the Parliament to legislate is limited.
   2. In India, matters related to the constitutionality of the Amendment of an act of the Parliament are referred to the Constitution bench by the Supreme Court.

   Select the correct answer using the codes given below:
   (a) 1 only (b) 2 only (c) Both 1 and 2 (d) Neither 1 nor 2

   Solution: (c)

   Explanation: In Britain, the Parliament is supreme whereas in India, the Constitution is supreme as discussed in various chapters. Hence, Statement 1 is correct. As per Article 145 that deals with regulating the procedure of the Supreme Court, any case involving substantial question of law as regards interpretation of the Constitution should be heard by a Constitution Bench consisting of minimum 5 judges and hence Statement 2 is also correct and the correct answer is (c).

2. With reference to the Indian Judiciary consider the following statements: [2021]
   1. Any retired judge of the Supreme Court of India can be called back to sit and act as a Supreme Court judge by the Chief Justice of India with prior permission of the President of India.
   2. A High Court in India has the power to review its own judgement as the Supreme Court does.

   Which of the statements given above is/are correct?
   (a) 1 only (b) 2 only (c) Both 1 and 2 (d) Neither 1 nor 2

   Solution: (a)

   Explanation: As discussed under Section 12.3.3, Statement 1 is correct as per Article 128. However, review jurisdiction that provides the power to review its own judgements is provided only to the Supreme Court under Article 137 and hence Statement 2 is incorrect and the correct answer is (a).

3. Which one of the following factors constitutes the best safeguard of liberty in a liberal democracy [2021]

   (a) A committed judiciary (b) Centralisation of powers
   (c) Elected government (d) Separation of powers

   Solution: (d)

   Explanation: As discussed in Section 12.7, the Constitution has imposed definite limitations upon each organ of the State and it is based on effective checks and balance. The judiciary will strike down any law or action that is unconstitutional or violates the fundamental rights, including liberty. Separation of powers has been declared as a 'Basic structure' of our constitution. Thus, the correct answer is (d).

4. Consider the following statements: **[2019]**

1. The 44th amendment to the Constitution of India introduced an article placing election of the Prime Minister beyond judicial review.
2. The Supreme Court of India struck down the 99th amendment of the Constitution of India as being violative of the independence of judiciary.

Which of the statements given above is/are correct?

(a) 1 only (b) 2 only (c) Both 1 and 2 (d) Neither 1 nor 2

Solution: (b)

Explanation: As discussed in Section 12.3.1.4, the NJAC amendment with respect to appointment of judges (99th amendment) was struck down by the Supreme Court as being violative of independence of judiciary. Hence, statement 2 is correct. It was not the 44th amendment act after emergency was lifted but the 39th amendment act during emergency that introduced an article placing the election of the Prime Minister beyond judicial review. The 44th amendment act omitted that article. Hence, statement 1 is incorrect and the correct answer is (b).

UPSC Previous Years' Questions of Main Examination

1. Explain the reasons for the growth of public interest litigation in India. As a result of it, has the Indian Supreme Court emerged as the world's most powerful judiciary? [2024]

Approach: The reasons for the growth of PIL and Judicial activism to be discussed in the first part. The resulting impact of Supreme Court judgements and how it has become one of the most powerful judiciary needs to be discussed in the second part.

MODEL ANSWER

The Indian constitution works on the principle of broad separation of powers between the legislature/executive and the judiciary. The role of legislature and executive is to frame laws and implement them, while the judiciary interprets the laws and delivers justice.

Judicial activism believes that judges assume a role as independent policy makers or independent 'trustees' on behalf of society, that goes beyond their traditional role as the interpreters of the Constitution and laws. This is primarily exercised through the Public interest litigations (PILs) that can be filed in courts by any person in respect of a matter where public interest is involved.

Reasons for growth of PIL/Judicial activism

(a) Non-responsiveness of government.

(b) Pressure on judiciary to step in due to incompetence of the executive.

(c) Judicial enthusiasm to participate in social reform and change.

(d) Legislative vacuum left open – The Parliament and State legislature have been hesitant or have delayed the passage of various laws with changing times. For example, it was the Supreme Court judgement that resulted in decriminalisation of homosexuality even amongst consenting adults since the Parliament was reluctant to amend the law.

(e) Authority to make final declaration as to the validity of a law.
(f) Role of Judiciary as the guardian of fundamental rights.
(g) Public confidence in the judiciary.

Increased power of Judiciary

(a) Judicial activism through PILs as well as many other cases have been instrumental in providing justice to the poor and the needy.
(b) It has also acted as a check and balance on the legislative and executive organs of the State.
(c) Some of the examples of judicial activism resulting in constructive intervention in public issues include: (a) Announcement of ex-gratia for COVID 19 victims by Central Government (2021) (b) Framing of guidelines known as Vishaka guidelines that ensured proper treatment of women at workplace (1997) (c) Formation of SIT for probe into black money (2014), etc. (d) Various electoral reforms like NOTA, declaring of criminal antecedents, etc.
(d) Thus, while it has made the Judiciary powerful, it is ultimately aimed at securing public interest and justice.

2. Constitutionally guaranteed judicial independence is a prerequisite for democracy. Comment. [2023]

Approach: The points relating to the independence of judiciary provided in Section 12.5 need to be reproduced. The Mnemonics 2C4R will be helpful in recalling and reproducing all the points.

MODEL ANSWER

An independent Judiciary is a vital requirement for a functional democracy. The Judiciary acts as an independent branch that keeps a check and balance on the other two organs, viz., Executive and Legislature.

Constitutional provisions for Judicial independence

The following provisions of the Constitution guarantee the independence of the Supreme Court and High Courts:

(a) Appointment of Judges to higher judiciary is through the collegium process as laid down in the Second and Third Judges case.
(b) Judges can be removed only by the Parliament, on the grounds of proved misbehaviour or incapacity, after a detailed inquiry and by a special majority of both houses in the same session.
(c) Financial independence is ensured as the salaries and allowances of Judges as well as the expenditure of these courts are charged on the Consolidated Fund of India/State, respectively.
(d) There is restriction on discussion of a conduct of a Judge in the Parliament except when it is on a motion for his/her removal. Similarly, a Supreme Court Judge, after ceasing to hold office, cannot plead or act in any court or authority in India and a High Court Judge cannot plead or act except in Supreme Court and other High Courts.

The above provisions ensure complete independence of the Judiciary with respect to appointment, removal and also financial matters. However, the collegium process of appointment needs to be streamlined by revising the Memorandum of Procedure to ensure greater transparency in the process.

CHAPTER 13

High Courts

LEARNING OUTCOMES

1. Understanding the structure of High Courts, qualifications required for judges, and conditions of office
2. Comparing the appointment and removal process with that of Supreme Court judges and understanding the procedure for transferring judges between High Courts
3. Identifying provisions that ensure judicial independence of High Courts
4. Describing different types of jurisdictions exercised by High Courts, including writ, appellate, and supervisory jurisdiction
5. Comprehending the hierarchy, qualifications, and appointment procedures for judges in subordinate courts
6. Discussing the composition, jurisdiction, and benefits of Lok Adalats, along with eligibility for free legal aid under the justice system

Articles 214 to 231 in Part VI of the Constitution deals with the organisation, independence and power of the High Courts. The Supreme Court is the Union judiciary while the various High Courts are part of the State judiciary. However, as discussed in the introduction to the Supreme Court, the Indian judiciary is not federal in setup but is an integrated judicial setup. The High Courts are part of the higher judiciary at the State level.

The key provisions of the State Judiciary i.e., the High Courts can be summarised as below.

High Courts		
Composition	**Appointment and Removal**	**Functioning**
• Composition of the High Courts • Qualification for being a Judge of a High Court • Conditions of office of the High Court judges	• Appointment of Judges • Removal of Judges	• Independence of High Courts • Jurisdiction of a High Court • Superintendence over subordinate courts

The provisions in the Constitution with respect to the High Courts are similar in some aspects to the Supreme Court and differ in certain aspects.

13.1 COMPOSITION OF THE HIGH COURTS

13.1.1 Composition

There shall be a High Court for each State [Art 214]. The Parliament may by law establish a common High Court for two or more States or for two or more States and a Union territory [Art 231]. At present (2024) there are 25 High Courts in the country.

Every High Court shall consist of a Chief Justice and such other judges as the President may from time to time deem it necessary to appoint [Art 216]. Thus, the Constitution does not lay down the number of judges for every High Court but it is decided by the Central Government from time to time.

The High courts which handle a large number of cases in a particular region, have permanent benches (or a branch of the court) established there. For example, the Madras High Court has a bench in Madurai; the Bombay High Court has benches at Nagpur and Aurangabad.

Benches are also present in States which come under the jurisdiction of a court outside its territorial limits. For example, the Bombay High Court has a bench in Panaji (Goa) over which its territorial jurisdiction extends. Similarly, the Guwahati High Court has benches in Kohima (Nagaland), Aizawl (Mizoram) and Itanagar (Arunachal Pradesh) over which its territorial jurisdiction extends.

Smaller States with few cases may have circuit benches established. Circuit benches are temporary courts which hold proceedings for a few selected months in a year.

Every High Court shall be a court of record and shall have all the powers of such a court including the power to punish for contempt of the Court [Art 215].

13.1.2 Qualification for a High Court Judge

As per Article 217(2), a person shall be qualified for appointment as a Judge of a High Court if he/she fulfils the following conditions:

1. He/she is a citizen of India and,
2. For at least 10 years held a judicial office in the territory of India; or
3. Has for at least 10 years been an advocate of a High Court or of two or more such Courts in succession.

13.1.3 Conditions of Office

Every Judge of a High Court shall be appointed by the President by warrant under his/her hand and seal after consultation with the Chief Justice of India, the Governor of the State, and, in the case of appointment of a Judge other than the Chief Justice, the Chief Justice of the High Court, and shall hold office until he/she attains the age of 62 years [Art 217].

Provided further that –

(a) A Judge may, by writing under his/her hand addressed to the President, resign his/her office;

(b) A Judge may be removed from his/her office in the manner provided in the Constitution.

Every person appointed to be a Judge of a High Court shall, before he/she enters upon his/her office, make and subscribe before the Governor of the State, or some person appointed in that behalf by him/her, an oath or affirmation according to the form set out for the purpose in the Third Schedule [Art 219].

There shall be paid to the Judges of each High Court such salaries as may be determined by the Parliament by law [Art 221]. As per The High Court Judges (Salaries and Conditions of Service) Act, 1954 (as amended in 2018), the Chief Justice of a High Court draws a salary of ₹2,50,000 per month and other Judges ₹2,25,000 per month.

It may be noted that the Constitution neither provides for minimum age as a condition for qualification of the Judges of the High Court nor a fixed number of years of office (like 6 years for constitutional authorities like SPSC members). They serve from their date of appointment till they attain the age of 62 years.

13.2 APPOINTMENT, TRANSFER AND REMOVAL OF JUDGES

13.2.1 Appointment of Judges

As per Article 217(1) of the Constitution every Judge of a High Court shall be:

(a) appointed by the President by warrant under his/her hand and seal;

(b) after consultation with the Chief Justice of India, the Governor of the State, and, in the case of appointment of a Judge other than the Chief Justice, the Chief Justice of the High Court;

(c) and shall hold office until he/she attains the age of 62 years.

The procedure for appointment of judges to the higher judiciary has been subject to various cases before the Supreme Court. We have already discussed these cases in detail in the chapter on the Supreme Court.

As per the 3rd Judges case and Memorandum of Procedure, the Collegium process for appointment of the High Court Judges is summarised below:

- The Collegium for appointment of the Chief Justice of a High Court and High Court judges consists of the Chief Justice of India and other two seniormost Judges of the Supreme Court.
- The process for filling up any vacancy in a High Court shall be initiated by the Chief Justice of the concerned High Court in consultation with other two senior Judges of the High Court. The proposed list of names for appointment is sent by the Chief Justice of the High Court to the Governor of the State, the Union Government and the Supreme Court Collegium.
- The State Government may provide its inputs on the proposed list of names to the Union Government. The Union Government with its comments forwards the same to the Supreme Court Collegium. The Supreme Court Collegium consisting of the Chief Justice of India and other two seniormost Judges then make the final recommendation for appointment of Judges to a High Court.
- The President appoints the Judges to a High Court.

MNEMONICS

Concept or Provisions	Shortcut or Mnemonics	Details to Remember
Collegium for appointments and transfers	• Same for SC and HC transfer • Different for HC appointments	• For SC judges' appointment and transfer of judges from one HC to another – Chief Justice of India (CJI) + 4 seniormost judges • For HC Chief Justice and judges, appointment – CJI + 2 seniormost judges

13.2.2 Transfer of Judges

The President may, after consultation with the Chief Justice of India, transfer a Judge from one High Court to any other High Court [Art 222].

This process of transfer is also based on recommendation of the Supreme Court Collegium. The Collegium for transfer of Judges consists of the Chief Justice of India and four seniormost judges of the Supreme Court. The Chief Justice of India shall also consult the Chief Justices of concerned High Courts i.e., the High Court from which the transfer is to be made and the High Court to which the transfer is to be made before recommending transfer of a Judge to the President. It is only the Judge being transferred who can request the Collegium to review its decision.

13.2.3 Additional and Retired Judges

- When the office of the Chief Justice of a High Court is vacant, or when the Chief Justice is unable to perform his/her duties, the President may appoint any of the other Judges as acting Chief Justice [Art 223].
- If by reason of any temporary increase in the business of a High Court or by reason of arrears of work therein, it appears to the President that the number of the Judges of that Court should be for the time being increased, the President may appoint duly qualified persons to be additional Judges of the Court for such period not exceeding 2 years as he/she may specify [Art 224].
- When any Judge of a High Court is absent or unable to perform his/her duties or is appointed to act temporarily as the Chief Justice, the President may appoint a duly qualified person as acting Judge of that Court until the permanent Judge has resumed his/her duties [Art 224].
- An additional or acting Judge of a High Court shall not hold office after attaining the age of 62 years [Art 224].
- The Chief Justice of a High Court may at any time, with the previous consent of the President, request any person who has held the office of a Judge of that High Court or any other High Court to sit and act as the Judge of the High Court [Art 224A].
- In January 2025, the Supreme Court (SC) relaxed the conditions it had earlier imposed for appointing retired judges as ad hoc judges of the High Courts. In April 2021, the SC had held that retired judges may be appointed only if the vacancy at the High Court exceeded 20% of the sanctioned strength. However, to address the growing pendency of cases in High Courts, the SC had kept this requirement in abeyance in its January 2025 order. It held that High Courts can appoint upto 2 to 5 retired judges subject to a maximum of 10% of the sanctioned strength. These judges will sit in a Bench presided over by a sitting Judge and decide on pending criminal cases.

13.2.4 Removal of Judges

A Judge of the High Court may be removed from his/her office by the President in the manner provided in Article 124(4) for removal of a Judge of the Supreme Court [Art 217]. The provisions for removal of Judges of the Supreme Court [under Art 124 (4) and (5)] shall apply for removal of Judges of a High Court as well with the substitution of references to the High Court for references to the Supreme Court [Art 218].

The provisions under the Constitution as well as procedure under the Judges (Inquiry) Act, 1968 for removal of the Supreme Court Judges have been discussed in detail in Section 12.4 in the chapter on the Supreme Court. The same provisions and procedure are applicable for removal of a High Court Judge.

13.3 INDEPENDENCE OF THE HIGH COURTS

An independent Judiciary is a vital requirement for a functional democracy. While the executive is accountable to the legislature and the legislature gets elected by the people every 5 years, it is the Judiciary that upholds the Constitution and Rule of law on a day-to-day basis. The Judiciary acts as an independent branch that keeps a check and balance on the other two organs. In order to protect the Judiciary from wrongful interference by the executive as well as to ensure the financial independence of Judges, the Constitution contains various provisions to secure the independence of Judiciary. The following provisions ensure independence of the High Court:

(a) Every Judge of a High Court shall be appointed by the President by warrant under his/her hand and seal after consultation with the Chief Justice of India, the Governor of the State, and, in the case of appointment of a Judge other than the Chief Justice, the Chief Justice of the High Court, and shall hold office until he/she attains the age of 62 years [Art 217]. Now, with the Collegium system in place, the independence of the Judiciary with respect to appointments has increased even further.

(b) A Judge of a High Court shall be removed from his/her office, on the grounds of proved misbehaviour or incapacity, only by both the Houses of Parliament passing a resolution with special majority in the same session [Art 217].

(c) Every Judge shall be entitled to such privileges and allowances and to such rights in respect of leave of absence and pension as may from time to time be determined by or under law made by the Parliament. Neither the privileges nor the allowances of a Judge nor his/her rights in respect of leave of absence or pension shall be varied to his/her disadvantage after his/her appointment (except during a Financial emergency) [Art 221].

(d) The Salaries and allowances of Judges of any High Court shall be charged on the Consolidated Fund of that State [Art 202]. The pension in respect of the High Court Judges shall be charged on the Consolidated Fund of India [Art 112].

(e) The administrative expenses of a High Court, including all salaries, allowances and pensions payable to or in respect of the officers and servants of the Court, shall be charged upon the Consolidated Fund of the State [Art 229].

(f) Restriction on discussion in the State Legislature - No discussion shall take place in the Legislature of a State with respect to the conduct of any Judge of the Supreme Court or of a High Court in the discharge of his/her duties [Art 211].

(g) No person who has held the office as a permanent Judge of a High Court shall plead or act in any court or before any authority in India except the Supreme Court and other High Courts [Art 220]. This restriction is laid because they should not feel obliged during the period of holding the position as a judge to any other potential employers. The other reason is that they may influence their former colleagues in the same High Court if they can appear before them as lawyers.

(h) Transfer of judges between the High Courts is carried out by the President only based on the recommendation of the Supreme Court Collegium.

(i) The officers and servants of High Courts are appointed by the Chief Justice of the High Courts or any other Judge or officer whom he/she may direct. The Chief Justice of High Court also prescribes the conditions of their service [Art 229].

(j) The jurisdiction of the High Courts cannot be curtailed by the Parliament or State legislature.

MNEMONICS

Concept or Provisions	Shortcut or Mnemonics	Details to Remember
Independence of Judiciary	**2C4R**	Similar to independence of Supreme Court with two modifications: **C** – **C**harged on consolidated fund of the State – Salaries of HC judges and expenses of HC. Pensions of HC judges are charged on Consolidated fund of India. **R** – **R**estriction on further practice for HC judges except Supreme Court and other High Courts.

13.4 JURISDICTION OF THE HIGH COURTS

The High Courts have various powers and jurisdiction as per the Constitution and various laws made by the Parliament and the State legislatures. The jurisdiction of the High Courts as per the Constitution primarily consists of its writ jurisdiction (Art 226) and supervisory jurisdiction (Art 227). The important jurisdiction of the High Courts as per the Constitution and various laws are discussed here.

13.4.1 Original Jurisdiction

As per the Constitution, original jurisdiction refers to the exclusive jurisdiction of the Supreme Court in certain matters under Article 131. There is no corresponding provision similar to that for the High Courts. However, as per various laws, the High Courts hear disputes directly in respect of some matters as listed below:

(a) Contempt of the High Court

(b) Disputes relating to election of members of the Parliament and State legislature as per provisions of Representation of the People Act, 1951

(c) Regarding certain revenue matters

13.4.2 Writ Jurisdiction

> **THINK ABOUT IT**
>
> The writ jurisdiction of High Courts is wider than the Supreme Court. Comment.

Every High Court shall have power, throughout the territories in relation to which it exercises jurisdiction, to issue to any person or authority, including in appropriate cases, any Government, within those territories, directions, orders or writs, including writs in the nature of habeas corpus, mandamus, prohibition, quo warranto and certiorari, or any of them, for the enforcement of any of the rights conferred by Part III and for any other purpose [Art 226].

The writ jurisdiction of the High Courts is wider in scope than the Supreme Court. As per Article 32, the Supreme Court can issue writs only for the enforcement of Fundamental Rights. However, the High Courts can issue writs not only for the enforcement of Fundamental Rights but for any other purpose which includes enforcement of ordinary legal rights. The writ jurisdiction of the Supreme Court and High Courts is part of the basic structure of the Constitution.

The High Courts can issue such writs to any authority, person or government within its territorial jurisdiction as well as to other authorities or governments if the cause of action arises within its territorial jurisdiction.

13.4.3 Appellate Jurisdiction

A High Court is primarily a court of appeal. It hears appeals against the judgments of the subordinate courts functioning in its territorial jurisdiction. It has appellate jurisdiction in both civil and criminal matters.

Civil Matters

Appeals from orders and judgements of district courts, additional district courts and other subordinate courts lie with the High Court, exercising jurisdiction over those courts on both questions of law and fact. Appeals from the decisions of administrative and other tribunals also lie with the High Courts.

Criminal Matters

Appeals from judgements of sessions court and additional sessions court lie with the High Court if the sentence of imprisonment is for more than seven years. Further, a death sentence awarded by sessions or additional sessions court should be confirmed by the High Court before it can be executed.

13.4.4 Supervisory Jurisdiction

Every High Court shall have superintendence over all courts and tribunals throughout the territories in relation to which it exercises jurisdiction. The High Court may:

- call for returns from such courts;
- make and issue general rules and prescribe forms for regulating the practice and proceedings of such courts;
- prescribe forms in which books, entries and accounts shall be kept by the officers of any such courts [Art 227].

Scan QR code for conceptual video on High Courts

Any High Court can withdraw a case pending in a subordinate court, if it has to decide on a substantial question of law as to the interpretation of the Constitution. The High Court can then either dispose off the case itself or determine the said question of law and return the case to the subordinate court for further action as per such judgement [Art 228].

Apart from the above, every High Court is also a court of record (Art 215) and has the power to punish for contempt. It can also review its own judgement or order though there is no express review jurisdiction conferred on High Courts under the Constitution unlike the Supreme Court. High Courts also have the power of judicial review to examine the constitutional validity of (a) Constitutional amendments and (b) legislative and executive action of both the Centre and State(s) over which they exercise jurisdiction.

13.5 SUBORDINATE COURTS AND LOK ADALATS

13.5.1 Subordinate Courts

The appointments, postings and promotion of the district judges in any State shall be made by the Governor of the State in consultation with the High Court exercising jurisdiction in relation to such State [Art 233].

Structure of Sub-ordinate Judiciary

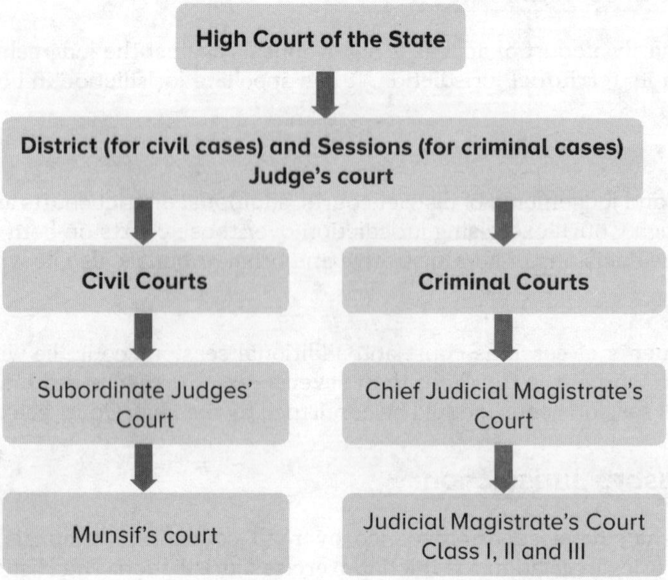

District Judge would include the city civil court judge, additional or joint or assistant district judge, sessions or additional or assistant sessions judge etc. Qualification for being appointed as a district judge is as follows:

- ❑ He/she should not be in the service of the Central or the State government;
- ❑ He/she should have been an advocate for at least 7 years and recommended by the High Court.

Appointments of persons other than district judges to the judicial service of a State shall be made by the Governor of the State in consultation with the State Public Service Commission and with the High Court exercising jurisdiction in relation to such State [Art 234].

The High Court shall have control over the district and other subordinate courts including posting, promotion and leave of persons belonging to the judicial services of the State [Art 235].

The High Courts shall have the power of superintendence over all courts as provided below [Art 227]:

- ❑ Every High Court shall have superintendence over all courts and tribunals throughout the territories in relation to which it exercises jurisdiction.

- The High Court may – (a) call for returns from such courts; (b) make and issue general rules and prescribe forms for regulating the practice and proceedings of such courts; and (c) prescribe forms in which books, entries and accounts shall be kept by the officers of any such courts.

13.5.2 Lok Adalats

Legal Service Authorities

National Legal Services Authority of India (NALSA) has been formed under the Legal Services Authorities Act, 1987.

The composition of NALSA shall be as follows:

- The Chief Justice of India is the Patron-in-Chief of NALSA.
- A serving or a retired judge to be nominated by the President, in consultation with the Chief Justice of India, shall be the Executive Chairman.
- Such number of other members, possessing requisite experience and qualifications as prescribed by the Central Government, to be nominated by the government in consultation with the Chief Justice of India.
- There is also a Supreme Court Legal Services committee that is constituted to administer and implement legal services programmes.

THINK ABOUT IT

Lok Adalats are an effective alternate dispute redressal mechanism. Elucidate based on their jurisdiction and benefits. What are the issues faced in effective organisation and utilisation of Lok Adalats?

There is a provision for similar mechanism at the State and the District level also to be headed by the Chief Justice of the High Courts and the Chief Judges of the District Courts respectively. The State Legal Services Authority (SLSA), the District Legal Service Authorities, the High Court Legal Service Committees and the Taluk Legal Service Committees are constituted under the Act.

The functions of SLSA are as follows:

- Provide free legal services to eligible persons as defined in the Act.
- Organise the Lok Adalats for speedy resolution of cases.
- Undertake preventive and strategic legal aid programmes for creating awareness.

Persons eligible for free legal aid under the Act include:

(a) Member of Scheduled Caste or Scheduled Tribe;

(b) A victim of trafficking in human beings or begar as referred in Article 23 of the Constitution;

(c) A woman or a child up to 18 years of age;

(d) A mentally ill or otherwise disabled person;

(e) A victim of mass disaster, ethnic violence, caste atrocity, flood, drought, earthquake or industrial disaster;

(f) An industrial workman;

(g) A person in receipt of annual income less than the limit specified under the Act. This limit varies from State to State (in most States, the limit is ₹1,00,000). In respect of cases before the Supreme Court, the limit is ₹5,00,000.

The Act and its provisions relating to free legal services are also to give effect to Article 39A of the Constitution that provides a directive to the State to make provisions for free legal aid.

Lok Adalats

The Lok Adalats are constituted under the Legal Services Authorities Act, 1987. It is an Alternate Dispute Redressal Mechanism (ADR) and provides cheap and prompt justice to the people.

The State/District Legal Services Authority or the Supreme Court/High Court/Taluk Legal Services Committee may organise the Lok Adalats at such intervals and places and for exercising such jurisdiction and for such areas as it thinks fit. The Lok Adalats organised shall consist of the serving or retired judicial officers and other persons.

A Lok Adalat shall have jurisdiction to determine and to arrive at a compromise or settlement between the parties to a dispute in respect of:

- Any case pending before any court, or
- Any matter which falls within the jurisdiction of any court and is not brought before such court for which the Lok Adalat is organised.

However, the Lok Adalat shall have no jurisdiction in respect of any case or matter relating to an offence that is not compoundable under any law. Compoundable offences are those where the complainant or victim (i.e., one who has filed the case), enters into a compromise, and agrees to have the charges dropped against the accused.

Any case pending before a court can be referred to the Lok Adalat for settlement if:

- Parties agree to settle the dispute in the Lok Adalat; or
- one of the parties makes an application for referring the case to the Lok Adalat for settlement; or
- the Court is satisfied that the matter is appropriate to be taken up by a Lok Adalat.
- In the case of a pre-litigation dispute (i.e., before a case is filed), the matter can be referred to the Lok Adalat on receipt of an application from any one of the parties to the dispute.

Matters such as matrimonial/family disputes, criminal cases (which are compoundable), land acquisition cases, labour disputes, bank recovery cases, etc., are usually taken up in the Lok Adalats.

The proceedings in a Lok Adalat are deemed to be judicial proceedings and it has the powers of a civil court in its proceedings. The award made by the Lok Adalat in any case shall be final and no appeal shall lie against such award in any court.

The benefits of the Lok Adalat include procedural flexibility and speedy trial, direct interaction with the judges by the parties through their counsel and speedy final settlement of disputes. However, the main challenge with Lok Adalats is that since it is based on compromise between parties to the dispute; if no compromise is reached, the case returns to the courts. Also, in majority of cases, poor litigants are pitted against powerful entities like insurance companies and banks, and they are forced to accept the compromise settlement.

In 2002, the Legal Services Authorities Act was amended to provide for establishment of the Permanent Lok Adalats for dealing with cases pertaining to public utility services like transport services; postal, telegraph or telephone; supply of power, light or water; sanitation; hospital or dispensary and insurance services.

MAINS STARTER

Area	Building Blocks For Model Introductions
Appointment of High Court Judges	Judges to a High Court are appointed by the President (executive) after consultation with the Chief Justice of India (judiciary), Chief Justice of the High Court and Governor of the State [Art 217]. This process has been subject to various case laws in the court that has resulted in the creation of the collegium system.
Removal of Judges	The Constitution provides a stringent process for the removal of judges of higher judiciary to ensure their independence. They may be removed on the grounds of proved misbehaviour or incapacity after a resolution with special majority is passed in both the houses in the same session [Art 218].
Writ Jurisdiction of High Court	The writ jurisdiction of the High Court is wider in scope and can be exercised by the High Courts for enforcement of fundamental rights guaranteed in Part III as well as for enforcement of other legal rights [Art 226].
Lok Adalats	Lok Adalats are alternate dispute redressal mechanism constituted under the Legal Services Authorities Act, 1987. They are aimed at providing speedy settlement of disputes based on compromise between the parties.

UPSC PREVIOUS YEARS' QUESTIONS OF PRELIMINARY EXAMINATION

1. With reference to the Constitution of India, consider the following statements: [2019]

1. No High Court shall have the jurisdiction to declare any central law to be constitutionally invalid.
2. An amendment to the Constitution of India cannot be called into question by the Supreme Court of India.

Which of the statements given above is/are correct?

(a) 1 only (b) 2 only (c) Both 1 and 2 (d) Neither 1 nor 2

Solution: (d)

Explanation: As discussed in Section 12.7, both Supreme Court and High Courts have power of judicial review including reviewing constitutional amendments. Hence both the statements are incorrect and the answer is (d).

UPSC Previous Years' Questions of Main Examination

1. Explain and distinguish between Lok Adalats and Arbitration Tribunals. Whether they entertain civil as well as criminal cases? **[2024]**

Approach: Explain Lok Adalats and Arbitration tribunals in the first part of the answer. Then, conclude by stating Lok Adalats can try both civil and criminal cases (that are compoundable) while arbitration tribunals are for civil matters.

MODEL ANSWER

Lok Adalats and Arbitration tribunals are both Alternate Dispute Redressal (ADR) mechanisms. While Lok Adalats are set up under the Legal Services Authority Act, 1987, arbitration tribunals are set up under the Arbitration and Conciliation Act, 1996.

Lok Adalats

(a) These are people's court organised at Supreme Court, High Court and district court levels.

(b) They entertain civil and minor criminal cases that are compoundable (like criminal case for dishonoured cheques). Serious criminal cases that are not-compoundable cannot be tried by Lok Adalats.

(c) Cases pending before courts or even in pre-litigation stage may be referred to Lok Adalat based on application by the parties to the dispute.

(d) Usually, no appeal lies against the order of Lok Adalats as the parties reach a settlement in an informal and amicable manner.

Arbitration Tribunals

(a) These are set up as per contractual terms for settling commercial and contractual disputes. They do not entertain criminal cases.

(b) It is a formal process and the award is binding on the parties.

(c) However, appeal can lie with higher courts.

Thus, Lok Adalats can entertain civil and minor criminal cases that are compoundable while arbitration tribunals only hear civil disputes.

2. Who are entitled to receive free legal aid? Assess the role of the National Legal Service Authority (NALSA) in rendering free legal aid in India. **[2023]**

Approach: The details provided in grey shaded box in Section 13.5.2 needs to be reproduced for the first part of the answer. The role of NALSA and Lok Adalats as discussed in that section should form the second part of the answer.

MODEL ANSWER

National Legal Services Authority of India (NALSA) has been formed under the Legal Services Authorities Act, 1987.

Persons eligible for free legal aid under the Act include:

(a) Member of Scheduled Caste or Scheduled Tribe;

(b) A victim of trafficking in human beings or begar as referred in Article 23 of the Constitution;

(c) A woman or a child up to 18 years of age;

(d) A mentally ill or otherwise disabled person;

(e) A victim of mass disaster, ethnic violence, caste atrocity, flood, drought, earthquake or industrial disaster;

(f) An industrial workman;

(g) A person in receipt of annual income less than limit specified under the Act. This limit varies from State to State (in most States the limit is ₹1,00,000). In respect of cases before the Supreme Court, the limit is ₹5,00,000.

Role of NALSA in rendering free legal aid

As per the directions of NALSA, the State Legal Services Authorities, constitute Lok Adalats to provide speedy trial and also free legal aid to eligible persons.

Matters such as matrimonial/family disputes, criminal cases (which are compoundable), land acquisition cases, labour disputes, bank recovery cases, etc., are usually taken up in Lok Adalats.

The benefits of Lok Adalat include procedural flexibility and speedy trial, direct interaction with the judges by the parties through their counsel and speedy final settlement of disputes.

CHAPTER 14

Fundamental Rights

LEARNING OUTCOMES

1. Understanding Natural, Fundamental, Constitutional and Legal Rights and their significance
2. Defining Fundamental rights and explaining their role in safeguarding individual liberties
3. Interpreting the constitutional definition of 'State' and examining the limitations imposed on it
4. Understanding in detail the six broad categories of Fundamental Rights, and doctrines and case laws relating to their interpretation
5. Recognising the exceptions to Fundamental Rights
6. Analysing Constitutional rights and their importance

14.1 INTRODUCTION TO FUNDAMENTAL RIGHTS

A right is essentially an entitlement or a reasonable claim. It denotes what we are entitled to as citizens and as human beings.

Rights place an obligation upon the State to act in certain kinds of ways. Each right indicates what the State must do as well as what it must not do. For example, the right to life creates a duty on the State to make laws that protects people from harm by others. Similarly, the right to liberty of a person, for instance, suggests that the State cannot simply arrest someone at its own will without reasonable procedure. Thus, rights are essentially claims of citizens or persons against the State and it creates duties on the State to protect those rights.

14.1.1 Various Types of Rights

Rights can be broadly classified into four categories – Natural, Fundamental, Constitutional and Legal. A brief description of these rights, examples for the same and also their enforceability in a court of law in the Indian context is summarised in the table, next page.

Type of Rights	Description	Examples	Enforceability in India
Natural Rights	These are inalienable human rights that a person is born with.	Right to Life, Liberty and Property.	Not enforceable by itself in a court of law in India. However, right to life and liberty are guaranteed as a Fundamental Right. Right to Property is a constitutional right.
Fundamental Rights	These are enumerated and guaranteed in Part III of the Constitution.	Right to equality, right to life and liberty, freedom of religion, etc.	Directly enforceable in the Supreme Court under Article 32 and also in High Courts under Article 226.
Constitutional Rights	These are provided in the Constitution but outside of Part III.	Right to property, right to vote and contest elections, etc.	Enforceable as per the law that provides for these constitutional rights. May also be directly enforceable in a High Court under Article 226.
Legal Rights	These are provided by ordinary laws of the Parliament or the State Legislature.	Right to work, Right to Maternity Benefit, Forest Rights Act, etc.	Enforceable in the courts as per the law that provides these legal rights. May also be directly enforceable in a High Court under Article 226.

In this chapter, we shall be discussing the Fundamental and Constitutional rights in detail.

14.1.2 Fundamental Rights in Indian Constitution

The Fundamental Rights are enshrined in Part III of the Constitution from Articles 12 to 35. These are modelled on the basis of 'Bill of Rights' of the US Constitution.

They are called 'fundamental' because of the following reasons:

1. They guarantee the basic political rights of equality and liberty that is enshrined in the Preamble to the Constitution;
2. They are essential for the all-round development of an individual; they are also favourable conditions and guarantees to be provided by the State to its citizens to live a dignified life;
3. They are guaranteed and protected by the fundamental law of the land i.e., the Constitution itself.

Originally, the Constitution provided for seven categories of Fundamental Rights:

1. Right to Equality (Art 14–18)
2. Right to Freedom (Art 19–22)
3. Right against Exploitation (Art 23–24)
4. Right to Freedom of Religion (Art 25–28)
5. Cultural and Educational Rights (Art 29–30)
6. Right to Property (Art 31)
7. Right to Constitutional Remedies (Art 32)

However, the Right to Property was deleted from Fundamental Rights by the 44th Constitutional Amendment Act in 1978. It is now a constitutional right under Article 300A. Hence, at present, we have the other six categories of Fundamental Rights.

It must be noted that Articles 14–18 that deal with the Right to Equality are aimed to guarantee equality of status and of opportunity as enshrined in the Preamble. Similarly, Articles 19–30 are aimed to guarantee liberty as enshrined in the Preamble.

We shall discuss about these six categories of Fundamental Rights in detail in this chapter. But before that, the following provisions and conceptual points relating to the Fundamental Rights need to be understood:

(a) The Constitution guarantees the Fundamental Rights of individuals against the State. Some of them are guaranteed against actions of other individuals as well. It also guarantees the rights of minorities.

(b) The Rights under Articles 15, 16, 19, 29 and 30 are available only to citizens. The rest of fundamental rights are available to all persons.

(c) Fundamental rights are not absolute in character. It means that there can be reasonable restrictions that can be placed by the State on these rights in the interest of the society.

(d) Fundamental rights are negative in character – One of the functions of the Constitution is to set limits on what a government can impose on its citizens. The part on Fundamental Rights, while guaranteeing the basic rights of equality and liberty, also places restriction on the State from making any laws that contravene these fundamental rights. Hence, they are negative in character as they place restriction on the State. Thus, they establish a 'government of laws and not of men'.

(e) Rights are claims of citizens and other persons against the State. They are also correlative with duties as they create duties on the State to protect these rights of individuals.

(f) They are not sacrosanct or permanent. However, they can be amended only by an amendment of the Constitution without affecting the 'basic structure'.

(g) They can be suspended during the proclamation of national emergency (except Articles 20 and 21).

(h) They are directly enforceable in the Supreme Court under Article 32. Most of them are self-executory (directly enforceable), while a few of them can be enforced on the basis of law for giving effect to them (like Articles 17, 23). Such a law can be made only by the Parliament, and not State legislatures, to ensure uniformity throughout the country (Art 35).

14.2 DEFINITION OF STATE AND RESTRICTIONS ON STATE

14.2.1 Definition of State

Article 12 defines 'the State' for the purpose of Fundamental Rights. Accordingly, the State includes:

(a) the Government and the Parliament of India,

(b) the Government and the Legislature of each of the States,

(c) all Local or other authorities within the territory of India or under the control of the Government of India.

Scan the QR code for conceptual video on 'Introduction to Fundamental Rights'

McGraw Hill edge

As we had discussed in the earlier section, rights are claims of citizens primarily against the State. Hence, the definition of State includes the legislative and the executive organs at both the Union and the State level. It also includes local bodies like the panchayats and the municipalities as well as any other statutory or non-statutory authorities under the control of the Government. The Supreme Court has also held that even a private body may be included within the definition of the State if it acts as an agency of the Government.

The definition of the State is important as the Constitution places restriction on the State from making any laws that contravene the Fundamental Rights.

14.2.2 Laws Inconsistent with Fundamental Rights to be Void

Article 13 places restriction on the State from making any laws that contravene the Fundamental Rights guaranteed in Part III. It provides that any law that contravenes the rights guaranteed in Part III can be declared void. Thus, it provides for the judicial review.

Judicial review is the power of the judiciary to declare any Act of the State as ultra vires (beyond the competence of the legislature or the executive to make the law) and void (not valid). This power of judicial review, though not explicitly mentioned in the Constitution, is implicitly conferred on the Supreme Court (through Article 32) and on the High Courts (through Article 226).

> **THINK ABOUT IT**
>
> Fundamental Rights in Part III lay the foundation for a constitutional government. Elucidate.

Article 13 provides for the following:

Provisions	Explanation/Example
All laws in force in the territory of India immediately before the commencement of the Constitution, in so far as they are inconsistent with the provisions of Part III, shall, to the extent of such inconsistency, be void [Art 13(1)].	For example, Section 377 of the Indian Penal Code, 1860 was in force from before the commencement of the Constitution. It criminalised homosexuality, even amongst consenting adults. However, after right to privacy was declared as an intrinsic right under Article 21, the Supreme Court, in ***Navtej Singh Johar case*** (2018), struck down section 377 of the IPC as unconstitutional. This is by virtue of power of judicial review under Article 32 read with this provision under Article 13.
The State shall not make any law which takes away or abridges (diminishes) the rights conferred by Part III and any law made in contravention of this clause shall, to the extent of the contravention, be void [Art 13(2)].	For example, Section 66A of the Information Technology Act, 2000 provided that sending 'offensive' information through a computer or mobile device can result in conviction and punishment for up to three years. However, the Supreme Court, in ***Shreya Singhal case*** (2015), held that this provision was an unreasonable restriction on the freedom of speech and expression guaranteed under Article 19(1)(a). Hence, it declared section 66A of IT Act as unconstitutional and void. This is again by virtue of power of judicial review under Article 32 read with this provision under Article 13.
Law includes any ordinance, order, bye-law, rule, regulation, notification, custom or usages having in the territory of India the force of law [Art 13(3)].	Since the 'State' includes both the legislature and the executive, law has been defined to include not only the ordinary laws passed by the Parliament or the State legislatures, but the executive instruments like ordinance, order, rules, regulations etc. Even a custom that has the force of law is considered to be part of law for the purpose of Article 13. Thus, none of these legislative laws, executive instruments or even customary practices should violate the Fundamental rights guaranteed in Part III.

Provisions	Explanation/Example
Nothing in this article shall apply to any amendment of the Constitution made under Article 368 [Art 13(4)].	The Supreme Court in the ***Golak Nath case*** held that even a constitutional amendment is a law within the meaning of Article 13 and hence Fundamental Rights cannot be amended at all even through a constitutional amendment. In order to overturn that decision of the Supreme Court, the Parliament amended Article 13 through the 24th Constitutional Amendment in 1971 and added this clause. The Supreme Court in ***Kesavananda Bharti case*** had upheld this amendment but also held that any constitutional amendment of the Fundamental Rights cannot violate the 'Basic structure' of the Constitution.

The following doctrines (principles) with respect to interpretation of the fundamental rights, as decided by the Supreme Court in various cases, need to be briefly understood.

Doctrine of Severability

- It means that if a part of an amendment or law is unconstitutional, that part alone can be declared void by severing (cutting off) it from the rest of the amendment or law. This will ensure that the rest of the amendment or law is valid and enforceable, while declaring the part that violates the Fundamental Rights to be void.
- It is a very important principle to protect the Fundamental Rights of every citizen.
- The substance of the law, and not its mere form, will be considered for the purpose of applying this doctrine. Further, after the invalid portion is struck down, if the remaining portion of the law cannot be meaningfully enforced, then the entire law is to be struck down as void. The courts will consider the history of the legislation, its object and preamble while deciding.
- This principle has been applied in *A.K. Gopalan case, Kihoto Hollohan case* and *Minerva Mills case* by the Supreme Court.

Doctrine of Eclipse

- This is primarily applicable to the pre-constitutional law [as referred to in Art 13(1) above]. If such a law or any of its part is in conflict with a Fundamental Right, it does not automatically become a dead letter, but only remains dormant and inoperative i.e., it is eclipsed by the provisions of the Fundamental Rights guaranteed in Part III.
- If there is any amendment to the Fundamental Right in future that removes this conflict, it will automatically make such law operative.
- This principle has been applied in *Bhikaji Vs State of M.P. case.*
- Originally, this doctrine was applied only for pre-constitution law. However, in Ambica Mills case and Dulare Lodh Case, the Supreme Court applied this doctrine even to a post-Constitution law made after 1950.

Doctrine of Waiver

- This doctrine is based on the premise that a person is his/her best judge and has the liberty to waive the enjoyment of rights conferred on him/her, either through a law or a contract. Such a person can no longer claim that right once he/she has waived off that right.
- However, this is applicable only to a legal right or rights under any contract. This doctrine is not applicable to the Fundamental Rights guaranteed under Part III and other constitutional rights as they are a matter of public policy. Moreover, the Constitution creates an obligation on the

State to protect these rights and hence the Fundamental rights and other constitutional rights cannot be waived off under this doctrine by any individual.

- This principle has been applied in Behram Khurshed Pesikaka Vs The State of Bombay, Basheshar Nath Vs The Commissioner of Income Tax of Delhi & Rajasthan, Olga Tellis & Ors Vs Bombay Municipal Corporation.

14.3 RIGHT TO EQUALITY

14.3.1 Concept of Equality

Equality invokes the idea that all human beings have an equal worth regardless of their colour, gender, race or nationality. Equality also implies no discrimination of the citizens by the State.

The concept of equality implies that all persons are entitled to the same rights and opportunities to develop themselves. There may be natural inequalities due to differences in skill and talent. For example, every person who plays cricket cannot claim a right to be part of the national cricket team. This is due to inherent difference in skill and talent. This natural inequality is not considered as lack of equality in the society. But it is the inequalities in peoples' access to basic goods such as education, health care and safe housing that makes an unequal society. The State aims to ensure that such societal inequality does not exist by guaranteeing equal access and rights.

Equality can be broadly classified under the following three categories:

- Political equality – Granting equal citizenship to all members of the State/Country with basic rights.
- Social equality – People belonging to different groups and communities also have a fair and equal chance to compete for goods and opportunities. For example, underprivileged castes, women etc.
- Economic equality – Trying to bridge inequality in income and wealth and providing equal opportunities in economic activities.

Affirmative actions are designed to correct the cumulative effects of past inequalities. The aim of this differential treatment is to ensure that a set of people can enjoy the same rights as the rest of the society.

Articles 14–18 under the category 'Right to Equality' primarily aims at guaranteeing political equality (Articles 14 to 16) and social equality (Articles 17 and 18) to all citizens or persons. However, it also provides for affirmative action in order to achieve social justice.

14.3.2 Equality before Law or Equal Protection of the Laws

Article 14 guarantees that the State shall not deny to any person equality before the law or the equal protection of the laws within the territory of India. It applies to both citizens and foreigners and is part of the basic structure. The term 'persons' also includes legal persons like corporations, companies, registered societies etc.

THINK ABOUT IT

Compare and contrast the principles of 'equality before law' and 'equal protection of the laws' under the Indian Constitution.

Equality before the law

It is a British concept and a component of Rule of Law propounded by the British jurist *A. V. Dicey*. This implies that all citizens are equal in the eyes of law. It means that:

- There will be absence of any special privileges in favour of any person;
- Everyone is subject to same set of laws; and
- There will be no person above the law, irrespective of their status in the society.

It is negative in nature as it restricts the State from making any discrimination between citizens.

Various criminal laws in the country are an example for equality before the law.

Rule of Law

'Rule of Law' is a concept propounded by the British jurist A.V. Dicey. There are three main principles behind this concept:

1. No man is punishable unless he/she has violated a law and has been tried in a court;
2. In terms of equality before law, no man is above the law;
3. Principle of supremacy of law, which is a result of the ordinary law of the land as interpreted by the British courts.

While the first two aspects are applicable as it is even in India, the third aspect is different in the Indian context as it is the Constitution that is supreme and is the source of all rights.

Equal protection of the Law

This is an American concept. It is a positive concept as it implies that people who are in similar circumstances shall be treated similarly. It implies that the State should ensure that every citizen gets equal protection of law and no one should be deprived of justice because of poverty or any other reason.

- It means that there will be equality of treatment under equal circumstances, both in privileges conferred and liabilities imposed by the laws.
- The like shall be treated alike without any discrimination.

Laws like the Income Tax Act, which provide for differential slabs of taxation based on income of an individual; certain special concessions for women in public transport etc., are examples of equal protection of the laws.

However, it must be noted that the classification for equal protection of the laws should not be arbitrary or irrational. It must be based on intelligible and reasonable distinction. Further, the classification must have reasonable relation to the objective or purpose of the legislation.

Exceptions to Equality

Equality before law is subject to a few exceptions as per the Constitution and certain conventions:

1. Protection to the President and the Governor in performing their duties [Art 361].
   - No criminal proceedings against the President or the Governor during their term of office;
   - No process for arrest or imprisonment of the President or the Governor during their term of office;
   - No civil proceedings against the President or the Governor except until expiration of 2 months' notice.

   These privileges were available to the Governor General and the Governors during the British rule. They have continued to exist under our Constitution for the President and the Governor.
2. Privileges of Members of the Parliament and the State Legislature under Articles 105 and 194, respectively.

3. Diplomats and ambassadors of other nations enjoy immunity from the civil and the criminal jurisdiction under Vienna convention. This is an international treaty that is applicable in more than 190 countries on a reciprocal basis in order to facilitate smooth functioning of diplomatic relations.

14.3.3 Prohibition of Discrimination

Article 15 guarantees that the State shall not discriminate against any citizen on grounds only of religion, race, caste, sex, place of birth or any of them [Art 15(1)]. This is applicable for any action by the State i.e., the legislative or the executive action. It must also be noted that this protection under Article 15 is available only for citizens.

This means that no citizen shall be treated unfavourably by the State when compared to others only because of religion, race, caste, sex or place of birth. The significance of the word 'only' is that if there is any other ground, along with any of the grounds specified in the article, the discrimination shall not be unconstitutional. For example, let us assume that the State requires help for evacuation of a hilly village that has been affected by floods. If it makes an order specifying that only men above the age of 18 years will be enrolled for the activity considering the nature of the terrain and hardships involved, that will not be considered as discrimination 'only' on the basis of sex, since it is also considering the physical demands of the work involved.

While clause (1) of Article 15 prohibits discrimination by the State, clause (2) provides protection even against discrimination by private individuals.

No citizen shall, on grounds only of religion, race, caste, sex, place of birth or any of them, be subject to any disability, liability, restriction or condition with regard to

- access to shops, public restaurant, hotels and places of public entertainment; or
- the use of wells, tanks, bathing ghats, roads and places of public resort maintained wholly or partly out of State funds or dedicated to the use of the general public [Art 15(2)].

This protection is considering the historical practices in Indian society where certain sections of depressed classes (like Scheduled Castes) were not allowed access to public places including wells and tanks. This clause guarantees the fundamental right of every citizen to public places like restaurants, hotels, wells, tanks etc., even if they are maintained by private individuals or the community as long as they are for use of general public.

Exceptions to non-discrimination

The following clauses in Article 15 provide the exceptions to this right against discrimination:

(3) The State can make any special provision for women and children.

(4) The State can make special provisions for the advancement of any socially and educationally backward classes of citizens or for the Scheduled Castes and the Schedule Tribes [added through the 1st Amendment of the Constitution in 1951].

(5) The State can make special provisions, by law, for the advancement of any socially and educationally backward classes of citizens or for the Scheduled Castes or the Scheduled Tribes in so far as such special provisions relate to their admission to educational institutions including the private educational institutions, whether aided or unaided by the State, other than the minority educational institutions established under Article 30(1). [added through the 93rd Amendment of the Constitution in 2005].

- This amendment was upheld by the Supreme Court in 2008.

(6) The State can make any special provisions for the advancement of any economically weaker sections of citizens including special provisions in relation to their admission to educational institutions including private educational institutions, whether aided or unaided by the State, other than the minority educational institutions established under Article 30(1), which in the case of reservation would be in addition to existing reservations and subject to a maximum of 10% [added through the 103rd Amendment of the Constitution in 2019].

- This amendment was upheld by the Supreme Court in 2022.

Scan the QR code for conceptual video on Right to Equality

The above exceptions are affirmative actions aimed at correcting the historical disadvantage of backward classes, in order to achieve social justice.

We shall discuss the reservation for the Other Backward Classes, the Scheduled Castes, the Scheduled Tribes and the Economically Weaker Sections, as well as the various case laws relating to these reservations together after discussion on Article 16.

14.3.4 Prohibition of Discrimination in Public Employment

While Article 15 guarantees the right against discrimination in all matters, Article 16 provides against discrimination specifically in the matter of public employment with the State.

Article 16 provides for the following rights:

(1) There shall be equality of opportunity for all citizens in matters relating to employment or appointment to any office under the State.

(2) No citizen shall, on grounds only of religion, race, caste, sex, descent, place of birth, residence or any of them, be ineligible for, or discriminated against in respect of, any employment or office under the State.

The following are the exceptions provided in Article 16 to this right against discrimination in matters relating to public employment:

(3) The Parliament can make any law prescribing, in regard to a class or classes of employment any requirement as to residence within that State or the Union territory prior to such employment or appointment –

a. The Public employment (Requirement as to Residence Act), 1957 was enacted by the Parliament which repealed any residence requirement for employment in any State laws.

b. Exceptions made for Andhra Pradesh, Himachal Pradesh, Manipur and Tripura were effective for 15 years till 1974.

c. It must be noted that it is only the Parliament (and not State legislatures) that can provide for residence as a requirement considering the local or regional requirements.

(4) The State can make any provision for the reservation of appointments or posts in favour of any backward class of citizens which, in the opinion of the State, is not adequately represented in the services under the State.

(5) A law can provide that the incumbent of an office in connection with the affairs of any religious or denominational institution shall be a person professing a particular religion or belonging to a particular denomination.

a. For example, the government can specify that the governing body member of a Hindu religious trust should be a Hindu or of a Shia Wakf Board should be a Shia Muslim.

(6) The State can make any provision for the reservation of appointments or posts in favour of any economically weaker sections of citizens, in addition to the existing reservation and subject to a maximum of 10% [added through the 103rd Amendment of the Constitution in 2019].

Brief history of reservation policy in India

- The reservation of seats in educational institutions and government jobs was initially provided to the Scheduled Castes (SC) and the Scheduled Tribes (ST). In 1982, the reservation for the Scheduled Castes was fixed at 15% and for the Scheduled Tribes at 7.5% in both the central educational institutions and the public sector undertakings. The reservation percentages vary from State to State according to their demographic profile and policy of the State.
- The first Backward Classes Commission was set up under Article 340 of the Constitution in 1953 under the chairmanship of Shri Kaka Kalelkar. The Commission recommended reservation for the Socially and Educationally Backward Classes (SEBC) in the central government educational institutions and jobs. However, no action was taken on the report by the Central government.
- The second Backward Classes Commission was set up in 1979 under the chairmanship of *Shri B. P. Mandal.* This was famously known as the Mandal Commission. The commission submitted its report in 1980 and recommended 27% reservation for SEBC or the Other Backward Classes (OBC) thereby fixing the total reservation (for OBC, SC and ST) at 50%.
- It was in 1990, when Shri V. P. Singh was the Prime Minister, that 27% reservation for OBC was implemented.

Important Case laws relating to reservation in public employment

a. **Indra Sawhney Case – 1992 – also known as 'Mandal' Case**

- This case challenged the 27% reservation for the OBCs that was introduced in 1990.
- The Supreme Court in this judgement upheld the 27% reservation of seats for the OBC.
- It opined that caste is a determinant of class in Indian context and the backwardness cannot be determined solely based on economic criteria.
- Schedule Castes and Schedule Tribes are 'backward' without doubt and there is no need to quantify/demonstrate the same.
- It fixed the cap of reservation at 50% unless there are exceptional circumstances to breach it.
- It also provided for exclusion of creamy layer amongst the OBC in the matters of reservation. The criteria for identifying 'creamy layer' are based on the recommendations of **Justice Ram Nandan Prasad Committee (1993)**. Children of (a) persons holding constitutional posts; (b) Group A/Class I and Group B/Class II officers of Central and State services and equivalent posts in PSUs, Banks, etc; (c) persons holding rank of colonel and above in army or equivalent in Navy, Air force and paramilitary forces; (d) persons having gross annual income of ₹8 lakhs or above (excluding salary and agricultural income); (e) persons holding agricultural land above certain limits or land/buildings in urban areas, etc., are excluded as belonging to 'creamy layer.'
- It held that reservations can be provided only in appointments and not in promotions. Consequently, the Parliament through 77th and 81st Amendments, added Articles 16(4A) and 16(4B), respectively.
- A permanent commission to be set up to examine the inclusion of the Backward Classes in OBC list. The National Commission for Backward Classes was set up in 1993 as a statutory body for this purpose and also for advising the government with respect to welfare of the Backward Classes. This commission has now been given constitutional status through the 102nd Constitutional amendment.

b. Constitutional amendments for reservation in promotions for SC and ST

- In the Indra Sawhney case, the Supreme Court held that reservations can be provided only in appointments and not in promotions. Further, it held that reservation for any year including backlog vacancies from previous years cannot exceed 50%. In order to overcome this, the Constitution was amended to include clause (4A) and clause (4B) as follows through the 77th and 81st Amendments, respectively.
- Article 16 (4A) – The State can make provision for reservation in matters of promotion, with consequential seniority, to any class or classes of posts in favour of the Scheduled Castes and the Scheduled Tribes which, in the opinion of the State, are not adequately represented in the services under the State.
- Article 16 (4B) – The State can consider any unfilled vacancies of a year which are reserved, in appointments or promotions, as a separate class of vacancies to be filled up in any succeeding year or years and such class of vacancies shall not be considered together with the vacancies of the year in which they are being filled up for determining the ceiling of 50% reservation on total number of vacancies of that year.

Scan the QR code for discussion on recent judgement of the Supreme Court with respect to sub-classification of Scheduled Castes and Scheduled Tribes

McGraw Hill edge

c. M. Nagaraj Case – 2006

- This case upheld the above amendments – 16(4A) and 16(4B) – with respect to reservation in promotions and backlog vacancies, but laid down the following three conditions:
  i. State must show the backwardness of the class.
  ii. Second, it must show that the class is inadequately represented in the position/service for which reservations in promotion will be granted. So, for the SC and the ST, there must be quantifiable data to demonstrate lack of representation.
  iii. It must show that the reservations are in the interest of administrative efficiency.

d. Jarnail Singh case – Review of Nagaraj judgement in 2018

- Many States found it difficult to satisfy the conditions that were laid down in the *Nagaraj case* judgement. There were many petitions seeking review of this judgement, as some of the conditions were in contradiction to the judgement in the Indra Sawhney case.
- The Supreme Court heard all these petitions together in the *Jarnail Singh case* and gave its judgement in 2018:
  - It struck down the demonstration of backwardness for the SC and the ST as laid down in the *Nagaraj case* (as it is against the judgement in the Indra Sawhney case).
  - There is no need for any quantifiable data to provide for promotions for the SC and the ST.
  - However, it introduced the creamy layer exclusion principle for the SC and the ST in reservation for promotions. However, the Central Government or various States have not implemented this aspect (as of 2024).

e. Sub-classification of Scheduled Castes (SC) and Scheduled Tribes (ST) for reservation – 2024

- A seven-judge bench of the Supreme Court by a majority of 6:1 held that States can pass laws to create sub-classification of SC and ST in their reservation. This case was relating to review of constitutional validity of certain State laws that provided sub-classification within SC for reservation benefits. The court held that this power flows from Articles 15(4) and 16(4) of the Constitution.

- This judgement overruled the earlier judgement of the court in E.V. Chinnaiah case (2005) that had held that State legislatures cannot provide any sub-classification within the Presidential list of SC and ST.
- In this 2024 judgement, four judges also impressed upon the government to frame suitable policies for exclusion of 'creamy layer' from SC and ST reservation. However, the Central government in a cabinet meeting asserted and reaffirmed that creamy layer does not apply to reservations for SC and ST.

Reservation for Economically Weaker Sections (EWS)

- The 103rd Constitutional amendment introduced reservation for the EWS that are not part of the OBC, the SC or the ST. In other words, EWS reservation is applicable for persons who belong to the General (unreserved) Category and do not enjoy any reservation benefits as OBC, SC or ST.
- This reservation can be extended by the State in educational institutions as well as public employment. The amendment suitably introduced clause (6) in Article 15 and clause (6) in Article 16.
- The maximum reservation for the EWS shall not exceed 10%. This will be over and above the existing reservation of 50% for the OBC, the SC and the ST.
- The Central and State governments can provide their respective eligibility criteria for EWS reservation. The criterion at the Centre is that persons whose family income is below ₹8 lakh per annum are eligible. This includes all sources of income and family includes the person who seeks reservation benefit; his/her parents and siblings below 18 years; and his/her spouse and children below 18 years. Further, persons who own or possess agricultural land, residential plot or flat above the specified thresholds are excluded.
- The Supreme Court by a majority of 3:2 upheld the constitutional validity of this EWS reservation in November 2022 ***[Janhit Abhiyan Vs Union of India]***. All the 5 judges agreed that the economic criteria can be a basis for reservation but differed in their views on other aspects of the amendment. The summary of key points of majority and minority view in this judgement is summarised below.
    - Majority view
        (a) Reservation for the EWS only on the basis of economic criteria does not violate the basic structure of equality under the Constitution.
        (b) The SC, ST and OBC are a separate category covered under existing reservations under Article 15(4), 15(5) and Article 16(4). Excluding them from the EWS reservation is not arbitrary and this 10% reservation is for a separate category of EWS amongst 'General category' that is not covered by existing reservation.
        (c) The ceiling of 50% for reservation set in the Mandal case is not inflexible. That limit was set for the backward classes and this 10% reservation is for a new category of the EWS.
    - Minority view
        (a) The exclusion of the SC, the ST and the OBC from this quota of 10% is violative of equality as a basic structure.
        (b) Breach of ceiling of 50% for reservation set in the Mandal case can provide a gateway for further infractions (violations).

THINK ABOUT IT

Critically evaluate the 103rd constitutional amendment that provided 10% reservation for the Economically Weaker Sections.

The above provisions for reservation may be viewed as 'Differentiated Citizenship' in our country. The concept of 'Differentiated Citizenship' advocates the incorporation of members of certain (cultural) groups not only as individuals, but also as members of groups, their rights depending in part on this group membership catering to their special needs. This is provided in the Indian Constitution (under Articles 15 and 16 of Fundamental Rights, Articles 330 and 332, etc.) that provides for special provisions including reservations to be made for SEBC, SC, ST and EWS.

14.3.5 Abolition of Untouchability

- Untouchability is abolished and its practice in any form is forbidden. The enforcement of any disability arising out of untouchability shall be an offence punishable in accordance with law [Art 17].
- The Constitution has not defined the term 'untouchability' but there are laws that have been enacted to punish the practice of untouchability.
- Untouchability (offences) Act, 1955, has been amended and renamed as the 'Protection of Civil Rights Act, 1955'. This act makes the practice of untouchability punishable either by imprisonment up to 6 months or by fine up to ₹500 or both.
- The Scheduled Castes and the Scheduled Tribes (Prevention of Atrocities) Act, 1989 also provides for punishment for any atrocities that is committed against the Scheduled Castes or Scheduled Tribes.
- This is a right which is not only enforceable against the State but against any private person violating the law which prohibits untouchability. This view was upheld by the Supreme Court in ***People's Union for Democratic Rights*** case (1982).

14.3.6 Abolition of Titles

Article 18 abolishes conferring of titles by the State. It also places restrictions on citizens or persons accepting titles from the foreign state. The provisions of Article 18 are summarised below:

- The State shall not confer any title, except a military or academic distinction. So, for example, (a) military ranks like General, Major, Captain, Admiral etc.; (b) gallantry titles like Param Vir Chakra (PVC), Maha Vir Chakra (MVC); and (c) Doctorate by universities can be conferred by the State.
- A citizen of India shall not accept any title from any foreign State.
- Any person who is not a citizen of India, while he/she holds any office of profit or trust under the State, shall not accept without the consent of the President, any title from any foreign State.
- Any person (citizen or foreigner) holding any office of profit or trust under the State shall not, without the consent of the President, accept any present, emolument, or office of any kind from any foreign State.

In the Balaji Raghavan case, the Supreme Court allowed the State to give the Bharat Ratna and the Padma awards, but made it clear that these should not be used as a title. These National Awards were instituted in 1954. The Janata Party government headed by Morarji Desai discontinued them in 1977. But they were again revived in 1980 by the Indira Gandhi government. These awards were again suspended between 1992 and 1995 due to litigation in some of the High Courts. However, the Supreme Court in 1995 again reiterated that these awards are not titles within the meaning of Article 18 and hence can be awarded by the State. The total number of Padma awards and Bharat Ratna awards in a year shall not be more than 120 and 3 respectively. It is based on a note of Ministry of Home Affairs that mentions that the maximum number of Bharat Ratna awards in a year is restricted to 3. However, in 1999, 4 Bharat Ratna awards were conferred and in 2024, 5 Bharat Ratna awards were conferred. The recipients for Bharat Ratna are recommended by the Prime Minister to the

President. For the Padma Awards, the selection is carried out by the Padma Awards Committee, which is constituted annually by the Prime Minister. It is headed by the Cabinet Secretary and includes Home Secretary, Secretary to the President and four to six eminent persons as members.

MNEMONICS

Concept or Provisions	Shortcut or Mnemonics	Details to Remember
Article Numbers of Fundamental Rights from Article 14 to 18	END^2 AT	• **E**quality before law or Equal protection of the laws – 14 • **N**o **D**iscrimination – 15 • **N**o **D**iscrimination in Public employment – 16 • **A**bolition of untouchability – 17 • **T**itles abolition– 18

14.4 RIGHT TO FREEDOM

14.4.1 Concept of Liberty

- The Fundamental Rights under Articles 19–30 aim at securing the liberty of thought, expression, belief, faith and worship that is enshrined in the Preamble. They have been classified into different categories viz., Right to Freedom (Art 19–22), Right against Exploitation (Art 23 and 24), Right to freedom of religion (Art 25–28) and Cultural and educational rights (Art 29 and 30).
- Freedom means absence of constraints. It is important for all round development of the individuals. It is of two types:

1. Freedom is said to exist when the external constraints on an individual are absent – 'Negative Liberty' or 'Freedom from'.

   'Negative liberty' seeks to define and defend an area in which the individual would be inviolable. This is an area in which any external authority cannot unreasonably interfere. It is a minimum area that is sacred and in which whatever the individual does, is not to be interfered with. For example, Articles 20 and 22 reflect this concept of 'Negative liberty.'
2. Freedom is also the condition in which people can develop their creativity and capabilities – 'Positive Liberty' or 'Freedom to'.

   The individual to develop his/her capability must get the benefit of enabling positive conditions in material, political and social domains. That is, the person must not be constrained by poverty or unemployment; they must have adequate material resources to pursue their wants and needs. To develop their mind and intellect, individuals must have access to education and other associated opportunities necessary to lead a reasonably good life. For example, Article 19 reflects this concept of 'Positive liberty.'

Both are important and they complement each other.

- Liberty focuses on individual rights over family, society and community. The reasonable restriction to ensure no harm to others is the primary difference between absolute freedom and Liberty.

- This is eloquently explained by John Stuart Mill in his essay 'On Liberty' as the 'Harm Principle.' Any action or choice that affects only one's self, should not have any restriction or interference by the State. In contrast, actions that have consequences for others and may cause them harm, can have external restrictions by the State. This is provided in our constitution in the form of 'reasonable restrictions' that can be placed by the State on individual freedom in the interest of society.

14.4.2 Protection of Certain Liberties

Article 19(1) provides that all citizens shall have the fundamental right to:

(a) freedom of speech and expression;

(b) assemble peaceably and without arms;

(c) form associations or unions or cooperative societies;

(d) move freely throughout the territory of India;

(e) reside and settle in any part of the territory of India; and

(f) omitted

(g) practise any profession, or to carry on any occupation, trade or business.

- The right to acquire, hold and dispose of property that was a fundamental right under Article 19(1)(f) was omitted through the 44th Constitutional Amendment Act in 1978. It is now a constitutional-cum-legal right under Article 300A.

14.4.2.1 Freedom of Speech and Expression

This clause provides every citizen the right to express his/her views, opinions, beliefs and thoughts in any manner. The Supreme Court has held in various cases that the freedom of speech and expression includes the following:

- Right to propagate one's views
- Freedom of the press and media [upheld in *Romesh Thapar case* by the Supreme Court in 1950]
- Right to know about government activities
- Right against imposition of pre-censorship on newspaper
- Right to demonstration but not the right to strike
- Right against bandh called by political party or organisation
- Freedom of silence
- Freedom of commercial advertisements and exhibiting films
- Right to post information/videos on internet/social media (*Shreya Singhal* case)
- Right to access to information on the internet (*Anuradha Bhasin* case)

Article 19(2) provides that the State can impose reasonable restrictions on the exercise of the freedom of speech and expression on the grounds of sovereignty and integrity of India, security of the State, friendly relations with foreign states, public order, decency or morality, contempt of court, defamation and incitement to an offence.

It must be noted that the most important word with respect to restrictions is the word 'reasonable'. The courts can strike down any restriction that is unreasonable. For example, Section 66A of the Information Technology Act, 2000 provided that sending 'offensive' information through a computer or mobile device can result in conviction and punishment for up to 3 years. However, the Supreme

Court held that this provision was an unreasonable restriction on freedom of speech and expression guaranteed under Article 19(1)(a). Hence, it declared Section 66A of IT Act as unconstitutional and void. (*Shreya Singhal* case – 2015)

14.4.2.2 Freedom of Assembly

- Under this clause, every citizen has the right to assemble peaceably and without arms. It includes the right to hold public meetings, demonstrations and take out processions.
- This freedom can be exercised only on public land.
- Article 19(3) provides that the State can impose reasonable restrictions on the exercise of right of assembly on two grounds, namely, sovereignty and integrity of India, and public order.
- For example, Section 163 of Bharatiya Nagarik Suraksha Sanhita authorises a magistrate to place restrictions on assembly, meeting of people etc., in any area if there is a risk of obstruction to public order. However, any such restriction should be reasonable.

14.4.2.3 Freedom of Association

- Under this clause, every citizen has the right to form associations or unions or cooperatives (cooperatives was added through the 97th amendment).
- It includes the right to form political parties, societies, clubs, organisations or any association of persons.
- Article 19(4) provides that the State can impose reasonable restrictions on the exercise of right of association on the grounds of sovereignty and integrity of India, public order and morality.

14.4.2.4 Freedom of Movement

- Under this clause, every citizen can move freely throughout the territory of India.
- This right reflects that India is one nation and there cannot be any regionalism as far as movement of citizens within the country is concerned.
- Article 19(5) provides that the State can impose reasonable restrictions on this freedom in the interests of general public and the protection of interests of any Scheduled Tribe.
- The restriction in the interest of Scheduled Tribes is to protect their unique culture and to protect them from exploitation. This will be understood further when the provisions of the Fifth and Sixth schedules to the Constitution are discussed in later chapters.

14.4.2.5 Freedom of Residence

- Under this clause, every citizen has the right to temporarily reside in or permanently settle down in any part of the territory of India.
- This right reflects that India is one nation and there cannot be any regionalism as far as residence of citizens within the country is concerned.
- Article 19(5) provides that the State can impose reasonable restrictions on this freedom in the interests of general public and the protection of interests of any Scheduled Tribe.
- The restriction in the interest of the Scheduled Tribes is to protect their unique culture and to protect them from exploitation. This will be understood further when the provisions of the Fifth and Sixth schedules to the Constitution are discussed in later chapters.

14.4.2.6 Freedom of Profession

- Under this clause, all citizens are given the right to practise any profession or to carry on any occupation, trade or business.
- Article 19(6) provides that the State can impose reasonable restrictions on the exercise of this right in the interest of the general public. Further, the State is empowered to:
  - Prescribe professional or technical qualifications necessary for practising any profession or carrying on any occupation, trade or business. Thus, to practice medicine, the State can specify MBBS as qualification; to practice law, the State can specify a legal degree as a qualification etc.
  - Carry on by itself any trade, business, industry or service whether to the exclusion (complete or partial) of citizens or otherwise. Thus, the State can nationalise any trade or business partially or fully. For example, the Railways is a nationalised industry in our country.
- In 2023, the Punjab and Haryana High Court had struck down a law enacted by the Haryana assembly in 2021 that guaranteed 75% reservation to locals in private sector jobs in Haryana as violative of Article 19(1)(g). In 2020, in *Anuradha Bhasin* case, the Supreme Court held that freedom to carry on trade, business or occupation over the internet medium is integral to Article 19(1)(g). Similarly, in *Internet and mobile association of India Vs Reserve Bank of India* (2020), the court declared the circular that banned trading in virtual currencies (crypto currency) as unconstitutional and violative of Article 19(1)(g).

The following additional points need to be understood with respect to these six rights:

- These six rights are protected primarily against State action. However, in Kaushal Kishor Vs State of Uttar Pradesh (2023), the Supreme Court had held that Article 19 can be enforced even against private persons other than the State on a case to case basis.
- These rights are only applicable to Indian citizens and not to foreigners.
- This Article can be suspended only when National Emergency under war or external aggression is declared and not under armed rebellion.

MNEMONICS

Concept or Provisions	Shortcut or Mnemonics	Details to Remember
Article 19(1) (a) to (g)	SAw Ur MRP	• **S**peech & expression – 19(1)(a) • **A**ssemble without arms – 19(1)(b) • **U**nion & Associations – 19(1)(c) • **M**ovement within India – 19(1)(d) • **R**esidence in India – 19(1)(e) • **P**rofession – 19(1)(g)

14.4.3 Protection in Respect of Conviction for Offences

Article 20 guarantees protection against arbitrary and excessive punishment to all persons. This right is applicable to citizens, foreigners and even legal persons like corporations. This Article reflects some of the basic principles of criminal jurisprudence and has the following four important protection in respect of conviction for offences to any person accused of a crime:

1. No person shall be convicted of any offence except for violation of a law in force at the time of the commission of the Act charged as an offence [Art 20(1)].
   - This means there can be no ex post facto criminal law or there can be no criminal law with retrospective effect. A law is said to be retrospective when it is effective from a back date. A civil law can have retrospective effect but not a criminal law.
2. No person shall be subjected to a penalty greater than that which might have been inflicted under the law in force at the time of the commission of the offence [Art 20(1)].
   - The punishment for an offence cannot be more than what might have been awarded under the law on the date of commission of the crime.
   - For example, the punishment for theft under section 303 of Bharatiya Nyaya Sanhita, 2023 is imprisonment up to 3 years. Let us assume a person named 'X' commits a theft and is arrested as an accused for the same. Even if the Parliament subsequently increases the maximum period of imprisonment to 5 years, this person 'X' can be sentenced to a maximum of only 3 years in prison as it was the punishment that can be inflicted at the time of commission of the offence.
3. No person shall be prosecuted and punished for the same offence more than once [Art 20(2)].
   - This is famously known as protection against 'double jeopardy' in the United States.
   - It protects a person from being punished more than once for the same offence. However, it must be noted that this is applicable for only judicial punishment or prosecution. Departmental proceedings or other civil disqualifications due to conviction cannot be considered as punishment more than once. For example, a person convicted of a criminal offence and sentenced to minimum 2 years of imprisonment is disqualified from contesting elections for 6 years from the date of release. This disqualification from contesting in elections will not be considered as 'double jeopardy'. However, he/she cannot be criminally prosecuted for the same offence again once he/she has served his/her punishment.
4. No person accused of any offence shall be compelled to be a witness against himself/herself [Art 20(3)].
   - This protects an individual from 'self-incriminating' evidence. The burden of proof lies on the prosecution to prove the guilt of a person accused of a crime. Any person accused of a crime is presumed to be innocent until proven guilty beyond reasonable doubt. For this purpose, the accused cannot be forced to be a witness against himself/herself.
   - However, DNA or blood samples can be drawn from an accused and this is not considered to be a violation of this protection.

14.4.4 Right to Life and Personal Liberty

Article 21 stipulates that no person shall be deprived of his/her life or personal liberty except according to procedure established by the law. This right is available to citizens as well as foreigners.

THINK ABOUT IT

'Due process of law' is a stronger protection for life and liberty than 'procedure established by law.' Comment with important Supreme Court judgements in this regard.

14.4.4.1 'Procedure Established by Law' versus 'Due Process of Law'

- This right is a check on arbitrary powers of the State. The State must act according to a procedure established by law while depriving any individual of his/her liberty. The procedure established by the law has been borrowed from the British tradition. It checks whether the law is procedurally correct and whether such procedure established by the law has been followed by the executive while performing its action. However, the judiciary is not allowed to challenge the intentions of the law. In essence, 'procedure established by law' protects the life and liberty of an individual from arbitrary executive action.

- On the other hand, 'due process of law' is a facet of the American judiciary. Under this concept, the judiciary can challenge the law not only on the procedural grounds but also on the basis of its reasonableness. It implies that the law has to be fair and reasonable i.e., it should follow the principles of natural justice. If it does not, then it is liable to be struck down even if the prescribed procedure is followed. In essence, 'due process of law' safeguards an individual's life and liberty not only from arbitrary executive actions but also from arbitrary legislation.
- The Constituent Assembly after deliberations, decided to retain 'procedure established by law' for the purpose of protection under this article. However, this has been subject to interpretation and judgements of the Supreme Court in subsequent cases.

Important Case Laws

Scan the QR code for conceptual video on Right to Freedom and Right against exploitation

(1) A. K. Gopalan Case (1950)

The Supreme Court literally interpreted Article 21 and held that the due process of law is not available in India. Hence, it implied that the right under Article 21 only protects life and liberty of an individual from arbitrary executive action, and not from the legislative action. Further, it was enough if the procedure was followed and the courts could not inquire into the reasonableness of the procedure.

(2) Maneka Gandhi Case (1978)

The Supreme Court over turned its decision in the A. K. Gopalan case and accepted that the due process is inherent in procedure established by the law. The Supreme Court in this case applied the principle of the 'due process of law' for the first time. It applied the following arguments:

- Articles 19 and 21 can't be understood as watertight compartments and the same criteria of reasonableness as applicable in Article 19 must be applied for Article 21 as well.
- Merely following the procedure established by the law is not enough. The courts have the right to review and question the reasonableness of the procedure itself.
- Restrictions must be reasonable, just and fair and shouldn't be arbitrary.

In India, traditionally we followed the principle of 'procedure established by law', as it prevailed in Britain. However, since 1978 after the Maneka Gandhi case, the courts have held that the procedure established by the law has to be reasonable and follow the principles of natural justice. Further, the Supreme Court in various cases has held that the right to life as enshrined in Article 21 is more than mere survival and animal existence. It would include the right to live with dignity. Thus, though Article 21 is in the form of a negative liberty that casts a duty on the State not to interfere in life and liberty of an individual, yet various decisions of the Supreme Court have now imposed positive obligations on the State.

Rights as interpreted by the Supreme Court as rights covered under Article 21

The Supreme Court has read several rights into Article 21 in its various judgements. Some of the important ones are as follows:

- Right to live with human dignity
- Right to clean environment
- Right to work under safe conditions
- Right to privacy (declared as an integral part of Article 21 in the Puttaswamy case)
- Right to shelter

- Right to basic primary health
- Right to free legal aid
- Right to information
- Right to speedy and fair trial
- Right to travel abroad
- Right against bonded labour
- Right to emergency medical aid and timely medical treatment
- Right to die with dignity (passive euthanasia – *Common Cause Vs Union of India*)
- Right against Climate change (integral to Articles 14 and 21)

In 2018 in *Hadiya case*, the Supreme Court had ruled that the right to marry a person of one's choice is protected under Article 21 as it is part of Right to Privacy. However, in Supriyo case in 2023, that declined to legalise same-sex marriage, the Supreme Court held that the Constitution does not recognise marriage as a fundamental right and it is a legal right provided by statutes.

Doctrine of Proportionality

This doctrine was originally laid down by the Supreme Court in *Om Kumar Vs Union of India* case (2000) and further elaborated in the *Puttaswamy* case that upheld right to privacy. This doctrine seeks to balance the means and outcomes of government action. When a government body makes a decision, it should keep its goal in mind and use appropriate methods to achieve them. There should be a rational nexus between the objects and the means adopted to achieve them. This doctrine was also applied in *Vivek Narayan Sharma Vs Union of India* (case that upheld the demonetisation of ₹500 and ₹1000 notes) and in *Anuradha Bhasin Vs Union of India* (case that dealt with legality of internet shutdown).

14.4.5 Right to Education

- The State shall provide free and compulsory education to all children of the age of 6–14 years in such manner as the State may, by law, determine. It was added through the 86th Constitutional Amendment Act of 2002 after the Supreme Court in *Unni Krishnan* case (1993) had recognised right to primary education as a fundamental right under Article 21.
- The 86th Amendment Act brought about the following changes to the Constitution:
  - Under Article 21A, every child between the age of 6 and 14 has a fundamental right to education.
  - Early childhood care and protection (for children in the age group of 0–6) is provided for as a Directive Principle of State Policy under Article 45 of the Constitution.
  - Article 51A(k) provides a duty on parent or guardian, to provide opportunities for education to his/her child or ward between the age of 6 and 14.
- The Parliament has enacted the Right to Education Act, 2009 to supplement the Fundamental Right under Article 21A.

14.4.6 Protection against Arrest and Detention

Article 22 provides for protection in case of arrest and detention. While Article 20 deals with protection in case of conviction (i.e., punishment for a crime), Article 22 deals with protection in case of arrest in a criminal matter. The summary of protection under Article 22 is provided below [Art 22(1) and (2)]:

- A person who is arrested shall not be detained in custody without being informed of the grounds for such arrest;
- He/she shall not be denied the right to consult, and to be defended by, a legal practitioner of his/her choice;
- He/she shall be produced before the nearest magistrate within a period of 24 hours of such arrest excluding time taken for travel;
- He/she shall not be detained in custody beyond 24 hours without the order of a magistrate.

When a person is arrested and detained by the police, it is known as 'police custody'. When a magistrate orders the person to be sent to jail it is known as 'judicial custody'. The police have to obtain permission from the court for any further investigation of the accused person once he/she is sent to judicial custody.

Further, the following are the various categories of bail that may be granted to an accused under criminal laws:

- Regular bail which is granted under section 478 of The Bharatiya Nagarik Suraksha Sanhita, 2023 (BNSS).
- Anticipatory bail which is a pre-arrest legal process granted under section 482 of BNSS.
- Interim Bail – This is not explicitly provided in any statute but is granted by courts for a short period until a final decision on their regular or anticipatory bail plea is heard and disposed of under BNSS.
- Default bail or Statutory bail – This is granted when the police or investigating agency fails to submit a full charge sheet within the specified period of time (60 or 90 days depending on the nature of the offence). This is provided under section 187(3) of BNSS.

Exceptions to above protection

Article 22(3) provides that the above protection in case of arrest and detention shall not apply to the following set of persons:

(a) to any person who for the time being is an enemy alien (i.e., a foreigner in our country with which India is at war); or

(b) to any person who is arrested or detained under any law providing for preventive detention.

The detention for which protection under Article 22 is applicable is known as punitive detention i.e., arresting and detaining a person who is suspected of having committed a crime. On the other hand, preventive detention is to prevent a person from committing a crime.

The British provided for such detention in India before independence in various laws like the Bengal Regulation Act, 1818 and the Rowlatt Act, 1919. This is considered to be a draconian provision that affects the liberty of an individual. However, after deliberations, the Constituent Assembly adopted this provision.

Article 22(4) provides certain protection for the persons who are preventively detained:

- No law that provides for preventive detention shall authorise the detention of a person for a period more than 3 months unless an advisory board authorises detention for a longer period.
- Such an Advisory Board shall consist of persons who are, or are qualified to be appointed as, Judges of a High Court.

Article 22(5) provides that when any person is preventively detained under any law, the authority making the order shall, as soon as may be, communicate to such person the grounds on which the order has been made and shall afford him/her the earliest opportunity of making representation against the order. Article 22(6), however, provides that the authority need not disclose facts which such authority considers to be against public interest. The Supreme Court, in the case of *Mohammed Shaji* (2024), set stringent standards for authorities imposing preventive detention, making it mandatory to furnish all relevant documents and statements to the person being detained, that too in the language the detainee is conversant with.

The Constitution authorises both the Parliament and the State Legislature to pass laws providing for preventive detention. Parliament has exclusive powers to make law in this regard for reasons connected with defence, foreign affairs and security of India while both the Parliament and State legislatures can concurrently make laws for preventive detention for reasons connected with the security of a State, maintenance of public order and maintenance of supplies and services essential to the community. However, it is only the Parliament that can pass a law providing for preventive detention beyond 3 months without the opinion of an advisory board. Parliament can also make laws prescribing the maximum period for which any person may be detained under any preventive detention law and the procedure to be followed by the advisory board constituted under Article 22(4).

Some of the preventive detention laws made by the Parliament are as follows:

(a) Maintenance of Internal Security Act (MISA), 1971 (Repealed in 1978).
(b) Conservation of Foreign Exchange and Prevention of Smuggling Activities Act (COFEPOSA), 1974.
(c) National Security Act (NASA), 1980.
(d) Unlawful Activities (Prevention) Act (UAPA), 1967.

14.5 RIGHT AGAINST EXPLOITATION

14.5.1 Prohibition of Traffic in Human Beings and Forced Labour

Article 23 prohibits trafficking in human beings and all forms of forced labour.

- Traffic in human beings and *begar* and other similar forms of forced labour are prohibited and any contravention of this provision shall be an offence punishable in accordance with law [Art 23(1)].
- Article 23(1) abolishes any form of bonded labour, forced labour and trafficking in human beings. It has special significance for the SC/STs and women. Traffic in human beings includes selling and buying of men, women and children; *devadasi* system etc. '*Begar*' is described as labour or service, which a person is forced to give without receiving any remuneration for it.
- Various laws like Immoral Traffic (Prevention) Act, 1956; Bonded Labour System (Abolition) Act, 1976 have been enacted by the Parliament to prohibit trafficking and forced labour as well as to punish persons committing these offences.
- Article 23(2) provides an exception that the State can impose compulsory service for public purpose if there is a need for the same. However, there shall be no discrimination by the State while imposing such compulsory service only on the grounds of religion, race, caste or class.

14.5.2 Prohibition of Employment of Children in Factories etc.

- Article 24 provides that children below the age of 14 years shall not be employed to work in any factory or mine or engaged in any other hazardous employment.
- The Child Labour (Prohibition and Regulation) Act, 1986 was enacted to list down the hazardous activities in which children below the age of 14 years cannot be employed. However, it did not prohibit children from being employed in harmless work.

- However, with the right to education between the age of 6 and 14 becoming a fundamental right under Article 21A, children have a right to attend school till the age of 14.
- In order to resolve this difference, the recent amendment to the Child Labour (Prohibition and Regulation) Act, 2016 has made it mandatory that no child below the age of 14 can be employed in any occupation or process. The principal Act has been renamed as Child and Adolescent Labour (Prohibition and Regulation) Act and it also stipulates that adolescent children between the age of 14 and 18 shall not be employed in hazardous employment like mining, explosives and occupations in Factories Act.
- The only exceptions for children below the age of 14 are as follows:
  - They can provide help in family enterprise after school hours or during vacation i.e., enterprises run by close relatives of the child like parents, brother, sister, uncle or aunt.
  - If they are 'child artist', they can work for not more than 5 hours in a day without affecting their education.

MNEMONICS

Concept or Provisions	Shortcut or Mnemonics	Details to Remember
Articles 20 to 24	CLEArLy	• **C**onviction protection – 20 • **L**ife & Liberty – 21 • **E**ducation – 21A • **Ar**rest and detention (protection) – 22 • **L**abour – Forced Labour – 23 & Child Labour – 24 (protection)

14.6 RIGHT TO FREEDOM OF RELIGION

14.6.1 Freedom of Conscience and Free Profession, Practice and Propagation of Religion

Subject to public order, morality and health and to the other provisions of part III, all persons are equally entitled to freedom of conscience and the right freely to profess, practice and propagate religion [Art 25(1)].

> **THINK ABOUT IT**
>
> What is protected under freedom of religion are 'essential religious practices.' Explain with support of recent case laws decided by the Supreme Court.

The following points need to be noted with respect to an individual's right to practice religion:

- Article 25 guarantees the freedom of conscience (inner beliefs), freedom to profess (declaration of belief), practice (ways of worship, rituals and ceremonies) and propagate (spread or preach about one's religion to others) any religion of a person's choice.
- It aims to secure the liberty of belief, faith and worship as enshrined in the Preamble.
- It is available to both citizens and foreigners.

- While the right to propagate includes the right to preach, it does not include the right to convert another individual into one's religion. Conversion through fraud, coercion or allurement does not come under the right to propagate. This was decided by the Supreme Court in the *Stanislaus case* in 1977.
- Right to freedom of religion is subject to reasonable restrictions by the State on the grounds of public order, morality and health as well as other provisions relating to the fundamental rights.

Article 25(2) permits the State to regulate the secular activities of any religious practice and also provide for social reform. It permits the State to make laws for the following:

(a) regulating or restricting any economic, financial, political or other secular activity which may be associated with religious practice;

(b) providing for social welfare and reform or the throwing open of Hindu religious institutions of a public character to all classes and sections of Hindus.

It further provides that wearing and carrying of kirpans shall be deemed to be included in the profession of the Sikh religion. Further, for the purposes of sub-clause (b) above, the reference to Hindus and the Hindu religious institutions shall be construed as including a reference to the Sikh, Jains or Buddhist and their institutions.

This clause (b) was specifically added considering the practice that was prevalent in pre-independence India, wherein persons belonging to certain depressed classes were not allowed entry into various temples. In order to ensure that such discriminatory and wrongful practice was not claimed as part of freedom to practice religion, this power has been conferred on the State.

Essential religious practice

As per Article 25(2)(a), the State can regulate or restrict secular activities associated with religious practice. As per various Supreme Court and High Court judgements, regulations should not interfere with essential religious practices. However, the classification of any religious practice as secular or essential part of a particular religion is not a straightforward task. The difference between the two may be blurred and it is for the courts to determine whether a practice is an essential part of religion or only a secular practice.

Some of the recent important cases in this regard are briefly discussed below:

1. **Entry of women in Sabarimala – 2018 *(Indian Young Lawyers Association case)***
   - As per the practice in Lord Ayyappa shrine in Sabarimala, women between the age group of 10 and 50 are restricted from entering the shrine.
   - The Travancore Devaswom Board that regulates the temple submitted that this practice is an essential religious practice.
   - However, the Supreme Court in a verdict in 2018 (by a majority of 4:1) held that this practice, of restricting menstruating women between 10 and 50 years of age, is not an essential religious practice. It held that this practice is violative of Articles 14, 15 and 25.
   - It also referred to Article 25(2) and held that the State has the responsibility to carry out social reform in the matters of religious practices.
   - However, this judgement has been referred to a seven-judge bench for review in 2019 and this is pending in the Supreme Court at present (2024).

2. **Triple Talaq case – 2017 *(Shayara Bano case)***
   - The 5 judge bench of the Supreme Court had in August 2017 (by a majority of 3:2) declared the practice of 'Instant Triple Talaq' or 'Talaq-e-biddat' as unconstitutional. It was a practice

under Section 2 of Muslim Personal Law under which a man can pronounce 'Talaq' thrice in one sitting and divorce his wife. This was also irrevocable as per the Muslim Law.

- The majority ruling held that this practice of Instant Triple Talaq is violative of Article 14 (equality before law) and held it unconstitutional.
- It held that this practice of Instant Triple Talaq is not an essential practice under Islam religion.

3. **Hijab in Karnataka schools and colleges – 2022**
   - In February 2022, the Karnataka Government made an order stating that school and college uniforms have to be strictly adhered to without any exception. This was in response to the demands by some Muslim girl students that they be allowed to wear the Hijab, a customary head scarf worn by Muslim women.
   - The Karnataka High Court upheld the Government order in March 2022 and ruled that wearing of Hijab is not an essential religious practice of Islam.
   - This judgement of the High Court was appealed against in the Supreme Court. In October 2022, a division bench (two judges) of the Court gave a split verdict with one judge upholding the Karnataka High Court order and the other judge setting it aside on the grounds that wearing of Hijab is a personal choice. It is now referred to a larger bench.

14.6.2 Freedom to Manage Religious Affairs

While Article 25 guarantees freedom of religion for individuals, Article 26 guarantees certain rights to religious groups and denominations.

Under Article 26, every religious denomination or any section thereof shall have the right:

(a) to establish and maintain institutions for religious and charitable purposes;
(b) to manage its own affairs in matters of religion;
(c) to own and acquire movable and immovable property; and
(d) to administer such property in accordance with law.

These rights are subject to reasonable restrictions by the State on the grounds of public order, morality and health.

As per judgements of the Supreme Court, a religious denomination is a religious sect or body having (a) common faith, (b) common organisation and (c) a distinctive name.

For example, under above criteria the Supreme Court has ruled that 'Ramakrishna Mission' is a religious denomination under Hindu religion while 'Sri Aurobindo Society' is not.

The proposed amendment to the Waqf Act in 2025 brings in certain significant changes to the Waqf Act, 1995. It enhances the government's regulatory authority over waqf properties. It allows for inclusion of non-Muslims in key waqf institutions.

As per the Central Government, these reforms are meant to streamline the administration of waqf properties. However, the political parties in opposition and many Muslim organisations have alleged that these amendments infringe on the Fundamental rights guaranteed under Articles 25 and 26.

14.6.3 Freedom from Taxation for Promotion of any Religion

- ❑ Article 27 stipulates that no person shall be compelled to pay any taxes, the proceeds of which are specifically appropriated in payment of expenses for the promotion or maintenance of any particular religion or religious denomination.

- Article 27 prohibits the State from spending any public money collected by way of tax for promotion of any particular religion. It is one of the essential consequences of secularism.
- This provision prohibits the State from favouring or supporting one religion over the other. However, tax money can be used for the promotion or maintenance of all religions without favouring any particular religion.

14.6.4 Freedom from Attending Religious Instruction

Article 28 lays down the following provisions with respect to religious instruction in educational institutions:

- No religious instruction shall be provided in any educational institution wholly maintained out of the State funds.
- However, this provision does not apply to institutions administered by the State but established under any endowment or trust, which requires imparting religious instructions.
- Further, in an educational institution recognised by the State or receiving aid out of State funds, religious instructions can be provided to a person but only with his/her consent. In case he/she is a minor, his/her guardian's consent is required.

14.6.5 Indian Secularism versus Western Secularism

The fundamental rights under Articles 25–28, reflect the secular values of our Constitution and country. Further, Articles 15 and 16 that prohibit discrimination by the State only on the basis of religion in public matters and employment, is also a reflection of secular nature of our polity.

Secularism is a concept that evolved in the Medieval Europe during the period of 'Renaissance' or enlightenment. Before this period, the Kings were heavily influenced and controlled by religion and Church even in the matters of public administration. Secularism originally signified non-interference of the Church in governance and public affairs of the State. Subsequently, it also came to signify the non-interference of the State in matters of religion and a complete separation of religion and the State.

> **THINK ABOUT IT**
> How is Indian secularism different from western secularism?

However, Indian secularism differs from the Western secularism on account of the following factors:

1. Western secularism primarily signifies separation of the State from all religions and opposes any discrimination on the basis of religion. The Indian secularism is not only opposed to inter-religious discrimination but also opposed to intra-religious discrimination. Thus, it provides for protection to Dalits and women against oppression in Hinduism as well as protection to women in other faiths.
2. Indian secularism not only deals with religious freedom of individuals but also with religious freedom of minority communities. Thus, religious and linguistic minorities have the right to protect their distinct culture and language [Art 29] and also establish educational institutions [Art 30].
3. Western secularism is mutual non-interference of the State and the Religion in each other's domain. But Indian secularism has made room for

> Scan the QR code for conceptual video on Right to freedom of religion, cultural and educational rights and constitutional remedies
>
> McGraw Hill edge

the State-supported religious reform. The following provisions are examples for the same – (a) Abolition of untouchability [Art 17], (b) the State can regulate secular practices of religion [Art 25(1)], (c) the State can provide for social welfare and reform [Art 25(2)].

Thus, Indian secularism is unique and can also be termed as 'positive secularism'.

14.7 CULTURAL AND EDUCATIONAL RIGHTS

14.7.1 Protection of Interest of Minorities

Article 29 provides the following rights to citizens:

(1) Any section of the citizens residing in the territory of India or any part thereof having a distinct language, script or culture of its own shall have the right to conserve the same.

(2) No citizen shall be denied admission into any educational institution maintained by the State or receiving aid out of the State funds on grounds only of religion, race, caste, language or any of them.

Article 29(1) recognises the right of an individual to preserve his/her culture, language and script. Article 29(2) prohibits the State from discriminating while granting access to educational institutions. This is the reason that the exceptions under Articles 15(4) and 15(6) that enable the State to make special provisions for socially and educationally backward classes, the Scheduled Castes, the Scheduled Tribes and the economically weaker sections draws a reference to Article 29(2).

Article 29 grants protection to both linguistic and religious minorities. The Supreme Court has however held that the scope of this article is not restricted to minorities alone and is available to 'any section' of the population including majority with a distinct language or culture like various Scheduled Tribes. This article reflects the protection of minority interests that is a feature of the Indian secularism.

14.7.2 Right of Minorities to Establish and Administer Educational Institutions

Article 30(1) provides the right to all minorities, whether based on religion or language, to establish and administer educational institutions of their choice.

The following points need to be understood with respect to this right available to minorities:

- This right is available to citizens who belong to religious or linguistic minorities. The term 'minority' has not been defined in the Constitution.
- As per Section 2(c) of the National Commission for Minorities Act, 1992, the Central government has notified Muslims, Christians, Sikhs, Buddhists, Zoroastrians (Parsis) and Jains as minority community.
- The Supreme Court in the *TMA Pai foundation case* in 2002 had ruled that the unit for determining linguistic and religious minorities should be at the State level. In July 2022, the Supreme Court has again reiterated in a PIL that the unit for determining linguistic and religious minorities shall be at the State level.
- The Supreme Court in the case relating to the minority status of Aligarh Muslim University (2024), laid down three tests for determining the minority status of an institution:

1. The first test is to trace the genesis of the institution. This involves identifying the "origin of the idea of the establishment" and other preliminary sources indicating a minority community member's involvement in the institution's ideation.
2. The second test is to determine the purpose of establishing the institution. It need not be primarily for the benefit of the religious or linguistic community, nor is it necessary for the education provided to be "in the language spoken by the minority or on the religion of the minority."
3. The third test is to examine the steps taken to implement the establishment, such as who provided the funds, land, etc.

It also held that it is not necessary to prove that administration vests with the minority to prove that it is a minority educational institution. Even for institutions established before the Constitution, the Court must determine if the institution was established to further the interests of the minority community. The fact that an institution is now administered under a central or State law will not automatically result in that institution losing its minority status.

- This right to establish and administer educational institutions consists of the following rights: (a) To appoint a governing body of its choice, (b) To appoint teaching and non-teaching staff, (c) To admit eligible students of their choice and determine its own reasonable fee structure and (d) To own and use its properties for the institution.
- However, this right is subject to reasonable regulations by the State in the interest of welfare of the students and staff of such institutions. These institutions need to follow all the statutory regulations with respect to working hours, employee welfare, industrial relations, public order etc. The Supreme Court in 2024, while upholding the validity of Uttar Pradesh Board of Madrasa Education Act, 2004, has stressed the need to balance the interests of religious minorities in running educational institutions and the state's interest in regulating standards.
- Any scheme of reservation, for the Scheduled Castes, the Scheduled Tribes, the socially and educationally backward classes and the economically weaker sections, in educational institutions under Articles 15(5) and 15(6) cannot be extended to minority educational institutions set up under Article 30(1).
- This article reflects the protection of minority interests that is a feature of the Indian secularism.

Article 30(1A) lays down that while making any law providing for the compulsory acquisition of any property of an educational institution established and administered by a minority, the State shall ensure that the amount fixed by or determined under such law for the acquisition of such property is such as would not restrict or abrogate the right guaranteed under Article 30(1). In other words, the right to property of a minority educational institution continues to be a fundamental right.

This clause was added through the 44th Constitutional amendment. In this amendment, the right to property of citizens was deleted from being a fundamental right under Article 19(1)(f) and introduced as a constitutional right under Article 300A. However, the 'protection of minority interest' has been declared as a 'basic structure' of the Constitution that cannot be adversely amended. Hence, this clause was added to protect the right to property and fair compensation in case of compulsory acquisition of any property of any minority educational institution as a fundamental right.

Article 30(2) further provides that the State shall not, in granting aid to educational institutions, discriminate against any minority educational institution.

MNEMONICS

Concept or Provisions	Shortcut or Mnemonics	Details to Remember
Articles 25 to 30	Prime **M**inister gave **Tax Instruction**; for developing **Culture & Education**	• **P**rofess & Practise Religion – 25 • **M**anage Religious activities – 26 • **T**axation not allowed in the name of religion – 27 • Religious **Instructions** not allowed – 28 • **Cultural** Rights of minorities – 29 • **Educational** Rights of minorities – 30

14.8 RIGHT TO CONSTITUTIONAL REMEDIES

14.8.1 Remedies for Enforcement of Fundamental Rights

Part III guarantees various sets of fundamental rights as discussed in the previous sections of this chapter. However, without an effective mechanism for their enforcement, these rights will only remain as ideals without any force. This aspect is addressed through Article 32, which guarantees the right to move the Supreme Court for enforcement of the rights conferred by Part III. Dr Ambedkar referred to this article as the heart and soul of the Constitution. Article 32 has been declared as a 'basic structure' of the Constitution by the Supreme Court.

Article 32 provides for the following:

(1) Right to move the Supreme Court by appropriate proceedings for the enforcement of the fundamental rights conferred by Part III.

(2) The Supreme Court shall have power to issue directions or orders or writs, including writs in the nature of habeas corpus, mandamus, prohibition, quo-warranto and certiorari whichever may be appropriate, for the enforcement of any of the fundamental rights conferred by Part III.

(3) The Parliament may by law empower other lower courts to issue writs, orders or directions within the local limits of its jurisdiction without prejudice to the powers conferred on the Supreme Court under Article 32.

(4) This right (except for enforcement of Articles 20 and 21) can be suspended only during declaration of National Emergency as per Article 359.

(5) In M.C. Mehta Vs Union of India (1986), the Supreme Court held that its power under Article 32 is not only for preventing the infringement of fundamental rights, but also remedial where it can provide relief against the breach of fundamental rights.

14.8.2 Various Types of Writs

We have already discussed briefly about the writ jurisdiction of the Supreme Court and the High Courts. The key difference between the writ jurisdiction of the Supreme Court and the High Court is as follows:

- The Supreme Court can issue writs only for enforcement of Fundamental Rights while the High Court can issue them for enforcement of Fundamental Rights and for any other purpose including enforcement of legal rights. Thus, the scope of writ jurisdiction of High Courts is wider than the Supreme Court.
- The Supreme Court can issue writs throughout the territory of India while the High Courts can issue them for the area under its territorial jurisdiction. Thus, the territorial jurisdiction of the Supreme Court for issuing writs is larger than the High Courts.
- Finally, the writ jurisdiction of the Supreme Court is itself a fundamental right under Article 32 while the writ jurisdiction of the High Courts under Article 226 is not a fundamental right. However, both these articles have been declared as part of the 'basic structure' of the Constitution. Further, the Supreme Court has observed, while hearing certain petitions under Article 32, that it would encourage the petitioners to first approach the High Courts for appropriate relief under Article 226 wherever possible.

We shall now briefly understand the meaning and scope of various types of writs. The literal meaning of these 'prerogative writs' that have Latin names are as follows:

1. Habeas Corpus = 'to have the body of'
2. Mandamus = 'we command'
3. Prohibition = 'to forbid'
4. Certiorari = 'to be certified'
5. Quo Warranto = 'by what authority'

> **THINK ABOUT IT**
>
> Article 32 is the heart and soul of the Indian Constitution. Briefly explain the various writ jurisdictions of the Supreme Court for the enforcement of fundamental rights.

Habeas Corpus

- It is issued by the court to examine the legality of detention of a person. It is the most important writ issued under Articles 21 and 22 to protect against deprivation of liberty and illegal detention. The grounds for issuance include unlawful detention, violation of fundamental rights, and absence of legal justification.
- It can be issued against the State as well as private individuals. However, the writ is not issued if the detention is lawful; or it is under a proceeding for contempt of court; or the detention is as per orders of a competent court; or if the detention is outside the jurisdiction of the court.

Mandamus

- It is issued by the court to a public official asking him/her to carry out something he/she has failed or refused to perform. This may also be issued to a lower court or any other government body. The grounds for issuance include failure to perform duty, failure to discharge a legal obligation and in circumstances where there is no discretion to the authority but for discharging the duty.
- It cannot be issued against private individuals. It also cannot be issued (a) to enforce departmental instructions that do not have statutory force; (b) when the duty is discretionary or based on contract; (c) against the President or Governors; and (d) against the Chief Justice of a High Court acting in judicial capacity.
- Let us take a hypothetical example. It is a fundamental right under Article 19(1)(g) to carry on any trade or business. Suppose a citizen is carrying on a business and he/she needs to renew his/her licence for continuing the same. If the public authority responsible for renewing the licence is unduly delaying such renewal, a writ of Mandamus can be issued by the court directing the authority to complete the renewal without delay.

Prohibition

- While mandamus is issued to command a particular action, the writ of prohibition is issued against a lower court or tribunal to prevent it from passing a wrongful order or exceed its jurisdiction. The grounds of issuance include jurisdictional error where a lower court or tribunal has gone beyond its limit, procedural irregularity where the principles of natural justice have not been adhered to, and violation of law.
- This is usually issued only against judicial and quasi-judicial authorities.
- In the same hypothetical example as discussed under 'Mandamus' above, let us assume that there is a case filed against the business in a district court seeking cancellation of the licence. The citizen carrying on the business may approach the Supreme Court or the High Court and seek a writ of Prohibition to be issued to the local court to prevent it from passing a wrongful order.

Certiorari

- This is similar to higher appeal against the order of a lower court. The higher court may quash the order of a lower court if there is an error or lack of jurisdiction. This is issued after an order is passed by a lower court or authority. In addition, the higher court may also ask the lower court or tribunal to transfer the concerned case to the higher court. Thus, certiorari is both curative and preventive.
- This was earlier issued only against the judicial bodies but since 1991, is also issued against administrative authorities.
- In the same hypothetical example as above, let us assume that the lower court has passed an order cancelling the business licence. The Supreme Court or the High Court can issue a writ of certiorari and quash the order of the lower court to grant relief.

Quo Warranto

- This is issued by the Court to enquire into the legality of claim of a person to a public office, thereby preventing wrongful occupation of a public office by any person. The conditions for this writ to be issued include that the office must be a substantive one created by the constitution or a statute and open to the public; and the holder of that office occupies it unlawfully.
- This writ can be sought by any public minded person and not necessarily the aggrieved person. In ***B.R.Kapoor Vs State of Tamil Nadu*** (2001), the Supreme Court had set aside the appointment of Ms J Jayalalitha as Chief Minister of Tamil Nadu as not legal and valid.

14.9 MISCELLANEOUS PROVISIONS

14.9.1 Fundamental Rights and Armed Forces

- Article 33 empowers the Parliament to restrict or abrogate the application of fundamental rights in relation to members of the armed forces, paramilitary forces, intelligence agencies, police and people employed in communication systems that serve these forces.
- It is only the Parliament that is authorised to make such laws and not the State Legislatures.
- Such legislation by the Parliament of India may restrict the operation of any fundamental rights such as equality, freedom of expression, freedom of association, personal liberty etc.
- The Army Act, Navy Act and Air Force Act all enacted in 1950, Police Forces (Restriction of Rights) Act, 1966 are examples of such legislation by the Parliament.

- This is to ensure the proper discharge of duties and the maintenance of discipline among such forces.

14.9.2 Fundamental Rights and Martial Law

- Article 34 pertains to the restrictions on the fundamental rights while martial law is in force in any area. Martial law is not defined in the Constitution but it means 'military rule'.
- The article provides that the Parliament by law may indemnify any public servant or any other person in respect of acts done during operation of martial law.
- Here we have to note that the Constitution does not have any specific provision of authorising the proclamation of martial law. It may be imposed in any specific area that has been disturbed due to war, riots or rebellion, in order to bring it under control and maintain public order. It must also be noted that martial law has never been imposed in independent India till date.
- The article simply means that if there is a government servant on duty or any other person, then he/she is indemnified for the acts done by him/her in connection with maintenance of law and order in the area where martial law is in force. This act of indemnity cannot be challenged in any court on the ground of contravention of any fundamental rights. However, the Supreme Court has observed that imposition of martial law will not automatically result in suspension of the writ of Habeas Corpus.

14.9.3 Legislation to Give Effect to Certain Provisions

Article 35 vests the power to make laws to give effect to certain provisions of Part III only in the Parliament and not the State Legislatures. This would ensure that there is uniformity throughout the territory of India in both the laws made and the punishments prescribed for offences violating the Fundamental Rights.

The Parliament shall have the power to make laws to give effect to the following provisions of Part III:

- Article 16(3) – Prescribing residence as a criterion for employment in a State or Union Territory or local authority;
- Article 32(3) – Empowering lower courts to issue writs or orders for enforcement of the Fundamental Rights;
- Article 33 – Restricting or abrogating the application of the fundamental rights in relation to members of the armed forces, paramilitary forces, intelligence agencies and police.
- Article 34 – Indemnifying a government servant or any other person for acts done during the operation of martial law in any area.
- Prescribing punishment for those acts that are declared to be offences under Part III like untouchability (Art 17), traffic in human beings and forced labour (Art 23).

14.10 EXCEPTIONS TO FUNDAMENTAL RIGHTS

We have already understood that the fundamental rights are not absolute rights. They are subject to (a) reasonable restrictions in the interest of society, and (b) exceptions to achieve social justice. The exceptions in Articles 15 and 16 that provide for reservations is to secure social justice.

It must be noted that till 1978, the right to property was a fundamental right under Article 19(1)(f). Article 31 (since omitted in 1978), provided a fundamental right for fair compensation in case of compulsory acquisition of property by the State.

Agricultural land and estates were the most important property at the time of our independence. In order to achieve social and economic justice as provided for in the Preamble and Directive Principles of State Policy, it was essential for the State to acquire these properties from big landlords and redistribute them amongst various poorer sections and landless labourers. Further, land was also required to be acquired for industrial and infrastructural development. However, the resources available with the governments at both the centre and the States was insufficient to provide fair compensation at market rates for acquisition of property. Hence, exceptions were incorporated through amendments to Part III in order to enable the State to acquire property without any violation of the fundamental rights, especially of Article 14 (equality) and Article 19 (various liberties which included the right to property till 1978).

We shall be discussing about Articles 31A, 31B and 31C in further detail in the next two chapters viz., Amendment of the Constitution and Directive Principles of State Policy. However, the key points with respect to these articles that provide exceptions to the fundamental rights are discussed below.

14.10.1 Saving of Laws Providing for Acquisition of Estates, etc.

Article 31A

- It saves five categories of laws related to (a) acquisition of estates and related rights by the State; (b) taking over the management of properties by the State; (c) amalgamation of corporations; (d) extinguishment or modification of rights of directors or shareholders of corporations; (e) extinguishment or modification of mining leases, from being challenged or invalidated on grounds of contravention of Article 14 and Article 19.
- It also provides for payment of compensation at market value when the State acquires the land of a person under his/her personal cultivation and such land is within statutory ceiling limit.
- The provisions of this article shall not apply to a State law unless it has been reserved for the President's consideration and received his/her assent.

14.10.2 Validation of Certain Acts and Regulations

Article 31B

- It saves the Acts and regulations that are placed in the Ninth Schedule from being declared void on the ground that it violates any of the fundamental rights in Part III.
- This is a very wide exception, as any law placed in the Ninth Schedule through a constitutional amendment is protected under this article from all the fundamental rights. There are 282 laws at present (2024) in the Ninth Schedule. Many of the State laws placed in the Ninth Schedule relate to land reforms while the Parliamentary laws deal with other matters. The Supreme Court in ***Waman Rao case*** (1981), upheld the validity of Articles 31A and 31B.
- However, in the ***Coelho case*** (2007) the Supreme Court ruled that there could not be any blanket immunity from judicial review as it is a basic feature of the Constitution. Hence, any Act included in the Ninth Schedule after 24 April 1973 is now subject to judicial review (since judicial review was established as a basic structure of the Constitution in the ***Kesavananda Bharati*** case in April 1973).

14.10.3 Saving of Laws Giving Effect to Certain Directive Principles

Article 31C

- Any law that seeks to implement the socialistic directives specified in Article 39 (b) or (c) shall not be void on the ground that it contravenes any of the rights conferred by Article 14 or Article 19.
- This provision was added by the 25th amendment. The 42nd amendment extended the scope of this article to include all directive principles specified in Part-IV. However, this extension was declared as unconstitutional by the Supreme Court in the *Minerva Mills case.*
- The provisions of this article shall not apply to a State law unless it has been reserved for the President's consideration and received his/her assent.

14.11 SIGNIFICANCE AND CRITICISM OF FUNDAMENTAL RIGHTS

14.11.1 Significance of Fundamental Rights

The importance and significance of Fundamental rights in our Constitution and polity cannot be overemphasised. It lays the foundation for a democratic society and guarantee the basic rights of equality and liberty to all citizens of the country. The significance of fundamental rights can be listed as follows:

1. It lays down the foundation for a democratic society by establishing 'Rule of law'.
2. It aims at securing the basic human rights of equality and liberty for all individuals, and also securing fraternity amongst citizens.
3. It also provides for securing justice.
4. It strengthens the secular fabric of our country.
5. It protects the interest of the minorities and the weaker sections of the society.
6. It limits the powers of the Government and also provides strength to every individual against the State.

14.11.2 Criticism of Fundamental Rights

While the fundamental rights are significant for the reasons stated in previous section, there are also certain criticisms against the way in which the fundamental rights are provided and implemented in our Constitution. The below table summarises the important criticisms and also the protection to balance such criticism.

Heading	Key Criticism	Balancing Protection
Excessive limitations	The liberties that are granted under Articles 19, 25, 26, 29 and 30 are subject to restrictions under various grounds. These are considered to be excessive limitations on the liberties guaranteed.	While there are various grounds under which restrictions can be placed by the State, the most important protection available is that these restrictions should be reasonable. The courts can decide on the reasonableness of any restriction and strike down as unconstitutional any restriction that is unreasonable.

Heading	Key Criticism	Balancing Protection
No social and economic rights	The fundamental rights guaranteed in Part III are mainly political rights of equality and liberty. It does not provide for any social or economic rights like right to work, right to social security, right to leisure etc., that are required for development of an individual and the society.	Equality and liberty are the two basic rights that are guaranteed through Part III. However, Part IV of the Constitution that lays down directives to the State is to provide for various social and economic rights. These have been operationalised as legal rights through various laws made by the Parliament and the State Legislatures.
Ambiguity	Terms like 'minorities', 'public order', 'reasonable restrictions', 'morality', 'public interest' etc., are ambiguous and vague. They are also not clearly defined in the Constitution.	The courts through their various judgements over many years have tried to lay down a consistent interpretation of these terms to reduce the ambiguity and increase the safeguards for citizens.
No permanency	Fundamental rights are not sacrosanct and they can be amended by the Parliament. Right to property that was a fundamental right till 1978 was omitted in the 44th Amendment Act. Hence, there is no permanency for the fundamental rights.	After the ***Kesavananda Bharati*** judgement in 1973, an amendment of the Constitution cannot violate basic structure. While right to property was omitted from the fundamental rights and moved as a constitutional right, the essence of almost all other fundamental rights have already been declared as basic structure of the Constitution in various judgements.
Suspension during Emergency	Enforcement of the Fundamental Rights can be suspended whenever National Emergency is declared. This again reduces the efficacy of the fundamental rights.	Articles 20 and 21 that protect individual liberty cannot be suspended even during emergency after the 44th Constitutional amendment.
Expensive remedy	Article 32 allows any person to approach the Supreme Court directly for enforcement of the Fundamental Rights. Further, Article 226 allows the High Courts to hear any case of violation of the Fundamental Rights. However, these remedies are expensive and time-consuming for an ordinary citizen.	Article 32 provides for a speedy remedy as any aggrieved person can directly approach the Supreme Court. With the advent of judicial activism, the poorer sections can also get justice through Public Interest Litigations.
Preventive Detention	Article 22 provides for preventive detention of any person by the State. This negates the individual liberty that is guaranteed in various other articles.	This is indeed a very valid criticism as this provision can be misused by the State. However, there are few safeguards that have been provided in Article 22 itself against arbitrary misuse of this preventive detention powers of the State.

14.12 CONSTITUTIONAL RIGHTS

The Fundamental Rights are enumerated and guaranteed in Part III of the Constitution. Apart from these rights, there are few other rights that are provided in the Constitution but outside of Part III. These are commonly known as the 'Constitutional Rights'.

The following points with respect to the constitutional rights need to be understood:

- While both the fundamental rights and the constitutional rights are provided in the Constitution, there is a difference between the two. The Fundamental Rights are enforceable by directly approaching the Supreme Court under Article 32. However, there is no remedy under Article 32 if any constitutional right is violated. The aggrieved person can approach the High Court under Article 226 or enforce his/her right as per the legal process that is laid down in the laws that provide for these constitutional rights. That is why these rights are also referred to as 'constitutional-cum-legal rights'.
- However, these constitutional rights are also equally important as they provide political rights that lay down the democratic values in our Constitution.

We shall now discuss the constitutional rights under two sections viz., (a) Right to Property and (b) Other constitutional rights.

14.12.1 Right to Property

No person shall be deprived of his/her property save by authority of law [Art 300A].

The Right to property was a fundamental right under Article 19(1)(f) till 1978. Article 31 further provided that the State shall provide fair compensation for any compulsory acquisition of property.

However, this resulted in excessive litigation by zamindars and other landlords in the Supreme Court whenever any land reforms were sought to be implemented by the State. While exceptions were provided under Articles 31A, 31B and 31C, there were still many cases that were filed directly in the Supreme Court for protection of right to property guaranteed under Article 19(1)(f) read with Article 31. In order to avoid this situation, Article 19(1)(f) and Article 31 were omitted through the 44th Constitutional Amendment Act in 1978. The same amendment introduced Article 300A that made right to property a constitutional right for all persons.

THINK ABOUT IT

Though 'Right to Property' is no longer a fundamental right, it continues to be an important constitutional right. Discuss highlighting the key sub-rights as enumerated by the Supreme Court under 'Right to Property.'

The significance of this amendment and other points with respect to the Right to property are as follows:

- Right to property can be regulated by ordinary law of the Parliament or the State Legislature. An aggrieved person cannot directly approach the Supreme Court under Article 32 in case of any violation but can approach the High Court under Article 226 or as per the procedure laid down in the law.
- But the Supreme Court has held in many cases that while a law can provide for acquisition of property, it cannot be by force and the purpose has to be for public welfare. The process as well as compensation should be just, fair and reasonable.

- The Supreme Court has reiterated in many cases that the Right to property remains an important constitutional-cum-legal right. In January 2025, the Supreme Court reiterated that it is a constitutional right as well as a human right in a welfare State like India.
- The Supreme Court in State of H.P. & Ors. Vs Karam Singh & Ors. (May 2024) held that the constitutional right to property contains 7 sub-rights as follows:
    1. Right to notice – Individuals must be informed about the intention to acquire the property
    2. Right to be heard – Individuals have right to voice objections
    3. Right to reasoned decision – Justification for acquisition with a reasoned decision
    4. Public purpose – Acquisition should be for a public purpose
    5. Right to fair compensation
    6. Right to an efficient process adhering to set timelines
    7. Right to conclusion – Process concludes with physical transfer of property

However, the Right to Property continues to be a fundamental right under the following two provisions of Part III:

- When the State acquires property of a minority education institution, the institution has a fundamental right to get fair compensation [Art 30(1A)].
- When the State acquires personal cultivation land of a person and the land is within the statutory ceiling limits, he/she has a fundamental right to adequate compensation [Art 31A].

Scan the QR code for discussion on recent Supreme Court judgement on Right to Property

14.12.2 Other Constitutional Rights

The following are the other constitutional rights provided in our Constitution:

(a) No tax shall be levied or collected except by authority of law [Art 265]. It means that the executive both at the centre and at the States can levy or collect any tax only with the approval of the Parliament and the State Legislatures.

(b) The elections to the House of the People and to the Legislative Assembly of every State shall be on the basis of adult suffrage i.e., every citizen above 18 years of age who is not disqualified under any law shall be entitled to be registered as a voter [Art 326]. There shall be one general electoral roll for every constituency and no person shall be excluded only on the grounds of religion, race, caste, sex or any of them [Art 325]. Right to vote has also been declared as a constitutional right by the Supreme Court in the ***Rajbala case*** [2015]. The right to contest elections has also been declared as a constitutional right by the Supreme Court in the same case.

(c) Trade, commerce and intercourse throughout the territory of India shall be free [Art 301].

14.13 TABULAR SUMMARY OF FUNDAMENTAL RIGHTS

Art No.	Fundamental Right	Applicability	Explanation/ Remarks	Exceptions/ Restrictions
14	Equality before the law or equal protection of the laws	All persons	• Equality before Law connotes the absence of any special privileges. • Equal protection of the laws means the equality of treatment under equal circumstances. • The principle of equality is part of the basic structure of the Constitution.	Equality has the following exceptions: • Privilege of members of the Parliament and the State Legislatures. • Protection to the President/ Governor from arrest and criminal proceedings. • Diplomatic immunity under Vienna convention.
15	Prohibition of discrimination on certain grounds	Citizens	• Prohibits discrimination on grounds only of religion, race, caste, sex or place of birth. • Access to well, tanks, roads and places of public resort is a fundamental right guaranteed even against private persons and not just the State.	Non-discrimination is subject to the following exceptions: • Special provisions can be made for women and children. • Special provisions can be made for the socially and educationally backward classes (SEBC), the Scheduled Castes (SC) and the Scheduled Tribes (ST). • Special provision for SEBC, SC and ST for admission to educational institutions except minority educational institutions. • Reservation for the Economically Weaker Sections (EWS) up to 10%.
16	Equality of Opportunity in Public Employment	Citizens	• Prohibits discrimination on grounds only of religion, race, caste, sex, place of birth, residence or descent.	Non-discrimination in public employment is subject to the following exceptions: • The Parliament can provide residence as an exception. • Reservation in favour of backward classes i.e., SEBC, SC and ST. • Reservation for the EWS up to 10%.
17	Abolition of Untouchability		• Practice of untouchability in any form is an offence punishable as per law. • The term 'Untouchability' has not been defined in the Constitution. • The SC has held that the right is also available against private individuals.	There are no exceptions to this right. However, the enforcement of this right can be suspended when a National emergency is declared.

Art No.	Fundamental Right	Applicability	Explanation/ Remarks	Exceptions/ Restrictions
18	Abolition of Titles		• Hereditary titles of nobility are banned, since they are against the principle of equal status for all. • The SC has upheld the constitutional validity of National Awards i.e., Bharat Ratna and Padma awards, and ruled that these awards do not amount to 'titles' within the meaning of Article 18.	
19	19(1)(a) – Freedom of speech and expression 19(1)(b) – Assemble peaceably and without arms 19(1)(c) – Form associations, unions and co-operative societies 19(1)(d) – move freely throughout the territory of India 19(1)(e) – Reside and settle in any part of the territory of India 19(1)(g) – practice any profession, trade or business	Citizens	• These six rights form the essence of 'liberty' that is guaranteed to citizens. • These rights can be suspended only if an emergency is declared due to war or external aggression. • The reasonable restrictions to the rights provided by the Constitution attempts to strike a balance between individual liberty and social control.	Reasonable restrictions can be placed by the State on these rights on the following grounds: 19(2) – Reasonable restriction on freedom of speech and expression under 19(1)(a) on the grounds of sovereignty and integrity of India, security of State, friendly relations with foreign states, public order, decency and morality, contempt of court, defamation, and incitement to an offence. 19(3) – Reasonable restrictions on freedom of assembly under 19(1)(b) on the grounds of sovereignty and integrity of India, Public order. 19(4) – Reasonable restrictions on freedom of association under 19(1)(c) on the grounds of sovereignty and integrity, public order and morality. 19(5) – Reasonable restrictions on freedom of movement under 19(1)(d) and freedom of settlement under 19(1)(e) on the grounds of interests of general public, protection of interests of any Scheduled Tribe. 19(6) – Reasonable restrictions to freedom of profession, trade and business on ground of interests of general public. Further the State can prescribe professional or technical qualification for any profession and also nationalise any business.

Art No.	Fundamental Right	Applicability	Explanation/ Remarks	Exceptions/ Restrictions
20	Protection in respect of conviction for offences	All persons	• No person shall be convicted of any offence except for violation of a law in force at the time of the commission of the Act charged as an offence. • No person shall be subjected to a penalty greater than that which might have been inflicted under the law in force at the time of the commission of the offence. • No person shall be punished for the same offence more than once. • No person shall be compelled to be a witness against himself/herself.	
21	Protection of life and personal liberty	All persons	• In the ***Maneka Gandhi*** case (1978), the Supreme Court held that procedure established by law has to be reasonable, fair and just.	
21A	Right to Education	All persons	• Every child between the age of 6 and 14 years shall be provided free and compulsory elementary education by the State. • This provision was added by the 86th Constitutional Amendment Act in 2002.	
22	Protection against arrest and detention in certain cases	All persons	• A person who is arrested shall not be detained in custody without being informed of the grounds for such arrest. • He/she shall not be denied the right to consult, and to be defended by, a legal practitioner of his/her choice. • He/she shall be produced before the nearest magistrate within a period of 24 hours of such arrest excluding time taken for travel. • He/she shall not be detained in custody beyond 24 hours without the order of a magistrate.	These protections are not available to: • Enemy aliens. • Persons detained under law providing for preventive detention. However, the period of preventive detention shall not exceed 3 months unless authorised by an advisory board.

Art No.	Fundamental Right	Applicability	Explanation/ Remarks	Exceptions/ Restrictions
23	Prohibition of traffic in human beings and forced labour	All persons	• Traffic in human beings and forced labour are prohibited and is an offence punishable in accordance with law. • It protects the individual not only against the State but also against private persons.	The State can impose compulsory service for public purposes.
24	Prohibition of employment of children in factories etc.	All persons	• No child below the age of 14 years shall be employed in factory, mine or other hazardous employment. • The recent amendment to the Child and Adolescent Labour (Prohibition and Regulation) Act, 2016 has made it mandatory that no child below the age of 14 can be employed in any occupation or process.	
25	Freedom of conscience and free profession, practice and propagation of religion	All persons	• It guarantees the freedom of conscience (inner beliefs), freedom to profess (declaration of belief), practice (ways of worship, rituals and ceremonies) and propagate (spread or preach about one's religion to others) any religion of a person's choice.	• It is subject to Public Order, Morality and Health. • The State can make laws regulating the secular, political, economic activities associated with religious practices. • The State can provide for social welfare and reform
26	Freedom to manage religious affairs.	All persons	Religious denominations or any section thereof, have the right to – • establish and maintain religious and charitable institutions; • manage its own affairs in matters of religion; • own, acquire and administer property.	• It is subject to public order, morality and health.
27	Freedom from taxation for promotion of a religion	All persons	No person shall be compelled to pay any taxes, the proceeds of which are specifically appropriated for the promotion or maintenance of any particular religion or religious denomination.	

Art No.	Fundamental Right	Applicability	Explanation/ Remarks	Exceptions/ Restrictions
28	Freedom from attending religious instruction.	All persons	• No religious instructions shall be provided in institutions maintained wholly out of State funds. • No person attending any educational institution recognised by the State or receiving the State funds shall be required to take part in any religious instruction without his/her own consent or his/her guardian's consent (for minors).	This provision does not apply to an educational institute recognised by the State and established under any endowment or Trust, requiring imparting of religious instructions.
29	Protection of interests of minorities.	Citizens	• Any section of the citizens having distinct, language, script, or culture of its own, shall have the right to conserve the same. • It also protects the rights of an individual against any discrimination in admission to educational institutions on grounds only of religion, race, caste or language.	
30	Rights of minorities to establish and administer educational institution	Citizens	• All minorities, whether based on religion or language, can establish and administer educational institutions of their choice. • While making any law providing for the compulsory acquisition of any property of an educational institution established and administered by a minority, the State should provide for fair compensation.	
32	Remedies for enforcement of rights conferred by Part III	All persons	• The right to move the Supreme Court for enforcement of any fundamental right is guaranteed. • The Supreme Court can issue orders, directions or writs in the nature of Habeas Corpus, Mandamus, Prohibition, certiorari, Quo Warranto.	The President can suspend the right to move any court for the enforcement of Fundamental Rights (except Articles 20 and 21) during National Emergency.

MAINS STARTER

Area	Building Blocks For Model Introductions
Fundamental Rights	Fundamental rights in the Constitution are guaranteed under Part III from Articles 14 to 32. These rights guarantee the basic rights of equality and liberty enshrined in our Preamble. It also places restrictions on the State from making any laws violating these rights.
Equality	Equality invokes the idea that all human beings have equal worth. It implies no discrimination of citizens by the State. Articles 14 to 18 of Part III guarantee equality in the Indian Constitution.
Rule of law	Rule of law is a concept propounded by British Jurist A.V. Dicey. It brings out the principle that all men are equal before the law that governs them.
Reservation in India	Reservations are a kind of affirmative action in India to provide equal opportunities to underprivileged sections like Socially and educationally backward classes, Scheduled Castes, Scheduled Tribes and Economically Weaker Sections. They are aimed at securing social justice. Articles 15 and 16 provide for the same.
Liberty	Liberty is freedom from wrongful interference in personal domain by the State. It is also the freedom to develop oneself fully. The fundamental rights under Articles 19 to 30 guarantee such individual liberty. It is subject to reasonable restrictions in the interest of the society.
Right to Privacy	Right to Privacy is an integral part of Article 21 that guarantees right to life and liberty. This was declared so by the Supreme Court in Puttuswamy case.
Due Process of law	Due process of law is a legal process under which the judiciary can review a law not only for procedural grounds but also on the basis of its reasonableness. It implies that the law has to be fair and follow the principles of natural justice.
Freedom of Religion	The Indian Constitution guarantees freedom to practise any religion for an individual under Article 25. It also guarantees religious rights to groups under Article 26. These articles bring out the secular nature of our Constitution.
Indian Secularism	Secularism is a basic structure of the Constitution as declared in the S R Bommai case. Indian secularism is 'positive secularism' that treats all religions with equal respect without discriminating against any religion. It also provides for state-supported religious reforms.
Right to Property	Right to property in India is a constitutional-cum-legal right available to all persons under Article 300A. The Supreme Court has also opined that it is a basic human right in a welfare state like India.

UPSC Previous Years' Questions of Preliminary Examination

1. Under which of the following Articles of the Constitution of India, has the Supreme Court of India placed the Right to Privacy? **[2024]**
   (a) Article 15 (b) Article 16
   (c) Article 19 (d) Article 21

   Solution: (d)

   Explanation: Right to Privacy has been declared as a fundamental right under Article 21 in the Puttaswamy judgement. Hence, the correct answer is (d).

2. A writ of Prohibition is an order issued by the Supreme Court or High Courts to: **[2024]**
   (a) a government officer prohibiting him from taking a particular action.
   (b) the Parliament/Legislative Assembly to pass a law on Prohibition.
   (c) the lower court prohibiting continuation of proceedings in a case.
   (d) the Government prohibiting it from following an unconstitutional policy.

   Solution: (c)

   Explanation: As discussed in Section 14.8.2, writ of prohibition is issued against a lower court or tribunal to prevent it from passing a wrongful order and hence prohibiting continuation of proceedings in a case. Hence, the correct answer is (c).

3. In essence, what does 'Due Process of Law' mean? **[2023]**
   (a) The principle of natural justice (b) The procedure established by law
   (c) Fair application of law (d) Equality before law

   Solution: (a)

   Explanation: As discussed in Section 14.4.4.1, Due process of law is procedure established by law that is reasonable and follows principle of natural justice. Hence, the most appropriate answer is (a).

4. Consider the following statements: **[2023]**

Statement-I: The Supreme Court of India has held in some judgements that the reservation policies made under Article 16(4) of the Constitution of India would be limited by Article 335 for maintenance of efficiency of administration.

Statement-II: Article 335 of the Constitution of India defines the term 'efficiency of administration'.

Which one of the following is correct in respect of the above statements?

(a) Both Statement-I and Statement-II are correct and Statement-II is the correct explanation for Statement-I.
(b) Both Statement-I and Statement-II are correct and Statement-II is not the correct explanation for Statement-I.
(c) Statement-I is correct but Statement-II is incorrect.
(d) Statement-I is incorrect but Statement-II is correct.

Solution: (c)

Explanation: As discussed in Section 14.3.4, the Supreme Court in M. Nagaraj case and Jarnail Singh case has held that reservation in public employment should be in the interest of administrative efficiency as specified in Article 335. Hence, Statement I is correct. However, Article 335 does not define the term 'efficiency in administration' and hence Statement II is incorrect. Hence, the answer is (c).

5. Consider the following statements: **[2023]**
   1. According to the Constitution of India, the Central Government has a duty to protect States from internal disturbances.
   2. The Constitution of India exempts the States from providing legal counsel to a person being held for preventive detention.
   3. According to the Prevention of Terrorism Act, 2002, confession of the accused before the police cannot be used as evidence.

How many of the above statements are correct?

(a) Only one (b) Only two (c) All three (d) None

Solution: (b)

Explanation: Under Article 355, Statement 1 is correct (discussed in Chapter 21). As discussed in Section 14.4.6, the protection in case of arrest and detention with respect to consultation with a legal counsel of choice is not available to a person being held under preventive detention. Hence, Statement 2 is correct. Under POTA, 2002 (that was subsequently repealed in 2004), confession of the accused before a police officer not below the rank of Superintendent of Police, can be used as evidence and Statement 3 is incorrect. Hence, the answer is (b).

6. With reference to the writs issued by courts in India, consider the following statements: **[2022]**
   1. Mandamus will not lie against a private organisation unless it is entrusted with a public duty.
   2. Mandamus will not lie against a Company even though it may be a government company.
   3. Any public minded person can be a petitioner to move the court to obtain the writ of quo warranto.

Which of the statements above is/are correct?

(a) 1 and 2 only (b) 2 and 3 only (c) 1 and 3 only (d) 1,2 and 3

Solution: (d)

Explanation: As discussed in Section 14.8.2, Mandamus cannot be issued against a private body unless it is tasked with public duty. Statement 3 is correct as any person can move a court to obtain a writ of quo warranto against a person who has wrongfully occupied a public office. With respect to Statement 2, there is ambiguity. If a government company is performing a public duty, then mandamus will lie against it, but if a government company is not performing any statutory public duty, mandamus will not lie against it. It is likely that UPSC took the second interpretation and has made statement 2 also correct and hence the answer provided is (d).

UPSC Previous Years' Questions of Main Examination

1. Right to privacy is intrinsic to life and personal liberty and is inherently protected under Article 21 of the constitution. Explain. In this reference discuss the law relating to D.N.A. testing of child in the womb to establish its paternity. **[2024]**

Approach: Discussion on Right to Privacy and Puttaswamy case that declared right to privacy as part of Article 21. Various judgements and enactments as a result of this judgement need to be discussed. The D.N.A testing of child in a womb was a case law decided by the Supreme Court in February 2023. The decision of the court in this case needs to be mentioned in the conclusion.

MODEL ANSWER

The Supreme Court in *Puttaswamy* case (2017) declared Right to Privacy as a fundamental right under Article 21 of Part III.

Impact of the judgement on the scope of Fundamental Rights

(a) This judgement has enlarged the scope of fundamental rights, especially right to life and liberty under Article 21.

(b) The Supreme Court had in 2018 struck down Section 377 of IPC that criminalised homosexuality even amongst consenting adults as unconstitutional. This has been a fallout of the Right to privacy judgement since this section violated the privacy of the individual's sexual choice.

(c) Similarly, in the *Aadhaar* judgement in 2018, while the Supreme Court upheld the validity of the Aadhaar Act, it struck down certain provisions that authorised private parties to collect Aadhaar data of individuals. This is again due to the violation of privacy that was declared as a fundamental right in the Puttaswamy case.

(d) As per the direction of the Supreme Court in Aadhaar case, the Parliament has enacted 'The Digital Personal Data Protection Act, 2023' that provides safeguards for personal data obtained and stored by government and other data fiduciaries.

(e) Thus, this judgement has strengthened and widened the scope of fundamental rights.

D.N.A. testing of child in the womb to establish its paternity

In the case of ***Aparna Ajinkya Firodia v. Ajinkya Arun Firodia*** (2023), the Supreme Court held that DNA test of a child in womb cannot be ordered routinely as it violated the right to privacy of the child.

DNA tests of children born during the subsistence of a valid marriage may be directed, only when there is sufficient prima-facie material to dislodge the presumption under Section 112 of the Indian Evidence Act which presumes that a child born out of subsisting marriage or within 280 days of its dissolution is a legitimate child of the husband.

2. Discuss India as a secular state and compare with the secular principles of the US constitution. [2024]

Approach: Bring out the secular provisions of the Constitution in the first part of the answer. The second part of the answer can compare based on differences between Indian Secularism and Western Secularism, which is the basis for secularism as per US Constitution.

MODEL ANSWER

India is a secular country, and secularism has been declared as a basic structure of the Constitution by the Supreme Court in the S R Bommai case.

Nature of Indian Secularism

(a) The State does not have any religion and gives equal respect to all religions.
(b) The Fundamental rights under Articles 15 and 16 guarantee no discrimination on the basis of religion by the State.
(c) The Right to freedom of religion (Articles 25–28) guarantee fundamental right to practise any religion of one's choice.
(d) There can be no discrimination on the basis of religion in right to contest elections and right to vote that are constitutional rights.

Comparison with secularism as per U.S. Constitution

Indian secularism is different from Anglo-Saxon secularism that is the basis for U.S. Secularism as well. That is the reason why the word 'secular' was not added in the Preamble during the adoption of the Constitution but later added in 1976. The similarities are that (a) both nations give equal rights to all citizens irrespective of religion and do not discriminate on the basis of religion and (b) both nations do not have a state religion. The differences are summarised below.

Indian Secularism	U.S. Secularism
Not only opposed to inter-religious discrimination but also opposed to intra-religious discrimination. Thus, it provides for protection to Dalits and women against oppression in Hinduism as well as protection to women in other faiths.	Primarily signifies separation of the State from all religions and opposes any discrimination on the basis of religion.
Deals specifically with religious freedom of minority communities. Thus, minorities have the right to protect their distinct culture and language [Art 29] and also establish educational institutions [Art 30].	There are no such specific provisions for minorities.
Provides for State-supported religious reform. Examples – (a) Abolition of untouchability [Art 17], (b) State can regulate secular practices of religion [Art 25(1)], (c) State can provide for social welfare and reform [Art 25(2)].	Mutual non-interference of State and Religion in each other's domain.
Positive Secularism	Negative Secularism

3. **The Constitution of India is a living instrument with capabilities of enormous dynamism. It is a constitution made for a progressive society. Illustrate with special reference to the expanding horizons of the right to life and personal liberty.** [2023]

Approach: The introduction should be about Article 21 that deals with life and personal liberty. Then, the discussion about various case laws that have expanded the scope of this article needs to be summarised.

MODEL ANSWER

Article 21 of the Constitution provides that no person shall be deprived of his life or personal liberty except as per the procedure established by law.

The expanding horizon of this right can be summarised through the following judgements of the Supreme Court:

(a) In A K Gopalan vs State of Madras (1950), the Supreme Court held that due process of law is not available in India and Article 21 protects people only from arbitrary executive action.

(b) However, in Maneka Gandhi case (1978), the Supreme Court overturned its decision in A K Gopalan case and held that due process is inherent in the procedure established by law. It held that Articles 19 and 21 cannot be understood as watertight compartments and the same criteria of reasonableness as applicable in Article 19 must be applied for Article 21 as well.

(c) Further, the Supreme Court in various cases has held that the right to life as enshrined in Article 21 is more than mere survival and animal existence. It would include the right to live with dignity. It includes the right to a clean environment, free legal aid, health etc.

(d) In 2017, the Supreme Court in the Puttaswamy case held that Right to Privacy is an integral part of Article 21. This has led to further expansion of the scope of life and personal liberty as follows:
- Section 377 of IPC that criminalised homosexuality and Section 497 that criminalised adultery have been struck down as unconstitutional.
- The Digital Personal Data Protection Act has been enacted in 2023 by the Parliament to provide a robust 'Data protection framework' in order to protect the personal liberty of individuals.

4. **Right of movement and residence throughout the territory of India are freely available to Indian citizens, but these rights are not absolute. Comment.** **[2022]**

Approach: Explain the fundamental rights under Article 19(1)(d) and (e) in the introductory part of the answer and provide the reasonable restrictions that can be placed on them in the concluding part.

MODEL ANSWER

Freedom of movement and Residence

Article 19(1)(d) provides for freedom of movement throughout the territory of India and Article 19(1)(e) provides for freedom of residence anywhere in the territory of India.

Both these rights are important fundamental rights as it reflects that India is one nation and there cannot be any regionalism as far as movement or residence of citizens within the country is concerned.

Reasonable restrictions

- Article 19(5) provides that the State can impose reasonable restrictions on both these freedoms in the interests of general public and the protection of interests of any Scheduled Tribe.
- Examples of restrictions in the interest of general public are the recent lockdowns and restrictions on travel that were imposed during the COVID-19 pandemic.
- The restrictions in the interest of Scheduled Tribes are due to the provisions of Fifth and Sixth schedule. Under these schedules, there can be restrictions placed on transfer of land and settling down of non-tribals in Scheduled areas (Fifth Schedule) and Tribal areas (Sixth Schedule), to protect the unique culture of tribals and to protect them from exploitation.

Thus, while these are important fundamental rights, they are subject to reasonable restrictions.

5. 'Constitutional Morality' is rooted in the Constitution itself and is founded on its essential facets. Explain the doctrine of 'Constitutional Morality' with the help of relevant judicial decisions. **[2021]**

Approach: Discuss about Constitutional morality that is different from personal morality. Then explain the same with help of some case laws.

MODEL ANSWER

Constitutional morality is adherence to the constitutional principles and values. Constitutional values include Rule of law, equality, liberty, fraternity etc. Constitutional morality should be practiced and inculcated amongst the citizens to uphold these values. These are different from personal morality which may change from person to person.

Constitutional morality is inherent in the constitution itself. This was highlighted by the Supreme Court in the Kesavananda Bharati case in which the 'Basic Structure' doctrine was propounded thereby restricting the Parliament from amending those 'basic features' of the constitution that reflect its morality.

Apart from the above, some other judgements in which the courts highlighted the concept of constitutional morality in recent past are as follows:

(a) In Puttaswamy case (2017) that declared 'Right to privacy' as a fundamental right, the Supreme Court held that constitutional morality ensures that the courts must strike down any executive or legal action that is unconstitutional.

(b) In Sabarimala case (2018), the court held that constitutional morality requires equal treatment of women.

(c) In Government of NCT of Delhi case (2018), the court held that constitutional morality acts as a check on arbitrary use of power.

Thus, through various judgements the Supreme Court has reiterated the importance of constitutional morality in order to uphold the constitutional values.

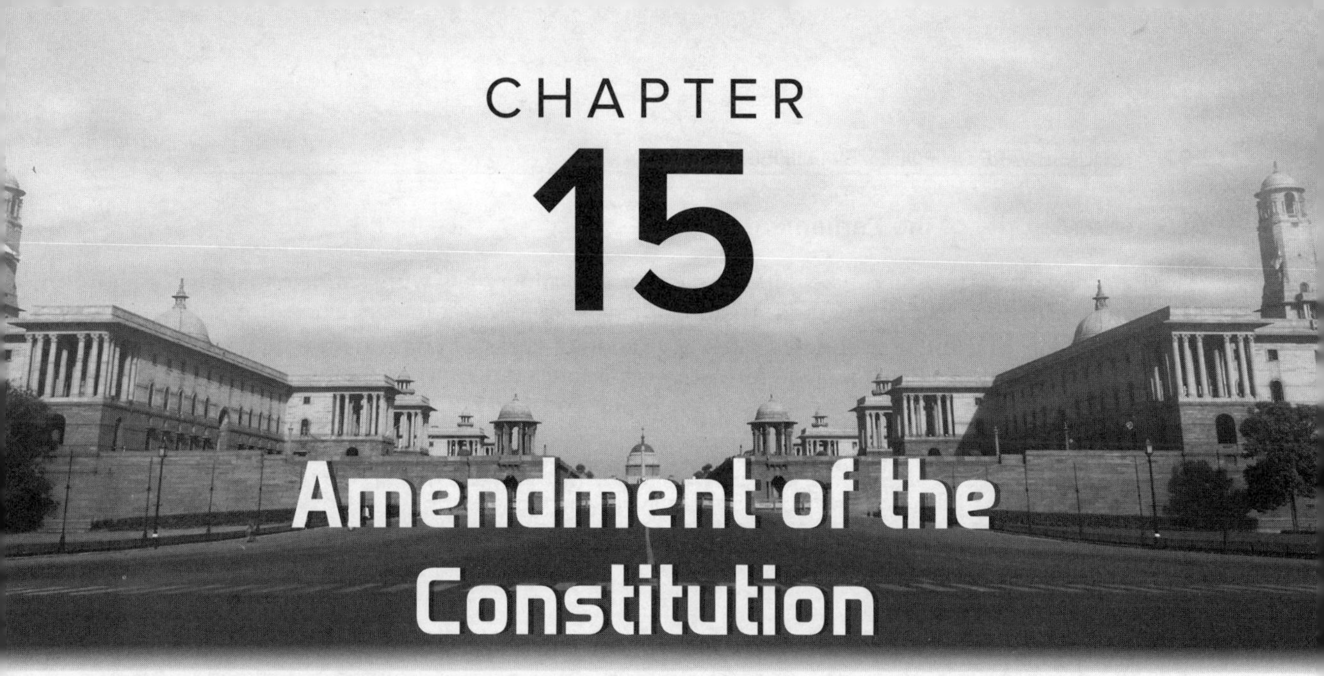

CHAPTER 15

Amendment of the Constitution

LEARNING OUTCOMES

1. Familiarising with various types of amendments as envisaged in the Constitution
2. Understanding the detailed procedure for amendment under Article 368 of the Constitution
3. Examining the basic structure doctrine – Various case laws of the Supreme Court with respect to amending power of the Parliament finally culminating in the 'Basic structure' doctrine
4. Listing and explaining the constitutional features recognised by the judiciary as part of the Basic Structure

Like other Constitutions of the world, the Indian Constitution also provides for its amendment to meet the changing times and exigencies.

Article 368 in Part XX of the Constitution lays down the procedure for the amendment of the Constitution. It states that the Parliament may, in exercise of its constituent power, amend by way of addition, variation or repeal any provision or feature of the Constitution, in accordance with the procedure laid down for the purpose.

15.1 PROCEDURE FOR AMENDMENT

15.1.1 Types of Amendment

The amendment procedure in our Constitution is a combination of rigidity and flexibility.

There are three types of amendment as follows:

1. Amendment by simple majority of the Parliament. This is in fact not deemed to be an amendment of the Constitution under Article 368 though it has the effect of changing the respective provisions of the Constitution.
2. Amendment by special majority of the Parliament i.e., majority of total membership of the House and a majority of two-thirds of the members of the House present and voting.
3. Amendment by special majority of the Parliament followed by ratification by at least half of the State Legislatures.

A. Simple Majority of the Parliament

The following modifications can be done by passing an ordinary law with a simple majority in both the Houses of the Parliament (without treating it as an amendment under Article 368):

(a) Formation or admission of new States, alteration of areas or changing the names of existing States. Recent examples include formation of Telangana (2014), reorganisation of Jammu & Kashmir into two Union Territories of J & K and Ladakh (2019). This will also have the effect of modifying the First and the Fourth Schedule as required.
(b) Abolition or creation of the Legislative Councils in States.
(c) Changes to the Fifth and the Sixth Schedules of the Constitution.
(d) Rules of Procedure in the Parliament.
(e) Parliamentary privileges.
(f) Quorum in the Parliament.
(g) Salaries and allowances of members of the Parliament.
(h) Number of judges of the Supreme Court and conferment of additional jurisdiction on the Supreme Court.
(i) Use of official languages.
(j) Citizenship – acquisition and termination.
(k) Election to the Parliament and the State Legislatures.
(l) Administration of the Union territories.
(m) Extending $1/3^{rd}$ reservation for women in Lok Sabha and State Legislative Assemblies after initial period of 15 years.

MNEMONICS

Concept or Provisions	Shortcut or Mnemonics	Details to Remember
Provisions that can be changed by Ordinary law of Parliament through simple majority (without being considered an amendment under Article 368)	**RAC 5 & 6** travel was **CLEAN** for **Women** due to **PQRS** (**P**lasser **Q**uick **R**elaying **S**ystem)	• **R** – **R**eorganisation of a State or Union Territory • **AC** – **A**bolition or **C**reation of Legislative council • **5 & 6** – Changes to Fifth and Sixth Schedules Following matters: • **C** – **C**itizenship • **L** – Official **L**anguages • **E** – **E**lections to Parliament and States • **A** – **A**dministration of Union Territories • **N** – **N**umber of judges of Supreme Court **Women** – Extending 1/3rd reservation for women in Lok Sabha and State Legislative Assemblies after initial period of 15 years. Following matters with respect to Parliament: • **P** – **P**rivileges • **Q** – **Q**uorum • **R** – **R**ules of procedure • **S** – **S**alaries and allowances

B. Special Majority of the Parliament

Amendment of almost all the other provisions of the Constitution, except like the ones listed above, will require a special majority in both the houses of the Parliament i.e., a majority of total membership of the House and a majority of not less than two-thirds of the members of the House present and voting [Art 368].

Examples of provisions that can be amended with special majority include (a) the Fundamental Rights, (b) the Directive Principles of State Policy and (c) All provisions other than those listed in A (above) and C (below).

THINK ABOUT IT

The amendment of the Indian Constitution is a blend of rigidity and flexibility. Elucidate.

C. Special Majority of the Parliament and Ratification by States

In respect of the following amendments, Article 368 of the Constitution stipulates that apart from special majority in the Parliament, the amendment should also be ratified by not less than half of the State legislatures (with a simple majority). This is considering the federal character of these provisions. There is no time limit specified for the States to ratify such amendments.

(a) Election of the President
(b) Extent of the executive power of the Union and the States, High Court for Union territories and GST Council
(c) Supreme Court and High Courts
(d) Distribution of legislative powers between the Union and the States and the lists in the Seventh Schedule
(e) Representation of States in the Parliament
(f) Provisions of Article 368 itself

MNEMONICS

Concept or Provisions	Shortcut or Mnemonics	Details to Remember
Federal items that require ratification by at least half of the States	**SHEEP GST Distribute itself**	• **SH** – **S**upreme Court and **H**igh Court – changes to judiciary • **E** – **E**lection of President • **E** – **E**xtent of Executive power of the Union and States • **P** – Representation of States in **P**arliament • **GST** – GST Council • **Distribute** – **Distribution** of legislative powers and changes to Seventh Schedule • **Itself** – Any changes to Article 368 itself

15.1.2 Procedure for Amendment under Article 368

Procedure for amendment of the Constitution as laid down in Article 368:

1. Amendment of the Constitution can be initiated only by introduction of a Bill in either House of the Parliament, by a minister or a private member.
2. The bill must be passed in each House of the Parliament by a special majority, i.e., a majority of total membership of the House and a majority of not less than two-thirds of the members of the House present and voting.
3. Each House of the Parliament must pass the bill separately. In case of disagreement between the two Houses, there is no provision for calling a joint-sitting of both the Houses.
4. If the bill attempts to amend the federal provisions of the Constitution, it must also be ratified by the legislatures of at least half the States by a simple majority.
5. After getting passed by both the Houses and the State Legislatures where necessary, the bill is sent to the President for his/her assent.
6. The President must give his/her assent to the bill. He/she cannot withhold the bill or send the bill back to the Parliament for reconsideration. Once the President gives his/her assent, the bill becomes a Constitutional Amendment Act.

Some of the criticisms against the amendment procedure of our Constitution is as follows:

- It is only the Parliament that can initiate any amendment to the Constitution and not any of the State Legislatures unlike in the United States.
- Most of the Constitution can be amended by the Parliament itself without any ratification by the States. It is only few federal provisions that require ratification by at least half of the States.
- Some of the important provisions like reorganisation of a State can be carried out by the Parliament through an ordinary law.

Scan the QR code for conceptual video on 'Amendment of the Constitution and Basic Structure'

However, despite the above criticisms, the different types of amendment procedure as discussed above have been effective in meeting changing circumstances and needs. As opined by various legal experts, these procedures are diverse and strike a good balance between rigidity and flexibility.

15.2 BASIC STRUCTURE DOCTRINE

The main conflicts in the past with respect to the constitutional amendments have been when such amendments had modified the provisions with respect to the Fundamental Rights in Part III.

As discussed in the previous chapter on the Fundamental Rights, Article 13 places restriction on the State from making any law that violates the fundamental Rights guaranteed in Part III. As discussed in Section 14.10 (Exception to Fundamental Rights), right to property and adequate compensation in the event of acquisition of property by the State was a Fundamental Right until 1978. In order to achieve social and economic justice and also to fulfil the directive principles, amendments were made to Part III by adding Articles 31A, 31B and 31C at various points of time. This curtailed the fundamental right to equality (Article 14) and liberty (Article 19), especially right to property that existed as a fundamental right till 1978.

The question before the Supreme Court in various important case laws was whether a constitutional amendment is also to be considered as 'law' within the meaning of Article 13, which will have an effect on the Parliament's power to amend Part III even through constitutional amendments. This question and eventually the 'basic structure' doctrine evolved through important case laws as discussed below.

Shankari Prasad Vs Union of India (1951)

- This case was filed challenging the 1st Constitutional Amendment that added Articles 31A and 31B. This curtailed right to property, which was a fundamental right at that time.
- *The Supreme Court in this case ruled that 'law' within the meaning of Article 13 included only ordinary laws passed by the Parliament or the State Legislatures.* The court held that it does not include a constitutional amendment under Article 368.
- Hence, *the Parliament through a constitutional amendment can modify any part of the Constitution including the fundamental rights in Part III.*

Golak Nath Vs State of Punjab (1967)

- This case was filed in the wake of some land-related Acts in Punjab, which fixed a ceiling on the extent of agricultural land that can be held by a person. The 17th Amendment of the Constitution, also amended Article 31A to specify that the right to property and fair compensation at market rates, shall be applicable only for land within the ceiling limit as per State laws. This was challenged on the ground that it violated the fundamental right to property and fair compensation.
- *The Supreme Court in this judgement reversed the earlier stand it had taken in the Shankari Prasad case.*
- In this case, the Supreme Court held that even a Constitutional Amendment Act will be included within the meaning of law for the purpose of Article 13. The Fundamental Rights have been given a transcendental (i.e., above all other provisions) and immutable (i.e., unchangeable) position. Hence, *even a constitutional amendment cannot take away any fundamental rights guaranteed in Part III.*
- The Court also introduced the **'Doctrine of Prospective Overruling'** in this case. If any amendment is struck down retrospectively, it would create chaos and will affect several transactions that were carried out under the old regime. However, in the 'Doctrine of Prospective Overruling', constitutional amendments or laws already in place would not be affected by the decisions of the court and only future amendments or laws would have to follow the judgement laid down by the court in a case. In other words, under the 'Doctrine of Prospective Overruling', the law declared by the Court applies only to future cases, and its applicability to cases that have reached finality is preserved because repeal would otherwise cause hardship to those who had relied on it.
- This introduction of 'doctrine of prospective overruling' is also an example of 'creative interpretation' by the Supreme Court under which the courts evolve new concepts and new procedures to meet the requirements of changing circumstances. Similarly, the creation of 'basic structure doctrine' in the Kesavananda Bharati case is also an example of 'creative interpretation.' This is different from (a) 'literal interpretation' where the courts interpret the provisions in their plain, ordinary, natural and grammatical meaning or (b) 'purposive interpretation' where the courts look into the purpose of incorporating a provision in the Constitution.
- The Supreme Court has held that the Constitution should be interpreted in a broad and liberal manner, and not in a narrow and pedantic manner. This is the doctrine of 'liberal interpretation.' This reflects the fact that the Constitution is a living document and should be interpreted as the machinery by which laws are made and not as a mere law itself. This ensures that the part of Fundamental rights is interpreted in a broad sense, and not by a restricted approach.

24th Constitutional Amendment Act (1971)

- The decision in the *Golak Nath case* resulted in the Parliament amending the Constitution by the 24th Constitutional Amendment Act in 1971. The Parliament amended Articles 13 and 368.
- Article 13(4) was added to provide that nothing in that article shall apply to any amendment of the Constitution made under Article 368.
- Article 368(3) was added to provide that nothing in Article 13 shall apply to any amendment made under Article 368 in the Constitution.
- This amendment made it clear that the Parliament has the power to amend any part of the Constitution including the Fundamental Rights and the word 'law' as used in Article 13 does not include a Constitutional Amendment Act.

Kesavananda Bharati Vs State of Kerala (1973)

- The 24th Amendment Act was challenged in the *Kesavananda Bharati case.*
- In this case, the Supreme Court over ruled its judgement in the *Golak Nath* case. It upheld the 24th Amendment Act that allowed amendment of even the fundamental rights through a Constitutional amendment Act. However, it created the 'basic structure' doctrine and held that basic structures of the Constitution cannot be violated through any amendment.
- In the *Kesavananda Bharati case*, the Supreme Court propounded that the Constitution of India has certain basic features that cannot be altered or destroyed through amendments by the Parliament of India.
- The doctrine thus forms the basis for the Supreme Court of India to review and strike down the constitutional amendments and Acts enacted by the Parliament or State Legislatures which violate or alter the 'basic structure' of the Constitution.
- The basic features of the Constitution have not been explicitly defined in the Constitution or by the Judiciary, and these are determined by the Court in various cases that comes before it.
- In Indira Nehru Gandhi Vs Raj Narain case (1975), the Supreme Court reaffirmed the doctrine of basic structure of the Constitution.

42nd Amendment Act and the Minerva Mills Case

- In order to nullify the judgement of the Supreme Court in the *Kesavananda Bharati* case, the Parliament through the 42nd Amendment Act in 1976 added clauses (4) and (5) to Article 368. It declared that no constitutional amendment can be called into question in any court on any ground [368(4)]. It also declared that there shall be no limitation on the constituent power of the Parliament to amend any provision of the Constitution [368(5)].
- However, in the *Minerva Mills case*, the Supreme Court struck down clauses (4) and (5) of Article 368 as unconstitutional as it violates the basic structure of judicial review.
- It also held that ***the Parliament's power to amend the Constitution is limited and it cannot grant itself unlimited power to destroy the basic structure of the Constitution.***

SUMMARY OF IMPORTANT SUPREME COURT JUDGEMENTS W.R.T BASIC STRUCTURE DOCTRINE

Case Law	Key Judgement
Shankari Prasad	• Constitutional Amendment Act is not a law within the meaning of Article 13. • Hence, Parliament can modify even fundamental rights through constitutional amendment.

Case Law	Key Judgement
Golak Nath	• Reversed the decision in Shankari Prasad. • Even a Constitutional Amendment Act is a law within Article 13. So, Parliament cannot modify fundamental rights even through constitutional amendment.
Kesavananda Bharati	• Reversed the decision in Golak Nath. • Parliament can amend any part of the Constitution including fundamental rights without violating the 'Basic structure.'
Minerva Mills	• Judicial review is a basic structure. • Parliament cannot destroy the 'basic structure' through constitutional amendment.

Various Features declared as part of 'Basic Structure'

The 'basic structure' doctrine evolved with the judgement in the *Kesavananda Bharati* case. This concept has since been developed by the Supreme Court in various subsequent cases like the Minerva Mills case, the Central Coal Fields Limited case, the S. P. Sampath Kumar case, the Indra Sawhney or Mandal case, the Kihoto Hollohon case, the S. R. Bommai case, the Coelho case etc.

Some of the important 'basic features' as declared by the Supreme Court in various cases are as follows:

1. Supremacy of the Constitution
2. Rule of law
3. The principle of separation of powers
4. The objectives specified in the Preamble to the Constitution of India
5. Judicial review
6. Articles 32 and 226
7. Federalism
8. Secularism
9. The sovereign, democratic, republican structure
10. Unity and integrity of the nation
11. The principle of equality, not every feature of equality, but the quintessence of equal justice
12. The 'essence' of other fundamental rights in Part III
13. The concept of social and economic justice – to build a welfare state: Part IV of the Constitution
14. The harmonious balance between the fundamental rights and the directive principles
15. The parliamentary system of government
16. The principle of free and fair elections
17. Limitations upon the amending power conferred by Article 368
18. Independence of the judiciary

THINK ABOUT IT

The 'basic structure' doctrine brings out the supremacy of the Constitution in our country. Explain with various case laws that finally culminated in the creation of 'basic structure' by the Supreme Court.

Scan the QR code for latest Supreme Court ruling on interpretation of 'Basic Structure' Doctrine

Mc Graw Hill edge

19. Effective access to justice
20. Powers of the Supreme Court of India under Articles 32, 136, 141 and 142

The Supreme Court in 2024, while upholding the validity of Uttar Pradesh Board of Madrasa Education Act, 2004, has opined that a legislation cannot be struck down by just making a blanket statement that it violates the 'basic structure' without specifying the violation of an express provision of the Constitution.

Criticism against 'Basic Structure' doctrine

There have been certain criticisms against the 'basic structure' doctrine as follows:

1. It is not supported by any explicit provision of the Constitution.
2. It is undemocratic as the decisions of unelected judges overrides the will of elected representatives.
3. It lacks clarity and inherently subjective based on individual judges' interpretation.
4. By allowing the judiciary to intervene in the legislative and constituent power of Parliament, the doctrine violates the principle of separation of powers.

However, the 'basic structure' doctrine has been instrumental in striking down amendments/legislations by which the Parliament has tried to wield unlimited powers without any restraint. It is aimed at establishing 'constitutional sovereignty' and 'constitutionalism' in our democracy.

15.3 PARLIAMENTARY SOVEREIGNTY, JUDICIAL SUPREMACY AND CONSTITUTIONAL SOVEREIGNTY

The doctrine of Parliamentary sovereignty is associated with the British Parliament. This is because there is no written constitution in the U.K. and Parliamentary laws are supreme for governance of the country. On the other hand, the concept of judicial supremacy is associated with the U.S. It is because the American Supreme Court has wide powers in interpreting their constitution as per 'due process of law.'

The Indian Constitutional scheme is basically a synthesis of Parliamentary Sovereignty and Judicial Supremacy. The Parliament can amend any part of the Constitution through its constituent power under Article 368. However, the courts can, through their power of judicial review, strike down any law or constitutional amendment as unconstitutional. The Parliament may override such decisions through further amendments. For example, the 24th amendment was passed to override the decision in Golak Nath case. But such amendments are again subject to judicial review – like the 24th amendment that was subjected to review in the Kesavananda Bharati case.

> **THINK ABOUT IT**
>
> Indian polity is a blend of parliamentary sovereignty and judicial supremacy. But they are both subject to the overall constitutional sovereignty. Comment.

Finally, it can be said that through the 'Basic structure doctrine' propounded by the Supreme Court in Kesavananda Bharati judgement, that has been reiterated in subsequent cases, the court has reinforced 'Constitutional sovereignty' in the governance of our country. Parliament's amending power is not unlimited and should not violate the 'basic features' of the Constitution as held by the judiciary.

Various Types of Majority		
Types of Majority	**Calculation**	**Applicability**
Highest Special Majority – 2/3rd of total membership of the house	Lok Sabha = 543 × 2/3 = 362 Rajya Sabha = 245 ×2/3 = 164 Irrespective of number of members present and voting, the above number of votes required in the respective house for passing the resolution.	Only for impeachment of the President.
Effective – Majority of all the then members of the house	All the then members = Total membership (Less) Vacancies including due to death, resignation, disqualification, etc. Please refer section 8.5.2 for calculation with example.	For removal of Officers of Parliament & State legislature i.e., Speaker & Deputy Speaker (in Lok Sabha and Legislative Assembly), Chairman & Deputy Chairman (in Rajya Sabha and Legislative Council). Only for removal of Vice President (Chairman of Rajya Sabha), the resolution for removal also needs to be approved by simple majority in Lok Sabha.
Special – Majority of total membership and not less than two-thirds of members present and voting	Please refer section 12.4.1 for calculation with example.	Important provisions requiring special majority: • Removal of Judges and authorities like CAG, Chief Election Commissioner, State Election Commissioner. • Constitutional amendment bills. • State Legislative Assembly resolution recommending creation or abolition of Legislative Council.
Unique Special majority – Only two-thirds of members present and voting	Please refer section 19.2.3.1 for calculation with example.	Only in Rajya Sabha in the following two situations: • Authorising Parliament to legislate on a subject in the State list in National interest. • Authorising Parliament to create All India service.
Simple – Majority of members present and voting	For example, in Lok Sabha, if 500 members are present and voting, simple majority is 251. Similarly, in Rajya Sabha, if 200 members are present and voting, simple majority is 101.	• Passage of ordinary bills, resolutions, motions in both the houses. • All matters as mentioned in Section 15.1.1 - A.

MAINS STARTER

Area	Building Blocks For Model Introductions
Amendment power of the Parliament	The Parliament enjoys the constituent power to amend by way of addition, variation or repeal, any of the provisions of the Constitution under Article 368. However, the basic structure cannot be violated in any such amendment as laid down in the Kesavananda Bharati case.
Unitary bias in amendment of the Constitution	The Constitution can be amended by the Parliament as per the provisions of Article 368. It must be noted that it is only the Parliament that can initiate an amendment of the Constitution, and not the States. Further, amendment of only a few federal aspects requires ratification by at least half of the States and majority of the Constitution can be amended by the Parliament itself. There are also a few areas that can be changed by just an ordinary law of Parliament.
Basic Structure	'Basic structure doctrine' was created by the Supreme Court in Kesavananda Bharati case and reiterated in many subsequent cases including Minerva Mills case. It provides that the Parliament's amending power is not unlimited and certain basic features of the Constitution cannot be violated even by a constitutional amendment. Various features have been declared as part of the 'Basic structure' in different cases.
Constitutional Sovereignty	The Indian Constitutional scheme is basically a synthesis of Parliamentary Sovereignty and Judicial Supremacy. However, through the 'Basic structure doctrine' propounded by the Supreme Court in Kesavananda Bharati judgement, the court has reinforced 'Constitutional sovereignty' in the governance of our country. Parliament's amending power is not unlimited and should not violate the 'basic features' of the Constitution as held by the judiciary.

UPSC Previous Years' Questions of Preliminary Examination

1. As per Article 368 of the Constitution of India, the Parliament may amend any provision of the Constitution by way of: [2024]
   1. Addition
   2. Variation
   3. Repeal

   Select the correct answer using the code given below:
   (a) 1 and 2 only (b) 2 and 3 only
   (c) 1 and 3 only (d) 1, 2 and 3

   Solution: (d)

   Explanation: Article 368 provides that Parliament may, in exercise of its constituent power, amend by way of addition, variation or repeal any provision of the Constitution. Hence, all 3 are correct and the answer is (d).

2. Consider the following statements: [2022]
   1. A Bill amending the Constitution requires a prior recommendation of the President of India.
   2. When a Constitutional Amendment Bill is presented to the President of India, it is obligatory for the President of India to give his/her assent.
   3. A Constitution Amendment Bill must be passed in both Lok Sabha and Rajya Sabha by a special majority and there is no provision for joint sitting.

   Which of the statements given above is/are correct?
   (a) 1 and 2 only (b) 2 and 3 only (c) 1 and 3 only (d) 1, 2 and 3

   Solution: (b)

   Explanation: As discussed in Section 15.1.2, as per the procedure for constitutional amendment bill, statements 2 and 3 are correct. Such a bill does not require prior recommendation of the President and hence statement 1 is incorrect and the answer is (b).

3. Consider the following statements: [2020]
   1. The Constitution of India defines its 'basic structure' in terms of federalism, secularism, fundamental rights and democracy.
   2. The Constitution of India provides for 'judicial review' to safeguard the citizens' liberties and to preserve the ideals on which the Constitution is based.

   Which of the statements given above is/are correct?
   (a) 1 only (b) 2 only (c) Both 1 and 2 (d) Neither 1 nor 2

   Solution: (d)

   Explanation: As discussed in Section 15.2, 'Basic Structure' is not defined in the Constitution but has evolved through various judgements of the Supreme Court starting with the *Kesavananda Bharati* case. Hence, Statement 1 is incorrect. Statement 2 is subject to interpretation. But technically the constitution does not explicitly provide for 'Judicial Review' in any article and it is implied through various articles like Article 13, Article 32, Article 226, Article 136 etc. Hence, Statement 2 is also considered as incorrect and the answer is (d).

UPSC Previous Years' Questions of Main Examination

1. Parliament's power to amend the constitution is limited power and it cannot be enlarged into absolute power. In light of this statement explain whether parliament under Article 368 of the constitution can destroy the Basic structure of the constitution by expanding its amending power? **[2019]**

Approach: The procedure for amendment of the Constitution in Article 368 needs to be part of the introduction. Then, the discussion on 'Basic structure' along with relevant case laws needs to be provided.

MODEL ANSWER

The amendment procedure of the Constitution is provided in Article 368. Any amendment requires to be passed by a special majority in both the houses of Parliament and later assented to by the President. If the amendment affects any of the federal characteristics of the Constitution, then it also needs to be ratified by at least half of the State legislatures before being assented by the President.

Amendment power and Basic structure

- The power of the Parliament to amend the Constitution has come in conflict with the Fundamental rights guaranteed in Part III.
- Article 13 of the Constitution stipulates that any law shall not violate the Fundamental rights guaranteed in Part III. The question before the Supreme Court in various cases has been whether a constitutional amendment under Article 368 will also be subject to restriction imposed by Article 13.
- In *Shankari Prasad case*, the court held that a constitutional amendment act is not a law within the meaning of Article 13. However, in ***Golak Nath case***, the court held that even a constitutional amendment act is a law within Article 13 and hence the Parliament cannot amend any part of Fundamental rights.
- This led to the 24th amendment which made it clear that Parliament has the power to amend any part of the Constitution including Fundamental Rights and the word 'law' as used in Article 13 does not include a Constitutional Amendment Act.
- While upholding the 24th amendment, the court finally arrived at the 'Basic structure' doctrine in the *Kesavananda Bharati case* in 1973. It held that while the Parliament can amend any part of the Constitution including Fundamental Rights, it cannot violate the 'Basic structure' of the Constitution. In *Minerva Mills* case, the Supreme Court reiterated that the Parliament's power of amendment is limited and it cannot assume such power to destroy the basic structure of the Constitution.

Several aspects like Judicial review, independence of judiciary, rule of law, federalism, secularism, principle of equality, essence of fundamental rights, harmonious balance between fundamental rights and directive principles etc., have been declared as 'basic structure' of the Constitution that cannot be violated through amendments.

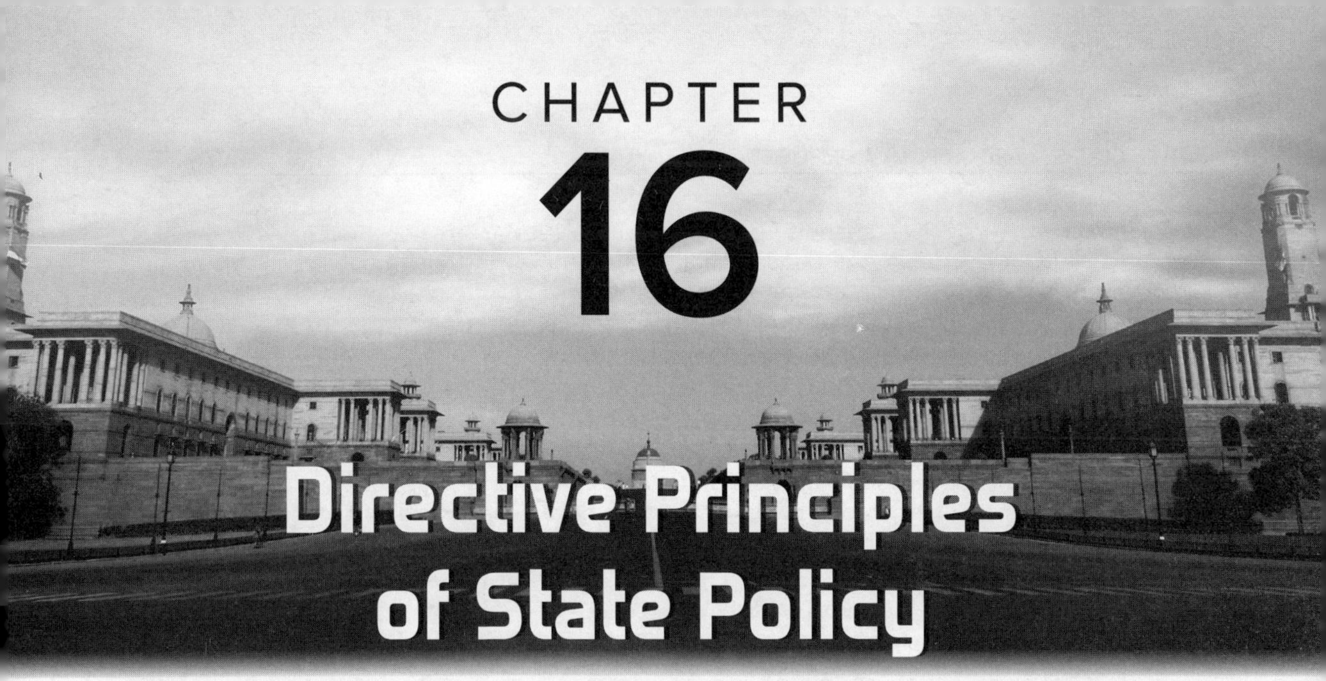

CHAPTER 16

Directive Principles of State Policy

LEARNING OUTCOMES

1. Understanding the Concept and Objectives of Directive Principles
2. Analysing the non-enforceability of DPSPs, but recognising that DPSPs play a crucial role in governance and policymaking
3. Examining various legislations enacted by the State to implement DPSPs
4. Analysing the interplay between Fundamental Rights and DPSPs, including the doctrine of harmonious balance
5. Exploring constitutional directives outside Part IV that the State is obligated to follow for effective governance

16.1 INTRODUCTION TO DIRECTIVE PRINCIPLES OF STATE POLICY

16.1.1 Introduction

We have seen in the previous chapter on Fundamental Rights as to how it primarily aims at securing equality and liberty enshrined in the Preamble. These are the basic rights that citizens of any democratic republic must enjoy and these are guaranteed in Part III.

Equally important is 'justice' that is enshrined in the Preamble. The social, economic and political justice are the foundation for a fair society and that is why these have been placed on top in the Preamble. The Directive Principles of State Policy (DPSP) are instructions to the State authorities to secure to all citizens justice – social, economic and political.

We shall discuss about the various principles in this chapter in detail. We shall then discuss about the relationship between the Fundamental Rights and the DPSP as it evolved through various judgements of the Supreme Court.

Before we get into the detailed discussion, the following provisions and conceptual points relating to the DPSP need to be understood:

- It is contained in Part IV of the Constitution of India in Articles 36–51. The concept of the DPSP was borrowed from the Irish Constitution. The Indian Constitution was also influenced by the United Nations Universal Declaration of Human Rights. Dr Ambedkar described these principles as a novel feature of the Indian Constitution.

- The Directive Principles are non-justiciable in nature i.e., they are not enforceable by themselves in a court of law unlike the Fundamental Rights. However, though non-justiciable in nature, they help the courts in determining the constitutional validity of a law.
- The term 'Directive Principles of State Policy' indicates the ideals that the State should have while formulating its policies. They embody the concept of a 'welfare state'. They are fundamental in the governance of the country as per the Constitution.
- The Directive Principles resemble the 'Instrument of Instructions' enumerated in the Government of India Act of 1935. They were instructions that were issued by the British Crown to the Governor General of India and Governors of provinces. The DPSP in our Constitution are instructions or directives that have been issued to the legislature and the executive branches of government.
- The DPSP do not constitute any limitations upon the legislative or the executive functions of the State unlike the Fundamental Rights.
- In short, the DPSP can be summarised as consisting of the following three important aspects:
  1. Goals and objectives, we as a society should adopt – like (a) social, economic and political justice (b) raising the standard of living (c) equitable distribution of resources (d) promotion of international peace;
  2. Certain social and economic rights that individuals should enjoy apart from fundamental rights – like (a) adequate means of livelihood (b) equal pay for equal work (c) right against economic exploitation (d) right to work (e) right to early childhood care;
  3. Certain policies that the government should adopt – like (a) Uniform Civil Code (b) prohibition of liquor (c) promotion of cottage industries (d) prevention of cow slaughter (e) promotion of village panchayats.

16.1.2 Definition of State and Application of Principles

16.1.2.1 Definition of State

In Part IV, the State shall have the same definition as in Part III [Art 36]. The State for the purposes of DPSP as well includes the legislature and the executive at the Union and State level. It also includes all local authorities within the territory of India and any authority under the control of the Government of India.

THINK ABOUT IT

Though directive principles are not enforceable in a court of law, they are, nevertheless, fundamental in the governance of the country. Discuss.

16.1.2.2 Non-enforceability of DPSP in Courts

Article 37 lays down the following with respect to application of the principles contained in DPSP and their non-enforceability:

- *The provisions contained in Part IV shall not be enforceable by any court;*
- *But these principles are nevertheless fundamental in the governance of the country; and*
- *It shall be the duty of the State to apply these principles in making laws.*

The reason for making the directives non-enforceable in a court of law is due to the following reasons:

- Implementation of these directive principles depends on availability of financial resources with the State. Since our country did not have the financial resources at the time of independence to fund the implementation of various schemes to fulfil these principles, these were made non-enforceable in a court of law.

- The vastness and diversity would have posed a challenge in their strict implementation across the country.
- The order and timing of their implementation also had to take into account various considerations. Hence, these were provided as directives to the State rather than enforceable rights for citizens.

One of the important criticisms against DPSP is its non-enforceability in courts. Many leading jurists have opined that these are mere aspirations that have been placed in the Constitution without any real power behind them. Further, it mixes up important social and economic issues with relatively unimportant ideals.

However, the following points lend strength to the utility of the DPSP:

- It has been given importance by specifying that these principles are fundamental in the governance of the country.
- The public opinion and their awakening play an important role in fulfilment of these principles as the governments are answerable to the people in regular elections. As Dr Ambedkar summed up in his concluding Constituent Assembly speech, these directive principles may not be enforceable in a court of law but are enforceable in the highest court in a democracy i.e., the Court of People.
- Successive governments both at the Centre and various States have implemented laws and schemes to fulfil these principles thereby providing social and economic rights to the citizens. Suitable examples for the same will be provided along with discussion on individual principles in subsequent section.

16.1.3 Classification of Directive Principles

The Constitution has classified the Fundamental Rights into six different categories as discussed in the previous chapter on Fundamental Rights. However, it does not have a formal classification of the Directive Principles. Nonetheless, the DPSP can be classified broadly into three categories based on their content as follows:

(a) Socialistic principles – Those principles that primarily provide for social and economic justice for poorer and weaker sections of the society.

(b) Gandhian principles – Those principles that primarily deal with Gandhian values of prohibition of alcohol, self-sustainable villages, cooperative movement, ban on cow-slaughter.

(c) Liberal–Intellectual principles – Those liberal principles that deal with protection of environment and historical monuments, uniform civil code, friendly international relations.

While discussing each of the principles in the subsequent section, the relevant classification will also be mentioned for the same.

16.2 DISCUSSION ON DIRECTIVE PRINCIPLES

We shall now discuss the principles contained in Articles 38–51. Along with a brief discussion as required for each article, suitable examples of laws and schemes that have been implemented by the State to fulfil the principles will also be provided. The classification of each principle as a Socialistic, Gandhian or Liberal–Intellectual principle will also be provided.

Article 38 – State to secure a social order for the promotion of welfare of the people

(1) The State shall strive to promote the welfare of the people and a social order in which justice, social, economic and political, shall prevail in all the institutions of national life.

(2) The State shall minimise inequalities in income, and try to eliminate inequalities in status, facilities and opportunities, amongst (a) individuals, (b) groups of people residing in different areas and (c) engaged in different professions.

This is a socialistic principle.

This principle reflects the objective in the Preamble of securing social, economic and political justice for citizens. It also directs the State to frame policies that will reduce the inequalities not just amongst individuals but also amongst various regions and different professions.

Schemes like Hill Area Development Programme (1960), Drought Prone Area Programme (1973) have been launched in the past for this purpose. Schemes like Mahatma Gandhi National Rural Employment Guarantee Programme (MNREGA, 2006) for individuals and Aspirational Districts Programme (2018) for development of the backward districts are also examples of policies aimed at fulfilling this principle.

Article 39 – Certain principles of policy to be followed by the State

The State shall, in particular, direct its policy towards securing:

(a) that men and women equally have the right to an adequate means of livelihood;

(b) that the ownership and control of material resources of the community are distributed to subserve the common good;

(c) that the operation of the economic system does not result in the concentration of wealth and means of production to the common detriment (harmful);

(d) that there is equal pay for equal work for both men and women;

(e) that the health and strength of workers and children are not abused and that citizens are not forced to enter occupations unsuited to their age or strength;

(f) that children are given opportunities to develop in a healthy manner and are protected against exploitation and against moral and material abandonment.

Scan the QR code for discussion on recent Supreme Court judgment interpreting Article 39(b)

McGraw Hill edge

This is a socialistic principle.

- These principles are policies to be adopted by the State while framing its schemes and laws.
- There have been many laws made for fulfilling the principles under Article 39(b) and (c) that provide for economic justice. Various States have enacted laws for land reforms aimed at abolishing zamindari and other intermediary systems and also for redistribution of land amongst landless labourers. Laws for nationalising banking and insurance are also examples of laws aimed for securing these principles.

THINK ABOUT IT

The ownership and control of material resources should be so distributed to serve the common good. Comment on this important directive principle contained in Part IV drawing reference to supreme court judgements in this regard.

- In *Property owners' association versus State of Maharashtra* case reference (2024), a nine-judge Constitution Bench of the Supreme Court, in a majority judgement (8:1), held that every private resource cannot be considered a 'material resource of the community' to be used by the government to subserve the 'common good.' It held that to qualify as a 'material resource of the community,' a resource must be 'material' and 'of the community.' The 'public trust doctrine' and context-specific key factors that would determine this are

(a) nature and inherent characteristics of the resource;

(b) its impact on community well-being;

(c) its scarcity and consequence of its concentration in private hands.

Hence, certain resources like forests, ponds, spectrum, mines and minerals may fall within the scope of Article 39(b) even if they are privately held. However, not every private resource automatically qualifies just because it meets material needs. The term 'distribute' in Article 39(b) also carries a wide meaning that can include both government acquisition and redistribution to private players, as long as it serves the common good.

- Various laws like Payment of Wages Act, Minimum Wages Act, Equal Remuneration Act, Factories Act, Industrial Disputes Act, Bonded Labour Abolition Act, have all been enacted to fulfil the principles under clauses (a), (d) and (e). Many of these labour laws have now been reframed and replaced in 2020 under the four new codes for labour and wages i.e., Code on Wages, Industrial Relations Code, Social Security Code, and Health and Working Conditions Code. All the States and Union Territories are expected to complete harmonisation and pre-publication of draft rules under these four codes by March 2025, after which they are expected to be implemented through out the country.
- Laws like Child and Adolescent Labour (Prohibition and Regulation) Act have also been enacted to fulfil the principle under clause (f).

Article 39A – Equal justice and free legal aid

The State shall secure

- legal system that promotes justice, on a basis of equal opportunity, and
- provide free legal aid, by suitable legislation or schemes to the poor.

This is a socialistic principle. This was added through the 42nd Constitutional Amendment Act in 1976.

The Legal Services Authorities Act, 1987 constitutes legal service authorities at the National and the State level that aims to provide free legal aid for the poor. The Lok Adalats are organised under this law for speedy settlement of disputes. The Supreme Court has also referred to this article to justify Public Interest Litigations (PIL) filed for securing justice for the poor and needy.

Article 40 – Organisation of village panchayats

The State shall take steps to organise village panchayats and endow them with such powers and authority as may be necessary to enable them to function as units of self-government.

This is a Gandhian principle.

Various States enacted laws since commencement of the Constitution, starting from the Rajasthan Panchayat Act, 1953, that created elected panchayats in those States. It must be noted that with the 73rd Constitutional Amendment Act in 1992, three-tier panchayats in rural areas have been given a constitutional status. The powers and authority of these panchayats is as per devolution by respective State laws.

MNEMONICS

Concept or Provisions	Shortcut or Mnemonics	Details to Remember
Articles 39, 39A and 40	**PEP** talk	**P** – **P**olicies to be followed by State (39) **E** – **E**qual justice and free legal aid (39A) **P** – **P**anchayats (40)

Article 41 – Right to work, to education and to public assistance in certain cases

The State shall make effective provision for securing the right to work, to education and to public assistance in cases of unemployment, old age, sickness and disablement, and in other cases of undeserved want.

This is a socialistic principle.

The MNREGA Act (2006) is a Parliamentary law enacted to secure right to work as a legal right. Similarly, there are schemes for unemployment allowance as well as old age and disability pension that is provided by the centre as well as various State governments. 'Undeserved want' would mean being a victim of a mass disaster, ethnic violence, flood, earth quake, etc. The Central and State governments provide assistance to such victims to fulfil this directive.

THINK ABOUT IT

The well-being of labour is an important principle in Part IV of the Constitution. Discuss in light of recent debates surrounding the number of working hours per week in the Indian industry.

Article 42 – Provision for just and humane conditions of work and maternity relief

The State shall make provision for securing just and humane conditions of work and for maternity relief.

This is a socialistic principle.

As discussed under Article 39, the various labour laws have provisions to ensure humane conditions of work for workers. Similarly, the Maternity Benefit Act (as amended in 2017) mandates 26 weeks of maternity leave for working women.

Scan the QR code for discussion on labour rights in DPSP in light of recent debate on working hours in industry

McGraw Hill edge

Article 43 – Living wage, etc., for workers

(i) The State shall endeavour to secure to all workers (a) living wage, (b) conditions of work ensuring a decent standard of life and (c) full enjoyment of leisure and social and cultural opportunities.

(ii) The State shall endeavour to promote cottage industries on an individual or cooperative basis in rural areas.

Point (i) is a socialistic principle, while point (ii) can be considered a Gandhian principle.

As discussed under Article 39, the various labour laws have provisions to ensure that the principles contained in (i) above are fulfilled. Similarly, Khadi and Village Industries Commission, Handicrafts Board, Handloom Board, Silk Board etc., have been set up for the development of cottage industries.

Article 43A – Participation of workers in management of industries

The State shall take steps to secure the participation of workers in the management of undertakings, establishments or other organisations engaged in any industry.

This is a socialistic principle. This was added through the 42nd Constitutional Amendment Act in 1976.

For example, the Industrial Relations Code, 2020 provides for constitution of Works Committee that will have equal representation from both the employer and the employees in any industrial establishment in which more than 100 workers are employed.

MNEMONICS

Concept or Provisions	Shortcut or Mnemonics	Details to Remember
Articles 41 to 43A (DPSPs related to work and labour)	**W4**	**W1** – Right to **W**ork (41) **W2** – Humane conditions of **W**ork (42) **W3** – Living **W**age (43) **W4** – Participation of **W**orkers in management (43A)

Article 43B

The State shall endeavour to promote voluntary formation, autonomous functioning, democratic control and professional management of cooperative societies.

This is a Gandhian Principle. This was added through the 97th Constitutional Amendment Act in 2011.

Various States have enacted laws for formation, elections and functioning of cooperative societies. Recently (2021), the central government has created Ministry of Cooperation to strengthen cooperative movement in the country and reaching it up to the grassroots.

Article 44 – Uniform civil code for the citizens

The State shall endeavour to secure for the citizens a uniform civil code (UCC) throughout the territory of India.

This is a Liberal-Intellectual principle.

A UCC administers the same set of secular personal laws to govern all people irrespective of their religion, caste and tribe. This supersedes the right of citizens to be governed under different personal laws based on their religion or caste or tribe. Such codes are in place in most modern nations.

In India, we have uniform criminal laws that are applicable to all citizens irrespective of their religion. Even in civil laws, with respect to various matters like taxation, contract laws etc., we have common laws applicable to all citizens.

However, in matters such as marriage, divorce, inheritance of property, various religious communities in India followed their personal laws that is based on their religious doctrines and scriptures. It continues to be governed by such religion-specific laws. For example, the Hindus are governed by laws such as the Hindu Marriage Act (1955) and the Hindu Succession Act (1956). Jains, Buddhists and Sikhs are covered by the Hindu laws. The Sikh marriages can also be registered under the Anand Marriage Act (2012). Similarly, the Christians have their own personal laws on these matters and the Muslims are governed by the Muslim Personal Law (Shariat) Application Act (1937).

The Constitution makers were divided about the inclusion of the UCC in the Constitution. There were some members who wanted it to be made as a Fundamental Right that will ensure uniformity in all civil laws and secure equal rights for women. However, some members were not in favour of including it in the Constitution at all as they felt that a UCC will violate the fundamental right to religion that is guaranteed in Part III. Finally, it was included as a directive principle in Part IV.

The need for a UCC has always been a discussion point in the Indian polity. While the personal laws of Hindus and Christians have been amended after independence to provide for gender equality, the personal laws of Muslims are yet to be substantially amended.

The key arguments in favour of the UCC are as follows:

- The UCC will make India secular in the true sense where all are subject to same personal laws.
- So long as different communities continue to practice different personal laws, they will continue to remain conscious of their separate identities that will weaken national integration. Hence, a UCC is essential for a strong integrated nation.
- While the above reasons are important, the most vital argument in favour of the UCC is gender justice. It will ensure that all women irrespective of their religion have equal rights when it comes to personal laws relating to marriage, divorce and inheritance.

THINK ABOUT IT

Why is Uniform Civil Code important for a secular, democratic country like India? What are the challenges in its implementation?

The key issues in implementing the UCC are as follows:

- There can be potential conflict between the provisions of the UCC and freedom of religion under Articles 25 and 26, and freedom to conserve one's culture under Article 29.
- Issue of the UCC is vast and its potential repercussions remain untested. Change should be done in a manner which can protect and preserve the diversity and plurality which forms the socio-cultural fabric of the nation.
- Mere legislation does not automatically result in gender equality in societal setup, though it is the first step.

A UCC is required to ensure equality for women. However, this should not be politicised as a religious issue. The best way out is to remove discrimination within various personal laws, or enact a uniform law for all religions after wide consultation, to achieve uniformity and equality for women.

Goa, which merged with the Indian Union in 1961, continues to have the civil code based on Portugese civil code introduced in 1870. It is largely a UCC for all Goans with a few exceptions. Uttarakhand State has become the first State to enact the Uniform Civil Code of Uttarakhand Act, 2024, which came into effect from January 2025. It implements a UCC for all residents of the State with exemption for Scheduled Tribes and their practices.

Article 45 – Provision for early childhood care and education

The State shall endeavour to provide early childhood care and education for all children until they complete the age of 6 years.

This is a Liberal–Intellectual principle.

At the time of commencement of the Constitution, Article 45 provided that the State shall endeavour to provide free and compulsory education for children until the age of 14 years. However, in the 86th Constitutional Amendment Act in 2002, this was incorporated as a Fundamental Right under Article 21A. Hence, Article 45 was amended to provide for early childhood care and education till the age of 6 years.

THINK ABOUT IT

Childcare is provided a significant impetus in Part IV of the Constitution. Elucidate.

The National Food Security Act, 2013 provides a legal right that children up to 6 years of age shall be provided free nutritious meals in the *Anganwadi* centres set up under the Integrated Child Development Services Scheme.

Article 46 – Promotion of interests of SC, ST and other weaker sections

The State shall promote with special care the educational and economic interests of the weaker sections of the people, and, in particular, of the Scheduled Castes and the Scheduled Tribes, and shall protect them from social injustice and all forms of exploitation.

This is a Gandhian principle as it is meant for protection of the SC, the ST and the weaker sections that is a Gandhian philosophy. To the extent that it provides for promotion of educational and economic interests of weaker sections, it can also be viewed as a socialistic principle.

The Fundamental Right under Article 15 was amended in 1951 and 2005 that enabled the State to provide for reservations for the OBC, the SC and the ST in educational institutions. Similarly, the Fundamental Right under Article 16 was amended in 1995 that enabled the State to provide for reservations for the SC and the ST in promotions. In 2019, the Fundamental Rights under Articles 15 and 16 were amended to provide for reservations for the Economically Weaker Sections (EWS).

Article 47 – State to raise the level of nutrition and improve public health

(i) The State shall regard the raising of the level of nutrition and the standard of living of its people and the improvement of public health as among its primary duties.

(ii) The State shall endeavour to bring about prohibition of the consumption except for medicinal purposes of intoxicating drinks and of drugs which are injurious to health.

Point (i) is a socialistic principle, while point (ii) is a Gandhian principle.

Primary Health Centres (PHC) and hospitals have been established across the country by the State governments and the Central government for providing health care and improving the delivery of public health. Various health programmes have been launched like polio vaccination, eradication of diseases like TB, leprosy, AIDS etc. There are also public health insurance schemes like Ayushman Bharat that have been launched.

Prohibition of alcohol was a contentious issue in the Constituent Assembly debates. While many of the members, inspired by Gandhian ideals, wanted total prohibition in the country, some of the members opposed it on the grounds that it is against individual liberty. Further, total prohibition results in smuggling and consumption of spurious liquor. Finally, it was included as directive principle.

Some of the States have imposed prohibition and have also rolled it back due to loss of revenue as well as issues associated with consumption of spurious liquor. For example, Tamil Nadu imposed prohibition in 1952 and reversed it in 1971. Andhra Pradesh imposed it in 1994 and reversed it in 1997. Kerala imposed it in 2014 which was reversed in 2017. Gujarat continues to impose prohibition till date (2024). Bihar imposed prohibition in 2015. The courts have upheld decisions imposing prohibition by States as it is to give effect to this directive principle.

MNEMONICS

Concept or Provisions	Shortcut or Mnemonics	Details to Remember
Articles 44 to 47	**Uniform Childcare** for **Weaker sections** with **Nutrition**	**Uniform** – UCC (44) **Childcare** – Childcare till the age of six (45) **Weaker sections** – Promotion of interest of SC, ST and weaker sections (46) **Nutrition** – Health and Nutrition; prohibition of alcohol (47)

Article 48 – Organisation of agriculture and animal husbandry

- The State shall endeavour to organise agriculture and animal husbandry on modern and scientific lines.
- It shall take steps for preserving and improving the breeds, and prohibiting the slaughter, of cows, calves and cattle.

This is a Gandhian principle.

Various schemes have been announced for development of agriculture on modern and scientific lines. Many States have also enacted laws that prohibit cow, bullock and buffalo slaughter.

Article 48A – Protection and improvement of environment

The State shall endeavour to protect and improve the environment and to safeguard the forests and wild life of the country.

This is a Liberal-Intellectual principle. This was added through the 42nd Constitutional Amendment Act in 1976.

Various laws like the Environment Protection Act (1986), the Wildlife (Protection) Act (1972) and the Forest (Conservation) Act (1980) have been enacted for protecting and safeguarding the environment and wildlife. Further, the Water (Prevention and Control of Pollution) Act (1974) and the Air (Prevention and Control of Pollution) Act (1981) provide for setting up of the Central and State pollution control boards.

Article 49 – Protection of monuments and places and objects of national importance

The State shall protect every monument or place or object of artistic or historic interest, from spoilation, destruction, removal etc.

This is a Liberal-Intellectual principle.

The Ancient Monuments and Archaeological Sites & Remains Act, 1958 has been enacted to protect ancient and historic monuments of national importance.

Article 50 – Separation of judiciary from executive

The State shall take steps to separate the judiciary from the executive in the public services of the State.

This is a Liberal–Intellectual principle.

Before 1973, the executive magistrates like District Collector, Sub-Divisional Officer etc., also enjoyed judicial powers. But in the Criminal Procedure Code, 1973, which has now been replaced by the Bharatiya Nagarik Suraksha Sanhita, 2023, these judicial powers have been vested in judicial magistrates.

MNEMONICS

Concept or Provisions	Shortcut or Mnemonics	Details to Remember
Articles 48 to 50	**AIMS**	**A** – **A**griculture and animal husbandry (48) **I** – Protection and **I**mprovement of environment (48A) **M** – Protection of **M**onuments (49) **S** – **S**eparation of judiciary from executive (50)

Article 51 – Promotion of international peace and security

The State shall endeavour to:

a. promote international peace and security;
b. maintain just and honourable relations between nations;
c. foster respect for international law and treaty obligations in the dealings of organised peoples with one another; and
d. encourage settlement of international disputes by arbitration.

Scan the QR code for conceptual video on DPSP

This is a Liberal–Intellectual principle.

India has traditionally followed the principle of Non-alignment and Panchsheel to maintain friendly relations with other countries throughout the world and neighbourhood, respectively. India is also a signatory to various international treaties. In recent years, there have been consistent efforts from the Central Government to maintain friendly relations with all countries.

16.3 FUNDAMENTAL RIGHTS VERSUS DIRECTIVE PRINCIPLES

THINK ABOUT IT

The Constitution exists on a harmonious balance between Part III and IV of the Constitution. Analyse with reference to the various case laws in this regard.

There has always been conflict between the Fundamental Rights guaranteed in Part III and Directive Principles laid down in Part IV. The DPSP aims to achieve social and economic justice for the society as a whole. However, the laws made for the purpose of achieving these objectives for the society, have come in conflict with individual liberty and equality that are guaranteed in Part III.

It must also be noted that till 1978, the right to property was a fundamental right under Article 19(1)(f). Article 31 (since omitted in 1978), provided a fundamental right for fair compensation in case of compulsory acquisition of property by the State. Exceptions were incorporated in Part III to enable the State to acquire property for public purposes. These laws for acquisition of property were also to fulfil the directive principles, especially the principles contained in Article 39(b) and 39(c). Such laws also came in conflict with the fundamental rights guaranteed in Part III.

Since 1950, there have been various cases that have come up before the Supreme Court due to this conflict between the Fundamental Rights and the DPSP. These judgements have finally resulted in the principle of harmonious balance between Fundamental Rights and the DPSP. We shall now discuss the important cases over the years that have shaped the relationship between the Fundamental Rights and the DPSP.

Champakam Dorairajan Vs State of Madras (1952)

- This conflict between the Fundamental Rights and the DPSP came to the Supreme Court for the first time in the Champakam Dorairajan case (1952).
- Smt Champakam Dorairajan was a woman from the State of Madras. In 1951, she was not admitted to a medical college because of a Government Order (GO), which had provided caste-based reservation in government jobs and college seats. This GO was passed in 1927 in the Madras Presidency.
- The conflict was between the Fundamental Rights under Articles 16(2), 29(2) and the DPSP under Article 46 of the Constitution.
- Article 16(2) states that no citizen shall be discriminated against only on the basis of caste in respect of any employment under the State. Article 29(2) states that no citizen shall be discriminated against only on the basis of caste in respect of admission to educational institutions run by the State. These are guaranteed fundamental rights that are enforceable in a court.
- Article 46, on the other hand, provides a directive to the State to promote the educational and economic interests of the weaker sections of the people, and, in particular, of the Scheduled Castes and the Scheduled Tribes. This is part of the DPSP that is not enforceable in a court.
- The Supreme Court held that Article 37 expressly says that the directive principles are not enforceable by the court. The Supreme Court mandated that the chapter on Fundamental Rights in the Constitution is sacrosanct and the directive principles have to conform to and run subsidiary to the chapter on Fundamental Rights.
- Champakam Dorairajan case led to the first amendment of the Indian Constitution. The amendment added Article 15(4) that provided for an exception that nothing in Article 15 or in Article 29(2) shall prevent the State from making any special provision for the advancement of any socially and educationally backward classes of citizens or for the Scheduled Castes and the Scheduled Tribes.

Golak Nath Vs State of Punjab (1967)

- The court in this case laid down that Fundamental Rights cannot be abridged or diluted to implement the directive principles.
- Article 13(2) provides that the State shall not make any law which takes away or abridges the Fundamental Rights and any law made in contravention of this clause shall, to the extent of the contravention, be void.
- In the *Golak Nath* case, the Supreme Court held that even a Constitutional Amendment Act will be included within the meaning of law for the purpose of Article 13. The Fundamental Rights have been given a transcendental (i.e., above all other provisions) and immutable (i.e., unchangeable) position. Hence, even a constitutional amendment cannot take away any fundamental rights guaranteed in Part III.

24th and 25th Constitutional Amendments (1971)

- The decision in the *Golak Nath* case resulted in the Parliament amending the Constitution by the 24th Constitutional Amendment Act in 1971. This amendment provided that the Parliament has the power to amend any part of the Constitution including the Fundamental Rights and the word 'law' as used in Article 13 does not include a Constitutional Amendment Act.
- Apart from the above, the Parliament also added Article 31C through the 25th Amendment Act. Article 31C provided that, laws giving effect to the policy of the State towards securing the principles specified in Article 39, clause (b) or (c), shall not be deemed to be void on the ground that it violates any of the rights conferred by Articles 14, 19 or 31. It also provided that any law containing a declaration that it is for giving effect to such policy shall not be called into question in any court on the ground that it does not give effect to such policy.

Kesavananda Bharati Vs State of Kerala (1973)

- The 24th and 25th amendments were challenged in the Kesavananda Bharati case.
- In this case, the Supreme Court over ruled its judgement in the *Golak Nath* case. It upheld the 24th Amendment Act that allowed amendment of even the Fundamental Rights through a Constitutional Amendment Act. However, it created the 'basic structure' doctrine and held that basic structures of the Constitution cannot be violated through any such amendment.
- It also upheld the first part of the 25th Amendment Act, which gave primacy to the Directive Principles under Article 39(b) or (c) over the Fundamental Rights under Articles 14, 19 and 31. However, it struck down the second part of the 25th Amendment Act, which provided that any such law containing a declaration to that effect is immune from judicial review as violative of the basic structure.

42nd Constitutional Amendment Act (1976)

- To nullify the *Kesavananda Bharati* judgement, the 42nd amendment further amended Article 31C and provided that any law giving effect to the policy of the State towards securing all or any of the principles laid down in Part IV shall not be void on the ground that it violates any of the rights conferred by Articles 14, 19 or 31.
- So not only Articles 39(b) or (c), but all Directive Principles were given primacy over the Fundamental Rights under Articles 14, 19 and 31 by the 42nd Amendment Act.

Scan the QR code for conceptual video on Fundamental Rights Vs DPSP

McGraw Hill edge

Minerva Mills Vs Union of India (1980)

- In the *Minerva Mills* case, the Supreme Court struck down the provisions of the 42nd Amendment Act that gave primacy to all Directive Principles over the Fundamental Rights under Articles 14, 19 and 31, on the ground that it violated the basic structure of the Constitution.
- The Supreme Court held that the Constitution exists on the harmonious balance between Part III and Part IV and that giving absolute primacy to one over other will disturb the harmony of the Constitution.
- This took Article 31C to its prior condition that a law would be protected by Article 31C only if it has been made to implement the principles in Article 39(b) or (c) and not any of the principles included in Part IV.

The summary of the above judgements by the Supreme Court and amendments to the Constitution, with respect to the relationship between the Fundamental Rights and the Directive Principles is tabulated below:

Judgement/Amendment	Key Points
Champakam Dorairajan Case	• The Fundamental Rights are enforceable in a court while the DPSP is not. • Hence, the Fundamental Rights are superior to the DPSP and provisions of the DPSP have to conform and run subsidiary to the chapter on the Fundamental Rights.
Golak Nath Case	• The Fundamental Rights cannot be abridged or diluted to implement the directive principles.
25th Constitutional Amendment	• Article 31C was added which provided that, laws giving effect to the policy of the State towards securing the principles specified in Article 39, clause (b) or (c), shall not be deemed to be void on the ground that it violates any of the Fundamental Rights conferred by Articles 14, 19 or 31.
Kesavananda Bharati Case	• Upheld the 25th Amendment as mentioned above but also held that any such law shall be subject to judicial review.
42nd Constitutional Amendment	• All Directive Principles [and not just Article 39(b) and (c)] were given primacy over the Fundamental Rights.
Minerva Mills Case	• The Constitution exists on the harmonious balance between Part III and Part IV and that giving absolute primacy to one over other will disturb the harmony of the Constitution.

The present status is that the Parliament can amend the Fundamental Rights for giving effect to implementation of the Directive Principles but without affecting the basic structure. In short, the DPSP and the Fundamental Rights complement each other and together form the heart and soul of the Constitution.

However, some of the key points of difference between the Fundamental Rights and the Directive Principles are summarised below:

Characteristics	Fundamental Rights	Directive Principles
Nature	These are negative in nature as they place restrictions on the State.	These are positive in nature as they require the State to provide certain things.
Objective	They aim to secure political rights and thereby establish political democracy. They are individualistic as they guarantee liberty and equality to an individual.	They aim to secure social and economic rights and thereby establish social and economic democracy. They are societal as they promote welfare of the society at large.
Enforceability	These are enforceable in a court of law directly and do not require any separate legislation for their implementation.	These are not enforceable in a court of law. They require legislation by the State for their implementation.
Effect of violation	Any law that violates the Fundamental Rights have to be declared void by the courts as unconstitutional.	No law can be declared void for violating any of the directive principles. However, a law can be upheld by the courts for giving effect to directive principles.

16.4 DIRECTIVES OUTSIDE OF PART IV

Apart from the Directive Principles that are provided in Part IV, there are few other directives provided to the State in other parts of the Constitution.

(1) Article 335 – Claims of the Scheduled Castes and the Scheduled Tribes to services and posts

The claims of the members of the Scheduled Castes and the Scheduled Tribes shall be taken into consideration, consistently with the maintenance of efficiency of administration, in the making of appointments to services and posts in connection with the affairs of the Union or of a State. Through the 82nd Amendment Act in 2000, a provision was added to Article 335 that enables the State to make any provision in favour of SCs and STs for relaxation in qualifying marks or lowering the standards of evaluation in matters of reservation in promotions.

(2) Article 350A – Facilities for instruction in mother-tongue at primary stage

It shall be the endeavour of every State and of every local authority within the State to provide adequate facilities for instruction in the mother-tongue at the primary stage of education to children belonging to linguistic minority groups.

(3) Article 351 – Directive for development of the Hindi language

It shall be the duty of the Union to promote the spread of the Hindi language, to develop it so that it may serve as a medium of expression for all the elements of the composite culture of India.

MAINS STARTER

Area	Building Blocks For Model Introductions
DPSP	The DPSPs contained in Part IV are aimed at securing the social, economic and political justice enshrined in our Preamble. Though not enforceable by itself in a court of law, these principles are fundamental in the governance of the country as per Article 37 and the State implements these principles through various laws and policies.
Important components of DPSP	The DPSP in Part IV primarily consists of goals and objectives that the society should aim for, social and economic rights over and above fundamental rights in Part III that citizens should enjoy, and certain policies to be followed by the government.
Distribution of resources/ Economic justice	The DPSP in Article 39 contains important provisions for securing economic justice. Article 39(b) stipulates that the material resources of the community should be distributed to subserve the common good while 39(c) provides that the operation of economic system should not result in the concentration of wealth. The Supreme Court has also recently provided its judgement with respect to the interpretation of 39(b) in line with the market-oriented economy at present.
Labour well-being in DPSP	The DPSP contains significant provisions between Articles 41 and 43A for the well-being of labour in various industries who form the backbone of the economy. It provides for right to work, just and humane conditions of work, a minimum living wage and participation of workers in management.

Area	Building Blocks For Model Introductions
Women welfare in DPSP	The DPSP contains significant provisions for welfare of women. These include equal pay for equal work, adequate means of livelihood for women, maternity relief for women, implementation of Uniform Civil Code for gender justice etc.
Childcare in DPSP	The DPSP contains important provisions in Articles 39 and 45 that deal specifically with children and their well-being. It stipulates that children should be free from exploitation and that they should receive adequate care till the age of 6 before going to school.
Uniform Civil Code	Uniform Civil code is an important policy that the State should endeavour to implement as per DPSP (Article 44). This is required primarily to ensure gender justice so that women enjoy equal rights in all civil matters like marriage, divorce, custody of children, inheritance, etc. It is also important to foster unity in our secular nation amongst different communities.
Fundamental Rights Versus Directive Principles	The Supreme Court in Minerva Mills case has held that the Constitution rests on a harmonious balance between Part III and Part IV of the Constitution and it is part of the basic structure. Providing absolute primacy to one over the other will disturb this balance.

UPSC Previous Years' Questions of Preliminary Examination

1. Under the Indian Constitution, concentration of wealth violates **[2021]**

(a) the Right to equality
(b) the Directive Principles of State policy
(c) the Right to Freedom
(d) the concept of welfare

Solution: (b)

Explanation: As discussed in Section 16.2, Article 39 provides a directive to the State that the operation of the economic system does not result in concentration of wealth. Hence, the correct answer is (b).

2. In India, separation of judiciary from the executive is enjoined by [2020]
   (a) Preamble of the Constitution (b) Directive Principles of State Policy
   (c) Seventh Schedule (d) Conventional Practice

Solution: (b)

Explanation: As discussed in Section 16.2, Article 50, deals with separation of judiciary from the executive and hence the correct answer is (b).

3. Which part of the Constitution declares the ideal of 'Welfare State'? [2020]
   (a) Directive Principles of State Policy (b) Fundamental Rights
   (c) Preamble (d) Seventh Schedule

Solution: (a)

Explanation: As discussed in Section 16.1, the purpose of DPSP is to secure social and economic justice in the society which is the hallmark of a welfare state. Hence, the correct answer is (a).

4. With reference to provisions contained in Part IV of the Constitution of India, which of the following statements is/are correct [2020]
   1. They shall be enforceable by courts.
   2. They shall not be enforceable by any court.
   3. The principles laid down in this part are to influence the making of laws by the State.

   Select the correct answer using the code given below:
   (a) 1 only (b) 2 only (c) 1 and 3 only (d) 2 and 3 only

Solution: (d)

Explanation: As discussed in Section 16.1, Statements 2 and 3 are correct and hence, the correct answer is (d).

UPSC Previous Years' Questions of Main Examination

1. Explain the Constitutional perspectives of Gender justice with the help of relevant Constitutional provisions and case laws. [2024]

Approach: The introduction may highlight the fundamental right to freedom from discrimination based on sex. Then various provisions for empowerment and development of women in Part III, IV and IVA along with 106th amendment that has provided for $1/3^{rd}$ reservation to women can form part of the answer.

MODEL ANSWER

Articles 15 and 16 guarantee no discrimination only on the basis of sex as a fundamental right, which is the foundation for gender justice.

Other Constitutional provisions & case laws for gender justice

Apart from the guaranteed fundamental right, there are specific provisions that uphold gender justice in order to provide adequate opportunities for women as well as to provide them with social and economic rights as follows:

(1) Special provisions can be made for the upliftment of women and children [Art 15(3)].

(2) In Part IV, DPSP provides for equal pay for equal work [Art 39(d)], adequate means of livelihood for both men and women [Art 39(a)], maternity relief for women [Art 42], etc., that provide for gender justice. These have been operationalised through various laws. Article 44, which deals with Uniform Civil Code, also aims at equal rights for women in civil matters.

(3) The Fundamental Duties [Art 51A] provide that citizens should renounce practices derogatory to the dignity of women.

(4) Minimum $1/3^{rd}$ reservation for women in Panchayats and Municipalities both in members and chairpersons. Further, in September 2023, the Constitution has been amended (106th amendment) to provide $1/3^{rd}$ reservation of seats for women in Lok Sabha and Legislative Assemblies.

Some of the important case laws for Gender Justice include:

(a) Vishaka case that laid down guidelines for the prevention of sexual harassment of women at work place.

(b) Triple Talaq case that declared instant Triple Talaq as unconstitutional.

(c) Sabarimala case which provided that women of all ages should be allowed inside the Ayyappa Temple (though it has been referred to a larger bench for review now).

CHAPTER

17

Fundamental Duties

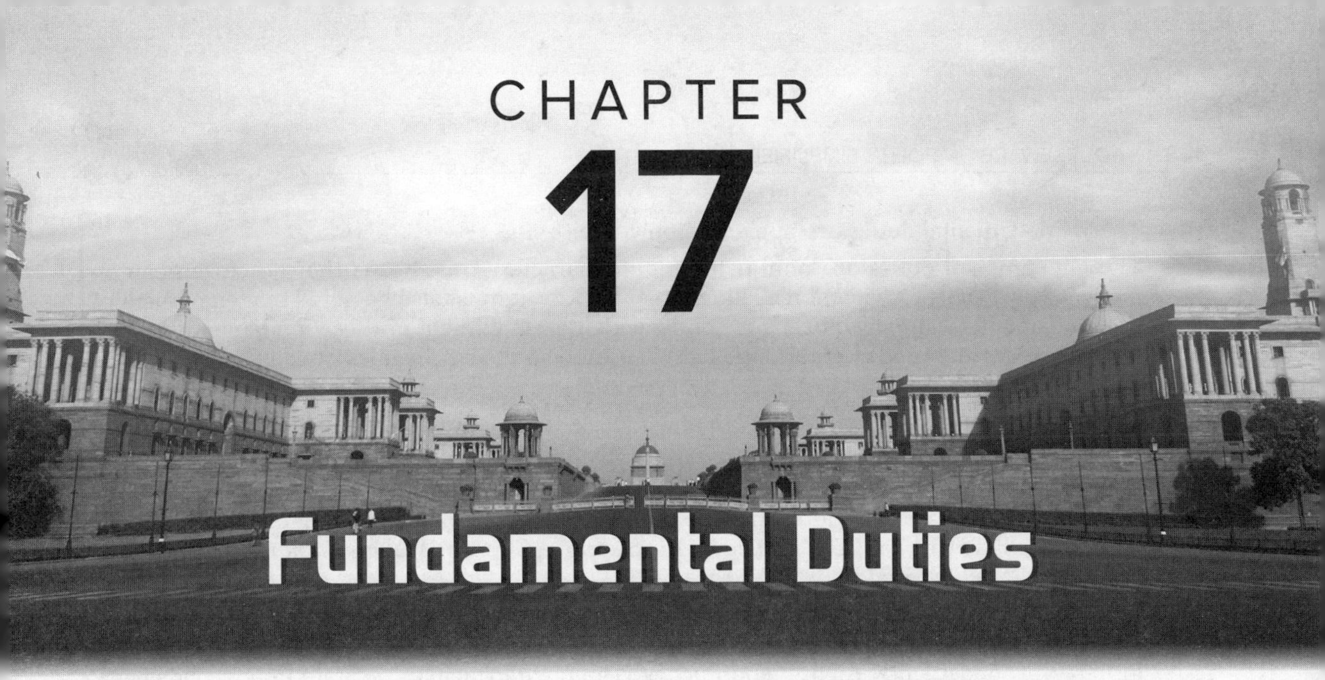

LEARNING OUTCOMES

1. Understanding the characteristics of Fundamental Duties
2. Learning about the Fundamental Duties in Part IVA
3. Analysing the significance and criticisms of Fundamental Duties
4. Examining initiatives taken to promote awareness and encourage adherence to Fundamental Duties among citizens

17.1 INTRODUCTION AND CHARACTERISTICS OF FUNDAMENTAL DUTIES

17.1.1 Introduction

Fundamental duties are an integral part of the Constitutions of countries such as the erstwhile USSR and Japan. These duties remind the citizen that apart from enjoying the fundamental rights, he/she also has an obligation towards the society. By performing the duties, the citizens contribute to strengthening the social fabric of the country and its overall development in all spheres of life.

The Constitution of the world's first socialist country that of the Soviet Union contained a list of the fundamental rights immediately followed by a list of the fundamental duties. It was clearly asserted that the enjoyment of the fundamental rights is conditional on the satisfactory performance of the fundamental duties.

Originally, the Constitution of India did not contain any list of fundamental duties. In other words, enjoyment of the fundamental rights was not conditional on the performance of the fundamental duties.

17.1.2 Characteristics of Fundamental Duties

- The Fundamental Duties of citizens were added to the Constitution by the 42nd Amendment Act in 1976, upon the recommendations of the *Swaran Singh Committee*. Part IVA and Article 51A were added through this amendment. Originally 10 in number, the Fundamental Duties were increased to 11 by the *86th Amendment Act in 2002.*

- These Fundamental duties are applicable only to citizens.
- The Fundamental duties are non-justiciable in character. This means that no citizen can be punished by a court for violation of a fundamental duty. It must also be noted that enjoyment of the fundamental rights by citizens is not dependent on fulfilment of these fundamental duties. In this respect the fundamental duties are like the Directive principles of the Constitution in part IV.
- The Directive principles lay down some high ideals to be followed by the State. Similarly, the fundamental duties in Article 51A, lay down some high ideals to be followed by the citizens. In both cases, violation does not invite any punishment.
- However, the fundamental duties may be used by the courts in determining the constitutional validity of a law. This has been opined by the Supreme Court in ***Mohan Kumar Singhania*** case (1991) and ***Ramlila Maidan Incident*** case (2012).
- The Universal Declaration of Human Rights (UDHR) provides for individual rights of liberty and equality as well as social, economic and cultural rights for the society. These are reflected in Part III (Fundamental Rights) and Part IV (Directive Principles of State Policy). However, the last three articles of UDHR also provides for mutual duties of every individual to one another and to society. This is reflected in Part IVA – Fundamental Duties.

17.2 LIST OF FUNDAMENTAL DUTIES

Article 51A provides the list of fundamental duties to be followed by citizens:

(a) To abide by the Constitution and respect its ideals and institutions, the National Flag and the National Anthem;

(b) To cherish and follow the noble ideals which inspired our national struggle for freedom;

(c) To uphold and protect the sovereignty, unity and integrity of India;

(d) To defend the country and render national service when called upon to do so;

(e) To promote harmony and the spirit of common brotherhood amongst all the people of India transcending religious, linguistic and regional or sectional diversities; to renounce practices derogatory to the dignity of women;

(f) To value and preserve the rich heritage of our composite culture;

(g) To protect and improve the natural environment including forests, lakes, rivers and wild life, and to have compassion for living creatures;

(h) To develop the scientific temper, humanism and the spirit of inquiry and reform;

(i) To safeguard public property and to abjure violence;

(j) To strive towards excellence in all spheres of individual and collective activity, so that the nation constantly rises to higher levels of endeavour and achievement;

(k) To provide opportunities for education by the parent or guardian, to his/her child, or a ward between the age of 6 and 14 years (This was added by the 86th Amendment Act in 2002).

17.3 SIGNIFICANCE AND CRITICISM OF FUNDAMENTAL DUTIES

While the fundamental duties are not enforceable in a court, they still are significant in the following ways:

1. They serve as ideals that the citizens should follow while enjoying their fundamental rights.

2. They serve as a source of inspiration for the citizens and promote discipline and a commitment towards national cause amongst them.
3. Though non-justiciable in nature, it still helps the court in examining the constitutional validity of a law.
4. The Parliament can provide for the imposition of appropriate penalty or punishment for failure to fulfil any of them through appropriate legislation.

THINK ABOUT IT

The fundamental duties can inspire the citizens to strive for a disciplined and fulfilling life, which, in turn, would result in the development of the country. Critically analyse the significance and criticisms of Fundamental duties in this regard.

However, the fundamental duties are also subject to the following criticisms:

1. The list of fundamental duties is not exhaustive i.e., it doesn't contain other important duties like casting vote, paying taxes, etc.
2. Some of the duties mentioned like 'composite culture', 'scientific temper' etc., are ambiguous and difficult to understand for the common man.
3. It cannot be enforced in a court of law. So, it is of no use even if it is included in the Constitution.

But the previous discussion about their significance makes it an important part of the Constitution.

Verma Committee (1999) on Fundamental Duties

Justice J. S. Verma Committee was constituted in the year 1998 to operationalise a countrywide programme for teaching fundamental duties. The Committee submitted its report in 1999.

It identified the legal provisions that are existing in various laws that have the effect of enforcing fundamental duties. Some examples are as follows:

1. In order to ensure that no disrespect is shown to the National Flag, the Constitution of India and the National Anthem, the Prevention of insults to National Honour Act, 1971 was enacted.
2. In order to ensure that the correct usage regarding the display of the National Flag is well understood, the instructions issued from time to time on the subject have been embodied in the Flag Code of India.
3. There are a number of provisions in the existing criminal laws, to ensure that the activities which encourage enmity between different groups of people on grounds of religion, race, place of birth, residence, language, etc. are adequately punished.
4. A Communal Organisation can be declared unlawful association under the provisions of Unlawful Activities (Prevention) Act 1967.
5. Representation of the People Act, 1951 declares that soliciting of vote on the ground of religion and the promotion or attempt to promote feelings of enmity or hatred between different classes of citizens of India on the grounds of religion, race, caste, community or language is a corrupt practice. A person indulging in a corrupt practice can be disqualified from being a Member of the Parliament or a State Legislature under the Act.

THINK ABOUT IT

The focus of our governance has been only on Fundamental Rights of citizens with little importance given to fundamental duties. Why are fundamental duties important? What measures can be taken to popularise them to ensure voluntary adherence by the citizens?

Further, the Committee also suggested certain actions for wide publicity and implementation of the fundamental duties as follows:

1. Radio and video spots highlighting important messages related to the Fundamental Duties on All India Radio, Doordarshan and other channels.
2. Display of the text of Article 51A prominently in the government publications, diaries, calendars, offices and at public places.
3. Setting up an autonomous body to act like ombudsman on citizenship values and for overseeing operationalisation or effectuation of the Fundamental Duties.
4. Publication of small booklets on various aspects of the Fundamental Duties written in simple language.
5. Activist role by the electronic and the print media in the matter of Fundamental Duties like protection of the environment.
6. Media should avoid the glorification of acts of violence, armed robberies and terrorist activities.
7. The State machinery ensuring the effectuation of the Fundamental Duties, where necessary, by prompt legislation.

Scan the QR code for conceptual video on Fundamental Duties

MAINS STARTER

Area	Building Blocks For Model Introductions
Fundamental Duties	The Fundamental Duties were added in Part IVA through the 42nd Constitutional amendment in 1976. This was based on the recommendations of the Swaran Singh Committee. The aim is to instil a sense of responsibility amongst the citizens, towards the society while enjoying their rights.
Enforceability of Fundamental Duties	The Fundamental Duties contained in Part IVA are not enforceable in a court of law. However, they can be used by the courts in examining constitutional validity of a law. Further, Parliament, through appropriate legislation, can provide for penalty or punishment for failure to fulfil them.

UPSC PREVIOUS YEARS' QUESTIONS OF PRELIMINARY EXAMINATION

1. Other than the Fundamental Rights, which of the following parts of the Constitution of India reflect/reflects the principles and provisions of the Universal Declaration of Human Rights (1948)? **[2020]**
   1. Preamble
   2. Directive Principles of State Policy
   3. Fundamental Duties

   Select the correct answer using the code given below:
   (a) 1 and 2 only (b) 2 only (c) 1 and 3 only (d) 1,2 and 3

   Solution: (d)

   Explanation: Preamble and DPSP reflect the human rights that include liberty, equality, social and economic rights. Further, as discussed in Section 17.1.2, the last 3 articles of UDHR also provides for mutual duties of every individual to one another and to society. This is reflected in Part IVA – Fundamental Duties. Hence, the correct answer is (d).

2. Which of the following statements is/are true of the Fundamental Duties of an Indian citizen? **[2017]**
   1. A legislative process has been provided to enforce these duties.
   2. They are correlative to legal duties.

   Select the correct answer using the code given below:
   (a) 1 only (b) 2 only (c) Both 1 and 2 (d) Neither 1 nor 2

   Solution: (d)

   Explanation: As discussed in Section 17.1.2, the Fundamental duties are not enforceable and hence statement 1 is incorrect. Fundamental duties are not legal duties but ideals that citizens should follow. Example of legal duties are payment of taxes, following laws made by legislature etc. Hence statement 2 is also incorrect and the answer is (d).

3. 'To uphold and protect the sovereignty, unity and integrity of India' is a provision made in the **[2015]**

   (a) Preamble of the Constitution (b) Directive Principles of State policy
   (c) Fundamental Rights (d) Fundamental Duties

   Solution: (d)

   Explanation: As discussed in Section 17.2, this is one of the fundamental duties of Indian citizen and hence the answer is (d). These wordings in fundamental duties should not be confused with the words in the Preamble that declare India to be a sovereign country.

CHAPTER 18

Constitutional Authorities

LEARNING OUTCOMES

1. Understanding the roles, appointment procedures, removal processes, and functions of key independent constitutional authorities, including the ECI, CAG, UPSC, and SPSC
2. Analysing the constitutional provisions ensuring the independence of these authorities, identifying related challenges, and suggesting measures to strengthen their autonomy
3. Explaining the composition and functions of the Finance Commission and GST Council
4. Knowing the structure, appointment process, power, and functions of the National Commissions for SCs, STs, and SEBCs
5. Outlining the appointment, qualification and duties of Attorney General and Advocate General
6. Examining the objectives and functions of special officer for Linguistic Minorities

18.1 INTRODUCTION

All the authorities who are mentioned in the Constitution are Constitutional authorities. So, the office of the President, the Vice-President, the Prime Minister, the Governor, the Chief Minister, the Speaker, the Chairman, the Judges of the Supreme Court and the High Courts are all Constitutional authorities. However, the term 'constitutional authorities' in common parlance is usually used to refer to those independent constitutional bodies like the Election Commission, the Comptroller and Auditor General and the Public Service Commissions. We shall be discussing in detail about these bodies in this chapter. There are other constitutional bodies that advise the government on various matters like National Commission for Scheduled Castes, National Commission for Scheduled Tribes, National Commission for Backward classes, Finance Commission, Goods and Services Tax Council, Attorney General, Advocate General etc., that will also be covered in this chapter.

18.2 ELECTION COMMISSION OF INDIA

18.2.1 Introduction

India is a democratic republic and the largest democracy in the world. To ensure free and fair elections, the Constitution has provided for the Election Commission of India (ECI).

The superintendence, direction and control of (a) preparation of the electoral rolls and (b) conduct of all elections

- to the Parliament and to the Legislature of every State
- to the offices of the President and the Vice-President held under the Constitution shall be vested in the Election Commission [Art 324].

Thus, the Election Commission of India is responsible for conduct of elections to the Union Parliament as well as the State Legislatures. This is a unitary or non-federal feature of our Indian Constitution.

18.2.2 Composition of ECI

Article 324 provides for the composition of the ECI. The key provisions with respect to the composition are as follows:

(a) It shall consist of the Chief Election Commissioner (CEC) and such number of other Election Commissioners (EC) as the President may fix from time to time.

(b) The appointment of the CEC and EC shall be made by the President. The Supreme Court in a judgement in 2023 ***(Anoop Baranwal vs Union of India)***, had stipulated that the CEC and EC be appointed based on the recommendation of a committee comprising the Prime Minister, the Chief Justice of India and the Leader of Opposition in the Lok Sabha. If no Leader of Opposition is available, the leader of the largest opposition party in the Lok Sabha shall be part of the committee. This shall be the process till the Parliament enacts a law on this aspect as per the Supreme Court judgement.

The Parliament enacted 'The Chief Election Commissioner and other Election Commissioners (Appointment, Conditions of Office and Terms of Office) Act, 2023' during December 2023. It provides for the procedure for the appointment of the Chief Election Commissioner (CEC) and other two Election Commissioners (ECs).

The key provisions with respect to appointment process are summarised below:

- The CEC and other ECs shall be appointed from persons who are holding or have held a post equivalent to the rank of Secretary to the Government of India. They must be persons of integrity and should have knowledge and experience in the conduct of elections.
- There shall be a search committee headed by the Minister of Law and Justice, who shall prepare a panel of five persons for consideration of Selection Committee.
- The CEC and EC shall be appointed by the President on the recommendation of a Selection Committee consisting of the Prime Minister, Leader of Opposition (or the largest Opposition Party) in the Lok Sabha and a Union Cabinet Minister to be nominated by the Prime Minister.

Analysis of the new law

The Dinesh Goswami Committee on Electoral Reforms (1990) and the Law Commission in its 255th report on 'Electoral Reforms' (2015), had suggested that the CEC and ECs should be appointed by a committee consisting of the Prime Minister, the Chief Justice of India and the Leader of the Opposition or the largest opposition party in the Lok Sabha. It is considering these recommendations that the Supreme Court, in Anoop Baranwal case, had stipulated a similar committee.

The international practices for the selection and appointment of members to the Electoral body vary between different democracies. In South Africa, the President of the Constitutional Court, representatives of the Human Rights Court and Gender equality are involved. In the United Kingdom, the House of Commons approves the candidates, whereas in the USA, the appointment is by the President and confirmed by the Senate.

While the new law moves the appointment process from just an executive decision to a committee-based selection, it is still tilted in favour of an incumbent Government. It would be laudable and instil a great deal of confidence in the public about the functioning of the ECI, if at least the selections under the new law are made by unanimous decisions by the proposed selection committee.

(c) When any additional EC is appointed, the CEC shall act as the Chairman of the Election Commission.

(d) There is also a provision for appointment of Regional Commissioners by the President in consultation with the Election Commission. However, at present there are no Regional Commissioners who are appointed. Regional Commissioners were appointed during the first general elections in 1951 for 6 months in Bombay and Patna. After that, there have been no Regional Commissioners who have been appointed.

(e) The conditions of service and tenure of Election Commissioners and Regional Commissioners, at present, is specified in "The Chief Election Commissioner and other Election Commissioners (Appointment, Conditions of Office and Terms of Office) Act, 2023.' *As per the provisions of this Act, they hold office for a term of 6 years or until the age of 65 years, whichever is earlier. The CEC and ECs receive equal salary and allowances, which are similar to those of a Supreme Court judge.*

(f) Originally, the Commission had only a Chief Election Commissioner. It currently consists of a Chief Election Commissioner and two Election Commissioners.

(g) For the first time, two additional Commissioners were appointed in October 1989, but they had a very short tenure till December 1989. Later, in October 1993, two additional Election Commissioners were appointed. The concept of multi-member Commission has been in operation since then, with decision making by the majority.

18.2.3 Removal of CEC and other ECs

Article 324 of the Constitution provides the following provisions with respect to removal of CEC and other ECs:

- The CEC can be removed from his/her office only in the same manner and on the same grounds as a Judge of the Supreme Court of India.
- The other election commissioners can be removed by the President on the recommendation of the CEC.

CEC versus Other ECs

As discussed above, the government has the power to appoint the Election Commissioners to the ECI apart from the CEC. However, the protection available to CEC in the matter of removal is not available to the other two ECs. Further, when other ECs are appointed to the Commission, the CEC shall act as the Chairman of the ECI.

The relationship between the CEC and other ECs was elaborated by the Supreme Court in the *T. N. Seshan Vs Union of India case* in 1995. The key observations of the Supreme Court in this case are summarised below:

- The provision that the ECs once appointed cannot be removed from office before the expiry of their tenure except on the recommendations of the CEC ensures their independence. It is so because this privilege has been conferred on the CEC to ensure that the ECs are not at the mercy of political or executive bosses of the day. The CEC must exercise this power only when there exist valid reasons, which affect the efficient functioning of the Election Commission.

- The CEC must so conduct himself/herself at the meetings chaired by him/her, that he/she is able to win the confidence of his/her colleagues of the Commission and carry them with him/her. The CEC cannot exercise his/her power ***suo motu*** because the members of the Commission are of equal status. Hence, if there is any disagreement between the CEC and other ECs, the decisions have to be taken by majority.

18.2.4 Independence of the ECI

In the performance of its functions, the Election Commission is insulated from executive interference. It is the ECI, which decides the election schedules for the conduct of elections, location of polling stations, assignment of voters to the polling stations, location of counting centres, arrangements to be made in and around polling stations and counting centres and all allied matters. To ensure independent functioning of the Commission, the Constitution provides for the following provisions:

- The Chief Election Commissioner is provided with security of tenure. He cannot be removed from his/her office except in the same manner and on the same grounds as a Judge of the Supreme Court of India.
- Any other Election Commissioner cannot be removed from his/her office, except on the recommendation of the Chief Election Commissioner.

THINK ABOUT IT

The independence of the Election Commission is paramount for democracy. In light of recent controversies surrounding the functioning of Election Commission, enumerate the provisions in the Constitution for ensuring its independence. What more reforms are required to strengthen the institution?

18.2.5 Powers and Functions

The Election Commission has power to supervise, direct and control the preparation of electoral rolls as well the conduct of elections to the Parliament and the State Legislatures, and for the office of the President and the Vice-President.

The powers and functions of the ECI can be classified into (a) Administrative, (b) Advisory and (c) Quasi-judicial.

Administrative Powers

- To define the territorial boundaries for constituencies for various elections on the basis of the Delimitation Commission.
- To prepare and periodically revise electoral rolls and to register all eligible voters.
- To notify dates and schedules of elections, to appoint returning officers and observers for conduct of elections.
- To implement the Model Code of Conduct to be observed by parties and candidates at the time of elections and to pass appropriate orders for enforcement of the same.
- To cancel polls in the event of rigging, booth capturing, violence and other irregularities.
- To request the Central and the State governments for staff necessary for conducting elections.
- To register political parties under the Representation of the People Act, 1951 and allot election symbols to them for contesting elections.
- To grant the status of recognised National or State parties, on the basis of poll performance.
- To work for voter education and electoral participation.

Advisory Powers

- Under the Constitution, the Commission also has advisory jurisdiction in the matter of post-election disqualification of sitting members of the Parliament and the State Legislatures. The opinion of the Commission in all such matters is binding on the President or, as the case may be, the Governor to whom such opinion is tendered.
- The Commission has the power to disqualify a candidate, who has failed to lodge an account of his/her election expenses within the time and in the manner prescribed by law.
- Further, in respect of cases of persons found guilty of corrupt practices in elections by the courts, such orders are referred to the Commission for its opinion on the question as to whether such person shall be disqualified and, if so, for what period.
- It advises the President on whether elections can be held in a State under the President's rule, in order to extend the period of the President's rule beyond one year.

Quasi-judicial Powers

- It has the authority to settle disputes related to granting of recognition to political parties and allotment of election symbols to them.
- The Commission also has the power for removing or reducing the period of disqualification under the provisions of the Representation of the People Act, 1951.

18.2.6 Reforms for Strengthening the ECI and Electoral Process

The Election Commission of India had submitted a memorandum to the Government of India in 2016 that listed the key reforms that are required for strengthening the ECI as well to implement certain electoral reforms for enhancing the quality of our democracy. The key recommendations of this memorandum are listed below:

- Equal protection for Election Commissioners like CEC with respect to removal. The Supreme Court in its judgement in 2023 (*Anoop Baranwal vs Union of India*) has suggested that it is desirable that this reform is given effect to.
- Budget of ECI to be charged on the Consolidated Fund of India like other independent bodies like CAG, UPSC etc. In the same judgement of the Supreme Court mentioned above, the Court has made a fervent appeal to the Government of India/the Parliament to make necessary changes to place a permanent Secretariat for the Election Commission of India and charging its expenditure to the Consolidated Fund of India to protect the independence of the ECI.
- Overseas electors may be provided postal voting or proxy voting.
- Increase punishment for filing false affidavits during nomination from 6 months to 2 years. Further, filing such false affidavits should be included under 'corrupt electoral practice' under Section 123 of the Representation of the People Act, 1951.
- Election to seats of the Legislative Councils by MLAs of the State ($1/3^{rd}$) may also be conducted through open ballot just like the Rajya Sabha elections.
- Use of totaliser machines for clubbing votes from EVMs – This will ensure voting pattern of each booth is not known and kept a secret.
- One candidate to be allowed to contest from only one constituency – Presently the law allows contesting from two constituencies.
- Persons charged with cognisable offences should be de-barred from contesting in the elections,

- at the stage when the charges are framed by the competent court provided the offence is punishable by imprisonment of at least 5 years,
- and the case is filed at least 6 months prior to the election in question.

- Power to ECI to de-register a party if it does not contest elections.
- Tax relief only for political parties that win seats in elections.
- Cap on political party spending on a candidate and also ceiling on expenditure by political parties.
- Ban on the Government advertisements 6 months before elections.

SUMMARY OF PROVISIONS FOR ECI

Provisions	Details
Appointment of CEC and ECs	• As per 'The Chief Election Commissioner and other Election Commissioners (Appointment, Conditions of Office and Terms of Office) Act, 2023', the CEC and ECs shall be appointed by the President on the recommendation of a Selection Committee consisting of the Prime Minister, Leader of Opposition (or the largest Opposition Party) in the Lok Sabha and a Union Cabinet Minister to be nominated by the Prime Minister.
Tenure	• 6 years or 65 years whichever is earlier.
Removal	• The CEC can be removed from his office only in the same manner and on the same grounds as a Judge of the Supreme Court of India. • The other Election Commissioners can be removed by the President on the recommendation of the CEC.
Expenditure	• The Expenditure of ECI is NOT charged on the consolidated fund of India.

18.3 COMPTROLLER AND AUDITOR GENERAL

18.3.1 Appointment and Term of Office

- The Comptroller and Auditor General (CAG) of India is one of the most important officers under the Constitution of India. As mentioned by Dr Ambedkar, he/she is to be the guardian of the public purse and it is his/her duty to see that not a rupee is spent out of the Consolidated Fund of India or of a State without the authority of the appropriate Legislature.

- The CAG is appointed by the President of India and holds office for a period of 6 years or up to the age of 65 years, whichever is earlier [Art 148 and CAG Act, 1971].
- He/she can resign by addressing his/her resignation to the President. He/she can be removed by the Parliament on the same grounds and procedure for removal of a Judge of the Supreme Court [Art 148 and CAG Act, 1971].

- The CAG is paid salary which is equal to the salary of a Judge of the Supreme Court [Art 148 and CAG Act, 1971].
- The CAG takes an oath to bear true faith and allegiance to the Constitution; to uphold the sovereignty and integrity of India; to perform his/her duties to the best of his/her ability without fear or favour and affection or ill-will; and to uphold the Constitution and laws [form of oath as per the Third Schedule].

18.3.2 Independence of the CAG

The CAG is required to audit the accounts of the Union as well as the State Governments and bring out the irregularities, if any. Hence, the Constitution provides for various safeguards to ensure the independence of the CAG. The key provisions that provide for independence of the CAG under Article 148 are as follows:

- **Security of tenure** – The Comptroller and Auditor General of India shall only be removed from office in like manner and on the like grounds as a Judge of the Supreme Court.
- **Financial security** – Neither the salary of a Comptroller and Auditor General nor his/her rights in respect of leave of absence, pension or age of retirement shall be varied to his/her disadvantage after his/her appointment. The Salary, allowances and pension payable to the CAG shall be charged on the Consolidated Fund of India.
- The administrative expenses of the office of the Comptroller and Auditor General, including all salaries, allowances and pensions payable to persons serving in that office, shall be charged upon the Consolidated Fund of India.
- **Restriction on further employment** – The Comptroller and Auditor General shall not be eligible for further office either under the Government of India or under the Government of any State after he/she has ceased to hold his/her office. This is to ensure that the CAG is not unduly influenced by any post-retirement employment opportunity while he/she discharges his/her functions as the CAG.

18.3.3 Duties and Powers

Article 149 specifies the duties and powers of the Comptroller and Auditor General as follows:

(a) The Comptroller and Auditor General shall perform such duties and exercise such powers in relation to the accounts of the Union and of the States and of any other authority or body as may be prescribed by any law made by the Parliament, and

(b) Until provision in that behalf is so made, shall perform such duties and exercise such powers exercisable by the Auditor General of India immediately before the commencement of the Constitution.

CAG (Duties, Powers, and Conditions of Service) Act, 1971

This Act has been passed by the Parliament as per provisions of Article 149. This Act lists down the powers and duties of the CAG apart from laying down the conditions of service.

The key powers and duties of the CAG under this Act are as follows:

(a) It shall be the duty of the Comptroller and Auditor General –

1. To audit all expenditure from the Consolidated Fund of India, of each State and of each Union Territory having a Legislative Assembly and to ascertain whether:
   - The moneys shown in the accounts as having been disbursed were legally available for and applicable to the service or purpose to which they have been applied or charged;
   - The expenditure conforms to the authority which governs it.

   The above two aspects fall in the category of 'Regulatory audit' which means that the CAG verifies whether the money was legally available and was spent by the authorised person.

   But the audit scope at present has moved from just being a 'regulatory audit' to 'propriety audit'.

The 'propriety audit' extends beyond scrutinising the mere formality of expenditure to its wisdom and economy and to bring to light cases of improper expenditure or waste of public money.

For example, the irregularities during conduct of the Commonwealth Games in 2010 was brought to light due to the propriety audit conducted by the office of the CAG.

2. To audit all transactions of the Union and of the States relating to the Contingency Funds and Public Accounts (like Postal savings);
3. To audit all trading, manufacturing, profit and loss accounts and balance-sheets and other subsidiary accounts kept in any department of the Union or of a State;
4. To audit accounts of all Government companies and corporations like ONGC, SAIL etc., – some directly audited, some through private auditors appointed by the CAG office;
5. Where any authority or body is substantially financed by Government, the Comptroller and Auditor General shall audit all receipts and expenditure of that body or authority – like IIT, IIM, State Health Societies;
6. Accounts of any authority or body on request of the President/the Governor – like local authorities.

(b) It shall be the duty of the Comptroller and Auditor General to audit all receipts of the Central and the State Government and to satisfy himself/herself that the rules and procedures in that behalf are designed to secure an effective check on the assessment, collection and proper allocation of revenue and are being duly observed.

For example, the CAG report on 2G spectrum allocation (2011) and Coal block allocation (2012) had highlighted the irregularities in assessment as well as method of allocation of these resources, that resulted in loss to the Government exchequer.

CAG Reports

1. The reports of the Comptroller and Auditor General of India relating to the accounts of the Union shall be submitted to the President, who shall cause them to be laid before each House of the Parliament.
2. The reports of the Comptroller and Auditor General of India relating to the accounts of a State shall be submitted to the Governor of the State, who shall cause them to be laid before the Legislature of the State [Art 151].
3. He/she acts as a friend, philosopher and guide to the Public Accounts Committee of the Parliament which exercises detailed financial control on the behalf of the Parliament.

CAG Role in Maintenance of Accounts

The accounts of the Union and of the States shall be kept in such form as the President may, on the advice of the Comptroller and Auditor General of India, prescribe [Art 150].

Accordingly, there are 'Government accounting rules' that have been prepared as per provisions of Article 150. The key aspects with respect to these rules and role of the CAG in preparation and maintenance of accounts are provided below:

- The CAG is assisted by Indian Audit and Accounts department.
- There is an Accountant General for Audit and an Accountant General for Accounts in each State.
- Accounts of States and Union Territories with Legislative Assembly is prepared and compiled by the Accountant Generals under CAG.

- Accounts of Central Government is prepared under supervision of the Controller General of Accounts.
- So, CAG is not involved in preparing accounts of Central Government but involved in preparation of accounts for the State Governments and Governments of Union Territories with an Assembly.

CAG Activism

- CAG plays an important role in auditing the accounts of the Union and the States. As discussed earlier, it is not just restricted to a formal regulatory audit but also includes a propriety audit to report on the wisdom and efficiency in government revenue collection as well as expenditure.
- The CAG also assists the Public Accounts Committee while it scrutinises the reports submitted by the CAG. This has led to many significant financial issues being highlighted and debated in the Parliament by the opposition parties.
- The reports of CAG act as a check and balance on the executive in financial matters.

> **THINK ABOUT IT**
>
> CAG activism is as important as judicial activism to hold the executive responsible. Critically evaluate citing examples of active role played by the Comptroller and Auditor General in analysing government policies in the last decade.

- However, there have been criticisms in the past about the scope and extent to which the CAG can scrutinise the policy decisions of the Government. This is sometimes referred to as 'CAG activism' similar to 'judicial activism' where judiciary gives directions or decisions on policy matters.
- For example, there have been questions raised about the reporting of irregularities in 2G spectrum allocation and coal block allocations, where the CAG found fault with the policy decision of the government in the manner of allocation of these licences. Critics have argued that the CAG had exceeded his/her scope by commenting on the policy decisions, which are the prerogative of the elected executive.
- However, it must be noted that based on these reports, the Supreme Court had cancelled the licences that were originally allotted and ordered fresh auction for allotment. This led to significant increase in revenue of the government. Recently, in 2023, the CAG report had raised concerns surrounding the steep increase in the Dwarka Expressway Project's construction cost.
- Thus, the CAG and its audit report act as an effective check and balance on the executive.

Indian CAG versus UK CAG

- The office of the CAG has been modelled on the basis of the Auditor General under the Government of India Act, 1935. After independence, this was created as the Comptroller and Auditor General in the Constitution, in line with the CAG office of the United Kingdom.
- However, while the nomenclature (term used) is CAG in India, the Indian CAG differs from the CAG in the UK on the following grounds:
  - The Indian CAG is just Auditor General and not Comptroller and Auditor General, whereas CAG England does both controlling and audit functions.
  - The CAG England controls the receipt of public money and issue of public money from the Public Exchequer. Thus, he/she can prevent withdrawal for any unauthorised purpose.
  - The CAG India does not have control over the issue of money from the Consolidated Fund of India. He/she only does an audit once expenditure is incurred or revenue is collected.

SUMMARY OF PROVISIONS FOR CAG

Provisions	Details
Appointment	• Appointed by the President.
Tenure	• 6 years or 65 years whichever is earlier.
Conditions of service	• Conditions of service specified in CAG (Duties, powers and conditions of service) Act, 1971'. • The CAG receives salary and allowances, which are similar to those of a Supreme Court judge. • After ceasing to hold office, CAG cannot be employed by Government of India or any State.
Removal	• The CAG can be removed from his office only in the same manner and on the same grounds as a Judge of the Supreme Court of India.
Expenditure	• The Expenditure of CAG and its office is charged on the consolidated fund of India.
Reports	• The reports of the CAG relating to the accounts of the Union shall be submitted to the President, who shall cause them to be laid before each House of Parliament. • The reports of the CAG relating to the accounts of the States shall be submitted to the Governor of the State, who shall cause them to be laid before State Legislature.

18.4 PUBLIC SERVICE COMMISSION

18.4.1 Historical Details

- The first Public Service Commission was established in 1926 as per provisions of the Government of India Act, 1919.
- The Government of India Act, 1935 provided for the setting up of the Federal Public Service Commission and the same was set up under this Act.
- Under the Constitution of India, the Union Public Service Commission (UPSC) has been set up for the Union and similarly State Public Service Commissions (SPSC) have been set up for the States.

The provisions with respect to composition, appointment, terms of office, removal and functions are very similar for the UPSC and the SPSCs with only a few differences. We shall discuss them in detail here and also summarise the same in a tabular form after the discussion.

18.4.2 Composition

Article 315 provides for the composition of the Public Service Commissions as follows:

- There shall be a Public Service Commission for the Union and a Public Service Commission for each State.
- Two or more States may agree for a Joint Public Service Commission for that group of States, if a resolution to that effect is passed by the House(s) of the Legislature of each of those States, and then the Parliament by law provides for the appointment of a Joint State Public Service Commission (JPSC) to serve the needs of those States.
    - At present (2024) there is no JPSC that is functioning. After the creation of Haryana out of Punjab in 1966, the two States had a JPSC for a short period of time.

- It must also be noted that any JPSC is a statutory body formed by a law of the Parliament and not a Constitutional body like UPSC or SPSC.

- The Public Service Commission for the Union, if requested so to do by the Governor of a State, may, with the approval of the President, agree to serve all or any of the needs of the State.

18.4.3 Appointment and Term of Office

Article 316 provides for appointment of members to the Public Service Commissions and their term of office:

Appointment

- The Chairman and other members of the UPSC and the JPSC (if formed) shall be appointed by the President.
- The Chairman and members of the SPSCs shall be appointed by the Governors of the respective States.
- There is no individual qualification for becoming a member of the UPSC, the JPSC or the SPSC. However, as nearly as may be one-half of the members of every Public Service Commission (UPSC, JPSC or SPSC) shall be persons who at the time of their appointments have been in office for at least 10 years either under the Government of India or under the Government of a State.

Tenure

- The Chairman and members of the UPSC hold office for a term of 6 years or until they attain the age of 65 years, whichever is earlier.
- The Chairman and members of the SPSC and the JPSC (if formed) hold office for a term of 6 years or until they attain the age of 62 years, whichever is earlier.
- A member of the UPSC or the JPSC may resign by writing to the President, while a member of the SPSC may resign by writing to the Governor.
- A member of the UPSC, the JPSC or the SPSC shall on the expiration of his/her term be ineligible for reappointment to the same office.

Regulations relating to Conditions of Service of Public Service Commission

Article 318 contains provisions relating to power to make regulations as to conditions of service of members and staff of the Commission as follows:

- The Constitution has not specified the strength of the Public Service Commissions.
- In respect of the UPSC and the JPSC (if formed), the number of members and their conditions of service; the number of staff and their conditions of service, are determined as per regulations made by the President. Usually, the UPSC consists of nine to eleven members, including the Chairman.
- Similarly, in respect of SPSCs, the number of members and their conditions of service; the number of staff and their conditions of service are made by the Governors.
- The conditions of service of a member of a Public Service Commission shall not be varied to his/her disadvantage after his/her appointment.

18.4.4 Removal of Members

Article 317 provides for the grounds on which the Chairman or member of a Public Service Commission can be removed from his/her office.

(a) Removal on grounds of misbehaviour

The Chairman or members of the UPSC, the JPSC or the SPSC can be removed by the President on the grounds of misbehaviour. However, in such a case the President has to refer the matter to the Supreme Court for an inquiry and they can be removed only if the Supreme Court reports after the inquiry that the Chairman or such other member ought to be removed. The advice tendered by the Supreme Court is binding on the President [Art 317(1)].

If the Chairman or any other member of the UPSC, the JPSC or the SPSC has interest in any government contract or derives benefit from any such contract, he/she shall be deemed to be guilty of misbehaviour [Art 317(4)].

The President in case of the UPSC (or the JPSC if formed) and the Governor in case of the SPSC may suspend the Chairman or any other member in respect of whom a reference has been made to the Supreme Court for conducting an inquiry [Art 317(2)].

(b) Other grounds for removal

The Chairman or a member of the UPSC, the JPSC or the SPSC can be removed from office by the President under the following circumstances (without any referral to the Supreme Court):

- If he/she is adjudged an insolvent;
- If he/she engages in paid employment outside his/her office; or
- If he/she is unfit to continue in office by reason of infirmity of mind or body.

It must be noted that while the appointing authority for the UPSC (and the JPSC if formed) is the President and for the SPSC is the Governor, the authority to remove the Chairman or member of either the UPSC, the JPSC or the SPSC is only the President.

18.4.5 Independence of Public Service Commission

The UPSC and the SPSC are key constitutional bodies that ensure merit while recruiting for various government positions. To ensure its independent functioning the following provisions have been provided in the Constitution.

- There is stability of tenure and members of the UPSC and the SPSC can be removed only by the President after an inquiry by the Supreme Court in case of misbehaviour, or by the President on advice of council of ministers under specific circumstances like insolvency or infirmity.
- The conditions of service of a member of a Public Service Commission shall not be varied to his/her disadvantage after his/her appointment [Art 318].
- The entire expense including the salaries, allowances and pensions of the members and staff of the UPSC is charged on the Consolidated Fund of India. Similarly, the entire expense including the salaries, allowances and pensions of the members and staff of the SPSCs is charged on the Consolidated Fund of the State [Art 322].
- There is prohibition on holding offices by members of the Public Service Commission after ceasing to be members [Art 319]. They cannot hold any employment under the Government of India or Government of any State except appointments within the Public Service Commissions as tabulated in the next page. This is to maintain the independence of the members while they are discharging their duties as members of the Public Service Commission.

Position	Further Appointments Allowed after Ceasing to Hold Office
Chairman of UPSC	No further employment allowed with the Government of India or any State.
Chairman of any SPSC	Eligible for appointment as the Chairman or any other member of UPSC or the Chairman of any other SPSC but no other employment allowed with the Government of India or any State.
Member of UPSC	Eligible for appointment as the Chairman of UPSC or the Chairman of any SPSC but no other employment allowed with the Government of India or any State.
Member of any SPSC	Eligible for appointment as the Chairman or any other member of UPSC or the Chairman of that or any other SPSC but no other employment allowed with the Government of India or any State.

18.4.6 Functions and Responsibilities of Public Service Commission

The primary duty of the UPSC and the SPSCs is to conduct examinations for appointments to the services of the Union and the services of the State respectively [Art 320].

The UPSC shall also, if requested by any two or more States, assist those States in framing and operating schemes of joint recruitment for any services for which candidates possessing special qualifications are required [Art 320].

> **THINK ABOUT IT**
>
> Enumerate the important functions and responsibilities of public service commissions.

Article 320 further lists down the following matters in respect to which the UPSC and the SPSCs shall be consulted by the Union Government and the State Governments respectively:

(a) Methods of recruitment to civil services and posts;

(b) Principles to be followed and suitability of candidates while making appointments, promotions and transfers;

(c) Disciplinary matters affecting a person serving under the government;

(d) Reimbursement/Payment of any claim of a person who has served in the government with respect to costs incurred in defending any legal proceedings instituted against him/her in respect of any act done while performing his/her duties as a government servant;

(e) Award of any pension for a person who has suffered any injuries while performing his/her duties as a government servant.

The UPSC and the SPSCs shall advise the Union and the State governments, respectively, on any of the above matters that are referred to them.

However, the UPSC or the SPSC need not be consulted as respects the following matters:

- Manner in which any provision referred to in Article 16(4) may be implemented (reservation in public employment);
- Manner in which effect may be given to the provisions of Article 335 (reservation for Scheduled Castes and Scheduled Tribes not to affect the efficiency in administration).

Limitations on Role of the UPSC and the SPSC

In respect of All-India services and the central cervices, the President and in respect of the State services, the Governor, can lay down regulations specifying the matters in respect of which it shall not be necessary for the UPSC or the SPSC to be consulted. However, such regulations shall be laid before the Parliament or the State Legislature for at least 14 days and is subject to such modifications made by the Parliament or the State Legislature.

The recommendations made by UPSC and SPSC are only of advisory nature and not binding on the government. However, if any of the advice of the Public Service Commission is not accepted by the Union or the State governments, the reasons for such non-acceptance have to be laid while submitting the annual report of the Public Service Commission before the Parliament or the State Legislature respectively.

18.4.7 Miscellaneous Provisions

- The Parliament or, as the case may be, a State Legislature may by law extend the service of the UPSC or the SPSCs by providing additional functions as respects the services of the Union or the State and also as respects the services of any local authority.
- The UPSC presents an annual report to the President regarding its performance, which is placed by the President before the Parliament. Along with such report, the government also presents a memorandum explaining reasons for non-acceptance of any advice of the UPSC.
- Similarly, the SPSC (and the JPSC if formed) presents an annual report to the Governor regarding its performance, which is placed by the Governor before the State Legislature. Along with such report, the government also presents a memorandum explaining reasons for non-acceptance of any advice of the SPSC.

Scan the QR code for conceptual video on ECI, CAG and PSC

Mc Graw Hill edge

18.4.8 Comparison Table of the UPSC and SPSC

Provisions	UPSC	SPSC
Appointment	• Appointed by the President	• Appointed by the Governor of the State
Tenure	• 6 years or 65 years whichever is earlier	• 6 years or 62 years whichever is earlier
Conditions of service	• Conditions of service determined by the President • After ceasing to hold office, the Chairman of the UPSC cannot be employed by the Government of India or any State • After ceasing to hold office, member of the UPSC can be appointed only as the Chairman of the UPSC or the Chairman of any SPSC	• Conditions of service determined by the Governor • After ceasing to hold office, the Chairman of a SPSC can be appointed only as member or the Chairman of the UPSC or the Chairman of any other SPSC • After ceasing to hold office, a member of SPSC can be appointed only as a member or the Chairman of the UPSC or the Chairman of any SPSC
Removal	• Can be removed only by the President ◦ after an inquiry by the Supreme Court on charges of misbehaviour or ◦ on grounds of insolvency, paid employment outside of office or infirmity of mind or body. • Can be suspended by the President pending inquiry by the Supreme Court.	• Can be removed only by the President ◦ after an inquiry by the Supreme Court on charges of misbehaviour or ◦ on grounds of insolvency, paid employment outside of office or infirmity of mind or body. • Can be suspended by the Governor pending inquiry by the Supreme Court.

Provisions	UPSC	SPSC
Expenditure	• Expenditure on salaries, allowances and pension of members and staff are charged on the Consolidated Fund of India.	• Expenditure on salaries, allowances and pension of members and staff are charged on the Consolidated Fund of the State.
Annual report	• Annual report submitted to the President who causes it to be laid before the Parliament.	• Annual report submitted to the Governor who causes it to be laid before the State Legislature.

MNEMONICS

Concept or Provisions	Shortcut or Mnemonics	Details to Remember
Provisions for ensuring independence of authorities like ECI, CAG and Public Service Commission	**TRFR** (short form for Transfer in Banking transactions)	• **T** – **T**enure stability – All authorities 6 years or 65 years of age (SPSC members up to 62 years) • **R** – **R**emoval procedure is rigid for CEC & ECs, CAG and PSC members. • **F** – **F**inancial independence as expenditure charged on consolidated fund. Except **ECI** whose expenditure is **NOT E**xpenditure **C**harged on consolidated fund (So, **EC NOT EC**). • **R** – **R**estriction on further employment with government for CAG and PSC members.

18.5 ISSUES COMMON TO INDEPENDENT CONSTITUTIONAL AUTHORITIES

We have discussed about the three independent constitutional authorities viz., the Election Commission of India (ECI), the Comptroller & Auditor General (CAG) and the Public Service Commission (UPSC and SPSC) in detail in the previous three sections.

Since these bodies are responsible for (a) conduct of free and fair elections (ECI), (b) ensuring accountability of the governments with respect to public finance (CAG) and (c) ensuring transparent and meritorious process of recruitment to public posts and services (PSC), their independence is of paramount importance. This is vital for efficiency, transparency and accountability in our democracy.

We have discussed about the provisions that have been made in the Constitution in order to ensure and protect the independence of these constitutional authorities in the previous sections. As discussed earlier, there are provisions that ensure independence of tenure after appointment as well as financial independence during their tenure.

However, the following can be summarised as the key issues common to all these constitutional authorities that may affect their independent functioning:

- The power of appointment to these constitutional posts is with the executive. There are various statutory posts like the Central Vigilance Commissioner, the Members and the Chairman of

Human Rights Commission, the Lokpal etc., which are appointed through a committee that consists of the judiciary and/or the leader of opposition in the Lok Sabha. This increases the transparency in their appointments. At present, the CEC and EC of the Election Commission are appointed by a committee consisting of the Prime Minister, Leader of Opposition in the Lok Sabha and a cabinet minister. However, CAG and Public Service Commission members continue to be appointed by the executive alone. A similar committee-based appointment may be provided for these authorities also by amending the Constitution.

- While there are restrictions on further employment with the Government of India or any State for the CAG and the Public Service Commission members, there are no restrictions on them from joining political parties and contesting elections or getting nominated to the Rajya Sabha. This may raise questions about their independence while they discharged their functions in the constitutional post.
- In a democracy there cannot be any restriction on any individual from holding a political position. The Election Commission had in fact in 2012 recommended to the Union government to provide for a cooling off period for top bureaucrats after their retirement before they could join political parties and contest elections. However, the Government had rejected this recommendation based on opinion of the Attorney General that this may not be in line with the constitutional provisions and democratic values. It is pertinent to note that the Chairperson and members of Lokpal are not permitted to contest any elections for a period of 5 years from the date of relinquishing their post. However, there can be at least restrictions placed on nomination to posts or appointment to any other position in the Government for a cooling-off period, after these independent constitutional authorities relinquish their posts.

18.6 FINANCE COMMISSION

Article 280 of the Constitution of India provides for a Finance Commission as a constitutional body. It is constituted by the President of India every 5 years to make recommendations on financial allocations of resources between the Centre and the States.

18.6.1 Composition and Qualification

The Finance Commission consists of a chairman and four other members who are appointed by the President. They hold office for such period as may be specified in the order of the President appointing them and are eligible for reappointment. They can resign from their office by a letter addressed to the President.

The Constitution does not provide any qualifications for being appointed as a member of the Finance Commission but has authorised the Parliament to stipulate the same. Accordingly, as per 'The Finance Commission (Miscellaneous Provisions) Act, 1951', the Parliament has specified the following qualifications for the Chairman and the members of the Commission:

- The Chairman should be a person having experience in public affairs;
- Four other members shall be selected from amongst the following persons:
    - a judge of High Court or qualified to be appointed as one;
    - have specialised knowledge of finance and accounts of the government;
    - have had wide experience in financial matters and in administration;
    - have special knowledge of economics.

The Finance Commission shall be deemed to be a civil court and has the powers of a civil court with respect to (a) summoning and enforcing attendance of witnesses, (b) requiring the production of any document, (c) requisitioning any public record from any court or office, and (d) receiving evidence on affidavits. Hence, it is also a quasi-judicial body apart from being a constitutional body.

18.6.2 Functions of the Finance Commission

As per Article 280, the Finance Commission makes recommendations to the President on the following areas:

1. The distribution of the net proceeds of taxes to be shared between the Centre and the States (vertical devolution), and the allocation between the States of the respective share of such proceeds (horizontal devolution);
2. The principles that should govern the grants-in-aid to the States by the centre out of Consolidated Fund of India;
3. The measures needed to augment the Consolidated Fund of a State to supplement the resources of the panchayats and the municipalities on the basis of the recommendations made by the State Finance Commission;
4. Any other matter referred to it by the President in the interest of sound finance.

Under the terms of reference for the 16th Finance Commission (constituted for giving recommendations for the period 2026–2031), the Commission may review the present arrangements of financing Disaster Management initiatives, with reference to the funds constituted under the Disaster Management Act, 2005 and make appropriate recommendations thereon.

The Finance Commission submits its report to the President who lays it before both the Houses of the Parliament along with an explanatory memorandum as to the action taken on its recommendations [Art 281].

Though the Finance Commission is only an advisory body and its recommendations are not binding on the Government, the Government usually accepts most of its recommendations. Thus, the Finance Commission is a very significant policy making body. Earlier, the Finance Commission was undermined by the role of the powerful Planning Commission, an extra-constitutional, non-statutory body responsible for formulating plan-based development. Now, with the dismantling of the Planning Commission, the Finance Commission has become significant again.

MNEMONICS

Concept or Provisions	Shortcut or Mnemonics	Details to Remember
Functions of Finance Commission	**DGCA** (**D**irector **G**eneral of **C**ivil **A**viation)	• **D** – **D**istribution of net tax proceeds principles • **G** – **G**rants-in-aid principles • **C** – **C**onsolidated fund of States – measures needed to augment • **A** – **A**ny other matter referred to by the President

18.7 GOODS AND SERVICES TAX (GST) COUNCIL

Article 279A of the constitution provides for formation of the GST Council for making recommendations to the Union and the State Governments on issues related to GST. This was created through the 101st Constitutional Amendment Act in 2017.

Scan the QR code for conceptual video on Finance Commission and GST Council

The following points need to be noted with respect to the GST Council created through the 101st amendment:

- This amendment was ratified by more than half of the State Legislatures as per the requirement of Article 368 before assented to by the President
- Any amendment to Article 279A in future will also require ratification by not less than half of the State legislatures.

18.7.1 Composition

The Goods and Services Tax Council shall consist of the following members:

(a) The Union Finance Minister – Chairperson
(b) The Union Minister of State in charge of Revenue or Finance – Member
(c) The Minister in charge of Finance or Taxation or any other Minister nominated by each State Government – Members

One-half of the total number of members of the GST Council shall constitute the quorum at its meetings.

Every decision of the Council has to be taken by a majority of not less than three-fourth of the weighted votes of the members present.

- The vote of the central government has a weightage of one-third of the total votes cast, and
- The votes of all the State governments together have a weightage of two-thirds of the total votes cast.

Therefore, the GST Council is hailed as a classic example for cooperative federalism since neither the centre nor all States together can take any decision unilaterally.

THINK ABOUT IT

GST council is a classic example of co-operative federalism. Elucidate detailing the composition, decision making process and functions of the GST council.

18.7.2 Functions

The Goods and Services Tax Council shall make recommendations to the Union and the States on:

- The taxes, cesses and surcharges levied by the Union, the States and the local bodies which may be subsumed in the goods and services tax.
- The goods and services that may be subjected to, or exempted from the goods and services tax.
- Model Goods and Services Tax Laws, principles of levy, apportionment of Goods and Services Tax levied on supplies in the course of inter-State trade or commerce under article 269A and the principles that govern the place of supply.

- The threshold limit of turnover below which goods and services may be exempted from goods and services tax.
- The rates including floor rates with bands of goods and services tax.
- Any special rate or rates for a specified period, to raise additional resources during any natural calamity or disaster.
- Special provision with respect to the States of Arunachal Pradesh, Assam, Jammu and Kashmir, Manipur, Meghalaya, Mizoram, Nagaland, Sikkim, Tripura, Himachal Pradesh and Uttarakhand.
- Any other matter relating to the goods and services tax, as the Council may decide.
- Goods and Services Tax Council shall recommend the date from which the goods and services tax be levied on petroleum crude, high speed diesel, petrol, natural gas and aviation turbine fuel.

18.8 NATIONAL COMMISSION FOR SC, ST AND SEBC/OBC

The Constitution of India has established constitutional bodies for the protection and welfare of the Scheduled Castes (SC), the Scheduled Tribes (ST) and the Socially and Educationally Backward Classes (SEBC or OBC).

Originally, Article 338 provided for appointment of special officer for the SCs and the STs to investigate all matters relating to the constitutional safeguards for the SCs and the STs and report to the President on their working.

- Through the 65th Constitutional Amendment in 1990, there was a National Commission for Scheduled Castes (NCSC) that was created by amending Article 338. This NCSC was required to perform functions for investigating matters relating to constitutional safeguards and also suggest measures for the welfare and development of the SCs, the STs, the OBCs and the Anglo-Indians.
- Subsequently through the 89th Constitutional Amendment in 2003, the National Commission for Scheduled Tribes (NCST) was created by adding Article 338A. This NCST (established in 2004) is required to perform similar functions for the STs and the NCSC continues to perform it constitutionally for the SCs and the Anglo-Indians.
- After the ***Indra Sawhney*** case judgement in 1992, there was a National Commission for Backward Classes (NCBC) that was created in 1993 through the National Commission for Backward Classes Act, 1993. This National Commission for Backward Classes has been made a constitutional body by adding Article 338B in 2018 through the 102nd Constitutional Amendment. This NCBC is required to perform similar functions for the SEBCs.

Hence, at present there is NCSC that takes care of the interest of the SCs and the Anglo-Indians (Art 338), there is NCST that takes care of the interest of the STs (Art 338A) and there is NCBC that takes care of the interest of the SEBC or the OBC (Art 338B). The provisions of all these constitutional bodies are similar.

We will summarise the appointment, composition and tenure which is the same for three bodies. Then we will understand their functions that are similar. After understanding their functions as per the Constitution, we shall also discuss the issues that surround the effective functioning of these bodies and suggestions for improvement of the same.

18.8.1 Appointment, Composition, Tenure and Qualification

In respect of the NCSC (Art 338), the NCST (Art 338A) and the NCBC (Art 338B), the following similar provisions are provided in the respective articles and rules that govern them with respect to appointment, composition, tenure and qualification of members.

Apart from the above specified articles of the Constitution, the following rules are made for the conditions of service and tenure of Chairperson and members of these constitutional bodies:

(a) The National Commission for Scheduled Castes Chairperson, the Vice-Chairperson and the Members (Conditions of Service and Tenure) Rules, 2004
(b) The National Commission for Scheduled Tribes Chairperson, the Vice-Chairperson and the Members (Conditions of Service and Tenure) Rules, 2004
(c) The National Commission for Backward Classes Chairperson, the Vice-Chairperson and the Members (Conditions of Service and Tenure) Rules, 2018

Particulars	Provisions as per the Constitution and Rules for NCSC, NCST and NCBC
Appointment	The Chairperson and other members are appointed by the President by warrant under his/her hand and seal as per the Constitution.
Composition	All the three Commissions consist of a Chairperson, a Vice-Chairperson and three other members as per the Constitution.
Tenure	Conditions of service and tenure of office are to be determined by the President as per the Constitution. As per above rules, the Chairperson, the Vice-Chairperson and members of all three commissions hold office for a period of 3 years. They are not eligible for reappointment for more than two terms.
Qualification	As per the above rules, the qualification requirements for all the three commissions are similar as follows: (a) The members are to be appointed from amongst persons of ability, integrity and standing who have had record of selfless service to the cause of justice of the SCs or the STs or the SEBCs for the respective commission. (b) The Chairperson to be an eminent socio-political worker belonging to the SC or the ST or the SEBC for the respective commission. (c) The Vice-Chairperson and at least two members shall be appointed from amongst persons belonging to the SC or the ST or the SEBC for the respective commission. (d) At least one member of the all the three commissions shall be a woman.

18.8.2 Functions, Powers and Reports

Functions of the NCSC, the NCST and the NCBC

In respect of the NCSC (Art 338), the NCST (Art 338A) and the NCBC (Art 338B), the following similar provisions are provided in the respective articles with respect to their functions towards the protection and welfare of the SCs, the STs and the SEBCs respectively.

(a) To investigate and monitor all matters relating to the safeguards provided for the SCs or the STs or the SEBCs (respectively) under the Constitution or under any other law for the time being in force or under any order of the Government and to evaluate the working of such safeguards;

(b) To inquire into specific complaints with respect to the deprivation of rights and safeguards of the SCs or the STs or the SEBCs (respectively);

(c) To participate and advise on the socio-economic development of the SCs or the STs or the SEBCs (respectively) and to evaluate the progress of their development under the Union and any State;

(d) To present to the President, annually and at such other times as the Commission may deem fit, reports upon the working of those safeguards;

(e) To make in such reports the recommendations as to the measures that should be taken by the Union or any State for the effective implementation of those safeguards and other measures for the protection, welfare and socio-economic development of the SCs or the STs or the SEBCs (respectively); and

(f) To discharge such other functions in relation to the protection, welfare and development and advancement of the SCs or the STs or the SEBCs (respectively) as the President may, subject to the provisions of any law made by the Parliament, by rule specify.

Apart from the above, the NCST has been assigned certain additional functions through rules made by the President in 2005. These functions are for the protection, welfare, development and advancement of the STs. These include measures to be taken for conferring ownership rights on minor forest produce, safeguarding rights of tribals over mineral and water resources, improvement of relief and rehabilitation measures for tribals displaced due to development projects, ensuring full implementation of the provisions of PESA Act, 1996 etc.

Powers of the NCSC, the NCST and the NCBC

In respect of the NCSC (Art 338), the NCST (Art 338A) and the NCBC (Art 338B), the following similar provisions are provided in the respective articles with respect to their powers.

- All the three Commissions are vested with the power to regulate their own procedure.
- All the three Commissions while investigating any matter or inquiring into any complaint have all the powers of a civil court. They can summon and enforce the attendance of any person from any part of India and examine him/her on oath. They also have the power to receive evidence on affidavits and requisitioning any public record from court or office.
- The Central and State governments are required to consult the commissions on all major policy matters affecting the SCs or the STs or the SEBCs respectively.

Reports of the NCSC, the NCST and the NCBC

In respect of the NCSC (Art 338), the NCST (Art 338A) and the NCBC (Art 338B), the following similar provisions are provided in the respective articles with respect to the reports to be submitted by these three commissions.

- The three Commissions present a report annually, and at such other times as it deems fit, to the President upon the working of the safeguards for protection of the SCs or the STs or the SEBCs respectively.
- The President places all such reports before the Parliament, along with a memorandum explaining the action taken on recommendations made by the Commissions. The memorandum should also contain the reasons for non-acceptance of any such recommendations.
- Also, reports relating to States are forwarded by the President to the Governor, who then places it before the State legislatures along with similar action taken report.

MNEMONICS

Concept or Provisions	Shortcut or Mnemonics	Details to Remember
Functions of National Commission for SC, ST and OBC	SSS RRR	• **S** – **S**afeguards provided – working of such safeguards to be investigated and monitored • **S** – **S**pecific complaints regarding deprivation of rights to be inquired • **S** – **S**ocio-economic development – to participate and advise • **R** – **R**eport annually or when deemed fit • **R** – **R**ecommendation for safeguards, welfare and development • **R** – as per **R**ules, such other functions

SC, ST and SEBC List

- The President may by public notification specify the castes, races or tribes that shall be deemed to be Scheduled Castes with respect to any State or Union Territory. Any inclusion or exclusion to this list can be done only through a Parliamentary law [Art 341].
  - In pursuance of this article, 'The Constitution (Scheduled Castes) Order, 1950' has been notified that provides the list of the Scheduled Castes in various States and Union Territories.
  - As per the order, only persons professing Hinduism, Sikhism and Buddhism shall be deemed to be members of the Scheduled Caste. A Commission of inquiry under the chairmanship of former CJI K G Balakrishnan had been set up by the Central government to examine if SC reservation can be granted to Dalits who convert to religions other than Sikhism and Buddhism (mainly Islam and Christianity). This commission was set up in October 2022 and will submit its report by October 2025.
- The President may by public notification specify the tribes or tribal groups that shall be deemed to be Scheduled Tribes with respect to any State or Union Territory. Any inclusion or exclusion to this list can be done only through a Parliamentary law [Art 342].
  - In pursuance of this article, 'The Constitution (Scheduled Tribes) Order, 1950' has been notified that provides the list of Scheduled Tribes in various States and Union Territories.
- A State government / Union Territory government or administration may choose to recommend certain communities for inclusion or omission from the list of Scheduled Castes or Scheduled Tribes. Such proposals of the State Governments / Union Territory Administrations concerned is forwarded to the Registrar General of India (RGI). The proposals which have been agreed to by the RGI and NCSC, in the case of SCs, and RGI and NCST in the case of STs, are further processed in accordance with the provisions of Articles 341 and 342 by the Union government to seek Parliamentary approval. Once approved by Parliament houses and assented to by the President, the list is accordingly amended.
- The President may by public notification specify the socially and educationally backward classes (SEBC) that shall be deemed to be SEBC in the Central list for the purposes of the Central Government. Any inclusion or exclusion to this list can be done only through a Parliamentary law [Art 342A].
  - Every State and Union Territory, may by law, prepare and maintain its own list of SEBC for its own purposes [105th Constitutional Amendment].

18.8.3 Key Challenges and Suggestions

In respect of the NCSC, the NCST and the NCBC, while they are all advisory constitutional bodies, they are expected to play an autonomous role in order to ensure the working of the constitutional safeguards provided to the SCs, the STs and the SEBCs and also suggest measures for their development.

However, the key challenges and suggestions for improving their composition and functioning can be summarised as below:

- The members to these three commissions are appointed solely by the Union government. There are various statutory posts like members and Chairman of Human Rights Commission, Lokpal etc., which are appointed through a committee that consists of judiciary and/or leader of opposition in the Lok Sabha. This increases the transparency in their appointments. Hence, the Constitution may be amended to provide that the members to these three commissions will be appointed through a committee that represents various stake holders including the leader of opposition.
- They may be given the powers to grant financial awards to victims during the course of their inquiry into any violations.

> **THINK ABOUT IT**
>
> The National Commission for Scheduled Tribes plays an important role in protection, welfare and development of the Scheduled Tribes. Discuss the unique functions assigned to this commission in this regard. What further reforms are required to strengthen its functioning?

18.9 ATTORNEY GENERAL OF INDIA

18.9.1 Appointment, Qualification and Term of Office

Article 76 of the Constitution deals with the office of the Attorney General:

- The Constitution has provided for the office of the Attorney General, as the highest law officer in the country. The Attorney General is appointed by the President of India.
- He/she must be a person who is qualified to be a Judge of the Supreme Court. However, even a person above 65 years of age (who fulfils the qualification to be appointed as a Judge of the Supreme Court) can be appointed as the Attorney General.
- He/she holds office during the pleasure of the President and receives remuneration as determined by the President. This means that he/she may be removed by the President at any time. Conventionally, he/she resigns when the government changes, as he/she is appointed on its advice.
- The Attorney General does not fall in the category of government servants. Further, he/she is not debarred from private legal practice though there are restrictions on the kind of cases in which he/she can appear.

18.9.2 Duties

Article 76 of the Constitution lists down the duties of the Attorney General as follows:

- To give advice to the Government of India upon such legal matters, and to perform such other legal duties, as may from time to time be referred or assigned to him/her;
- To discharge the functions conferred on him/her as per the Constitution or any other law;

- In the performance of his/her duties the Attorney General shall have right of audience in all courts in the territory of India i.e., he/she can appear before any court within the territory of India.

As per the existing practice, the Attorney General performs the following duties assigned to him/her:

- To appear on behalf of the Government of India in all cases in the Supreme Court in which the Government of India is concerned.
- To appear (when required by the Government of India) in any High Court in any case in which the Government of India is concerned.
- To represent the Government of India in any reference made by the President to the Supreme Court under Article 143 of the Constitution.

Scan the QR code for conceptual video on National Commissions for SC/ST/SEBC and Attorney General

The Attorney General has the right to speak and to take part in the proceedings of both the Houses of the Parliament or their joint sitting and any committee of the Parliament of which he/she may be named a member, but without a right to vote [Art 88]. He/she also enjoys the privileges enjoyed by the Members of Parliament.

Restrictions on the Private Practice of Attorney General

The Attorney General is not a full-time government servant and he/she is allowed to carry on with his/her private legal practice. He can advise or appear in any civil case between private parties. However, the following restrictions are placed on his/her practice in order to avoid any conflict with his/her official role as Attorney General under the Constitution:

- He/she should not advise or hold brief against the Government of India;
- He/she should not defend accused persons in criminal prosecutions without the permission of the Government of India;
- He/she should not accept appointment as a director in any company or corporation without the permission of the Government of India.

18.9.3 Solicitor General and Additional Solicitors General

- The Solicitor General and the Additional Solicitor General are other law officers of the Government of India.
- There is one Solicitor General and around 10–15 Additional Solicitors General who are appointed by the Government from time of time. They are also law officers who assist the Attorney General in fulfilment of his/her official duties.
- It should be noted here that only the office of the Attorney General is created by the Constitution under Article 76 and the offices of the Solicitor General and the Additional Solicitor General are not mentioned in the Constitution but are governed by the Law Officers (Conditions of Service) Rules, 1987. The private practice of these law officers is also subject to similar restrictions as mentioned above for the Attorney General.

18.10 ADVOCATE GENERAL

- There is an Advocate General for each State under Article 165, who performs similar duties with respect to the government of the States, which the Attorney General performs for Government of India.

- The Advocate General is appointed by the Governor of a State.
- He/she must be a person who is qualified to be a Judge of the High Court. However, even a person above 62 years of age (who fulfils the qualification to be appointed as a judge of a High Court) can be appointed as the Advocate General.
- He/she holds office during the pleasure of the Governor and receives remuneration as determined by the Governor. This means that he/she may be removed by the Governor at any time. Conventionally, he/she resigns when the government changes, as he/she is appointed on its advice.

Article 165 of the Constitution lists down the duties of the Advocate General as follows:

- To give advice to the Government of a State upon such legal matters, and to perform such other legal duties, as may from time to time be referred or assigned to him/her;
- To discharge the functions conferred on him/her as per the Constitution or any other law.

The Advocate General has the right to speak and to take part in the proceedings of the House(s) of State Legislature and any Committee of the State Legislature of which he/she may be named a member, but without a right to vote [Art 177]. He/she also enjoys the privileges enjoyed by the Members of State Legislature.

18.11 SPECIAL OFFICER FOR LINGUISTIC MINORITIES

The States Reorganisation Commission (1953–55) made a recommendation for creation of an officer for linguistic minorities. Accordingly, the Seventh Constitutional Amendment Act of 1956 added Article 350-B in the Constitution. This article contains the following provisions:

- There shall be a Special Officer for Linguistic Minorities who is to be appointed by the President.
- It would be the duty of the Special Officer to investigate all matters relating to the safeguards provided for linguistic minorities under the Constitution. He/she would report to the President upon those matters at such intervals as the President may direct. The President should place all such reports before each House of the Parliament and send to the governments of the States concerned.

In pursuance of the provision of Article 350-B of the Constitution, the office of the Special Officer for Linguistic Minorities was created in 1957. It is designated as the Commissioner for Linguistic Minorities under the Ministry of Minority Affairs.

The Commissioner for Linguistic Minorities performs the following functions:

- Takes up all the matters pertaining to the grievances arising out of the non-implementation of the constitutional and other safeguards provided to linguistic minorities and recommends remedial actions to be taken.
- Submits to the President of India, the reports on the status of implementation of the constitutional and the nationally agreed safeguards for the linguistic minorities.
- Monitors the implementation of safeguards through various review mechanisms.

The office of the Commissioner for Linguistic Minorities has the following objectives:

1. To provide equal opportunities to the linguistic minorities for inclusive development and national integration.
2. To spread awareness amongst the linguistic minorities about the safeguards available to them.

3. To ensure effective implementation of the safeguards provided for the linguistic minorities in the constitution and other safeguards.
4. To handle the representations for redressal of grievances related to the safeguards for linguistic minorities.

MAINS STARTER

Area	Building Blocks For Model Introductions
Election Commission of India	The ECI is an independent constitutional authority that is tasked with the function of conducting free and fair elections (Art 324), which is a basic feature of our Constitution.
Appointment of Election Commissioners	The Supreme Court in Anoop Baranwal case (2023), had stipulated that the CEC and other ECs should be appointed by a committee consisting of Prime Minister, the CJI and Leader of Opposition in the Lok Sabha. The Parliament by a law has reconstituted this committee to comprise PM, LOP and a cabinet minister to be nominated by PM.
Comptroller and Auditor General	CAG is an important constitutional authority who audits the accounts of Union and States (Articles 148 & 149) and holds the executive to financial accountability before the legislature.
Propriety Audit of CAG	The role of CAG is not restricted to just 'regulatory audit' where the formal correctness of expenditure incurred is audited. It also includes 'propriety audit' where the expenditure is scrutinised for its wisdom and economy and bring to light cases of improper expenditure and waste of public money.
CAG activism	CAG activism can be equated to judicial activism where the authority goes beyond its stipulated function of auditing the accounts and reporting thereof. In CAG activism, the authority provides its views on policy decisions of the government.
Union Public Service Commission/ State Public Service Commission	The UPSC/SPSC is an independent constitutional authority that is responsible for conducting examinations for appointments to the services of the Union/ States (Art 320). It also advises the Union government/State government on various matters relating to appointment, promotion and disciplinary matters of government servants.
Independence of Constitutional authorities	The independence of various constitutional bodies like ECI, CAG and UPSC/ SPSC is ensured in the Constitution. They have stability of tenure – 6 years or 65/62 years whichever is earlier; stringent removal procedure; and financial independence. There are also restrictions on further employment with government for CAG and PSC members.
Finance Commission	Finance Commission is constituted every 5 years by the President consisting of a chairperson and 4 members (Article 280). It makes recommendations on financial allocation of resources between Centre and States, principles that should govern grants-in-aid, and measures to improve the financial position of States and local bodies.

Area	Building Blocks For Model Introductions
GST Council	The GST council is a constitutional body consisting of the Union Finance Minister, Minister of State for revenue or finance, and Finance minister or a minister nominated by each State government as its members (Article 279A). It advises the Union and the States on various matters relating to GST. It is hailed as a classic example of co-operative federalism.
National Commission for SC/ST/SEBC (OBC)	The National Commission for SC/ST/SEBC are constitutional advisory bodies that are constituted for protecting/monitoring the constitutional safeguards provided to SC/ST/SEBC. It also advises the government on socio-economic development of SC/ST/SEBC.
Attorney General	The Attorney General is the highest law officer of the country appointed by the President (Article 76). He/She provides advice to the government on legal matters and discharges such other functions as provided by the Constitution or any law. He/She has the right of audience in any court of India and is also authorised to speak in Parliament when called upon to do so under Article 88.

UPSC Previous Years' Questions of Preliminary Examination

1. Consider the following statements: [2024]
   1. It is the Governor of the State who recognises and declares any community of that State as a Scheduled Tribe.
   2. A community declared as a Scheduled Tribe in a State need not be so in another State.

   Which of the statements given above is/are correct?

   (a) 1 only (b) 2 only
   (c) Both 1 and 2 (d) Neither 1 nor 2

   Solution: (b)

Explanation: As discussed in Section 18.8.2.4, it is the President who may, by public notification, specify the tribes or tribal groups (communities) that shall be deemed to be ST with respect to any State or UT. Any change to this can be done only by Parliament. Hence, Statement 1 is incorrect. The SC and ST are notified State/UT wise and hence a community declared as ST in one State need not be so in another State. Hence, Statement 2 is correct, and the answer is (b).

2. Consider the following organizations/bodies in India: **[2023]**

1. The National Commission for Backward Classes
2. The National Human Rights Commission
3. The National Law Commission
4. The National Consumer Disputes Redressal Commission

How many of the above are constitutional bodies?

(a) Only one (b) Only two (c) Only three (d) All four

Solution: (a)

Explanation: As discussed in Section 18.8, the National Commission for Backward classes has been made a constitutional body by the 102nd constitutional amendment by adding Article 338B. 2 and 4 are statutory bodies and 3 is an executive body. Hence, the correct answer is (a).

3. Consider the following statements: **[2022]**

1. Attorney General of India and Solicitor General of India are the only officers of the Government who are allowed to participate in the meetings of the Parliament of India.
2. According to the Constitution of India, the Attorney General of India submits his resignation when the Government which appointed him resigns.

Which of the statements given above is/are correct?

(a) 1 only (b) 2 only (c) Both 1 and 2 (d) Neither 1 nor 2

Solution: (d)

Explanation: As discussed in Section 18.9.2, it is only Attorney General who can participate in meetings of the Parliament under Article 88 and hence Statement 1 is incorrect. As discussed in Section 18.9.1, the Attorney General holds office during the pleasure of the President. This means that he/she may be removed by the President at any time as per the Constitution. Conventionally, he/she resigns when the government changes, as he/she is appointed on its advice and it is not as per the provisions of the Constitution and hence Statement 2 is also incorrect and the answer is (d).

UPSC Previous Years' Questions of Main Examination

1. "The duty of the Comptroller and Auditor General is not merely to ensure the legality of expenditure but also its propriety." Comment. **[2024]**

Approach: Discussion needs to be around the role of CAG and importance of propriety audit. Examples to be provided to bring out the importance of 'propriety audit' as given in Section 18.3.3.

MODEL ANSWER

The Comptroller and Auditor General (CAG) of India is one the most important officers under the Constitution of India. As mentioned by Dr Ambedkar, he is to be the guardian of the public purse and it is his duty to see that not a rupee is spent out of the Consolidated Fund of India or of a State without the authority of the appropriate Legislature.

Powers of CAG and Propriety audit

1. The CAG audits the consolidated fund of India and of every State to ascertain whether:
   - the moneys shown in the accounts as having been disbursed were legally available for and applicable to the service or purpose to which they have been applied or charged;
   - the expenditure conforms to the authority which governs it.
2. But the audit scope at present has moved from just being a 'regulatory audit' to 'propriety audit'. 'Propriety Audit' extends beyond scrutinising the mere formality of expenditure to its wisdom and economy and to bring to light cases of improper expenditure or waste of public money. For example, the irregularities during conduct of Commonwealth Games in 2010 were brought to light due to the propriety audit conducted by the office of CAG. Recently in 2023, the CAG had raised concerns surrounding the steep increase in the Dwarka Expressway Project's construction cost.
3. Apart from expenditure audit, the CAG also audits the receipts of Central and State Governments. In this aspect as well, the 'propriety audit' helps in assessing whether the policies are designed to secure an effective check on assessment and collection of revenue. For example, the CAG report on 2G spectrum allocation (2011) and Coal block allocation (2012) had highlighted the irregularities in assessment as well as method of allocation of these resources that resulted in loss to Government exchequer.

Thus, the CAG plays a very vital role in maintaining a check and balance on the executive with respect to financial transactions.

2. Discuss the role of National Commission for Backward classes in the wake of its transformation from a statutory body to a constitutional body. **[2022]**

Approach: This is a static question in which the functions and powers of NCBC is to be discussed. The constitutional provisions can form the body of the answer with recommendations for its improvement in the conclusion.

MODEL ANSWER

National Commission for Backward Classes (NCBC) was created in 1993 through the National Commission for Backward Classes Act, 1993. This statutory body has been made a constitutional body by adding Article 338B in 2018 through the 102nd constitutional amendment.

Role of NCBC

The NCBC shall consist of Chairperson, a Vice-Chairperson and three other members as per the Constitution. The key functions of NCBC are as follows:

(a) To investigate and monitor all matters relating to the safeguards provided for the Socially and Educationally Backward Classes (SEBC) and to evaluate the working of such safeguards;

(b) To inquire into specific complaints with respect to the deprivation of rights and safeguards of SEBCs;

(c) To participate and advise on the socio-economic development of the SEBCs and to evaluate the progress of their development under the Union and any State;

(d) To present to the President, annually and at such other times as the Commission may deem fit, reports upon the working of those safeguards;

(e) To make recommendations as to the measures that should be taken by the Union or any State for the effective implementation of those safeguards and other measures for the protection, welfare and socio-economic development of the SEBCs.

Issues and Suggestions

- While NCBC has been given a constitutional status, it requires autonomy in its functioning and also empowerment from the top political leadership to make it an effective body.
- The constitution may be further amended to provide that the members to NCBC will be appointed through a committee that represents various stake holders including leader of opposition. This will bring more transparency and credibility to the body.
- They may be given the powers to grant financial awards to victims during the course of their inquiry into any violations.

CHAPTER

19

Union and State Relations

LEARNING OUTCOMES

1. Comprehending various dimensions of Centre-State relations – Legislative, Administrative and Financial
2. Analysing Legislative relations – territorial jurisdiction, distribution of powers, Parliament's power to legislate on State list, doctrines relating to interpretation
3. Examining administrative relations – Restrictions on States, directions from Centre, mutual delegation, and Centre's control during emergencies
4. Understanding financial relations – Learning about taxation powers, the distribution of revenues, the role of the GST Council and Finance Commission, etc.
5. Understanding trends in Centre-State relations – Sarkaria Commission and Punchhi Commission
6. Analysing Inter-State relations, mechanisms for resolution of issues and steps towards co-operative federalism

19.1 INTRODUCTION TO UNION/CENTRE AND STATE RELATIONS

India is a federal country and its constitution is a federal constitution. The provisions of the executive and the legislative branches of the Union as well as the States are modelled on the basis of this federal structure.

In this chapter, we shall discuss the relations between the Union and the States. It must be noted that the Constitution uses the term 'Union–State relations' in Parts XI and XII that deal with these relations. However, it is quite common to refer to them as Centre–State relations as well. Hence, both these terms may be used interchangeably in this chapter.

The Constitution of India divides the legislative, administrative and financial powers between the Centre and the States. This division of powers is essential for harmonious coordination between them. The Centre–State relations can be studied in the following manner that are covered in Parts XI and XII:

- ❑ Legislative relations (Art 245–255)
- ❑ Administrative relations (Art 255–263)
- ❑ Financial relations (Art 265–293)

Apart from the above, there are also provisions relating to trade and commerce that are provided in Part XIII, which will be covered in this chapter.

19.2 CENTRE–STATE LEGISLATIVE RELATIONS

There is distribution of subjects between the Union and the States in the Seventh Schedule of the Constitution. The Centre–State legislative relations need to be understood from the following perspectives:

1. Territorial jurisdiction of the Parliament and State Legislatures
2. Distribution of subjects and residuary power
3. Parliament's power to legislate on State list and federal supremacy

19.2.1 Territorial Jurisdiction of Parliament and State Legislatures

Article 245 lays down the territorial jurisdiction of laws made by the Parliament and State Legislatures as follows:

- The laws made by the Parliament apply to the whole or any part of the territory of India.
- The laws made by the State Legislature apply to the whole or any part of territory of the State.
- Only the Parliament has extra-territorial jurisdiction i.e., it can make laws that are applicable to Indian citizens and their properties abroad. Example of such a law recently enacted is the Fugitive Economic Offenders Act (2018), which allows declaration of any Indian citizen who has fled the country as a fugitive economic offender and allows confiscation of his/her property situated in India or abroad.

19.2.2 Distribution of Legislative Subjects and Residuary Power

Article 246 (read with the Seventh Schedule) lays down the distribution of legislative subjects between the Parliament and State Legislatures as follows:

- The Parliament has the exclusive powers to make laws related to 98 matters in List I of the Seventh Schedule (Union List). Examples of subjects in the Union list include defence, banking, railways, foreign affairs, citizenship, currency, communication etc.
- The State legislature has powers to make laws related to 59 matters in List II of the Seventh Schedule (State List). Examples of subjects in the State list include public order, police, health, agriculture, land, local governments, fisheries, betting and gambling etc.
- Both the Parliament and the State Legislature have power to make laws related to 52 matters in List III of the Seventh Schedule (Concurrent List). However, the powers of State legislature in the Concurrent list are subject to powers of the Parliament. Examples of subjects in the Concurrent list include criminal law and procedure, civil procedure, marriage and divorce, prevention of cruelty to animals, education, forests etc. The 42nd amendment transferred the following five subjects from the State list to the Concurrent list – (i) education, (ii) forests, (iii) weights and measures, (iv) protection of wild animals and birds and (v) administration of justice; constitution and organisation of all courts except the Supreme Court and the High Courts.
  - In respect of any subject on the Concurrent list, the Parliamentary law made before or after any State law on the same subject will prevail over such State law if there is any inconsistency between the Parliament and the State laws [Article 254].
  - However, if such a State law with provisions that are inconsistent, has been reserved for consideration of the President and receives the assent, then it shall prevail in that State.

The following additional points need to be understood with respect to distribution of subjects:

- As per Article 246A (the 101st GST amendment), the Parliament and State Legislatures have the power to make laws with respect to Goods and Services Tax (GST). However, it is the Parliament that has exclusive powers to legislate with respect to GST where the supply of goods or services takes place in the course of inter-State trade or commerce (this will be discussed in Centre–State financial relations in more detail).
- The Parliament has the power to legislate on matters in the 'State list' with respect to the Union Territories or acquired territories (if any). The Union territories with a Legislative Assembly viz., Delhi, Puducherry and Jammu & Kashmir will have the powers to legislate on the matters in the 'State list' and the 'Concurrent list' subject to certain exceptions. However, the Parliamentary law will prevail over the laws made by such UT Assemblies in case of any repugnancy.
- The Constitution expressly provides in Article 246 that the Union list prevails over the State list. So, in the event of any overlap between the two lists, the Union list shall prevail over the State list. Similarly, in the event of overlapping between the Concurrent list and the State list, the Concurrent list shall prevail.

Residuary Power with Parliament

Article 248 lays down that the residuary power i.e., the legislation on any of the matters not listed in any of the three lists, shall lie with the Parliament. In federations like the United States and Australia, the powers of the Federal government are enumerated and all the residuary powers lie with the States. However, our Constitution has followed the Canadian model where the residuary powers lie with the Centre.

For example, if there is a law that needs to be made with respect to 'Cryptocurrency' like the Bitcoin. This is a matter that cannot be fitted into any of the entries in the three lists, as it is a matter of recent development. In such a scenario, it is the Parliament that has the power under Article 248 to legislate on this subject.

19.2.2.1 Doctrines Relating to Distribution of Subjects

The Supreme Court has provided certain doctrines (rules or principles), in the cases that it has decided, which are to be used while interpreting the extent of the legislative powers and the distribution of subjects between the Centre and the States. The most important of them are discussed below.

1. **Doctrine of 'Pith and Substance'**

   'Pith and substance' means 'true nature and character'. It is used by the courts to determine the true nature or substance of an enactment over its mere legal form and thereby decide as to which list or legislative domain it falls under.

   To determine the true nature, the court looks at the enactment as a whole, its main objects and the scope of its provisions. If a legislature encroaches on the field of another legislature, the court looks at whether this encroachment is in substance or merely incidental to the statute. If it is only incidental, then it will not render the law invalid. This doctrine allows some flexibility to the scheme of distribution of powers in the Indian Constitution. The rationale provided is that if every slight or incidental encroachment is struck down, the legislature's power would be severely reduced and it would not be able to carry out its duties. Case laws relating to this doctrine include ***Krishna Vs State of Madras*** (1956) and ***State of Bombay Vs Narottamdas*** (1950).

2. **Doctrine of 'Harmonious construction'**

   The doctrine of harmonious construction applies to cases where (a) provisions of the same law seem to contradict each other and (b) provisions of the law of a State seem to contradict the provisions of the law made by the Union.

The courts should construct in such a way that (a) avoids inconsistency between various sections of the law and (b) avoids inconsistency between the central and the State laws. When it is impossible to completely reconcile the differences in contradictory provisions, the courts must interpret them in such a way so that effect is given to both the provisions as much as possible. Case laws relating to this doctrine include ***Shankari Prasad Vs Union of India*** (1951) and ***Shri Krishna Rangnath Vs Gujarat University*** (1963).

3. **Doctrine of 'Colourable Legislation'**

   The doctrine of Colourable Legislation is based on the maxim 'what cannot be done directly, cannot be done indirectly'. It restricts legislatures from indirectly doing something, which they cannot do directly. In the case of indirect encroachment, it is known as 'colourable legislation'.

   The courts employ the doctrine of 'Pith and Substance' to determine if the legislature is competent to enact the disputed statute. The extent of encroachment is a relevant factor while determining if the enactment is colourable legislation. Case laws relating to this doctrine include ***State of Bihar Vs Kameshwar Singh*** (1952).

4. **Doctrine of 'Territorial Nexus'**

   A State law cannot have operation outside the territory of the State. This doctrine of 'Territorial Nexus' is invoked to find out if a law in question has an operation beyond its jurisdiction. This doctrine provides that while there needs to be territorial nexus between the State enacting the law and subject matter, the object to which the law applies does not have to be located within the strict territory of the State. For example, in ***State of Bombay Vs RMDC*** (1957), a tax levied by the State of Bombay on lotteries conducted through newspapers that were in circulation even outside the State was held to be valid as there was sufficient 'territorial nexus'.

   This doctrine is not only limited to taxation laws but to other kinds of laws also as held by the Supreme Court in ***Charusila Dasi*** case (1959) that allowed a Bihar law to regulate trust property situated in West Bengal, and ***Shrikant*** case (1994) that allowed the State of Gujarat to determine land ceiling based on land held in other States.

5. **Doctrine of Incidental and Ancillary Powers**

   It provides that every entry in the Seventh schedule carries with it the incidental and ancillary powers which is necessary to execute that power. The entries in the three lists are not to be read in a narrow or restricted sense but should be held to extend to all incidental and ancillary matters related to it. For example, the power to levy tax would include the power to check tax evasion as held in ***Commissioner of commercial taxes Vs R. S. Jhaver.*** However, the scope should not be extended to any unreasonable extent. For example, the power to levy tax cannot be held to include the power to confiscate goods as held in ***Check Post officer Vs K P Abdulla.***

   The doctrine of liberal interpretation with respect to the entries in the Seventh schedule is closely related to this doctrine of incidental and ancillary powers.

6. **Doctrine of Occupied Field**

   This doctrine states that when Parliament enacts a law on a specific subject and thereby occupies the legislative field, the State legislature is prohibited from making laws on the same subject.

   This doctrine can be applied only to entries in the concurrent list as held in ***State of Rajasthan Vs Vatan Medical and General Store.*** This leads to the doctrine of repugnancy under Article 254 which specifies that if there is repugnancy between Parliamentary law and State law for a matter in the concurrent list, the former will prevail.

19.2.3 Parliament's Power to Legislate on State List and Federal Supremacy

19.2.3.1 Parliament Legislation on State Subjects

The Parliament has the power to legislate over the subjects in the State list under the following circumstances.

Normal Circumstances	Emergency Circumstances
• When the Rajya Sabha passes resolution, with two-thirds of members present and voting, authorising the Parliament [Art 249]. • When two or more States pass resolution authorising the Parliament [Art 252]. • To implement any international or bilateral agreements, treaties or conventions entered into by Government of India [Art 253].	• When there is a Proclamation of National emergency [Art 250]. • When there is President's rule in a State [Art 356].

Normal circumstances when Parliament can legislate on State list

1. **When the Rajya Sabha passes resolution [Art 249]**

> If the Council of States (Rajya Sabha) has declared by resolution, supported by not less than two-thirds of the members present and voting, that the Parliament can legislate on a matter in the State list in National interest, then the Parliament can legislate on that matter in the State list.

This is a unique type of special majority that is provided only in Article 249 and Article 312 (with respect to creation of All-India services). We have discussed about special majority for removal of judges (Section 12.4.1) and for the amendment of the Constitution. However, that special majority is different from this special majority mentioned in Article 249. Here, the majority required is only two-thirds of members present and voting. Taking the same scenarios in the example provided under Section 12.4.1, let us understand this majority as below.

Scenario	No of Members Present and Voting	Majority Required – 2/3rd of Members Present and Voting
I	240	160
II	210	140
III	180	120

Such resolution passed by the Rajya Sabha and the laws made by the Parliament by virtue of such resolution are not permanent. The following points in this regard need to be noted:

- The Rajya Sabha resolution shall remain in force for a maximum of 1 year and can be renewed any number of times for a further period of 1 year at a time.
- The laws made by the Parliament by virtue of such resolution shall be in effect for a maximum period of 6 months after the resolution has ceased to be in force.
- The State legislature can still pass a law on the subject, when the Parliamentary law is in force. However, if there

> **THINK ABOUT IT**
>
> Parliament's power to legislate on the State list is a reflection of strong unitary features in our Constitution. Critically evaluate.

is any repugnancy between the Parliamentary law and State laws, the Parliamentary law will prevail till such time it is in effect [Art 251].

2. **When two or more States pass resolution [Art 252]**

According to Article 252, when the legislatures of two or more States pass resolutions requesting the Parliament to enact laws on any of the matters in the State list, then the Parliament can pass a law for regulating such matter.

The following points need to be noted with respect to this:

- The resolution authorising the Parliament should be passed by at least two or more States. Hence, one single State cannot authorise the Parliament under Article 252.
- Any State can subsequently adopt a similar resolution and make the Act of the Parliament apply to it.
- However, this is a permanent surrender of the powers by the State Legislatures that pass such a resolution. Once the Parliament enacts a law by virtue of resolution under Article 252, it is only the Parliament that can amend or repeal such an Act. The State Legislatures of the concerned States to which such law applies cannot amend or repeal such an Act.

Scan the QR code for conceptual video on Centre-State legislative relations

Mc Graw Hill edge

Examples of Acts passed by the Parliament under this provision includes Prize Competition Act, 1955 (with respect to entry 34 in the State list – Betting and Gambling), Urban Land (Ceiling and Regulation) Act, 1976 (with respect to entry 17 in the State list – Land).

3. **To implement international agreements, treaties and conventions [Art 253]**

The Parliament has the power to make any law, on any matter even in the State list, for implementing any treaty, agreement or convention with any other country or countries or any decision made at any international conference, association or other body. There is no requirement of approval by the States for enacting such laws by the Parliament.

Examples of Acts passed by the Parliament under this provision includes the United Nations (Privileges and Immunities) Act, 1947 (to give effect to the Convention on Privileges and immunities of the United Nations); Geneva Convention Act, 1960 (to give effect to the Geneva Convention); Lokpal and Lokayuktas Act, 2013 (to give effect to the United Nations Convention Against Corruption).

Emergency circumstances when Parliament can legislate on State list

1. **During proclamation of National Emergency [Art 250]**

The Parliament is empowered to make laws on any matters included in the State list for the whole or any part of India while a proclamation of National Emergency (under Article 352) is in operation. Such laws will have effect up to 6 months after the emergency has ceased to operate.

2. **During proclamation of President's rule in a State [Art 357]**

When the President's rule is imposed in a State (under Article 356), the Parliament is empowered to make any laws on any matters included in the State list with respect to that State. Such laws will continue to have effect even after the President's rule is revoked until it is altered or repealed or amended by the State Legislature subsequently.

MNEMONICS

Concept or Provisions	Shortcut or Mnemonics	Details to Remember
Parliament's power to legislate on State list	**RTI Emergency**	• **R** – **R**ajya Sabha passes resolution (authorising the Parliament) with 2/3rd of members present and voting in National interest • **T** – **T**wo or more states pass resolution authorising the Parliament • **I** – **I**nternational or bilateral treaty or agreement or convention entered into by Central government – to implement the same. **Emergency** – Whenever National emergency or State emergency is declared

19.2.3.2 Federal Supremacy

We have already discussed in the previous section the circumstances when the Parliament can legislate on a subject in the State list. Further, the Union list prevails over the State list if there is any overlap. Similarly, a Union law on any matter in the Concurrent list will prevail over a State law on the same matter in case of any repugnancy between the two. This is 'federal supremacy' in built in our Constitution. Apart from the above, the following provisions in the Constitution also provide for 'federal supremacy':

- Reservation of bills passed by the State Legislature by the Governor for consideration of the President.
- Certain bills can be introduced in the State Legislature only with the previous approval of the President – For example, under Article 304, any State bill imposing restrictions on freedom of trade and commerce can be introduced in the State Legislature only with the previous approval of the President.
- The Centre can direct the States to reserve Money bills and Financial bills passed by the State Legislature for consideration of the President when a financial emergency is declared.

Centre-State Legislative Relations (Seventh Schedule)		
Territorial Extent	**Distribution of Powers**	**Parliament Power on State list**
(a) Parliament law – whole or part of India (b) State law – whole or part of the State (c) Only Parliament has extra-territorial jurisdiction i.e., making a law applicable overseas to Indian citizens and their properties	(a) Parliament – exclusive power on Union list (98) (b) State – power on State list (59) subject to Parliament's power (c) Concurrent (52) – Both have powers (d) Residuary power – Parliament	(a) Normal – (i) Rajya Sabha resolution with 2/3rd of members present and voting (ii) 2 or more States resolution (iii) To implement international treaty or agreement (b) Emergency – During National or State emergency

19.3 CENTRE–STATE ADMINISTRATIVE RELATIONS

- The executive power of the Union extends to the matters in respect of which the Parliament can make laws and the executive power of the State extends to the matters in respect of which the State legislature can make laws.
- Thus, the Union executive carries out all administrative activities for subjects in the Union list while the State executive does the same for the subjects in the State list. In respect of matters in the Concurrent list, the executive power of the State shall be subject to, and limited by, the executive power expressly conferred upon the Union. Thus, for a law on a Concurrent list matter, the States usually execute the law even if it is enacted by the Parliament unless the law confers such executive power on the Union government.
- While the above is the administrative or the executive powers of the Union and States, the Constitution contains provisions for administrative relations between the Centre and the States in Part XI [Articles 256–261]. This can be broadly classified under the following categories:
  - Overall restrictions on the executive powers of the States
  - Directions from the Centre to the States in certain cases
  - Mutual entrustment of functions between the Centre and the States

We shall discuss the provisions under the above three categories in this section. Apart from these, there are provisions in the Constitution under other parts that provide for administrative relations between the Centre and the States. For example – (a) All-India Services and Public Service Commission (under Part XIV); (b) Emergency provisions (under Part XVIII) (discussed in this section); (c) various other unitary provisions like appointment of Governor by the Centre, appointment of Judges to the High Courts by the Centre; (d) issuing directions to States for providing instruction in mother tongue etc. These have been, or will be suitably, discussed in the relevant chapters that deal with these matters.

19.3.1 Overall Restrictions on the Executive Power of the States

While the Centre and the States carry out their respective executive functions as per the Constitution, the following are the overall restrictions on the executive power of the States:

1. The executive power of every State shall be so exercised as to ensure compliance with the laws of the Parliament. Also, the Union executive power extends to the giving of such directions to the States as may appear to the Government of India to be necessary for the purpose [Art 256]. So, the executive action of any State government should not violate any law made by the Parliament.
2. The executive power of every State shall be so exercised as not to impede (interfere) or prejudice (harm) the exercise of the executive power of the Union. The executive power of the Union shall extend to the giving of such directions to the States as may appear to the Government of India to be necessary for that purpose [Art 257(1)]. So, the executive action of any State government should not interfere with, or create trouble for, the Union to exercise its executive functions.
3. Article 365 of the Constitution provides that where any State has failed to comply with any directions given by the Centre, it shall be lawful for the President to hold that there is a break-down of the constitutional machinery. This may result in imposition of the President's rule under Article 356. However, after the judgement of the Supreme Court in the *S. R. Bommai case*, Article 356 can be used only sparingly.

19.3.2 Directions from Centre to States in Certain Cases

Apart from the above two general restrictions on the executive power of the States, the executive power of the Union also extends to giving directions to the States for the following matters:

1. Construction and maintenance of means of communication declared in the direction to be of national or military importance [Art 257(2)];
2. Measures to be taken for the protection of the railways within the State [Art 257(3)].

19.3.3 Mutual Delegation of Functions between the Centre and the States

The Seventh Schedule provides the distribution of legislative subjects between the Centre and the States. This is a clear demarcation for legislative matters. However, the implementation of laws by the executive can result in overlap of functions between the Centre and the States. It also may result in conflicts that need to be avoided. Hence, the Constitution provides the following scheme for mutual delegation of functions between the Centre and the States:

1. The President (Union government) may, with the consent of the Government of a State, entrust any executive functions of the Centre to such State government [Art 258(1)].
2. A Parliamentary law may confer powers and impose duties, or authorise the conferring of powers and the imposition of duties, upon a State or officers and authorities thereof with respect to any union executive function [Art 258(2)]. In this case, the consent of the State government is not necessary.
3. The Governor of a State (State government) may, with the consent of the Government of India, entrust any executive function of the State to the central government [Art 258A].

Further, the Constitution also provides that full faith and credit shall be given throughout the territory of India to public acts, records and judicial proceedings of the Centre and every State [Art 261]. It provides for the recognition and enforcement of any public act, record or judicial proceeding by the Centre or any State within the territory of India. Further, final judgements and orders of civil courts in any part of India are capable of execution anywhere within the territory of India.

THINK ABOUT IT

Explain the mechanisms in the Constitution for relations between Union and State governments. Is it tilted in favour of the Centre?

19.3.4 Centre's Complete Control during Emergencies

The extent of the Centre's control over the States in respect of the executive functions during emergencies is provided below:

1. Whenever a proclamation of national emergency is in operation, the executive power of the Union shall extend to giving directions to any State as to the manner in which the executive power of the State is to be exercised [Art 353]. Thus, while under normal circumstances the Union executive can give directions to the States only on specific matters, whenever there is a national emergency, the Union executive can give directions on any matter to the States.
2. Whenever the President's rule is imposed in a State under Article 356, the Union government will take over all the executive functions of the State.
3. Whenever a financial emergency is in operation, the Centre can direct the States to observe canons of financial propriety and can give directions including the reduction of salaries of State government employees [Art 360].

Centre-State Administrative Relations	
Overall restrictions	• Executive power of every State to be in compliance with Parliamentary laws. • Executive power of every State not to impede or prejudice executive power of the Union.
Directions	• Union can give instructions for (a) construction and maintenance of communication networks; (b) protection of Railways within the State • During emergency on any matter
Mutual Delegation	• Centre may entrust any of its function to State and vice-versa with mutual consent • Parliamentary law may confer powers and duties on State authorities w.r.t Union executive functions

19.4 CENTRE–STATE FINANCIAL RELATIONS

In continuation of the legislative and the administrative relations, the financial relations between the Centre and the States are also provided in the Constitution. It is covered in Part XII between Articles 264 and 293.

The financial relations need to be understood broadly under the following headings:

(a) Taxation powers and scheme for distribution of tax revenues
(b) Distribution of non-tax revenues
(c) Grants-in-Aid from the Centre to the States
(d) Composition and functions of the Finance Commission and GST Council
(e) Borrowing powers of the Centre and the States
(f) Inter-Governmental tax immunities
(g) Trade and commerce within India and restrictions that can be placed in public interest (Part XIII)

19.4.1 Taxation Powers and Scheme for Distribution of Tax Revenues

The Constitution gives a detailed scheme of distribution of financial resources between the Union and the States. The Constitution makes a broad distinction between the power to levy (impose) and collect a tax, and the power to appropriate (use/distribute) the proceeds of a tax. Thus, the legislature which levies a tax is not necessarily the authority which retains the proceeds of a tax levied.

The Constitution grants the Union Parliament exclusive power to levy taxes on several items in the Union list (from entry 82 to 92B and 96 in the Seventh Schedule). The State Legislatures enjoy similar power of taxation with regard to items specified in the State list (from entry 46 to 63 and 66 in the Seventh Schedule).

The main articles that provide for levy and distribution of taxes and duties are Articles 268, 269, 269A and 270. Of these, after the commencement of GST regime, Article 269A is very important for levy of GST as well as Article 270 for distribution of tax revenue between the Centre and the States. We shall now discuss briefly about these articles.

Duties levied by the Union but collected and appropriated by the States – Article 268

Stamp duties that are mentioned in the Union list are levied by the Government of India but are collected and appropriated by the States where they are collected. Such proceeds (taxes received) do not form part of the Consolidated Fund of India but are assigned to that State.

Entry 91 of the Union list in the Seventh Schedule deals with stamp duties in respect of bill of exchange, cheques, promissory notes, policies of insurance, transfer of shares and debentures etc. These duties will fall under this category of Article 268.

For example, let us assume that a person purchases a policy of insurance for his/her two-wheeler in the city of Mumbai. In such a case, the stamp duty on this policy of insurance shall be levied by the Government of India but it will be collected and appropriated by the Government of Maharashtra.

Goods and Services Tax (GST) and the 101st Constitutional Amendment

Before we discuss the provisions of Articles 269 and 269A, it is important to understand the GST system that was introduced in July 2017 through the 101st Constitutional Amendment. Let us briefly summarise the key points with respect to the GST system that will help us understand the provisions of revised Articles 269 and 269A.

1. The GST was introduced to subsume (include or absorb) various indirect taxes levied by the Centre as well the States. This was done in order to avoid cascading effect of taxes i.e., taxes being levied on taxes, and to create a national market for goods and services with uniform taxes.
   - The important indirect taxes levied by the Centre that were subsumed into GST include (i) Excise duty, (ii) Customs duty, (iii) Service tax, (iv) Central Sales tax etc.
   - The important indirect taxes levied by the States that were subsumed into GST include (i) Value-added taxes or State sales tax, (ii) Octroi and entry tax, (iii) Entertainment tax etc.
   - There are four types of GST that are levied
     (a) Central GST (CGST) – This is levied by the Centre that replaced earlier excise duty (on manufacture) or service tax (on services).
     (b) State GST (SGST) – This is levied by the States that replaced earlier sales tax and other local taxes.
     (c) Integrated GST (IGST) – This is levied by the Centre for sale of goods or services during inter-State trade. Earlier, there used to be excise duty or service tax that was levied by the Centre initially and then the Centre used to levy Central Sales tax on such inter-State sale. However, under the GST system, it is replaced by IGST that is levied by the Centre.
     (d) Union Territory GST (UTGST) – This is levied by the Centre w.r.t. sale of goods and services in the Union Territories.
2. GST is a 'destination-based tax' rather than the earlier system of sales tax that was an 'origination-based tax'. This is to ensure that there is no cascading effect of taxes as goods and services may have multiple movements from origination, but finally will have one destination where they are consumed. Also, it is based on the principle of equity as the tax revenues are assigned to the State where the demand for the goods or services have been created.
   - For example, let us assume that a car is manufactured in Tamil Nadu and sold within Tamil Nadu. Earlier, there used to be an excise duty on manufacture which is now levied as CGST. The sale within Tamil Nadu would have attracted sales tax within the State which is now levied as SGST. It must be noted that the GST rate for a product is same across the country. It is divided as CGST and SGST equally for sale within a State. For example, if the GST rate on a car is 28%, the same is levied as CGST (by the Centre) at 14% and SGST (by the State) at 14% in the given example.
   - On the other hand, let us assume that the sale happens from Tamil Nadu to Bihar. Earlier, the excise duty would have been levied by the Centre. Thereafter, for such inter-State sale, there was Central Sales Tax (CST) that was levied and collected by the Centre but assigned to the State where it was collected. So, in our example, the CST would have been levied

and collected by the Centre but assigned to Tamil Nadu that was the 'origination' place. However, this would have resulted in cascading effect of taxes as there was no uniformity in the rates of taxes across the States and the mechanism to claim credit of input tax was also very inefficient.

- Now, under the GST system for the above example of inter-State sale from Tamil Nadu to Bihar, the Centre would levy IGST at 28% (which is the GST rate for car in our example). Thereafter, 50% of the same i.e., 14% would form part of the Centre's tax proceeds and the balance 14% would be apportioned (distributed) to the consuming State i.e., Bihar. This is the reason that GST is known as 'destination-based' tax and this ensures that any input tax credit is efficiently claimed. Further, it is also based on the principle of equity as the Government of the State that created the demand i.e., Bihar in our example, gets the share of taxes for its spending. Similarly, the tax on a good or service produced in Bihar and consumed in Tamil Nadu will be appropriated between the Government of India and Tamil Nadu government.
- However, the new GST system resulted in loss of revenue for the industrialised States like the Southern and Western States that were net exporters of goods and services out of their States. In order to ensure that this does not affect the finances of the States, the 101st Constitutional Amendment provided that any loss in revenue for 5 years i.e., from July 2017 to June 2022 between the earlier system and the new GST system, for any State shall be compensated by the Centre. This loss was arrived at taking the tax revenue of every State for the year 2015–16 as the base year and compounding it at 14% per annum. Any shortfall in actual revenue of any State under the GST system was compared with this computed amount and the shortfall has been compensated by the Central Government.

Taxes levied and collected by the Union but assigned to the States – Article 269

This article was applicable for both the inter-State sale of goods and the inter-State consignment of goods before the GST system. However, after the introduction of GST, this is applicable primarily for taxes on consignment of goods.

Consignment of goods is when the principal seller sends the goods to his/her agent on a consignment basis. The agent will then make the final sale to the end customer. For instance, in the example discussed in previous section, let us assume that instead of outright sale of car from Tamil Nadu to Bihar, the car is sent on consignment from Tamil Nadu to Bihar. This is sent by the seller (in Tamil Nadu) to his/her agent (in Bihar). The agent (in Bihar) will then make the final sale to end customer (in Bihar) and in turn will earn a commission on such sale.

As per the GST system for such inter-State consignment of goods, the GST is levied and collected by the Government of India at the time of sending the goods on consignment. However, this GST is assigned to the State where it is levied i.e., in our example, this is assigned to the State of Tamil Nadu.

Levy and collection of GST in course of inter-State trade – Article 269A

As explained in the previous section on GST, before the introduction of GST system, the Centre levied and collected Central Sales tax on any inter-State sale of goods. This tax was assigned to the State where it was collected.

After the introduction of GST system, the Centre continues to levy and collect GST on inter-State sale of goods and services. This is the IGST levied and collected by the Centre. However, this is distributed as per the provisions of law made by the Parliament on the recommendation of the GST Council. This law is the IGST Act enacted by the Parliament and as per this Act, the IGST collected is distributed between the Centre and the destination State. Imports shall also be deemed to be in the course of inter-State trade or commerce for this purpose.

Taxes levied and distributed between the Union and the States – Article 270

The following taxes are levied and collected by the Government of India. They are distributed between the Union and the States as per the recommendation of the Finance Commission:

(a) All taxes and duties referred in the Union list (except duties and taxes referred in Articles 268, 269 and 269A) – Examples of such taxes include income tax, corporation tax etc.

(b) CGST on sale of goods and services within a State.

(c) Centre's share of IGST on goods and services in the course of inter-State trade or commerce under Article 269A.

Scan the QR code for conceptual video on Centre-State Administrative and Financial relations

Mc Graw Hill edge

The following are levied and collected by the Government of India but they are not shared with the States and are used only by Government of India:

- Cess levied for a particular purpose like the Swachh Bharat Cess. This is levied, collected and used by Government of India for the purpose for which it is collected.
- Surcharge on taxes (Art 271) like surcharge on income tax for persons with taxable income above certain limits. This is levied, collected and used by the Government of India.

Taxes levied, collected and retained by the States

As discussed earlier, the State GST on the sale of goods and services within a State is levied, collected and retained by the respective States. Similarly, the taxes in respect of items in the State list like excise duty on alcohol, land revenue, taxes on land and building, taxes on vehicles and luxuries etc., are levied, collected and retained by the States.

Further, taxes on the sale of petrol, diesel, natural gas, aviation turbine fuel; taxes on minerals; taxes on professions and employment; taxes, if any, on agricultural income; estate duty in respect of agricultural land; taxes on animals and boats; tolls; fees on matters enumerated in State list are also levied, collected and retained by the respective States.

19.4.2 Distribution of Non-tax Revenues

Non-tax revenues are the revenues of the Central Government and the State Governments from various sources as per the distribution of subjects between them under the Constitution.

Thus, the main sources of non-tax revenues for Central Government includes railways, post & telegraphs, banking, insurance, broadcasting, coinage and currency, central public sector undertakings etc.

The main sources of non-tax revenues of the States include irrigation, forests, fisheries, State public sector undertakings etc.

19.4.3 Grants-in-aid from Centre to States

Article 275 of the Constitution provides for grants-in-aid from the Centre to the States. Grants-in-aid are monies that are provided by the Parliament for meeting various developmental needs of States. This is over and above the distribution of tax revenues between the Centre and the States. Following are the key points under Article 275 with respect to grants-in-aid.

- Grants-in-aid are provided to various States as the Parliament may determine to be in need of assistance, and different sums may be fixed for different States. Such sums shall be charged on the Consolidated Fund of India in each year.
- These grants-in-aid are provided after considering the recommendations of the Finance Commission.

- Additionally, grants-in-aid may also be paid out of the Consolidated Fund of India to enable any State to meet the costs of schemes for development of the Scheduled Tribes in the State or raising the level of administration of the Scheduled areas in that State.
- Further, the Centre and the States may make discretionary grants for any public purpose, even if that purpose is not within their legislative powers [Art 282]. Under this provision, the Centre may make grants to various States to help them financially and also to coordinate their actions.

19.4.4 Composition and Functions of Finance Commission and GST Council

We have discussed about the composition and functions of the Finance Commission and the GST Council in the previous chapter on Constitutional Authorities (Sections 18.6 and 18.7 and the previous sections of this chapter). We will discuss about the recommendations of the 15th Finance Commission, the current issues raised regarding devolution of funds, as well as the recent developments related to the GST in this section.

Recommendations of the 15th Finance Commission

The Finance Commission is constituted once every 5 years by the President [Art 280]. It provides its recommendations on distribution of taxation revenues and grants-in-aid between the Centre and the States.

The 14th Finance Commission that provided its recommendations for the period 2015–2020 had proposed significant changes in the (a) percentage of devolution from the Centre to States (vertical devolution) and (b) distribution of the States' share amongst the States (horizontal devolution).

> **THINK ABOUT IT**
>
> The Finance Commission is progressively devolving more funds to the States over the years. However, the criteria still provide higher weightage for equity over efficiency. Discuss.

The key recommendations of the 14th Finance Commission can be summarised as follows:

- The transfer from the Centre to the States consist of tax-devolution, grants for various Centrally Sponsored Schemes and grants-in-aid according to the needs of certain States.
- The 14th Finance Commission was of the view that tax devolution should be the primary mechanism of resources to the States. Since this tax devolution is formula driven, it is conducive for sound fiscal federalism and provides flexibility to the States to utilise their resources according to their local requirements and priorities. Hence, it increased the tax devolution from the Centre to the States from 32% (as per recommendation of the 13th Finance Commission) to 42%.
- It introduced forest cover as a criterion for the horizontal devolution amongst the States.

> Scan the QR code for video on recent issues with respect to devolution of funds from Centre to States
>
> McGraw Hill edge

The 15th Commission was constituted for providing its recommendations for the period 2020–2025 under the chairmanship of Shri N. K. Singh. The Commission first submitted recommendations for 1 year (2020–21) and then submitted its final recommendation for the 5-year period of 2021–2026.

Terms of reference of the 15th Finance Commission

Apart from the standard terms of reference (i.e., areas on which recommendations will be submitted), as per Article 280 of the Constitution, the following were the key additional terms of reference for the 15th Finance Commission based on which they could consider proposing performance-based incentives for States:

(a) Efforts made by the States in expansion and deepening of tax net under GST;
(b) Efforts and progress made in achieving replacement rate of population growth;
(c) Achievements in implementation of flagship schemes of Government of India;
(d) Progress made in increasing capital expenditure and reducing the losses of power sector;
(e) Promoting digital economy and direct benefit transfers;
(f) Control or lack of it in incurring expenditure on populist measures;
(g) Progress made in sanitation, solid waste management and bringing change to end open defecation.

Further, the Commission was required to use the population data as per Census 2011 alone for making its recommendation.

Some of the above terms of reference like (a) Efforts for deepening GST, (b) Achievements in implementation of the central government schemes, (c) promoting digital economy and (d) controlling expenditure on populist measures, created a controversy at the time of notification as these parameters are vaguely definable and they were against the spirit of cooperative federalism. Further, some of the Southern States objected to the use of 2011 Census population as the sole criterion for population, since it could act against their interest when they have controlled their population. However, the Finance Commission also included 'Demographic performance' as one of the criteria to address this issue.

Key recommendation of the 15th Finance Commission

(a) Devolution of taxes to States:
- The share of States in the Centre's taxes was recommended to be decreased from 42% during the 2015–20 period to 41% for 2021–26.
- The 1% decrease is to provide for the newly formed Union Territories of Jammu & Kashmir, and Ladakh from the resources of the central government.

(b) Criteria for devolution:
- ***The Finance Commission reintroduced performance-based incentives to States on two parameters – demographic performance and taxation efforts***

Criteria	14th Finance Commission 2015–20	15th Finance Commission 2021–26
Income distance	50.0	45.0
Population (1971)	17.5	–
Population (2011)	10.0	15.0
Area	15.0	15.0
Forest cover	7.5	–
Forest and ecology	–	10.0
Demographic Performance	–	12.5
Tax effort	–	2.5
Total	100	100

- Income distance is the distance of the State's income from the State with the highest income. The States with lower per capita income would be given a higher share to maintain equity among States.
- The demographic performance criterion has been introduced to reward efforts made by the States in controlling their population. States with a lower fertility ratio will be scored higher on this criterion.
- Forest and ecology consider share of dense forest of each State in the aggregate dense forest of all the States.
- Tax effort as a criterion has been used to reward States with higher tax collection efficiency.

(c) Grants-in-aid
- The following grants will be provided to States: (i) revenue deficit grants, (ii) grants to local bodies and (iii) disaster management grants.

(d) Recommendations on fiscal roadmap
- The Commission noted that the tax revenue is far below the estimated tax capacity of the country.
- The Commission recommended: (i) broadening the tax base, (ii) streamlining tax rates and (iii) increasing capacity and expertise of tax administration in all tiers of the government.
- It also suggested the limits for the fiscal deficits of the Centre and the States.
- States need to take steps for expanding the GST base and ensuring compliance

(e) Other recommendations
- A State should increase spending on health to more than 8% of their budget.
- A dedicated fund called the 'Modernisation Fund for Defence and Internal Security' to be constituted to bridge the gap for funds for capital expenditure in defence and internal security.

Recent issues surrounding devolution of funds

The criteria for horizontal devolution of funds amongst the States over the last 5 Finance Commissions are provided below.

Criteria for horizontal devolution amongst the States over last 5 FCs

Criteria	11th FC 2000–05	12th FC 2005–10	13th FC 2010–15	14th FC 2015–20	15th FC 2021–26
Income Distance	62.5	50	47.5	50.0	45.0
Population (1971)	10	25	25	17.5	-
Population (2011)	-	-	-	10.0	15.0
Area	7.5	10	10	15.0	15.0
Forest Cover	-	-	-	7.5	-
Forest and Ecology	-	-	-	-	10.0
Infrastructure index	7.5	-	-	-	-
Fiscal Discipline	7.5	7.5	17.5	-	-
Demographic Performance	-	-	-	-	12.5
Tax Effort	5	7.5	-	-	2.5
Total	**100**	**100**	**100**	**100**	**100**

Recently, various opposition ruled States, especially from South India, have claimed that they have not been receiving their fair share under the present scheme of financial devolution. They have raised issues about their less than proportionate share of receipt in tax revenue when compared to their contribution towards tax collection.

The key reasons for this issue are as follows:

- Cess and surcharge collected by the Centre is estimated at around 23% of its gross tax receipts for 2024–25, which does not form part of the divisible pool and hence not shared with the States.
- Amount each State gets back for every rupee they contribute to central taxes shows steep variation. This is partly due to the fact that many corporations are headquartered in industrially developed State capitals where they would remit their direct taxes. However, this variation can also be attributed to the difference in GST collection amongst various States.
- Higher weightage being given for equity (income gap) and needs (population, area and forest) than efficiency (demographic performance and tax effort).

It is essential that the States that are betteroff financially support the poorer States to ensure equitable development across the nation. Further, the poorer States supply raw materials and labour for businesses across the country, which helps in the GSDP growth of industrially developed States. However, it is also essential that the distribution appears fair, and the following steps may be taken in this regard.

- The divisible pool can be enlarged by including some portion of cess and surcharge in it. The Centre should also gradually discontinue various cesses and surcharges it imposes by suitably rationalising the tax slabs.
- Weightage for efficiency criteria in horizontal devolution should be increased. States' contribution to the country's GDP, relative GST contribution from States etc., may be considered as criteria by providing suitable weightage.
- Formal arrangement for participation of States in the constitution and working of Finance Commission should be considered.

GST Council and recent developments

- We have discussed about the composition and functions of GST Council in Section 18.7 in the previous chapter and previous sections of this chapter. Article 279A provides that the GST Council shall establish a mechanism to settle any dispute arising out of the recommendations of the Council or in its implementation – (a) between the Government of India and one or more State governments and (b) between two or more State governments.
- In *Mohit Minerals case* in 2022, the Supreme Court in its judgement had specified that the recommendations of the GST Council are recommendatory in nature on the Union and the States. It had specified that the GST Council recommendations cannot be considered as binding on the Union and the States based on the interpretation of Articles 246A and 279A and that both the Union and the States have concurrent powers to legislate on the GST. However, it must be noted that the decisions of the GST Council are abided by the Union as well as all States even after this judgement.

GST Compensation from Centre to States

- The imputed shortfall in tax collection for States on account of implementation of the GST has been compensated by the Centre to the States for 5 years from July 2017 to June 2022.
- Due to the COVID-19 pandemic, there has been significant reduction in economic activity during the period from March 2020 to March 2022. Many of the States have been demanding

that the compensation for shortfall be extended by a further period of 2 to 5 years. However, the Centre has not acceded to this demand considering the overall fiscal position of the Central Government.

- The Central government has been levying a GST compensation cess in order to meet the shortfall payment to the States. It is only the levy of this cess that has been extended till March 2026, in order to repay the loans that have been availed by the Central Government for payment of shortfall to the States during the COVID-19 pandemic period.

SUMMARY OF IMPORTANT PROVISIONS FOR CENTRE–STATE FINANCIAL RELATIONS

Provisions	Art 268	Art 269	Art 269A	Art 270
Nature of tax	Stamp duties mentioned in the Union list.	GST on inter-State consignment of goods.	GST on inter-State sale of goods and services.	All other taxes in Union list like direct taxes, CGST, Centre's share of IGST.
Levied by	Government of India.	Government of India.	Government of India.	Government of India.
Collected by	State where levied.	Government of India.	Government of India.	Government of India.
Apportionment/ Assignment	Assigned to State where levied.	Assigned to State where levied.	Apportioned between Centre and destination State as per IGST Act.	Distributed between Centre and States as per recommendations of the Finance Commission.

19.4.5 Borrowing Power of Centre and the States

The Constitution contains the following provisions with respect to borrowing by the Central and the State governments:

(a) The Central Government can borrow upon the security of the Consolidated Fund of India, or provide guarantees for such borrowing, subject to such limits as may be fixed by the Parliament [Art 292].
- It must be noted that no such law has been made by the Parliament till date (2024), and hence the executive power of the Union extends to borrowing monies without any limit for meeting any budgetary deficit.
- The Fiscal Responsibility and Budget Management Act (FRBM) that was passed in 2003 has set limits for the government with respect to the fiscal deficit and the debt (as a percentage of GDP). However, these limits have been breached during the COVID-19 pandemic and expected to be brought within limits in the coming years.

(b) The State Government can borrow upon security of consolidated fund of the State, within the territory of India, subject to such limits as may be fixed by the State Legislature [Art 293].
- Thus, the State governments can borrow only within the territory of India.

(c) If there is any outstanding debt/guarantee of the State to the Central Government, it cannot borrow further without the consent of the Central Government [Art 293].
- The consent may be granted by the Central Government subject to such conditions as it may impose.

19.4.6 Inter-Governmental Tax Immunities

The Constitution provides for mutual exemption from taxation on properties and incomes of the Union and the States as follows:

- Exemption of the central property from the State taxation – The property of the Centre is exempted from all taxes imposed by a State or any authority within a State like municipalities, district boards, panchayats and so on [Art 285].
- Exemption of the State property or income from the central taxation – The property and income of a State is exempted from the central taxation [Art 289].
- It must however be noted that the exemption is only in respect of property or income related to the functions of Government. Any corporation or company that is a separate legal entity, which is owned by the Central or the State governments are subject to taxation.

19.4.7 Trade and Commerce

The provisions with respect to trade, commerce and intercourse within the territory of India is provided in Part XIII of the Indian Constitution. 'Trade' refers to the action of buying and selling goods and services, 'Commerce' refers to all forms of transportation such as land, air or water, and 'intercourse' refers to movement of goods from one place to another.

The summary of key provisions with respect to trade, commerce and intercourse is as follows:

- Trade, commerce and intercourse throughout the territory of India shall be free [Art 301].
- The Parliament may by law impose restrictions on the freedom of trade, commerce or intercourse between one State and other or within any part of territory of India as may be required under public interest, but no preference can be given to one State over other except by the Parliament to deal with a situation of scarcity of goods [Art 302 and 303].
- The Legislature of a State may,
  - impose on goods imported from other States or the Union Territories, any tax to which similar goods manufactured or produced in that State are subject [Art 304]. After the introduction of the GST regime that provides for uniform tax rates across the country, this provision has very little relevance at present except for goods that are outside the purview of the GST like liquor.
  - impose such reasonable restrictions on freedom of trade, commerce or intercourse with that State or within that State in public interest. However, such a bill cannot be introduced, in the State legislature, without previous sanction of the President [Art 304].

19.5 TRENDS IN CENTRE–STATE RELATIONS

19.5.1 Committees on Centre–State Relations

There have been various commissions/committees that have been set up by the Central government for improving the Centre–State relations. Three important commissions and their recommendations are summarised in this section.

1st Administrative Reforms Commission (ARC), 1966

The Central government appointed a six-member ARC in 1966 under the chairmanship of *Shri. Morarji Desai*. It submitted its report in 1969 with the following important recommendations:

- Establishment of an Inter-State Council under Article 263 of the Constitution.
- Appointment of persons having long experience in public life and administration and non-partisan attitude as governors.
- Delegation of powers to the maximum extent to the States.
- Transferring of more financial resources to the States to reduce their dependency upon the Centre.

However, no action was taken by the Central government on the recommendations of the 1st ARC.

Sarkaria Commission, 1983

This is one of the important commissions on Centre–State relations that was set up by the Central government in the year 1983 under the chairmanship of retired Supreme Court Judge Shri R. S. Sarkaria. It submitted its report in 1987 with 247 recommendations to improve the Centre–State relations. We have already discussed, some of the important recommendations of the Sarkaria Commission with respect to appointment of the Governor and discretionary powers to be exercised by the Governor. Following are the important recommendations for improving the Centre–State relations:

- A permanent Inter-State council should be set up under Article 263.
- Article 356 should be used very sparingly. Governors should not dismiss the Council of Ministers as long as they command a majority in the Assembly.
- The procedure of consulting the Chief Minister of a State in appointment of the Governor should be prescribed in the Constitution itself. Governor's term of 5 years should not be disturbed except for compelling reasons.
- Zonal Council should be constituted afresh and re-activated to promote federalism.
- All-India Services should be further strengthened.
- The Centre should consult the States before making any law on a subject in the Concurrent list.
- The President should decide on bills reserved for his/her consideration within a period of 6 months. Whenever the President withholds assent to the State bills, the reasons should be communicated to the State government.
- The residuary powers of taxation should remain with the Parliament, while other residuary powers should be placed in the Concurrent list.
- Steps should be taken to implement the three-language formula in true spirit.

The Central Government has over the years implemented various recommendations of the Sarkaria Commission. However, some of the most important recommendations with respect to Governor appointment; consultation by the Centre with the States before enacting on a Concurrent list subject; providing reasons for withholding assent to State bills have not been implemented till date [2024].

Punchhi Commission, 2007

The Central government had set up one more commission for providing recommendations with respect to Centre–State relations in 2007 under the chairmanship of Shri M.M. Punchhi. This commission submitted its report in 2010. It relied extensively on the reports of Sarkaria Commission, the National Commission to review the working of the Constitution and the 2nd ARC while finalising its report. The important recommendations of the commission are as follows:

- Broad agreement to be reached between the Centre and the States before legislation by Parliament on a subject in the Concurrent list.

- Governors should grant assent or reserve bill for consideration of the President within a period of 6 months. The President should assent or withhold assent to a State bill reserved for his/her consideration within a period of 6 months.
- State Chief Ministers should be consulted before appointment of the Governors and they should be given a fixed tenure of 5 years. The Governor cannot be removed by the Centre but only impeached by the State Legislature, similar to the impeachment procedure laid down for the President.
- Article 356 to be suitably amended to incorporate the guidelines as per the S. R. Bommai judgement.
- New All-India Services in sectors like health, education, engineering and judiciary should be created.
- A balance of power between States is desirable and this can be achieved through the constitutional amendment that provides equality of representation to all States in the Rajya Sabha irrespective of their population size.
- There should be an effective mechanism to involve the States in the finalisation of 'Terms of Reference' of the Finance Commissions.

Many of these recommendations have not been implemented till date [2024].

It must be noted that even the States have set up such committees in the past like the Rajamannar Committee in Tamil Nadu in 1969, Anandpur Sahib resolution in Punjab in 1973, and the West Bengal Memorandum in West Bengal in 1977. However, the recommendations of these committees set up in the States have not been considered by the Central governments.

Some common unresolved issues

As can be seen from the recommendations of various commissions, there is a need to strengthen the federal nature of our country by strengthening the powers of the States. However, the following issues remain unresolved:

- Appointment of Governors and the relationship between the Governor and the elected government of a State remains an issue, especially with respect to States that are ruled by political parties different from the party in power at the Centre. Delay in granting assent to the bills passed by State legislatures as well as reserving such bills for the consideration of the President when it is not required are also issues that have arisen in the recent years in opposition ruled States. The role of Governor as chancellor of universities and higher powers provided to them with respect to the appointment of Vice-Chancellors and administration of State universities under UGC regulations have also created tussle between State governments and Governors in opposition ruled States.
- Passage of bills on subjects in the Concurrent list by the Parliament without discussion with the States. Recent example (2020) is that of Farm-related enactments that were passed by the Parliament that was objected to by many States. Finally, the Central Government had to repeal these laws in December 2021 after prolonged demonstrations by farmers against the laws.
- There have been issues raised by the Southern States about lower devolution of tax proceeds from the Centre to those States.

19.5.2 Towards Cooperative and Competitive Federalism

There are unitary features in the Constitution that lean towards a strong Centre. However, 'Federalism' is a basic structure of the Constitution. While in the legislative sphere the demarcation between the Centre and the States is mostly clear, it is in the administrative and the financial relations that the federal principles need to be followed the most in order to avoid conflicts. In this regard, there are various initiatives that have been taken towards achieving 'cooperative' federalism. Some of the most important ones are listed below:

- NITI Aayog for cooperation between the Centre and the States formed in 2015 (replacing the erstwhile Planning Commission).
- GST Council which is a constitutional body formed in 2017.
- Inter-State Council which is a constitutional body formed in 1990.
- Zonal Councils which are statutory bodies.

THINK ABOUT IT

The aim of the governments at the Centre and States should be to move towards co-operative and competitive federalism by shunning confrontation. Discuss the issues that plague Centre-State relations and measures to achieve co-operation.

Apart from the above, there is also a thrust towards 'competitive federalism'. NITI Aayog endeavours to promote competitive federalism amongst various States and Union Territories to improve their performance in various fields of governance. This is done through transparent rankings in various sectors that enables healthy competition. Some of the examples of such indices launched by the NITI Aayog and the Central Government ministries include State Health index, Composite Water Management index, Good Governance index, Sustainable Development Goals index, Export Competitiveness index, India Innovation Index etc.

19.6 INTER-STATE RELATIONS

Since the States, in every federation, normally act as independent units in the exercise of their internal autonomy, conflicts of interest between the States are sure to arise. Hence, in order to maintain the strength of the Union, it is essential that there should be an adequate provision for (a) judicial determination of disputes between the States; (b) settlement of disputes by extra-judicial bodies; and (c) their prevention by consultation and joint action. The provisions relating to the Inter-State relations in the Constitution can be studied under these three categories as summarised below.

Judicial Determination	Extra-judicial Tribunal	Consultation
Original jurisdiction of the Supreme Court under Article 131 for settling any disputes between two or more States.	For settling any river water dispute between two or more States under Article 262.	• Inter-State Council [Art 263] • Zonal Councils

We have already discussed about the 'Original Jurisdiction' of the Supreme Court, which is the judicial mechanism for settling disputes between two or more States. Let us discuss about the other two mechanisms for settling river water disputes as well as cooperation amongst the States.

19.6.1 Inter-State River Water Disputes and Tribunals

India has many rivers that flow across various States. Under the Seventh Schedule to the Constitution, while 'Water and its storage' is a subject in the State list (entry 17 of the State list), it is subject to entry 56 in the Union list that deals with 'Regulation and development of inter-State rivers and river valleys by the Parliamentary law in public interest'.

Article 262 of the Constitution empowers the Parliament to enact a law that provides for adjudication of any dispute with respect to the use, distribution or control of waters in any inter-State river or river valley. Considering the sensitive nature of such disputes and the technical aspects that may be involved in their resolution, the Constitution further provides that the Parliament by law can exclude the jurisdiction of the Supreme Court or any other court in such disputes.

The Inter-State River Water Disputes Act, 1956 (IRWD Act) is an Act of the Parliament enacted under Article 262 of the Constitution, on the eve of reorganisation of States on linguistic basis, to resolve the water disputes that would arise in the use, control and distribution of an inter-State river or river valley.

The key provisions of this IRWD Act, 1956 are as follows:

(1) Under the 1956 Act, when a complaint is received from a State government regarding a water dispute, the central government may ask the affected States to undertake negotiations to settle the dispute. If the dispute cannot be settled through negotiations, the central government must set up a Water Disputes Tribunal within a year of receiving such a complaint.

(2) Water Disputes Tribunal must give its decision on a dispute within a period of 3 years. This period is extendable by a maximum of 2 years.

(3) If the decision is again referred to the Tribunal by a State for further consideration, the Tribunal must submit its report to the central government within a period of 1 year. This period of 1 year can be extended by the central government for such a period as it may consider necessary.

(4) The decision of the Tribunal must be published by the central government in the official gazette. After publication, the decision has the same force as that of an order of the Supreme Court.

List of tribunals set up under this Act are as follows:

S.No.	Name	Year	States Involved	Status as of 2024
1	Krishna Water Disputes Tribunal – I	1969	Maharashtra, Karnataka and Andhra Pradesh	Closed
2	Godavari Water Disputes Tribunal	1969	Maharashtra, Karnataka, Andhra Pradesh, Madhya Pradesh and Odisha	Closed
3	Narmada Water Disputes Tribunal	1969	Rajasthan, Gujarat, Madhya Pradesh and Maharashtra	Closed
4	Ravi and Beas Water Disputes Tribunal	1986	Punjab, Haryana and Rajasthan	Active
5	Cauvery Water Disputes Tribunal	1990	Karnataka, Kerala, Tamil Nadu and Puducherry	Closed
6	Krishna Water Disputes Tribunal – II	2004	Maharashtra, Karnataka, Telangana and Andhra Pradesh	Active
7	Vansadhara Water Disputes Tribunal	2010	Odisha and Andhra Pradesh	Closed
8	Mahadayi Water Disputes Tribunal	2010	Goa, Karnataka and Maharashtra	Active
9	Mahanadi Water Disputes Tribunal	2018	Odisha and Chhattisgarh	Active

The jurisdiction of the Supreme Court has been excluded by Section 11 of the Act for any such dispute referred to a tribunal. It must, however, be noted that the Supreme Court had allowed appeal against the order of Cauvery River Water Tribunal under its appellate jurisdiction (Article 136). It also passed final orders in this case in 2018. Similarly, the award of Vansadhara water disputes tribunal has been challenged in the Supreme Court in 2019 and is sub-judice as on date (2024). In respect of other disputes as well, various State governments have filed appeals in the Supreme Court at different points of time.

The Central government had introduced an amendment bill to the IRWD Act in the year 2019. This bill proposed the constitution of one single tribunal for all disputes and setting up separate benches within the tribunal for individual disputes. It also proposed reduction in timelines for grant of awards by the tribunal. However, with the dissolution of the 17th Lok Sabha in June 2024, this bill has lapsed.

19.6.2 Consultative Process for Inter-State Relations

19.6.2.1 Inter-State Council

Article 263 of the Constitution provides that the President can set up an Inter-State Council in public interest for effective coordination amongst the States and between the Centre and the States. The duties that can be assigned to the Council as per the provisions of Article 263 are as follows:

- inquiring into and advising upon disputes which may have arisen between States;
- investigating and discussing subjects in which some or all of the States, or the Union and one or more of the States, have a common interest; or
- making recommendations upon any such subject and, in particular, recommendations for the better coordination of policy and action with respect to that subject.

The 1st ARC and the Sarkaria Commission had recommended the setting up of the Inter-State Council. The Inter-State Council was finally set up vide the Presidential Order dated 28 May 1990. The composition of the Inter-State Council as set out in the above-mentioned Presidential Order included the Prime Minister, the Chief Ministers of all States, the Chief Ministers of Union territories having Legislative Assemblies and Administrators of Union territories not having Legislative Assemblies, Governors of States under President's Rule, six Ministers of Cabinet rank in the Union Council of Ministers to be nominated by the Prime Minister and two Ministers of Cabinet rank in the Union Council of Ministers to be nominated by the Prime Minister as permanent invitees.

THINK ABOUT IT

The Inter-State Council is an important constitutional body that has been given scant importance. Comment. What steps have been taken recently by the Central government to revitalise this body?

The duties of the Council are:

1. To investigate and discuss subjects of common interest;
2. Make recommendations for the better coordination of policy and actions on such subjects; and
3. Deliberate on such matters of general interest to the States as may be referred by the Chairman.

Working of Inter-State Council

While the Council has been established in 1990 with a mandate that it may meet at least 3 times a year, it has met only 12 times since inception (as of 2022). The Inter-State Council has not been effective in addressing the issues between

Scan the QR code for conceptual video on Trends in Centre-State relations and Inter-State relations

Mc Graw Hill edge

various States. This is due to lack of political importance given to this Constitutional body when compared to the executive bodies like the erstwhile Planning Commission or the present NITI Aayog. However, considering its constitutional status, it can be effectively utilised along with bodies like the NITI Aayog for resolving various issues between States and between the Centre and the States.

In May 2022, the Central Government had reconstituted the composition of the Inter-State Council as follows:

- Prime Minister as Chairman
- Chief Ministers of all States and Union Territories with Legislative Assembly; administrators of the Union Territories not having a Legislative Assembly; six Union ministers as members.
- Ten Union ministers will be permanent invitees to the Council.
- Standing Committee of the Inter-State Council with Union Home Minister as Chairman, some union ministers and Chief Ministers of certain States as members.
- The Standing Committee will perform the following functions:
    - Continuous consultation and process matters for consideration of the Council, process all matters pertaining to the Centre–State relations before they are taken up for consideration in the Inter-State Council;
    - Monitor implementation of the decisions taken on the recommendation of the Council;
    - Invite experts and persons eminent in specific fields to have the benefit of their views while deliberating on the related subjects.

19.6.2.2 Zonal Council

- Zonal Councils have been established by the States Reorganisation Act, 1956 to advise on matters of common interest to each of the five zones into which the territory of India has been divided – Northern, Southern, Eastern, Western and Central.
- Each Zonal Council consists of the Chief Minister and two other ministers of each of the States in the zone and the administrator in the case of a Union Territory. The Union Home minister has been nominated to be the common chairman of all the Zonal Councils.
- These Zonal Councils owe their origin to an Act of the Parliament, having been introduced by the States Reorganisation Act, with a view to securing cooperation and coordination as between the States, the Union Territories and the Union, particularly in respect of economic and social development.
- If properly worked, these Councils could foster the federal sentiment by resisting the separatist tendencies based on language and regionalism.

The zones covered by these Councils are as follows:

- The Central Zone, comprising the States of Uttar Pradesh, Uttarakhand, Madhya Pradesh and Chhattisgarh. (Headquarters – Prayagraj)
- The Northern Zone, comprising the States of Haryana, Himachal Pradesh, Punjab, Rajasthan, and the Union Territories of Delhi, Chandigarh, Jammu & Kashmir and Ladakh. (Headquarters – New Delhi)
- The Eastern Zone, comprising the States of Bihar, Jharkhand, West Bengal and Odisha. (Headquarters – Kolkata)
- The Western Zone, comprising the States of Gujarat, Maharashtra, Goa and the Union Territory of Dadra & Nagar Haveli and Daman & Diu. (Headquarters – Mumbai)
- The Southern Zone, comprising the States of Andhra Pradesh, Telangana, Karnataka, Kerala, Tamil Nadu and the Union Territory of Puducherry. (Headquaters – Chennai)

- Besides these, there is the North-Eastern Council set up in 1971, to deal with Assam, Meghalaya, Manipur, Nagaland, Tripura, Arunachal Pradesh, Mizoram and Sikkim. The Home Minister is the ex-officio chairperson of this North-Eastern Council. The members consist of Governor of the constituent States, Chief Ministers of the States and 3 members to be nominated by the President.

The Zonal Councils discuss matters of common concern to the States and the Union Territories in each Zone, such as, economic and social planning, border disputes, inter-State transport, matters arising out of the re-organisation of States and the like and give advice to the Governments of the States concerned as well as the Government of India.

MAINS STARTER

Area	Building Blocks For Model Introductions
Centre-State relations	India is a federal country, and federalism has been declared as a basic structure of our Constitution in S R Bommai case. The Constitution provides for relations between Centre and State on legislative, administrative and financial matters. Though there are unitary features in this distribution, the aim is to foster co-operative federalism.
Centre-State legislative relations	The Constitution contains the scheme under the Seventh Schedule for distribution of legislative subjects between the Centre and States. The Parliament's power is larger when compared to the States under this scheme of distribution. (Articles 246–254)
Centre-State administrative relations	The Constitution provides for the relations between the Union government and State governments. It includes the Union government's power to issue instructions for specific matters as well as mutual entrustment of functions between the Centre and the States. (Articles 256–258)
Centre-State financial relations	The scheme for distribution of tax proceeds between Centre and States forms the most important aspect of their financial relations. Apart from this, it also includes grants-in-aid from Centre to States as well as provisions for borrowings by the Centre and the States. (Articles 264–293)
Co-operative federalism	While the Constitution contains 'unitary' bias that provides more powers to the Centre, federal principles are equally important and part of the basic structure. The aim is to foster co-operative federalism through institutions like NITI Aayog, GST council, Inter-State council and Zonal councils.
Competitive federalism	Various rankings released by NITI Aayog and ministries aim at instilling competitive federalism amongst various States. This would help in the development of various States that strive to improve their performance, thereby contributing to the development of the country as a whole.
Inter-State relations	The Constitution provides the mechanism for Inter-State relations through judicial determination of disputes, extra-judicial determination of inter-State river water disputes by tribunals, and consultative process through Inter-State council.

UPSC Previous Years' Questions of Preliminary Examination

1. Which one of the following statements is correct as per the Constitution of India? **[2024]**
(a) Inter-State trade and commerce is a State subject under the State List
(b) Inter-State migration is a State subject under the State List
(c) Inter-State quarantine is a Union subject under the Union List
(d) Corporation tax is a State subject under the State List

Solution: (c)

Explanation: Inter-State quarantine is a Union subject under entry 81 of the Union list and hence the answer is (c). The other 2 inter-state matters are also under Union list (entries 42 and 81) and Corporation tax is also under Union list (entry 85).

2. The North Eastern Council (NEC) was established by the North Eastern Council Act, 1971. Subsequent to the amendment of NEC Act in 2002, the council comprises which of the following members? **[2024]**
1. Governor of the Constituent State
2. Chief Minister of the Constituent State
3. Three Members to be nominated by the President of India
4. The Home Minister of India

Select the correct answer using the code given below:
(a) 1, 2 and 3 only
(b) 1, 3 and 4 only
(c) 2 and 4 only
(d) 1, 2, 3 and 4

Solution: (a)

Explanation: As per the amendment to the NEC Act in 2002, the North Eastern Council consists of Governor of the constituent States, Chief Ministers of the States and 3 members to be nominated by the President. For other 5 Zonal councils that have been formed as per the States reorganisation Act, 1956, Home Minister is a member and Chairman of these councils. However, the Home Minister is not a member of North Eastern Council though he/she is the ex-officio chairperson. Hence, by eliminating point 4, the answer can be arrived at which is (a).

UPSC Previous Years' Questions of Main Examination

1. What changes has the Union Government recently introduced in the domain of Centre-State relations? Suggest measures to be adopted to build the trust between the Centre and the States and for strengthening federalism. **[2024]**

Approach: The federal features of the Indian constitution can be the introduction to the answer. Then the various steps taken by the Union government in recent years to strengthen Centre-State relations need to be listed. The issues surrounding Centre-State relations and suggestions from the Sarkaria and Punchhi commissions can be the second part of the answer.

MODEL ANSWER

India is a federal country with dual governments at the Centre and States for which the powers are distributed as per the Constitution. Federalism has been declared as a 'basic structure' of the Constitution by the Supreme Court in S R Bommai case.

Recent initiatives of Union government for Centre-State relations

There are various initiatives that have been taken towards achieving 'co-operative' federalism. Some of the most important ones are listed below:

(a) NITI Aayog for co-operation between the centre and the states formed in 2015 (replacing the erstwhile Planning Commission). NITI Aayog endeavours to promote co-operative federalism amongst various states and union territories to improve their performance in various fields of governance.

(b) There is also a thrust towards 'competitive federalism.' This is done through transparent rankings in various sectors that enables healthy competition. Some of the examples of such indices launched by NITI Aayog and Central Government ministries include State Health index, Composite Water Management index, Good Governance index, Sustainable Development Goals index, Export Competitiveness index, etc.

(c) GST council which is a constitutional body formed in 2017.

(d) Inter-State council which is a constitutional body formed in 1990 and has been recently reconstituted in 2022.

(e) Zonal councils which are statutory bodies for cooperation amongst the states in 6 zones of the country.

Issues and Suggestions for improvement

(a) There are also confrontations between centre and States on various issues like appointment of Governors, legislating on matters in the concurrent list (like the recently enacted and subsequently repealed farm laws), etc.

(b) Similarly, there are inter-State river water disputes as well as border disputes between various States. These affect the federal character and also the unity of the nation.

(c) The recommendations of the Sarkaria Commission and Punchhi Commission with respect to the appointment of governors in consultation with Chief Minister, consultation with States before enactment of laws in the concurrent list, etc. can be followed to avoid such confrontation.

(d) There have also been issues with respect to devolution of finances by the Finance Commission. This can be addressed by reducing the cess and surcharge levied by Central government and thereby increasing the divisible pool of tax proceeds.

(e) The aim should be to avoid confrontation and foster co-operative and competitive federalism that can result in the overall growth of the Nation and our States.

2. Explain the significance of the 101st Constitutional Amendment Act. To what extent does it reflect the accommodative spirit of federalism? **[2023]**

Approach: Discuss the significant provisions of GST amendment as given in Section 19.4.1. Then the discussion on GST council as a classic example of co-operative federalism.

MODEL ANSWER

The 101st constitutional amendment is the Goods and Services Tax (GST) amendment that is aimed at ushering in a uniform tax rate and structure for the entire country.

Significance of GST Amendment

1. The GST was introduced to subsume (include or absorb) various indirect taxes levied by the Centre as well the States. This was done in order to avoid cascading effect of taxes, i.e., taxes being levied on taxes, and to create a national market for goods and services with uniform taxes.
   - The important indirect taxes levied by the Centre that were subsumed into GST include (i) Excise duty (ii) Customs duty (iii) Service tax (iv) Central Sales tax, etc.
   - The important indirect taxes levied by the States that were subsumed into GST include (i) Value added taxes or State sales tax (ii) Octroi and entry tax (iii) Entertainment tax, etc.
2. GST is a 'destination-based tax' rather than the earlier system of sales tax that was an 'origination-based tax.' This is to ensure that there is no cascading effect of taxes as goods and services may have multiple movements from origination, but finally will have one destination where they are consumed. Also, it is based on the principle of equity as the tax revenues are assigned to the state where the demand for the goods or services has been created.

GST Council & Co-operative federalism

Every decision of the council has to be taken by a majority of not less than three-fourths of the weighted votes of the members present.

- The vote of the central government has a weightage of one-third of the total votes cast, and
- The votes of all the state governments together have a weightage of two-thirds of the total votes cast.

Therefore, the GST council is hailed as a classic example for co-operative federalism since neither the centre nor all States can take any decision unilaterally.

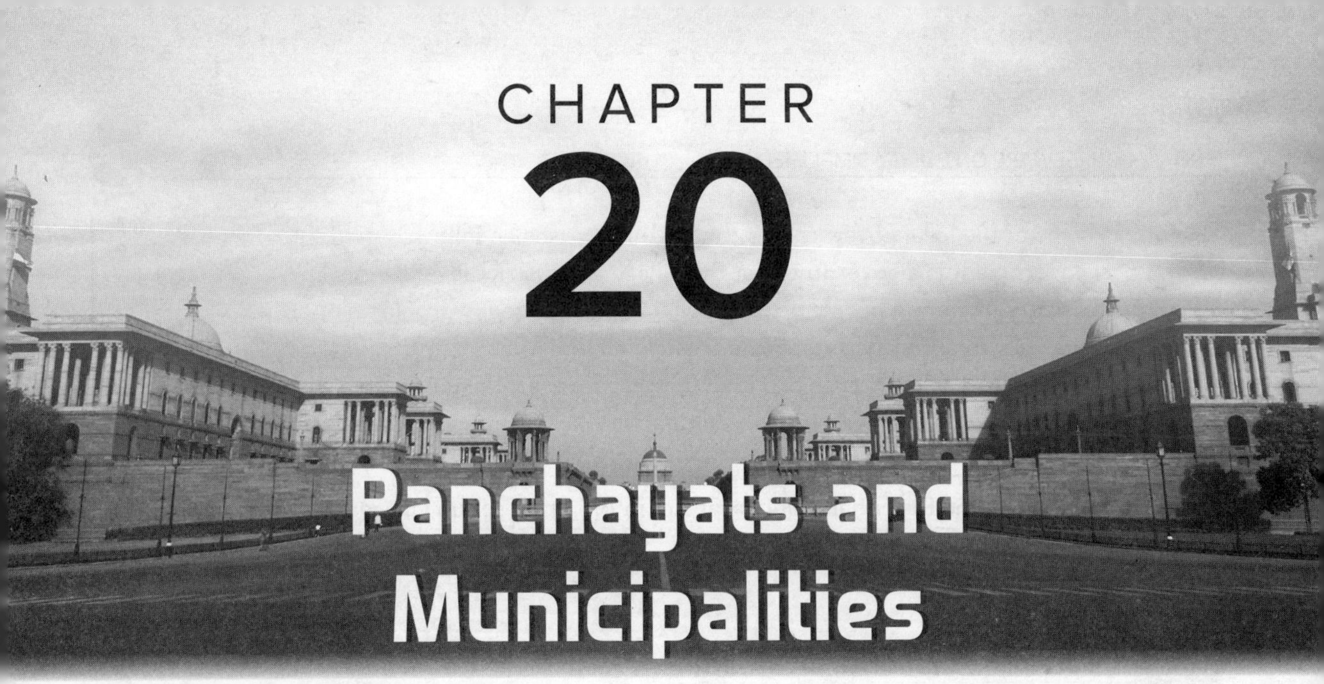

CHAPTER 20

Panchayats and Municipalities

LEARNING OUTCOMES

1. Tracing the evolution of Panchayati Raj Institutions in independent India
2. Explaining the key provisions of the 73rd Constitutional Amendment for Panchayats – composition, power, finance and elections
3. Understanding the essential features of Panchayat (Extension to Scheduled Areas) Act, 1996 and Gram Nyayalayas Act, 2008
4. Comparing the 74th Constitutional Amendment for Municipalities with the 73rd Amendment in terms of composition, powers, finances, and elections, along with the role of District and Metropolitan Planning Committees
5. Analysing the achievements, key issues and potential solutions for strengthening local government bodies

The passage of the Constitution (73rd Amendment) Act, 1992 marks a new era in the democratic setup of the country. It added Panchayats under Part IX in the Constitution of India and accorded them a Constitutional status as institutions of local self-government for rural India. It also added the Eleventh Schedule to the Constitution that contains 29 functional items for the Panchayats.

In this chapter, we shall discuss first about the evolution of the Panchayati Raj system followed by the constitutional provisions with respect to composition and functioning of the Panchayati Raj institutions. Similar to panchayats for rural India, the municipalities are local self-government institutions for urban India. The provisions with respect to composition and functioning of the municipalities is similar to the panchayats with few differences. We shall summarise the similarities in a tabular form (like similarities between the Union and the State executive, the Union Parliament and the State Legislature) and discuss the area of differences. Finally, we shall discuss the issues surrounding the functioning of these local self-government institutions and steps to be taken to improve their performance.

20.1 EVOLUTION OF PANCHAYATI RAJ INSTITUTIONS (PRI)

Article 40 of the Constitution provided a directive to the State to organise village panchayats and endow them with such powers and authority as may be necessary to enable them to function as units of self-government.

The importance of the local governments can be summarised as follows:

- Local government is a government at the village and district level.
- It is closest to common people as it involves the day-to-today problems of ordinary citizens.
- It is necessary for efficient and people-friendly administration.
- It believes that local knowledge and local interest are essential for democratic decision making.
- Strong local governments also ensure both active participation and purposeful accountability.

Starting from 1950s, various States started enacting laws for the setting up of PRIs in their respective States. It started with the Rajasthan Panchayat Act in 1953 that set up village panchayats throughout the State of Rajasthan. The Central government had set up various committees from time to time to recommend on setting up of PRIs. The key committees and their recommendations are discussed below.

20.1.1 Balwant Rai Mehta Committee

Initially, the Government of India had started Community Development Programme in 1952. The major aim of this programme was to bring an integrated development in the rural society that covers social and economic aspects of the lives of people. Under this programme, the districts in the country were divided into blocks for effective implementation and monitoring. Subsequently, in 1953 the National Extension Service programme was launched with an idea of having a wider coverage at lesser cost and more peoples' participation. Both these programmes were in the nature of bureaucratic decentralisation.

The Balwant Rai Mehta Committee was a committee appointed by the Government of India in January 1957 to examine the working of the Community Development Programme (1952) and the National Extension Service (1953) and to suggest measures for their better working. The committee submitted its report in November 1957. It recommended the establishment of the scheme of 'democratic decentralisation' which finally came to be known as Panchayati Raj.

Recommendations of the Balwant Rai Mehta Committee

- Establishment of a three-tier Panchayati Raj System – Gram Panchayat at the village level, Panchayat Samiti at the block level and Zila Parishad at the district level.
- The Village Panchayat should be constituted with directly elected representatives, whereas the Panchayat Samiti and Zila Parishad should be constituted with indirectly elected members.
- All planning and developmental activities should be entrusted to these bodies. The Panchayat Samiti should be the executive body while the Zila Parishad should be the advisory, coordinating and supervisory body.
- The District Collector should be the Chairman of the Zila Parishad.
- There should be a genuine transfer of power and responsibility to these democratic bodies.

These recommendations were accepted by the National Development Council in January 1958.

20.1.2 Ashok Mehta Committee

This Committee was appointed by the Janata Party government in 1977 to revive the declining Panchayati Raj institutions in the country. The key recommendations of this committee were as follows:

- The three-tier system of Panchayati Raj should be replaced by the two-tier system – Zila Parishad at the district level, and below it, the Mandal Panchayat.
- A district should be the first point for decentralisation under popular supervision below the State.
- Zila Parishad should see an official participation of political parties at all levels of Panchayat elections. Seats for the SCs and the STs should be reserved based on their population.
- The Panchayai Raj institutions should have compulsory powers of taxation to mobilise their own financial resources.
- The Nyaya Panchayats should be kept as separate bodies from that of development Panchayats. They should be presided over by a qualified judge.
- The Chief Electoral Officer of the State in consultation with the Chief Election Commissioner should organise and conduct the Panchayati Raj elections. Development functions should be transferred to the Zila Parishad and all development staff should work under its control and supervision.
- A minister for Panchayati Raj should be appointed in the State Council of Ministers to look after the affairs of the Panchayati Raj institutions.

However, due to the fall of Janata Government in 1979, no action was taken on the Ashok Mehta Committee recommendations.

20.1.3 G. V. K. Rao Committee

The G. V. K. Rao Committee was appointed by the Planning Commission to look at various aspects of PRIs once again in 1985. The key recommendations of the Committee were as follows:

- PRIs must play a central role in handling people's problems.
- A post of District Development Commissioner should be created who will act as CEO of Zila Parishad.
- PRIs must be activated and provided with all the required support to become effective organisations.
- PRIs at district level and below should be assigned the work of planning, implementation and monitoring of rural development programmes.

20.1.4 L. M. Singhvi Committee

This committee was appointed in 1986 by the Central government to prepare a concept paper on 'Revitalisation of Panchayati Raj for Democracy and Development'. The key recommendations of the committee were as follows:

- Local self-government should be constitutionally recognised, protected and preserved by the inclusion of a new chapter in the Constitution.
- Nyaya panchayats to be established for a cluster of villages.
- It emphasised the importance of Gram Sabha that would be a reflection of direct democracy.
- The village panchayats should have more financial powers.

Subsequently, Thungon Committee and Gadgil Committee were also constituted in 1988 that gave recommendations for strengthening the Panchayati Raj system. These committees recommended for constitutional recognition of PRIs, fixed tenure of 5 years, reservation for SC, ST and women, establishment of State Election Commission and State Finance Commission, etc.

20.1.5 Constitutional Status for Panchayats

64th and 65th Amendment Bills

Late Prime Minister Rajiv Gandhi, introduced the 64th Constitutional Amendment Bill in 1989 to provide constitutional status to PRIs (65th Amendment Bill was for Municipalities). The 64th Amendment Bill was passed in the Lok Sabha, but it got defeated in the Rajya Sabha. The opposition parties felt that the provisions of the bill would result in more centralisation bypassing the State Legislatures.

73rd and 74th Amendment

Finally, the Constitutional (73rd Amendment) Act, was passed in 1992 by the Narasimha Rao government, that came into force on 24 April 1993 (the 74th Amendment was for Municipalities). The aim of the amendment was to provide constitutional sanction to establish 'democracy at the grassroots level as it is at the State level or National level'. It added Part IX to the Constitution consisting of Article 243 to Article 243-O.

The main features of the Panchayati Raj institutions as per Part IX is summarised below in tabular form. The details will be discussed in the subsequent sections.

Key Feature	Provisions under Part IX
Constitution [Art 243B]	• A three-tier system of Panchayati Raj for all States having population of over 20 lakhs i.e., village level, intermediate level and district level. • In States having population less than 20 lakhs, intermediate level may not be constituted.
Composition [Art 243C]	• All seats in all the three-tiers to be filled by persons chosen by direct election. • Chairperson of village panchayat shall be elected in direct or indirect manner as provided by the State law. • Chairperson of intermediate and district level shall be elected indirectly from amongst the elected members.
Reservation [Art 243D]	• Reservation for SCs and STs (in seats and chairpersons) in proportion to their population at each tier (1/3rd of the same to be reserved for women). • Out of the total number of seats to be filled by the direct elections and chairpersons, minimum 1/3rd must be reserved for women. • State legislature can additionally provide reservation in favour of the backward classes in seats or offices of Chairpersons of Panchayats.
Duration [Art 243E]	• Panchayats will have duration of 5 years. • If earlier dissolved, elections to be held within 6 months and the newly constituted Panchayat will serve for the remainder of the term.
Qualification and Disqualification [Art 243F]	• A person shall have the same disqualifications that is applicable for a member of the State Legislature. However, age requirement for being a member of Panchayat is 21. • State legislature can provide any additional grounds for disqualification.
Powers and responsibilities [Art 243G]	• State legislature may endow the Panchayats with such powers as may be necessary to enable them to function as institutions of self-government.

Key Feature	Provisions under Part IX
Finance for Panchayats [Art 243H]	• State legislature may authorise panchayats to levy and collect taxes, assign taxes collected by the State government to panchayats and provide grants-in-aid to panchayats.
State Finance Commission [Art 243 I]	• State Finance Commission is constituted every 5 years for making recommendations with respect to distribution of revenues between the State government and the panchayats.
State Election Commission [Art 243K]	• Elections to Panchayats are conducted by the State Election Commission in each State consisting of the State Election Commissioner. • The State Election Commissioner is appointed by the Governor but can be removed only by the Parliament like a Judge of a High Court.

20.2 PRIs – COMPOSITION, POWERS, FINANCES AND ELECTIONS

20.2.1 Composition of Panchayats

The Gram Sabha would consist of all the persons registered as voters in a Village Panchayat area [Art 243]. Its powers and functions are decided by law made by the State Legislature [Art 243A]. The Gram Sabha is a body that takes decisions through direct participation of all voters in the village panchayat area and reflects direct democracy at the grass root level.

The three-tier PRI system is representative democracy. It is a mechanism for local self-government through democratic decentralisation.

Constitution and Composition

All States now have a uniform three-tier Panchayati Raj structure as explained below [Art 243B]:

- At the base is the 'Gram Panchayat'. A Gram Panchayat covers a village or group of villages.
- The intermediary level is the Mandal. These bodies are called by different names in different States like Mandal or Taluka Panchayats or Panchayat unions. The intermediary level body may not be constituted in smaller States with population less than 20 lakhs.
- At the apex is the District Panchayat (also known as Zila Panchayat) covering the entire rural area of the district.

The composition of Panchayats shall be as follows [Art 243C]:

- The State Legislature may make laws for composition of panchayats by dividing the panchayat areas at all three levels into territorial constituencies. This is done through Delimitation Commissions set up at the State level by a law of the State Legislature.
- All the seats at all levels of panchayat shall be filled through direct election by the eligible voters.
- Additionally, the State Legislature may, by law, provide for representation of Members of Parliament and Members of the State Legislature at intermediate and district level of panchayats.
- The Chairperson of Panchayat at village level shall be elected in such manner as provided in the State law. For example, the Chairperson of Village Panchayat in States like Assam, Bihar, Andhra Pradesh, Tamil Nadu etc., are elected directly by the people. In States like Karnataka,

Kerala, West Bengal etc., they are elected indirectly from amongst the elected members of the Panchayat.

- The Chairperson of Panchayat at intermediate and district level in all the States, shall be elected indirectly from amongst the elected members of the respective panchayats as per the Constitution.

Reservation of Seats

Article 243D provides for reservation in panchayat seats at all levels as follows:

- Reservation for the SCs and the STs (in seats for members) in proportion to their population at each level (1/3rd of the same to be reserved for women).
- Out of the total number of seats to be filled by the direct elections, minimum 1/3rd must be reserved for women.
- Reservation for the SC and the ST in proportion to their population and minimum 1/3rd for women (including 1/3rd for the SC and the ST women) in the post of Chairpersons.
    - As of 2024, 21 States and 2 Union Territories have provided 50% reservation for women in PRIs.
- State legislature can additionally provide reservation in favour of the backward classes.
    - States like Maharashtra and Madhya Pradesh have provided reservation for Backward Classes (BC) in their State's PRIs.
    - The Supreme Court has allowed such reservations for BCs subject to the 'Triple-Test' being satisfied.
    - The Triple-Test Formula, laid down by the Supreme Court in 2010 (in ***Krishnamoorthy Vs Union of India case***) and later reiterated in March 2021 (in ***Vikas Kishanrao Gawali*** case), required the States to
        a. appoint a dedicated commission to conduct rigorous inquiry into the nature of backwardness and collecting quantifiable data,
        b. making recommendations by the commission on the number of seats to be reserved for BCs, and
        c. ensuring total reservation for the SC, the ST and the BC does not exceed 50%.

Duration

According to Article 243E, duration of panchayats is as follows:

- Every panchayat, unless sooner dissolved, shall have a term of 5 years from the date appointed for its first meeting.
- An election to constitute a Panchayat shall be completed before the expiry of 5 years or before expiration of 6 months from the date of its dissolution.
- A panchayat constituted upon dissolution of a panchayat before the expiration of its duration shall continue only for the remainder of the period. For example, if a panchayat is dissolved within 2 years and fresh elections are held immediately, it will continue only for balance 3 years.

Disqualification

According to Article 243F, the qualification and disqualification criteria for becoming a member of a Panchayat is as follows:

- A person shall have the same disqualifications that is applicable for the purpose of election as a member of the State Legislature.
- However, age requirement for being a member of Panchayat is 21 (and not 25 as required for Legislative Assembly of a State).

- State legislature can provide any additional grounds for disqualification.

20.2.2 Powers and Finances of Panchayats

Powers, authority and responsibilities

The powers, authority and responsibilities of PRIs can be summarised as follows [Art 243G]:

- State legislature may, by law, endow (provide) the Panchayats with such powers and authority as may be necessary to enable them to function as institutions of self-government.
- Such a law may contain provisions for devolution of powers and responsibilities upon Panchayats at appropriate level (i.e., village, intermediate or district) with respect to
  - The preparation of plans for economic development and social justice;
  - The implementation of schemes for economic development and social justice as may be entrusted to them including those in relation to the matters listed in the Eleventh Schedule.

The Eleventh Schedule to the Constitution was added by the 73rd Constitutional Amendment. This Schedule consists of 29 items that include (a) Agriculture, (b) Animal husbandry, dairying and poultry, (c) Fisheries, (d) Khadi, village and cottage industries, (e) Rural housing, (f) Drinking water, (g) Maintenance of community assets, (h) Markets and fairs etc. The PRIs may be provided with powers and responsibilities at the appropriate level for the purpose of preparation and implementation of schemes with respect to these areas.

Financial powers

The financial powers of PRIs can be summarised as follows [Art 243-H]:

The State Legislatures have been empowered to enact laws:

(i) to authorise a Panchayat to levy, collect and appropriate certain taxes, duties, tolls and fees;

(ii) to assign to the Panchayat, certain taxes, duties, tolls that are levied and collected by the State Government;

(iii) to provide for making grants-in-aid to the Panchayats from the Consolidated Fund of the State; and

(iv) to provide for the Constitution of such funds for Panchayats for crediting all money received by or on behalf of Panchayats and the withdrawal of such moneys.

> **THINK ABOUT IT**
>
> The key aspect in empowering panchayats is to endow them with adequate power and finance. Explain the constitutional provisions in this regard and the challenges faced with respect to this aspect. What can be done to improve the situation?

State Finance Commission

Similar to Finance Commission constituted once every 5 years under Article 280 for making recommendations with respect to distribution of revenues between the Union and the States, Article 243-I requires the Constitution of a State Finance Commission once every 5 years for making recommendations with respect to distribution of revenues between the States and the local self-government institutions – i.e., Panchayats and Municipalities.

The State Finance Commission is constituted by the Governor of a State. State law may provide for the composition of the commission and qualification of its members. The Commission shall make recommendations as to the following:

(a) the principles which should govern
  (i) the distribution between the State and the Panchayats of the net proceeds of the taxes, duties, tolls and fees leviable by the State, which may be divided between them (vertical devolution) and the allocation between the Panchayats at all levels of their respective shares of such proceeds (horizontal devolution);
  (ii) the determination of the taxes, duties, tolls and fees which may be assigned to, or appropriated by, the Panchayats;
  (iii) the grants-in-aid to the Panchayats from the Consolidated Fund of the State;

(b) the measures needed to improve the financial position of the Panchayats;

(c) any other matter referred to the Finance Commission by the Governor in the interests of sound finance of the Panchayats.

The report of the State Finance Commission shall be submitted to the Governor, who shall cause every recommendation made by the Commission together with an explanatory memorandum as to the action taken thereon to be laid before the State Legislature.

20.2.3 Elections to Panchayats

State Election Commission

Article 243K provides for the Constitution of a State Election Commission in each State with a State Election Commissioner for conduct of elections to the Panchayats. The key provisions with respect to the same are as follows:

- The superintendence, direction and control of the preparation of electoral rolls and the conduct of all elections to the panchayats is vested in the State Election Commission consisting of State Election Commissioner (SEC) who is appointed by the Governor.
- The conditions of service and tenure of SEC is determined by the Governor subject to any law of the State Legislature.
- The SEC shall not be removed from his/her office except in like manner and on the like grounds as a Judge of the High Court and the conditions of his/her service shall not be varied to his/her disadvantage after his/her appointment.
- Thus, the SEC has the same protection with respect to removal like the CEC i.e., he/she can be removed only by the Parliament. However, the State Election Commissioner is an independent office and is not under the control of the Election Commission of India.
- The Governor of the State shall provide such staff as may be necessary for the SEC to discharge its functions.

Further, there is bar on interference by the courts in electoral matters relating to Panchayats [Art 243-O]:

- Any law relating to the delimitation of constituencies shall not be called into question in a court of law.
- Any question relating to election to any Panchayat shall be called into question only through an election petition before an appropriate authority as provided in any law made by the State

Legislature – usually the State laws provide that such election petitions can be filed with the High Court having jurisdiction over the State.

20.2.4 Miscellaneous Provisions

- The Legislature of a State may, by law, make provisions with respect to the maintenance of accounts by the Panchayats and the auditing of such accounts [Art 243J].
- Provisions of Part IX are applicable to the Union Territories as they are applicable to States. However, the President may specify that the provisions shall be applicable to any Union Territory subject to such modifications and exceptions [Art 243L].
- The provisions of Part IX are not applicable to States of Nagaland, Meghalaya, Mizoram; Scheduled and Tribal areas in various States; hill areas in Manipur and Darjeeling district in West Bengal.
- The Parliament may by law extend the provisions of Part IX to Scheduled and Tribal areas referred to in the Fifth and the Sixth Schedules of the Constitution respectively. The Parliament has enacted 'Panchayat (Extension to Scheduled Areas) Act, 1996' or PESA Act, 1996 that extends the provisions of Part IX to Scheduled areas under the Fifth Schedule.

Thus, Part IX creates certain compulsory provisions for the States that includes organising Gram sabha at the village level; constitution of 3-tier panchayats; elections every 5 years for these panchayats; reservation of seats for SC, ST and women; constitution of State Election Commission and State Finance Commission.

It also provides for certain voluntary provisions which includes extent of powers to be endowed on Gram Sabha and panchayats; giving representation to members of State legislature and MPs in intermediate and district panchayats; reservation of seats for OBCs in panchayats; extent of financial powers to be devolved on panchyats.

20.2.5 Panchayat (Extension to Scheduled Areas) Act or PESA Act, 1996

The provisions of Part IX are not applicable to the Scheduled areas under the Fifth Schedule and Tribal areas under the Sixth Schedule. However, the Parliament may by law extend the provisions of Part IX to these areas subject to such modifications and exceptions.

The Parliament has enacted 'Panchayat (Extension to Scheduled Areas) Act, 1996' or PESA Act, 1996 that extends the provisions of Part IX to Scheduled areas under the Fifth Schedule.

The Fifth Schedule of the Constitution deals with the administration and control of Scheduled Areas as well as of Scheduled Tribes residing in any State other than the States of Assam, Meghalaya, Tripura and Mizoram. At present, the Fifth Schedule areas exist in 10 States i.e., Andhra Pradesh, Chhattisgarh, Gujarat, Himachal Pradesh, Jharkhand, Madhya Pradesh, Maharashtra, Odisha, Rajasthan and Telangana.

The following points must be noted in this regard:

- The Scheduled Areas in these various States were mainly the 'Partially-Excluded' areas during the British rule under the Government of India Act, 1935. These tribal pockets had their own unique culture, dispute redressal mechanism, economic activity based on forest produce etc.
- While the 'Tribal Areas' in the North-Eastern States under the Sixth Schedule have locally elected bodies in the form of District Councils and Regional Councils, the 'Scheduled Areas' in

the Fifth Schedule had no such locally elected bodies. Hence, the Parliament has extended the provisions of Part IX with respect to PRIs to these areas.

- However, considering that these are usually hilly or forest areas where the Scheduled Tribes reside in smaller hamlets (a small settlement with a group of houses), the PESA Act provides for modifications to create Gram Sabha at hamlet level and enables the State Legislatures to empower these Gram Sabhas.

20.2.5.1 Key Provisions of the PESA Act

Definition of Village and Gram Sabha

- Under the PESA Act, a village shall ordinarily consist of a habitation or a group of habitations or a hamlet or a group of hamlets comprising a community and managing its affairs in accordance with traditions and customs.
- Every village shall have a Gram Sabha consisting of persons whose names are included in the electoral rolls for the Panchayat at the village level.

PESA and Gram Sabha

The Act exclusively empowers Gram Sabha:

- to safeguard and preserve the
  a. traditions and customs of the people, and their cultural identity;
  b. community resources;
  c. customary mode of dispute resolution.
- carry out the executive functions to
  a. approve plans, programmes and projects for social and economic development;
  b. identify persons as beneficiaries under the poverty alleviation and other programmes;
  c. issue a certificate of utilisation of funds by the Panchayat for the plans, programmes and projects.

PESA empowers Gram Sabha/Panchayat at appropriate level with the following matters in the Scheduled Areas:

- right to mandatory consultation in land acquisition, resettlement and rehabilitation of displaced persons;
- planning and management of minor water bodies;
- recommendations for prospective licences/lease for mines and concession for the exploitation of minor minerals;
- regulate sale/consumption of intoxicants;
- ownership of minor forest produce;
- prevent land alienation and restore alienated land;
- manage village markets;
- control over money lending to the STs;
- control over institutions and functionaries in social sector, local plans including Tribal sub-plans and resources.

20.2.5.2 Importance of the PESA Act

Effective implementation of PESA Act will not only bring development but will also deepen democracy in the Fifth Schedule Areas. Importance of PESA Act can be summarised as below.

- It will enhance people's participation in decision making.
- PESA will reduce alienation of tribals as they will have better control over the utilisation of public resources.
- PESA will reduce poverty and out-migration among tribal population as they will have control and management of natural resources that will improve their livelihoods and incomes.
- PESA will minimise exploitation of tribal population as they will be able to control and manage money lending, consumption and sale of liquor and also village markets.
- Effective implementation of PESA will check illegal land alienation and restore unlawfully alienated tribal land.
- Most importantly PESA will promote cultural heritage through preservation of traditions, customs and cultural identity of tribal population.

THINK ABOUT IT

The Panchayat (Extension to Scheduled Areas) Act, 1996 is yet to achieve its full purpose. Comment on the importance of this law and the issues that still hamper its effective implementation.

However, effective implementation of PESA Act suffers from the following issues that need to be addressed.

- State laws have not been amended in line with PESA or only partially amended.
- Many powers to be delegated to Gram Sabhas have been delegated only to Gram Panchayats. This violated cardinal principle of PESA Act which required that the Scheduled areas should be subject to Gram Sabha decisions that are formed at the hamlet or village level.
- Minor Forest Produce is still under control of State governments and not Gram Sabhas.
- Lack of awareness and grievance redressal mechanism in the Scheduled areas.

20.2.6 Gram Nyayalayas Act 2008

Gram Nyayalayas Act was enacted in the year 2008 in order to provide access to justice to citizens at their door steps. It must be noted that Gram Nyayalayas (GN) are judicial bodies that settle civil and criminal cases within the limits provided in the Act. This is an alternate dispute redressal mechanism at the Panchayat level in order to deliver speedy justice to citizens. The salient features of the Act are provided below:

(a) GN is established at intermediate level of Panchayat or for contiguous Gram Panchayats where intermediate level is not established.

(b) State Government in consultation with the High Courts will determine the area under the jurisdiction of GN.

(c) State Government in consultation with the High Court appoints Nyayadikari (qualified to be appointed as Judicial Magistrate – First class) for every GN.

(d) GN shall have jurisdiction over both the civil and the criminal matters to the extent provided under the Act.

(e) A person accused of an offence can file an application for plea bargaining in GN.

Scan the QR code for conceptual video on Panchayats and Municipalities

Mc Graw Hill edge

(f) The Act provides for appointment of conciliators which shall be based on a list prepared by the District Court in consultation with District Magistrate consisting of names of social workers at Village level having the required integrity.

(g) No appeal from order of GN if it is based on plea bargaining or where the fine is less than 1000 rupees.

As per information made available by the Department of Justice (as of 2024), 494 Gram Nyayalayas have been notified so far by 16 States/UTs. Out of these 324 are operational in 12 States. These Gram Nyayalayas should be further established and made operational in all States to achieve its aim of being an effective alternative dispute redressal mechanism.

THINK ABOUT IT

Gram Nyayalayas can be an effective alternative dispute redressal mechanism if they function effectively. Discuss the extent of powers of Gram Nyayalayas and the issues faced in its effective functioning.

20.3 MUNICIPALITIES – URBAN LOCAL BODIES

20.3.1 Historical Background and Constitutional Status

- The establishment of Madras Municipal Corporation in 1688 was the commencement of urban local governance in India. Later, similar corporations were formed in Calcutta and Bombay in 1726.
- In 1882, Lord Ripon – the Viceroy of India – passed a resolution of local self-government which laid the foundation for democratic form of municipal governance in India. In the Government of India Act, 1919, local government became a transferred subject in the provinces under the system of 'dyarchy.' Under the Government of India Act, 1935, which established a federal set-up with provinces, it became a subject in the provincial list.
- Indian independence ushered a new era of local governance in India. The Constitution of India allotted the local self-government to the State list of functions. Various States created their own laws for establishment of urban local self-government institutions within their States.
- In 1986, the Central Government appointed the National Commission on Urbanisation, which gave its report in 1988. This was the first commission to study and give suggestions on all aspects of urban management. Also, several committees were appointed in different States in order to improve the municipal organisations and administration. Finally, it was the Constitution (74th Amendment) Act, 1992 that gave constitutional status to the Urban Local bodies or the Municipalities in India.

20.3.2 Similarities between Panchayats and Municipalities

The provisions for Municipalities in Part IXA of the Constitution added through the 74th Amendment provide for three levels of urban local bodies. The provisions with respect to composition, reservation, duration, qualification and disqualification, powers and duties, finances, elections, and other miscellaneous provisions are similar for Municipalities as they are for Panchayats that has been covered in detail in the previous section. We shall first understand the constitution of Municipalities at three levels and then understand the rest of the provisions that are similar to Panchayats in a tabular form. The other miscellaneous provisions will be summarised at the end of this section.

20.3.2.1 Constitution of Municipalities

Article 243Q provides for three levels of Municipalities to be set up in each State.

- 'Nagar Panchayat' (by whatever name called) for transitional areas i.e., an area in transition from a rural area to an urban area;
- 'Municipal Council' for a smaller urban area; and
- 'Municipal Corporation' for a larger urban area.

The classification of urban areas into 'transitional area', 'a smaller urban area' or 'a larger urban area' shall be done by the Governor of a State (i.e., the State government) having regard to the population and its density, revenue generated for local administration, percentage of employment in non-agricultural activities, economic importance and such other factors as deemed fit.

It must be noted that Panchayats are constituted in three-tiers one above the other for rural areas while Municipalities are constituted at three levels one after the other. This can be pictorially represented as per below diagrams for ease of understanding.

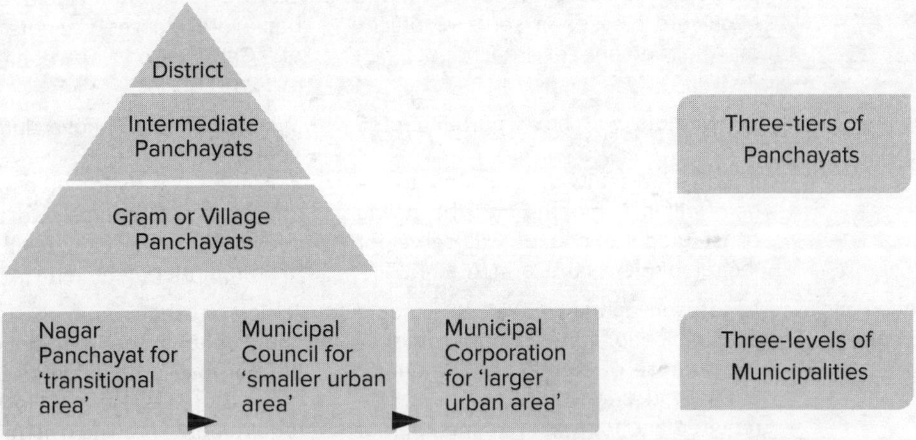

20.3.2.2 Similarities between Municipalities and Panchayats

The provisions with respect to composition, reservation, duration, qualification and disqualification, powers and duties, finances, elections, and other miscellaneous provisions are similar for Municipalities as they are for Panchayats and summarised in the table below.

Key Feature	Provisions under Part IX for Panchayats	Similar Provisions under Part IXA for Municipalities
Constitution	• A three-tier system of Panchayati Raj i.e., village level, intermediate level and district level [Art 243B].	• Three levels of Municipalities namely Nagar Panchayat, Municipal Council and Municipal Corporation [Art 243Q].
Composition	• All seats in all three-tiers to be filled by persons chosen by direct election. • Chairperson of village panchayat shall be elected in direct or indirect manner as provided by State law.	• All seats in all three levels to be filled by persons chosen by direct election. • State law can provide for representation of MPs, MLAs, MLCs and experts in Municipalities at three levels.

Key Feature	Provisions under Part IX for Panchayats	Similar Provisions under Part IXA for Municipalities
	• Chairperson of intermediate and district level shall be elected indirectly from amongst the elected members [Art 243C].	• State law can provide for the manner of election of the Chairperson of Municipalities at all three levels – Direct or Indirect [Art 243R].
Reservation	• Reservation for the SCs and the STs (in seats and chairpersons) in proportion to their population in each tier (1/3rd of the same to be reserved for women). • Out of the total number of seats to be filled by the direct elections and chairpersons, minimum 1/3rd must be reserved for women. • State legislature can additionally provide reservation in favour of the backward classes in seats or offices of Chairpersons of Panchayats [Art 243D].	• Reservation for the SCs and the STs (in seats and chairpersons) in proportion to their population at each level (1/3rd of the same to be reserved for women). • Out of the total number of seats to be filled by the direct elections and chairpersons, minimum 1/3rd must be reserved for women. • State legislature can additionally provide reservation in favour of the backward classes in seats or offices of Chairpersons of Municipalities [Art 243T].
Duration	• Panchayats will have duration of 5 years. • If earlier dissolved, elections to be held within 6 months and the newly constituted Panchayat will serve for the remainder of the term [Art 243E].	• Municipalities will have duration of 5 years. • If earlier dissolved, elections to be held within 6 months and the newly constituted Municipality will serve for the remainder of the term [Art 243U].
Qualification and Disqualification	• A person shall have the same disqualifications that is applicable for the purpose of election as a member of the State Legislature. However, age requirement for being a member of Panchayat is 21. • State legislature can provide any additional grounds for disqualification [Art 243F].	• A person shall have the same disqualifications that is applicable for the purpose of election as a member of the State Legislature. However, age requirement for being a member of Municipality is 21. • State legislature can provide any additional grounds for disqualification [Art 243V].
Powers and responsibilities	• State legislature may endow the panchayats with such powers as may be necessary to enable them to function as institutions of self-government. • The State law may endow Panchayats with powers to prepare plans for economic development and social justice and implement schemes for matters listed in the Eleventh Schedule [Art 243G].	• State legislature may endow the Municipalities with such powers as may be necessary to enable them to function as institutions of self-government. • The State law may endow Municipalities with powers to prepare plans for economic development and social justice and implement schemes for matters listed in the Twelfth Schedule [Art 243W].

Key Feature	Provisions under Part IX for Panchayats	Similar Provisions under Part IXA for Municipalities
	• The Eleventh Schedule to the Constitution was added by the 73rd Constitutional Amendment. This Schedule consists of 29 items that include (a) Agriculture, (b) Animal husbandry, dairying and poultry, (c) Fisheries, (d) Khadi, village and cottage industries, (e) Rural housing, (f) Drinking water, (g) Maintenance of community assets, (h) Markets and fairs etc.	• The Twelfth Schedule to the Constitution was added by the 74th Constitutional Amendment. This Schedule consists of 18 items that include (a) Urban planning including town planning, (b) Regulation of land use and construction of buildings, (c) Water supply, (d) Public health, sanitation conservancy and solid waste management, (e) Slum improvement and upgradation, (f) Urban poverty alleviation, (g) Provision of urban amenities, (h) Public amenities etc.
Finance	• State legislature may authorise the Panchayats to levy and collect taxes, assign taxes collected by the State government to panchayats and provide grants-in-aid to panchayats [Art 243H].	• State legislature may authorise the Municipalities to levy and collect taxes, assign taxes collected by the State government to municipalities and provide grants-in-aid to municipalities [Art 243X].
State Finance Commission	• State Finance Commission is constituted every 5 years for making recommendations with respect to distribution of revenues between the State government and the panchayats [Art 243-I].	• State Finance Commission constituted under Article 243-I shall also make recommendations with respect to distribution of revenues between the State government and the municipalities [Art 243Y].
State Election Commission	• Elections to Panchayats are conducted by State Election Commission in each State consisting of State Election Commissioner. • The State Election Commissioner is appointed by the Governor but can be removed only by the Parliament like a Judge of a High Court [Art 243K].	• Elections to Municipalities are conducted by the State Election Commission referred to in Article 243K [Art 243ZA].
Miscellaneous	• The Legislature of a State may, by law, make provisions with respect to the maintenance of accounts by the Panchayats and the auditing of such accounts [Art 243J]. • Provisions of Part IX are applicable to the Union Territories as they are applicable to States. However, the President may specify that the provisions shall be applicable to any Union territory subject to such modifications and exceptions [Art 243L].	• The Legislature of a State may, by law, make provisions with respect to the maintenance of accounts by the Municipalities and the auditing of such accounts [Art 243Z]. • Provisions of Part IXA are applicable to the Union Territories as they are applicable to States. However, the President may specify that the provisions shall be applicable to any Union territory subject to such modifications and exceptions [Art 243ZB].

Key Feature	Provisions under Part IX for Panchayats	Similar Provisions under Part IXA for Municipalities
	• The provisions of Part IX are not applicable to States of Nagaland, Meghalaya, Mizoram; Scheduled and Tribal areas in various States; hill areas in Manipur and Darjeeling district in West Bengal. • Certain compulsory and voluntary provisions provided for States under Part IX with respect to Panchayats (Refer Section 20.2.4).	• The provisions of Part IXA are not applicable to Scheduled and Tribal areas in various States; Darjeeling Gorkha Hill Council constituted for the hill areas of Darjeeling district. • Similar compulsory and voluntary provisions provided for States under Part IXA with respect to Municipalities.

20.3.3 Additional Provisions for Municipalities

> **THINK ABOUT IT**
>
> Unless the plans of panchayats and municipalities are effectively synchronised, the effectiveness of local governance bodies is bound to be sub-optimal. Discuss the role of District Planning Committees in combining the plans of panchayats and municipalities.

- **Wards Committees [Art 243S]** – The Constitution provides for Wards Committees to be constituted, consisting of one or more wards, within the territorial area of a Municipality having a population of three lakhs or more. The State Legislature may provide for the composition, territorial area and the manner in which the seats are to be filled. A member of a Municipality representing a ward within the territorial area of a Wards Committee shall be a member of such committee. One of such ward members elected by the Wards Committee shall be the Chairperson of that Committee.
- **Committee for District Planning [Art 243ZD]** – The Constitution provides for a District Planning Committee (DPC) to consolidate the plans prepared by the Panchayats and the Municipalities in the district and to prepare a draft development plan for the district as a whole. The State Legislature may provide for (a) the composition of the DPC, (b) the manner in which the seats are to be filled in the DPC, (c) the functions relating to district planning which may be assigned to DPC and (d) the manner in which Chairpersons of DPC shall be chosen.

  Every DPC shall, in preparing the draft development plan:
  - have regard to matters of common interest between the Panchayats and the Municipalities including spatial planning, sharing of water and other physical and natural resources, the integrated development of infrastructure and environmental conservation;
  - have regard to the extent and type of available resources whether financial or otherwise;
  - consult such institutions and organisations as the Governor may, by order, specify.
- Some of the issues with respect to DPC are: (a) it is non-functional in many states; (b) political interference; (c) lack of coordination and financial resources. These need to be addressed to make them effective.
- **Committee for Metropolitan Planning [Art 243ZE]** – The Constitution provides for a Metropolitan Planning Committee (MPC) in every metropolitan area to prepare a draft development plan for the Metropolitan area as a whole. The State Legislature may provide for (a) the composition of the MPC, (b) the manner in which the seats are to be filled in the MPC, (c) the representation in such committees of the Government of India and the Government of the State, (d) the functions relating to planning and coordination for the Metropolitan area which may be assigned to MPC and (e) the manner in which Chairpersons of MPC shall be chosen.

Every Metropolitan Planning Committee shall, in preparing the draft development plan,

(a) have regard to –
- the plans prepared by the Municipalities and the Panchayats in the Metropolitan area;
- matters of common interest between the Municipalities and the Panchayats, including coordinated spatial planning of the area, sharing of water and other physical and natural resources, the integrated development of infrastructure and environmental conservation;
- the overall objectives and priorities set by the Government of India and the Government of the State;
- the extent and the nature of investments likely to be made in the Metropolitan area by agencies of the Government of India and of the Government of the State and other available resources whether financial or otherwise;

(b) consult such institutions and organisations as the Governor may, by order, specify.

20.4 ACHIEVEMENTS, KEY ISSUES AND SOLUTIONS

20.4.1 Achievements of PRIs and Municipalities

The local self-government institutions i.e., Panchayats and Municipalities for rural and urban areas, respectively, have made significant achievements in the following ways:

- Democratic decentralisation at the grass root levels.
- Empowerment of women due to minimum reservation of one-third seats for women. Many States have increased the reservation for women to 50%.
- Empowerment of the Scheduled Castes and the Scheduled Tribes through reservation.

20.4.2 Key Issues

The 73rd and the 74th Amendments provided constitutional status to local body institutions. The provisions with respect to constitution, elections, reservation, duration etc., have been made mandatory through these amendments. However, with respect to functioning and finances, the provisions in the Constitution are not compulsory in nature. They are dependent on the extent of devolution of powers and finances by the State Legislatures. The functioning of local self-government institutions suffers due to the following issues:

- Lack of adequate devolution of powers and funds by the State Legislatures and the State governments. States like Kerala and Karnataka have devolved more powers while many other States have not devolved adequate powers.
- Parastatal agencies like DRDA, District Health Society, Water Agencies, Smart city SPVs etc., affect the functioning of PRIs and Municipalities.
- Lack of adequately trained manpower for performing various functions.
- Excessive control by bureaucracy over elected representatives.
- Caste rivalry and group clashes resulting in electoral violence.

20.4.3 Way Forward

The 2nd Administrative Reforms Commission provided the following suggestions for improving the powers and functioning of the PRIs and the Municipalities. However, it must be noted that these recommendations have not yet been implemented. Implementation of the following recommendations will significantly improve the functioning of these local self-government institutions and also increase their accountability towards the people.

- The State Legislature should devolve powers to local bodies for making plans and implementation of schemes for the matters listed in the Eleventh and the Twelfth Schedules. At present, it is not obligatory for the State Legislature and it may devolve such powers as it deems necessary. This should be replaced with compulsory devolution.
- The devolution of powers should be based on the principle of 'subsidiarity', which means that what can be done at a lower level should be done at that level itself.
- Legislative Councils to be constituted in all States with more representation from members elected by local bodies.
- Ward or Area sabhas should be constituted in urban local bodies similar to Gram Sabhas in Panchayats. There is model law that has been passed by the Parliament, Model Nagar Raja Bill Act in 2010, but all States have not enacted and implemented the same.

MAINS STARTER

Area	Building Blocks For Model Introductions
Panchayati Raj Institutions (PRI)/ Municipalities	Panchayats/Municipalities are rural/urban local governance bodies that are established as per the provisions of Part IX/IXA of the Constitution that was added through the 73rd/74th constitutional amendment. It is aimed at achieving democratic decentralisation at the grassroots level.
Achievements of PRI/ Municipalities	The PRI and Municipalities have resulted in democratic decentralisation as envisaged in Article 40 of the DPSP. They have also empowered women, Scheduled Castes and Scheduled Tribes through the scheme of reservations.
Issues of PRI/ Municipalities	Despite its various achievements, PRIs/Municipalities suffer from issues like lack of devolution of powers and finance, excessive control by bureaucracy and lack of trained manpower.
Gram Nyayalayas	The Gram Nyayalayas are a mode of alternative dispute redressal mechanism set up under the Gram Nyayalayas Act, 2008. They have jurisdiction over both civil and criminal matters to the extent provided under the Act. However, they have not been set up in many States and not functioning effectively wherever set up.

Register on **McGraw Hill Edge** for the following:
- Articles at a glance for this chapter
- Additional Data point for types of urban local bodies
- Practice questions for Preliminary examination including PYQ of 2014–24
- Model answers for Mains PYQ of 2014–24
- Attend regular webinars by the author including discussion on **'Think about It'** questions

UPSC Previous Years' Questions of Preliminary Examination

1. Local self-government can be best explained as an exercise in [2017]
   (a) Federalism
   (b) Democratic decentralisation
   (c) Administrative delegation
   (d) Direct democracy

Solution: (b)

Explanation: As discussed in section 20.1.5, the main purpose of constitutional status to PRIs through the 73rd Amendment was to bring democracy at the grass root level as it exists at the State and National level. Hence, the correct answer is (b).

UPSC Previous Years' Questions of Main Examination

1. Analyse the role of local bodies in providing good governance at local level and bring out the pros and cons merging the rural local bodies with the urban local bodies. [2024]

Approach: The importance of local elected bodies in providing governance at the grassroots levels, as provided in grey shaded box in Section 20.1, needs to be discussed in the first part. The pros and cons of merging rural and urban local bodies to be discussed. Conclusion can bring out reforms required for strengthening the District Planning Committee.

MODEL ANSWER

The 73rd and 74th amendments provided constitutional status to Panchayats (Part IX) and Municipalities (Part IXA). It also added eleventh and twelfth schedules for providing the areas of governance for these bodies, respectively.

Role and importance of local bodies in providing good governance at local level

The importance of local governments can be summarised as follows:

1. It is closest to common people as it deals with the day-to-today problems of ordinary citizens.
2. Believes local knowledge and interest are essential for democratic decision making.
3. Strong local governments also ensure both active participation and purposeful accountability.

The panchayats and municipalities have strengthened governance and democracy through grassroots participation; reservation for women, SC and ST in members and chairpersons.

Pros and Cons of merging Panchayats and Municipalities

Various districts in India are getting urbanised fast. In this respect, the pros and cons of merging rural and urban local bodies:

(a) Merger of local bodies can result in more holistic planning and resource allocation.

(b) It can reduce bureaucratic delays and improve service delivery.

(c) However, the demands of rural and urban areas are different. Merger may result in one set of issues dominating the other, depending on the extent of such areas in the district. This can result in loss of local identity and redressal of grievances.

Rural areas getting transformed into urban areas are anyway merged into or changed to Municipalities. This process can continue and District Planning Committees in each district should be strengthened for effective coordination between rural and urban bodies in a district.

2. The states in India seem reluctant to empower urban local bodies both functionally as well as financially. Comment. **[2023]**

Approach: The issues for Panchayats and Municipalities discussed in Section 20.4 are broadly similar. Hence, these need to be highlighted with respect to Municipalities. Then, suggestions as per 2nd ARC for their improvement need to be part of the conclusion.

MODEL ANSWER

The 74th Constitutional Amendment provided constitutional status to urban local bodies or Municipalities.

Key provisions with respect to Municipalities as per the Constitution – Part IXA

(a) Three levels of Municipalities, namely, Nagar Panchayat, Municipal Council and Municipal Corporation.

(b) State legislature may endow the Municipalities with such powers as may be necessary to enable them to function as institutions of self-government especially for matters listed in the Twelfth Schedule like urban planning, water supply, public health, sanitation and waste management, etc.

(c) State legislature may authorise Municipalities to levy and collect taxes.

Key issues and way forward

(a) Lack of adequate devolution of powers and funds by the State legislatures and State governments.

(b) Due to this lack of empowerment, urban local bodies are unable to discharge their functions. The reasons for non-devolution are:
- Parastatal agencies like District Health society, Water agencies, Smart city SPVs being given more powers.
- Lack of adequately trained manpower for performing various functions.
- Excessive control by bureaucracy over elected representatives.

As recommended by the 2nd ARC, the Constitution should be amended to provide that the State legislature should devolve powers to urban local bodies for making plans and implementation of schemes for the matters listed in the Twelfth schedule.

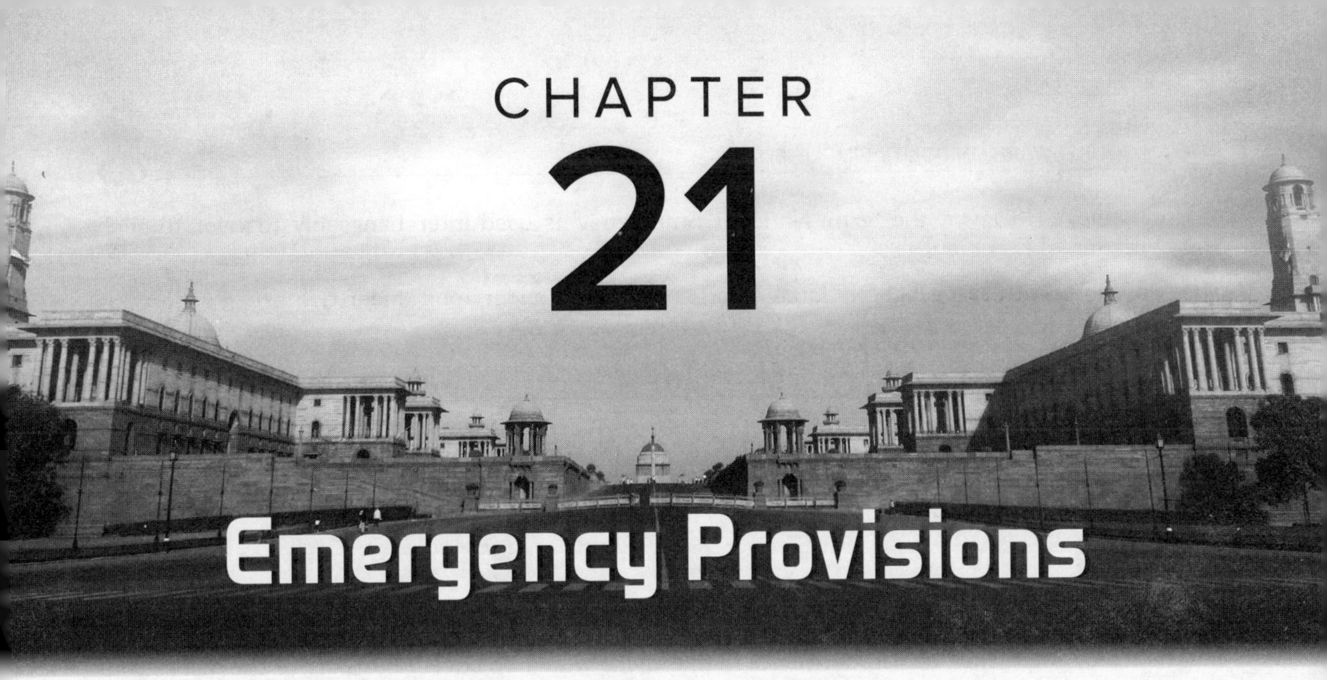

CHAPTER 21

Emergency Provisions

LEARNING OUTCOMES

1. Comprehending the history and significance of emergency provisions
2. Explaining the procedure for the proclamation and approval of a National Emergency, along with key amendments introduced by the 44th Amendment
3. Understanding impact of National emergency on Centre-State relations and Fundamental Rights
4. Analysing the procedure, significance, and judicial interpretation of State Emergency, with a focus on the S R Bommai judgement
5. Understanding the proclamation and approval process of a Financial Emergency and its implications on Centre-State financial relations

The Constitution of India has provided certain emergency provisions to enable the Union in dealing with any emergency and abnormal situation in an effective manner. They allow the Union to defend the sovereignty, unity, integrity and security of the country. The emergency provisions are part of the unitary features of the Indian Constitution.

It converts the federal structure into unitary one without a formal amendment to the Constitution. These provisions are included in Part XVIII, from Articles 352 to 360. These principles are borrowed from the Government of India Act 1935.

The Constitution provides for three types of emergencies as below:

National Emergency (352)	State Emergency* (356)	Financial Emergency (360)
An emergency due to war, external aggression or armed rebellion.	An emergency due to the failure of the constitutional machinery in the States.	An emergency due to a threat to the financial stability or credit of India.

*The word 'emergency' is not used in Article 356 and it is popularly known as 'President's rule'.

21.1 NATIONAL EMERGENCY

Article 352 of the Constitution enumerates the various provisions regarding National emergency. The word 'National Emergency' is not used in the Constitution and it employs the term 'Proclamation of Emergency'. However, the term 'National Emergency' is used interchangeably to refer to such 'Proclamation of Emergency'.

The provisions with respect to National emergency can be understood under two broad aspects as given below.

Procedure for Proclamation	Effect of National Emergency
• Grounds for declaration and procedure • Territorial extent of proclamation • Approval by the Parliament • Procedure for continuation • Revocation by the President	• On Centre–State relations • On Fundamental rights • On duration of the Lok Sabha and the State Legislative Assembly

We shall now discuss the key provisions for the above two aspects. Further, there have been significant amendments to these aspects through the 44th Amendment Act in 1978 based on the experience of emergency declared in 1975. While these would be covered as part of the discussion, a comparative table between the provisions as it existed at the time of declaration of emergency in 1975 and the amendments made through the 44th Amendment Act will be provided at the end of the section for easy reference.

21.1.1 Procedure for Proclamation

The grounds for declaration and its procedure, territorial extent, initial approval and continuation by the Parliament etc., are provided in Article 352 that are summarised below.

21.1.1.1 Grounds for Declaration and Procedure

- The President can declare a national emergency, when the security of India or a part of it is threatened by war, external aggression or armed rebellion. When a national emergency is declared on the grounds of 'war' or 'external aggression', it may be also called as 'External Emergency' and when it is declared on the ground of 'armed rebellion', it may be called as 'Internal Emergency'.
- The 44th Amendment Act of 1978 substituted the words 'armed rebellion' for 'internal disturbance'.
- The President can declare a national emergency even before the actual occurrence of war or external aggression or armed rebellion, if he/she is satisfied that there is an imminent danger.
- The President can also issue different proclamations on grounds of war, external aggression, armed rebellion, or imminent danger thereof, whether or not there is a proclamation already issued by him/her and such proclamation is in operation.
- The President can proclaim a national emergency only after receiving a written recommendation from the cabinet. This means that the emergency can be declared only on the concurrence of the cabinet and not merely on the advice of the Prime Minister. The 44th Amendment Act of 1978 introduced this safeguard to eliminate any possibility of the Prime Minister alone taking a decision in this regard as it had happened during 1975. Article 352 also defines 'cabinet' as the council consisting of the Prime Minister and other Ministers of the cabinet rank. It may be noted that the word 'cabinet' is used in the Constitution only in Article 352 and the term used to denote the executive in all other places is 'council of ministers'.

21.1.1.2 Territorial Extent of Proclamation

A proclamation of national emergency may be applicable to the entire country or only a part of it. The 42nd Amendment Act of 1976 enabled the President to limit the operation of a national emergency to a specified part of India.

21.1.1.3 Approval by Parliament

- The proclamation of national emergency must be approved and ratified by both the Houses of the Parliament within 1 month from the date of its issue by a special majority i.e., majority of total membership of the House and by a majority of not less than two-thirds of members present and voting.
- Originally, the period allowed for approval by the Parliament was 2 months by a simple majority. But it was reduced to 1 month by the 44th Amendment Act of 1978 and the majority required was made as special majority.
- However, if the proclamation of emergency is issued at a time when the Lok Sabha has been dissolved or the dissolution of the Lok Sabha takes place during the period of 1 month without approving the proclamation, then the Rajya Sabha needs to approve it within 1 month. The reconstituted Lok Sabha must approve the proclamation within 30 days from its first sitting, failing which the proclamation will cease to have effect.

21.1.1.4 Procedure for Continuation

- Once approved by the Parliament, the proclamation of emergency continues for 6 months (from the date of passing of the second of the resolutions by Parliament approving the proclamation) unless revoked earlier. It can be extended for a further period of 6 months at a time by an approval of the Parliament. Such resolutions for continuation must also be passed by a special majority.
- This provision was also added by the 44th Amendment Act of 1978. Earlier, the proclamation of emergency once approved would continue to be in force until revoked by the President. However, the 44th Amendment Act added this requirement that it needs to be approved every 6 months, by a special majority, for its continuation.
- However, if the Lok Sabha has been dissolved or the dissolution of the Lok Sabha takes place during the period of 6 months without approving the continuation of proclamation, then the Rajya Sabha needs to approve it within that period. The reconstituted Lok Sabha must approve the continuation of proclamation within 30 days from its first sitting, failing which the proclamation will cease to have effect.

21.1.1.5 Revocation of Proclamation

The Proclamation of Emergency can be revoked in two ways:

1. The Lok Sabha has the power to pass a resolution for disapproving the proclamation of emergency or its continuation.
    - A notice for moving a resolution for disapproving the proclamation or its continuance needs to be signed by not less than one-tenth of the total members of the Lok Sabha. Such a notice shall be issued to the Speaker (if the House is in session) or to the President (if the House is not in session).

- A special sitting of the Lok Sabha shall be held within 14 days from the date on which such notice is received for the purpose of considering such a resolution. The resolution must be passed by a simple majority i.e., majority of members present and voting, to disapprove the emergency.
- If such a resolution is passed in the Lok Sabha, the President shall immediately revoke the proclamation of emergency.
- This provision was added by the 44th Amendment Act in 1978. It must be noted that after the 44th Amendment, any approval of proclamation of emergency or its continuance requires a special majority in both the Houses. However, it can be revoked by a resolution passed by a simple majority in the Lok Sabha alone.

2. It can be revoked by the President on the advice of the Council of Ministers any time.

21.1.2 Effect of National Emergency

The Proclamation of Emergency has an effect on (a) Centre–State relations [Art 353 and 354], (b) Fundamental rights [Art 358 and 359] and (c) tenure of the Lok Sabha and the Legislative Assemblies of States [Art 83 and 172].

21.1.2.1 Effect on Centre–State Relations

The Proclamation of Emergency has an effect on the administrative and the legislative relations between the Centre and the States [Art 353], as well on the financial relations [Art 354]. The key provisions in this regard are summarised below:

- The executive power of the Union shall extend to the giving of directions to any State as to the manner in which the executive power thereof is to be exercised while a National Emergency is in operation. Thus, while under normal circumstances, the Union executive can give instructions to the States only on specific matters, during an emergency it can be in respect of any matter.
- The power of the Parliament to make laws with respect to any matter shall include the power to make laws, conferring power and imposing duties, notwithstanding that it is one which is not enumerated in the Union list. Thus, the State list will act like a Concurrent list during National Emergency. Such a law made by the Parliament on a subject in the State list, shall cease to have effect on the expiration of 6 months after the emergency has ceased to operate.
- Where a Proclamation of Emergency is in operation only in any part of the territory of India, – (i) the executive power of the Union to give directions to the State government and (ii) the power of the Parliament to make laws in State list, shall also extend to any State other than a State in which or in any part of which the Proclamation of Emergency is in operation if and in so far as the security of India is threatened by activities in or in relation to the part of the territory of India in which the Proclamation of Emergency is in operation.
- The President may, while a Proclamation of Emergency is in operation, by order direct that all or any of the provisions of Articles 268–279 shall have effect subject to such exceptions or modifications as he/she thinks fit. Articles 268–279 contain provisions primarily relating to distribution of tax revenues between the Centre and the States as well as Grants-in-aid from the Centre to the States. These may be given effect subject to modifications or exceptions as required by the central government during an emergency. However, such order shall not extend beyond the end of the financial year in which the proclamation ceases to operate. For example, the emergency that was declared in June 1975 had ceased to operate on 21 March 1977. Hence, any order that was made under this clause would not have extended beyond 31 March 1977.

21.1.2.2 Effect on Fundamental Rights

The Proclamation of Emergency results in suspension of provisions of Article 19 [Art 358] and suspension of enforcement of the rights conferred by Part III [Art 359]. The key provisions in this regard are summarised below:

- While a Proclamation of Emergency is declared on the grounds of war or external aggression, nothing in Article 19 shall restrict the power of the State (as defined in Part III) to make any law or to take any executive action which the State would but for the provisions contained in that Part be competent to make or to take. It means that while during ordinary circumstances, the State can place only 'reasonable restrictions' on the rights conferred by Article 19(1), there are no such limits for restrictions that can be placed during emergency. However, any law so made shall, to the extent of incompetency, cease to have effect as soon as the emergency ceases to operate. Article 358 also allows laws or executive actions to be implemented in a State or Union Territory where the emergency is not in effect, if the security of India or any part of its territory is threatened due to activities linked to the region under emergency. Additionally, the suspension of Article 19 shall apply only to:
  - (a) Laws which contain a recital to the effect that it is in relation to the Proclamation of emergency in operation when it is made (i.e., explicitly state their connection to the ongoing Proclamation of Emergency at the time of enactment); or
  - (b) Executive actions taken under such laws

  However, it must be noted that this suspension of provisions of Article 19 is not applicable when an emergency is declared on the ground of 'armed rebellion'.
- Where a Proclamation of Emergency is in operation, the President may by order declare that:
  - The right to move any court for the enforcement of the rights conferred by Part III (except Articles 20 and 21) as may be mentioned in the order; and
  - All proceedings pending in any court for the enforcement of the rights so mentioned;

  shall remain suspended for the period during which the Proclamation is in force or for such shorter period as may be specified in the order. Every such order shall be laid before the Houses of Parliament.
  - If the Proclamation of Emergency is in operation only in a part of the territory of India, any such order shall not extend to any other part of the territory of India unless extended by the President in the interest of security of India.
- While any such Presidential order, as mentioned above, is in force, the State can make any law or take any executive action abridging or taking away the fundamental rights specified in such order. When the order ceases to operate, any law made to the extent of inconsistency with specified fundamental rights, will cease to have effect. Further, these provisions shall apply only to laws that contain a recital that it is in relation to the emergency in operation or executive actions taken under such laws.
- Suspension of enforcement of Fundamental rights by moving the courts during an emergency was applicable to all rights before 1978. Hence, the right to move a 'habeas corpus' petition against violation of Fundamental Rights in Articles 20 and 21 was suspended during the operation of an emergency. In ADM Jabalpur case (1976), the Supreme Court had upheld this provision with a majority of 4:1. Only Justice H. R. Khanna had dissented to the majority view on the ground that right to life and liberty is an inalienable right of every individual and hence these rights should not be suspended even during emergency.
- The 44th Amendment Act made an exception to Articles 20 and 21, the enforcement of which cannot be suspended even during an emergency.

21.1.2.3 Effect on Duration of Legislatures

As discussed in the chapters on Parliament and State Legislature, while a National Emergency is in operation, the life of the Lok Sabha and the Legislative Assembly of a State can be extended by a Parliamentary law for 1 year at a time. However, such extension cannot continue beyond 6 months after the Emergency has ceased to operate.

21.1.3 Key Changes through 44th Amendment Act

There have been significant changes in the provisions with respect to emergency that were carried out through the 44th Amendment Act in 1978. It was in order to make the procedure for proclamation more stringent and the effect on the fundamental rights to be less severe. These changes are summarised in the comparison table below for easy reference.

Particulars	Provision before 1978	44th Amendment Act
Proclamation of Emergency	No specific mention of written recommendation from the cabinet.	President can proclaim an emergency only based on the written recommendation from the cabinet.
Grounds	'Internal disturbance' was a ground for declaring emergency.	'Internal disturbance' was amended to 'armed rebellion' (though this is not defined in the Constitution).
Time period for approval	A proclamation needs to be approved by both the Houses of Parliament within 2 months.	A proclamation needs to be approved by both the Houses of Parliament within 1 month.
Resolution for continuation	No requirement of any resolution for continuation at periodic intervals. Proclamation once approved continued to be in force till it was revoked.	Both Houses of Parliament need to pass a resolution for approving the continuation of emergency, every 6 months. Otherwise, the proclamation will cease to operate.
Majority for approval and continuation	The Proclamation of Emergency was required to be approved by a simple majority in both the Houses. Further, there was no requirement of any approval for continuation at periodic intervals.	The approval of Proclamation as well as the approval for its continuation (every 6 months) needs to be approved by a special majority in both the Houses.
Revocation by the Lok Sabha	No provision for revocation of proclamation based on resolution by the Lok Sabha.	If the Lok Sabha passes a resolution, with a simple majority, disapproving the proclamation or its continuance, then the President should revoke the emergency.
Suspension of provisions of Article 19	Suspended when emergency was declared on any ground i.e., war, external aggression or internal disturbance.	Suspended only when emergency is declared on the grounds of war or external aggression. Does not get suspended if it is declared due to 'armed rebellion'.
Suspension of enforcement of Fundamental rights in courts	Enforcement (in courts) of all Fundamental rights can be suspended through the Presidential order during emergency period.	Enforcement of Articles 20 and 21 cannot be suspended even during emergency.

21.1.4 Declarations made so far

Emergency under Article 352 has been proclaimed on three occasions:

1. October 1962 – at the time of Chinese aggression this emergency was proclaimed for the first time and continued till January 1968.
2. December 1971 – at the time of Indo-Pak war and it continued up to March 1977.
3. President declared it in June 1975 on the ground of 'internal disturbance' on account of internal political crisis that continued till March 1977.

THINK ABOUT IT

Emergency provisions are a colonial relic and not desirable in a democracy like India. Comment highlighting the significant amendments brought in by the 44th amendment to safeguard democracy and citizen rights.

SUMMARY OF NATIONAL EMERGENCY PROVISIONS

Proclamation of National Emergency (Art 352–354, 358, 359)		
Grounds	**Approval**	**Effect**
(a) Security of India or any part threatened by War, External Aggression or Armed Rebellion*. (b) President to declare only based on written recommendation from the Cabinet for the whole or part of India. *Internal disturbance changed to 'Armed Rebllion' in 1978	(a) Within 1 month of the proclamation by special majority in both houses. (b) Approval every 6 months by special majority for continuation. (c) Lok Sabha can pass resolution for revocation by simple majority.	(a) On Centre–State relations – Centre gets more powers in legislative, administrative and financial relations. (b) On Fundamental rights – Right to move courts for enforcement can be suspended (except 20 & 21); Art 19 can be suspended only if declaration due to war or external aggression. (c) Lok Sabha & Legislative Assembly – Duration can be extended by 1 year at a time.

Criticisms about the emergency provisions

- The emergency provisions were carried over from the Government of India Act, 1935. In the Constituent Assembly, some of the members objected to the inclusion of these provisions as it would be against the democratic polity of our independent nation. Even Dr Ambedkar remarked that these provisions can be misused or abused for political purposes.
- The key criticisms against the emergency provisions, that were on display during the emergency imposed in 1975 are as follows:
  - Federal character of the Constitution will be destroyed and the Union executive and the Parliament would become all powerful.
  - Financial autonomy of the States would be in trouble.
  - Fundamental rights will be suspended that will take away the individual rights and democratic foundation of our country.

Scan the QR code for conceptual video on National emergency

McGraw Hill edge

However, after 1977, no such emergency has been proclaimed. The 44th Amendment to the Constitution introduced further safeguards with regard to the emergency provisions as discussed in the earlier section.

21.2 STATE EMERGENCY

Article 356 of the Constitution enumerates the various provisions regarding the Presidential proclamation with respect to a State. The word 'State emergency' is not used in the Constitution and it employs the term 'Proclamation by President'. However, the term 'State emergency' and 'President's rule' is used interchangeably to refer to such Proclamation.

21.2.1 Procedure for Presidential Proclamation

The grounds for declaration and its procedure, initial approval and continuation by the Parliament etc., are provided in Article 356 that are summarised below.

21.2.1.1 Grounds for Declaration of State Emergency and Procedure

- The President can declare a State emergency, when the Government of a State cannot be carried on in accordance with the provisions of the Constitution. This is also known as breakdown of 'Constitutional machinery'.
- The President can make such a proclamation based on receipt of report from the Governor of a State or otherwise.
- Article 355 of the Constitution states that it shall be the duty of the Union to protect every State against external aggression and internal disturbance and to ensure that the Government of every State is carried on in accordance with the provisions of the Constitution.
- Article 365 further states that where any State has failed to comply with, or to give effect to, any directions given by the Union under any of the provisions of the Constitution, it shall be lawful for the President to hold that a situation has arisen in which the Government of the State cannot be carried on in accordance with the provisions of the Constitution.
- Thus, the above two articles provide a precursor for imposition of the President's rule in a State by the President. A report from the Governor of a State with respect to breakdown of constitutional machinery can also form the basis for such a proclamation.
- The past issues with respect to misuse of Article 356 and the Supreme Court judgement in the *S. R. Bommai case* that stopped such misuse will be discussed in Section 21.2.3.

21.2.1.2 Approval by the Parliament

- The proclamation of President's rule must be approved and ratified by both the Houses of the Parliament within 2 months from the date of its issue by a simple majority.
- However, if the proclamation is issued at a time when the Lok Sabha has been dissolved or the dissolution of the Lok Sabha takes place during the period of 2 months without approving the proclamation, then the Rajya Sabha needs to approve it within 2 months. The reconstituted Lok Sabha must approve the proclamation within 30 days from its first sitting, failing which the proclamation will cease to have effect.

21.2.1.3 Procedure for Continuation

- Once approved by the Parliament, the President's rule continues for 6 months (from the date of issue of proclamation) unless revoked earlier. It can be extended for a further period of 6 months at a time by an approval of the Parliament. Such resolutions for continuation must also be passed by a simple majority. The President's rule cannot extend beyond a period of 3 years in total.

- However, if the Lok Sabha has been dissolved or the dissolution of the Lok Sabha takes place during the period of 6 months without approving the continuation of proclamation, then the Rajya Sabha needs to approve it within that period. The reconstituted Lok Sabha must approve the continuation of proclamation within 30 days from its first sitting, failing which the proclamation will cease to have effect.

- The 44th Amendment Act of 1978 introduced a new provision to restrain the power of the Parliament to extend a proclamation of the President's rule beyond 1 year. No such approval shall be given, continuing the operation of a Proclamation beyond 1 year from the date of its issue except under certain conditions as mentioned below:
  - Proclamation of Emergency (National emergency) is in operation in the State concerned or in the whole of India; and
  - Election Commission has certified that it is difficult to conduct general elections to the Legislative Assembly of the State concerned.

21.2.1.4 Revocation of Proclamation

The Proclamation imposing the President's rule can be revoked by the President on the advice of the Council of Ministers any time.

21.2.2 Effect of Presidential Proclamation

The President acquires the following powers when the President's rule is imposed in a State:

- He/she can take up the functions of the State government and powers vested in the Governor or any other executive authority in the State.
- He/she can declare that the powers of the State Legislature are to be exercised by the Parliament.
- He/she can take all other necessary steps including the suspension of the constitutional provisions relating to any authority or body in the State. However, the powers of High Court or the constitutional provisions with respect to the High Courts are not affected by a Presidential Proclamation.

When the President's rule is imposed in a State, the following consequences follow:

- The President dismisses the State Council of Ministers, headed by the Chief Minister or the President's rule is imposed when the council of ministers resign. The State Governor, on behalf of the President, carries on the State administration with the help of the Chief Secretary of the State, or the advisors appointed by the President.
- State Assembly may be dissolved or kept under suspended animation (suspended) depending upon prevailing circumstances.
- Such a Proclamation may declare that the powers of the State Legislature shall be exercisable by or under the authority of the Parliament.
- As per Article 357, the Parliament may confer this legislative power on the President and authorise him/her to further delegate it to any other authority.
- The Parliament can authorise the President to sanction expenditure from the Consolidated Fund of the State when the Lok Sabha is not in session, pending approval by the Parliament.
- A law made (with respect to a State) by the Parliament or the President or any authority authorised during the President's rule, shall continue to remain in force even after the revocation of the proclamation until altered or repealed by a competent Legislature i.e., usually the State Assembly constituted after fresh elections after the State emergency has been revoked.

SUMMARY OF STATE EMERGENCY PROVISIONS

Ground	• Breakdown of constitutional machinery. • Based on report of the Governor or otherwise. • Presidential proclamation based on advise of council of ministers.
Approval	• Approval by both houses within 2 months and approval for continuation every 6 months by simple majority. • Maximum period – 3 yrs; beyond 1 yr approval only on specific circumstances.
Effect	• Executive powers of the State will be vested in the Central government. • Legislative powers of the State will be exercised by or under the authority of Parliament.

21.2.3 Issues with State Emergency and the S. R. Bommai Judgement

The provision of Article 356 is modelled on the basis of similar provisions in the Government of India Act, 1935. This is one of the unitary features of the Constitution that affects the federal setup. There were Constituent Assembly members who opposed the inclusion of this provision in our independent Constitution as it is undemocratic and against the federal spirit. However, considering the security of the nation and stability of its polity, it was felt necessary to include the provisions of Article 356 in our Constitution.

THINK ABOUT IT

The imposition of President's rule is anathema to the federal spirit of our constitution. Critically evaluate. What constitutional and judicial safeguards have developed to prevent its misuse?

21.2.3.1 Misuse of Article 356

Dr Ambedkar, while appreciating the concerns of some Constituent Assembly members against the inclusion of Article 356, argued that no provision is immune from abuse and misuse. He expected that there would be adequate precautions taken by the President before imposition of President's rule and that the provisions of Article 356 would remain a dead letter in the Constitution.

However, there have been innumerable instances when they have been misused in the past. Between 1950 and 1994, Article 356 was used on more than 90 occasions. On several of these occasions, the State governments were dismissed even when they enjoyed majority in the Assembly. On some occasions, they were dismissed without giving them an opportunity to prove their strength on the floor of the House i.e., inside the Legislative Assembly.

The Sarkaria Commission was of the view that the extraordinary provisions contained in Article 356 should be called into operation rarely, in extreme cases, as a last resort when all other alternatives fail.

21.2.3.2 S. R. Bommai Judgement

The misuse of Article 356 as stated above dramatically reduced after the landmark judgement of the Supreme Court in the S. R. Bommai case in 1994. The following are the key points of the Supreme Court judgement in this case:

- The imposition of the President's rule under Article 356 is subject to judicial review.
- The satisfaction of the President for invoking Article 356 should be based on relevant material. The burden to prove the relevance of the material lies on the Central Government. The Court cannot review the correctness of the material but will review its relevance.

- If the imposition of the President's rule is declared unconstitutional, the Court can restore the position as it existed before the invocation of Article 356.
- Till the Parliament approves the imposition of the President's rule, the Legislative Assembly should not be dissolved and it can be only kept under suspended animation.
- The State Government losing its majority should be proved only in the floor of the House i.e., inside the Legislative Assembly.
- Article 356 cannot be used for political reasons and should be used only as an exception. It should not be used for failure of the law-and-order machinery but only for failure of the 'constitutional machinery'.
- It also declared secularism and federalism as the basic features of the Constitution.

While Article 356 has been used even after 1994, it was almost always when its use was inevitable when no party or coalition enjoyed majority to form a stable government necessitating imposition of the President's rule till fresh elections were conducted; or any other combination was formed that provided a stable government. Any arbitrary use of Article 356 has been struck down by the Supreme Court as unconstitutional.

The National Commission to review the working of the Constitution (2002) and the Punchhi Commission (2010) had suggested that Article 356 should be amended to bring it in line with judgement of the Supreme Court in the S. R. Bommai case and to increase the safe guards against its misuse. However, Article 356 has not been amended in line with these recommendations.

21.2.4 President's Rule in Union Territories with Assembly

The above provisions of Article 356 are applicable to the States in the country. There are three Union Territories (UT) with a Legislative Assembly and elected government viz., National Capital Territory (NCT) of Delhi, Puducherry and Jammu & Kashmir. The provisions for the President's rule in these three UTs are provided in the respective acts for governing these UTs. These provisions are summarised below.

Union Territory	Relevant Act	Provision with respect to President's Rule
NCT of Delhi	The Government of NCT of Delhi Act, 1991 (Section 50) and Article 239AB	• The President, on receipt of a report from the Lieutenant Governor or otherwise, can impose President's rule in NCT of Delhi under Article 239AB. • The Government of NCT of Delhi Act provides that such order shall be valid for 1 year. The provisions of Article 356 with respect to approval within 2 months by both Houses of the Parliament shall apply to such order. • The duration of such order imposing the President's rule may be extended beyond 1 year for a further period not exceeding 2 more years. Every such extension has to be approved by both Houses of Parliament. Thus, the maximum tenure for President's rule cannot exceed 3 years.
Puducherry	The Government of Union Territories Act, 1963 (Section 51)	• The President, on receipt of a report from the Lieutenant Governor or otherwise, can impose the President's rule in Puducherry. • The President may by such order suspend the operation of all or any of the provisions of this Act for such period as he/ she thinks fit.

Union Territory	Relevant Act	Provision with respect to President's Rule
		• The President may make such incidental and consequential provisions for administering the Union Territory during such period.
Jammu & Kashmir	Jammu & Kashmir Reorganisation Act, 2019 (Section 73)	• The President, on receipt of a report from the Lieutenant Governor or otherwise, can impose the President's rule in Jammu & Kashmir. • The President may by such order suspend the operation of all or any of the provisions of this Act for such period as he/she thinks fit. • The President may make such incidental and consequential provisions for administering the Union Territory during such period.

21.3 FINANCIAL EMERGENCY

21.3.1 Procedure for Financial Emergency

The grounds for declaration and its procedure, approval by the Parliament etc., are provided in Article 360 that are summarised below. It must, however, be noted that Financial emergency has never been declared in India till date (2024).

21.3.1.1 Grounds for Declaration of Financial Emergency and Procedure

- The President proclaims Financial emergency under Article 360, if he/she is satisfied that a situation has arisen whereby the financial stability or credit of India, or any part thereof is threatened.

21.3.1.2 Approval by the Parliament

- The proclamation of Financial emergency must be approved and ratified by both the Houses of the Parliament within 2 months from the date of its issue by a simple majority.
- However, if the proclamation is issued at a time when the Lok Sabha has been dissolved or the dissolution of the Lok Sabha takes place during the period of 2 months without approving the proclamation, then the Rajya Sabha needs to approve it within 2 months. The reconstituted Lok Sabha must approve the proclamation within 30 days from its first sitting, failing which the proclamation will cease to have effect.

Scan the QR code for conceptual video on State and Financial emergency

21.3.1.3 Procedure for Continuation

Once approved by the Parliament, the Financial emergency continues to be in force till it is revoked.

21.3.1.4 Revocation of Proclamation

The Proclamation imposing the Financial emergency can be revoked by the President on the advice of the Council of Ministers any time.

21.3.2 Effect of Financial Emergency

- During the period of Financial emergency, the Union government can give directions to the States to observe canons (rules) of financial propriety as may be specified in the directions.
- Such directions may require (a) reduction of the salaries and allowances of all or any class of persons serving under a State and (b) reservation of all money and financial bills passed by the State Legislature for consideration of the President.
- The President may also issue directions for reduction of salaries and allowances of persons serving under the Union including the Judges of the Supreme Court and the High Courts.

SUMMARY OF FINANCIAL EMERGENCY PROVISIONS

Ground	• If a situation has arisen whereby the financial stability or credit of India, or any part thereof is threatened. • Proclamation based on advise of the council of ministers.
Approval	• Approval by both houses within 2 months by simple majority. • President can revoke the emergency at any point of time
Effect	• Union government can give directions to States to observe canons of financial propriety. • President may issue directions for reduction of salaries of persons serving under the Union including the Judges of the Supreme Court and High Courts.

MAINS STARTER

Area	Building Blocks For Model Introductions
Emergency provisions	Emergency provisions are a relic of GOI Act, 1935. It converts the federal nature of our constitution into a unitary one which gives enormous powers to the Centre.
National emergency	A proclamation of national emergency can be made on the grounds of war, external aggression or armed rebellion. It requires approval by special majority of the Parliament (Art 352). It impacts Centre–State relations and fundamental rights of citizens (Art 358–359).
State emergency	President's rule or State emergency is imposed when the government of a State cannot be carried on in accordance with the provisions of the Constitution (Art 356). Though this was misused in the past by central governments, its imposition has been curtailed after the Supreme Court judgement in S R Bommai case.
Financial emergency	Financial emergency may be imposed if the financial stability or credit of India is threatened (Art 360). It affects the Centre–State financial relations. It has never been imposed in India till date.

UPSC Previous Years' Questions of Preliminary Examination

1. If the President of India exercises his power as provided under Article 356 of the Constitution in respect of a particular State, then **[2018]**
   (a) the Assembly of the State is automatically dissolved
   (b) the powers of the Legislature of that State shall be exercisable by or under the authority of the Parliament
   (c) Article 19 is suspended in that State
   (d) the President can make laws relating to that State

   Solution: (b)

   Explanation: As discussed in Section 21.2.2, on declaring President's rule under Article 356 in a State, the President may declare that the powers of the Legislature of that State shall be exercisable by or under the authority of the Parliament. Hence, the answer is (b).

2. Which of the following are not necessarily the consequences of the proclamation of the President's rule in a State? **[2017]**
   1. Dissolution of the State Legislative Assembly
   2. Removal of the Council of Ministers in the State
   3. Dissolution of the local bodies

   Select the correct answer using the codes given below:
   (a) 1 and 2 only (b) 1 and 3 only (c) 2 and 3 only (d) 1, 2 and 3

   Solution: (b)

   Explanation: As discussed in Section 21.2.2, the primary effect of imposing President's rule in a State is dismissal/removal of council of Ministers and the President assuming all the executive powers vested in the Governor. So, statement 2 is necessarily a consequence of proclamation of President's rule and once it is eliminated, the answer is (b).

   Further, the assembly of the State need not be dissolved in order to explore alternate government formation. Further, as discussed in Section 21.2.3, after the S R Bommai judgement, the assembly should not be dissolved till the President's rule is approved by Parliament within 2 months. The local bodies have their tenure as per constitution and are not affected by imposition of President's rule under Article 356. Hence 1 and 3 are not necessarily the consequences and the answer is (b).

UPSC PREVIOUS YEARS' QUESTIONS OF MAIN EXAMINATION

1. Account for the legal and political factors responsible for reduced frequency of using Article 356 by the Union Governments since mid-1990s. **[2023]**

Approach: The introduction about State emergency needs to be provided. The legal factor is the S R Bommai judgement and the political factor is coalition governments. This needs to be explained in the body of the answer.

MODEL ANSWER

President's rule or State emergency is imposed when the government of a State cannot be carried on in accordance with the provisions of the Constitution (Art 356). It needs to be approved by Parliament within 2 months by a simple majority. The continuation should be approved every 6 months by a simple majority and President's rule cannot exceed beyond 3 years. This provision was used on more than 90 occasions during the period 1950–94, mainly for political reasons.

Legal factors resulting in reduced use – S R Bommai Judgement (1994)

The misuse of Article 356, dramatically reduced after the landmark judgement of the Supreme Court in S R Bommai case in 1994. The following are the key points of the SC judgement in this case:

- The imposition of President's rule under Article 356 is subject to judicial review.
- The satisfaction of President for invoking Article 356 should be based on relevant material. Court cannot review the correctness of the material but will review its relevance.
- If the imposition of President's rule is declared unconstitutional, the court can restore the position as it existed before the invocation of Article 356.
- Till Parliament approves the imposition of President's rule, the Legislative Assembly should not be dissolved and it can be only kept under suspended animation.
- The State Government losing its majority should be proved only on the floor of the House, i.e., inside the Legislative Assembly.
- Article 356 cannot be used for political reasons and should be used only as an exception.

Political factors

Since mid-1990s, India has seen coalition governments at the centre till 2014. This included various regional parties that have always opposed use of Article 356 by the Centre for political reasons. This is also a factor for reduced use of Article 356.

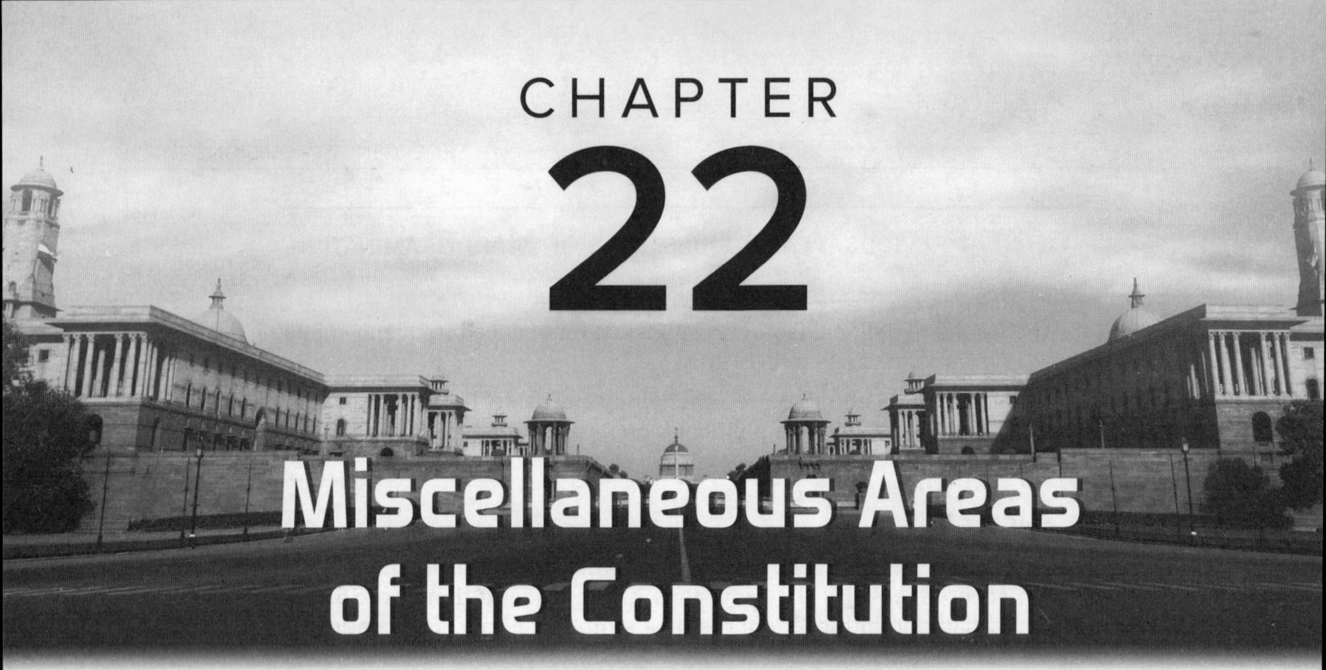

CHAPTER 22

Miscellaneous Areas of the Constitution

LEARNING OUTCOMES

1. Understanding provisions for the administration of Union Territories, including UTs with Legislative assemblies
2. Analysing special provisions for certain States that result in asymmetrical federalism
3. Summarising various schedules to the Constitution
4. Understanding other miscellaneous areas of the Constitution

22.1 UNION TERRITORIES

A Union Territory (UT) is a type of administrative division in the Republic of India. Article 1 of the Constitution provides that the territory of India shall also comprise the Union Territories specified in the First Schedule. Unlike the States of India, which have their own governments, the Union Territories are federal territories governed, in part or in whole, by the Government of India.

There are currently eight Union Territories in India, namely Andaman and Nicobar Islands, Chandigarh, Dadra and Nagar Haveli and Daman and Diu (merged into one UT with effect from January 2020), National Capital Territory (NCT) of Delhi, Jammu & Kashmir, Ladakh, Lakshadweep and Puducherry. Of these, three Union Territories i.e., the NCT of Delhi, Puducherry and Jammu & Kashmir have a Legislative Assembly.

The reasons for creation of Union Territories ranges from strategic importance to cultural distinctiveness. The Union Territories of Andaman and Nicobar Islands, Lakshadweep were formed and maintained as such for strategic reasons. It is due to political and administrative considerations that Delhi and Chandigarh are maintained as Union Territories. The State of Jammu & Kashmir was bifurcated into two Union Territories in 2019 due to administrative reasons (Ladakh) and the prevailing internal security situation (Jammu & Kashmir). The rest of the Union Territories have their cultural distinctiveness.

22.1.1 Administration of Union Territories

Part VIII of the Constitution (Articles 239–241) deals with administration of the Union Territories. We shall first summarise the provisions with respect to all the Union Territories. We shall then discuss the separate provisions that are applicable for the NCT of Delhi, Puducherry and Jammu & Kashmir.

Key provisions with respect to administration of the Union Territories are as follows:

- Every Union Territory shall be administered by the President acting through an administrator to be appointed by him/her with such designation as he/she may specify. The designation is Lieutenant Governor for the NCT of Delhi, Jammu & Kashmir, Ladakh, Puducherry and Andaman and Nicobar Islands. It is Administrator for Chandigarh, Lakshadweep, Dadra and Nagar Haveli and Daman and Diu.
- The President may appoint the Governor of a State as the administrator of an adjoining Union Territory, and where a Governor is so appointed, he/she shall exercise his/her functions as such administrator independently of his/her Council of Ministers. For example, if the Governor of Punjab is appointed as the Administrator of Chandigarh, he/she would exercise his/her functions as the Administrator of Chandigarh independent of the advice of the Council of Ministers of Punjab.
- The Parliament has the power to make laws on any subject including the subjects in the State list with respect to Union Territories. However, the Union Territories of Delhi, Puducherry and Jammu & Kashmir that have their own Legislative Assemblies have the power to make laws on subjects in the State and Concurrent lists subject to certain exceptions. However, the Parliamentary law will prevail over the laws made by such UT Assemblies in case of any repugnancy.
- The President may make regulations for the peace, progress and good government of the Union Territories of Andaman and Nicobar Islands, Lakshadweep, Dadra and Nagar Haveli and Daman and Diu and Puducherry. However, in respect of Puducherry, the President can make such regulations only when its Assembly is dissolved or suspended.
- The Parliament may by law constitute a High Court for a Union Territory or place it under the jurisdiction of the High Court of a State. The below table lists down the Union Territories with the High Court exercising jurisdiction over them.

Union Territory	High Court
NCT of Delhi	The High Court of Delhi
Jammu & Kashmir, Ladakh	The High Court of Jammu & Kashmir and Ladakh
Puducherry	The High Court of Madras
Andaman and Nicobar Islands	The Calcutta High Court
Lakshadweep	The Kerala High Court
Chandigarh	The Punjab and Haryana High Court
Dadra and Nagar Haveli and Daman and Diu	The High Court of Bombay

22.1.2 Union Territories with Legislative Assembly

22.1.2.1 National Capital Territory (NCT) of Delhi

Articles 239AA and 239AB of the Constitution, added through the 69th Amendment Act in 1991, contain special provisions for the NCT of Delhi. The Parliament has also enacted 'The Government of NCT of Delhi Act, 1991' to supplement the provisions of the Constitution.

Special provisions with respect to Delhi

Under the Constitution, the following are the special provisions applicable to Delhi:

- The Union Territory of Delhi shall be called the National Capital Territory of Delhi and the Administrator thereof appointed under Article 239 shall be designated as the Lieutenant Governor.
- The Legislative Assembly of Delhi shall have power to make laws for the whole or any part of the National Capital Territory with respect to any of the matters enumerated in the State list or in the Concurrent list in so far as any such matter is applicable to the Union Territories except matters with respect to Entries 1 (Public order), 2 (Police) and 18 (Land) of the State list. The Parliament however, shall continue to have the power to make laws on any matter for a Union Territory including the NCT of Delhi.
- There shall be a Council of Ministers consisting of not more than 10% of the total number of members in the Legislative Assembly including the Chief Minister. The total number of members of Delhi Assembly as on date (2024) is 70. Hence, the total number of ministers in the Delhi's Council of Ministers shall not exceed 7.
- As per the 106th Constitutional Amendment Act, as nearly as may be, 1/3rd of the seats in the Legislative Assembly of NCT of Delhi (including 1/3rd of the seats reserved for Scheduled Castes), shall be reserved for Women. This will be implemented based on the first census after commencement of the 106th Constitutional Amendment Act.
- The Chief Minister shall be appointed by the President and other Ministers shall be appointed by the President on the advice of the Chief Minister and the Ministers shall hold office during the pleasure of the President.
- In the case of difference of opinion between the Lieutenant Governor and his/her Ministers on any matter, the Lieutenant Governor shall refer it to the President for decision and act according to the decision given thereon by the President.
- Ordinance can be promulgated by the Lieutenant Governor (based on advice of the Council of Ministers) only after obtaining instructions from the President.
- The NCT of Delhi can be placed under the President's rule if the President is satisfied based on a report from the Lieutenant Governor or otherwise that the administration of the NCT of Delhi cannot be carried on in accordance with the provisions of the Constitution or the Government of NCT of Delhi Act.

The Government of NCT of Delhi Act, 1991 contains various provisions relating to the legislature and executive of the Government of Delhi. These provisions are similar to the provisions under Part VI of the Constitution with respect to States with few modifications.

Issues between Lieutenant Governor (LG) and Government of NCT of Delhi

There have been issues between the LG (representing the Central government) and the elected government in Delhi whenever the Central government and Delhi government were run by different political parties. While many of the issues may be political in nature, the constitutional and legal issues between the two governments arise because of the following two contentious areas.

1. Demand for full Statehood

- The Delhi Assembly and government do not have any authority with respect to police, public order and land. These subjects have been kept under the control of the Central government and the Parliament as Delhi is not just a Union Territory but also consists of the National Capital that houses all Central government offices as well the embassies/high commissions of foreign countries.

- However, the MLAs of Delhi and its government is elected directly by the people to whom they are accountable for any issue in the NCT. This is the reason that all political parties that have come to power in the NCT of Delhi have demanded full Statehood for Delhi at various points of time.
- One possible solution to this issue can be to reduce the area that comes under the control of the Central government. The NCT of Delhi is more than 1450 square kilometres. However, 'New Delhi' area that is the capital of India and which houses all the Central government offices and foreign government offices is only around 45 square kilometres. In the United States, Washington DC which is the capital district is only spread around 177 square kilometres. A similar approach can be implemented where the area in 'New Delhi' of less than 50 square kilometres can be under the complete control of the Central government. The rest of the areas in the NCT of Delhi may be brought under the powers of Delhi Assembly and government including police, public order and land.

2. LG role in Services

- The Constitution specifies that in the case of difference of opinion between the Lieutenant Governor and his/her Ministers on any matter, the Lieutenant Governor shall refer it to the President for decision and act according to the decision given thereon by the President.
- This has also resulted in conflict between the LG and the elected government of NCT of Delhi. There was a case that was filed in the Delhi High Court by the Delhi Government in this regard. The Delhi High Court ruled in August 2016 that the LG has full powers with respect to administration of the NCT of Delhi. However, the Supreme Court in 2018 on appeal gave a judgement that the LG should act as per the advice of the Council of Ministers except for the entries of public order, police and land. He should refer any difference of opinion to the President not as a matter of routine but only under exceptional circumstances. This judgement would have ideally settled the issue between the LG and the elected government in Delhi.

THINK ABOUT IT

Does the recent amendment to the Government of National Capital Territory of Delhi Act in 2023 undermine the role of the elected government? Critically analyse.

- However, the Government of the NCT of Delhi Act was again amended by the Parliament, in 2021. It required the council of ministers to obtain the opinion of LG before any executive action on matters, as may be indicated by the LG. An order was made in April 2021, pursuant to this amendment that required the council of ministers to obtain the clearance of LG on various items. This amendment and the order tilted the balance again in favour of the LG that created rift with the elected government of Delhi.
- A constitution bench of the Supreme Court in May 2023 had held that the Government of NCT of Delhi shall have legislative and executive powers over 'services' except in relation to Public Order, Police and Land. 'Services' mainly deals with the appointment and transfer of officers to various posts in the government, as well as initiation of disciplinary proceedings against officers. As part of its judgement, the Supreme Court mentioned that there is a triple chain of accountability in a democracy. The officials are accountable to the ministers; the council of ministers are collectively responsible to the legislative assembly; and the legislative assembly members are accountable to the people.
- The Central government had promulgated an ordinance immediately after this judgement to vest the power of 'services' with the LG. Subsequently in

Scan the QR code for conceptual video on Union Territories

McGraw Hill edge

August 2023, the Parliament passed, The Government of NCT of Delhi (Amendment) Act, 2023 with the following significant provisions:

1. It created the National Capital Civil Service Authority for deciding and recommending to the LG, on various matters relating to 'Services' in the NCT of Delhi.
2. This authority will consist of the Chief Minister, the Chief Secretary and the Home Secretary of Delhi. The decisions will be taken by a majority vote. This has the effect of reducing the importance of the elected Chief Minister in decisions relating to 'Services'.
3. Further, in case of any difference of opinion between the recommendations of the authority and the LG, the decision of the LG shall be final.

- The stated objective of the amendment is to maintain democratic and administrative balance in the NCT of Delhi. However, it must be noted that in a democracy, the elected government is accountable to the people. Hence, the essence of the Supreme Court judgement in 2018 and 2023 should be followed.

22.1.2.2 Puducherry

The Union Territory of Puducherry was formed on 1 July 1963. The provisions for Puducherry are contained in Articles 239A–239B of the Constitution, read along with 'The Government of Union Territories Act, 1963'.

The special provisions for Puducherry are as follows:

- The Parliament may by law create a body to function as the legislature of Puducherry or a Council of Ministers or both for the Union Territory of Puducherry. As per this provision, 'The Government of Union Territories Act, 1963' provides for a Legislative Assembly with 30 members and the Council of Ministers. The Legislative Assembly also has 3 members who are nominated by the Central government. $1/3^{rd}$ of the seats in the Legislative Assembly of Puducherry will be reserved for women (in a manner and time-frame similar to Lok Sabha and other State assemblies).
- The Chief Minister is appointed by the President and all other ministers are appointed by the President on the advice of the Chief Minister.
- Ordinance can be promulgated by the Lieutenant Governor (based on the advice of Council of Ministers) only after obtaining instructions from the President.

22.1.2.3 Jammu & Kashmir

The State of Jammu & Kashmir had special status under Article 370 of the Constitution. As per this special status, the State had its own constitution. There was a presidential order issued in 1954 under Article 370. It had special provisions with respect to residence and ownership of property within the State. Many of the provisions of the Indian Constitution were made applicable to the State while many others were not applicable to that State.

In August 2019, the Indian Parliament reorganised the State of Jammu & Kashmir into two Union Territories namely Jammu & Kashmir and Ladakh.

J & K Reorganisation in August 2019

The Parliament carried out the following reorganisation in August 2019:

- The Constitution (Application to Jammu & Kashmir) Order, 2019 – issued by the President of India to supersede the 1954 order related to Article 370.
- Resolution for repeal of Article 370 of the Constitution of India.

- Jammu & Kashmir (Reorganisation) Act, 2019.

Key Changes

- The President had used his/her powers under Article 370 to fundamentally alter the provision, extending all Central laws, instruments and treaties to Jammu & Kashmir.
- While the Union Territory of Jammu & Kashmir will have a legislature, the Union Territory of Ladakh will be without a legislature.
- The notification by the President has effectively allowed the entire provisions of the Constitution, with all its amendments, exceptions and modifications, to apply to the area of Jammu & Kashmir.
- All Central laws and State laws of J&K would apply to the new Union Territories of J&K and Ladakh.
- The subjects of police and public order are to be with the Centre with respect to the Union Territory of Jammu & Kashmir.

Legislative powers of the Union Territory of Jammu & Kashmir

- The Legislative Assembly may make laws for the whole or any part of the Union Territory of Jammu & Kashmir with respect to any of the matters enumerated in the State list except on subjects 'public order' and 'police' which will remain in the domain of the Centre through the Lieutenant Governor (LG).
- In case of inconsistencies between laws made by the Parliament and laws made by the Legislative Assembly, the Parliamentary law shall prevail and law made by the Legislative Assembly shall be void.
- The role of the Chief Minister will be to communicate to the LG all decisions of the Council of Ministers relating to the administration of affairs of the Union Territory and proposals for legislation and to furnish such information relating to the administration of affairs as the LG may call for.

Role and powers of the Lieutenant Governor

- Appointment of LG in Ladakh: The President shall appoint the LG under Article 239. The LG will be assisted by advisors appointed by the Centre since the Union Territory will not have a Legislative Assembly.
- In the case of Union Territory of Jammu & Kashmir, the LG shall 'act in his/her discretion' on issues which fall outside the purview of powers conferred on the Legislative Assembly, in which he/she is required to exercise any judicial functions, and/or matters related to All-India Services and the Anti-Corruption Bureau.
- ***The Chief Minister shall be appointed by the LG who will also appoint other ministers as per advice of the CM.*** The total number of ministers, including the Chief Minister, shall not exceed 10% of the total membership of the Legislative Assembly.
- The LG will have the power to promulgate ordinances which shall have the same force and effect as an Act of the Legislative Assembly assented by the LG.
- 1/3rd of the seats in the Legislative Assembly of J&K will be reserved for women (in a manner and time-frame similar to Lok Sabha and other State assemblies).
- There can be a total of 5 members whom the LG can nominate to the J&K assembly – (a) Up to 2 women members if, in the opinion of the LG, women are not adequately represented in the Legislative Assembly; (b) 2 members from the Kashmiri migrant community (of whom one shall be woman); (c) one member representing the displaced persons from Pakistan-occupied Kashmir.

Rationale behind this move

- Article 370 had prevented J&K to merge with India rather than being a basis of its merger. It was seen as discriminatory on the basis of gender, class, caste and place of origin.
- Post the repeal of the Article 370, doors to private investment in J&K would be opened, which would in turn increase the potential for development there.
- Increased investments would lead to increased job creation and further betterment of socio-economic infrastructure in the State.
- Opening of buying of lands would bring in investments from private individuals and multinational companies and give a boost to the local economy.

Supreme Court judgement on J&K reorganisation

The Supreme Court, in December 2023, upheld the actions taken by the Central Government and Parliament in August 2019 with respect to reorganisation of Jammu & Kashmir into two Union Territories. The summary of the Supreme Court judgement is as follows:

- Article 370 was a temporary provision and there was no internal sovereignty for J&K. It held that Article 370 was a feature of 'asymmetric federalism.'
- It held that President can unilaterally issue an order to make Article 370 ineffective after the abolition of the Constituent Assembly of J&K.
- It upheld the carving out of Ladakh as a separate Union Territory without a Legislative Assembly.
- The Court stated that J&K's statehood should be restored as soon as possible.

Elections to the J&K assembly were held in September 2024 and a democratically elected government is in place at present. As opined by the Supreme Court, statehood should be restored at the earliest to Jammu & Kashmir.

22.2 SPECIAL CATEGORY STATES

We have already discussed that the Indian Constitution is quasi-federal in nature due to the presence of unitary features that provide more powers to the centre when compared to the States. This aspect has also been explained under legislative, executive and financial relations between the Centre and the States.

THINK ABOUT IT

Indian federalism is 'asymmetrical federalism.' Elucidate with reference to special provisions for certain States in Part XXI.

> Apart from being quasi-federal with unitary bias, the Indian federalism is also 'asymmetrical' in nature. Asymmetrical federalism is where different States possess different powers and some of the States have more autonomy than others. A classical federation like the United States or Australia is a symmetrical federation as all States enjoy the same set of powers and autonomy under their Constitution. In the Indian context, there are few States that enjoy more autonomy or special provisions under the Constitution than the other States.

Scan the QR code for conceptual video on Special category States

McGraw Hill edge

The special category States are under Articles 371–371J of the Constitution in Part XXI. These provisions can be broadly classified under the following two categories:

1. Special status for States of North-East India – These provisions are made to (a) protect the cultural interests of tribal and local people of the region and (b) deal with the law-and-order situation in some of the border States of the region.
2. Special provisions for certain other States like Maharashtra, Gujarat, Andhra Pradesh, Telangana and Karnataka – to fulfil the aspirations of people belonging to the backward regions within these States.

The key provisions for these special category States are summarised below in a tabular form.

Article No.	State(s) for which Applicable	Key Special Provisions
371	Maharashtra and Gujarat	• The President may by order made with respect to the State of Maharashtra or Gujarat, provide for any special responsibility of the Governor: ◆ to establish separate development boards for Vidarbha and Marathwada (in Maharashtra); Saurashtra and Kutch (in Gujarat) with a provision that a report on the working of these boards be placed each year before the State Assembly; ◆ for equitable allocation of funds for development expenditure over said areas; ◆ for an equitable arrangement providing adequate facilities for technical education and vocational training, and adequate opportunities for employment in respect of the said areas.
371A	Nagaland	• No Act of Parliament shall apply to the State of Nagaland unless the Legislative Assembly of Nagaland by a resolution so decides in respect of – ◆ religious or social practices of the Nagas, ◆ Naga customary law and procedure, ◆ administration of civil and criminal justice involving decisions according to Naga customary law, ◆ ownership and transfer of land and its resources. • The Governor of Nagaland shall have special responsibility with respect to law and order in the State of Nagaland and after consulting the Council of Ministers, he/she can exercise his/her individual judgment as to the action to be taken.
371B	Assam	The President is empowered to provide for the creation of a committee of the Assam Legislative Assembly consisting of the members elected from the 'Tribal Areas' (i.e., the areas specified in the Sixth Schedule) of the State and such other members as he/she may specify.
371C	Manipur	• The President may, by order made with respect to the State of Manipur, provide for the Constitution and functions of a committee of the Legislative Assembly of the State consisting of members of that Assembly elected from the Hill Areas of that State. • The Governor shall annually, or whenever so required by the President, make a report to the President regarding the administration of the Hill Areas in the State of Manipur and the executive power of the Union shall extend to the giving of directions to the State as to the administration of the said areas.

Article No.	State(s) for which Applicable	Key Special Provisions
371D	Andhra Pradesh & Telangana	The President may by order made with respect to the State of Andhra Pradesh or Telangana, provide for equitable opportunities and facilities for the people belonging to different parts of such State, in the matter of public employment and in the matter of education, and different provisions may be made for various parts of the States.
371E	Andhra Pradesh	The Parliament may by law provide for the establishment of a Central University in the State.
371F	Sikkim	• The Legislative Assembly of the State of Sikkim shall consist of not less than 30 members. • The Parliament may, for the purpose of protecting the rights and interests of the different sections of the population of Sikkim make provision for the number of seats in the Legislative Assembly of the State of Sikkim which may be filled by candidates belonging to such sections. • The Governor of Sikkim shall have special responsibility for peace and for an equitable arrangement for ensuring the social and economic advancement of different sections of the population of Sikkim and in the discharge of his/her special responsibility under this clause, the Governor of Sikkim shall, subject to such directions as the President may, from time to time, deem fit to issue, act in his/her discretion.
371G	Mizoram	• No Act of Parliament shall apply to the State of Mizoram unless the Legislative Assembly of Mizoram by a resolution so decides in respect of – ◆ religious or social practices of the Mizos, ◆ Mizo customary law and procedure, ◆ administration of civil and criminal justice involving decisions according to the Mizo customary law, ◆ ownership and transfer of land and its resources. • The Legislative Assembly of the State of Mizoram shall consist of not less than 40 members.
371H	Arunachal Pradesh	• The Governor of Arunachal Pradesh shall have special responsibility with respect to law and order in the State of Arunachal Pradesh and in the discharge of his functions in relation thereto, the Governor shall, after consulting the Council of Ministers, exercise his/her individual judgment as to the action to be taken. • The Legislative Assembly of the State of Arunachal Pradesh shall consist of not less than 30 members. It actually consists of 60 members as on date.
371-I	Goa	• The Legislative Assembly of the State of Goa shall consist of not less than 40 members.

Article No.	State(s) for which Applicable	Key Special Provisions
371J	Karnataka	• The President may by order made with respect to the State of Karnataka, provide for any special responsibility of the Governor: ◆ to establish separate development boards for Hyderabad–Karnataka region with a provision that a report on the working of these boards be placed each year before the State Assembly; ◆ for equitable allocation of funds for development expenditure over said region; ◆ for equitable opportunities and facilities for people belonging to the said region in matters of public employment, education and vocational training; ◆ for reservation of seats in educational and vocational training for students who belong to that region; ◆ for reservation in State government posts in the region for persons who belong to the region.

22.3 SCHEDULES TO THE CONSTITUTION

Schedules to the Constitution are like annexures that form part of the Constitution. They supplement or elaborate on the aspect mentioned in a relevant part/article of the Constitution. We have already discussed the relevant Schedules under the respective areas.

This section is a tabular summary of the Schedules and the areas they deal with. The chapter/section where they have been discussed in relevant chapters have also been provided for reference. The Fifth and Sixth Schedules that deal with protection of interest of the Scheduled Tribes in Scheduled and Tribal areas will be discussed at the end of this section.

Scan the QR code for conceptual video on Schedules to the Constitution

Schedule No.	Article Reference	Key Provisions	Chapter/Section Reference
First	1 and 4	List of States and Union Territories	Chapter 6 – Section 6.1
Second	Various Articles	It provided for salaries and allowances to be paid to various constitutional authorities like the President, the Governor, Judges, the CAG etc.	This Schedule is no longer relevant as all those emoluments have been modified through various Parliamentary laws
Third	Various Articles	Forms of Oaths or Affirmations to be taken by various constitutional authorities before entering office	Chapter 10 – Section 10.5.2.1 and also in other sections of different chapters as applicable
Fourth	4(1) and 80(2)	Allocation of seats in the Council of States	Chapter 10 – Section 10.3.2

Schedule No.	Article Reference	Key Provisions	Chapter/Section Reference
Fifth	244(1)	Administration of Scheduled Areas in various States	Discussed below
Sixth	244(2) and 275	Administration of Tribal Areas in the States of Assam, Meghalaya, Tripura and Mizoram	Discussed below
Seventh	246	Distribution of powers between the Union and the States	Chapter 19 – Section 19.2.2
Eighth	344(1) and 151	List of official languages	Discussed in Section 22.4 below.
Ninth	31B	Protection of laws that may be inconsistent with Fundamental rights	Chapter 14 – Section 14.10.2
Tenth	102(2) and 191(2)	Disqualification on ground of defection	Chapter 10 – Section 10.4.3.2
Eleventh	243G	Areas for Panchayats to prepare development plans	Chapter 20 – Section 20.2.2
Twelfth	243W	Areas for Municipalities to prepare development plans	Chapter 20 – Section 20.3.2.2

The Fifth and Sixth Schedules have been modelled on the basis of 'Partially Excluded' and 'Excluded' areas under the Government of India Act, 1935. These provisions are aimed at protecting the interest of the Scheduled Tribes. The key provisions with respect to these two schedules are discussed below.

Fifth Schedule

This Schedule is applicable to all 'Scheduled areas' that are declared by the President. Key provisions of the Fifth Schedule are as follows:

- 'Scheduled areas' means such areas as the President by order declare to be Scheduled Areas. The guiding norms for declaring an area as a 'Scheduled area' include preponderance of tribal population, compactness of the area, a viable administrative unit like a district or block, and economic backwardness.
- Ten States at present have Fifth Schedule areas – Andhra Pradesh, Chhattisgarh, Gujarat, Himachal Pradesh, Jharkhand, Madhya Pradesh, Maharashtra, Odisha, Rajasthan and Telangana.
- The Governor of a State with Scheduled areas has to make a report to the President annually or whenever required by the President about administration of Scheduled areas. The executive power of the Union shall extend to giving of directions to a State in respect of administration of such areas.
- Tribes advisory Council (TAC)
    - Tribes Advisory Council to be set up in each State having Scheduled areas.
    - It shall consist of not more than 20 members of whom 3/4th shall be from tribal MLAs of the State. If tribal MLAs are not sufficient, then other members of those tribes shall be made members of TAC.
    - Duty of the Council to advise on such matters pertaining to the welfare and advancement of the Scheduled Tribe (ST) in the State as may be referred to them by the Governor.

- Governor shall make rules prescribing and regulating meetings of the TAC.

❑ Law applicable to Scheduled areas
- Governor may direct that a particular Act of Parliament or State Legislature shall not apply or apply with such modifications to the Scheduled areas.
- Governor may make regulations for
  - Prohibiting or transferring of land by or among members of ST in such area;
  - Regulating the allotment of land to members of ST in such area;
  - Regulating the business as money-lender by persons who lend money to ST in such area.
- All such regulations shall be submitted to the President and until assented to by him/her shall have no effect.
- In case there is a TAC, no regulation shall be made without consulting such Council.

❑ The Parliament can amend the Fifth Schedule by an ordinary law and no such law shall be deemed to be an amendment of the Constitution under Article 368.

Sixth Schedule

❑ This is applicable to 'Tribal areas' in the States of Assam, Meghalaya, Tripura and Mizoram.

❑ Autonomous districts are formed in each of these four States. If there are different Scheduled Tribes in an autonomous district, the Governor may divide the area or areas inhabited by them into autonomous regions.

❑ There shall be a district council for each autonomous district consisting of not more than 30 members, of whom 4 persons shall be nominated by the Governor and rest shall be elected on the basis of adult suffrage.

❑ If regional council is present, then administration shall be vested in such council for such region.

❑ Governor will make rules for constitution and election to the District and Regional Councils.

❑ District and Regional Councils shall have powers to make laws with respect to –
- Allotment, occupation or setting apart of land other than reserve forest land for agriculture;
- Management of any forest not being a reserved forest;
- Use of canal or water resource for agriculture;
- Regulation of Jhum or shifting cultivation;
- Establishment of village or town councils;
- Appointment or succession of Chiefs or Headman;
- Inheritance of property;
- Marriage and divorce;
- Social customs.

All such laws are to be submitted to the Governor for his/her approval and shall have no effect unless approved by the Governor.

Scan the QR code for video on recent demands for inclusion in Sixth Schedule

McGraw Hill edge

❑ For the above matters, laws made by the State Legislature as the case may be will not be applicable in the Tribal Areas unless extended by the District Councils.

❑ Similarly the Parliamentary and State laws (for matters other than those above) may be made not applicable or applicable with modifications/exceptions through notification by the President/Governor.

❑ The Parliament can amend the Sixth Schedule by an ordinary law and no such law shall be deemed to be an amendment of the Constitution under Article 368.

- Arunachal Pradesh assembly for the entire State and the Manipur Hill Area Committee for the 'Hill areas' in the State had passed resolutions in recent years for inclusion in the Sixth Schedule. There is a growing demand for inclusion of Union territory of Ladakh as well in the Sixth Schedule. These demands have to be examined promptly and necessary decisions taken at the earliest to protect the interest of tribals in these areas.

MNEMONICS

Concept or Provisions	Shortcut or Mnemonics	Details to Remember
Schedules to the Constitution	**TEARS OF OLD PM**	• **T** – **T**erritories of India – First Schedule • **E** – **E**moluments and allowances of constitutional authorities – Second Schedule • **A** – **A**ffirmations and Oaths – Third Schedule • **R** – **R**ajya Sabha – allocation of seats – Fourth Schedule • **S** – **S**cheduled Areas – Fifth schedule • **O** – **O**ther Tribal areas in Assam, Tripura, Meghalaya and Mizoram (ATM Money) – Sixth Schedule • **F** – **F**ederal set up – Distribution of powers – Seventh Schedule • **O** – **O**fficial Languages – Eighth Schedule • **L** – **L**and reforms and exception to fundamental rights under Art 31B – Ninth Schedule • **D** – **D**isqualification due to defection – Tenth Schedule • **P** – **P**anchayats – Eleventh Schedule • **M** – **M**unicipalities – Twelfth Schedule

22.4 OFFICIAL LANGUAGES

The provisions related to official languages are provided in Part XVII of the Constitution. The key provisions of this part are summarised below.

22.4.1 Language of the Union

1. Hindi in *Devanagari* script shall be the official language of the Union. The form of numerals to be used for official purposes shall be the international form of Indian numerals (i.e., 1, 2, 3 etc.) [Art 343].

2. English would continue to be used for official purposes for 15 years from the commencement of the Constitution. Thereafter, the Parliament by law may provide for the continued use of English language [Art 343]. Accordingly, the Parliament has enacted the Official Languages Act, 1963. This Act provides for the continued use of English, in addition to Hindi, for all official purposes of the Union and transaction of business in the Parliament (without any time limit).
3. English language shall be used for communication between the Union and a State which has not adopted Hindi as its official language. Further, for any communication between one ministry/department/corporation or company of the Central government and another, the official communication shall be provided in both Hindi and English.
4. The Official Languages Act, 1963 also provides for the setting up of a committee of Parliament on official language to review the progress made in the use of Hindi for official purposes of the Union. This committee shall consist of 30 members – 20 from the Lok Sabha and 10 from the Rajya Sabha. As a convention, the Union Home Minister is elected as the Chairman of the committee from time to time. This Committee was set up in 1976 and is required to submit its report from time to time to the President. It has submitted the 12th volume of its report in September 2023 to the President. The theme of the 12th volume is 'Simplification'.

22.4.2 Regional Languages

1. The Legislature of a State may adopt any one or more of the languages in use in the State or Hindi as the official language(s) to be used for official purposes of that State [Art 345]. Various States have adopted Hindi or their major regional language as their official language. Some of the North-Eastern States (like Meghalaya, Arunachal Pradesh and Nagaland) have adopted English as their official language. It is not necessary that the official language has to be one of the languages listed in the Eighth Schedule.
2. English would be the official language of communication between one State and another [Art 346]. Further, as per the Official Languages Act, 1963, any communication in Hindi from a State that has adopted Hindi as its official language to a State that has not adopted Hindi as its official language, shall also be accompanied by an English translation.
3. Two or more States are free to agree to use Hindi for communication amongst themselves [Art 346]. Rajasthan, Uttar Pradesh, Bihar and Madhya Pradesh are some of the States that have entered into such agreements.
4. When the President, based on a demand, is satisfied that a substantial proportion of the population of a State desire the use of any language spoken by them to be recognised by that State, he/she may direct that such language shall also be officially recognised in that State [Art 347].

22.4.3 Language of the Judiciary and Text of Laws

- Until the Parliament by law otherwise provides, the following shall be in English language only [Art 348]:
  - (a) All proceedings in the Supreme Court and the High Courts.
  - (b) The authoritative texts of all bills, acts, ordinances, rules, orders, regulations and bye-laws at both the Union and State levels.

- The Governor of a State may, with the previous consent of the President, authorise the use of Hindi or any other official language of the State in proceedings in the High Court of the State except for judgements, orders or decrees [Art 348].
- A State Legislature can prescribe the use of any language, other than English, with respect to bills, acts, ordinances, rules, orders, regulations and bye-laws. However, an English translation is also to be published [Art 348].
- The Official Languages Act, 1963 provides that every bill introduced in the Parliament is to be accompanied by a Hindi translation. Further, the Hindi translation of acts, ordinances, rules, orders, regulations and bye-laws published under the authority of the President are deemed to be authoritative texts. Further, under the Authorised Translations (Central Laws) Act, 1973, a translation in any regional language specified in the Eighth Schedule of central acts, ordinances, rules, orders, regulations and bye-laws, published under the authority of the President shall be deemed to be the authoritative texts in such language.

22.4.4 Special Directives

- Every aggrieved person has the right to submit a representation for redressal of any grievance to the government authority in any language used in the Union or the State [Art 350].
- It shall be the endeavour of every State and of every local authority within the State to provide adequate facilities for instruction in the mother-tongue at the primary stage of education to children belonging to linguistic minority groups [Art 350A].
- The President shall appoint a special officer for linguistic minorities to investigate all matters relating to the constitutional safeguards for linguistic minorities and to report to him/her. The President shall place all such reports before the Parliament and to the State governments concerned [Art 350B].
- It shall be the duty of the Union to promote the spread of the Hindi language, to develop it so that it may serve as a medium of expression for all the elements of the composite culture of India [Art 351].

22.4.5 Classical Languages

In 2004, the Government of India created a new category of languages called 'classical languages.' This is not as per the Constitution or any law but conferred by the executive.

The 6 languages conferred with classical language status between 2004 and 2014 are Tamil (2004), Sanskrit (2005), Telugu and Kannada (2008), Malayalam (2013) and Odia (2014). In October 2024, the Centre conferred classical language status on 5 more languages – Marathi, Pali, Prakrit, Assamese and Bengali. This takes the total classical languages to 11.

The conferment of 'classical language' status is based on the recommendation of the ***Linguistic Expert Committee (LEC)*** which comprises representatives of the Union Ministries of Home, Culture and four to five linguistic experts at any given time. ***It is chaired by the president of the Sahitya Akademi. The Sahitya Akademi is the nodal agency for LEC for which the nodal ministry is Ministry of Culture.***

The criteria for conferring classical language status have been revised in 2024. The revised criteria are as follows:

1. High antiquity of early texts/recorded history over a period of 1500–2000 years.
2. A body of ancient literature/texts, which is considered a heritage by generations of speakers.

3. Knowledge texts, especially prose texts in addition to poetry, epigraphical and inscriptional evidence. (revised in 2024)
4. The Classical Languages and literature could be distinct from its current form or could be discontinuous with later forms of its offshoots.

The benefits of classical languages include financial assistance for setting up a centre of excellence, two major awards for scholars of eminence and creation of professional chairs in central universities supported by the UGC. The Government has also established the Centre for Excellence for studies in Classical Languages at the Central Institute of Indian Languages in Mysore. This comes under the Ministry of Education.

22.5 TRIBUNALS

Tribunals in India have been a long-standing feature of the judicial system, beginning with the setting up of the Income Tax Appellate Tribunal as early as 1941. The 42nd Amendment Act in 1976, added Part XIV-A which inserted Articles 323A–323B to the Constitution. It empowered both the Parliament and the State Legislatures to establish administrative and other tribunals. With this insertion, tribunals, as an alternate method of adjudication, received constitutional legitimacy.

Article 323A: Provides for the establishment of Administrative Tribunals for adjudication or trial of disputes and complaints with respect to recruitment, conditions of service of persons appointed to public services and posts in Union and in States/Local authority. The Parliament has power to enact any law under Article 323A.

Article 323B: Makes provision for the creation of Tribunals for adjudication or trial of disputes, complaints or offences connected with tax, foreign exchange, industrial and labour disputes, land reforms, ceiling on urban property, election to Parliament and State Legislatures, etc. Both the Parliament and the State Legislatures can make laws on matters under Article 323B, subject to their legislative competence.

Administrative Tribunals

The Parliament has passed the Administrative Tribunals Act, 1985 under the provisions of Article 323A.

Under this law, there is a Central Administrative Tribunal (CAT) that has been set up. The jurisdiction of this tribunal extends to All-India services, central services and civilian employees of defence services. The Act also empowers the Central government to establish State Administrative Tribunals (SAT) on request of the concerned State governments. Just like CAT has jurisdiction over recruitment and service matters of the Union government employees, the SAT has jurisdiction on these matters of the State government employees.

Tribunals for other matters

Both the Parliament and the State Legislatures can make laws on matters under Article 323B, subject to their legislative competence. These matters are taxation, foreign exchange, industrial and labour disputes, land reforms, ceiling on urban property, election to the Parliament and the State Legislatures, food stuffs, rent and tenancy rights etc. There can also be a hierarchy of tribunals for these matters under the law that establishes them.

In the *Chandra Kumar case* (1997), the Supreme Court held that the provisions of Articles 323A and 323B that excluded the jurisdiction of the High Courts for matters decided by these tribunals as unconstitutional. Hence, judicial remedies are available against the orders of these tribunals at both the High Courts and the Supreme Court.

Critical analysis of Tribunals

Advantages of Tribunals can be summarised as follows:

- Tribunals are composed of technical experts thereby allowing for niche jurisprudence.
- They are less expensive when compared to courts and also have the effect of reducing the burden on the ordinary courts.
- They follow principles of natural justice but are not bound by procedures under the Civil Procedure Code and The Bharatiya Sakshya Adhiniyam, 2023. Hence, they can provide speedier justice.
- Their decisions are legally binding on the parties, subject to appeal.

However, Tribunals also have some limitations that are summarised below:

- Their statutory nature and inadequate safeguards against executive influence means that they compromise the principle of separation of powers.
- Since the government is the largest litigator in the country, setting up tribunals whose members are appointed by the government creates conflict of interest.
- Tribunals were set up to expedite justice delivery but have failed to deliver on that promise over time.

Law Commission recommendations with respect to Tribunals

The Law Commission submitted its report on 'Assessment of Statutory Frameworks of Tribunals in India' in October 2017. The report examined issues related to (i) constitution of tribunals, (ii) appointment of the chairman and members of tribunals and (iii) service conditions of members of tribunals.

It recommended various measures for improved functioning of the tribunals:

- Qualification of judges to be appropriate for the jurisdiction under their care.
- Selection of members to be done by an impartial selection committee formed for the purpose.
- Appointment of the chairman and members of tribunal to be uniform and smooth with the process of appointment initiated before the retirement of predecessors.
- It should be possible to challenge any order of the tribunal or its appellate tribunal in the division bench of the High Court having territorial jurisdiction over such tribunal.

Tribunal Reforms Act, 2021

The Parliament passed the Tribunal Reforms Act, 2021. The key provisions with respect to this Act are as follows:

- It seeks to dissolve certain existing appellate tribunals and transfer their functions to the High Courts and the civil courts. Film Certification Appellate Tribunal, Airports Appellate Tribunal, Authority for Advance Rulings, Intellectual Property Appellate Board and the Plant Varieties Protection Appellate Tribunal are the tribunals which are sought to be abolished by the Act.
- It seeks to empower the Central Government to make rules for qualifications, appointment, term of office, salaries and allowances, resignation, removal and other terms and conditions of service of Members of Tribunals.
- It provides that the Chairperson and Members of the Tribunals will be appointed by the Central Government on the recommendation of a Search-cum-Selection Committee.

- Minimum age for appointment as a member or a Chairman is 50 years.
- Maximum tenure for the members and the Chairman is 4 years.

22.6 PUBLIC SERVICES

Articles 308–314 of Part XIV contain provisions regarding All-India Services, central services and State services. They are summarised below:

1. The Parliament and the State Legislatures can regulate the recruitment and conditions of service of persons appointed to public services and posts under the Union and the States respectively [Art 309].
2. The members of defence service, civil services of the Union, All-India Services, persons holding defence post or civil post under the Union, hold their office during the pleasure of the President. Similarly, members of civil services of a State or persons holding civil posts under a State, hold their office during the pleasure of the Governor [Art 310].
3. There are two safeguards to civil servants against arbitrary dismissal from their posts: (a) A civil servant cannot be dismissed or removed by an authority subordinate to that by which he/she has been appointed; (b) A civil servant cannot be dismissed or removed or reduced in rank except after an inquiry in which he/she has been informed of the charges against him/her and given a reasonable opportunity of being heard in respect of those charges [Art 311].
4. All-India Services including All-India judicial services can be created by the Parliament by law based on a resolution passed by the Rajya Sabha with two-thirds of members present and voting [Art 312]. The Indian Administrative Service, the Indian Police Service and the Indian Forest Service are the existing All-India Services. Though the Constitution enables creation of All-India Judicial Service, it has not been created till date (2024).

22.7 RIGHTS AND LIABILITIES OF GOVERNMENT

Articles 294–300 in Part XII and few other articles/conventions determine the rights and liabilities of the Government. Some of the important provisions with respect to rights and liabilities of the Government under the Constitution are summarised below:

- All lands, minerals and other things of value underlying the ocean within the territorial waters, continental shelf and exclusive economic zone of India shall vest in the Union [Art 297]. India's territorial waters extend to 12 nautical miles and exclusive economic zone extends up to 200 nautical miles as per Parliamentary laws.
- All contracts made in the exercise of executive power of the Union or a State shall be expressed to be made by the President or by the Governor of a State. Neither the President nor the Governor shall be personally liable in respect of any such contract or assurance made or executed [Art 299].
- The Government of India may sue or be sued (i.e., filing of cases) by the name of the Union of India and the Government of a State by the name of that State [Art 300].
- Earlier as per the British convention, the governments in India (Union or State), were liable for torts (civil wrongs) committed by its officials only in the exercise of its non-sovereign functions. In respect of sovereign functions like administering justice, commanding during war etc., there was no liability of the government and it could not be sued against. However, in subsequent

judgements the Supreme Court has held that governments can be sued and would be liable for all torts of its employees, whether done in exercise of sovereign or non-sovereign powers.

- Protection to the President and the Governor in performing their duties [Art 361].
  - No criminal proceedings against the President or the Governor during their term of office;
  - No process for arrest or imprisonment of the President or the Governor during their term of office;
  - No civil proceedings against the President or the Governor except until expiration of 2 months' notice.
- The Ministers are not liable in the courts for their official acts. However, they do not enjoy any immunity for their personal acts, and can be sued for crimes as well as civil wrongs in the ordinary courts like other citizens.
- Judicial officers i.e., judges, magistrate, collector or any other person acting in a judicial capacity shall not be liable for any act done by them in the discharge of their official duty.
- The civil servants are not personally liable in respect of any official contract of the government. Civil proceedings can be initiated against them for anything done in their official capacity after giving 2 months' notice. Criminal proceedings can be initiated against them for acts done in official capacity after permission from the President or the Governor as the case may be.

22.8 CO-OPERATIVE SOCIETIES

The 97th Constitutional amendment of 2011 provided constitutional status to co-operative societies. The main changes by virtue of this amendment are:

- Under Article 19(1)(c), the right to form co-operative societies was included as a Fundamental Right.
- Article 43B was added under the Directive Principles of State Policy for promoting voluntary formation, autonomous functioning, democratic control and professional management of co-operative societies.
- 'Part IXB – The Co-operative Societies' was added with Articles 243-ZH to 243-ZT.

Part IXB and Constitutional Validity

Part IXB contained provisions with respect to (a) incorporation, regulation and winding-up of co-operative societies, (b) number of members of the Board of such societies and their term, (c) elections of members of the Board of such societies, (d) audit of accounts of co-operative societies etc. The Constitution provided that these will be governed by laws made by State legislature subject to the overall provisions contained in Part IXB.

Article 243ZR provided that the provisions of Part IXB shall also apply to the Multi-State co-operative societies (that operate in more than one State) subject to laws made by Parliament.

'Co-operative societies' is under Entry 32 of the State list in the Seventh Schedule. The matter of multi-state co-operative societies that operate in more than one State is covered under Entry 44 of the Union list in the Seventh Schedule.

The Gujarat High Court in ***Rajendra N Shah case*** (2013) had struck down the constitutional validity of Part IXB on the ground that the 97th Amendment was not ratified by at least half of the State legislatures as required under Article 368, since the amendment concerned an entry in the State list.

The Supreme Court on appeal, in 2021, partially upheld the judgement of the Gujarat High Court. It held that Part IXB was violative of the powers conferred on the State legislatures for enacting laws relating to the local co-operative societies that operated within a State. However, applying the doctrine of severability, it held that the provisions of Part IXB shall be applicable insofar as it concerns multi-state co-operative societies both within the various States and in the Union territories of India.

Multi-State Co-operative Societies (Amendment) Act, 2023 was passed in August 2023, by the Parliament to amend the original act passed in 2002. The key provisions of the amendment that aim to enhance transparency, accountability and governance of these Multi-State Co-operative societies (MSCS) are as follows:

- Creation of a co-operative election authority by the Central government that will ensure that elections are conducted in a fair, free and timely manner, thus reducing complaints and malpractices.
- Appointment of co-operative ombudsman that will establish a structured system for grievance redressal.
- Appointment of co-operative information officers that will improve transparency by providing members with timely access to information.
- Creation of a digital ecosystem through the provision for electronic submission and issuance of documents.
- It provides for issuance of non-voting shares in MSCS that will aid them in raising funds. It also proposes for creation of rehabilitation, reconstruction and development fund to rejuvenate struggling co-operative societies.
- It restricts the voting rights of directors in contracts or arrangements in which the director himself/herself or any of his/her relative is directly or indirectly interested. This will improve the transparency and independence of the Board.

MAINS STARTER

Area	Building Blocks For Model Introductions
Asymmetrical federalism	The provision for special category States under Articles 371-371J is a reflection of the 'asymmetrical federalism' in our Constitution. These provisions are primarily aimed at the development of backward regions in certain States, and protecting the local culture and maintaining law and order in North Eastern States.
Tribunals	Tribunals are alternate dispute redressal mechanism that are set up to ensure speedy delivery of justice as well as to reduce the burden of ordinary courts.

UPSC Previous Years' Questions of Preliminary Examination

1. The Constitution (71st Amendment) Act, 1992 amends the Eighth Schedule to the constitution to include which of the following languages? **[2024]**
   1. Konkani
   2. Manipuri
   3. Nepali
   4. Maithili

   Select the correct answer using the code given below:
   (a) 1, 2 and 3
   (b) 1, 2 and 4
   (c) 1, 3 and 4
   (d) 2, 3 and 4

   Solution: (a)

   > ***Explanation:*** Konkani, Manipuri and Nepali were added through 71st amendment. Maithili was added through 92nd amendment in 2004. By eliminating Maithili (4), the answer can be arrived at.

2. With reference to 'Scheduled Areas' in India, consider the following statements: **[2023]**
   1. Within a State, the notification of an area as Scheduled Area takes place through an Order of the President.
   2. The largest administrative unit forming the Scheduled Area is the District and the lowest is the cluster of villages in the Block.
   3. The Chief Ministers of the concerned States are required to submit annual reports to the Union Home Ministry on the administration of Scheduled Areas in the States.

   How many of the above statements are correct?
   (a) Only one
   (b) Only two
   (c) All three
   (d) None

   Solution: (b)

   > ***Explanation:*** As discussed in Section 22.3 (under the Fifth Schedule), Statement 1 is correct. However, Statement 3 is incorrect as the Governor is required to submit annual reports to the President. Statement 2 is also correct and hence the answer is (b).

3. If a particular area is brought under the Fifth schedule of the Constitution of India, which one of the following statements best reflects the consequence of it? **[2022]**
   (a) This would prevent the transfer of land of tribal people to non-tribal people.
   (b) This would create a local self-governing body in that area.
   (c) This would convert that area into a Union Territory.
   (d) The State having such areas should be declared a Special category State.

   Solution: (a)

   > ***Explanation:*** As discussed in Section 22.3, the provisions in Fifth Schedule are made for protection of interest of Scheduled Tribes. The Governor can make regulations for prohibiting or transfer of land by or among members of Scheduled Tribes in such Scheduled areas and transfer to non-tribal private parties can be declared void. Hence, the correct answer is (a).

UPSC PREVIOUS YEARS' QUESTIONS OF MAIN EXAMINATION

1. How far do you agree with the view that tribunals curtail the jurisdiction of ordinary courts? In view of the above, discuss the constitutional validity and competency of the tribunals in India? **[2018]**

   Likely context to the question: The Law Commission submitted its report on 'Assessment of Statutory Frameworks of Tribunals in India' in October 2017. This could be the likely context to the question.

   Approach: Discussion on tribunals and how they do not curtail but supplement the efforts of judiciary in speedy delivery of justice can be discussed in the first part. The recommendations of the Law Commission report can be the second part of the answer.

MODEL ANSWER

Article 323A authorises the Parliament to set up administrative tribunals for adjudication of disputes relating to recruitment and conditions of service of Central and State government employees. Article 323B authorises both Parliament and State legislature to set up tribunals for adjudication of disputes relating to tax, foreign exchange, industrial and labour disputes, land reforms etc., according to their legislative competence.

Constitutional validity and competency

Tribunals are an alternate dispute redressal mechanism that do not necessarily curtail the powers of ordinary courts but help in reducing their burden by adjudicating on matters within their jurisdiction.

The key advantages of Tribunals are:

- Tribunals are composed of technical experts thereby allowing for niche jurisprudence.
- They are less expensive when compared to courts and also have the effect of reducing the burden on the ordinary courts.
- They can provide speedier justice.

However, Tribunals also have some limitations that are summarised below:

- Their statutory nature and inadequate safeguards against executive influence means that they compromise the principle of separation of powers.
- Since the government is the largest litigator in the country, setting up tribunals whose members are appointed by the government creates conflict of interest.

The Law Commission submitted a report in 2017 for improved functioning of the tribunals with following key recommendations:

- Qualification of judges to be appropriate for the jurisdiction under their care.
- Selection of members to be done by an impartial selection committee formed for the purpose.
- It should be possible to challenge any order of the tribunal or its appellate tribunal in the division bench of the High Court having territorial jurisdiction over such tribunal.

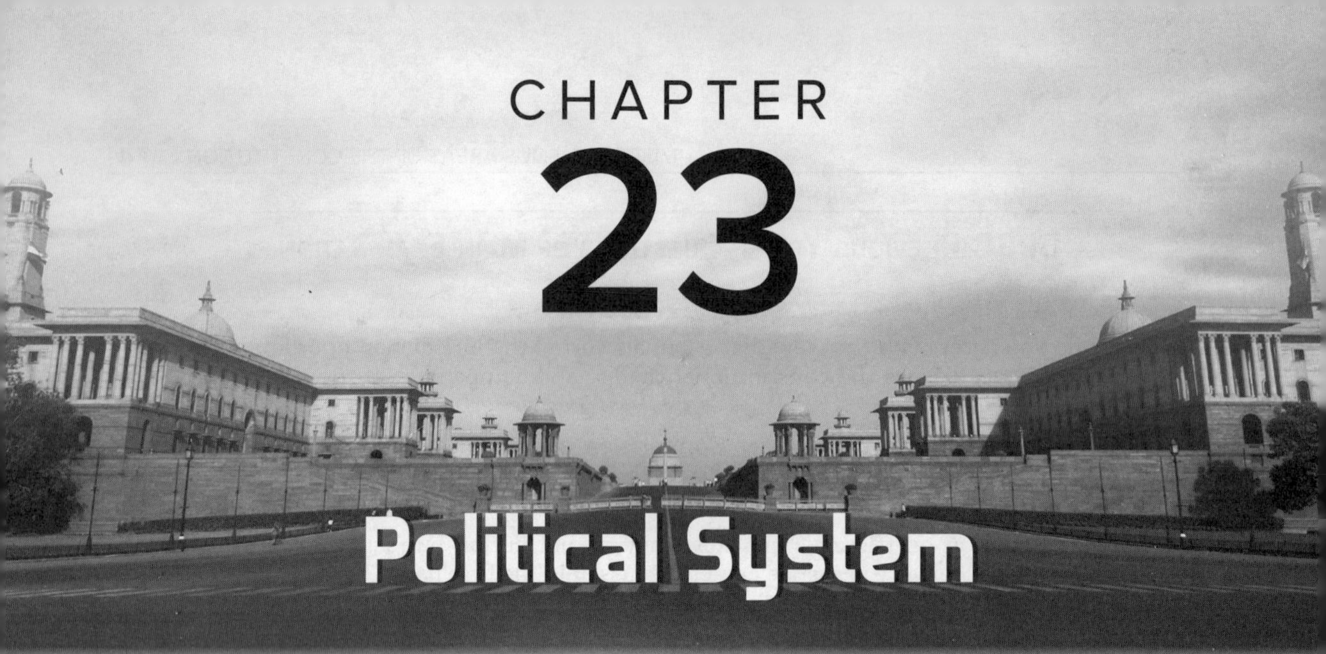

CHAPTER 23

Political System

LEARNING OUTCOMES

1. Comprehending key provisions of the Representation of the People Act, 1950 and 1951, along with the Delimitation Acts passed over time
2. Understanding the election process, including the Model Code of Conduct, voting procedures, and the need for electoral reforms
3. Gaining knowledge of the criteria and process for registration and recognition of political parties in India
4. Analysing recent electoral developments, such as One Nation One Election, linking of the Election Identity Card with Aadhaar, and remote voting for NRIs and migrant workers

We have discussed about the constitutional provisions relating to the Election Commission of India. Apart from the constitutional provisions, certain other aspects related to political system in India can be covered under the following broad heads – (a) Election-related laws, (b) Election process and conduct of elections, (c) Political parties and their recognition and (d) Some recent developments in the election process. We shall discuss the various topics under these heads in this chapter.

23.1 ELECTION LAWS

We have discussed some of the important provisions in two election-related laws – (a) The Representation of the People Act, 1950 and (b) The Representation of the People Act, 1951 in Chapters 10 and 11 dealing with the Parliament and the State Legislature. We have discussed in these chapters about the allocation of seats in the Lok Sabha and the State Legislatures (provided in the Act of 1950), qualification and disqualification for Members of the Parliament and the State Legislatures (provided in the Act of 1951). Apart from these, the objectives of these laws and other key provisions are summarised in this section.

23.1.1 Representation of the People Act, 1950

- The objectives of the Act are as follows:
  - The allocation of seats in, and the delimitation of constituencies for the purpose of election to, the House of the People and the Legislatures of States;

i. First Schedule provides the allocation of seats in the Lok Sabha
ii. Second Schedule provides the allocation of seats in the Legislative Assemblies of States and the Union Territories with a Legislative Assembly
iii. Third Schedule provides the allocation of seats in the Legislative Council of States having such a council.

- The qualifications of the voters at such elections;
- The preparation of electoral rolls;
- The manner of filling seats in the Rajya Sabha to be filled by representatives of the Union Territories with a Legislative Assembly.

- Chief Electoral Officer – Appointed by the Election Commission in consultation with the State Government who shall supervise the preparation, revision and correction of all electoral rolls in a State.
- District Election Officer – Appointed by the Election Commission in consultation with the State Government for each District in a State.
- Apart from the above two, electoral registration officers and assistant electoral registration officers are also appointed for preparation and revision of electoral rolls.
- Qualifying date in relation to electoral roll means 1st January, 1st April, 1st July and 1st October of the respective year in which the electoral roll is prepared or revised. Thus, citizens who have completed 18 years of age on above qualifying dates are eligible for inclusion in the electoral roll.
- Qualification and disqualification for being an elector (voter)
  - Qualifications
    i. Not less than 18 years of age;
    ii. Ordinarily resident in a constituency;
    iii. In 2010, the Act was amended to allow NRIs to register themselves in the constituency which is mentioned as their place of residence in the passport. But, in order to vote they should be physically present in the constituency on the date of poll.
  - Disqualifications
    i. Not a citizen of India;
    ii. Unsound mind and so declared by a competent court;
    iii. Disqualified from voting under the provisions of any law relating to corrupt practices and other offences.

23.1.2 Representation of the People Act, 1951

- The objectives of the Act are as follows:
  - conduct of elections to the Houses of Parliament and to the House or Houses of the Legislature of each State,
  - the qualifications and disqualifications for membership of those Houses,
  - the corrupt practices and other offences at or in connection with such elections and
  - the decision of doubts and disputes arising out of or in connection with such elections.
- Only Armed forces personnel can have vote by proxy. People who are serving in the State police force outside their State or with the Government of India outside India can have a postal vote. Similarly, voters on election duty and electors subjected to preventive detention can have a postal vote. Further, media persons on election duty carrying authorisation from the Election Commission, and those working in essential services such as healthcare can also vote using postal ballots (introduced in General elections of 2024).

23.1.3 Delimitation Acts

- Delimitation literally means the Act or process of fixing limits or boundaries of territorial constituencies in a country or a province having a legislative body. The process of delimitation is assigned to a high-power body, known as Delimitation Commission or a Boundary Commission.
- In India, the Delimitation Commission consists of Judge of the Supreme Court or High Courts, the Election Commissioners of India and the State Election Commissioners as ex-officio members.
- In India, such Delimitation Commissions have been constituted four times – in 1952 under the Delimitation Commission Act, 1952, in 1963 under the Delimitation Commission Act, 1962, in 1973 under the Delimitation Act, 1972 and in 2002 under the Delimitation Act, 2002. The number of seats in the Lok Sabha and the Legislative Assembly in States is based on the Delimitation Act, 1972 (basis 1971 Census) while the boundaries of the constituencies and the number of seats reserved for the Scheduled Castes and the Scheduled Tribes is based on the Delimitation Act, 2002 (basis 2001 Census).
- The Delimitation Commission in India is a high-power body whose orders have the force of law and cannot be called in question before any court. These orders come into force on a date to be specified by the President of India in this behalf. The copies of its orders are laid before the House of the People and the State Legislative Assembly concerned, but no modifications are permissible therein by them.

THINK ABOUT IT

The task of the next delimitation commission of India is going to be a challenging one. Comment on the constitutional provisions with respect to delimitation and the issues surrounding the next delimitation exercise.

Ensuing Delimitation and Issues

The number of seats in Lok Sabha had been frozen as per 1971 census to encourage population control measures so that States with higher population growth do not end up having higher number of seats. This was done through the 42nd Amendment Act till 2000 and was extended by the 84th Amendment Act till 2026. This number will be readjusted based on the first census after 2026.

The population explosion that happened in our country during the last five decades has been uneven with some States like Uttar Pradesh, Bihar, Madhya Pradesh and Rajasthan having a greater increase than States like Kerala, Tamil Nadu, Karnataka and Andhra Pradesh. There are two options that are being discussed in public domain with respect to the revised delimitation exercise based on the projected population of various States as of 2026. The first is to continue with the existing 543 seats and their redistribution amongst various States and the second is to increase the number of seats with corresponding increase amongst various States.

Scan the QR code for video on issues surrounding Ensuing Delimitation Exercise

Mc Graw Hill edge

In both scenarios, Southern states, smaller Northern states like Punjab, Himachal Pradesh, and Uttarakhand, along with the Northeastern states, are likely to be at a disadvantage compared to larger Northern states such as Uttar Pradesh, Bihar, Madhya Pradesh and Rajasthan.

This may go against the federal principles of our country. It also goes against the philosophy for freezing the seats as per 1971 census with the States that have been better at controlling the population losing out on their political significance.

In a federation like USA, the number of seats in the House of Representatives (equivalent to our Lok Sabha) has been capped at 435 since 1913. As of 2024, the European Union (EU) Parliament comprises 720 members, with seats allocated to member countries based on the principle of 'degressive proportionality.' Under this principle, the ratio of population to number of seats shall increase as the population increases. For example, Denmark, with a population of around 60 lakh, has 15 seats (average population of 4 lakh per member) as against Germany, with a population of 8.3 crore, having 96 seats (average population of 8.6 lakh per member).

Issues are bound to arise as the democratic and federal principles seem to be at loggerheads in the next delimitation exercise. However, they can be harmoniously reconciled by giving equal importance to both. Some of the international practices as discussed above may be considered for this purpose. Mixed Member Proportional Representation that gives weightage to percentage of votes secured by political parties while filling seats in the elected houses may also be considered.

23.2 ELECTION PROCESS AND CONDUCT OF ELECTIONS

The election process is contained in the Representation of the People Act, 1951 (RP Act, 1951) and also rules made by the Government along with various orders of the Election Commission of India (ECI) pursuant to that Act and rules. The key provisions about the same are summarised in this section.

23.2.1 Conduct of Elections

- The ECI is vested with the overall power of superintendence, direction and control of the conduct of elections to the Houses of Parliament and the State Legislature.
- Subject to the superintendence, direction and control of the Election Commission, the Chief Electoral Officer of each State shall supervise the conduct of all elections in the State.
- Subject to the superintendence, direction and control of the Chief Electoral Officer, the District Election Officer shall coordinate and supervise all work in the district or in the area within his jurisdiction in connection with the conduct of all elections to the Parliament and the Legislature of the State.
- Observers
    - They are the appointees of the ECI working under the superintendence, control and discipline of the Commission for the period from their appointment until the process of elections is complete.
    - General Observers
        - i. IAS officers of the States other than the State in which the election is conducted are usually appointed as General Observers.
        - ii. They are eyes and ears of the ECI.
        - iii. Have recommendatory powers to the ECI and based on their reports the ECI takes the final decision.
        - iv. They are appointed to observe whether elections are conducted in a free and fair manner.
    - Expenditure Observers
        - i. The Expenditure Observers are usually from the Indian Revenue Service. They shall be appointed by the Commission for specified constituencies to observe the election expenses by the candidates.
        - ii. There shall be at least one Expenditure Observer for each district.
        - iii. They are appointed for monitoring day-to-day election expenses made by candidates.

iv. Details of election expenses will have to be submitted within 30 days of announcement of election results to the District Electoral Officer.

- Returning Officers
  The ECI appoints the Returning Officers and Assistant Returning Officers, respectively, in consultation with the State Government.
  - The duties of the Returning Officers are as follows:
    i. To accept and scrutinise the nomination forms of candidates and allot election symbols to the contesting candidates.
    ii. To prepare the final list of contesting candidates.
    iii. Printing of ballot papers and forwarding them to service voters, preparation of EVMs for the Lok Sabha and the Assembly elections.
    iv. Deputing polling officers to booths with election materials.
    v. To supervise the functions of the polling officers in his/her Assembly Constituency on the day of poll and forward the necessary report to the ECI and the Chief Electoral Officer.
    vi. To get the polling completed during the election in a fair and just manner and as per the statutory provisions.
    vii. To supervise the counting of votes and declare the results on counting day.
- Some important aspects of the election process that have been in the news in recent times:
  i. Form 17 C – It contains details regarding the total number of electors assigned to a polling station and the number of votes recorded as per EVM. This is signed by the Presiding officer of every booth and handed over to the polling agents of various parties. This is cross checked with the votes counted on the counting day.
  ii. Conduct of election rules, 1961 is for conduct of free and fair elections. It has been amended in December 2024 to restrict sharing of CCTV footages of inside of a polling station as part of the election papers and documents.
  iii. Registration of Electors rules, 1960 provides for the preparation and publication of electoral rolls.

23.2.2 Model Code of Conduct

- The Model Code of Conduct (MCC) for guidance of political parties and candidates is a set of norms which has evolved with the consensus of political parties who have consented to abide by the principles embodied in the said code and also binds them to respect and observe it in its letter and spirit. This code began to be implemented strictly in the 1990s and has been revised in 2013 by the ECI.

> **THINK ABOUT IT**
> The Model Code of Conduct, though high on its ideals, has been low on its effectiveness in ensuring free and fair elections. Discuss.

- The MCC is operational from the date on which the election schedule is announced until the date of announcement of result.

Key Provisions

- MCC lays down how political parties, contesting candidates and party(s) in power should conduct themselves during the process of elections i.e., on their general conduct during campaigning, holding meetings and processions, poll day activities and functioning of the party in power etc.
- General Conduct: Criticism of political parties must be limited to their policies and programmes, past record and work. Activities such as using caste and communal feelings to secure votes, bribing or intimidation of voters, etc. are prohibited.

- Meetings: Parties must inform the local police authorities of the venue and time of any meeting in time to enable the police to make adequate security arrangements.
- Polling Day: All authorised party workers at polling booths should be given suitable badges or identity cards.
- Polling Booths: Only voters, and those with a valid pass from the ECI are allowed to enter polling booths.
- Observers: The ECI will appoint observers to whom any candidates may report problems regarding the conduct of the election.
- Party in Power:
  - Ministers must not combine official visits with election work or use official machinery for the same.
  - The party must avoid advertising at the cost of the public exchequer or using official mass media for publicity on achievements to improve chances of victory in the elections.
  - Ministers and other authorities must not announce any financial grants, or promise any construction of roads, provision of drinking water, announce new projects etc.
  - Other parties must be allowed to use public spaces and rest houses and these must not be monopolised by the party in power.
- Election manifestos: Added in 2013, these guidelines prohibit parties from making promises that exert an undue influence on voters, and suggest that manifestos also indicate the financial means to achieve the poll promises. However, there has been an increasing trend of promising various welfare schemes and cash transfers to the women/students in election manifestos by all parties, without adequate discussion on the financial viability of such measures.
- Though MCC does not have any statutory backing, it has come to acquire strength in the past 3 decades because of its strict enforcement by the ECI.
- Certain provisions of the MCC may be enforced through invoking corresponding provisions in other criminal laws and The Representation of the People Act 1951. Further, under Paragraph 16A of the Symbols order, the ECI has the power to suspend or withdraw recognition of a recognised political party for its failure to observe MCC or follow lawful directions of the Commission.
- In 2013, the Standing Committee on Personnel, Public Grievances, Law and Justice, recommended making the MCC legally binding and recommended that the MCC be made a part of the Representation of the People Act, 1951.
- However, the ECI is not in favour of making the MCC legally binding. According to the ECI, elections must be completed within a relatively short period of around 45 days and judicial proceedings take longer. Therefore, it is not feasible to make it enforceable by law.

23.2.3 Voting Procedure and Reforms

THINK ABOUT IT

Is it time for India to move away from First Past the Post System (FPTP) to Proportional Representation (PR) system in conduct of elections to popularly elected houses? Critically evaluate.

Voting Method

Following are the various methods of voting in different elections held in India:

1. The President and the Vice-President elections are held in accordance with the system of proportional representation by means of the single transferable vote and the voting at such election shall be by secret ballot.
2. The election to the Rajya Sabha is held in accordance with system of proportional representation by means of the single transferable vote and the voting at such election is by open ballot.

3. The election to the Legislative Council in a State having such a council is held in accordance with system of proportional representation by means of the single transferable vote and the voting at such election is by secret ballot.
4. The election to the Lok Sabha and the Legislative Assembly in a State is held through secret ballot. The system for declaring the winner in such election is called the 'Plurality system' or the 'First-Past-the-Post system' (FPTP) where the candidate with maximum votes polled is declared the winner.

FPTP versus Proportional Representation (PR)

As mentioned above, we follow the FPTP in our elections for the Lok Sabha and the Legislative Assembly. This is the system that is followed for elections to the popular House in most of the larger democracies of the world like the United States, the United Kingdom, Canada, and in many other democracies across the world.

The advantages of FPTP system are as follows:

- It is the simplest and most feasible method in a large country like India where some of the voters are also illiterate. It is because of this reason that candidates are also allotted symbols in Indian elections.
- India is a Parliamentary democracy. The system of FPTP provides greater stability to the executive in such a system because the ruling government can enjoy a majority in the Lok Sabha/ the Legislative Assembly even without obtaining majority of the votes across the constituencies. For example, below is the summary of election results for the General elections conducted in 2014, 2019 and 2024 in India.

SUMMARY OF RESULTS OF GENERAL ELECTIONS – 2014 AND 2019

	2014		2019	
Political Party (predominant State)	%age of Votes	No. of Seats	%age of Votes	No. of Seats
Bharatiya Janata Party (All India)	31.0%	282	37.3%	303
Indian National Congress (All India)	19.3%	44	19.5%	52
Bahujan Samaj Party [BSP] (UP)	4.1%	0	3.6%	10
Samajwadi Party (UP)	3.4%	5	2.6%	5
All India Trinamool Congress [TMC] (WB)	3.8%	34	4.1%	22
Anna Dravida Munnetra Kazhagam [ADMK] (TN)	3.3%	37	1.4%	1
Dravida Munnetra Kazhagam [DMK] (TN)	1.7%	0	2.3%	24
Telugu Desam Party (AP)	2.6%	16	2.0%	3
YSR Congress Party (AP)	2.6%	9	2.5%	22
Shiv Sena (MH)	1.9%	18	2.1%	18
Biju Janata Dal [BJD] (OD)	1.7%	20	1.7%	12
All other parties/independents	24.6%	78	20.9%	71
Total	**100%**	**543**	**100%**	**543**

SUMMARY OF ELECTION RESULTS OF 2024 ELECTION

Political Formation	%age of Votes	Actual no. of Seats
National Democratic Alliance (NDA)	43.3%	293
Indian National Developmental Inclusive Alliance (I.N.D.I.A)	41.6%	234
Others/Independents	15.1%	16
Total	**100%**	**543**

- As can be seen from the above instances, the party/coalition with less than 50% of votes in the last three general elections, won more than the majority number of seats required (272) to form the government. Thus, it provides more stability in a Parliamentary democracy like India.

The shortcomings of the FPTP system are:

- Lack of representation of minor parties or skewed representation based on electoral alliances.

The Proportional Representation (PR) system ensures more representation of all parties. There are various types of PR system and some of the most commonly used ones are mentioned below:

- Party list PR – Where voters vote for the Party (and not individual candidates) and then parties get seats in proportion to their vote share – for example in Israel and Netherlands.
- Single transferable vote – Where voters rank candidates and the candidates with required quota/majority are elected.
- Mixed Member Proportional representation system (MMP) – Under this system, there is one candidate who is elected through FPTP system from each territorial constituency. However, there are some additional seats that are filled based on various parties' percentage of votes. In Germany, that follows the MMPR system, out of 598 seats in Bundestag (their equivalent to our Lok Sabha), 299 seats (50%) are filled from constituencies under FPTP system. The voters also provide their preference for a party in the ballots. The balance 299 seats (50%) are filled by apportioning them amongst parties, that secure at least 5% votes, based on their percentage of votes. Similarly, in New Zealand, out of the total 120 seats in House of Representatives, 72 seats (60%) are filled through FPTP system from territorial constituencies. The balance 48 seats (40%) are allotted to various parties, that secure at least 5% votes, based on their vote share. This system will provide the required stability in a Parliamentary democracy like India while also ensuring representation even for minor parties. Law commission, in its 170th report, 'Reform of the electoral laws' (1999), had also recommended the introduction of the MMPR system for 25% of the seats.

EVM and VVPAT

- In India, since the Lok Sabha elections of 2004, the ECI has been using Electronic Voting Machine (EVM) in all constituencies both for the Lok Sabha elections and the Legislative Assembly elections of the States. It has the following advantages:
  - It ensures that there are no invalid or doubtful votes. It also reduces the quantity of paper and cost of printing substantially.
  - It also makes the process of counting faster.
- However, there have been unsubstantiated doubts raised by political parties about the independence/reliability of EVMs at various points of time.
- In order to ensure voter confidence in the entire polling process, the system of Voter Verifiable Paper Audit Trail (VVPAT) was introduced. This has been introduced in all polling booths for

elections to the Lok Sabha or the Legislative Assembly since the General elections of 2019. Under this system, the voter will be able to verify the correctness of his/her vote by viewing a printed slip with the symbol for which he/she cast his/her vote. At the time of counting, the votes as per EVM are tallied with the VVPATs for five booths per Legislative Assembly segment on a random basis. In case of any discrepancy, the votes as per the printed slips is considered as final.

- The Supreme Court in April 2024 had dismissed PILs filed by Association of Democratic Reforms and other petitioners seeking return to paper ballots. It also dismissed the pleas seeking 100% verification of VVPAT with EVM count, and allowing the voter to get the VVPAT slip in their hand before depositing it in a box.
- The court also directed that the burnt memory of microcontrollers of 5% of EVMs can be checked and verified by a team of engineers of the EVM manufacturers in case of any suspicion of tampering. This exercise would be initiated on a written request, within seven days of declaration of results, from candidates who have come second or third in a constituency.

23.3 POLITICAL PARTIES

India is a multi-party democracy with parties at the national level as well as regional levels. The Representation of the People Act, 1951 provides for registration of political parties with the ECI. These are called as 'Registered parties' and enjoy benefits like tax exemption on their donations.

Scan the QR code for conceptual video on topics related to 'Political System'

Apart from the 'Registered unrecognised parties', a party is recognised as 'National' or 'State' party under the provisions of 'The Election Symbols (Reservation and Allotment) Order, 1968' by the ECI.

Recognition as State Party

- A registered party has to fulfil any of the following conditions for recognition as a State Party:
  - A party should win minimum 3% of the total number of seats or a minimum of three seats in the Legislative Assembly of the State whichever is higher.
  - A party should win at least 1 seat in the Lok Sabha for every 25 seats or any fraction thereof allotted to that State.
  - A political party should secure at least 6% of the total valid votes polled during general election to a Lok Sabha or a State Legislative Assembly and should, in addition, win at least one Lok Sabha, or two Legislative Assembly seats in that election as the case may be.
  - A party secures 8% or more of the total valid votes polled in the State in any Lok Sabha or Assembly election.

Recognition as National Party

- A registered party is recognised as a National Party only if it fulfils any one of the following three conditions:
  - The party wins 2% of seats in the Lok Sabha (as of 2014, 11 seats) from at least three different States.
  - At a general election to the Lok Sabha or the Legislative Assembly, the party polls 6% of votes in four States and in addition it wins 4 Lok Sabha seats from one or more States.
  - A party gets recognition as a State Party in four or more States.

At present (2024), there are 6 parties that have been recognised as National parties – Bahujan Samaj Party (BSP), Bharatiya Janata Party (BJP), Communist Party of India (Marxist) (CPIM), Indian National Congress (INC), National People's Party (NPP) and Aam Aadmi Party (AAP).

Allotment of symbols

Symbols are allotted to political parties and contesting candidates as per the provisions of 'The Election Symbols (Reservation and Allotment) Order, 1968' by the ECI.

- A National party will have a reserved symbol for its candidates throughout the country and it is not allotted to any other candidate in any constituency.
- A State recognised political party symbol will not be granted to any other party/candidate in that State or even in other States as per revised guidelines.
- For registered but unrecognised political parties, one of the free symbols is allotted throughout a State if that party contests 5% of seats to the Assembly or two Lok Sabha constituencies as the case may be. These parties have to submit audited accounts for the last three financial years, expenditure statement of the last two elections, and the signature of office-bearers to obtain such common symbol.

Apart from preference in symbol allotment as mentioned above, the Recognised political parties (both National and State) can appoint a maximum of forty 'Star campaigners' as against twenty by registered but unrecognised political parties. Star campaigners (or 'leaders of a political party' as officially mentioned in the RP Act, 1951), have to be members of the political party that appoints them. The expenditure incurred by 'leaders of a political party' (Star Campaigners) on account of travel by air or any other means of transport for propagating programme of their political party shall not be deemed to be part of the election expenditure of a candidate of such party. This is applicable as long as they limit themselves to general campaigning for the party without seeking votes in the name of contesting candidates.

23.4 RECENT DEVELOPMENTS

23.4.1 One Nation One Election

Scan the QR code for video on recent developments relating to 'One Nation One Election'

During the first four general election cycles i.e., in 1952, 1957, 1962 and 1967, the elections to the Lok Sabha and the State Legislative Assemblies were held simultaneously. However, subsequently due to premature dissolution of the Lok Sabha on various occasions and also due to premature dissolution of Legislative Assemblies, the elections to the Lok Sabha and various assemblies are held at different times. In 2024, along with the Lok Sabha election, only four States had their State Legislative Assembly election.

Desirability of Simultaneous Elections

- Firstly, it is estimated that the cost of holding general elections to the Lok Sabha is around ₹4,000 crores for the Central Government. Each State assembly election would also cost considerable amount of money according to the size of the State. While this is the official expenditure of the government, the expenditure by political parties and candidates are manifold times higher. Simultaneous elections would entail a reduction in these costs.

- Secondly, there are at least 5–6 State elections that happen every year. This results in 'Permanent campaign' mode for the political parties including ministers, acting as a hindrance to policy making and governance. Further, the Model Code of Conduct is enforced during the election process that ranges usually from 45–60 days when no new schemes or projects can be announced by the Central government and State governments concerned.

THINK ABOUT IT

Discuss the constitutional and political challenges in implementing simultaneous elections to the Lok Sabha and State legislative assemblies

Issues with Simultaneous Elections

The major issues with the implementation of One Nation One Election (ONOE) can be divided into political issues and constitutional issues.

Political issues around ONOE	Constitutional issues around ONOE
• Conducting elections simultaneously to Lok Sabha and all State assemblies would result in national issues overshadowing the regional and State specific issues.	• India is a parliamentary democracy where the governments at the Centre and a State need to enjoy majority in the Lok Sabha and Legislative Assembly, respectively. If the party or coalition in power loses majority and no alternative government can be formed, it leads to the dissolution of the houses and fresh elections.
• The national political parties would have a significant advantage over regional parties on account of this mechanism that affects the federal spirit of our democracy.	• Council of ministers enjoying majority may recommend early dissolution of the houses and seek fresh elections.
• Elections also serve as an effective feedback mechanism for the governments in power. If elections are held only once in 5 years, it can affect this process.	• Under Article 356, President's rule may be imposed and State assemblies dissolved.

Various Committee Recommendations and International Practices

The reports of Law Commission (1999) and the Parliamentary Standing Committee on Personnel, Public Grievances, Law and Justice (2015), have dealt with the issue of simultaneous elections. The Law Commission had also submitted a draft report in 2018. The highlights of all these discussions and recommendations can be summarised as follows:

- The elections to Lok Sabha and part of the State assemblies may be clubbed together in one cycle and the remaining State assemblies can be held in another cycle after two and a half years.
- Any 'No-Confidence motion' in Lok Sabha or Legislative Assembly should be mandatorily accompanied by a 'Confidence motion' for the formation of an alternative government. If for any unavoidable reasons, the Lok Sabha or State Assembly is to be dissolved prematurely, the duration of the newly constituted House should be only for the remainder period of the original house.

It may be noted that Parliamentary democracies like South Africa, Sweden and Germany have fixed tenure for their legislatures. The elections to National Assembly and provincial legislatures happen simultaneously in South Africa every five years and the President of the country is elected by the National Assembly. The Prime Minister of Sweden and the Chancellor of Germany are elected by the respective legislatures of these countries that are elected every four years. Any lack of confidence in the Chancellor in Germany can be moved only by electing a successor.

Ram Nath Kovind Committee Recommendations and Proposed Amendments

A High-Level Committee (HLC) headed by former President Shri Ram Nath Kovind was constituted to make its recommendations for implementing ONOE. The HLC submitted its report on ONOE to the President in March 2024. It recommended simultaneous elections to be held for both Lok Sabha and State legislative assemblies after necessary constitutional amendments. The elections to the local bodies – Panchayats and Municipalities – to be held within 100 days of such simultaneous general elections.

Proposed Constitutional Amendment

The Constitution (one hundred and twenty-ninth amendment) Bill, 2024 has been introduced in the Lok Sabha in December 2024 to give effect to the recommendations of the HLC for conducting simultaneous elections to Lok Sabha and State legislative assemblies.

The key highlights of this proposed amendment are summarised below:

- Insertion of Article 82A for transitional provisions:
    - After the General Election to the Lok Sabha, once it is constituted, the President shall issue a notification on the date of the House's first sitting to implement the provisions of simultaneous elections. This date shall be referred to as the 'Appointed Date.'
    - Once the transitional provisions are brought into play, the tenure of all State Legislative Assemblies constituted in any election after the 'Appointed Date' would come to an end on the expiry of the full term of the Lok Sabha, irrespective of when the Assembly was constituted.
    - This would result in the Lok Sabha and all State legislative assemblies being ready for simultaneous elections at the end of this term.
- Amendments to Articles 83 and 172 that deal with the duration of the Lok Sabha and State Legislative assemblies:
    - In the event of dissolution of Lok Sabha or any State Assembly before the end of its term, elections will happen, but the newly constituted house shall be only for the remainder of the term of the original house.
- It authorises the Parliament, by amending Article 327, to enact laws relating to conduct of 'simultaneous elections.'

This bill has been referred to a Joint Parliamentary Committee for its views (as of March 2025).

23.4.2 Electoral Bonds

The scheme of 'Electoral Bonds' was introduced in the Union budget of 2017. This was a mechanism for electoral funding. These bonds could have been purchased by any citizen of India or a body incorporated in India.

Features

- The bonds were available for purchase for a period of 10 days each in the beginning of every quarter, i.e., in January, April, July and October as specified by the Central Government.
- The donor would remain anonymous. The electoral bonds did not bear the name of the donor. The intention was that all the donations made to a party would be accounted for in the balance sheets without exposing the donor details to the public.

The Supreme Court, however, had declared the Electoral Bonds Scheme as unconstitutional in the case of *Association for Democratic Reforms Vs Union of India* (2024). The court held that the scheme violated the citizens' right to information about the sources of finances raised by political parties. With respect to the stated objective of curbing black money, the court applied a proportionality test, viz., whether curtailing the voters' right to know through donor anonymity was achieved through the least restrictive means. The Electoral Bond Scheme, to the extent that it infringed on this right to information by anonymising contributions through bonds, violated Article 19(1)(a). The corresponding amendments to the Income Tax Act (that exempted maintaining records for contributions received through electoral bonds), and Companies Act (that removed cap on donations and deleted disclosure requirements in annual reports) were also struck down as arbitrary and unconstitutional.

23.4.3 Linking of Electoral ID with Aadhaar

The Representation of the People Act, 1950 was amended in December 2021. It provided for the linking of Electors Photo Identity Card (EPIC) with Aadhaar number. The purpose of the same is to establish the identity of any person and for the purpose of authentication of entries in order to remove duplication. The Registration of Electors Rules, 1960 was also modified in line with the above amendment. It provides the format in which the Aadhaar information may be submitted to the Electoral Registration Officer by a new voter at the time of fresh registration (Form 6 – to establish identity) or an existing voter already included in the electoral roll (Form 6B – for the purpose of authentication). Any other listed document may be submitted only if the voter is unable to furnish their Aadhaar number because they do not have an Aadhaar number. Such individuals may furnish alternative documents like PAN card, Driving License, Indian Passport, Bank passbook, etc. While the above amendments were challenged in the Supreme Court, the ECI in September 2023 informed the court that the submission of Aadhaar number is not mandatory. In March 2025, the ECI has again initiated technical consultations with UIDAI (that issues Aadhaar cards), for the purpose of linking EPIC with Aadhaar.

Scan the QR code for video on linking EPIC with Aadhaar

Mc Graw Hill edge

Issues

Linking EPIC with Aadhaar number will help in weeding out duplicate entries that will ensure the sanctity of the electoral roll. However, the following issues need to be addressed:

- The issues surrounding violation of right to privacy as declared in the Puttaswamy judgement need to be considered as the Aadhaar number mentioned in EPIC or Electoral roll may result in its misuse since these rolls are widely circulated amongst political parties.
- Aadhaar is only a proof of residence and not a proof of citizenship. Thus, it may not help in removing voters who are not citizens from the electoral roll.
- There are errors in the Aadhaar database which can result in wrongful deletion of entries in the electoral roll.
- There must be wide publicity about the benefits of linkage between EPIC and Aadhaar database in cleaning up the electoral roll of duplicate entries, which, in turn, strengthens the electoral process. Any misplaced concern amongst voters about the secrecy of their vote being compromised because of this linking should be removed.

THINK ABOUT IT

There have been many allegations about the sanctity of the electoral rolls being compromised with duplicate and bogus voters. In this regard, explain whether the process of linking Electoral ID with Aadhaar will address the issue of duplicate entries in the electoral roll.

23.4.4 Remote Voting for NRIs and Migrant Workers

NRI Voters

- According to estimates, India has one of the largest diaspora populations, with nearly 1.5 crore non-resident Indians spread across the globe. Many of them are in the Gulf countries, the US and the UK.
- After the passing of the Representation of the People (Amendment) Act, 2010, eligible NRIs who had stayed abroad beyond 6 months can vote, but only in person at the polling station where they have been enrolled as an elector.
- The ECI formed a committee in 2014 to explore the options for overseas electors. The committee narrowed it down to two remote voting options – e-postal ballot and proxy voting.
- The Electronically Transmitted Postal Ballot System (ETPBS) is developed by the ECI with the help of Centre for Development of Advanced Computing (C-DAC). It involves the NRI voter sending an application to the returning officer in person or online. The returning officer will send the ballot electronically.
- The voter can then register their mandate on the ballot printout and send it back with an attested declaration. The voter will either send the ballot by ordinary post or drop it at an Indian Embassy where it would be segregated and posted.
- Proxy voting, meanwhile, enables voters to appoint proxies to vote on their behalf.
- Many political parties consulted by the ECI were against proxy voting as they felt it could never be guaranteed that the proxy would vote as per the actual voter's choice.
- In 2017, however, the government introduced a Bill to amend the Representation of People Act to remove the condition of in-person voting for NRIs and enable them to vote through proxies. The Bill was passed in the Lok Sabha in 2018 but never introduced in the Rajya Sabha, eventually lapsing with the dissolution of the 16th Lok Sabha.
- In 2020, the ECI wrote to the Law Ministry that it was technically and administratively ready to facilitate ETPBS for NRIs but the External Affairs Ministry flagged huge logistical challenges relating to identity verification of voters, absence of polling agents, the burden on embassy staff etc.

Migrant Voters

The overall voting percentage in general elections is usually in the range of 65%–70%. It is even lesser in States like Uttar Pradesh and Bihar where many voters would have migrated to other locations for work.

The Election Commission (EC) had formed a 'Committee of Officers on Domestic Migrants' to address this issue. The Committee's report submitted in 2016 suggested 'remote voting' to address this issue.

Remote Voting refers to all means which allow electors to vote from locations other than their assigned polling station where they are registered as voters. It comprises both electronic and non-electronic voting mechanisms. This mechanism will increase voter participation in elections that would further strengthen the electoral democracy and make it more representative.

However, remote voting systems are vulnerable to hacking, fraud and other manipulations. Further, all migrant voters may not have access to internet that may be necessary to participate in remote voting. Similarly, postal votes may not reach on time. It would also give an edge to larger parties and their candidates who could campaign outside their constituency and mobilise migrant and NRI voters.

Thus, before introduction of remote voting for NRIs and migrants, it is important that it gains acceptability and confidence of all stake holders including political parties. It should also be on a secure technology that is tamper-proof, which will ensure accuracy as well as secrecy of voting.

MAINS STARTER

Area	Building Blocks For Model Introductions
Delimitation Commission	Delimitation Commission is a statutory body set up under an Act of Parliament. It determines the number of constituencies for Lok Sabha and State assemblies as well as the boundaries of such constituencies. There have been four delimitation commissions till date in India.
Model Code of Conduct (MCC)	The MCC is a set of norms that have evolved based on consensus amongst political parties, which the parties have consented to follow during the electioneering or campaign period. It does not have statutory backing but acquires strength from its strict enforcement by the ECI.
Proportional Representation (PR) system of elections	The PR system is an election system which ensures more equitable representation of all parties that contest elections. There are various types of PR system that include Party list PR, Single transferable vote, and Mixed member proportional representation.
Simultaneous elections	The idea of simultaneous elections proposes conduct of general elections to the Lok Sabha and State legislative assemblies together once every 5 years. It also proposes synchronising all local body elections together.
Linking Electoral ID with Aadhaar	The process of linking Electoral ID with Aadhaar commenced in 2015. After the amendments to election laws that facilitated this linking were challenged in the Supreme Court, the ECI submitted that it is voluntary in nature. This process would help in weeding out duplicate entries that would ensure sanctity of the electoral roll.

UPSC PREVIOUS YEARS' QUESTIONS OF PRELIMINARY EXAMINATION

1. How many Delimitation Commissions have been constituted by the Government of India till December 2023? **[2024]**

(a) One (b) Two (c) Three (d) Four

Solution: (d)

Explanation: As discussed in Section 23.1.3, Delimitation Commissions have been constituted four times in 1952, 1963, 1973 and 2002.

UPSC PREVIOUS YEARS' QUESTIONS OF MAIN EXAMINATION

1. Examine the need for electoral reforms as suggested by various committees with particular reference to 'One Nation – One Election' principle. **[2024]**

Likely Context: A Committee under the Chairmanship of former President Ram Nath Kovind was formed for providing recommendations to implement 'One Nation – One Election'. The Committee submitted its report in March 2024.

Approach: It is only a ten-marks question but it asks about the need for electoral reforms with particular reference to 'One Nation-One Election'. So, focus on ONOE with specific reference to various committee recommendations on the same and in the conclusion summarise other electoral reforms briefly.

MODEL ANSWER

The Central Government has initiated discussion on the proposal of conducting simultaneous elections to the Lok Sabha, State legislative assemblies and local bodies.

Critical Analysis of Simultaneous Elections

1. It will reduce the 'Permanent campaign' mode in Indian polity. Model Code of Conduct is enforced during the election process that disrupts the governance machinery in States.
2. The cost to the exchequer for conducting elections would reduce significantly.
3. However, it can impact voter behaviour. It can also affect regional parties and regional issues during elections if held along with national elections.

Committee Recommendations

The key committee recommendations with respect to simultaneous elections are as follows:

1. Law Commission report in 1999 and its draft report of 2018 as well as Parliamentary Standing Committee on Personnel, Law and Justice (Nachiappan Committee 2015), had recommended conducting simultaneous elections in two phases, i.e., Lok Sabha and half the assemblies together and other half of State assemblies together after two and a half years.
2. The Ram Nath Kovind Committee set up in September 2023 had suggested simultaneous elections to Lok Sabha and all assemblies together once every 5 years. Local body elections to be held within 100 days of this election.
3. If the Lok Sabha or State Assembly is to be dissolved prematurely, the duration of the newly constituted House should be only for the remainder period of the original House.

The above recommendations will require constitutional amendments which need to be considered after a detailed discussion with all stakeholders. A constitutional amendment bill for the same has been introduced in December 2024 in the Parliament and referred to a Joint Parliamentary Committee.

2. Discuss the role of Election Commission of India in the light of the evolution of the Model code of conduct. **[2022]**

Approach: The evolution of MCC and its salient provisions can be discussed in the first part of the answer. The issues surrounding MCC and its implementation can be summarised in the conclusion.

MODEL ANSWER

Evolution of Model Code of Conduct (MCC)

- The Model Code of Conduct for guidance of political parties and candidates is a set of norms which has evolved with the consensus of political parties who have consented to abide by the principles embodied in the said code and also binds them to respect and observe it in its letter and spirit.
- This code began to be implemented in 1990s and has been revised recently in 2013 by the ECI.
- The MCC is operational from the date on which the election schedule is announced until the date of announcement of result.

Key provisions

- Model Code of Conduct lays down how political parties, contesting candidates and party(s) in power should conduct themselves during the process of elections i.e., on their general conduct during campaigning, holding meetings and processions, poll day activities and functioning of the party in power etc.
- Election manifestos: Added in 2013, these guidelines prohibit parties from making promises that exert an undue influence on voters, and suggest that manifestos also indicate the financial means to achieve the poll promises.

Issues and way forward

- The MCC does not have a legal backing and its enforcement is a challenge considering the use of money power in Indian elections in the recent past.
- However, the ECI has taken initiatives like joint task forces for enforcement, introduction of c-VIGIL mobile app for lodging complaints by citizens etc., for its effective implementation.

CHAPTER 24

Rights Issues

LEARNING OUTCOMES

1. Gaining insight into various legislative enactments that establish or enhance legal and fundamental rights
2. Examining recent developments and challenges in the effective implementation of these laws

The main areas for 'Rights issues' revolve around various types of rights. We have already discussed the provisions with respect to Fundamental and Constitutional rights as per the Constitution in Chapter 14.

There are several laws made by the Parliament and various State Legislatures that provide various legal rights to the citizens. In this chapter, we shall discuss some important legal rights that have been provided through laws made by the Parliament. Some of these laws have been made to supplement a fundamental right (this will be suitably explained under the relevant laws). Apart from the important laws discussed in this chapter; readers/candidates should also be aware of any important developments/judgements/amendments from time to time with respect to any other rights related enactments in the country.

24.1 RIGHT TO INFORMATION ACT, 2005

The Right to Information Act, 2005 (RTI Act) is an important legislation that provides a right to persons to obtain information from the government machinery and other public authorities. The right to information is derived from our fundamental right of freedom of speech and expression under Article 19(1)(a) of the Constitution. If we do not have information on how our government and public authorities function, we cannot express any informed opinion on it. This has also been read into Article 19(1)(a) and Article 21 of the Constitution by the Supreme Court in various judgements. Hence, while the Right to information is not specifically mentioned in Part III, it is implied as part of the fundamental rights under Article 19(1)(a) and Article 21, in various cases decided by the courts. It is undoubtedly a legal right that is provided under the RTI Act.

Salient Features of RTI Act

The salient features of the RTI Act are provided below:

- Persons can seek information from public authorities under the Act. Public authority means any authority or body or institution of self-government established or constituted by (a) the Constitution, (b) law of the Parliament or State Legislature, (c) body owned, controlled or substantially financed by the Central or State Government and (d) Non-Governmental Organisation (NGO) substantially financed directly or indirectly by the Central or State Government. Thus, all constitutional, statutory and executive bodies including corporations owned or controlled by the government is a public authority. Even NGOs that are substantially financed by the government can be considered as public authority under the Act.
- The Act requires suo-moto disclosures of some details by public authorities.
- Public Information Officer (PIO) and Appellate Public Information Officer (APIO) to be appointed by each public authority.
- Time limit for providing information is 30 days and if it is related to life or liberty of an individual, it is 48 hours. The following is the mechanism for appeals if the information is not provided or the provided information is not satisfactory:
    - Appeals against PIO with APIO in each Public authority within 30 days from the date of reply from PIO or expiry of time limit.
    - First Appellate authority (APIO) to pass orders within 30 days of appeal (or 45 days if reasons for delay are given in writing).
    - Appeal with the Central Information Commission (CIC) or State Information Commission (SIC) (as the case may be) within 90 days of receipt of orders of APIO or expiry of time limit.
- Specific exemptions provided under Section 8 and Section 9 of the Act deal with information relating to national security, sovereignty, relations with foreign states, trade secrets, individual safety and personal privacy. The Act will also not apply to security and intelligence organisations.
- Further, the DPDP Act passed in 2023, has amended Section 8 of the Act, that provides exemption for obtaining data from a public authority. The present amendment has provided for a blanket exemption of 'information which relates to personal information.'

24.2 NATIONAL FOOD SECURITY ACT, 2013

National Food Security Act, 2013 (NFS) provides a legal right to obtain subsidised food grains from the government. This is one of the landmark legislations that aims to provide food and nutritional security to the citizens throughout the human life cycle from pregnancy to old age.

24.2.1 Salient Features of NFS Act

The salient features of the NFS Act are as follows:

- 5 kg of food grains per person in a family to be provided at subsidised price – ₹3 per kg of rice, ₹2 per kg of wheat and ₹1 for coarse grains like jowar, bajra, ragi etc.
- 35 kg per family (irrespective of number of members) for those who are covered under Antyodaya Anna Yojana (AAY) scheme. This scheme targets the poorest of the poor who are identified as families that require special nutritional support.
- Food security to cover at least 75% of rural population and 50% of urban population.

- Free nutritious meals will be provided through Integrated Child Development Services (ICDS) centres during pregnancy and after 6 months of child birth.
- Maternity benefit of not less than six thousand rupees to be provided for first child. ₹5,000 is provided as Direct Benefit Transfer to the Bank/Post Office account under the Pradhan Mantri Matru Vandana Yojana (PMMVY) and the remaining cash incentive of around ₹1,000 under Janani Suraksha Yojana after institutional delivery. Cash incentive of ₹6,000 under PMMVY will also be provided for the second child if it is a girl child.
- Free meals at ICDS centres for the child till age of 6 and in schools till age of 14.
- Woman of 18 years of age in every eligible household shall be the head of the household for the purpose of issue of ration cards. If not available the male will be the head till a girl reaches 18 years of age.

- Central government is responsible for procurement of food grains and transporting it to States.
- State government is responsible for taking delivery and implementation of the provisions of the Act.
- In case of non-supply of entitled quantities, the State Governments have to pay Food security allowance.

24.2.2 One Nation One Ration Scheme (ONOR)

ONOR is a scheme that is implemented under the NFS Act to enable migrant beneficiaries to claim their quota of subsidised food grains from any Fair Price Shop (FPS) or Ration shop anywhere in the country. The system allows their family members to claim balance foodgrains on the same ration card in their place of origin. This is made possible through linking of ration card with Aadhaar/biometric authentication.

> **THINK ABOUT IT**
>
> One Nation One Ration is a noble scheme that needs to be implemented for achieving the aims of the National Food Security Act. Elucidate highlighting the importance and issues surrounding the implementation of this scheme.

Benefits

- It ensures that right to food reaches almost 30% of the population who belong to migrant workers category in India.
- It will result in reduction of leakages due to Aadhaar/biometric authentication.
- It will also ensure that there is no social discrimination in FPS. Earlier, a person was tagged to a specific FPS in his/her locality. The underprivileged sections and woman could be discriminated against in their locality and may not be provided the quota of foodgrains. But with the ONOR scheme, a person can access any FPS and obtain their quota of foodgrains.

Issues

- There are instances of exclusion errors due to the Aadhaar linkage especially for poor citizens who may not have an Aadhaar card.
- The FPS are allotted fixed quota of foodgrains as per the number of cards traditionally tagged to that shop. ONOR scheme can disrupt this allotment and supplies.
- These issues need to be effectively addressed based on experience and data gathered to ensure effective implementation of the scheme.

24.3 RIGHT TO EDUCATION ACT, 2009

Right to Education, between the age of 6 and 14, is a fundamental right under Article 21A of the Constitution. The Right of Children to Free and Compulsory Education Act, 2009 (RTE) is a law that supplements this fundamental right to elementary education.

24.3.1 Salient Features of RTE Act

The salient features of RTE Act are as follows:

- Every child between the age of 6 and 14 shall be entitled to get free elementary education. Elementary education means education from first class to eighth class.
- School includes (a) schools of Government or local authority, (b) schools aided by Government or local authority, (c) a specified category school like Kendriya Vidyalaya, Navodaya Vidyalaya etc. and (d) an unaided school i.e., a privately run school.
- Government or local authority schools [(a) mentioned above] shall provide free and compulsory elementary education to all children admitted therein.
- Government or local authority aided schools [(b) mentioned above], shall provide free and compulsory elementary education to children in proportion to the aid received by it subject to a minimum of 25%.
- Specified category schools [(c) mentioned above] and unaided schools [(d) mentioned above] shall admit in Class I, to the extent of at least 25% of the strength of the class, children belonging to weaker section and disadvantaged group in the neighbourhood and provide free and compulsory elementary education till completion.
- Child belonging to disadvantaged group means a child belonging to the Scheduled Caste, the Scheduled Tribe, Socially and Educationally Backward Class, or any disadvantaged group owing to social, cultural, economic, geographical, linguistic, gender or such other factor as per government notification.
- For unaided schools, expenditure incurred by the school (subject to maximum as spent by the Government in Government schools) on providing 25% free education shall be reimbursed. However, if due to allotment of land, building etc., if such school is obligated to provide free education, then there would be no reimbursement.
- No child shall be subjected to physical punishment or mental harassment.
- School Management Committee (SMC) is to be set up for all schools (except unaided schools) consisting of elected representatives of local authority, parents or guardians. $3/4^{th}$ of the members of SMC are to be parents or guardians (of children studying in such school), and proportionate representation to be provided to disadvantaged groups. At least 50% of the members of SMC have to be women.
- SMC shall have the following responsibilities:
  - Monitor working of the school;
  - Prepare and recommend school development plan;
  - Monitor utilisation of grants received.
- Teachers should have required minimum qualification as laid down by an academic authority. Pupil (Student)–Teacher ratio as prescribed in the schedule to the Act is to be followed.
- Teachers to be deployed only for Census, relief or elections. They should not engage in private tuitions or private teaching activity.

- Section 1(4) of the RTE Act, as amended in 2012, states that its provisions are subject to Articles 29 and 30 of the Constitution. Additionally, Section 1(5) exempts Madrasas, Vedic Pathshalas, and other institutions primarily focused on religious education from the Act's applicability.

24.3.2 No Detention Policy & Amendment

- Section 16 of the RTE Act, 2009 had the provision that no child admitted shall be held back in a class or expelled till completion of elementary education. This no-detention policy was aimed at preventing drop outs and ensuring that every child completes school till 8th class.
- However, this no-detention policy resulted in poor learning outcomes. Many States and schools had criticised this provision as it compromises with quality of education and does not encourage competency and excellence at elementary school level.
- Hence, in 2019, Section 16 of the RTE Act was amended to do away with this compulsory no-detention policy. It is now up to the appropriate government i.e., State or Central government to decide on detention policy for the schools being governed by them.
- The amendment to Section 16 in 2019 was as follows:
  - There shall be a regular examination in the fifth class and in the eighth class at the end of every academic year.
  - If a child fails in the examination referred to above, he/she shall be given additional instruction and granted opportunity for re-examination within a period of 2 months from the date of declaration of the result.
  - The appropriate Government may allow schools to hold back a child in the fifth class or in the eighth class or in both classes, in such manner and subject to such conditions as may be prescribed, if he/she fails in the re-examination as well. However, the appropriate Government may decide not to hold back a child in any class till the completion of elementary education.
  - No child shall, however, be expelled from a school till the completion of elementary education.
- In December 2024, the Centre announced the removal of the 'No-Detention Policy' for Classes 5 and 8 in schools under its jurisdiction. This decision aligns with the National Curriculum Framework following the implementation of the New Education Policy in 2020.

24.4 RIGHTS OF PERSONS WITH DISABILITIES ACT, 2016

- This Act replaced the Persons with Disabilities (Equal Opportunities, Protection of Rights and Full Participation) Act, 1995. Instead of seven disabilities specified in the earlier Act, the new Act covers 19 conditions.
- Persons with at least 40% of a disability are entitled to certain benefits such as reservations in education and employment, preference in government schemes, etc.
- The Act confers several rights and entitlements to disabled persons. These include disabled friendly access to all public buildings, hospitals, modes of transport, polling stations, etc.
- In case of mentally ill persons, district courts may award two types of guardianship. A limited guardian takes decisions jointly with the mentally ill person. A plenary guardian takes decisions on behalf of the mentally ill person, without consulting him/her.

24.5 FOREST RIGHTS ACT, 2006

The Act is named Scheduled Tribes and Other Traditional Forest Dwellers (Recognition of Forest Rights) Act, 2006 and is famously known as the Forest Rights Act, 2006. This Act recognises and vests various rights on the scheduled tribes and other forest dwellers that they are entitled to as part of their lifestyle over centuries.

The salient features of the Act are as follows:

- Section 3 lists down the rights of tribes and forest dwellers as below:
  - Right to hold and live in forest land;
  - Community rights over forest land;
  - Right of ownership, access to collect, use and dispose minor forest produce (like bamboo, honey etc.);
  - Other community rights of uses and entitlements such as fish and other products of water bodies;
  - Rights including community tenures of habitat and habitation for primitive tribal groups and pre-agricultural communities;
  - Rights for conversion of pattas or leases to title;
  - Right to protect, regenerate or conserve any community forest resource which they have been traditionally protecting and conserving for sustainable use;
  - Any other traditional right customarily held;
  - Right to in situ rehabilitation in case of wrongful eviction.
- Section 4(1) recognises and vests forest rights in the Scheduled Tribes and other traditional forest dwellers.
- Section 4(2) provides for safeguards even while rehabilitating tribes from wild life sanctuary areas.
- Rights conferred in the Act are heritable but not alienable or transferable and shall be registered jointly in the names of both spouses in case of married persons and single head in the case of a single household.
- Gram Sabha is empowered to take decisions for important aspects of the Act.

24.6 TRANSGENDER PERSONS (PROTECTION OF RIGHTS) ACT, 2019

This Act will benefit a large number of transgender persons. It will also be instrumental in mitigating the stigma, discrimination and abuse against the transgenders and help bring them into the mainstream of society.

Definition of Transgender

According to the definition (Section 2(k) of the Act), a transgender is a person whose gender does not match the gender assigned to that person at birth and includes trans-men or trans-women, persons with intersex variations, gender-queers, and persons having socio-cultural identities such as *kinnar, hijras, aravani* and *jogta*.

Highlights of the Act

- The Act aims to stop discrimination against a transgender person in various sectors such as education, employment and healthcare. It also directs the Central and the State governments to provide welfare schemes for them.
- It states that a person will be recognised as transgender on the basis of a certificate of identity issued by the District Magistrate. This certificate will be a proof of identity as transgender and confer rights under the Act.
- A person would have the right to choose to be identified as a man, woman or transgender, irrespective of sex reassignment surgery and hormonal therapy.
- It also requires transgender persons to be certified as a transperson through the District Magistrate and 'District Screening Committee'. This committee would consist of a medical officer, a psychologist or psychiatrist, a district welfare officer, a government official and a transgender person.
- There shall be a National Council for Transgender persons which shall be headed by the Union Minister in-charge of Ministry of Social Justice and empowerment as ex-officio Chairperson and various other members from different ministries, statutory commissions like NHRC and NCW, representatives of transgender community and experts.

Criticisms

- The Act does not grant reservations to transgender persons.
- It does not mention any punishments for rape or sexual assault of transgender persons as according to existing criminal laws, rape is only when a man violates a woman.

24.7 DIGITAL PERSONAL DATA PROTECTION ACT, 2023

After the judgement in Puttaswamy case (2017) that declared 'Right to Privacy' as a fundamental right, the government constituted a committee under the chairmanship of Justice Shri B. N. Srikrishna to deliberate and report on the 'Data protection framework'. The Committee submitted its report and a draft bill on data protection in July 2018. Subsequently, in August 2023, the Parliament passed 'The Digital Personal Data Protection Act, 2023' (DPDP Act).

> **THINK ABOUT IT**
>
> Analyse the salient features and issues surrounding the Digital Personal Data Protection Act, 2023.

Key Definitions under the DPDP Act

- Personal data – data about an individual who is identifiable by or in relation to such data.
- Digital Personal Data – Personal data in digital form.
- Data Principal – Person to whom data relates and includes parents or lawful guardian in case of a child and lawful guardian in case of a person with disability.
- Data Fiduciaries – Persons, companies and government entities who determine the purpose and means of processing of personal data.
- Data processing – collection, storage or any other operation on personal data.
- Data processor – person who processes personal data on behalf of Data Fiducuary.
- Data Protection Board of India – Board established under the Act consisting of Chairperson and such other members as the Central Government may notify.

Salient Features of the Act

The Salient features of the Act are as below:

- It is based on the following seven principles:
  - Consented, lawful and transparent use of personal data;
  - Purpose limitation (use of personal data only for the purpose specified at the time of obtaining consent of the Data Principal);
  - Data minimisation (collection of only as much personal data as is necessary to serve the specified purpose);
  - Data accuracy (ensuring data is correct and updated);
  - Storage limitation (storing data only till it is needed for the specified purpose);
  - Reasonable security safeguards; and
  - Accountability (through adjudication of data breaches and breaches of the provisions of the act and imposition of penalties for the breaches).
- It provides the following rights to Data Principals:
  - Access information about personal data processed;
  - Correction and erasure of data;
  - Grievance redressal;
  - Nomination of a person to exercise rights in case of death or incapacity;
  - Data of children can be processed only with parental consent.
- It places the following obligations on Data Fiduciaries:
  - To have security safeguards to prevent personal data breach;
  - To intimate personal data breaches to the affected Data Principal and the Data Protection Board;
  - To erase personal data when it is no longer needed for the specified purpose;
  - To erase personal data upon withdrawal of consent;
  - To have in place grievance redressal system and an officer to respond to queries from Data Principals; and
  - To fulfil certain additional obligations in respect of Data Fiduciaries notified as 'Significant Data Fiduciaries' (considering the volume of data processed, potential impact on sovereignty and integrity of India, risk to electoral democracy, security of the State etc.), such as appointing a data auditor and conducting periodic Data Protection Impact Assessment to ensure higher degree of data protection.
- The composition of the Data Protection Board shall be as follows:
  - Chairperson and other members shall be appointed by the Central government. They shall hold office for a period of 2 years and shall be eligible for re-appointment.
  - The Chairperson and members shall be persons of ability, integrity and standing who possess special knowledge or practical experience in the fields of data governance, consumer protection, dispute resolution, information and communication technology, digital economy etc. At least one of the members shall be an expert in the field of law.
  - A person shall be disqualified for being appointed or for continuing as Chairperson or member if he/she is adjudged insolvent, convicted of an offence involving moral turpitude, becomes physically or mentally incapable of acting as a member, acquired financial interest prejudicial to functioning as a member or abused position that renders continuance in office prejudicial to public interest.
  - The Chairperson or member shall not be removed by Central government unless he/she has been given an opportunity of being heard in the matter.
  - The Chairperson or any other member shall not for a period of one year from the date on which they cease to hold office, except with the previous approval of the central government, accept any employment with any Data Fiduciary against whom proceedings

were initiated by or before such Chairperson or member. They shall also disclose to the central government any subsequent acceptance (after one year) of employment with such Data Fiduciary.

- The key functions of the Data Protection Board are as follows:
  - To give directions for remediating or mitigating data breaches;
  - To inquire into data breaches and complaints and impose financial penalties;
  - To refer complaints for Alternate Dispute Resolution and to accept Voluntary Undertakings from Data Fiduciaries; and
  - To advise the Government to block the website, app etc. of a Data Fiduciary who is found to repeatedly breach the provisions of the Act.
  - The appeal against an order or direction by the Board shall lie with the Telecom Disputes Settlement and Appellate Tribunal under TRAI Act, 1997.
- Exemptions provided in the Act are as follows:
  - For notified agencies, in the interest of security, sovereignty, public order, etc.;
  - For research, archiving or statistical purposes;
  - For startups or other notified categories of Data Fiduciaries;
  - To enforce legal rights and claims;
  - To perform judicial or regulatory functions;
  - To prevent, detect, investigate or prosecute offences;
  - To process in India personal data of non-residents under foreign contract;
  - For approved merger, demerger etc.; and
  - To locate defaulters and their financial assets etc.

Key Issues and Analysis

- This law is the first comprehensive framework on data protection in our country. It is written in a simple language with illustrations at various places to make the meaning of the law clear. It is the first law that acknowledges women in Parliamentary law making by using the word 'she' instead of 'he'.
- Exemptions to data processing by the State on grounds such as national security may lead to data collection, processing, and retention beyond what is necessary. This may violate the fundamental right to privacy.
- The Act does not grant the right to data portability and the right to be forgotten to the Data principal.
- The Act allows transfer of personal data outside India, except to countries notified by the central government. This mechanism may not ensure adequate evaluation of data protection standards in the countries where transfer of personal data is allowed.
- The members of the Data Protection Board of India will be appointed for two years and will be eligible for re-appointment. The short term with scope for re-appointment may affect the independent functioning of the Board.
- Further, the DPDP Act has amended Section 8 of the Right to Information Act, 2005 (RTI) that provides exemption under that act for obtaining data from a public authority. The present amendment has provided for a blanket exemption of 'information which relates to personal information.'
  - Earlier, the RTI act stipulated that information which relates to personal information, the disclosure of which has no relationship to any public activity or interest, or which would cause unwarranted invasion of the privacy, of an individual need not be provided.

Scan the QR code for conceptual video on Rights Issues and Related Enactments

McGraw Hill edge

- However, if the Central Public Information officer or State Public Information officer or appellate authority was satisfied that larger public interest justified the disclosure of such information, the same could be provided.
- This ensured that public officials cannot get a blanket exemption from furnishing data on the ground that it is personal information. For example, the details of assets of a public official may be required to be obtained if there is a charge of accumulation of disproportionate wealth when compared to known sources of income.
- However, this amendment in 2023 (as part of the DPDP Act), has weakened the RTI Act by exempting all personal information without any exceptions.

24.8 OTHER RIGHTS RELATED ENACTMENTS/ISSUES

Apart from the above important laws, there are various other legislations that confer legal rights on citizens. Some of the laws/issues that have been in the news in recent past include:

- Maternity Benefit (Amendment) Act, 2017 – that increased the period of maternity leave to 26 weeks.
- The Medical Termination of Pregnancy (Amendment) Act, 2021 – (a) It covered even unmarried women under the Act (under the clause of failure of contraceptive) to provide access to safe abortion, (b) the gestation period for abortion of foetus was increased from 20 weeks to 24 weeks for rape survivors and beyond 24 weeks for foetal abnormalities. The opinion of only one registered medical practitioner will be required for the abortion of a foetus up to 20 weeks of gestation and of two practitioners for the termination of pregnancy from 20 to 24 weeks of gestation. The opinion of a state-level medical board is required for abortions over 24 weeks, in the case of suspected foetal abnormalities.
- Surrogacy Regulation Act, 2021 and Surrogacy Regulation Rules, 2022 that regulate the conditions for a couple to have a child through a surrogate mother.

Thus, as discussed in the introduction to this chapter, apart from the important laws discussed in this chapter, readers/candidates should also be aware of any important developments/judgements/amendments/issues from time to time with respect to any other rights related enactments in the country. Such developments/amendments/judgements in relation to the laws discussed in this chapter as well as other rights related enactments are captured and discussed in the Monthly current affairs update on the 'edge' platform as part of this courseware.

MAINS STARTER

Area	Building Blocks For Model Introductions
For any question from rights related enactments	Mention that it is a legal right (or a fundamental right supplemented by that specific law) and mention the name of the Act that provides the same. Briefly bring out the importance of such a right/Act. For example – The rights of Scheduled Tribes and other forest dwellers are legal rights provided under the Forest Rights Act, 2006. It recognises and confers various traditional rights enjoyed by tribals.

UPSC Previous Years' Questions of Preliminary Examination

1. At the National level which ministry is the nodal agency to ensure effective implementation of the FRA, 2006 **[2021]**
   (a) Ministry of environment, forest and climate change
   (b) Ministry of Panchayati Raj
   (c) Ministry of rural development
   (d) Ministry of Tribal affairs

   Solution: (d)

   Explanation: As discussed in Section 24.5, the FRA, 2006 is to recognise and protect the interest of Scheduled Tribes and other forest dwellers. So, the Ministry of Tribal affairs is the nodal agency for implementation of the act and correct answer is (d). A joint communication to States by Ministry of environment, forest and climate change and by Ministry of Tribal affairs under FRA, 2006 in July 2021, that was objected to by some activists, could have been the likely context for this question.

UPSC Previous Years' Questions of Main Examination

1. The Rights of Persons with Disabilities Act, 2016 (RPD Act) remains only a legal document without intense sensitisation of government functionaries and citizens regarding disability. Comment. **[2022]**
2. The Right of Children to Free and Compulsory Education Act, 2009 (RTE Act) remains inadequate in promoting incentive-based system for children's education without generating awareness about the importance of schooling. Analyse. **[2022]**

   Approach: The above two questions are related to the acts that have been discussed in Sections 24.3 (RTE Act) and 24.4 (RPD Act). The salient features of these acts can be summarised as the first part of the respective answers. The second part of the answers needs to discuss about current issues leading to poor implementation of these acts and possible solutions.

MODEL ANSWERS

1. **The RPD Act replaced the Persons with Disabilities (Equal Opportunities, Protection of Rights and Full Participation) Act, 1995. Instead of seven disabilities specified in the earlier act, the new Act covers 19 conditions.**

Salient Features

- Persons with at least 40% of a disability are entitled to certain benefits such as reservations in education and employment, preference in government schemes, etc.
- The Act confers several rights and entitlements to disabled persons. These include disabled friendly access to all public buildings, hospitals, modes of transport, polling stations, etc.

Issues in implementation

While the act has been enacted, it still remains largely on paper due to the following reasons:

(a) Lack of adequate disabled friendly facilities in public places and public transport.
(b) Government officials not adequately trained to be sensitive to the needs of persons with disability.
(c) Lack of awareness amongst citizens.

The above issues need to be addressed to make the act effective in meeting the needs of persons with disabilities.

2. **Right to Education, between the age of 6 and 14, is a fundamental right under Article 21A of the Constitution. The Right to Education Act, 2009 (RTE) is a law that supplements this fundamental right to elementary education.**

Salient Features

(a) Every child between the age of 6 and 14 shall be entitled to get free elementary education. Elementary education means education from first class to eighth class.
(b) Specified category schools [like Kendriya Vidyalaya & Navodaya Vidyalaya] and unaided schools [i.e., private schools] shall admit in Class I, to the extent of at least 25% of the strength of the class, children belonging to weaker section and disadvantaged group in the neighbourhood and provide free and compulsory elementary education till completion.
(c) Pupil-Teacher ratio to be maintained as provided in the act and School Management Committee to be established for monitoring the functioning of the schools.

Issues

While the act has been enacted to give effect to a fundamental right, it is inadequate in providing quality education to children due to following reasons:

i. Lack of awareness amongst the citizens about their fundamental right to education.
ii. Lack of effective implementation of 25% reservation for disadvantaged groups.
iii. Lack of availability of teachers in remote areas and non-maintenance of pupil-teacher ratio.

The above issues need to be addressed through campaigns and creating awareness for effective implementation of the RTE Act.

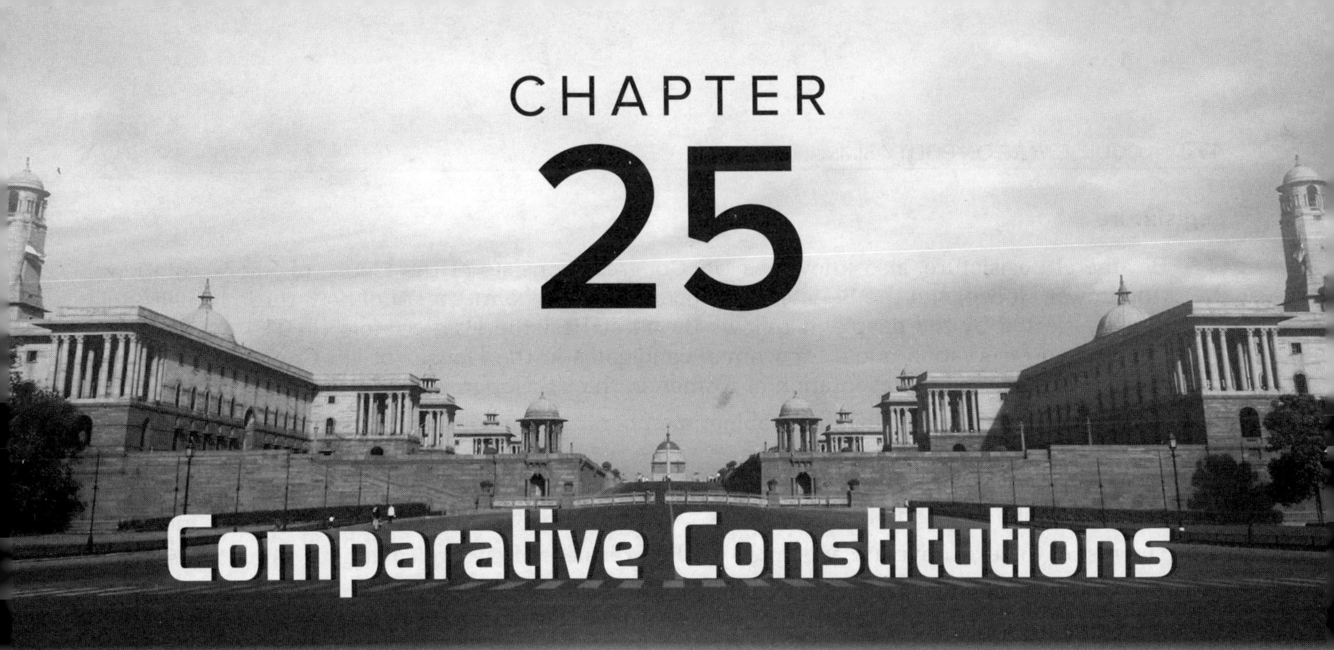

CHAPTER 25

Comparative Constitutions

LEARNING OUTCOMES

1. Understanding the key provisions of various democratic and federal constitutions
2. Exploring the comparison with important aspects of the Indian constitution

We have discussed the provisions of the Indian Constitution in detail in the previous chapters. We shall discuss the key provisions of some other Constitutions of major democracies of the world. This is not an exhaustive discussion but an overview with respect to a few comparative Constitutions. Apart from the Constitutions discussed in this chapter, the candidates should also keep themselves updated on current international affairs from time to time, relating to any big democratic and neighbouring countries and their Constitution.

25.1 US CONSTITUTION

25.1.1 Key Provisions

Significance

- It is the first written modern Constitution for a democracy (1789).
- It has been amended 27 times. The first 10 amendments are collectively known as the Bill of Rights.
- The amendments are appended to the end of the document (meaning, the original text of the Constitution remains unchanged).
- It is based on the doctrine of strict separation of powers between the three branches viz., Legislature, Executive and Judiciary.

Form of government

- It is a Presidential system of government in which the executive and the legislature are directly elected by the people.

Legislature

- Bicameral Legislature, also known as US Congress consists of the House of Representatives (the Lower House) and the Senate (the Upper House). The members of both these Houses are directly elected by the people. It follows the First Past the Post System (FPTP) in elections. There is no reservation quota for women candidates in the Houses of US Congress or within political parties. The representation of women in the US Congress stood at 29% as of 2024.
- Neither the President nor his/her Cabinet members are part of the legislature.

President and Executive

- The head of the State and the head of the Government is the President.
- The rest of the executive are appointed by the President after confirmation by the Senate.
- The President is independent in administration of the government and directly responsible to the people and can be impeached by the legislature.

Judiciary

- The President suggests the name of Judge to the Senate and only after confirmation by the Senate, the President appoints a Judge. The judiciary has no role in the appointment of Judges.
- Judicial Committee of the Senate evaluates the proposed judges, in a transparent and public fashion.
- Judges serve for a lifetime.

25.1.2 Comparison with Indian Constitution

The key similarities between the two Constitutions are as follows:

- Both are Republics with an elected head of the country. Both are federal Constitutions that have dual government, division of powers between the Centre and the States, and an independent judiciary to resolve disputes between the Centre and the States.
- The Fundamental Rights in the Indian Constitution is modelled on the basis of the 'Bill of Rights' in the US Constitution.
- The process of judicial review in India is modelled on the basis of such powers with the US Courts. However, the US Courts' judicial review powers are wider under a 'substantive due process' where the courts can review the validity of laws against unenumerated fundamental rights under the Constitution. In India, the scope of courts is a 'limited judicial review' where they can review the laws and the executive actions for constitutional validity and 'procedural due process'.

Key differences are as follows:

- While both the Constitutions are federal in character, the Indian Constitution has unitary bias that provides more power to the Centre on various matters.
- The system of government is Parliamentary democracy under the Indian Constitution whereas it is Presidential in the United States.
- The US Constitution is based on the doctrine of strict 'separation of powers' between the three branches. However, India being a Parliamentary democracy, the executive is part of the legislature and accountable to it. It is based on a system of 'checks and balance' where there are mechanisms for legislative control over the executive.

25.2 FRENCH CONSTITUTION

25.2.1 Key Provisions

Form of government

- It is a Semi-Presidential system of government in which the President is directly elected by the people who has military and diplomatic powers.
- It also has a Prime Minister, who is appointed by the President who is responsible for the domestic issues and policies of the government.

Legislature

- Bicameral Legislature, also called the National Assembly (the Lower House) and the Senate (the Upper House). However, it must be noted that though there are two Houses, France is not a federal country but a unitary country. National Assembly elections follow a two-round system if needed. A candidate winning over 50% of votes in the first round is elected outright. Otherwise, those securing more than 12.5% advance to the second round, where the candidate with highest votes is declared elected. While there is no women's reservation in the National Assembly, political parties have a quota for women candidates. As of 2024, women represented 36% of the Assembly.

President and Executive

- The President is the head of the State. He/she has military and diplomatic powers. He/she is directly elected by the people by majority of votes (in 1 or 2 rounds of election). If a candidate secures more than 50% of the votes cast in the first round, he/she is straight away elected as the President. Otherwise, the top two contenders have a run-off election in which the candidate who secures the majority of votes (i.e., more than 50%) is elected as the President.
- The President can call a referendum, dissolve the National Assembly, and can even propose a revision of the Constitution.
- The President appoints the Prime Minister and his/her Cabinet (on PM's advice). The Prime Minister is usually from the party that enjoys majority in the National Assembly. The Prime Minister is the head of the government and guides the Parliament and the nation in domestic matters.

Judiciary

- The courts are organised as follows:
  - Ordinary courts (judicial stream) that handle civil and criminal cases.
  - Administrative courts that supervise the government and handle complaints.
- Judges for the judicial stream are appointed by the President based on recommendation of a higher council of the judiciary.
- Judicial review is not given to regular courts, but to the Constitutional Council (semi-executive, semi-judicial body).

25.2.2 Comparison with Indian Constitution

- The principles of Liberty, Equality and Fraternity in the Indian Constitution are inspired by the French Constitution.

- France follows the principles of 'negative secularism'. It is known as '*Laicite*' in French, which is based on the division between private life and public affairs. The Constitution guarantees freedom of conscience and right to practice any religion for its citizens. However, the government is refrained from taking any position on matters of religion and maintains equal distance from all religions. There are no religious practices or symbols that are allowed in public affairs.
- In contrast, the Indian secularism is positive in nature.

25.3 JAPANESE CONSTITUTION

25.3.1 Key Provisions

Form of government

- It is a Parliamentary system of Government (similar to India).

Legislature

- Bicameral Legislature called the House of Representatives (the Lower House) and the House of Councillors (the Upper House). However, it must be noted that though there are two Houses, Japan is not a federal country but a unitary country. The House of Representatives follows a Mixed Member Proportional Representation (MMPR) system. Of its 465 members, 289 are elected through a First-Past-the-Post (FPTP) system in single-seat constituencies, while the remaining 176 are selected through Party-list Proportional Representation (PR). There is no women's reservation in the House or within political parties. As of 2024, women comprised 16% of the House of Representatives.

Executive

- The Emperor is the head of the State and hereditary in nature. He/she appoints the Prime Minister, the Chief Justice of Supreme Court, and promulgates statutes and treaties. However, he/she is only a nominal head like the Indian President and the British Monarch.
- The real executive power is vested in the Prime Minister and his/her Cabinet.

Judiciary

- All courts enjoy judicial review powers and can overrule statutes by the government if it fails to conform to the Constitution.
- Appointment of judges:
  - Chief Justice: Nominated by the Cabinet, appointed by the Emperor.
  - Other Justices: Nominated and appointed by the Cabinet, approved by the Emperor.

25.4 SOUTH AFRICAN CONSTITUTION

25.4.1 Key Provisions

Form of government

- It is a Parliamentary system of Government (similar to India).

Legislature

- Bicameral Legislature called the National Assembly (the Lower House) and the National Council of Provinces (the Upper House). South Africa is also a federal country like India and the United States. In South Africa, National Assembly and provincial legislature elections are held simultaneously every five years. While there is no women's reservation in the National Assembly, political parties have quotas for women candidates. As of 2024, women comprised 43% of the National Assembly.

Executive

- The President is the head of the State and Government. He/she is elected for a fixed term by the National Assembly. Once elected to the post of President, he/she resigns from the National Assembly and holds the post for a fixed term of 5 years unless impeached by the Parliament.
- The President appoints the members of his/her Cabinet from amongst the Members of the Parliament.

Judiciary

- Judicial Service Commission advises the President on the appointment of Judges. It is headed by the Chief Justice of South Africa and has representatives from the judiciary, the executive, the legislature, lawyers and law universities.
- It also advises the national government on all matters relating to judiciary and delivery of justice.

25.4.2 Comparison with Indian Constitution

- The important aspect in the South African Constitution that is relevant in the present Indian context is the manner of appointment of judges.
- There are differences of opinion between the judiciary and the Government of India as regards the manner of appointment of judges to higher judiciary. While the Parliament had enacted the National Judicial Appointments Commission (NJAC) by amending the Constitution in 2014, the same was struck down by the Supreme Court as violating the basic structure of 'independence of judiciary'. We continue to follow the collegium system of appointments till date. The pros and cons of both the system has already been discussed in the chapter on Supreme Court.
- A possible solution can be to follow the South African system. The NJAC may be broad-based like the Judicial Service Commission of South Africa that has representation of various stakeholders in the judicial system. This may make the entire process of appointment of judges more transparent and inclusive.

Scan the QR code for conceptual video on Comparative Constitutions

McGraw Hill edge

25.5 BRITISH CONVENTIONS

The British constitutional conventions are unwritten or uncodified. They are principles that are not legally enforceable but form part of the constitutional conventions that are followed by virtue of long practice and enforced politically and professionally.

- These include Parliamentary conventions with respect to the two Houses, Speaker's office, procedure in the Houses, collective responsibility of the council of ministers to the

THINK ABOUT IT

The FPTP system in India should be integrated with PR to more accurately represent the people's will. Comment comparing with election systems in other democracies.

House of Commons etc. The members to the House of Commons (equivalent to our House of the People) is elected by FPTP system. There is no women's reservation quota in the House of Commons, but there are quotas for women candidates within political parties. The representation of women in the House of Commons stood at 40% as of 2024.

- Judiciary is independent and it is a country governed by 'Rule of law'. Judges are appointed by the King on the advice of the Prime Minister, to whom names are recommended by a Selection Commission. The Selection Commission consists of judges and representatives of the Judicial Appointments Commission.

THINK ABOUT IT

The 106th amendment has introduced compulsory reservation of one-third seats for women in Lok Sabha and Legislative assemblies. Do you think it would lead to real women empowerment? Compare with systems in other democracies.

- Other provisions with respect to the Parliamentary privileges, office of Speaker etc., under the British system and its comparison with Indian Constitution have been discussed in the respective chapters.

25.6 OTHER DEMOCRATIC AND FEDERAL CONSTITUTIONS

Apart from the comparison with some important constitutions across the world in the previous sections, the table below summarises the key points with respect to some of the other democratic constitutions which are federal in character.

Country	Key Provisions of its Constitution
Canada	• The Constitution of Canada is an amalgamation of various codified acts, treaties, uncodified traditions, and conventions. One of the main parts of its constitution is the Constitution Act, 1982 (which itself is part of Canada Act, 1982). • Canada is a Parliamentary democracy. The Governor–General appointed by the British Crown is the nominal head of the country while the Prime Minister is the real executive head of the government. • Part I of the Constitution Act, 1982 is the Canadian Charter of Rights and Freedoms. The Charter guarantees civil rights and liberties to every citizen in Canada (similar to Part III – Fundamental Rights of the Indian Constitution). • The amendment of the Constitution Act is blend of rigidity and flexibility like the Indian Constitution. Amendments that affect the federal set up between the Federal Government and the Provinces require approval by the House of Commons & Senate in the Parliament and should also be approved by at least two-thirds of provincial legislatures (at least 7 out of 10) representing at least 50% of the population. Some of the amendments relating to use of official languages, amending formula itself or composition of the Supreme Court requires unanimous consent of all the 10 provinces. If the amendment affects only the federal government, it does not need approval of provinces and vice-versa. • There are no separate written constitutions for the provinces.
Germany	• The Constitution of Germany is called 'Basic law for the Federal Republic of Germany' (Basic Law). It provides a list of fundamental rights that are guaranteed to its citizens. • Germany is a Parliamentary democracy. The nominal head of the country is the Federal President while the real executive head is the Federal Chancellor. • The Federal Parliament consists of the *'Bundestag'* which is the popularly elected house (like our Lok Sabha) and *'Bundesrat'* which consists of delegates of respective

Country	Key Provisions of its Constitution
	State governments from the 16 States in Germany. The elections to the *'Bundestag'* happen every 4 years (unless earlier dissolved) and members are elected under the Mixed Member Proportional Representation system. There is no women's reservation quota in the *Bundestag*, but there is quota for women candidates within political parties. The women representation in *Bundestag* stood at 32% as of 2025. • The Federal Chancellor is elected by the *'Bundestag'* for its full term of 4 years and can be replaced only by electing a successor in a 'constructive vote of no confidence'. • States are called as *'Lander'* in Germany. • The legislative powers are listed under (a) Exclusive legislative powers of the Federation and (b) Matters under concurrent legislative powers of the Federation and *'Lander'*. The *'Lander'* can legislate on any matter insofar as the 'Basic Law' does not confer legislative power on the Federation. • Amendment to 'Basic Law' requires approval by 2/3rd of the members of *'Bundestag'* and 2/3rd of the votes of the *'Bundesrat'*.
Switzerland	• Switzerland's constitution is called 'The Federal Constitution of the Swiss Confederation'. • The legislature consists of the Federal Assembly that has two houses. The National Council (equivalent of our Lok Sabha) elected directly by the people by the voting system of 'Party-list proportional representation' and the Council of States (equivalent of our Rajya Sabha) with representatives from the 26 cantons of Switzerland. States in Switzerland are called as 'Cantons'. • The executive consists of Federal Council with seven members who are elected by the Federal Assembly. The President of the Confederation is also elected by the Federal Assembly every year. • The Cantons have their own constitution and have complete autonomy on all matters except for the matters on which the Federal Assembly can legislate. • The Cantons consist of various 'Communes' with their own elected local governments. The people of Switzerland support and treasure the freedom of their commune which can be equated to 'local republics'. • Any amendment to the Constitution, after approval in the Federal Assembly, should be approved by majority of the Cantons and also be approved by the People of Switzerland through a referendum.

The readers should also update themselves about important developments in constitutional scheme of things in our neighbouring countries and across the world from time to time. Such important developments would also be captured and discussed in the monthly current affairs update on 'edge' platform that is part of this courseware.

MAINS STARTER

Area	Building Blocks For Model Introductions
Any comparative constitution question	Begin by stating whether it is a federal or a unitary constitution. Highlight a key similarity between that Constitution and the Indian Constitution as appropriate for the question. For example – The Japanese constitution is a unitary constitution. It is a parliamentary democracy like India but with a nominal emperor as the head of the State.

UPSC Previous Years' Questions of Main Examination

1. Critically examine the procedures through which the Presidents of India and France are elected. **[2022]**

Approach: The likely context to this question could have been the Indian Presidential election in July 2022. The procedure for the election of Indian President and French President needs to be summarised in the first part of the answer and a comparison of the same can be the second part of the answer.

MODEL ANSWER

India and France are both republics with an elected President as the Head of the State. However, the Indian President is only a nominal head while the French President has real powers with respect to military and diplomatic matters.

Election of Presidents

India – The Indian President is elected by an electoral college consisting of elected MPs and elected MLAs by a system of proportional representation by means of the single transferable vote. The election is held every 5 years.

France – The French President is directly elected by the people by majority of votes (in 1 or 2 rounds of election). If a candidate secures more than 50% of the votes cast in the first round, he/she is straight away elected as the President. Otherwise, the top 2 contenders have a run-off election in which the candidate who secures the majority of votes (i.e., more than 50%) is elected as the President. This election is also held every 5 years.

Comparison

- The Indian President is a nominal head of the State and is elected indirectly, while the French President is the real head of the State and is elected by the people directly.
- The quota in the Indian Presidential election is more than 50% of votes polled for a candidate to be declared the winner. However, the preferences are transferred between surviving candidates after each round (in case of more than 2 contestants), if required, till any candidate gets the required quota. In France, the winner has to secure more than 50% of votes polled in the first round of the election or the run-off as explained above.

2. The judicial systems in India and the UK seem to be converging as well as diverging in recent times. Highlight the key points of convergence and divergence between the two nations in terms of their judicial practices. **[2020]**

Approach: The dependency of Indian legal system on the British system needs to be brought out in the introduction. Then the similarities and divergences need to be summarised.

MODEL ANSWER

The Indian legal system is part of the inheritance India received from the British after more than 200 years of their colonial rule. The same is evident from the many similarities the Indian legal system shares with the English Legal System.

Similarities between Indian and British judicial practices

- Both in India and Britain the independence of judiciary is ensured by having stringent provisions for removal of judges only through the Parliament.
- The courts in both the countries can declare any executive action that violates their legal limits as void.
- Both countries are governed by 'Rule of law' and follow 'Common law' system i.e., law as evolved through various judgements of the courts that are used as precedence.

Divergence between the two systems

- In Britain, the Parliament is sovereign and so the courts cannot strike down any law made by Parliament whereas in India, the Constitution is supreme and any law that violates the Constitution can be declared as void by the courts.
- The Indian courts have developed the doctrine of 'Basic structure' while reviewing various laws and constitutional amendments. There is no such practice in the British courts.
- In the UK, the judges are appointed based on recommendation of the Judicial Appointments Commission whereas in India, it is based on the recommendation of the Collegium.

Despite their differences, the judicial system in both the countries work towards upholding the 'Rule of law' and protecting individual liberties.

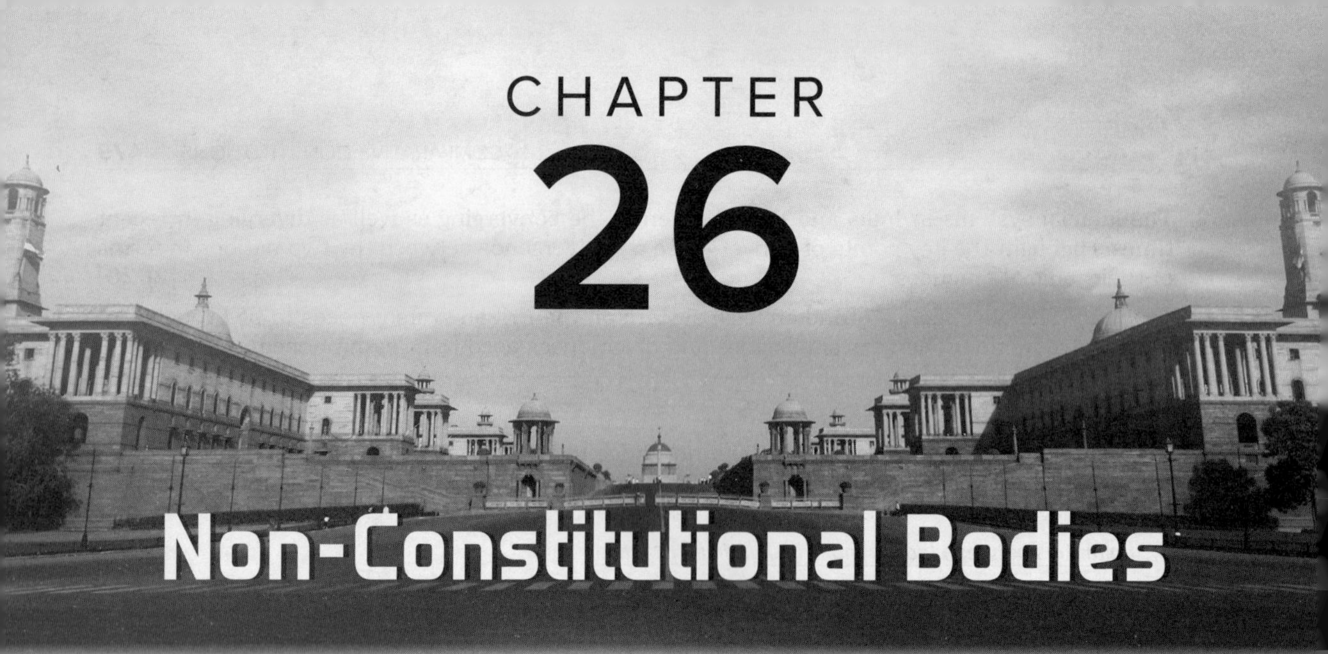

CHAPTER 26

Non-Constitutional Bodies

LEARNING OUTCOMES

1. Understanding various types of non-constitutional bodies
2. Analysing the composition and important functions of various statutory bodies
3. Understanding the composition and role of important executive bodies
4. Summarising the key aspects with respect to quasi-judicial and regulatory bodies

In this chapter, we shall discuss the important provisions relating to non-constitutional bodies that can be classified as statutory bodies and executive bodies. In the end, we will also understand about quasi-judicial bodies and regulatory bodies with few examples.

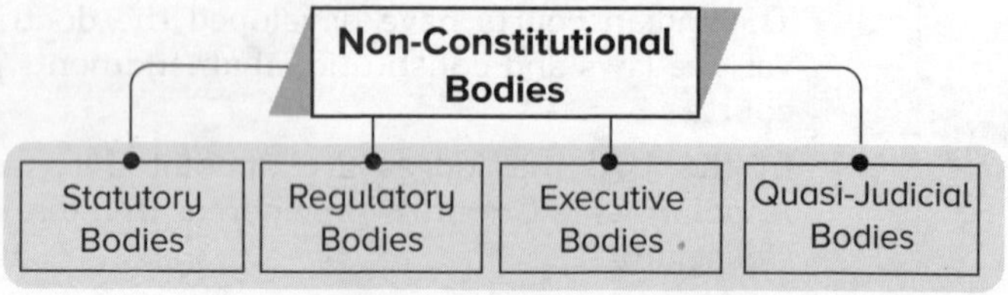

26.1 STATUTORY BODIES

Statutory bodies are those that are created by a law. Such bodies may be created by a Parliamentary law or law of a State Legislature. We shall discuss the important provisions with respect to statutory bodies created by a Parliamentary law.

26.1.1 Human Rights Commission

National Human Rights Commission (NHRC) and State Human Rights Commission (SHRC) are constituted under the provisions of 'The Protection of Human Rights Act, 1993'.

26.1.1.1 National Human Rights Commission

Composition of members

- The commission is a multi-member body consisting of a Chairperson and five members of which three persons (out of which at least one should be a woman) shall have knowledge or practical experience with respect to human rights.

- The ex-officio members of NHRC are the chairpersons of the National Commission for Minorities, the National Commission for SCs, the National Commission for STs, the National Commission for Women, the National Commission for BCs and the National Commission for Protection of Child Rights and the Chief Commissioner for Persons with Disabilities.

Appointment and tenure of members

- The Chairperson and members are appointed by the President on the recommendation of a six-member committee consisting of the Prime Minister, the Speaker of the Lok Sabha, the Deputy Chairman of the Rajya Sabha, leaders of the Opposition in both the Houses of Parliament and the Central Home Minister.
- The Chairperson and members hold office for a term of 3 years or until they attain the age of 70 years, whichever is earlier. They are eligible for re-appointment.

Qualification and Removal of members

- The Chairperson should be a retired Chief Justice of India or a Judge of the Supreme Court.
- One member who is a serving or a retired Judge of the Supreme Court and one member who is a serving or a retired Chief Justice of a High Court. Three other members, out of which at least one shall be a woman, who have knowledge or practical experience with respect to human rights.
- The President can remove the Chairperson or any member from the office under the following circumstances:
  - If he/she is adjudged an insolvent; or
  - If he/she engages, during his/her term of office, in any paid employment outside the duties of his/her office; or
  - If he/she is unfit to continue in office by reason of infirmity of mind or body; or
  - If he/she is of unsound mind and declared so by a competent court; or
  - If he/she is convicted and sentenced to prison for an offence that involves moral turpitude in the opinion of the President.
- The President can also remove the Chairperson or any member on the ground of proved misbehaviour or incapacity. However, in these cases, the President has to refer the matter to the Supreme Court for an inquiry and shall remove the Chairperson or any member, if the Supreme Court after the inquiry reports that such Chairperson or any member ought to be removed.

Important role of NHRC

- The NHRC is a statutory body. It was established in 1993 under a legislation enacted by the Parliament, namely, the Protection of Human Rights Act, 1993.
- The commission is the watchdog of human rights in the country, that is, the rights relating to life, liberty, equality and dignity of an individual guaranteed by the Constitution.
- The NHRC inquires into any violation of human rights or negligence in the prevention of such violation by a public servant, either suo motu or on a petition presented to it or on an order of a court.
- The commission is not empowered to inquire into any matter after the expiry of one year from the date on which the Act constituting violation of human rights is alleged to have been committed.
- It has no power to punish the violators of human rights, nor to award any relief including monetary relief to the victim.

- The commission has limited role, powers and jurisdiction with respect to the violation of human rights by the members of the armed forces.

26.1.1.2 State Human Rights Commission

Composition of members

The SHRC is a multi-member body consisting of a Chairperson and two members one of whom would be a person having knowledge or practical experience with respect to human rights.

Appointment and tenure of members

- The Chairperson and members are appointed by the Governor on the recommendations of a committee consisting of the Chief Minister, the Speaker of the Legislative Assembly, the State Home Minister and the Leader of the Opposition in the Legislative Assembly.
- In the case of a State having Legislative Council, the Chairman of the Council and the Leader of the Opposition in the Council would also be the members of the committee.
- The Chairperson and members hold office for a term of 3 years or until they attain the age of 70 years, whichever is earlier. They are eligible for reappointment.

Qualification and Removal of members

- The Chairperson should be a retired Chief Justice or a Judge of a High Court.
- One member should be a serving or retired Judge of a High Court or a District Judge in the State with a minimum of 7 years' experience as District Judge. One more member who has knowledge or practical experience with respect to human rights.
- Although the Chairperson and members of an SHRC are appointed by the Governor, they can be removed only by the President in the same way as NHRC.

Important role of SHRC

- The Protection of Human Rights Act of 1993 provides for the creation of SHRCs.
- An SHRC can inquire into violation of human rights only in respect of subjects mentioned in the State list (List-II) and the Concurrent list (List-III) in the Seventh Schedule of the Constitution.
- The Commission is not empowered to inquire into any matter after the expiry of 1 year from the date on which the Act constituting violation of human rights is alleged to have been committed.
- The Act also provides for the establishment of Human Rights Court in every district for the speedy trial of violation of human rights.
- These courts can be set up by the State government only with the concurrence of the Chief Justice of the High Court of that State.

26.1.2 Information Commission

The Central Information Commission (CIC) and the State Information Commissions (SIC) are constituted under the Right to Information Act, 2005 (RTI Act).

26.1.2.1 Central Information Commission

Composition of members

The Commission consists of a Chief Information Commissioner and not more than ten Information Commissioners.

Appointment and tenure of members

- The Chief Information Commissioner and other Information Commissioners are appointed by the President on the recommendation of a committee consisting of the Prime Minister as Chairperson, the Leader of Opposition in the Lok Sabha and a Union Cabinet Minister nominated by the Prime Minister.
- The Chief Information Commissioner and the Information Commissioners shall hold office for such term as prescribed by the Central Government or until they attain the age of 65 years, whichever is earlier. As per the RTI rules, 2019, they are appointed for a term of three years. They are not eligible for reappointment. Information Commissioner is eligible for appointment as Chief Information Commissioner, but the combined term in aggregate, as Information Commissioner and Chief Information Commissioner, shall not exceed five years.

Qualification and Removal of members

- They should be persons of eminence in public life with wide knowledge and experience in law, science and technology, social service, management, journalism, mass media or administration and governance.
- They should not be a Member of Parliament or a Member of the Legislature of any State or Union Territory.
- They should not hold any other office of profit or connected with any political party or carrying on any business or pursuing any profession.
- The President can remove the Chief Information Commissioner or any Information Commissioner from the office under the following circumstances:
  - if he/she is adjudged an insolvent; or
  - if he/she has been convicted of an offence which involves moral turpitude; or
  - if he/she engages during his/her term of office in any paid employment outside the duties of his/her office; or
  - if he/she is unfit to continue in office due to infirmity of mind or body; or
  - if he/she has acquired such financial or other interest as is likely to affect prejudicially his/her official functions.
- The President can also remove the Chief Information Commissioner or any Information Commissioner on the ground of proved misbehaviour or incapacity. However, in these cases, the President has to refer the matter to the Supreme Court for an inquiry and shall remove the Chairperson or any member, if the Supreme Court after the inquiry reports that such Chairperson or any member ought to be removed.

> **THINK ABOUT IT**
>
> The Information Commission requires as much autonomy as any other independent constitutional authority. Analyse. Is it time to make the Information Commission a constitutional body?

Important role of CIC

- The Central Information Commission is established under the provisions of the Right to Information Act, 2005.
- It entertains complaints and appeals pertaining to offices, financial institutions, public sector undertakings, etc., under the Central Government and the Union Territories.
- The Commission can order inquiry on its own into any matter if there are reasonable grounds (suo-moto power).

26.1.2.2 State Information Commission

Composition of members

A State Information Commission consists of a State Chief Information Commissioner and not more than ten State Information Commissioners.

Appointment and tenure of members

- The State Chief Information Commissioner and other State Information Commissioners are appointed by the Governor on the recommendation of a committee consisting of the Chief Minister as Chairperson, the Leader of Opposition in the Legislative Assembly and a State Cabinet Minister nominated by the Chief Minister.
- The Chief Information Commissioner and the Information Commissioners shall hold office for such term as prescribed by the Central Government or until they attain the age of 65 years, whichever is earlier. As per the RTI rules, 2019, they are appointed for a term of three years. They are not eligible for reappointment. A State Information Commissioner may be appointed as the State Chief Information Commissioner; however, their total tenure in both positions combined shall not exceed five years.

Qualification and Removal of members

- They should be persons of eminence in public life with wide knowledge and experience in law, science and technology, social service, management, journalism, mass media or administration and governance.
- They should not be a Member of the Parliament or a Member of the Legislature of any State or Union Territory.
- They should not hold any other office of profit or connected with any political party or carrying on any business or pursuing any profession.
- The Governor can remove the Chief Information Commissioner or any Information Commissioner from the office under the following circumstances:
  - if he/she is adjudged an insolvent; or
  - if he/she has been convicted of an offence which involves moral turpitude; or
  - if he/she engages during his/her term of office in any paid employment outside the duties of his/her office; or
  - if he/she is unfit to continue in office due to infirmity of mind or body; or
  - if he/she has acquired such financial or other interest as is likely to affect prejudicially his/her official functions.
- The Governor can also remove the Chief Information Commissioner or any Information Commissioner on the ground of proved misbehaviour or incapacity. However, in these cases, the Governor has to refer the matter to the Supreme Court for an inquiry and shall remove the Chairperson or any member, if the Supreme Court after the inquiry reports that such Chairperson or any member ought to be removed.

Important role of SIC

- The State Information Commissions are established under the provisions of Right to Information Act, 2005.
- It entertains complaints and appeals pertaining to offices, financial institutions, public sector undertakings, etc., under the concerned State Government.
- The Commission can order inquiry on its own into any matter if there are reasonable grounds (suo-moto power).

26.1.3 Central Vigilance Commission

Composition of members

The Central Vigilance Commission (CVC) is a multi-member body consisting of a Central Vigilance Commissioner (chairperson) and not more than two vigilance commissioners.

Appointment, tenure and removal of members

- The Central Vigilance Commissioner and other commissioners are appointed by the President by warrant under his/her hand and seal on the recommendation of a three-member committee consisting of the Prime Minister as its head, the Union Minister of Home Affairs and the Leader of the Opposition in the Lok Sabha.
- They hold office for a term of 4 years or until they attain the age of 65 years, whichever is earlier.
- The salary, allowances and other conditions of service of the Central Vigilance Commissioner are similar to those of the Chairman of the UPSC and that of the vigilance commissioners are similar to those of a member of the UPSC.
- The President can remove the Central Vigilance Commissioner or any vigilance commissioner from the office in the same manner and on same grounds as applicable to Chief Information Commissioner and other Information Commissioners of the Central Information Commission (discussed in previous section).

Important role of CVC

- The CVC is the main agency for preventing corruption in the Central government. It was established in 1964 by an executive resolution of the Central Government. Its establishment was recommended by the ***Santhanam Committee on Prevention of Corruption*** (1962–64). Now it has statutory backing through CVC Act, 2003.
- The CVC can inquire or cause an inquiry or investigation to be conducted on a reference made by the Central government wherein it is alleged that a public servant being an employee of the Central government or its authorities, has committed an offence under the Prevention of Corruption Act, 1988.
- It exercises superintendence over the functioning of the Delhi Special Police Establishment (CBI) insofar as it relates to the investigation of offences under the Prevention of Corruption Act, 1988.
- To exercise superintendence over the vigilance administration in the ministries of the Central government or its authorities.
- The Central Government is required to consult the CVC in making rules and regulations governing the vigilance and disciplinary matters relating to the members of Central Services and All-India Services.
- CVC has been designated as the agency to receive and act on complaints or disclosure on any allegation of corruption or misuse of office from whistle blowers under the 'Public Interest Disclosure and Protection of Informers' Resolution' (PIDPI), which is popularly known as 'Whistle Blowers' Resolution.
- CVC has been notified as a specific authority to receive information relating to suspicious transactions under the Prevention of Money Laundering Act, 2002.

26.1.4 Lokpal and Lokayuktas

The First Administrative Reforms Commission (ARC) of India (1966–1970) recommended the setting up of two special authorities designated as 'Lokpal' and 'Lokayukta' for the redressal of citizens' grievances. The Lokpal (for centre) and Lokayuktas (for States) are now set up under the Lokpal and Lokayuktas Act, 2013.

26.1.4.1 Lokpal

Composition of members

The Lokpal consists of a Chairperson with a maximum of eight members.

> **THINK ABOUT IT**
>
> The Lokpal was established after a powerful people's movement that was seen as a crusade against corruption in public life. However, its functioning leaves much to be desired. Analyse the important role of Lokpal and issues in its functioning.

Appointment and tenure of members

- The Chairperson and the members of the Lokpal shall be selected through a Selection Committee consisting of the Prime Minister, the Speaker of the Lok Sabha, the Leader of the Opposition in the Lok Sabha, the Chief Justice of India or a sitting Supreme Court Judge nominated by the Chief Justice of India and an eminent jurist to be nominated by the President of India on the basis of recommendation of the first four members of the selection committee.
- The Chairperson and members shall hold office for a period of 5 years or until the age of 70 years, whichever is earlier.

Qualification and Removal of members

- The Chairperson, who is or has been a Chief Justice of India or is or has been a Judge of the Supreme Court or an eminent person who is a person of impeccable integrity and outstanding ability having special knowledge and expertise of not less than 25 years in the matters relating to anti-corruption policy, public administration, vigilance, finance including insurance and banking, law and management.
- 50% of the members of the Lokpal shall come from amongst the SCs, the STs, the OBCs, minorities and women.
- 50% shall be judicial members i.e., is or has been a Judge of the Supreme Court or a Chief Justice of a High Court.
- They should not be a Member of Parliament or a Member of the Legislature of any State or Union Territory.
- They should not hold any other office of profit or connected with any political party or carrying on any business or pursuing any profession.
- They should not be convicted of an offence involving moral turpitude.
- They should not be less than 45 years of age.
- The President can remove the Lokpal or any member from the office under the following circumstances:
  - if he/she is adjudged an insolvent; or
  - if he/she engages during his/her term of office in any paid employment outside the duties of his/her office; or
  - if he/she is unfit to continue in office due to infirmity of mind or body.

- The President can also remove the Lokpal or any member on the ground of misbehaviour. However, in these cases, the President has to refer the matter to the Supreme Court for an inquiry and shall remove the Chairperson or any member, if the Supreme Court after the inquiry reports that such Chairperson or any member ought to be removed.
- After ceasing to hold office as Chairperson or a Member, they shall be ineligible for reappointment. They shall not hold any diplomatic assignment or any other appointment that is required to be made by the President by warrant under his hand and seal.
- They shall not be eligible for further employment under the Government of India or of a State.
- They shall not contest elections to the post of President or Vice-President; Member of Houses of Parliament or State Legislature or local bodies, for a period of 5 years from the date of relinquishing their post.

Important role of Lokpal

- The Lokpal will have the power of superintendence and direction over any investigating agency, including the CBI, for cases referred to them by the Lokpal.
- The Prime Minister has been brought under the purview of the Lokpal with subject matter exclusions and specific process for handling complaints against the Prime Minister.
- The Lokpal's jurisdiction will cover all categories of public servants, including Group A, Group B, Group C and Group D officers and employees of the Government.
- The first Lokpal was appointed only in 2019. However, in 5 years of its functioning, it has ordered probe only in 24 cases and granted prosecution sanction in only 6 cases. 90% of the complaints received have been rejected due to incorrect format. This indicates the need to strengthen the functioning of Lokpal.

26.1.4.2 Lokayukta

- In most of the States, the Lokayukta and the Upalokayukta are appointed by the Governor of the State (State government) in consultation with the Chief Justice of the State High Court and the Leader of the Opposition in the State Legislative Assembly.
- In most of the States, the term of office fixed for the Lokayukta is of 5 years duration or 65 years of age, whichever is earlier.
- There is no uniformity regarding the jurisdiction of the Lokayukta in all the States. In most of the States, the Lokayukta can initiate investigations either on the basis of a complaint received from the citizen against unfair administrative action or suo moto.

26.1.5 National Investigation Agency

- The National Investigation Agency (NIA) was constituted in 2009 under the provisions of the National Investigation Agency Act, 2008 (NIA Act). It is the central counter-terrorism law enforcement agency in the country.
- The NIA is headed by a Director-General appointed by the Central government.
- The NIA works under the administrative control of the Ministry of Home Affairs, Government of India. The NIA has a separate specialised cell known as Terrorist Financing and Financial Crimes (TFFC) Cell dealing with the subjects of fake currency notes and terror funding.
- The NIA is mandated to investigate and prosecute offences under the various Acts mentioned in the Schedule of the NIA Act.

- The NIA collects, collates and analyses counter-terrorism investigation and shares inputs with its sister intelligence agencies and law enforcement units both at Central and State governments level.
- The NIA has concurrent jurisdiction to investigate and prosecute the offences affecting the sovereignty, security and integrity of India, security of State, friendly relations with foreign States and offences under various Acts enacted to implement international treaties, agreements, conventions and resolutions of the UNO, its agencies and other international organisations.
- The 2019 Amendment of the NIA Act expanded its scope as follows:
  - The NIA is also empowered to probe the offences relating to human trafficking, counterfeit currency or bank notes, manufacture or sale of prohibited arms, cyber-terrorism and explosive substances.
  - It applied the provisions of the NIA Act also to persons who commit a scheduled offence beyond India against Indian citizens or affecting the interest of India.
  - It empowered the central government, with respect to a scheduled offence committed outside India, to direct the NIA to register the case and take up investigation as if such offence had taken place in India.

26.1.6 National Disaster Management Authority

The Disaster Management Act, 2005 provided for the creation of the National Disaster Management Authority (NDMA) to spearhead and implement a holistic and integrated approach to disaster management in the country.

The NDMA is the apex body for disaster management in the country. It works under the administrative control of the Union Ministry of Home Affairs.

Composition of members

- The Prime Minister is the ex-officio Chairperson of the NDMA. The NDMA consists of a Chairperson and other members, not exceeding nine.
- The other members are nominated by the Chairperson of the NDMA.
- The Chairperson of the NDMA designates one of the members as the Vice-chairperson of the NDMA.

Important functions

- To lay down policies on disaster management.
- To approve the National Plan.
- To approve plans prepared by the Ministries or Departments of the Government of India in accordance with the National Plan.
- To lay down guidelines to be followed by the State Disaster Management Authorities (SDMAs) in drawing up the State Plan.
- It exercises the general superintendence, direction and control of the National Disaster Response Force (NDRF). This force has been constituted for the purpose of specialist response to a threatening disaster situation or disaster.

There is also State Disaster Management Authority (SDMA) with the Chief Minister as the Chairperson set up at every State level with similar composition and functions at the State level. There is also District Disaster Management Authority with the Collector of a district as the ex-officio chairperson for coordinating disaster preparedness at the district level.

26.1.7 National Commission for Women

Women are considered the most vulnerable section of the society. They do not fall under minority group or backward classes but in a patriarchal society, they are disadvantaged. The National Commission for Women (NCW) is constituted under the National Commission for Women Act, 1990.

Composition of members

- The commission is a multi-member body consisting of a Chairperson, and five members to be nominated by the Central government from amongst persons of ability, integrity and standing who have had experience in law or legislation, trade unionism, management of an organisation committed to increasing the employment potential of women, women's voluntary organisations etc.
- There shall be at least one member each from the Scheduled Castes and the Scheduled Tribes.
- There shall be a member secretary who shall be adept in management, organisation, sociological movement or a member of the civil services of the Union.

Appointment and Removal of members

- The Chairperson and members are appointed by the Central government and hold office for a period not exceeding 3 years.
- The Central government can remove the Chairperson or any member from the office under the following circumstances:
    - becomes an undischarged insolvent; or
    - gets convicted and sentenced to imprisonment for an offence which in the opinion of the central government involves moral turpitude; or
    - becomes of unsound mind and declared so by a competent court; or
    - refuses to act or becomes incapable of acting; or
    - absent for three consecutive meetings of the commission without permission; or
    - has abused the position that render continuance in office detrimental to public interest.

Functions of NCW

- The Commission is expected to review development of women under the Union and the State governments.
- To study the reasons for deprived status of women and suggest remedial actions as necessary.
- To take up cases of violation of constitutional provisions provided for protection and development of women.
- To take part in the planning mechanism relating to social and economic development of women.
- Take 'suo moto' action or notice on matters relating to deprivation of women's rights.
- Section 10 of the NCW Act provides the functions to be performed by the Commission, which can be divided into four broad heads – (a) Safeguarding rights of women, (b) Study of problems faced by women, (c) Make recommendations to eradicate these problems and (d) Funding and fighting the cases for women with respect to violation of rights.

26.1.8 National Commission for Minorities

The National Commission for Minorities (NCM) is constituted under the National Commission for Minorities Act of 1992 and it derives its powers and functions from the Act.

Composition of members

- The Commission is a multi-member body consisting of a Chairperson, a Vice-Chairperson and five members to be nominated by the Central government from amongst persons of eminence, ability and integrity.
- The five members including the Chairperson shall be from amongst the minority communities.

Appointment and Removal of members

- The Chairperson and members are appointed by the Central government and hold office for a period of 3 years.
- The Central government can remove the Chairperson or any member from the office under the following circumstances:
  - becomes an undischarged insolvent; or
  - gets convicted and sentenced to imprisonment for an offence which in the opinion of the Central government involves moral turpitude; or
  - becomes of unsound mind and declared so by a competent court; or
  - refuses to act or becomes incapable of acting; or
  - absent for three consecutive meetings of the commission without permission; or
  - has abused the position that render continuance in office detrimental to public interest.

Functions of NCM

- Evaluate the progress of development of minorities under the Union and the States.
- Observe working of safeguards provided by the Constitution and laws enacted by the Parliament and the State Legislatures.
- Make recommendations for the effective implementation of safeguards.
- Attend to specific complaints regarding deprivation of rights and safeguards of minorities.
- Conduct studies, research and analysis on the issues relating to socio-economic and educational development of minorities.
- Make periodical or special reports on any matters pertaining to minorities.
- Any other matter which may be referred to it by the Central Government.

26.1.9 National Commission for Protection of Child Rights

The National Commission for Protection of Child Rights (NCPCR) is a statutory body constituted under the Commission for Protection of Child Rights Act, 2005 (CPRC, 2005). It works under the Ministry of Women and Child Development.

Composition of Members

- The Commission shall consist of a Chairperson who is a person of eminence and has done outstanding work for promoting the welfare of children.
- It shall consist of six members, out of which at least two shall be women, who shall be persons of eminence, ability, integrity and experience in the fields of education; childcare and development; juvenile justice or care of neglected, marginalised or disabled children; elimination of child labour or children in distress; child psychology or sociology; and laws relating to children.

Appointment and Removal of Members

- The Chairperson and members are appointed by the Central government and hold office for a period of 3 years. The Chairperson shall be appointed on the recommendation of a three-member selection committee constituted by the Central Government under the Chairmanship of Minister of Women and Child Development.
- The Chairperson and members shall not hold office for more than two terms. The age limit for the Chairperson is 65 years and for members it is 60 years.
- The Central government can remove the Chairperson or any member from the office under the following circumstances:
    - is adjudged an insolvent; or
    - engages during his/her term of office in any paid employment outside the duties of his/her office; or
    - gets convicted and sentenced to imprisonment for an offence which in the opinion of the Central government involves moral turpitude; or
    - becomes of unsound mind and declared so by a competent court; or
    - refuses to act or becomes incapable of acting; or
    - absent for three consecutive meetings of the commission without permission; or
    - has abused the position that render continuance in office detrimental to public interest.

Functions of NCPCR

- Examine and review the safeguards provided by or under any law for the protection of child rights and recommend measures for their effective implementation;
- Present to the Central government, annually and at such other intervals, as the commission may deem fit, reports upon working of those safeguards;
- Inquire into violation of child rights and recommend initiation of proceedings in such cases;
- Examine all factors that inhibit (prevent) the enjoyment of rights of children affected by terrorism, communal violence, riots, natural disaster, domestic violence, HIV/AIDS, trafficking, maltreatment, torture and exploitation, pornography and prostitution and recommend appropriate remedial measures;
- Look into the matters relating to the children in need of special care and protection including children in distress, marginalised and disadvantaged children, children in conflict with law, juvenile children without family and children of prisoners and recommend appropriate remedial measures;
- Study treaties and other international instruments and undertake periodical review of existing policies, programmes and other activities on child rights and make recommendations for their effective implementation in the best interest of children;
- Undertake and promote research in the field of child rights;
- Spread child rights literacy among various sections of the society and promote awareness of the safeguards available for protection of these rights through publications, the media, seminar and other available means;
- Inspect any juvenile custodial home, or any other place of residence or institution meant for children, under the control of the Central Government or any State Government or any other authority, including any institution run by a social organisation where children are detained or lodged for the purpose of treatment, reformation or protection and take up with these authorities for remedial action, if found necessary;
- Inquire into complaints and take suo moto notice of matters relating to (a) Deprivation and violation of child rights; (b) Non-implementation of laws providing for protection and development

of children; (c) Non-compliance of policy decisions for ensuring welfare of children and provide relief to children.

- The Commission may take any of the following steps on completion of inquiry held under the Act:
  - Recommend to concerned government or authority for initiation of proceedings for prosecution against concerned person(s);
  - Approach Supreme Court or High Court concerned for directions, orders or writs as necessary;
  - Recommend to concerned government or authority to grant interim relief to the victim or members of his/her family.

Scan the QR code for conceptual video on Non-constitutional bodies

State Commissions for Protection of Child Rights (SCPCR)

- A State government may constitute its own State Commission for Protection of Child Rights.
- The provisions relating to composition, appointment and removal of members of such commission; and functions of such commission at the State level are similar to NCPCR as discussed above. (The reference to Central Government in NCPCR to be replaced with 'State Government' for any SCPCR.)

26.2 EXECUTIVE BODIES

Executive bodies are those that are created by the Government through an order or notification.

26.2.1 NITI Aayog

The National Institution for Transforming India (NITI Aayog) was established via a Union Cabinet resolution on 1 January 2015 as a premier policy think tank of the Union Government. It replaced the erstwhile Planning Commission that was established in 1950.

Composition

- Chairperson – Prime Minister
- Governing Council – Its members are the Chief Ministers and the Administrators of the Union Territories.
- Regional Councils – These are created as per need and its members would be the Chief Ministers and the Administrators of UTs of respective regions.
- Vice Chairperson – The Vice-Chairperson is appointed by the Prime Minister.
- The Chief Executive Officer (CEO) is appointed by the Prime Minister. Apart from this it has full time members, part-time members and ex-officio members.
- Special invitees appointed by the Prime Minister.

Important roles of NITI Aayog

- To act as a resource centre and knowledge hub.
- Design policy and programme framework.
- Foster cooperative and competitive federalism.
- Monitoring and evaluation of implementation of programmes, and focus on technology upgradation and capacity building.

- The guiding principles of NITI Aayog are Antyodaya (uplifting the poor); Inclusion of vulnerable and marginalised sections; Village integration; Harnessing Demographic Dividend; People's participation; Transparent and accountable governance; and Sustainability.

26.2.2 Central Bureau of Investigation (CBI)

- The CBI was set up in 1963 by a resolution of the Ministry of Home Affairs. Later, it was transferred to the Ministry of Personnel. The Special Police Establishment (which looked into vigilance cases) set up in 1941 was also merged with the CBI.
- The CBI is not a statutory body. It derives its powers from the Delhi Special Police Establishment Act, 1946.
- The CBI is a multidisciplinary investigation agency of the Government of India and undertakes investigation of corruption-related cases, economic offences and cases of conventional crime.

Composition and tenure

- The Director of CBI is appointed by the Central government on the recommendation of a three-member committee consisting of the Prime Minister as Chairperson, the Leader of Opposition in the Lok Sabha and the Chief Justice of India or a Judge of the Supreme Court nominated by him/her. Where there is no recognised Leader of Opposition in the Lok Sabha, then the leader of the single largest opposition party in the Lok Sabha would be a member of that committee. This is as per the provisions of Delhi Special Police Establishment Act, 1946.
- The Director holds office for fixed tenure of 2 years. It can be extended further by one year at a time for up to 3 more years, based on the recommendation of the appointment committee as mentioned above, as per latest amendment made by the Parliament to the Delhi Special Police Establishment Act in 2021.
- The Directorate of Prosecution shall be appointed by the Central Government on the recommendation of the CVC.
- The officers of the rank of SP and above in the CBI are appointed by the Central government on the recommendation of a committee consisting of the Central Vigilance Commissioner as Chairperson, Vigilance Commissioners, Secretary of the Home Ministry and the Secretary of the Department of Personnel.

Important functions of CBI

- Combating corruption in public life, curbing economic and violent crimes through meticulous investigation and prosecution.
- Evolving effective systems and procedures for successful investigation and prosecution of cases in various law courts.
- Helping fight cyber and high technology crime.
- Playing a lead role in the war against national and transnational organised crime.
- In recent years, many opposition ruled States like Kerala, Jharkhand, West Bengal, Punjab and Karnataka have withdrawn general consent to CBI alleging bias in investigations by the agency.
- The above said issues of withdrawal of consent have arisen due to political differences between the ruling government at the centre and various states that are ruled by opposition parties. This issue should be settled through cooperative federalism and granting utmost autonomy to CBI in its functioning without any political interference.

26.2.3 Enforcement Directorate

The Directorate of Enforcement or ED is an executive body. It is a multi-disciplinary organisation mandated with investigation of economic crimes and violations of foreign exchange laws.

The history of ED can be summarised as below:

- An 'Enforcement Unit' was set up in 1956 in the Department of Economic Affairs, Ministry of Finance, for handling exchange control law violations under the then Foreign Exchange Regulation Act, 1947.
- In 1957, the unit was renamed as 'Enforcement Directorate' and in 1960, the administrative control was transferred from Department of Economic Affairs to Department of Revenue.

Composition and Tenure

- The ED is headed by a Director of Enforcement and consists of Special Directors, Joint Directors and Deputy Directors in charge of various departments and zones. The Director and all officials above the level of Deputy Directors are appointed as per the provisions of the Central Vigilance Commission Act, 2003.
- The Director of ED is appointed by the Central government on the recommendation of a committee consisting of the Central Vigilance Commissioner as Chairperson and Vigilance Commissioners, Secretaries to the Government of India in-charge of Home, Personnel and Department of Revenue as members.

> **THINK ABOUT IT**
>
> The CBI and Enforcement Directorate require autonomy from political interference in their functioning. Comment highlighting the procedure for appointment of heads of these bodies.

- The Director holds office for fixed tenure of 2 years. It can be extended further by 1 year at a time for up to 3 more years, based on the recommendation of the appointment committee as mentioned above, as per latest amendment made by the Parliament to the Central Vigilance Commission Act in 2021.
- The officers of the rank of Deputy Directors and above in the ED are appointed by the Central government on the recommendation of the above committee in consultation with the Director.

Functions of ED

The statutory functions of the ED include enforcement of the following Acts:

- The Prevention of Money Laundering Act, 2002 (PMLA) – It is a criminal law enacted to prevent money laundering and to provide for confiscation of property derived from money laundering and for matters connected therewith. ED has been given the responsibility to enforce the provisions of the PMLA by conducting investigation to trace the assets derived from proceeds of crime, to provisionally attach the property and to ensure prosecution of the offenders and confiscation of the property by a special court.
- The Foreign Exchange Management Act, 1999 (FEMA) – ED has been given the responsibility to conduct investigation into suspected contraventions of foreign exchange laws and regulations, to adjudicate and impose penalties on those adjudged to have contravened the law.
- The Fugitive Economic Offenders Act, 2018 (FEOA) – This law was enacted to deter economic offenders from evading the process of Indian law by remaining outside the jurisdiction of Indian courts. It is a law whereby ED is mandated to attach the properties of the fugitive economic offenders who have escaped from India warranting arrest and provide for the confiscation of their properties to the Central Government.

- Sponsoring agency under COFEPOSA – Under the Conservation of Foreign Exchange and Prevention of Smuggling Activities Act, 1974 (COFEPOSA), ED is empowered to sponsor cases of preventive detention with regard to contraventions of FEMA.

According to data presented in the Parliament in August 2024, only 40 people have been convicted in 5,297 cases registered under the Prevention of Money Laundering Act (PMLA) after the law was passed. The conviction rate is less than 1%.

In ***Vineet Narain case*** (1996), the Supreme Court had provided directions for strengthening the autonomy of CBI and ED. Panel-based selection of Director of CBI & ED, fixed tenure for Director of CBI & ED were all part of the directions in this case.

26.2.4 Law Commission of India

Law Commission of India is an executive body established by an order of the Government of India. The first Law Commission during the British rule was constituted in 1834 (under the Charter Act of 1833) and it was headed by Lord Macaulay. Subsequently, three more law commissions were constituted before independence in 1853, 1861 and 1879 respectively. They were instrumental in various important legislations like the Indian Penal Code (1860), Code of Criminal Procedure (1872), Transfer of Property Act (1882), Negotiable Instruments Act (1881), Indian Contract Act (1872), Indian Evidence Act (1872) etc.

The 1st Law Commission after independence was constituted in 1955 and the 23rd Law Commission was constituted in 2024 for the period of September 2024 to August 2027.

Composition and Tenure

- The Commission is constituted for a period of 3 years. The Chairperson and other members are appointed by the Central government.
- It is headed by a retired judge (of the Supreme Court or any of the High Courts) and consists of full-time and part-time members who are legal experts and a Member-Secretary.

Functions of Law Commission

- The vision of the Law Commission is to reform laws to maximise the spread of justice in society and promote good governance under the rule of law.
- The terms of reference/functions of the Law Commission (including the terms of reference while constituting the 23rd Law Commission) include the following:
  - Review/repeal of obsolete (out of date) laws.
  - Examination of laws affecting the poor and review of the system of judicial administration to ensure that it is responsive to reasonable demands of changing times.
  - Examine existing laws in the light of the Directive Principles of State Policy and suggest ways and means of reforming such laws through amendments.
  - Examine existing laws to promote gender equality and suggests amendments to achieve objectives set out in the Preamble to our Constitution.
  - To recommend measures as may be necessary to harness (make use of) law and legal process in the service of the poor.
  - Revise Central Acts of general importance to simplify them and remove anomalies, ambiguities and inequities.
  - Examine the impact of globalisation on food security, unemployment and recommend measures for the protection of the interests of the marginalised.

Reports of the Law Commission

- The Commission works on projects based on references received from the Central Government and/or the Supreme Court and High Courts. Sometimes, keeping in view the importance of the subject, the Commission initiates suo moto studies on specific subjects.
- The Commission makes every effort to ensure that the widest range of people/stakeholders are consulted in formulating proposals for law reforms. In this process, the Commission partners with professional bodies and academic institutions. The Commission submits its findings and recommendations in the form of reports to the Central Government.
- Various Law Commissions have submitted a total of around 280 reports as on date (2024). Some of the important reports and their recommendations have been highlighted below:
  - The 41st report submitted in 1969 resulted in the enactment of the new Code of Criminal Procedure, 1973.
  - The recommendations of the 165th report resulted in enactment of Right of Children to Free and Compulsory Education Act, 2009.
  - The National Green Tribunal Act, 2010 was enacted based on the recommendation of 186th report.
  - The 20th Law Commission (2013–2015) submitted four reports i.e., Report Nos. 248–251, recommending repeal of old and obsolete laws, which resulted in repeal of more than 1500 Central Acts.
  - 246th report provided inputs for amendment of Arbitration and Conciliation Act.
  - Report Nos. 244 and 255 recommended electoral reforms by strengthening the office of the Election Commission of India to provide greater independence and power to the institution.

26.3 QUASI-JUDICIAL AND REGULATORY BODIES

Quasi-judicial body

Quasi-judicial bodies are those bodies that can interpret the law and who pass orders on the matters they adjudicate upon, that are binding on parties concerned. These are not similar to courts of law. These bodies have the powers of a civil court while carrying out any investigation. They can summon and enforce the attendance of any person from any part of India and examine him/her on oath. They also have the power to receive evidence on affidavits and requisitioning any public record from court or office.

Examples of Quasi-judicial bodies in India include the Election Commission of India, the Central Information Commission, the Lok Adalats, various commissions like NCSC, NCST, NCBC, NHRC etc. Thus Quasi-Judicial bodies include Constitutional as well as Statutory bodies.

Regulatory bodies

Regulatory bodies are usually statutory bodies that are set up to monitor, guide and control various sectors like banking, insurance, telecom, food processing etc. Examples of such bodies in India include Reserve Bank of India (RBI), Securities and Exchange Board of India (SEBI), Telecom Regulatory Authority of India (TRAI), FSSAI, IRDAI, National Green Tribunal, Competition Commission of India etc. The readers should update themselves with important current events relating to all these regulatory bodies.

All significant current events relating to these Non-Constitutional bodies are captured and discussed in the Monthly current affairs update on 'edge' platform that is part of this courseware.

MAINS STARTER

Area	Building Blocks For Model Introductions
For any question relating to a statutory or executive body	Mention that it is a Statutory (or) Executive body and mention the name of the Act that has constituted it in the case of a Statutory body. Briefly explain the important role of the body. For example – The Central and State Information Commissions are statutory bodies constituted under the Right to Information Act, 2005. Its role is to entertain and decide on appeals under the Act that is aimed at bringing transparency and accountability in the functioning of public authorities.

UPSC Previous Years' Questions of Main Examination

1. Though the Human Rights Commissions have contributed immensely to the protection of human rights in India, yet they have failed to assert themselves against the mighty and powerful. Analysing their structural and practical limitations, suggest remedial measures. **[2021]**

Approach: The initial part of the answer can summarise the role of NHRC and SRHC. The second part can discuss the challenges of NHRC with suggestions for improvement in the conclusion.

MODEL ANSWER

National Human Rights Commission (NHRC) and State Human Rights Commission (SHRC) are constituted under the provisions of 'The Protection of Human Rights Act, 1993.'

Importance of Human Rights Commissions (HRC)

- The commissions are the watchdog of human rights in the country, that is, the rights relating to life, liberty, equality and dignity of the individual guaranteed by the Constitution.
- NHRC inquires into any violation of human rights or negligence in the prevention of such violation by a public servant, either suo moto or on a petition presented to it or on an order of a court.

- A State Human Rights Commission can inquire into violation of human rights only in respect of subjects mentioned in the State List (List-II) and the Concurrent List (List-III) in the Seventh Schedule of the Constitution.

Limitations of HRC

- These commissions are not empowered to inquire into any matter after the expiry of one year from the date on which the act constituting violation of human rights is alleged to have been committed.
- It has no power to punish the violators of human rights, nor to award any relief including monetary relief to the victim.
- These commissions have limited role, powers and jurisdiction with respect to the violation of human rights by the members of the armed forces.

Suggestions for improvement

- The one-year limit for inquiring into any violation may be removed.
- The commissions may be provided the power to grant financial awards for the victims of any human right violations.

2. The jurisdiction of the Central Bureau of Investigation (CBI) regarding lodging an FIR and conducting probe within a particular State is being questioned by various States. However, the power of the States to withhold consent to the CBI is not absolute. Explain with special reference to the federal character of India. **[2021]**

Likely context to the question: Starting from West Bengal in 2018, several opposition ruled States withdrew their general consent for CBI investigation in their States in 2019 and 2020. This is the likely context to this question.

Approach: Introduction to CBI and explanation of general and specific consent. Then discussion on the current affairs scenario (at that point of time) and explaining how the withdrawal of consent cannot be absolute. Finally conclude on a positive note to avoid confrontation in Indian federal set up.

MODEL ANSWER

The CBI was set up in 1963 by a resolution of the Ministry of Home Affairs. Later, it was transferred to the Ministry of Personnel. The CBI is not a statutory body. It derives its powers from the Delhi Special Police Establishment Act, 1946 (DPSE Act).

Investigation by CBI and withdrawal of general consent

The DPSE Act requires consent from the concerned State government for the CBI to lodge a FIR and investigate into any matter inside a State. This consent is of two types, viz. (a) General consent and (b) Specific consent.

General consent allows the CBI to file any case and carry out its investigation seamlessly within the State. However, if this is withdrawn, the CBI has to obtain specific consent on a case-by-case basis.

Starting from West Bengal in 2018, several opposition ruled States like Punjab, Chhattisgarh, Rajasthan, Kerala and Jharkhand withdrew their general consent for CBI investigation in their States in 2019 and 2020. They alleged that the agency has been misused by the central government for political purposes.

However, it must be noted that this power of the States to withhold consent is not absolute due to following reasons:

(a) The CBI can carry out its investigation without consent in 'Railway areas.'

(b) The Supreme Court and High Court can order a CBI probe in any State without its consent.

(c) Cases registered in another State in relation to which investigation leads to a State which has withdrawn general consent will not be affected by such withdrawal.

(d) The Central government will not be restricted in carrying out its investigation against its own employee by CBI even if it is within a State that has withdrawn general consent.

The above said issues of withdrawal of consent has arisen due to political differences between the ruling government at the centre and various states that are ruled by opposition parties. This issue should be settled through cooperative federalism and granting utmost autonomy to CBI in its functioning without any political interference.

3. Which steps are required for constitutionalisation of a Commission? Do you think imparting constitutionality to the National Commission for Women would ensure greater gender justice and empowerment in India? Give reasons. **[2020]**

Approach: The first part of the answer shall explain the procedure for constitutionalisation of a commission. The second part shall discuss about NCW and steps to be taken to empower NCW apart from constitutionalisation.

MODEL ANSWER

Steps for constitutionalisation of a Commission

Constitutionalisation of a Commission will require an amendment to the Constitution under Article 368. It will involve the following steps:

- Introduction of a constitutional amendment bill in Lok Sabha or Rajya Sabha.
- Passage of bill in both the houses by a special majority i.e., majority of the total membership of the house and by a majority of not less than two-thirds of members present and voting.
- It will then be presented to the President who shall give his/her assent to the bill and the Commission would become a Constitutional body.
- Recently in 2018, the National Commission for Backward Classes was made a constitutional body through the 102nd amendment.

National Commission for Women and Constitutional status

- The National Commission for Women (NCW) is a statutory body constituted under the NCW Act, 1990.
- NCW act provides the functions to be performed by the Commission, which can be divided into four broad heads – (a) Safeguarding rights of women (b) Study of problems faced by women (c) Make recommendations to eradicate these problems (d) Funding and fighting the cases for women with respect to violation of rights.
- Consitutionalisation of the NCW will definitely increase the stature of the body in line with other constitutional bodies and will be a step in the right direction.

- However, merely giving a constitutional status would not automatically result in greater gender justice and empowerment.
- The following additional powers need to be provided for empowering the NCW:
  - The body should have the highest support from the political executive to make it more powerful. There should also be more autonomy in its functioning without political interference.
  - The Commission should be provided with powers to award financial relief to victims during its investigation.

CHAPTER 27

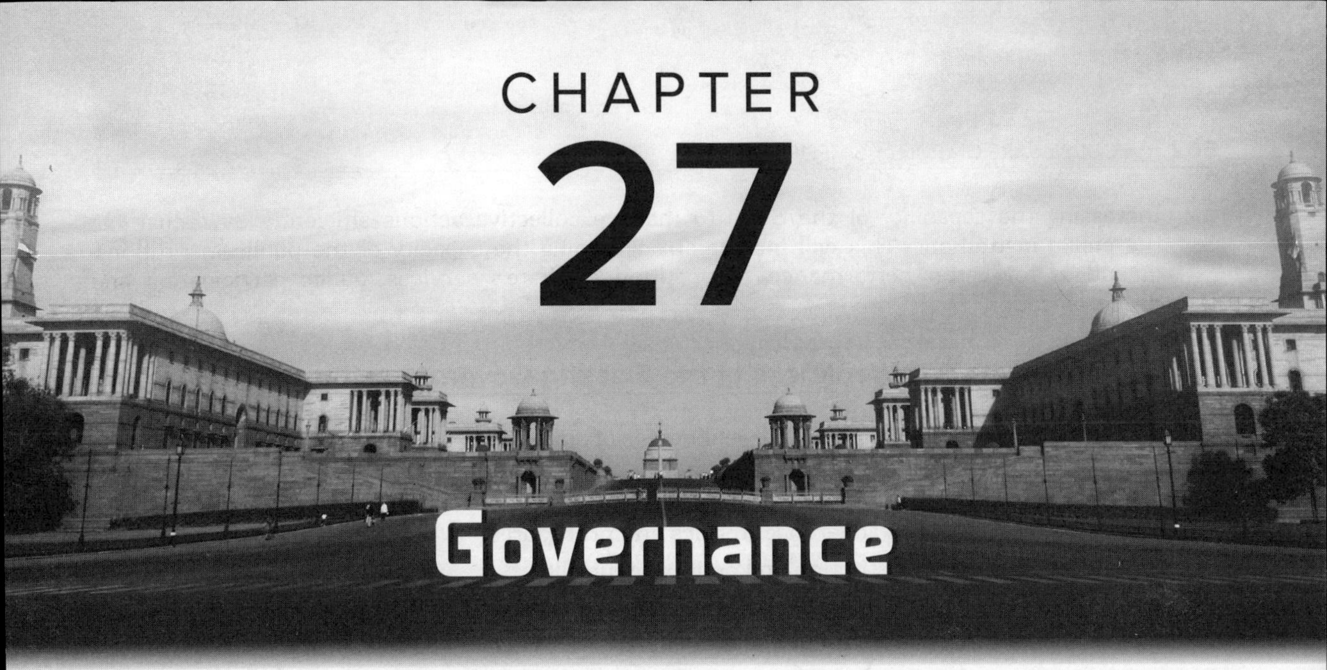

Governance

LEARNING OUTCOMES

1. Understanding the essential ingredients of good governance, transparency and accountability in governance
2. Knowing e-Governance – its importance, challenges and reforms required
3. Comprehending Citizen Charter – its characteristics, issues and suggestions for improving effectiveness
4. Exploring Pressure groups – its various types – formal and informal, role, methods adopted for influencing
5. Analysing 2nd ARC report recommendations on the above aspects

The Constitution is the basic legal framework based on which governance happens in our country. The legislature and the executive work within the framework provided by this supreme law of the country. In this chapter, we shall discuss briefly about governance and e-Governance; Citizens' charter and Pressure groups.

The 2nd Administrative Reforms Commission (2nd ARC) headed by ***Shri Veerappa Moily*** had submitted various reports on governance, e-governance, citizen charter, local bodies etc. The relevant content and recommendations of the 2nd ARC report on these subjects have been suitably discussed as part of this chapter.

27.1 GOVERNANCE – TRANSPARENCY AND ACCOUNTABILITY

Governance involves interaction between the formal institutions (like the legislature and the executive) and citizens in civil society. Governance refers to a process whereby the government enacts policies and decisions concerning public life and social upliftment.

Good governance has eight major characteristics. It is participatory, consensus oriented, accountable, transparent, responsive, effective and efficient, equitable and inclusive and follows the rule of law.

Two important measures to be taken for increasing the effectiveness of the Government are:

1. Narrowing the gap between the demands on the State and its abilities to meet these demands through greater selectivity in State's priorities. The priorities of the State action should be the maintenance of law and order, macro-economic stability, investment in basic social services, protection of vulnerable segments and the environment.

2. Increasing the capability of the State to manage collective actions efficiently by recharging the public institutions. This will include strengthening the capacity of the public institutions, incentives for better performance, competition to State's services, public participation and decentralisation.

27.1.1 Strengths and Weakness of the Existing Governance Structure

The 2nd ARC lists down the strengths and weaknesses of our existing governance structure as follows:

Strengths

- Time-tested system with adherence to rules and procedures
- Commitment to the Constitution and political neutrality
- Link between policy-making and implementation by permanent bureaucracy
- A national outlook amongst public functionaries

Weakness/Issues

- Undue emphasis on routine functions
- Proliferation of ministries and departments resulting in weak coordination
- Absence of team work
- Risk avoidance

The following are the barriers to good governance in our country:

- Attitude problem of the civil servants, who do not treat the citizens as their customers
- Lack of accountability with a poor record of disciplinary action against delinquent government servants
- Red tapism with focus on procedures rather than on outcomes
- Low levels of compliance with rules by the citizens also act as an impediment
- Ineffective implementation of laws and rules

27.1.2 Reforms for Increasing Efficiency, Transparency and Accountability

The important recommendations of the 2nd ARC for improving the efficiency, transparency and accountability in governance are listed below:

- Rationalising the functions of the Government based on the principles of subsidiarity – meaning what can be done at a lower level should be done at a lower level. This will include decentralisation/delegation.
- Rationalising and reorganising ministries.
- Recasting allocation of business rules – It should first provide the statement of mission of the department followed by a list of subjects and functions.

> **THINK ABOUT IT**
>
> Transparency and accountability are the hallmarks of good governance. In this regard, discuss the importance of the Right to Information Act in ushering in transparency and accountability.

- Ministries should focus on policy analysis and evaluation – Subordinate offices should carry out implementation.
- Creating effective regulatory framework – Like TRAI, FSSAI etc.

27.2 E-GOVERNANCE

e-Governance or 'electronic governance' is basically the application of Information and Communications Technology (ICT) to the processes of Government functioning in order to bring about 'Simple, Moral, Accountable, Responsive and Transparent' (SMART) governance.

27.2.1 e-Governance Initiatives

Various types of government interaction under e-Governance initiatives are as follows:

1. Government to Citizens (G2C)
2. Government to Business (G2B)
3. Government to Government (G2G)

The focus is to move towards Interactive Service Model that provides for a two-way communication between the government and the citizen.

Recent Initiatives of the Government

1. Direct Cash Transfer – NREGA wages, social security pension, disability and old age pension etc., of Central or any State governments are mostly transferred directly to the bank accounts, using the Aadhaar and authentication thereof as supported by the UIDAI.
2. Digital India Programme – The vision of the Digital India aims to transform the country into a digitally empowered economy.
3. MyGov Citizen Portal – PMO has launched an online platform mygov.nic.in to engage citizens in the task of 'good governance'.
4. e-Kranti Scheme – This consists of 44 Mission Mode Projects as part of the overall e-Governance plan.
5. e-Biz – Its vision is to 'transform the business environment in the country by providing efficient, convenient, transparent and integrated electronic services to investors, industries and business throughout the business life cycle'.
6. PM Gati Shakti – It is a scheme for multi-modal connectivity, with the aim of coordinated planning and execution of infrastructure projects.
7. e-Shram – It is a portal developed for registration of unorganised workers in industries such as construction, migrant labourers, street vendors and domestic workers. It will provide a unique identification number and also insurance cover in case of death or partial disability.

27.2.2 Challenges in e-Governance Implementation

The importance of e-Governance and ICT projects in the modern digital world cannot be over emphasised. However, the following issues are present in the implementation of e-Governance initiatives:

- Lack of adequate digital literacy amongst the citizens
- Poverty that prohibits access to digital infrastructure
- Inadequate connectivity in remote areas
- Lack of capacity amongst the administrators and government employees and their resistance to change

- Inadequate funding and lack of monitoring
- Delay in execution of projects

27.2.3 Reforms Required in e-Governance

The important recommendations of the 2nd ARC for effective implementation of e-Governance initiatives are listed below:

- Building a congenial environment for e-Governance within departments and providing political support at the highest level
- Identification of e-Governance projects and prioritisation
- Business process re-engineering of the government functions
- Capacity building for the government servants and creating awareness amongst citizens
- Effective monitoring and evaluation
- Mission mode projects for timely completion

> **THINK ABOUT IT**
>
> e-Governance is more about governance and less about electronic tools. Comment.

27.3 CITIZEN'S CHARTER

A Citizen's Charter is basically a set of commitments made by an organisation regarding the standards of service which it delivers. The principles of service delivery that must be reflected in a citizen charter include setting standards of service, consultation and involvement of citizens, being open and providing full information, encouraging access to citizens, treating all citizens fairly, effective use of resources, and innovation and improvement.

The aim of a citizen charter is to provide good and citizen-centric governance. It creates accountability for the government departments to provide timely service to the citizens and also serves as a feedback mechanism for improvement and innovation.

27.3.1 Issues with Citizen's Charter

The following are the important issues because of which many Citizen's Charter are ineffective:

- Lack of public awareness
- In majority of cases, charters are not formulated through a consultative process
- By and large, the service providers are not familiar with the philosophy, goals and main features of the Charter
- Charters are rarely updated and some documents date back from the inception of the Citizen's Charter Programme
- No funds for awareness generation on Citizen's Charter or for orientation of the staff on various components of the Charter

27.3.2 Making Citizen's Charter Effective

The important recommendations of the 2nd ARC for making Citizen's Charter effective are listed in the next page:

- One size does not fit all. The Citizen's Charter should be prepared for each independent unit under overall umbrella of Organisation's Charter
- Wide consultation with various stakeholders which includes civil society
- Firm commitments to be made and internal processes to be reformed to meet the commitments
- Redressal mechanism in case of default
- Regular evaluation of Citizen's Charter based on the feedback and changes as required including fixing of accountability
- Information and Communication Technology (ICT) and Artificial Intelligence (AI) tools may be effectively utilised and integrated in present circumstances to ensure time bound service delivery.

Scan the QR Code for Conceptual Video on various Governance Topics

27.4 PRESSURE GROUPS

A pressure group, also known as an 'interest group', is a group of people who are organised actively for promoting or defending their common interest. The term 'pressure group' is used as the group seeks to influence the public policy in a particular direction by exerting pressure on the government.

There are many formal/informal groups that influence the polity of any country, right from formation of the government to day-to-day governance issues. The pressure groups arise in different forms in different walks of life.

One of the characteristic features of any pressure group is that they try to influence or manipulate governmental affairs without any intention to have any direct control over it, which is one thing that differentiates it from a political party. Pressure groups do not contest elections unlike a political party and do not aim to capture power. Their aim is to influence public policy to meet their interests or needs.

27.4.1 Types of Pressure Groups

- After independence, a single political party was dominant over the government for a long time and the role of pressure groups was limited and perceived negative but today their role is taken to be constructive and democratic.
- Conventional Pressure Groups (PGs) based on caste, community, religion-based and regional groupings play a decisive role in Indian polity.
- Most political parties remain backed by certain groups especially religious and minority communities.
- Some groups keep on emerging and dissolving as per circumstances or for specific purposes like anti-dowry, anti-corruption movement etc.
- Pressure groups may be formal like the ones listed below or may be informal that are formed spontaneously for a particular purpose and dissolve on fulfilment of the purpose or otherwise. Examples include protest group formed for lifting the ban on Jallikattu (bull taming) sport in Tamil Nadu (2017), protest groups against farm laws (2021) etc.

Major Pressure Groups in India

- Business Groups – FICCI, CII, ASSOCHAM, AIMO, etc. (institutional groups)
- Trade Unions – AITUC, INTUC, HMS, CITU, BMS etc.

- Agrarian Groups – All India Kisan Sabha, Bharatiya Kisan Union etc.
- Student's Organisations – ABVP, AISF, NSUI etc.
- Religious Groups – RSS, VHP, Bajrang Dal, Jamaat-e-Islami etc.
- Caste Groups – Harijan Sevak Sangh, Nadar Caste Association etc.
- Linguistic Groups – Tamil Sangh, Andhra Maha Sabha etc.
- Tribal Groups – NSCN, TNU, United Mizo Federal Organisation, Tribal League of Assam etc.
- Ideology-based Groups – Narmada Bachao Andolan, Chipko Movement, Women Rights Organisation, India Against Corruption etc.
- Anomic Groups (socially disorganised or alienated) – ULFA, Naxalites, Jammu and Kashmir Liberation Front, etc.

27.4.2 Role of Pressure Groups

- Perform a role in educating citizens about specific issues.
- Groups can enhance democratic participation, pluralism and diversity.
- Groups raise and articulate issues that political parties perhaps won't touch because of their sensitivity.
- They offer an important access point for those seeking redress of grievance.
- They represent minorities who cannot represent themselves.
- Groups can be an important source of specialist information/expertise for an overloaded legislature and civil service.
- Many groups play a vital role in implementing changes to public policy.
- Pressure groups encourage decentralisation of power within the political system.
- They act as a check and balance to the power of the executive government.

THINK ABOUT IT

The proliferation of pressure groups has affected our democratic functioning. Critically evaluate.

The capacity of a pressure group is determined by its leadership, organisational abilities, mobilisation techniques and economic base. In the Indian context, the limitations of pressure groups are that they can be divisive if based on religious or caste lines. Further, they can be used for narrow political gains and also have short lives due to inadequate resources.

27.4.3 Techniques of Pressure Groups

Pressure groups primarily use one of the following three techniques:

- Electioneering – Campaigning and placing in public office persons who favour their interests
- Lobbying – Persuading public officers to adopt and enforce policies of their interest
- Propagandising – Influencing public opinion

Pressure groups may sometimes make use of media for dispersing their views in public and winning support. They may publish statistics in favour of their claims. However, sometimes they may even resort to illegitimate and illegal methods like strikes, violence or even bribes.

Overall, pressure groups in mobilising and organising masses have widened the base of political participation as well as creating a responsive political and administrative system. They provide a stabilising mechanism and form a crucial component of the structural equilibrium.

MAINS STARTER

Area	Building Blocks For Model Introductions
Governance, e-governance, transparency in governance	While the answer and content would depend on the demand of the question, a standard introduction to governance related topics can be as follows: Governance/e-governance is aimed at bringing citizen centric administration that is SMART – Simple, Moral, Accountable, Responsive and Transparent.
Citizen's charter	Citizen's charter is a mechanism for fixing accountability and citizen-centric governance. It declares the objectives and commitments of the government department/office towards the citizen with time-bound delivery of service.
Pressure groups	Pressure groups are formal or informal groups that champion the cause of a group/ issue. They spread awareness about the issue they advocate and try to influence government policies through various means.

UPSC Previous Years' Questions of Main Examination

1. e-governance is not just about the routine application of digital technology in service delivery process. It is as much about multifarious interactions for ensuring transparency and accountability. In this context, evaluate the role of the 'Interactive Service Model' of e-governance. **[2024]**

Approach: The importance of e-Governance and how digital technology has resulted in ICT being an integral part of service delivery needs to be discussed with examples of various government initiatives. Subsequently, the challenges in e-Governance implementation and measures for improvement can be summarised.

MODEL ANSWER

e-Governance or 'electronic governance' is basically the application of Information and Communications Technology (ICT) to the processes of Government functioning in order to bring about 'Simple, Moral, Accountable, Responsive and Transparent' (SMART) governance.

Interactive Service Model of e-Governance

'Interactive Service model' (ISM) refers to e-Governance initiatives that provide for a two-way communication between the government and the citizen. Various initiatives of the government that include government schemes for different sections, delivery of services, monitoring of implementation, etc. have been linked to digital technology through this model. It plays an important role in ensuring transparency as well as accountability of the government.

Some important recent initiatives of the Government that reflect how ISM and digitisation have become an integral part of governance are listed below:

1. Direct Cash transfer – NREGA wages, social security pension, Old Age Pension, etc., of any Central or State governments are mostly transferred directly to the bank accounts, using Aadhaar and authentication thereof as supported by UIDAI. Registration for such schemes and grievances are also raised and solved online.
2. MyGov citizen portal – PMO has launched an online platform mygov.nic.in to engage citizens in the task of 'good governance.'
3. e-Kranti Scheme – This consists of 44 Mission Mode Projects as part of the overall e-Governance plan.
4. PM Gati Shakti – It is a scheme for multi-modal connectivity, with the aim of coordinated planning and execution of infrastructure projects.
5. e-Shram – It is a portal developed for registration of unorganised workers in industries such as construction, migrant labourers, street vendors and domestic workers. It will provide a unique identification number and also insurance cover in case of death or partial disability.

However, lack of adequate digital literacy, inadequate connectivity in remote areas, lack of capacity amongst the administrators and government employees, resistance to change and delay in execution of projects are some of the problems in effective implementation of e-Governance projects. These need to be addressed through suitable measures and providing political support at highest levels for effective implementation.

2. The Citizens' charter has been a landmark initiative in ensuring citizen-centric administration. But it is yet to reach its full potential. Identify the factors hindering the realisation of its promise and suggest measures to overcome them. **[2024]**

Approach: The importance of citizens' charter, the issues with their effective use and suggestions for improvement as provided by the 2nd ARC need to be discussed in the answer.

MODEL ANSWER

1. A Citizens' Charter is basically a set of commitments made by an organisation regarding the standards of service which it delivers.
2. The aim of Citizens' charter is to provide good and citizen-centric governance.
3. It creates accountability on the government departments to provide timely service to the citizens and also serves as a feedback mechanism for improvement and innovation.

Issues/Limitations with Citizens' Charter

Following are the important issues because of which many citizens' charters are ineffective:

1. Lack of public awareness.
2. In majority of cases, charters are not formulated through a consultative process.

3. By and large, service providers are not familiar with the philosophy, goals and main features of the Charter.
4. Charters are rarely updated and some documents date back from the inception of the Citizens' Charter programme.
5. No funds for awareness generation on Citizen's Charter or for orientation of the staff on various components of the Charter.

Making Citizens' charter effective

The important recommendations of the 2nd ARC for making citizens' charter effective are listed below:

1. One size does not fit all. The Citizens' charter should be prepared for each independent unit under the overall umbrella of the Organisation's charter.
2. Wide consultation with various stakeholders which include civil society.
3. Firm commitments to be made and internal processes to be reformed to meet the commitments.
4. Redressal mechanism in case of default.
5. Regular evaluation of Citizens' charter based on feedback and changes as required, including fixing of accountability.
6. Use of ICT and AI tools for effective service delivery in the present circumstances.

3. e-Governance, as a critical tool of governance, has ushered in effectiveness, transparency and accountability in governments. What inadequacies hamper the enhancement of these features? **[2023]**

MODEL ANSWER

e-Governance or 'electronic governance' is basically the application of Information and Communications Technology (ICT) to the processes of Government functioning in order to bring about 'Simple, Moral, Accountable, Responsive and Transparent' (SMART) governance.

The various types of e-Governance initiatives include G2C (Government to Citizens), G2B (Government to Business) and G2G (Government to Government).

There are various recent initiatives like direct cash transfer, online monitoring of projects, online portal for migrant labourers, etc., that have been enabled through ICT projects and programmes.

Challenges in ICT/e-Governance initiatives

The following issues are present in the implementation of e-Governance initiatives:

- Lack of adequate digital literacy amongst the citizens.
- Poverty that prohibits access to digital infrastructure.
- Inadequate connectivity in remote areas.
- Lack of capacity amongst the administrators and government employees and their resistance to change.
- Inadequate funding and lack of monitoring.
- Delay in execution of projects.

Measures for effective implementation

The important recommendations of the 2nd ARC for effective implementation of e-Governance initiatives are listed below:

- Building a congenial environment for e-Governance within departments and providing political support at the highest level.
- Identification of e-Governance projects and prioritisation.
- Business process re-engineering of government functions.
- Capacity building for government servants and creating awareness amongst citizens.
- Effective monitoring and evaluation.
- Mission mode projects for timely completion.

4. Pressure groups play a vital role in influencing public policy in India. Explain how the business associations contribute to public policies. **[2021]**

Approach: The discussion in the first part can be an introduction to pressure groups and the role they play in influencing public policy. The second part of the answer can deal with how business groups contribute to policy-making.

MODEL ANSWER

Pressure group, also known as 'interest group', is a group of people who are organised actively for promoting or defending their common interest. The term 'pressure group' is used as the group seeks to influence the public policy in a particular direction by exerting pressure on the government.

Role of Pressure groups in influencing public policy

While pressure groups play a role in educating citizens about various issues, they play a role in public policy-making in the following important ways:

- Groups can enhance democratic participation, pluralism and diversity.
- Groups can be an important source of specialist information / expertise for an overloaded legislature and civil service.
- Many groups play vital role in implementing changes to public policy.

Business Groups and public policy

Business groups like CII, FICCI and ASSOCHAM are important pressure groups that work for the interest of businesses in our country. They contribute to public policy in the following ways:

(a) They provide valuable inputs based on their industry experience while the government makes laws or schemes for various sectors.

(b) They highlight the issues of various industries in the economy for the government to announce various measures for their upliftment.

(c) They provide valuable inputs during the discussion before Budget every year to the finance ministry.

CHAPTER 28

Civil Services in a Democracy

LEARNING OUTCOMES

1. Understanding the role and importance of civil services in governance
2. Analysing the issues in civil services and reforms needed
3. Understanding recent trends including lateral entry and Mission Karmayogi

The term 'Civil Service' refers to the administrative machinery of the Central and State governments (including local bodies), which is responsible for implementing policies made by the political executive, which constitutes the elected representatives in our democracy. The civil servants are also known as 'Permanent Executive'.

Civil services were established in modern India under the British rule. The main aim of civil servants under the British rule was maintenance of law and order. However, after independence the system was adopted with a view to enable the civil services not only in maintenance of law and order but also contribute for the development of the country.

28.1 CIVIL SERVICES IN INDIA

28.1.1 Role and Importance of Civil Service

The civil services perform the following important roles in our democracy:

- It is the administrative machinery for implementing various policies made by the elected governments.
- It not only implements the policies but also plays an important role in policy formulation. It is a source of facts, experience, ideas and solutions. It participates in policy making by giving advice to ministers and providing them the necessary information. The administrative tasks of public bureaucracy include formulation of policies and plans, executing and monitoring programmes, laying down laws, rules and regulations, which affect human actions in almost all walks of life.
- Civil services are responsible for implementing the laws and policies of the government. By carrying out laws, it regulates the behaviour of the people in society. By implementing public policies and programmes, it delivers the promised goods and services to the intended beneficiaries.

- Civil services act as a stabilising force in society. It settles social tensions and conflicts and thus creates social unity and harmony.
- Civil servants carry the role of governance even when the government changes after elections. Thus, they provide continuity in administration.
- They act as an instrument of social change and development.

28.1.2 Attributes of an Efficient Civil Service

Characteristics of Civil Service

(a) Structural characteristics

Characteristics	Brief description
Division of Labour	Total task is broken down into a number of specialised functions.
Hierarchy	Number of levels of differently graded functionaries with supervision.
System of rules	Rights and duties as well as modes of doing work governed by rules.
Specificity	Every role clearly earmarked with specific job descriptions.

(b) Behavioural characteristics

Characteristics	Brief description
Rationality	Decisions taken based on evidence, alternatives considered objectively.
Impersonality	Official business conducted without any regard for individual persons.
Rule orientation	Employees to follow rules strictly in discharge of duties.
Neutrality	Serves any kind of political regime without any bias.

(c) Development administration

Characteristics	Brief description
Change orientation	Unlike maintenance of status quo, aimed at socio-economic change.
Result orientation	Performance related to productivity in a time-bound manner.
Commitment	Involvement and emotional attachment to the job.
Client orientation	Satisfying the needs of specific target groups of citizens.

Issues in civil services

While the Indian Civil Services have played an important role in formulation and implementation of the government policies for the welfare of people, it has the following major issues:

- Lack of integrity.
- Lack of experienced leadership.
- Corruption at most levels.
- Complex relationship between politicians and bureaucrats.
- Bureaucrats care more about 'procedure' than 'outcome'.
- Arbitrary transfers.
- Lack of accountability and transparency.

In *Prakash Singh case* (2006), the Supreme Court issued various directions for police reforms. It held that the Director General of Police (DGP) of a State should be selected from amongst the three senior most officers of the department and should have a fixed tenure of 2 years. It also directed that a 'police establishment board' be set up in each State for deciding the working conditions related to police officers.

Further, the Supreme Court in *TSR Subramanian case* (2013) made the following two major rulings:

- Officers of All India Services and other civil servants were not bound to follow oral directives as they 'undermine credibility' of the services.
- Establishment of a Civil Services Board, headed by Cabinet Secretary at the national level and Chief secretaries at the State level to recommend transfers and postings of All India service officers (IAS, IPS and Indian Forest Service).

Reforms required for strengthening civil service

There are reforms required for strengthening and streamlining the civil services. The following are the attributes of an efficient civil service and reforms required:

- Insulating civil servants from undue political interference – The relationship between the political executive and the civil services needs to be transformed on the basis of mutual understanding, respect and recognition of each other's distinct roles and responsibilities.
- Professionalism with stability of tenure – There is need to recognise the complex challenges of modern administration in various spheres of activities. Meeting such challenges require domain expertise and long experience in the sectors concerned.
- The civil services should focus on citizen-centric administration.
- Outcome orientation – Monitoring in government is primarily through measurement of expenditure against outlays and at best through defined outputs. Clearly, there is need to move towards measurement of outcomes.
- Accountability – There is a general feeling that existing mechanisms of accountability are inadequate. On the one hand, there is no disincentive for non-performance and on the other, competence and integrity are not adequately recognised or rewarded. Therefore, innovative and effective mechanisms need to be put in place to protect public money, guarantee intended outcomes and enforce accountability.
- Promoting public service values and ethics – Apart from the traditional civil service values of efficiency, integrity, accountability and patriotism, it is necessary for civil servants to inculcate and adopt ethical and moral values including probity in public life, respect for human rights and compassion for the downtrodden and commitment to their welfare.
- Establishment of Civil Service Boards (CSBs) – The CSBs have not been set up in all States and even in States where set up, they are not empowered to take autonomous decisions with respect to postings and transfers. CSB should be set up and empowered in all States.
- Changes in Service rules – Specific rules may be added with respect to use of social media. This may include guidelines for the nature of official content that can be posted as well as the right to defend against any defamatory campaign concerning the official work. Officers should exercise 'responsible anonymity' while discharging their functions and disseminating information about the same.

28.2 RECENT TRENDS IN CIVIL SERVICES

28.2.1 Lateral Entry of Civil Servants

Lateral entry in civil services is when private sector or Public Sector Undertakings' specialists are appointed in government departments at the rank of Joint Secretary, Director, and Deputy Secretary. The Central government initiated this process in 2018.

Advantages of Lateral entry

- It will bring needed specialisation in civil services.
- It will make career bureaucrats more responsive and alert thereby bringing a positive change in work culture.
- Change in role of government from maintenance of law and order to development requires fresh ideas that can be brought in by lateral entrants.

Scan the QR code for video on recent developments with respect to lateral recruitments

McGraw Hill edge

Challenges of Lateral entry

- There can be coordination issues for the lateral entrants with career bureaucrats.
- Lack of field experience amongst lateral entrants.
- There can be conflict of interest while hiring recruits from private sector.

The way forward is to set objective criteria for recruitment and placing the lateral entrants in Mission mode projects. The selection process should be more transparent and there can be an orientation training programme for the recruits before they take up their roles. The process of appointment of lateral entrants should follow the principles of public policy, including suitable reservation for backward classes, while recruiting.

28.2.2 Mission Karmayogi

About the Programme

- Mission Karmayogi is a nationwide programme to lay the foundation for capacity building of civil servants. Officially called the 'National Programme for Civil Services Capacity Building', the mission plans to transform human resource management in the country.
- It will help the officers to learn about the best practices across the world.
- The fundamental focus of the reform is the creation of a 'citizen-centric civil service' capable of creating and delivering services conducive to economic growth and public welfare.
- Mission Karmayogi shifts the focus from 'Rule based training to Role based training'.
- Greater thrust has been laid on behavioural change.

Scan the QR code for conceptual video on Civil Services in a democracy

McGraw Hill edge

Unfolding of Mission Karmayogi

- Mission Karmayogi programme will be delivered by setting up a digital platform called iGOT Karmayogi.

- The platform will act as a launchpad for the National Programme for Civil Services Capacity Building (NPCSCB), which will enable a comprehensive reform of the capacity building apparatus at the individual, institutional and process levels.
- NPCSCB will be governed by the Prime Minister's Human Resource Council, which will also include the State Chief Ministers, the Union Cabinet ministers and experts. This council will approve and review civil service capacity building programmes.

THINK ABOUT IT

Career bureaucracy has outlived its utility. Critically examine.

- Besides this, there will be a Cabinet Secretary Coordination Unit comprising select secretaries and cadre controlling authorities.
- Also, there will be a Capacity Building Commission, which will include experts in related fields and global professionals. This commission will prepare and monitor annual capacity building plans and audit human resources available in the government.
- Also, there will be a wholly-owned Special Purpose Vehicle (SPV), which will govern the iGOT-Karmayogi platform.

MAINS STARTER

Area	Building Blocks For Model Introductions
Civil service	Civil service is 'permanent executive', which is the backbone, that provides stability and neutrality to the administration and political executive.
Lateral entry into civil services	Lateral entry is the mechanism by which officials for middle and senior bureaucracy are hired from the private sector and public sector undertakings. It is aimed at providing the required specialisation.

UPSC PREVIOUS YEARS' QUESTIONS OF PRELIMINARY EXAMINATION

1. In the context of India, which one of the following is the characteristic appropriate for bureaucracy [2020]

   (a) An agency for widening the scope of Parliamentary democracy
   (b) An agency for strengthening the structure of federalism
   (c) An agency for facilitating political stability and economic growth
   (d) An agency for the implementation of public policy

   Solution: (d)

Explanation: As discussed in Section 28.1.1, bureaucracy is the administrative machinery for implementing various policies made by the elected governments. Hence, correct answer is (d).

UPSC Previous Years' Questions of Main Examination

1. The Doctrine of Democratic Governance makes it necessary that the public perception of the integrity and commitment of civil servants becomes absolutely positive. Discuss. **[2024]**

Approach: The role of civil service and its importance for the overall development and democratic governance needs to be discussed first. The issues with civil services and measures for strengthening the same need to be the second part of the answer.

MODEL ANSWER

Civil services play an important role in the formulation and implementation of policies for social and economic development. The quality of civil service and its integrity are crucial for democratic governance.

Issues with Bureaucracy

At present, the civil services suffer from the following issues that weaken the democratic functioning, thereby reducing the perception in public:

(a) Lack of integrity and corruption at most levels.

(b) Complex relationship between politicians and bureaucrats. Arbitrary transfers, lack of accountability and transparency.

(c) Bureaucrats care more about 'procedure' than 'outcome'.

(d) Bureaucrats joining political parties after retirement or resignation.

Reforms required

- Insulating civil servants from undue political interference.
- Professionalism with stability of tenure and domain expertise.
- The civil services should focus on citizen-centric administration.
- Promoting public service values and ethics and a sense of accountability.

It must be noted that the central government has launched 'Mission Karmayogi' to lay the foundation for capacity building of civil servants. The fundamental focus of the reform is the creation of a 'citizen-centric civil service'.